"How Much Can I Make?"

Actual Sales, Expenses, and/or Profits on 77 Franchise Opportunities

2013 (13th) Edition

Robert E. Bond
Publisher

Annie Barbarika
Senior Editor

Zuzanna Gruca
Editor

Christopher Buenaventura
Graphic Design

Source Book Publications
Serving the Franchising Industry

1814 Franklin St., Suite 603
Oakland, CA 94612
(888) 612-9908

ISBN-10: 1-887137-89-0
ISBN-13: 978-1-887137-89-8

DISCLAIMER

The Financial Performance Representations in *"How Much Can I Make?"* are based on data submitted by the franchisors themselves to various state and/or federal regulatory agencies. The franchisor profiles are based on information submitted to Source Book Publications by the franchisors themselves. Every reasonable effort has been made to ensure that the information presented accurately reflects the original data submitted. Although the publisher and Source Book Publications feel confident that the information submitted is accurate and complete, they have not independently verified or corroborated the information. Accordingly, neither the publisher, Source Book Publications, nor the World Franchising Network assume any responsibility for errors or omissions. They strongly encourage any prospective franchisee to conduct an aggressive independent investigation into the sales and income potential of the franchises being considered. Readers should keep in mind that some of the franchisors may have terminated their franchising efforts since the submission of the original data. Others may have superseded the information contained herein with more current financial performance representations.

It is the intent of the author and publisher to annually update *"How Much Can I Make?"* To the extent that any franchisor making a Financial Performance Representation wishes to be included in subsequent editions, please forward a current copy of your FDD or Item 19 to Source Book Publications, 1814 Franklin St., Suite 603, Oakland, CA 94612 or email an electronic copy to info@worldfranchising.com.

This publication is designed to provide its readers with accurate and authoritative information with regard to the subject matter covered. It is sold with the understanding that neither the author nor the publisher is engaged in rendering legal, accounting, or other professional services. If legal advice or other expert assistance is required, the services of a competent professional person should be sought.

From a Declaration of Principles jointly adopted by a Committee of the American Bar Association and a Committee of Publishers.

Cover Design by Christopher Buenaventura.

ISBN-10: 1-887137-89-0
ISBN-13: 978-1-887137-89-8

Printed in the United States of America.
10 9 8 7 6 5 4 3 2 1

"How Much Can I Make?" is available at special discounts for bulk purchase. Special editions or book excerpts can also be created to specifications. For details, contact Source Book Publications, 1814 Franklin St., Suite 603, Oakland, CA 94612. Phone: (888) 612-9908 or (510) 839-5471; Fax: (510) 839-2104.

Preface

As a prospective franchisee, the single most important task ahead of you is to get an accurate and reliable sense of a business's potential sales, expenses, and profits. Without this analysis, you will have only a faint idea of how much you are going to earn as a result of your investment and considerable efforts.

Keep in mind that in acquiring a franchise, or any business for that matter, you are making an investment that has long-term responsibilities and consequences that are potentially far-reaching. If you find out 12 months after starting your business that you did not properly project the negative cash flows that would occur during the start-up phase, or didn't appreciate the magnitude of advertising/promotion costs, or assumed that revenues would be 30% higher than they actually are, then you have no one to blame but yourself. At that point, you can't re-negotiate your franchise contract. If you can't make the business work financially, the fact that you really enjoy being your own boss, really like the franchisor's management team and its vision, and really believe in the product/service is of secondary importance. If, six months after starting the business, you find yourself financially strapped, your options are severely limited. You can continue to limp along operating the business, working even harder, and most likely not enjoying what you are doing. You can borrow more money in the hopes of generating increased revenues. Or you can sell the business, most likely for substantially less than you invested.

Do yourself a favor. Take whatever time is necessary to do your homework. You will no doubt be under an inordinate amount of pressure from the franchisor to start your new business as soon as possible. Resist the temptation to do so until you are completely conversant with all facets of the particular business in which you are investing, as well as the dynamics of the industry itself. Spend the extra time and money to ensure that no stones are left unturned. In addition to the required research, make sure you fully understand what cash flow statements are about, the distinction between fixed and variable costs, and what industry operating standards are. Know where to go to get industry data. Call as many existing (and former) franchisees as are required to corroborate your projections. They will be able to tell you if your assumptions are either too optimistic or too pessimistic. Keep in mind that the existing franchisee base represents your best source of information on the business. You will only get one chance to perform your due diligence.

Given these alarmist warnings, it is incumbent on you to thoroughly research all aspects of the industry you are considering prior to making an irreversible investment. The risks are high. Your failure could well result in the loss of your investment (as well as any other property you may have pledged), your marriage (to the extent that your spouse was not equally committed to franchising and the inherent risks involved), and, possibly most important, your self-esteem. Contrary to much of the hype surrounding the industry, there are no guarantees. To think that you can simply pay a franchise fee and automatically step into a guaranteed money machine is naive at best, and financially fatal at worst. There is absolutely no substitute for extensive investigation. The burden is on you to do your homework and ensure that the choice is fully researched. Only you can maximize the likelihood of success and minimize the chances of failure or unfulfilled expectations.

"How Much Can I Make?" contains 77 financial performance representations in their entirety. The roster of franchisors runs from large, well-established operations like Burger King and McDonald's to newer, smaller franchises with only a handful of operating units. Keep in mind that the financial data presented below is based on actual, verifiable operating results that the franchisors must be able to document. Understanding these financial statements is only one step in a long and tedious process. They nevertheless provide an invaluable source of critical background information that you will not find in any other source.

One of the most important exercises you can do is to rigorously determine what the net earnings from your investment

3

will be. Realize that you have an "opportunity cost" associated with your investment in the business. If you invest $100,000 of equity, that money could probably earn a minimum of 5% if deployed elsewhere and with considerably less risk. Accordingly, the first $5,000 earned is not really a profit, but a return on your investment. Does the remaining "adjusted net cash flow" adequately reward you for the stress and strain of running your own business, including putting in long, hard hours at work, wearing 10 hats at a time, living with financial uncertainty, and giving up much of your discretionary time? On the other side of the ledger are the advantages of owning your own business: the pride and independence of running your own show, the chance to start something from scratch and sell it 5–10 years later at a multiple of your original investment, and the opportunity to take full advantage of your management, sales, and people skills. Clearly there is a balance, but make sure that you have a strong sense of how realistic your expectations are and if they have a solid chance of being achieved.

Although the level of detail and applicability to your own investment may differ substantially among the various financial performance representations, you can still learn a great deal by reviewing the data presented. Just because a financial performance representation is not in the same industry you are considering, do not assume that you should not read it. Reviewing a wide range of actual operating results provides an invaluable chance to become acquainted with basic accounting practices—how to get from gross sales to net income, how to differentiate between fixed expenses (such as rent, equipment rental, and utilities) and variable expenses (direct labor, shipping, and percentage rent), and how to determine a break-even point. Consider how various aspects of a totally different type of business might apply to your own. This is a great chance to avoid saying six months from now, "Why wasn't I aware of that expense?" Devoting even a minimal amount of time and energy will provide invaluable insights.

Presuming that you are committed to maximizing your chances for success, you have a great deal of work ahead of you. Because it is tedious, many people will opt for the easy way out and do only a modest amount of homework. Many of these will ultimately regret their lack of research and, accordingly, their investment decision. Others may be happy with the decision to enter franchising, but may wish they had joined another franchise system. Still others will go out of business. I strongly recommend that you commit the next several months to learning everything you can about the franchising industry in general, the specific industry you are considering in particular, all of the franchise opportunities within that industry, and, most importantly, the individual franchise you ultimately select.

You have a great deal at risk, and you don't get a second chance. Your cheapest form of insurance is the time you put into investigating a business before you invest. Take full advantage of the tools available to you. Do your homework.

Good luck, and Godspeed.

Table of Contents

30-Minute Overview | 1

There are three stages in the franchise selection process: investigation, evaluation, and negotiation. This book is intended to assist the reader in the first two stages by providing a framework for developing reasonable financial guidelines upon which to make a well-researched and properly-documented investment decision.

Understand at the outset that the entire franchise selection process should take many months, and can involve a great deal of frustration. I suggest that you set up a realistic timeline for signing a franchise agreement, and that you stick to that schedule. There will be a lot of pressure on you to prematurely complete the selection and negotiation phases. Resist the temptation. The penalties are too severe for a seat-of-the-pants attitude. A decision of this magnitude clearly deserves careful consideration.

Before starting the selection process, briefly review the areas covered below.

FRANCHISE INDUSTRY STRUCTURE

The franchising industry is made up of two distinct types of franchises. The first, and by far the larger, includes product and trade name franchising. Included in this group are automotive and truck dealers, soft drink bottlers, and gasoline service stations. For the most part, these are essentially distributorships.

The second group encompasses business format franchisors. This book only includes information on this latter category.

LAYMAN'S DEFINITION OF FRANCHISING

Business format franchising is a method of market expansion by which one business entity expands the distribution of its products and/or services through independent, third-party operators. Franchising occurs when the operator of a concept or system (the franchisor) grants an independent businessperson (the franchisee) the right to duplicate its entire business format at a particular location and for a specified period, under terms and conditions set forth in the contract (franchise agreement). The franchisee has full access to all of the trademarks, logos, marketing techniques, controls, and systems that have made the franchisor successful. In effect, the franchisee acts as a surrogate for a company-owned store in the distribution of the franchisor's goods and/or services. It is important to keep in mind that the franchisor and the franchisee are separate legal entities.

Classic Business Format Model

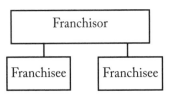

In return for a front-end franchise fee—which usually ranges from $15,000 – $35,000—the franchisor is obligated to "set up" the franchisee in business. This generally includes assistance in selecting a location, negotiating a lease, obtaining financing, building and equipping a site, and providing the necessary training, operating manuals, and start-up assistance. Once the training is completed and the store is open, the new franchisee should have a carbon copy of other units in the system and enjoy the same benefits they do, whether they are company-owned or not.

Business format franchising is unique because it is a long-term relationship characterized by an ongoing, mutually-beneficial partnership. Ongoing services include research and development, marketing strategies, advertising campaigns, group buying, periodic field visits, training updates, and whatever else is required to make the franchisee competitive and profitable. In effect, the franchisor acts as the franchisee's "back office" support organization. To reimburse the franchisor for this support, the franchisee pays the franchisor an ongoing royalty fee, generally 4 – 8% of gross sales. In many cases, franchisees also contribute an advertising fee to reimburse the franchisor for expenses incurred in maintaining a national or regional advertising campaign.

To work to maximum advantage, both the franchisor and the franchisees should share common objectives and goals. Both parties must accept the premise that their fortunes are mutually intertwined and that they are each better off working in a cooperative effort rather than toward self-serving goals. Unlike the parent/child relationship that has dominated franchising over the past 30 years, franchising is now becoming a true relationship of partners.

THE PLAYERS

1. The Franchisors

Source Book Publications routinely tracks approximately 3,000+ U.S. and Canadian franchisors. We believe this represents the number of legitimate, active franchisors in North America at any point in time. Profiles of these franchisors can be found in *Bond's Franchise Guide*, published annually by Source Book Publications. Copies of this 450+ page directory, which is considered the definitive directory in the field, are available for $34.95 plus $8.50 for shipping and handling ($45.50 + $12.00 in Canada). Call (888) 612-9908 or (510) 839-5471 or fax (510) 839-2104 to place a credit card order, or send a check to Source Book Publications, 1814 Franklin St., Suite 603, Oakland, CA 94612. There is an order form at the end of Chapter 3.

While you may already have your sights on a particular franchise opportunity, it would be short-sighted not to find out as much as you can about both the direct and indirect competition. You might discover that other franchises have similar products or services, but offer superior training and support, a reduced royalty fee, or vastly superior financing options. I strongly encourage you to read either *Bond's Franchise Guide* or one of the other franchise directories to fully explore the options open to you.

2. The Regulatory Agencies

The offer and sale of franchises are regulated at both the federal and state levels. Federal requirements cover all 50 states.

In addition, certain states have adopted their own requirements.

In 1979, after many years of debate, the Federal Trade Commission (FTC) implemented Rule 436. This rule requires that franchisors provide prospective franchisees with a disclosure statement (called an offering circular) containing specific information about a company's franchise offering. The rule has two objectives: to ensure that potential franchisees have sufficient background information to make an educated investment decision and to provide them with adequate time to do so.

The Franchise Rule was substantially updated (and improved) on July 1, 2008 as the FTC tried to make the disclosure document more consistent with various state regulations. Among other things, the Uniform Franchise Offering Circular (UFOC) became the Franchise Disclosure Document (FDD), and Item 19 of the new FDD morphed from an Earnings Claims Statement to a Financial Performance Representation. Overall, the revisions were positive and resulted in considerably more and better information being available to the prospective franchisee. Unfortunately, the revisions did not require all franchisors to provide a Financial Performance Representation from which potential franchisees could better determine the overall profitability of their potential investments.

Certain "registration states" require additional safeguards to protect potential franchisees. Their requirements are generally more stringent than the FTC's requirements. These states include California, Florida, Hawaii, Illinois, Indiana, Maryland, Michigan, Minnesota, New York, North Dakota, Oregon, Rhode Island, South Dakota, Virginia, Washington, and Wisconsin. Separate registration is also required in the province of Alberta.

The regulations require that the franchisor provide a prospective franchisee with the required information at their first face-to-face meeting or at least 14 days prior to the signing of the franchise agreement, whichever is earlier. Required information includes:

[1] The franchisor and any predecessors.

[2] Identity and business experience of persons affiliated with the franchisor.

[3] Litigation.

[4] Bankruptcy.

[5] Franchisee's initial fee or other initial payments.

[6] Other fees.

[7] Franchisee's initial investment.

[8] Obligations of franchisee to purchase or lease from designated sources.

[9] Obligations of franchisee to purchase or lease in accordance with specifications or from approved suppliers.

[10] Financing arrangements.

[11] Obligations of the franchisor; other supervision, assistance or services.

[12] Exclusive area or territory.

[13] Trademarks, service marks, trade names, logotypes, and commercial symbols.

[14] Patents and copyrights.

[15] Obligations of the participant in the actual operation of the franchise business.

[16] Restrictions on goods and services offered by franchisee.

[17] Renewal, termination, repurchase, modification, and assignment of the franchise agreement and related information.

[18] Arrangements with public figures.

[19] Actual, average, projected, or forecasted franchise sales, profits, or earnings.

[20] Information regarding franchises of the franchisor.

[21] Financial statements.

[22] Contracts.

[23] Acknowledgment of receipt by respective franchisee.

If you live in a registration state, make sure that the franchisor you are evaluating is, in fact, registered to sell franchises there. If not, and the franchisor has no near-term plans to register in your state, you should consider other options.

Keep in mind that neither the FTC nor any of the states has reviewed the disclosure document to determine whether the information submitted is true and accurate. They merely require that the franchisor make representations based upon a prescribed format. If the information provided is false, franchisors are subject to civil penalties. You should also be aware of the reality that neither the FTC nor the individual states have the staff or budget necessary to pursue a lengthy battle over possible misrepresentations. If you run into problems, your only real option is to retain an attorney and battle a franchisor, who may have an in-house legal staff and a bottomless war chest. While you might win the battle, you would most likely lose the war.

It is up to you to read and thoroughly understand all elements of the disclosure document and to take full advantage of the documentation that is available to you. Know exactly what you can expect from the franchisor and what your own obligations are. Under what circumstances can the relationship be unilaterally terminated by the franchisor? What is your protected territory? What are the terms of a renewal? Can you expand within your territory? While there is no question that the FDD is tedious reading, it nevertheless provides invaluable information. The penalties for not doing your homework are severe. You will have no one to blame but yourself. Hedge your bets by having a professional also review the FDD.

3. The Trade Associations

The International Franchise Association (IFA) was established in 1960 as a non-profit trade association to promote franchising as a responsible method of doing business. The IFA currently represents over 1,000 franchisors in the U.S. and around the world. It is recognized as the leading spokesperson for the industry. For most of its 40+ years, the IFA has represented the interests of franchisors only. In recent years, however, it has initiated an aggressive campaign to recruit franchisees into its membership and to represent their interests as well. The IFA's offices are located at 1501 K St., Suite 350, Washington, DC 20005. (202) 628-8000; Fax (202) 628-0812; www.franchise.org.

The Canadian Franchise Association (CFA), which has some 250+ members, is the Canadian equivalent of the IFA. Information on the CFA can be obtained by writing the group at 5399 Eglinton Ave. West, # 116, Toronto, ON M9C 5K6, Canada. (800) 665-4232 or (416) 695-2896; Fax (416) 695-1950; www.cfa.ca.

WHAT MAKES A WINNING FRANCHISE

Virtually every writer on the subject of franchising has his or her own idea of what determines a winning franchise. I believe there are five primary factors.

1. A product or service with clear advantages over the competition. These advantages may include brand recognition, a unique, proprietary product or service, or 30 years of proven experience.

2. A standardized franchise system that has been time-tested. A company that has operated numerous units, both company-owned and franchised, has usually worked out most of the bugs in the system. By the time a system has 30 or more operating units, it should be thoroughly tested.

3. Exceptional franchisor support. This includes not only the initial training program, but the ongoing support (research and development, refresher training, [800] help-lines, field representatives who provide on-site training, annual meetings, advertising and promotion, central purchasing, etc.).

4. The financial wherewithal and management experience to carry out any announced growth plans without short-changing its franchisees. Sufficient depth of management is often lacking in younger, high-growth franchises.

5. A strong mutuality of interest between franchisor and franchisees. Unless both parties realize that their relationship is one of long-term partners, the system will probably never achieve its full potential. A few telephone calls to existing and former franchisees can easily determine whether the necessary rapport between franchisor and franchisees exists.

THE NEGOTIATION PROCESS

Once you have narrowed your options down to your two or three top choices, you now have to negotiate the best deal you can with the franchisor. In most cases, the franchisor will tell you that the franchise agreement cannot be changed. Think twice before you accept the statement that the contract is non-negotiable. Notwithstanding the legal requirement that all of a franchisor's agreements be substantially the same at any point in time, there are usually a number of variables that are flexible. If the franchisor truly wants you as a franchisee, it may be willing to make concessions not available to the next applicant.

Will the franchisor take a short-term note for all or part of the franchise fee? Can you expand from your initial unit after you have proven yourself? If so, can the franchise fee on a second unit be eliminated or reduced? Can you get a right of first refusal on adjacent territories? Can the term of the agreement be extended from 10 to 15 years? Can you include a franchise cancellation right if the training and/or initial support do not meet your expectations or the franchisor's promises? The list goes on ad infinitum.

To successfully negotiate, you must have a thorough knowledge of the industry, the franchise agreement you are negotiating (and agreements of competitive franchise opportunities), and access to experienced professional advice. This can be a lawyer, an accountant, or a franchise consultant. Above all else, he or she should have proven experience in negotiating franchise agreements. Franchising is a unique method of doing business. Do not pay someone $100+ per hour to learn the industry. Make him or her demonstrate that he or she has been through the process several times before.

Negotiating a long-term agreement of this type is extremely tricky and fraught with pitfalls. The risks are extremely high. Do not think that you can handle the negotiations yourself, or that you can not afford outside counsel. In point of fact, you can not afford *not* to employ an experienced professional advisor.

THE 4 R'S OF FRANCHISING

At a young age, we are taught that the three R's of reading, 'riting, and 'rithmetic are critical to our scholastic success. Success in franchising depends on four R's: realism, research, reserves, and resolve.

1. **Realism**

At the outset of your investigation, be realistic about your strengths, weaknesses, goals, and capabilities. I strongly recommend you take the time necessary to do a personal audit—possibly with the help of outside professionals—before investing your life's savings in a franchise.

Franchising is not a money machine. It involves hard work, dedication, setbacks, and long hours. Be realistic about the nature of the business you are buying. What traits will ultimately determine your success? Do you have them? If it is a service-oriented business, will you be able to keep smiling when you know the client is a fool? If it is a fast-food business, will you be able to properly manage a minimum-wage staff? How well will you handle the uncertainties that will invariably arise? Can you make day-to-day decisions based on imperfect information? Can you count on the support of your partner after you have gone through all of your working capital reserves and the future looks increasingly cloudy?

Be equally realistic about your franchise selection process. Have you thoroughly evaluated all of the alternatives? Have you talked with everyone you can, leaving no stone unturned? Have you carefully and realistically assessed the advantages and disadvantages of the system offered, the unique demographics of your territory, the near-term market trends, and the financial projections? The selection process is tiring. It is easy to convince yourself that the franchise opportunity in your hand is really the best one for you before you have done all your homework. The penalties for such laziness, however, are extreme.

2. Research

There is no substitute for exhaustive research!

Bond's Franchise Guide contains over 900 franchise listings, broken into 29 distinct business categories. This represents a substantial number of options from which to choose. Other directories also cover the industry to varying degrees of thoroughness and accuracy. Spend the time required to come up with an optimal selection. At a minimum, you will probably be in the business for five years. More likely, you will be in it for 10 years or more. Given the long-term commitment, allow yourself the necessary time to ensure you will not regret your decision. Research is a tedious, boring process, but doing it carefully and thoroughly can greatly reduce your risk and exposure. The benefits are immeasurable.

First, determine which industry groups hold your interest. Do not arbitrarily limit yourself to a particular industry in which you have first-hand experience. Next, request information from all of the companies that participate in those industries.

The incremental cost of mailing (or calling) an additional 15 or 20 companies for information is insignificant in the big picture. Based on personal experience, you may feel you already know the best franchise. Step back. Assume there is a competing franchise out there with a comparable product or service, comparable management, etc., but which charges a royalty fee of sales that is 2% lower than your intuitive choice. Over a 10-year period, that could add up to a great deal of money. It certainly justifies your requesting initial information.

A thorough analysis of the literature you receive should allow you to reduce the list of prime candidates to six or eight companies. Aggressively evaluate each firm. Talking with current and former franchisees is the single best source of information you can get. Where possible, visit franchise sites. My experience is that franchisees tend to be candid in their level of satisfaction with the franchisor. However, since they do not know you, they may be less candid about their sales, expenses, and income. *"How Much Can I Make?"* should be of some assistance in filling this void. Go on the Internet or to the library and get studies that forecast industry growth, market saturation, industry problems, technical break-throughs, etc. Prevent finding out a year after becoming a franchisee of a coffee company that readily available reports suggested that the coffee market was over-saturated or that coffee was linked to some obscure form of colon cancer in rats.

3. Reserves

Like any new business, franchising is replete with uncertainty, uneven cash flows, and unforeseen problems. It is an imperfect world that might not bear any relation to the clean pro formas you prepared to justify getting into the business. Any one of these unforeseen contingencies could cause a severe drain on your cash reserves. At the same time, you will have fixed and/or contractual payments that must be met on a regular basis regardless of sales, such as rent, employee salaries, insurance, etc.

Adequate back-up reserves may be in the form of savings, commitments from relatives, bank loans, etc. Just make certain that the funds are available when and if you need them. To be absolutely safe, I suggest that you double the level of reserves recommended by the franchisor.

Keep in mind that the most common cause of business failure is inadequate working capital. Plan properly so you do not become a statistic.

4. Resolve

Let's assume for the time being that you have demonstrated exceptional levels of realism, thoroughly researched your options, and lined up ample capital reserves. You have picked an optimal franchise that takes full advantage of your strengths. You are in business and bringing in enough money to achieve a positive cash flow. The future looks bright. Now the fourth R—resolve—comes into play. Remember why you chose franchising in the first place: to take full advantage of a system that has been time-tested in the marketplace. Remember also what makes franchising work so well: that the franchisor and franchisees maximize their respective success by working within the system for the common good. Invariably, two obstacles arise.

The first is the physical pain associated with writing that monthly royalty check. Annual sales of $500,000 and a 6% royalty fee result in a monthly royalty check of $2,500 that must be sent to the franchisor every month. As a franchisee, you may look for any justification to reduce this sizable monthly outflow. Resist the temptation. Accept the fact that royalty fees are simply another cost of doing business. They are also a legal obligation that you willingly agreed to pay when you signed the franchise agreement. In effect, they are the dues you agreed to pay to belong to the club.

Although there may be an incentive, do not look for loopholes in the contract that might allow you to sue the franchisor or get out of the relationship. Do not report lower sales than actual in an effort to reduce royalties. If you have received the support that you were promised, continue to play by the rules. Honor your commitment. Let the franchisor enjoy the rewards it has earned from your success.

The second obstacle is the desire to change the system. You need to honor your commitment to be a "franchisee" and to live within the franchise system. What makes franchising successful as far as your customers are concerned is uniformity and consistency of appearance, product/service quality, and corporate image. The most damaging thing an individual franchisee can do is to suddenly and unilaterally introduce changes into a proven system. While these modifications may work in one market, they only serve to diminish the value of the system as a whole. Imagine what would happen to the national perception of your franchise if every franchisee had the latitude to make unilateral changes in his or her operations. Accordingly, any ideas you have on improving the system should be submitted directly to the franchisor for its evaluation. Accept the franchisor's decision on whether or not to pursue an idea.

If you suspect that you have a penchant for being an entrepreneur, or for unrestrained experimenting and tinkering, you are probably not cut out to be a good franchisee. Seriously consider this question before you get into a relationship, instead of waiting until you are locked into an untenable situation.

SUMMARY

I hope that I have been clear in suggesting that the selection of an optimal franchise is both time- and energy-consuming. Done properly, the process may take six to nine months and involve the expenditure of several thousand dollars. The difference between a hasty, gut-feel investigation and an exhaustive, well-thought-out investigation may mean the difference between finding a poorly-conceived or even fraudulent franchise and an exceptional one.

There is a strong correlation between the efforts put into the investigative process and the ultimate degree of success you enjoy as a franchisee. The process is to investigate, evaluate, and negotiate. Do not try to bypass any one of these elements.

Financial Performance Representations

The harsh reality is that you cannot tell—much less guarantee—how much you might make from a specific investment. Even the most successful business model, whether a franchise or not, simply cannot be replicated by someone who is not prepared to run the business the way it should be run. Area demographics, such as population, disposable per capita income, and education, are critical. For a retail business, a heavily trafficked location is critical. Adequate capital is critical. Management and decision-making skills are critical. Hard work is critical. The list goes on. It is up to you to ensure that all of these factors are optimized. If any one of these critical factors is missing or marginal, chances are the business will not meet your expectations.

This compendium of financial performance representations is meant to provide prospective franchisees with a better sense of what they might earn from their efforts. Without a sure understanding of potential sales, expenses and profits, an investor is inviting disappointment at best and failure at worst. I strongly encourage you to take whatever time is required to carefully review the following financial performance representations. Some are easy reading, others tedious and detail-oriented. But the better versed you are on the actual historical operating results of these 77 companies, however, the better positioned you will be to make an optimal franchise selection. You will be able to ask franchisors intelligent, penetrating questions when evaluating them. You will be better prepared to compare franchises within similar industries. You will have more credibility seeking the insights of existing franchisees. If you take the time to develop your own financial projections, you will not have to rely as heavily on expensive outside accountants and financial advisers. Most importantly, you will have a real understanding of the business before you commit your financial resources and your life. If your objective is to maximize your bottom line, taking full advantage of the financial performance representations in this book is an important start.

THE AVERAGE FRANCHISEE

The only in-depth study of actual franchisee earnings and satisfaction was conducted in 1997 by *Franchise Times* magazine. Based on answers from more than 1,000 franchisees, the Second Annual Franchisee Survey found that the average franchisee owned 3.5 units, had been in franchising for 8.9 years, and enjoyed net pre-tax earnings of $171,000, or roughly $50,000 per unit. Total annual household income before taxes averaged $118,000 for all franchisees. The median income, however, was $81,000. The initial start-up cost was $151,000 and the average loan size was $196,000, with a median of $88,000. Three-quarters of those surveyed answered that they were either "very" or "somewhat" satisfied with franchising. Just over 15% were "not too" satisfied, while only 9.8% were "not at all" satisfied. If you think that franchising is an automatic pot of gold, you should temper your enthusiasm with the facts of life brought out in the survey.

Whether these averages satisfy or alarm you, most prospective franchisees will probably be surprised to learn that even after 8+ years in the business, the average franchisee in the survey had pre-tax earnings of less than $50,000 per unit. Keep in mind, however, that the above statistics are only that—statistics. How well your earnings compare with those of the average franchisee is what counts. Yet if you hope to make $100,000 per year with your initial unit, you will have to be markedly more successful than the average franchisee. Picking up the right franchise in the right market is the first step.

THE MARKET VOID

The single most important factor in buying any business is calculating a realistic and verifiable projection of sales, expenses, and profits. Specifically, how much can you expect to earn after working 65 hours a week for 52 weeks a year? A prospective franchisee clearly does not have the experience to sit down and determine what his or her sales and profits will be over the next five years, especially if he or she has no applied experience in that particular business. The only source in a position to supply accurate information about a franchise opportunity is the franchisor itself.

It is unfortunate that not all franchisors are required to supply prospective franchisees with operating results. At a minimum, franchisors have information regarding net sales by all of their franchised units and certainly they have complete accounting information from any company-owned units. Similarly, if they have any sophistication, they must have developed computer models for outlets in various geographic and retail environments.

The sad reality, however, is that franchisors are not required to share this information, and roughly only 55% do. The likelihood that any such requirement will be implemented within the next couple of years is slim, leaving the franchisee to his or her own devices.

"How Much Can I Make?" has located and published 77 of these Item 19 documents for your review. Nowhere else can a potential franchisee find such a wealth of financial information on the industry. Any serious prospective investor would be short-sighted not to fully exploit this extraordinary resource.

GENERAL DISCLOSURE BACKGROUND

In 1979, the Federal Trade Commission adopted the "FTC Rule," which regulates the franchising industry. Titled "Disclosure Requirements and Prohibitions Concerning Franchising and Business Opportunities Ventures," the rule requires all franchisors to prepare and distribute a disclosure document or offering circular according to a format prescribed by the FTC. The document must be delivered to a prospective franchisee at either the first personal meeting or at least 14 days prior to the signing of any contract or the payment of any consideration, whichever is earlier. In addition, 15 states have adopted their own disclosure laws, which are generally more demanding than the FTC's requirements. Chapter 1 provides more information about the requirements of both the FTC and the 15 "registration states."

FINANCIAL PERFORMANCE REPRESENTATIONS DEFINED

Financial performance representations are covered under Item 19 of both the FTC and the state Franchise Disclosure Document (FDD) requirements. As defined by the FTC Rule, a financial performance representation is "any oral, written, or visual representation to a prospective franchisee, including a representation disseminated in the general media and Internet, that states or suggests a specific level or range of potential or actual sales, income, gross profits, or net profits. A chart, table, or mathematical calculation that demonstrates possible results based upon a combination of variables is a financial performance representation."

In the broadest sense, financial performance representations are defined as estimates or historical figures detailing the level of sales, expenses, and/or income a prospective franchisee might realize as the owner of a particular franchise.

However, it is important to remember that neither the FTC nor the state regulatory agencies check financial performance representations for accuracy or completeness. The document is voluntary and unverified, and the information's format and level of detail are left completely to each company's discretion.

The only requirement for any Item 19 is that the franchisor has a "reasonable basis" for the financial performance representation at the time the statement is prepared. The franchisor is merely required to deliver the document to the franchisee before the franchise can be sold. Although federal and state agencies suggest that you should let them know if something is amiss, they often do not have the manpower or budget to pursue any but the most flagrant and obvious violations. For the most part, you are on your own. In the next chapter, we will show you how to put financial performance representations and other related resources to good use.

SETTING REALISTIC EXPECTATIONS

You can learn a great deal by reviewing financial performance representations. Identifying the sales and costs that would be relevant to your own business, as well as to your skills and your experience, is invaluable. Do not be swayed by the profit margin alone, as you should also consider the cost of sales, payrolls, operating expenses, and rent and occupancy. Furthermore, you should also note that the historical data used as the basis for the claims do not apply to every geographic region, individual location, or franchisee, whose experience and business acumen may vary.

There is no universal way to measure and report on those variables. If you are evaluating how variations in revenue and expenses could affect your bottom line, then you are putting financial performance representations to good use. At best, these documents help you set realistic expectations. But, in reality, the actual earnings of any franchise will vary from individual to individual. Does the actual net cash flow adequately reward you for the stress and strain of running your own business, putting in long hours, wearing 10 hats at a time, living with financial uncertainty, and giving up much of your discretionary time?

On the other side of the ledger are the advantages of business ownership: the pride and independence of running the show, the chance to start something from scratch and sell it 5–10 years later for a multiple of your original investment, and the opportunity to take full advantage of your management, sales, and people skills. Clearly there is a balance, but make sure that you have a strong sense of how realistic your expectations are and if they have a solid chance of being achieved.

Presuming that you are committed to maximizing your chances for success, you have a great deal of work ahead of you. It is important to review a wide range of financial performance representations, including ones outside the industry you are considering. A sampling of financial performance representations will acquaint you with basic accounting practices—how to calculate net income from gross sales, how to differentiate between fixed expenses (rent, equipment rental and utilities) and variable expenses (direct labor, shipping and percentage rent), and how to determine a break-even point. Devoting even a minimal amount of time and energy to this research will provide invaluable insights and serve you well when making an investment decision.

HOW CAN I RESEARCH A FRANCHISE?

In addition to the financial performance representations/ earnings claims statements in this book, there are a number of sources for information on franchisors and franchise offerings.

1. Franchise Disclosure Documents (FDDs)

Although FDDs are public documents, many companies consider the information contained within them proprietary; thus, they do not make them readily accessible to the public. If you contact franchisors directly to request copies of FDDs, chances are they will not respond to your request, or they may wait weeks before granting it. Alternatively, you may try to purchase FDDs from the state (if the company has registered in that state).

What Items Are in an FDD? Every FDD contains the following 23 items:

Item 1	The Franchisor, and any Parents, Predecessors, and Affiliates
Item 2	Business Experience
Item 3	Litigation
Item 4	Bankruptcy
Item 5	Initial Fees
Item 6	Other Fees
Item 7	Estimated Initial Investment
Item 8	Restrictions On Sources Of Products And Services
Item 9	Franchisee's Obligations
Item 10	Financing
Item 11	Franchisor's Assistance, Advertising, Computer Systems, and Training
Item 12	Territory
Item 13	Trademarks
Item 14	Patents, Copyrights, and Proprietary Information
Item 15	Obligation To Participate In The Actual Operation Of The Franchise Business
Item 16	Restrictions On What The Franchisee May Sell
Item 17	Renewal, Termination, Transfer And Dispute Resolution
Item 18	Public Figures
Item 19	Financial Performance Representations
Item 20	Outlets and Franchisee Information
Item 21	Financial Statements
Item 22	Contracts
Item 23	Receipts

The easiest and quickest way to obtain FDDs and historical UFOCs is to purchase them directly from third-party companies that sell them. Among the various websites that sell FDDs directly online, one of the most popular is www.1-800-FDD-UFOC.com. Offering over 20,000 FDDs and UFOCs for roughly 3,000 North American franchisors, www.1-800-FDD-UFOC.com is the most comprehensive and up-to-date database of current FDD filings, as well as historical UFOCs dating back to 1997. In addition, every effort is made to provide all available financial performance representations (Item 19s), in their entirety, to the public. As a result, over 500 financial performance representations are available on www.Item19s.com, either as pre-selected packages or as individual statements.

All FDDs and historical UFOCs are available in PDF format and are delivered via email. Current-year FDD orders are typically processed in less than two hours. Prior year or unique orders may take longer. Item 19s and Item 19 packages are immediately available for download.

Price: Entire FDD/UFOC – $220 per statement; Partial FDD/UFOC – $150 per statement; All FDD/UFOC Exhibits – $150; Item 19 – $40 per statement; Food-Service Industry Package (156 earnings claims) – $300; Lodging Industry Package (51 earnings claims) – $150; Retail Industry Package (43 earnings claims) – $150; Service-Based Industry Package (281 earnings claims) – $450; All Four Industry Packages (531 earnings claims) – $750. Website: 1-800-FDD-UFOC.com.

2. Current and Former Franchisees

Without doubt, the most meaningful information that you can obtain on a particular franchise comes from existing franchisees, who tend to be very candid about their level of satisfaction with the franchisor, but less candid about their sales, expenses, and income. Depending on how well you have done your homework and your ability to ask meaningful questions that show a solid understanding of the basic business and its underlying economics, other franchisees should be willing to respond to your questions about: the major cost elements of the cash flow statement, the biggest surprises they encountered when they started their business, whether to buy supplies from the franchisor or from a third-party supplier, potential lenders, negotiable points in the franchise agreement, and more. In reviewing finances, pay particular attention to the major expense items and see if there are any

expense categories that you may have left out. Spend some time at a franchised unit to get a feel for the day-to-day operations of the business.

The FDD should include a list of current franchisees, as well as franchisees who left the system within the last year. Past UFOCs list franchisees that may no longer be in the system. Do not call only the franchisees specifically recommended by the franchisor. Contact as many as you can until you feel comfortable that you are hearing a consensus. You should also talk with as many former franchisees as you can. It is up to you to separate the truth from the fiction as to why they left the system. Too many disenchanted former franchisees should be a strong warning to be exceedingly cautious in your investigation and analysis.

3. State Franchise Regulators

If you are in a state with franchise registration requirements (see the section on Regulatory Agencies in Chapter 1), the state franchise regulators can tell you whether a franchisor is in good standing. They may also be able to tell you whether there are any pending complaints against a franchisor. The North American Securities Administrators Association, Inc. website (www.nasaa.org) contains a directory of each state's franchise regulators.

You can contact state franchise regulators to request a copy of the financial performance representation from any franchisor registered to do business in the state. Unfortunately, most of these state agencies cannot accommodate your request unless you are physically at their offices. The best bet is to call to learn your options. Some states are more helpful than others in providing access to their library of disclosure documents.

4. SEC

If a franchise is a publicly traded company, it is required to file certain information with the U.S. Securities and Exchange Commission. These filings are available online at www.edgar.gov.

5. *Bond's Franchise Guide*

Bond's Franchise Guide provides detailed profiles of approximately 900 North American franchisors resulting from an exhaustive 45-point questionnaire. The book also provides detailed profiles on leading franchise attorneys, consultants, and service providers. The data represents the most up-to-date, comprehensive and reliable information about the franchising industry.

The franchisor profiles are divided into 29 distinct industry categories and include the following information:

• Background—number of operating units, geographic distribution, and detailed description of the business.

• Capital requirements—initial cash investment and total investment, ongoing royalty and advertising fees, staffing levels, space needs, etc.

• Initial training and start-up assistance provided, as well as ongoing services.

• Franchisee evaluation criteria.

• Specific areas of geographic expansion: U.S., Canada and International.

• And much more…

6. Business and Industry Publications

The next best source of information is provided by various publications that compile general operating statistics on industries broken down by Standard Industrial Classification (SIC) codes. Three of the best-known annual industry surveys are 1) the *RMA Annual Statement Studies*, published by Robert Morris Associates of Philadelphia, PA, 2) *Almanac of Business and Industrial Financial Ratios*, edited by Leo Troy and published by Prentice Hall and 3) *Industry Norms and Key Business Rations*, published by Dun & Bradstreet Information Services. Although none of these publications provide detailed expense data, each is extremely helpful in determining industry averages/norms and key financial ratios. Based on actual tax returns for the entire spectrum of business categories (manufacturing, wholesaling, agriculture, service, and retailing), the composite financial data reflect actual operating results for major SIC code industries.

7. Franchise Attorneys

Franchising is a highly specialized field, and you should hire legal experts with experience representing franchisees or franchisors. www.franchisingattorney.com has a searchable directory that provides 25 fields of information about each attorney listed. Visit www.findlegalhelp.org, a site sponsored by the American Bar Association, to learn about referral services and issues you should address when consulting with a lawyer. Another source for examining an attorney's credentials is www.martindale.com. The franchise associations below may also provide referrals to experienced franchise attorneys.

8. Franchise Consultants and Service Providers

If you are using a franchise consultant or service provider, they can likely assist you with your franchisor research. www.franchisingsuppliers.com includes listings of firms that provide goods and services to the franchising community. These goods and services are designed to help franchisors and franchisees alike, and include advertising, consulting, translation, and Internet services.

9. Your Local Library

Industry trade associations publish composite financial statistics, usually on an annual basis. Consult the Directory of Trade Associations at your local business library for the address of the relevant trade association(s). Be prepared to pay reasonable fees to obtain as much industry-specific information as possible. Keep in mind that these statistics are made up solely of like-minded businesses that have similar expenses and competitive pressures.

Most industries are covered by one or more research houses that sell studies pertaining to the future of that industry. These cover new technology, industry trends, competitive trends, financial projections for various sales levels, and more. Even if these studies are somewhat outdated, it may be worthwhile to gather as much data as possible about an industry rather than risk your life savings based on incomplete information.

YOUR OWN CASH FLOW PROJECTIONS

Armed with financial performance representations, industry operating statistics and the information gathered from conversations with existing and former franchisees, as well as input from trusted colleagues and consultants, you can now prepare your own financial projections. This exercise is the most critical step in the process of evaluating and selecting a franchise. Without a solid understanding of the financial aspects of the business, you may be throwing your time and money away. Investors who do not do their homework because they say they do not understand an income statement or they are not a "numbers person" may soon regret their lack of motivation.

A number of well-written books about preparing financial projections are available. Most are written for the layman who has little or no formal understanding of the process. (Some are even written by laymen with little or no formal understanding of the process themselves.) Purchase a few of these books and become proficient in the rudiments of accounting and finance. Remember, you are playing with your own money and livelihood. Do not put yourself in a position where you have to pay your accountant $100+ per hour every time you have a question. Learn the distinction between income statements and cash flow statements. Realize that you have an "opportunity cost" associated with your investment, and that you must receive an annual return on this investment, as well as the return of the investment itself, before a true net profit can be determined. Put a value on the psychic income earned by being your own boss. This is especially important when comparing your near-term hourly income with what you might earn working for someone else. Ask yourself if you would invest in the business if you were an investor rather than an owner/operator. Alternatively, would you loan money to the business if you were a banker?

If you do not know how to develop a pro forma cash flow model on a computer, have someone help you. Perform "what if" calculations to see what would happen under best- and worst-case scenarios. This represents the cheapest insurance you can buy to fully understand the dynamics of your new business. You will probably be sorely handicapped in the operation of your business unless you are "computerized." Learn the basics of operating a computer before you have made your investment. Your discretionary time is likely to be minimal during the start-up phase of your new business.

Although the process of generating realistic cash flow statements may seem daunting without any prior business management experience, it is easier than you think. With a little common sense, you can learn it quickly.

To provide a starting point for your own financial projections, plug some numbers into the following tables. These tables are by no means complete and do not attempt to represent all possible scenarios. Each industry will have its own unique investment requirements and related operating expenses.

Table 1 lists Total Investment Requirements. In the second column, you should place the appropriate expenses listed by the franchisor in Item 7 of the disclosure document. In the third column, you should place your own well-researched estimate of what that expense or service will cost in your market. The sum of these various expenses represents the non-recurring expenses you will incur when starting the business. Some of the expenses, such as land and improvements, may not be appropriate if you can lease your space at an acceptable market rate over the term of your investment. Consult your financial advisor about the appropriate figures to include if you lease rather than purchase various expense items.

Table 2 is a Pro Forma Cash Flow Statement. The objective of a pro forma is to project monthly and annual sales over the next five years and deduct the corresponding operating expenses. The result is the pre-tax operating cash flow. From this number, deduct the non-cash items—depreciation and amortization—to determine pre-tax income. Further additions and subtractions determine net cash flow before taxes. It is worthwhile to construct a computer model that includes all of the items that will impact your business.

Hopefully, when the time comes, you can negotiate an agreement with a franchisor that allows you to extend the contract for successive 5 – 15 year periods, presuming you have performed satisfactorily. Over the next 7 – 15 years, you may attempt to build your business to its maximum potential. At some point, you may want to retire or try something else. The market value of your business will be a function of how much cash flow the business generates. Based on the current earnings potential, the prospective buyer will most likely use one of two valuation models. The first, and more simplistic, involves multiplying the current cash flow by some multiple (say three to five times) to arrive at a purchase price. The more sophisticated buyer will develop a 5 – 10 year cash flow statement, put in his or her own liquidation value and discount the annual cash flows at a rate that properly reflects the inherent risk of achieving those cash flows. As an example, if your business generates a legitimate cash flow of $150,000 after 10 years, you should be able to sell the business for $450,000 – $750,000. If you have done well selecting and managing the franchise, the real payoff will most likely come when you sell the business.

RECOMMENDATIONS REGARDING MANDATORY FINANCIAL PERFORMANCE REPRESENTATIONS

Virtually everyone agrees that the information included in a financial performance representation can be exceedingly helpful to a potential franchisee. Unfortunately, there are many reasons why franchisors do not willingly make their actual results available to the public. Many franchisors feel that prospective investors will be turned off if they have access to actual operating results and prefer to let them draw their own conclusions.

Other franchisors are understandably afraid of being sued for "misrepresentation." When publishing financial performance representations, franchisors face a considerable risk that it will be interpreted as a "guarantee" of sales or income for new units. Given today's highly litigious society and the propensity of courts to award large settlements to the little guy, it is not surprising that few franchisors provide such information.

Notwithstanding the potential problems, franchisors should be required to provide prospective franchisees with some form of earnings projection. To the extent that they are able to substantiate their claims, franchisors should be protected from frivolous and potentially devastating lawsuits filed by failed franchisees. Everyone should realize that the historical data used as the basis for the claims do not apply to every geographic region, individual location, or franchisee. Clearly, there is no universal methodology that covers all the variables. All parties involved—the franchisors, the franchisees, the regulatory agencies and the legal system—should rely on common business sense.

As it now stands, a franchisor is liable if it misrepresents its financial performance representation or any other items in the disclosure document. Normally, one would interpret this to mean that someone goes to jail if it is proven that he or she intentionally misled the prospective investor. Unfortunately,

neither the FTC nor any registration state has the budget, manpower, or technical expertise to enforce such a punishment. Unless a violation is particularly flagrant, there is little chance that a franchisor will be severely penalized. Accordingly, you should not assume that anyone is going to protect or support you if you decide that you have been misled.

However, if there are mandatory requirements, there must be some corresponding penalties for fraudulent financial performance representations. Specifically, franchisees must have a "right of action" that would give regulatory bodies the budget and staff to aggressively police fraud and deception. And this funding should come from the registration fees paid by the franchisors themselves. Alternatively, a portion of the initial franchise fee paid by franchisees could also supplement the super agency's budget.

At some point, registration states and the FTC (or its successor) will find common ground upon which to merge their efforts and require the filing of a single disclosure document acceptable to all parties. This will go a long way toward reducing the expense, effort, and frustration built into the now largely redundant registration process. At that time, mandatory financial performance representations should be instituted along with general, common sense guidelines for their preparation, substantiation, and presentation. Equally important is a standard set of rules for documenting and penalizing fraud and deception.

	TABLE 1	
	FRONT-END INVESTMENT REQUIREMENTS	
	Franchisor's Item VII	Actual in Your Area
Initial Franchise Fee	$	$
Land & Improvements		
Leasehold Improvements		
Architectural/Engineering Fees		
Furniture & Fixtures		
Vehicles Purchased		
Initial Inventory		
Initial Signage		
Initial Advertising Commitment		
Initial Training Fees		
Travel/Lodging/Etc. for Initial Training		
Rent Deposits		
Utility Deposits		
Telephone Deposits		
Initial Insurance		
In-Store Graphics		
Yellow Page Advertising		
Initial Office Supplies		
Prepaid Sales Taxes		
Initial Business Permits/Fees		
Office Equipment:		
Computer Hardware		
Computer Software		
Computer Installation		
Computer Training		
Point-of-Sales Computer		
Answering Machine		
Fax Machine		
Postage Meter		
Telephone System (Including Installation)		
Copier		
Security System		
Initial Loan Fees		
Due Diligence Expenses		
Attorney Fees		
Accounting Fees		
Consultant Fees		
Book Purchases/Courses/Etc.		
Travel Expenses		
Telephone/Mailing Expenses		
Total Non-Recurring Expenses	$	$
Working Capital Requirements		
FRONT-END INVESTMENT REQUIREMENTS	$	$

TABLE 2						
PRO FORMA CASH FLOW STATEMENT						
	Month	Month	Month	Month	Month	Month
	1	2	3	4	…	12
Gross Sales	$	$	$	$	$	$
Less Returns and Allowances						
Net Sales						
Less Cost of Goods Sold						
Gross Profit						
Gross Profits As A % Of Sales	%	%	%	%	%	%
Operating Expenses:						
Payroll:						
Direct Labor						
Indirect Labor						
Employee Benefits						
Payroll Taxes						
Owner Salary & Benefits						
Rent & Common Area Maintenance						
Equipment Rental/Lease Payments						
Advertising Fund Payments To Franchisor						
Yellow Page & Local Advertising						
Insurance						
Utilities:						
Telephone/Fax						
Gas & Electric						
Water						
Janitorial Expense						
Trash Removal						
Security						
Travel & Lodging						
Meals & Entertainment						
Delivery Charges						
Printing Expense						
Postage						
Operating Supplies						
Office Supplies						
Vehicle Expense						
Equipment Maintenance						
Uniforms & Laundry						
Professional Fees:						
Accounting						
Legal						
Consulting						
Repairs & Maintenance						
Business Licenses/Fees/Permits						
Dues & Subscriptions						

Property Taxes						
Business Taxes						
Bad Debt/Theft						
Bank Charges & Credit Card Fees						
Royalties to Franchisor						
Interest Expense						
Total Operating Expenses						
Pre-Tax Operating Cash Flow	$	$	$	$	$	$
Operating Cash Flow As A & Of Sales	%	%	%	%	%	%

ADJUSTMENT TO PRE-TAX NET CASH FLOW						
Pre-Tax Operating Cash Flow	$	$	$	$	$	$
Less Depreciation/Amortization						
Pre-Tax Income						
Plus Depreciation/Amortization						
Less Principal Payments						
Less Capital Expenditures						
Pre-Tax Net Cash Flow	$	$	$	$	$	$

ADJUSTMENT TO "REAL" CASH FLOW						
Pre-Tax Net Cash Flow						
Less Return On Invested Capital @ x%						
Pre-Tax "Real" Cash Flow						

Required Item 19 Preamble

The Federal Trade Commission requires that Financial Performance Representations begin with the following paragraph. This paragraph has been removed from all individual statements in this book in order to avoid redundancy.

The FTC's Franchise Rule permits a franchisor to provide information about the actual or potential financial performance of its franchised and/or franchisor-operated outlets, if there is a reasonable basis for the information, and if the information is included in the disclosure document. Financial performance information that differs from that included in this Item 19 may be given only if: (1) a franchisor provides the actual records of an existing outlet you are considering buying; or (2) a franchisor supplements the information provided in this Item 19, for example, by providing information about possible performance at a particular location or under particular circumstances.

How to Use the Data | 3

This book contains 77 financial performance representations/ earnings claim statements that are categorized into food-service, retail, and service-based industries. The information at the beginning of each company's earnings data is the result of a 45-point questionnaire sent out annually to the franchising community. It is intended as a brief overview of the company; the text that follows provides a more in-depth analysis of the company's requirements and advantages.

In some cases, an answer has been abbreviated to conserve room and to facilitate the comparison of different companies. When no answer was provided to an item within the profile, "N/A" is used to signify "Not Available."

Please take a few minutes to acquaint yourself with the composition of the questionnaire data. Supplementary comments have been added where some interpretation of the franchisor's response is required.

More than fast. More than signs.®

FASTSIGNS

2542 Highlander Way
Carrollton, TX 75006
Tel: (800) 827-7446; (214) 346-5679
Fax: (866) 422-4927
Email: mark.jameson@fastsigns.com
Website: www.fastsigns.com
Mark L. Jameson, SVP Franchise Support & Development

Signage has never been more important. Right now, businesses are looking for new and better ways to compete. Industries are revamping to meet compliance standards. Advertisers are expanding their reach into new media, like digital signage, QR codes, and mobile websites. Join the franchise that's leading the next generation of business communication. Now more than ever, businesses look to FASTSIGNS® for innovative ways to connect with customers in a highly competitive marketplace. Our high standards for quality and customer service have made FASTSIGNS the most recognized brand in the industry, driving significantly more traffic to the Web than any other sign company. We also lead in these important areas:

#1 Sign Franchise in Entrepreneur magazine Franchise 500, 2011; Franchise Business Review Best in Category 2006-2010; World Class Franchisee Satisfaction Recognition, 2011 Franchise Research Institute; Franchisees' Choice Designation, 2011 Canadian Franchise Association. FASTSIGNS is one of only a handful of franchises approved for the Franchise America Finance Program, with 6 million dollars in financing for approved franchise owners.

BACKGROUND

IFA Member:	Yes
Established & First Franchised:	1985; 1986
Franchised Units:	529
Company-Owned Units:	0
Total Units:	529
Dist.:	US – 451; CAN – 22; O'seas – 56
North America:	45 States, 6 Provinces
Density:	58 in TX, 45 in CA, 35 in FL
Projected New Units (12 Months):	25
Qualifications:	5, 5, 1, 3, 4, 5

FINANCIAL/TERMS

Cash Investment:	$75K
Total Investment:	$176 – $292.5K
Minimum Net Worth:	$250K
Fees (Franchise):	$34.5K

Fees (Royalty):	6%	Site Selection Assistance:	Yes
Fees (Advertising):	2%	Lease Negotiation Assistance:	Yes
Term of Contract (Years):	20/10	Co-operative Advertising:	No
Avg. # of Employees:	2 – 3 FT, 0 PT	Franchisee Assoc./Member:	Yes/Member
Passive Ownership:	Allowed	Size of Corporate Staff:	100
Encourage Conversions:	Yes	On-going Support:	C, D, E, G, H, I
Area Develop. Agreements:	Yes	Training:	2 Weeks Dallas, TX; 1 Week On-Site
Sub-Franchising Contracts:	No		
Expand in Territory:	Yes		
Space Needs:	1,200 – 1,500 SF	**SPECIFIC EXPANSION PLANS**	
		US:	All United States
		Canada:	All Canada except Quebec
SUPPORT & TRAINING		Overseas:	Australia, New Zealand, UK
Financial Assistance Provided:	Yes (I)		

ADDRESS/CONTACT

1. **Company name, address, telephone and fax numbers**

Comment: All of the data published in the book was current at the time the completed questionnaire was received or upon subsequent verification by phone. Over the 12-month period between annual publications, 10 – 15% of the addresses and/or telephone numbers become obsolete for various reasons. If you are unable to contact a franchisor at the address/telephone number listed, please call Source Book Publications at (510) 839-5471 or fax us at (510) 839-2104 and we will provide you with the current address and telephone number.

2. **(800) 827-7446; (214) 346-5679.** In many cases, you may find that you cannot access the (800) number from your area. Do not conclude that the company has gone out of business. Simply call the local number.

Comment: An (800) number serves two important functions. The first is to provide an efficient, no-cost way for potential franchisees to contact the franchisor. Making the prospective franchisee foot the bill artificially limits the number of people who might otherwise make the initial contact. The second function is to demonstrate to existing franchisees that the franchisor is doing everything it can to efficiently respond to problems in the field as they occur. Many companies have a restricted (800) line for their franchisees that the general public cannot access. Since you will undoubtedly be talking with the franchisor's staff on a periodic basis, determine whether an (800) line is available to franchisees.

3. **Contact.** You should honor the wishes of the franchisor and address all initial correspondence to the contact listed. It would be counter-productive to try to reach the president directly if the designated contact is the director of franchising.

Comment: The president is the designated contact in approximately half of the company profiles in this book. The reason for this varies among franchisors. The president is the best spokesperson for his or her operation, and no doubt it flatters the franchisee to talk directly with the president, or perhaps there is no one else around. Regardless of the justification, it is important to determine if the operation is a one-man show in which the president does everything or if the president merely feels that having an open line to potential franchisees is the best way for him or her to sense the "pulse" of the company and the market. Convinced that the president can only do so many things well, I would want assurances that, by taking all incoming calls, he or she is not neglecting the day-to-day responsibilities of managing the business.

4. **Description of Business.** The questionnaire provides franchisors with adequate room to describe their franchise and to differentiate it from the competition. In a few cases, some editing by the authors was required.

Comment: In instances where franchisors show no initiative or imagination in describing their operations, you must decide whether this is symptomatic of the company or simply a reflection on the individual who responded to the questionnaire.

BACKGROUND

1. **IFA.** There are two primary affinity groups associated with the franchising industry—the International Franchise Association (IFA) and the Canadian Franchise Association (CFA). Both the IFA and the CFA are described in Chapter One.

2. **Established: 1985.** FASTSIGNS was founded in 1985, and, accordingly, has 28 years of experience in its primary business. It should be intuitively obvious that a firm that has been in existence for over 28 years has a greater likelihood of being around five years from now than a firm that was founded only last year.

3. **1st Franchised: 1986.** 1986 was the year that FASTSIGNS's first franchised unit(s) were established.

   Comment: Over ten years of continuous operation, both as an operator and as a franchisor, is compelling evidence that a firm has staying power. The number of years a franchisor has been in business is one of the key variables to consider in choosing a franchise. This is not to say that a new franchise should not receive your full attention. Every company has to start from scratch. Ultimately, a prospective franchisee has to be convinced that 1) the franchise has been in operation long enough, and 2) its key management personnel have adequate industry experience to have worked out the bugs normally associated with a new business. In most cases, this experience can only be gained through on-the-job training. Do not be the guinea pig that provides the franchisor with the experience it needs to develop a smoothly running operation.

4. **Franchised Units: 529.** As of 6/1/13, FASTSIGNS had 529 franchisee-owned and operated units.

5. **Company-Owned Units: 0.** As of 6/1/13, FASTSIGNS had no company-owned or operated units.

   Comment: A younger franchise should prove that its concept has worked successfully in several company-owned units before it markets its "system" to an inexperienced franchisee. Without company-owned prototype stores, the new franchisee may well end up being the "testing kitchen" for the franchise concept itself.

If a franchise concept is truly exceptional, why does the franchisor not commit some of its resources to taking advantage of the investment opportunity? Clearly, a financial decision on the part of the franchisor, the absence of company-owned units should not be a negative in and of itself. This is especially true of proven franchises, which may have previously sold their company-owned operations to franchisees.

Try to determine if there is a noticeable trend in the percentage of company-owned units. If the franchisor is buying back units from franchisees, it may be doing so to preclude litigation. Some firms also "churn" their operating units with some regularity. If the sales pitch is compelling, but the follow-through is not competitive, a franchisor may sell a unit to a new franchisee, wait for him or her to fail, buy it back for $0.60 cents on the dollar, and then sell that same unit to the next unsuspecting franchisee. Each time the unit is resold, the franchisor collects a franchise fee, plus the negotiated discount from the previous franchisee.

Alternatively, an increasing or high percentage of company-owned units may well mean the company is convinced of the long-term profitability of such an approach. The key is to determine whether a franchisor is building new units from scratch or buying them from failing and/or unhappy franchisees.

6. **Total Units: 529.** As of 6/1/13, FASTSIGNS had a total of 529 operating units.

   Comment: Like a franchisor's longevity, its experience in operating multiple units offers considerable comfort. Those franchisors with over 15 – 25 operating units have proven that their system works and have probably encountered and overcome most of the problems that plague a new operation. Alternatively, the management of franchises with less than 15 operating units may have gained considerable industry experience before joining the current franchise. It is up to the franchisor to convince you that it is providing you with as risk-free an operation as possible. You do not want to be providing a company with its basic experience in the business.

7. **Distribution: US – 451; CAN – 22; Overseas – 56.** As of 6/1/13, FASTSIGNS had 451 operating units in the U.S., 22 in Canada, and 56 Overseas.

8. **Distribution: North America: 45 States, 6 Provinces.** As of 6/1/13, FASTSIGNS had operations in 45 states and 6 Canadian provinces.

Comment: It should go without saying that the wider the geographic distribution, the greater the franchisor's level of success. For the most part, such distribution can only come from a large number of operating units. If, however, the franchisor has operations in 15 states, but only 18 total operating units, it is unlikely that it can efficiently service these accounts because of geographic constraints. Other things being equal, a prospective franchisee would vastly prefer a franchisor with 15 units in New York to one with 15 units scattered throughout the U.S., Canada, and overseas.

9. **Distribution: Density: TX, CA, FL.** The franchisor was asked "what three states/provinces have the largest number of operating units." As of 6/1/13, FASTSIGNS had the largest number of units in Texas, California, and Florida.

Comment: For smaller, regional franchises, geographic distribution could be a key variable in deciding whether to buy. If the franchisor has a concentration of units in your immediate geographic area, it is likely you will be well-served.

For those far removed geographically from the franchisor's current areas of operation, however, there can be problems. It is both time consuming and expensive to support a franchisee 2,000 miles away from company headquarters. To the extent that a franchisor can visit four franchisees in one area on one trip, there is no problem. If, however, your operation is the only one west of the Mississippi, you may not receive the on-site assistance you would like. Do not be a missionary who has to rely on his or her own devices to survive. Do not accept a franchisor's idle promises of support. If on-site assistance is important to your ultimate success, get assurances in writing that the necessary support will be forthcoming. Remember, you are buying into a system, and the availability of day-to-day support is one of the key ingredients of any successful franchise system.

10. **Projected New Units (12 Months): 25.** FASTSIGNS plans to establish 25 new units over the course of the next 12 months.

Comment: In business, growth has become a highly visible symbol of success. Rapid growth is generally perceived as preferable to slower, more controlled growth. I maintain, however, that the opposite is frequently the case. For a company of FASTSIGNS's size, adding 25 new units over a 12-month period is both reasonable and achievable. It is highly unlikely, however, that a new franchise with only five operating units can successfully attract, screen, train, and bring multiple new units on-stream in a 12-month period. If it suggests that it can, or even wants to, be properly wary. You must be confident a company has the financial and management resources necessary to pull off such a Herculean feat. If management is already thin, concentrating on attracting new units will clearly diminish the time it can and should spend supporting you. It takes many months, if not years, to develop and train a second level of management. You do not want to depend on new hires teaching you systems and procedures they themselves know little or nothing about.

11. **Qualifications: 5, 5, 1, 3, 4, 5.** This question was posed to determine which specific evaluation criteria were important to the franchisor. The franchisor was asked the following: "In qualifying a potential franchisee, please rank the following criteria from Unimportant (1) to Very Important (5)." The responses should be self-explanatory:

Financial Net Worth (Rank from 1–5)
General Business Experience (Rank from 1–5)
Specific Industry Experience (Rank from 1–5)
Formal Education (Rank from 1–5)
Psychological Profile (Rank from 1–5)
Personal Interview(s) (Rank from 1–5)

FINANCIAL/TERMS

12. **Cash Investment: $75K.** On average, a FASTSIGNS franchisee will have made a cash investment of $75,000 by the time he or she finally opens the initial operating unit.

Comment: It is important that you be realistic about the amount of cash you can comfortably invest in a business. Stretching beyond your means can have grave and far-reaching consequences. Assume that you will encounter periodic set-backs and that you will have to draw on your reserves. The demands of starting a new business are harsh enough without adding the uncertainties associated with inadequate working capital. Trust the franchisor's recommendations regarding the suggested minimum cash investment. If anything, there is an incentive for setting the recommended level of investment too low, rather than too high. The franchisor will want to qualify you to the extent that you have adequate financing. No legitimate franchisor wants you to invest if there is a chance that you might fail because of a shortage of funds.

Keep in mind that you will probably not achieve a positive cash flow until you've been in business for at least six months. In your discussions with the franchisor, be absolutely certain that the calculations include an adequate working capital reserve.

13. **Total Investment: $176 – $292.5K.** On average, FASTSIGNS franchisees will invest a total of $176,000 – $292,500, including both cash and debt, by the time the franchise opens its doors.

Comment: The total investment should be the cash investment noted above plus any debt that you will incur in starting up the new business. Debt could be a note to the franchisor for all or part of the franchise fee, an equipment lease, building and facilities leases, etc. Make sure that the total includes all of the obligations that you assume, especially any long-term lease obligations.

Be conservative in assessing what your real exposure is. If you are leasing highly specialized equipment or a single-purpose building, it is naive to think that you will recoup your investment if you have to sell or sub-lease those assets in a buyer's market. If there is any specialized equipment that may have been manufactured to the franchisor's specifications, determine if the franchisor has any form of buy-back provision.

14. **Minimum Net Worth: $250K.** In this case, FASTSIGNS feels that a potential franchisee should have a minimum net worth of $250,000. Although net worth can be defined in vastly different ways, the franchisor's response should suggest a minimum level of equity that the prospective franchisee should possess. Net worth is the combination of both liquid and illiquid assets. Again, do not think that franchisor-determined guidelines somehow do not apply to you.

15. **Fees (Franchise): $34.5K.** FASTSIGNS requires a front-end, one-time-only payment of $34,500 to grant a franchise for a single location. As noted in Chapter 1, the franchise fee is a payment to reimburse the franchisor for the incurred costs of setting the franchisee up in business—from recruiting through training and manuals. The fee usually ranges from $15,000 – $30,000. It is a function of competitive franchise fees and the actual out-of-pocket costs incurred by the franchisor.

Depending on the franchisee's particular circumstances and how well the franchisor thinks he or she might fit into the system, the franchisor may finance all or part of the franchise fee. (See Section 32 below to see if a franchisor provides any direct or indirect financial assistance.)

The franchise fee is one area in which the franchisor frequently provides either direct or indirect financial support.

Comment: Ideally, the franchisor should do no more than recover its costs on the initial franchise fee. Profits come later in the form of royalty fees, which are a function of the franchisee's sales. Whether the franchise fee is $5,000 or $35,000, the total should be carefully evaluated. What are competitive fees and are they financed? How much training will you actually receive? Are the fees reflective of the franchisor's expenses? If the fees appear to be non-competitive, address your concerns with the franchisor.

Realize that a $5,000 differential in the one-time franchise fee is a secondary consideration in the overall scheme of things. You are in the relationship for the long-term.

By the same token, do not get suckered in by an extremely low fee if there is any doubt about the franchisor's ability to follow through. Franchisors need to collect reasonable fees to cover their actual costs. If they do not recoup these costs, they cannot recruit and train new franchisees on whom your own future success partially depends.

16. **Fees (Royalty): 6%.** Here, six percent of gross sales (or other measure, as defined in the franchise agreement) must be periodically paid directly to the franchisor in the form of royalties. This ongoing expense is your cost for being part of the larger franchise system and for all of the "back-office" support you receive. In a few cases, the amount of the royalty fee is fixed rather than variable. In others, the fee decreases as the volume of sales (or other measure) increases (i.e., 8% on the first $200,000 of sales, 7% on the next $100,000 and so on). In others, the fee is held at artificially low levels during the start-up phase of the franchisee's business, then increases

once the franchisee is better able to afford it.

Comment: Royalty fees represent the mechanism by which the franchisor finally recoups the costs it has incurred in developing its business. It may take many years and many operating units before the franchisor is able to make a true operating profit.

Consider a typical franchisor who has been in business for three years. With a staff of five, assume it has annual operating costs of $300,000 (including rent, travel, operating expenses, and reasonable owner's salaries). Assume also that there are 25 franchised units with average annual sales of $250,000. Each franchise is required to pay a 6% royalty fee. Total annual royalties under this scenario would total only $375,000. The franchisor is making a $75,000 profit. Then consider the personal risk the franchisor took in developing a new business and the initial years of negative cash flows. Alternatively, evaluate what it would cost you, as a sole proprietor, to provide the myriad services included in the royalty payment.

In assessing various alternative investments, the amount of the royalty percentage is a major ongoing expense. Assuming average annual sales of $250,000 per annum over a 15 year period, the total royalties at 5% would be $187,500. At 6%, the cumulative fees would be $225,000. You have to be fully convinced that the $37,500 differential is justified. While this is clearly a meaningful number, what you are really evaluating is the quality of management and the competitive advantages of the goods and/or services offered by the franchisor.

17. **Fees (Advertising): 2%.** Most national or regional franchisors require their franchisees to contribute a certain percentage of their sales (or other measure, as determined in the franchise agreement) into a corporate advertising fund. These individual advertising fees are pooled to develop a corporate advertising/marketing effort that produces great economies of scale. The end result is a national or regional advertising program that promotes the franchisor's products and services. Depending on the nature of the business, this percentage usually ranges from 2 – 6% and is in addition to the royalty fee.

Comment: One of the greatest advantages of a franchised system is its ability to promote, on a national or regional basis, its products and services. The promotions may be through television, radio, print medias or direct mail. The objective

its name recognition and, over time, the assumption that the product and/or service has been "time-tested." An individual business owner could never justify the expense of mounting a major advertising program at the local level. For a smaller franchise that may not yet have an advertising program or fee, it is important to know when an advertising program will start, how it will be monitored, and its expected cost.

18. **Term of Contract (Years): 20/10.** FASTSIGNS's initial franchise period runs for twenty years. The first renewal period runs for an additional ten years. Assuming that the franchisee operates within the terms of the franchise agreement, he or she has thirty years within which to develop and, ultimately, sell the business.

Comment: The potential (discounted) value of any business (or investment) is the sum of the operating income that is generated each year plus its value upon liquidation. Given this truth, the length of the franchise agreement and any renewals are extremely important to the franchisee. It is essential that he or she has adequate time to develop the business to its full potential. At that time, he or she will have maximized the value of the business as an ongoing concern. The value of the business to a potential buyer, however, is largely a function of how long the franchise agreement runs. If there are only two years remaining before the agreement expires, or if the terms of the extension(s) are vague, the business will be worth only a fraction of the value assigned to a business with 15 years to go. For the most part, the longer the agreement and the subsequent extension, the better. (The same logic applies to a lease. If your sales are largely a function of your location and traffic count, then it is important that you have options to extend the lease under known terms. Your lease should never be longer than the remaining term of your franchise agreement, however.)

Assuming the length of the agreement is acceptable, be clear under what circumstances renewals might not be granted. Similarly, know the circumstances under which a franchise agreement might be prematurely and unilaterally canceled by the franchisor. I strongly recommend you have an experienced lawyer review this section of the franchise agreement. It would be devastating if, after spending years developing your business, there were a loophole in the contract that allowed the franchisor to arbitrarily cancel the relationship.

19. **Average Number of Employees: 2 – 3 FT.** The questionnaire asked, "Including the owner/operator, how many employees are recommended to properly staff the average franchised unit?" In FASTSIGNS's case, two to three full-time employees are required.

Comment: Most entrepreneurs start a new business based on their intuitive feel that it will be "fun" and that their talents and experience will be put to good use. They will be doing what they enjoy and what they are good at. Times change. Your business prospers. The number of employees increases. You are spending an increasing percentage of your time taking care of personnel problems and less and less on the fun parts of the business. In Chapter 1, the importance of conducting a realistic self-appraisal was stressed. If you found that you really are not good at managing people, or you do not have the patience to manage a large minimum wage staff, cut your losses before you are locked into doing just that.

20. **Passive Ownership: Allowed.** Depending on the nature of the business, many franchisors are indifferent as to whether you manage the business directly or hire a full-time manager. Others are insistent that, at least for the initial franchise, the franchisee be a full-time owner/operator. FASTSIGNS allows franchisees to hire full-time managers to run their outlets.

Comment: Unless you have a great deal of experience in the business you have chosen or in managing similar businesses, I feel strongly that you should initially commit your personal time and energies to make the system work. After you have developed a full understanding of the business and have competent, trusted staff members who can assume day-to-day operations, consider delegating these responsibilities. Running the business through a manager can be fraught with peril unless you have mastered all aspects of the business and there are strong economic incentives and sufficient safeguards to ensure the manager will perform as desired.

21. **Conversions Encouraged: Yes.** This section pertains primarily to sole proprietorships or "mom and pop" operations. To the extent that there truly are centralized operating savings associated with the franchise, the most logical people to join a franchise system are sole practitioners who are working hard but only eking out a living. The implementation of proven systems and marketing clout could significantly reduce operating costs and increase profits.

Comment: The franchisor has the option of 1) actively encouraging such independent operators to become members of the franchise team, 2) seeking out franchisees with limited or no applied experience, or 3) going after both groups. Concerned that it may be very difficult to break independent operators of the bad habits they have picked up over the years, many franchisors choose the second option, thinking, "They will continue to do things their way. They won't, or can't, accept corporate direction." Other franchisors are simply selective in the conversions they allow. In many cases, the franchise fee is reduced or eliminated for conversions.

22. **Area Development Agreements: Yes.** This means that FAST-SIGNS offers an area development agreement, in this case, for two years. Area development agreements are more fully described in Chapter 1. Essentially, area development agreements allow an investor or investment group to develop an entire area or region. The schedule for development is clearly spelled out in the area development agreement.

Comment: Area development agreements represent an opportunity for the franchisor to choose a single franchisee or investment group to develop an entire area. The franchisee's qualifications should be strong and include proven business experience and the financial depth to pull it off. An area development agreement represents a great opportunity for an investor to tie up a large geographical area and develop a concept that may not have proven itself on a national basis. Keep in mind that this is a quantum leap from making an investment in a single franchise and is relevant only to those with development experience and deep pockets.

23. **Sub-Franchising Contracts: No.** FASTSIGNS does not grant sub-franchising agreements. (See Chapter One for a more thorough explanation.) Like area development agreements, sub-franchising allows an investor or investment group to develop an entire area or region. The difference is that the sub-franchisor becomes a self-contained business, responsible for all relations with franchisees within its area, from initial training to ongoing support. Franchisees pay their royalties to the sub-franchisor, who in turn pays a portion to the master franchisor.

Comment: Sub-franchising is used primarily by smaller franchisors who have a relatively easy concept and who are prepared to sell a portion of the future growth of their business to someone for some front-end cash and a percentage of the future royalties they receive from their franchisees.

24.**Expand in Territory: Yes.** Under conditions spelled out in the franchise agreement, FASTSIGNS will allow its franchisees to expand within their exclusive territory.

Comment: Some franchisors define the franchisee's exclusive territory so tightly that there would never be room to open additional outlets within an area. Others provide a larger area in the hopes that the franchisee will do well and have the incentive to open additional units. There are clearly economic benefits to both parties from having franchisees with multiple units. There is no question that it is in your best interest to have the option to expand once you have proven to both yourself and the franchisor that you can manage the business successfully. Many would concur that the real profits in franchising come from managing multiple units rather than being locked into a single franchise in a single location. Additional fees may or may not be required with these additional units.

25.**Space Needs: 1,200 – 1,500 SF.** The average FASTSIGNS retail outlet will require 1,200 – 1,500 square feet. Types of leased space might be a Storefront (SF), Strip Center (SC), a Free-Standing (FS) building, Convenience Store (C-store) location, Executive Suite (ES), Home-Based (HB), Industrial Park (IP), Kiosk (KI), Office Building (OB), Power Center (PC), Regional Mall (RM), or Warehouse (WH).

Comment: Armed with the rough space requirements, you can better project your annual occupancy costs. It should be relatively easy to get comparable rental rates for the type of space required. As annual rent and related expenses can be as high as 15% of your annual sales, be as accurate as possible in your projections.

SUPPORT & TRAINING

26.**Financial Assistance Provided: Yes (I)** indicates that FAST-SIGNS provides indirect financial assistance. Indirect (I) assistance might include making introductions to the franchisor's financial contacts, providing financial templates for preparing a business plan or actually assisting in the loan application process. In some cases, the franchisor becomes a co-signer on a financial obligation (such as equipment or space lease). Other franchisors are directly (D) involved in the process. In this case, the assistance may include a lease or loan made directly by the franchisor. Any loan would generally be secured by some form of collateral. A very common form of assistance is a note for all or part of the initial franchise fee. The level of assistance will generally depend on the relative strengths of the franchisee.

Comment: The best of all possible worlds is one in which the franchisor has enough confidence in the business and in you to co-sign notes on the building and equipment leases and allow you to pay off the franchise fee over a specified period of time. Depending on your qualifications, this could happen. Most likely, however, the franchisor will only give you some assistance in raising the necessary capital to start the business. Increasingly, franchisors are testing a franchisee's business acumen by letting him or her assume an increasing level of personal responsibility in securing financing. The objective is to find out early in the process how competent a franchisee really is.

27.**Site Selection Assistance: Yes.** This means that FASTSIGNS will assist the franchisee in selecting a site location. While the phrase "location, location, location" may be hackneyed, its importance should not be discounted, especially when a business depends on retail traffic counts and accessibility. If a business is home- or warehouse-based, assistance in this area is of negligible or minor importance.

Comment: Since you will be locked into a lease for a minimum of three, though probably five, years, optimal site selection is absolutely essential. Even if you were somehow able to sub-lease and extricate yourself from a bad lease or bad location, the franchise agreement may not allow you to move to another location. Accordingly, it is imperative that you get it right the first time.

If a franchisor is truly interested in your success, it should treat your choice of a site with the same care it would use in choosing a company-owned site. Keep in mind that many firms provide excellent demographic data on existing locations at a very reasonable cost.

28. **Lease Negotiations Assistance: Yes.** Once a site is selected, FASTSIGNS will be actively involved in negotiating the terms of the lease.

    Comment: Given the complexity of negotiating a lease, an increasing number of franchisors are taking an active role in lease negotiations. There are far too many trade-offs that must be considered—terms, percentage rents, tenant improvements, pass-throughs, kick-out clauses, etc. This responsibility is best left to the professionals. If the franchisor doesn't have the capacity to support you directly, enlist the help of a well-recommended broker. The penalties for signing a bad long-term lease are very severe.

29. **Co-operative Advertising: No.** This refers to the existence of a joint advertising program in which the franchisor and franchisees each contribute to promote the company's products and/or services (usually within the franchisee's specific territory).

    Comment: Co-op advertising is a common and mutually-beneficial effort. By agreeing to split part of the advertising costs, whether for television, radio, or direct mail, the franchisor is not only supporting the franchisee, but guaranteeing itself royalties from the incremental sales. A franchisor that is not intimately involved with the advertising campaign—particularly when it is an important part of the business—may not be fully committed to your overall success.

30. **Franchisee Association/Member: Yes, Member.** This response notes that the FASTSIGNS system includes an active association made up of FASTSIGNS franchisees and that, consequently, the franchisor is a member of such franchisee association.

    Comment: The empowerment of franchisees has become a major rallying cry within the industry over the past four years. Various states have recently passed laws favoring franchisee rights, and the subject has been widely discussed in congressional staff hearings. There are even political groups that represent franchisee rights on a national basis. Similarly, the IFA is now actively courting franchisees to become active members. Whether they are equal members remains to be seen.

Franchisees have also significantly increased their clout with respect with the franchisor. If a franchise is to grow and be successful in the long term, it is critical that the franchisor and its franchisees mutually agree they are partners rather than adversaries.

31. **Size of Corporate Staff: 100.** FASTSIGNS has 100 full-time employees on its staff to support its 529 operating units.

    Comment: There are no magic ratios that tell you whether the franchisor has enough staff to provide the proper level of support. It would appear, however, that FASTSIGNS' staff of 100 is adequate to support 529 operating units. Less clear is whether a staff of three, including the company president and his wife, can adequately support 15 fledgling franchisees in the field.

    Many younger franchises may be managed by a skeleton staff, assisted by outside consultants who perform various management functions during the start-up phase. From the perspective of the franchisee, it is essential that the franchisor have actual in-house franchising experience, and that the franchisee not be forced to rely on outside consultants to make the system work. Whereas a full-time, salaried employee will probably have the franchisee's objectives in mind, an outside consultant may not have the same priorities. Franchising is a unique form of business that requires specific skills and experience—skills and experience that are markedly different from those required to manage a non-franchised business. If you are thinking about establishing a long-term relationship with a firm that is just starting out in franchising, you should insist that the franchisor prove it has an experienced, professional team on board and in place to provide the necessary levels of support to all concerned.

32. **Ongoing Support:** C, D, E, G, H, I. Like initial training, the ongoing support services provided by the franchisor are of paramount importance. Having a solid and responsive team behind you can certainly make your life much easier and allow you to concentrate your energies on other areas. As is noted below, the franchisors were asked to indicate their support for nine separate ongoing services:

Service Provided	Included in Fees	At Add'l. Cost	N/A
Central Data Processing	A	a	N/A
Central Purchasing	B	b	N/A
Field Operations Evaluation	C	c	N/A
Field Training	D	d	N/A
Initial Store Opening	E	e	N/A
Inventory Control	F	f	N/A
Franchisee Newsletter	G	g	N/A
Regional or National Meetings	H	h	N/A
800 Telephone Hotline	I	i	N/A

If the franchisor provides the service at no additional cost to the franchisee (as indicated by letters A–I), a capital letter was used to indicate this. If the service is provided, but only at an additional cost, a lower case letter was used. If the franchisor responded with a N/A, or failed to note an answer for a particular service, the corresponding letter was omitted from the data sheet.

33. Training: 2 Weeks Dallas, TX; 1 Week On-Site.

Comment: Assuming that the underlying business concept is sound and competitive, adequate training and ongoing support are among the most important determinants of your success as a franchisee. The initial training should be as lengthy and as "hands-on" as necessary to allow the franchisee to operate alone and with confidence. Obviously, every potential situation cannot be covered in any training program. But the franchisee should come away with a basic understanding of how the business operates and where to go to resolve problems when they come up. Depending on the business, there should be operating manuals, procedural manuals, company policies, training videos, (800) help-lines, etc. It may be

helpful at the outset to establish how satisfied recent franchisees are with a company's training. It is also good to have a clear understanding about how often the company updates its manuals and training programs, the cost of sending additional employees through training, etc.

Remember, you are part of an organization that you are paying (in the form of a franchise fee and ongoing royalties) to support you. Training is the first step. Ongoing support is the second step.

SPECIFIC EXPANSION PLANS

34. **U.S.: All United States.** FASTSIGNS is currently focusing its growth on the entire United States. Alternatively, the franchisor could have listed particular states or regions into which it wished to expand.

35. **Canada: All Canada Except Quebec.** FASTSIGNS is currently seeking additional franchisees in all Canadian provinces except for Quebec. Specific markets or provinces could have also been indicated.

36. **Overseas: UK, Australia, New Zealand.** FASTSIGNS is currently expanding overseas with a focus on the United Kingdom, Australia, and New Zealand.

Comment: You will note that many smaller companies with less than 15 operating units suggest that they will concurrently expand throughout the U.S., Canada, and internationally. In many cases, these are the same companies that foresee a 50%+ growth rate in operating units over the next 12 months. The chances of this happening are negligible. As a prospective franchisee, you should be wary of any company that thinks it can expand throughout the world without a solid base of experience, staff, and financial resources. Even if adequate financing is available, the demands on existing management will be extreme. New management cannot adequately fill the void until they are able to fully understand the system and absorb the corporate culture. If management's end objective is expansion for its own sake rather than by design, the existing franchisees will suffer.

Note: The statistics noted in the profiles preceding each company's analysis are the result of data provided by the franchisors themselves by way of a detailed questionnaire. Similarly, the data in the summary comparisons in the Introduction Chapter were taken from the company profile data. The figures used throughout each company's analysis, however, were generally taken from the FDDs. In many cases, the FDDs, which are only printed annually, contain information that is somewhat out of date. This is especially true with regard to the number of operating units and the current level of investment. A visit to our website at worldfranchising.com should provide current data.

If you have not already done so, please invest some modest time to read Chapter 1: 30-Minute Overview.

The Franchise Bookstore
Order Form

Call (888) 612-9908 or (510) 839-5471; Fax (510) 839-2104; or email info@worldfranchising.com

Item #	Title	Price	Qty.	Total

Basic postage (1 Book)	$8.50
Each additional book add $4.00	
California tax (if CA resident)	
Total due in U.S. dollars	
Deduct 15% if total due is over $100.00	
Net amount due in U.S. dollars	

Please include credit card number and expiration date for all charge card orders. Checks should be made payable to Source Book Publications. All prices are in U.S. dollars.

□ Check enclosed
□ Charge my American Express
□ Charge my MasterCard
□ Charge my VISA

Mailing Information: All books are shipped by USPS Priority Mail (2nd Day Air). Please print clearly and include your phone number in case we need to contact you. Postage and handling rates are for shipping within the U.S. Please call for international rates.

Card #: _____

Expiration Date: _____

Signature: _____

Security Code: _____

Name: _____

Company: _____

Address: _____

City: _____

Title: _____

Telephone No.: (   ) _____

State/Prov.: _____

Zip: _____

Special Offer — Save 15%

If your total order exceeds $100.00,
deduct 15% from your bill.

Please send order to:
Source Book Publications
1814 Franklin St., Ste. 603, Oakland, CA 94612
Satisfaction Guaranteed. If not fully satisfied, return for a prompt, 100% refund.

Food-Service Franchises | 4

APPLEBEE'S

11201 Renner Blvd.
Lenexa, KS 66219
Tel: (888) 59-APPLE, (913) 890-0100
Fax: (913) 967-4135
Email: becky.johnson@applebees.com
Website: www.applebees.com
Becky Johnson, SVP Marketing

Everyone's favorite neighbor is definitely APPLEBEE'S Neighborhood Grill & Bar. This distinguished casual-dining restaurant has a comfortable individuality that reflects the neighborhood in which it is located, making the APPLEBEE'S concept appealing wherever it is built.

BACKGROUND
IFA Member:	Yes
Established & First Franchised:	1980; 1993
Franchised Units:	906
Company-Owned Units:	262
Total Units:	1,168
Distribution:	US – 1,155; CAN – 5; O'seas – 8
North America:	47 States, 3 Provinces
Density:	62 in FL, 54 in CA, 48 in OH
Projected New Units (12 Months):	125

Qualifications:	5, 5, 5, N/A, N/A, 5

FINANCIAL/TERMS
Cash Investment:	$1MM – 50% Liq.
Total Investment:	$1.7 – $3.1MM
Minimum Net Worth:	N/A
Fees (Franchise):	$35K/Unit
Fees (Royalty):	4%
Fees (Advertising):	3%
Term of Contract (Years):	20
Average Number of Employees:	75 – 100 FT
Passive Ownership:	Not Allowed
Encourage Conversions:	No
Area Development Agreements:	Yes
Sub-Franchising Contracts:	No
Expand in Territory:	Yes
Space Needs:	5,000 – 5,400 SF

SUPPORT & TRAINING
Financial Assistance Provided:	No
Site Selection Assistance:	Yes
Lease Negotiation Assistance:	Yes
Co-operative Advertising:	No
Franchisee Association/Member:	Yes/Member
Size of Corporate Staff:	300
On-going Support:	A, B, C, D, E, G, H, I
Training:	8-12 Weeks Certified Training Unit; 3 Days Headquaters

SPECIFIC EXPANSION PLANS
US:	AK, HI, LA, NY
Canada:	All Canada
Overseas:	All Countries

The average weekly domestic franchise unit sales for the 52 weeks ending December 31, 2011, was $46,084. Some Restaurants have achieved this sales level. There is no assurance that you will do as well. If you rely upon our figures, you must accept the risk of not doing as well.

Bases.

This sales figure was derived from the sales at all 1,674 franchise Restaurants operating in the United States for 52 weeks during 2011. Of those 1,674 franchise units, 729 attained at

34

least that stated average, which is 43.5% of all domestic franchise Restaurants.

Information that forms the basis for this representation is available to you on reasonable request.

If you are purchasing an existing outiet, we may provide you with the actual records of that outlet.

The financial results of your Restaurant may be directly affected by many factors, such as the Restaurant's size; geographic location; weather; the effectiveness of your regional and local marketing efforts; the level of existing brand awareness and acceptance in the market; the presence of other competing restaurants; and the quality of management and service at your Restaurant. Your individual financial results may vary substantial from the results stated in this financial performance representation.

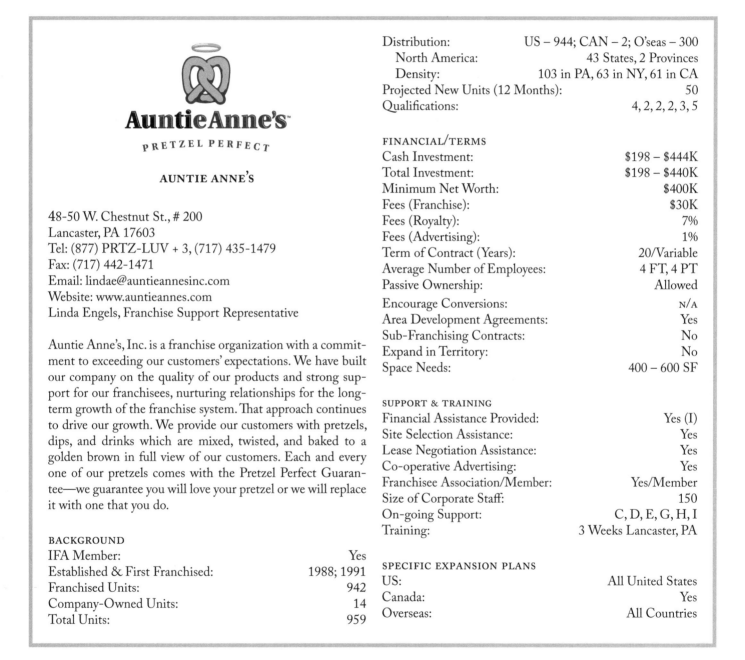

AUNTIE ANNE'S

48-50 W. Chestnut St., # 200
Lancaster, PA 17603
Tel: (877) PRTZ-LUV + 3, (717) 435-1479
Fax: (717) 442-1471
Email: lindae@auntieannesinc.com
Website: www.auntieannes.com
Linda Engels, Franchise Support Representative

Auntie Anne's, Inc. is a franchise organization with a commitment to exceeding our customers' expectations. We have built our company on the quality of our products and strong support for our franchisees, nurturing relationships for the long-term growth of the franchise system. That approach continues to drive our growth. We provide our customers with pretzels, dips, and drinks which are mixed, twisted, and baked to a golden brown in full view of our customers. Each and every one of our pretzels comes with the Pretzel Perfect Guarantee—we guarantee you will love your pretzel or we will replace it with one that you do.

BACKGROUND

IFA Member:	Yes
Established & First Franchised:	1988; 1991
Franchised Units:	942
Company-Owned Units:	14
Total Units:	959

Distribution:	US – 944; CAN – 2; O'seas – 300
North America:	43 States, 2 Provinces
Density:	103 in PA, 63 in NY, 61 in CA
Projected New Units (12 Months):	50
Qualifications:	4, 2, 2, 2, 3, 5

FINANCIAL/TERMS

Cash Investment:	$198 – $444K
Total Investment:	$198 – $440K
Minimum Net Worth:	$400K
Fees (Franchise):	$30K
Fees (Royalty):	7%
Fees (Advertising):	1%
Term of Contract (Years):	20/Variable
Average Number of Employees:	4 FT, 4 PT
Passive Ownership:	Allowed
Encourage Conversions:	N/A
Area Development Agreements:	Yes
Sub-Franchising Contracts:	No
Expand in Territory:	No
Space Needs:	400 – 600 SF

SUPPORT & TRAINING

Financial Assistance Provided:	Yes (I)
Site Selection Assistance:	Yes
Lease Negotiation Assistance:	Yes
Co-operative Advertising:	Yes
Franchisee Association/Member:	Yes/Member
Size of Corporate Staff:	150
On-going Support:	C, D, E, G, H, I
Training:	3 Weeks Lancaster, PA

SPECIFIC EXPANSION PLANS

US:	All United States
Canada:	Yes
Overseas:	All Countries

Tables 1 through 8 present net sales or average net sales, average expenses and average net operating income figures for the fiscal year ended December 31, 2010 for a majority of Auntie Anne's franchises that operated under the same ownership for the entire fiscal year, obtained from the unaudited profit and loss statements submitted by Auntie Anne's franchisees. All of the Auntie Anne's franchisees report financial information based upon a uniform reporting system. The Notes which follow each table apply to that table and should be read in conjunction with the information contained in the table.

As used throughout the following Tables 1- 8, the following definitions apply:

Net Sales - Net Sales includes the total of all sales of food products, beverages and other merchandise and products to your customers. Net Sales does not include sales taxes, use taxes or service taxes collected and paid to taxing authorities and customer refunds and sales discounts.

Cost of Goods Sold - Cost of Goods Sold (sometimes referred to as COGS) is a figure which reflects the cost of materials used to produce the products you sell to your customers. It includes the cost of food ingredients (pretzel mix, butter, beverages, etc.), paper products (cups, napkins, bags, straws, etc.) and retail items (Auntie Anne's At Horne® pretzel kits, etc.).

Gross Profit - Gross profit is Net Sales minus Cost of Goods Sold.

Operating Expenses - Operating expenses are the day-to-day costs incurred in conducting normal business operations.

Labor - Labor includes wages paid to your employees; payroll taxes paid for your employees; and actual wages and related expenses you pay to yourself.

Rent - Rent includes the base rent for your lease including extra charges, such as common area maintenance (CAM) charges, real estate taxes, percentage rents, etc.

Other Expenses - Other expenses include such things as utilities (electric, telephone), royalties, ad fund fees, advertising, insurance (Workers' Comp, property, casualty, liability, health, etc.), licenses, permits, repairs, uniforms, store supplies, etc.

Total Expenses - The total of Labor, Rent and Other Expenses

Net Operating Income - Gross Profit minus Total Expenses

Auntie Anne's includes the following Regions, and their respective states, in the information presented in Tables 1- 9:

a. Mid-Atlantic Region: (i) West Virginia; (ii) District of Columbia; (iii) Virginia; (iv) Maryland; (v) Pennsylvania; and (vi) Delaware.

b. Northeast Region: (i) New York; (ii) Connecticut; (iii) New Hampshire; (iv) Massachusetts; (v) New Jersey; (vi) Vermont; and (vii) Rhode Island.

c. Southeast Region: (i) North Carolina; (ii) Georgia; (iii) Alabama; (iv) Arkansas; (v) Tennessee; (vi) Florida; (vii) South Carolina; (viii) Louisiana; and (ix) Mississippi.

d. Midwest Region: (i) Kansas; (ii) North Dakota; (iii) Iowa; (iv) Kentucky; (v) Michigan; (vi) Illinois; (vii) Indiana; (viii) Missouri; (ix) Missouri; (x) Nebraska; (xi) Ohio; (xii) Minnesota; (xiii) Wisconsin; and (xiv) South Dakota

e. Western Region: (i) Nevada; (ii) Oregon; (iii) Texas; (iv) Oklahoma; (v) California; (vi) Washington; (vii) New Mexico; (viii) Colorado; and (ix) Arizona.

Table 1
Net Sales Range 2010 Fiscal Year — Various Venues
ALL REGIONS

2010	Enclosed Malls	Airports	Outlet Centers	Walmarts	Alternative Locations	Train Stations
Sample Size	474	25	29	26	25	6
High Sales	$2,491,813	$2,027,545	$952,456	$473,478	$615,297	$ 1,050,456
Low Sales	$59,840	$197,286	$102,542	$34,210	$101,609	$363,401
Average Sales	$516,409	$849.944	$496,407	$238,572	$267,028	$766,221
% of Stores at or Above Average	40.93%	36.00%	41.38%	46.15%	44.00%	50.00%
# of Stores at or Above Average	194	9	12	12	11	3

Median Sales	$467,348	$700,193	$471,064	$234,143	$237,427	$818,896
# of Stores at or Above Median	237	13	15	13	13	3
Total Number	526	30	32	28	34	6
Percent Included in Sample	90.11%	83.33%	90.63%	92.86%	73.53%	100.00%

Approximately 50% of Auntie Anne's franchises are located in enclosed malls. THE FOLLOWING TABLES RELATE ONLY TO AUNTIE ANNE'S FRANCHISES OPERATED IN ENCLOSED MALLS and do not include franchises operated in airports, outlet centers, Walmarts, alternative locations, train stations, casinos, concession trailers, farmer's markets, seasonal locations, strip malls and colleges and universities.

Table 2
Net Sales of Franchises In Operation For All 12 Months Of 2010
By Sales Range - Systemwide - Enclosed Malls
ALL REGIONS

Sales Range	Low	High	Number of Franchises
1	$700,000	and up	83
2	$550,000	$699,999	81
3	$400,000	$549.999	141
4	$250,000	$399.999	138
5	up to	$249.999	31

Average Net Sales: $516,409.51 (194 franchises, or 40.93%, were at or above this figure)
Median Net Sales: $467,348.50 (237 franchises were at or above this figure)

Notes to Table 2:

1. As of December 31, 2010, there were 587 enclosed mall Auntie Anne's locations. Of those 587, 526 Auntie Anne's locations within enclosed malls were open for business and under the same ownership from January 1, 2010 through December 31, 2010. This table does not include 61 enclosed mall locations which were neither under the same ownership nor open for the entire 2010 fiscal year. Of those 526 locations, 474 (representing 90.11% of the 526) are included within the information contained in Table 2.

2. Auntie Anne's has not included financial information in Table 2 for an enclosed mall location if: (i) the franchise was not in operation for the entire 2010 fiscal year; (ii) the ownership of the franchised location changed during the 2010 fiscal year; or (iii) the franchisee submitted late, incomplete, or illegible financial information or submitted such information in an unacceptable format.

Table 3
Average Net Sales and Net Operating Income as a percentage of Average Net Sales
for 2010 Fiscal Year - Systemwide - Enclosed Malls
ALL REGIONS

ALL REGIONS	Average	% of Net Sales	% of Stores at or Above Average	# of Stores at or Above Average
Net Sales	$516,409	100.00%	40.93%	194
Cost of Goods Sold	$ 96,923	18.77%	55.70%	264
Gross Profit	$419,486	81.23%	44.30%	210

Operating Expenses				
Labor	$ 136,o88	26.35%	55.70%	264
Rent	$77.746	15.06%	47.05%	223
Other Expenses	$ 83,952	16.26%	50.84%	241
Total Expenses	$297,738	57.66%	55.70%	264
Net Operating Income	$ 121,717	23.57%	44.30%	210

Average Net Sales: $516,409.51 (194 franchises, or 40.93%, were at or above this figure)
Median Net Sales: $467,348.50 (237 franchises were at or above this figure)

Notes to Table 3:

3.

1. As of December 31, 2010, there were a total of 587 Auntie Anne's locations operating within enclosed malls. Of those 587 locations, 526 operated under the same ownership from January 1, 2010 through December 31, 2010. This table does not include 61 enclosed mall locations which were neither under the same ownership nor open for the entire 2010 fiscal year. Of those 526 locations, 474 (representing 90.11% of the 526) are included within the information contained in Table

2. Auntie Anne's has not included financial information in Table 3 for an enclosed mall location if: (i) the franchise was not in operation for the entire 2010 fiscal year; (ii) the ownership of the franchised location changed during the 2010 fiscal year; or (iii) the franchisee submitted late, incomplete, or illegible financial information or submitted such information in an unacceptable format.

Table4

MID-ATLANTIC REGION

Average Net Sales and Net Operating Income as a percentage of Average Net Sales for 2010 Fiscal Year - Enclosed Malls

MID ATLANTIC REGION	Average	% of Net Sales	% ofStores at or Above Average	# of Stores at or Above Average
Net Sales	$579,554	100.00%	42.53%	37
Cost of Goods Sold	$107,860	18.61%	s6.32%	49
Gross Profit	$471,693	81.39%	43.68%	38
Operating Expenses				
Labor	$ 146,162	25.22%	62.07%	54
Rent	$ 79,186	13.66%	51.72%	45
Other Expenses	$ 93,924	16.21%	66.67%	s8
Total Expenses	$319,273	55.09%	72.41%	63
Net Operating Income	$152,419	26.30%	35.63%	31

Average Net Sales: $579,554.20 (37 franchises, or 42.53%, were at or above this figure)
Median Net Sales: $519,723 (44 franchises were at or above this figure)

Notes to Table 4:

contained in Table 4.

1. As of December 31, 2010, there were a total of 115 Auntie Anne's locations operating within enclosed malls in the Mid-Atlantic Region. Of those 115locations, 97 operated under the same ownership from January 1, 2010 through December 31, 2010. This table does not include 18 enclosed mall locations which were neither under the same ownership nor open for the entire 2010 fiscal year. Of those 97locations, 87 (representing 89.69% of the 97) are included within the information

2. Auntie Anne's has not included financial information in Table 4 for an enclosed mall location if: (i) the franchise was not in operation for the entire 2010 fiscal year; (ii) the ownership of the franchised location changed during the 2010 fiscal year; or (iii) the franchisee submitted late, incomplete, or illegible financial information or submitted such information in an unacceptable format.

Table 5

NORTHEAST REGION

Average Net Sales and Net Operating Income as a percentage of Average Net Sales
for 2010 Fiscal Year- Enclosed Malls

NORTHEAST REGION	Average	% of Net Sales	% of Stores at or Above Average	# of Stores at or Above Average
Net Sales	$688,046	100.00%	41.94%	26
Cost of Goods Sold	$128,164	18.63%	50.00%	31
Gross Profit	$559,881	81.37%	so.00%	31
Operating Expenses				
Labor	$ 173,713	25.25%	61.29%	38
Rent	$103,930	15.11%	59.68%	37
Other Expenses	$111,069	16.14%	74.19%	46
Total Expenses	$388,713	56.50%	43.55%	27
Net Operating Income	$171,117	24.87%	69.35%	43

Average Net Sales: $688,046.10(26 franchises, or 41.94%, were at or above this figure)
Median Net Sales: $573,205   (31 franchises were at or above this figure)

Notes to Table 5:

1. As of December 31, 2010, there were a total of 86 Auntie Anne's locations operating within enclosed malls in the Northeast Region. Of those 86 locations, 74 operated under the same ownership from January 1, 2010 through December 31, 2010. This table does not include 12 enclosed mall locations which were neither under the same ownership nor open for the entire 2010 fiscal year. Of those 74 locations, 62 (representing 83.78% of the 74) are included within the information contained in Table 5.

2. Auntie Anne's has not included financial information in Table 5 for an enclosed mall location if: (i) the franchise was not in operation for the entire 2010 fiscal year; (ii) the ownership of the franchised location changed during the 2010 fiscal year; or (iii) the franchisee submitted late, incomplete, or illegible financial information or submitted such information in an unacceptable format.

Table 6

SOUTHEAST REGION

Average Net Sales and Net Operating Income as a percentage of Average Net Sales
for 2010 Fiscal Year- Enclosed Malls

SOUTHEAST REGION	Average	% of Net Sales	% of Stores at or Above Average	# of Stores at or Above Average
Net Sales	$458,543	100.00%	39.56%	36
Cost of Goods Sold	$86,715	18.91%	62.64%	57
Gross Profit	$371,827	81.09%	37.36%	34
Operating Expenses				
Labor	$120,430	26.26%	57.14%	52
Rent	$71,803	15.66%	69.23%	63
Other Expenses	$74,681	16.29%	57.14%	52
Total Expenses	$266,853	58.20%	64.84%	59
Net Operating Income	$104,974	22.89%	35.16%	32

Average Net Sales: $458,543.38 (36 franchises, or 39.56%, were at or above this figure)
Median Net Sales: $442030 (46 franchises were at or above this figure)

Notes to Table 6:

1. As of December 31, 2010, there were a total of 109 Auntie Anne's locations operating within enclosed malls in the Southeast Region. Of those 109 locations, 97 operated under the same ownership from January 1, 2010 through December 31, 2010. This table does not include 12 enclosed mall locations which were neither under the same ownership nor open for the entire 2009 fiscal year. Of those 97 locations, 91 (representing 93.81% of the 97) are included within the information contained in Table 6.

2. Auntie Anne's has not included financial information in Table 6 for an enclosed mall location if: (i) the franchise was not in operation for the entire 2010 fiscal year; (ii) the ownership of the franchised location changed during the 2010 fiscal year; or (iii) the franchisee submitted late, incomplete, or illegible financial information or submitted such information in an unacceptable format.

Table 7

MIDWEST REGION
Average Net Sales and Net Operating Income as a percentage of Average Net Sales
for 2010 Fiscal Year- Enclosed Malls

MIDWEST REGION	Average	% of Net Sales	% of Stores at or Above Average	# of Stores at or Above Average
Net Sales	$466,826	100.00%	46.62%	62
Cost of Goods Sold	$86,490	18.53%	67.67%	90
Gross Profit	$380,336	81.47%	32.33%	43
Operating Expenses				
Labor	$123,415	26.44%	60.90%	81
Rent	$71,678	15.35%	54.89%	73
Other Expenses	$71,792	15.38%	54.89%	73
Total Expenses	$266,869	57.17%	60.90%	81
Net Operating Income	$113,438	24.30%	39.10%	52

Average Net Sales: $466,826.50 (62 franchises, or 46.62%, were at or above this figure)
Median Net Sales: $448,545 (67 franchises were at or above this figure)

Notes to Table 7

1. As of December 31, 2010, there were a total of 144 Auntie Anne's locations operating within enclosed malls in the Midwest Region. Of those 144 locations, 137 operated under the same ownership from January 1, 2010 through December 31, 2010. This table does not include 7 enclosed mall locations which were neither under the same ownership nor open for the entire 2010 fiscal year. Of those 144 locations, 137 (representing 97.08% of the population) are included within the information contained in Table 7.

2. Auntie Anne's has not included financial information in Table 7 for an enclosed mall location if: (i) the franchise was not in operation for the entire 2010 fiscal year; (ii) the ownership of the franchised location changed during the 2010 fiscal year; or (iii) the franchisee submitted late, incomplete, or illegible financial information or submitted such information in an unacceptable format.

Table 8

WESTERN REGION

Average Net Sales and Net Operating Income as a percentage of Average Net Sales
for 2010 Fiscal Year - Enclosed Malls

WESTERN REGION	Average	% of Net Sales	%of Stores at or Above Average	#of Stores at or Above Average
Net Sales	$474,085	100.00%	41.58%	42
Cost of Goods Sold	$91,259	19.25%	50.50%	51
Gross Profit	$382,826	80.75%	49.50%	50
Operating Expenses				
Labor	$ 135,109	28.50%	61.39%	62
Rent	$ 73,779	15.56%	59.41%	60
Other Ex:Q_enses	$ 82,864	17-48%	52.48%	53
Total Expenses	$291,819	61.55%	61.39%	62
Net Operating Income	$ 91,007	19.20%	38.61%	39

Average Net Sales: $474,085.76 (42 franchises, or 41.58%, were at or above this figure)
Median Net Sales: $428,690 (51 franchises)

Notes to Table 8:

1. As of December 31, 2010, there were a total of 133 Auntie Anne's locations operating within enclosed malls in the Western Region. Of those 133 locations, 121 operated under the same ownership from January 1, 2010 through December 31, 2010. This table does not include 12 enclosed mall locations which were neither under the same ownership nor open for the entire 2010 fiscal year. Of those 121 locations, 101 (representing 83-47% of the 121) are included within the informa-tion contained in Table 8.

2. Auntie Anne's has not included financial information in Table 8 for an enclosed mall location if: (i) the franchise was not in operation for the entire 2010 fiscal year; (ii) the ownership of the franchised location changed during the 2010 fiscal year; or (iii) the franchisee submitted late, incomplete, or illegible financial information or submitted such information in an unacceptable format.

Table 9

ALL REGIONS

Average Net Sales Per Transaction (NSPT) For 2011 for Enclosed Malls (EM)

Region	Average EMNSPT	Number of EM's open for all of 2011 used to calculate NSPT	Number of EM's open for all of 2011	% EM's used to calculate NSP-Tisto EM's open for all of 2011	Median EM NSPT	#/% of EM's that Met or Exceeded Average NSPT
Mid Atlantic	$4.93	110	125	88.oo%	$4.87	50/45.5%
Northeast	$5.15	79	96	82.29%	$4.92	35/44.3%
Southeast	$4.95	99	107	92.52%	$4.96	53/53.5%
Midwest	$5.08	113	136	83.09%	$4.99	58/43.6%
Western	$5.09	107	129	82.95%	$4.99	49/45.8%
Total All Regions	$5.04	528	593	89.04%	$4.97	245/46.4%

Notes to Table 9:

1. The above table shows Net Sales Per Transaction ("NSPT") averages experienced by Auntie Anne's enclosed mall locations which were open and reported sales for the entire fiscal year ended December 31, 2011. The NSPT averages are based on data received from 528 of 593 Auntie Anne's franchised locations that operated in enclosed malls and reported sales for all 52 weeks of 2011. Data from company-owned stores is not included in Table 9. These 528 locations represent 89.04% of the 593 total enclosed mall locations that were open for the entire fiscal year ended December 31, 2011. The NSPT average is obtained from the valid transaction count data as reported to us by Auntie Anne's franchisees based upon a uniform reporting system. The NSPT average is derived by dividing total Net Sales by the total number of cash register sales transactions as reported to us by Auntie Anne's franchisees for the fiscal year ended December 31, 2011. An average NSPT is determined for each Region and for the total of all the Regions.

Auntie Anne's has not included Net Sales or cash register sales transactions in Table 9 for an enclosed mall location if there was not a full 52 weeks' worth of data. Some reasons why there is not a full 52 weeks' worth of data include: (i) technical problems with cash application software, (ii) equipment problems such as cash register malfunctions, phone line failures, modem malfunction, power outages, and (iii) data validation problems such as receiving data that is incomplete or in an unacceptable format.

A new franchisee's individual financial results are likely to differ from the results stated in the financial performance representation.

Your sales will be affected by your own operational ability, which may include your experience with managing a business, your capital and financing (including working capital), continual training of you and your staff, customer service orientation, product quality, your business plan, and the use of experts, e.g.,

an accountant, to assist you with your business plans.

Your sales may be affected by franchise location and site criteria, including traffic count, local household income, residential and/or daytime populations, ease of ingress and egress, parking, visibility of your sign, physical condition of premises, number and type of other businesses around your location, competition, inflation, economic conditions, seasonal conditions (particularly in colder climates), inclement weather (e.g., hurricanes), changes in the Homeland Security threat level, etc.

Written substantiation for the financial performance representation will be made available to the prospective franchisee upon reasonable request.

We encourage you to consult with your own accounting, business, and legal advisors to assist you to prepare your budgets and projections, and to assess the likely or potential financial performance of your franchise. We also encourage you to contact existing franchisees to discuss their experiences with the system and their franchise business. Notwithstanding the information set forth in this financial performance representation, existing franchisees of Auntie Anne's are your best source of information about franchise operations.

Other than the preceding financial performance representation, Auntie Anne's Inc. does not make any financial performance representations. We also do not authorize our employees or representatives to make any such representations either orally or in writing. If you are purchasing an existing outlet, however, we may provide you with the actual records of that outlet. If you receive any other financial performance information or projections of your future income, you should report it immediately to the franchisor's management by contacting the Vice President, Legal and Compliance, Auntie Anne's Inc., Suite 200, 48-50 West Chestnut Street, Lancaster, PA 17603 (telephone number 717-435-1473).

BIG APPLE BAGELS

500 Lake Cook Rd., #475
Deerfield, IL 60015
Tel: (800) 251-6101, (847) 948-7520
Fax: (847) 405-8140
Email: tcervini@babcorp.com

Website: www.babcorp.com
Anthony Cervini, Director of Development

Bakery-cafe featuring three brands, fresh-from-scratch Big Apple Bagels and My Favorite Muffin, and freshly roasted Brewster's specialty coffee. Our product offering covers many day parts with a delicious assortment of made-to-order gourmet sandwiches, salads, soups, espresso beverages, and fruit smoothies. Franchisees can develop beyond their stores with corporate catering and gift basket opportunities, as well as wholesaling opportunities within their market area.

BACKGROUND		Passive Ownership:	Allowed
IFA Member:	Yes	Encourage Conversions:	Yes
Established & First Franchised:	1992; 1993	Area Development Agreements:	Yes
Franchised Units:	99	Sub-Franchising Contracts:	No
Company-Owned Units:	0	Expand in Territory:	Yes
Total Units:	99	Space Needs:	1,600 - 1,900 SF
Distribution:	US – 99; CAN – 0; O'seas – 0		
North America:	21 States, 0 Provinces	SUPPORT & TRAINING	
Density:	37 in MI, 19 in WI, 8 in IL	Financial Assistance Provided:	No
Projected New Units (12 Months):	10	Site Selection Assistance:	Yes
Qualifications:	3,4,3,3,3,5	Lease Negotiation Assistance:	Yes
		Co-operative Advertising:	No
FINANCIAL/TERMS		Franchisee Association/Member:	No
Cash Investment:	$100K	Size of Corporate Staff:	20
Total Investment:	$254.3 – $379.6K	On-going Support:	C, D, E, F, G, H, I
Minimum Net Worth:	$300K	Training:	2 Weeks IL
Fees (Franchise):	$25K	SPECIFIC EXPANSION PLANS	
Fees (Royalty):	5%	US:	All United States
Fees (Advertising):	1%	Canada:	All Canada
Term of Contract (Years):	10/10	Overseas:	All Countries
Average Number of Employees:	3 FT, 11 PT		

The information included in the Tables below is based on reports submitted to us by 90 fully-reporting franchised BAB Stores located in the United States that were operated for the entire 2011 Fiscal Year. The figures in Table 1 are for the 70 BAB Stores whose Primary Identifying Brand is "Big Apple Bagels." The figures in Table 2 are for the 20 BAB Stores whose Primary Identifying Brand is "My Favorite Muffin." The Franchised Stores include 87 BAB Production Stores and 3 BAB Satellite Stores (collectively the "Franchised Stores"). The Tables do not include any company-owned or affiliate-owned stores. Any franchised BAB Store that either opened or closed during the 2011 Fiscal Year, or failed to submit all 52 weeks of reporting during the 2011 Fiscal Year, has been excluded from the information contained in these Tables. The information was collected by us, but has not been independently audited or verified.

TABLE I

Gross Revenues1 of BAB Franchised Stores
By Quartile for 2011 Fiscal Year
Big Apple Bagels Stores

Quartile[2]	Gross Revenue Range[3]	# Franchisees Represented
1st	$482,595 - $738,632	18
2nd	$373,636 - $463,168	17
3rd	$233,944 - $354,741	18
4th	$53,106 - $233,295	17

TABLE 2
Gross Revenues1 of BAB Franchised Stores
By Quartile for 2011 Fiscal Year
My Favorite Muffin Stores

Quartile[2]	Gross Revenue Range[3]	# Franchisees Represented
1st	$515,688 - $824,817	5
2nd	$391,789 - $506,322	5
3rd	$314,002 - $390,173	5
4th	$258,398 - $282,149	5

Notes:

1. "Gross Revenues" is defined in the Franchise Agreement as the entire amount of all gross sales and business receipts, including direct or indirect barter transactions, catering accounts, proceeds of business interruption insurance policies, wholesale accounts (both on and off premises) arising out of the operation of the Store, or through or by means of the business conducted in connection therewith, whether for cash or credit, but excluding: (1) sales, use, or service taxes collected from customers and paid to the appropriate taxing authority; and (2) all bona fide customer refunds and approved rebates, discounts and allowances.

2. Quartile. "Quartile" refers to the relative performance of the Franchised Stores. Therefore, the "1st Quartile" refers to the top 25% performing Franchised Stores, based on Gross Revenues, the "2nd Quartile" refers to the next highest 25% performing Franchised Stores, and so on.

3. Gross Revenues Range. The Tables combine the Gross Revenues of all of the Franchised Stores for the 2011 Fiscal Year, and lists the high and low end of the Gross Revenues Range for each Quartile. For Big Apple Bagels there are 18 Franchised Stores in the 1st Quartile, 17 in the 2nd Quartile, 18 in the 3rd Quartile, and 17 in the 4th Quartile. For My Favorite Muffin there are 5 Franchised Stores in the 1st Quartile, 5 in the 2nd Quartile, 5 in the 3rd Quartile, and 5 in the 4th Quartile.

Material Bases and Assumptions

The Franchised Stores represented in the Table above are substantially similar to the concept being offered to you.

The Franchised Stores are primarily located in strip shopping centers, with a small percentage in free-standing locations.

The Gross Revenues are NOT net of costs of goods sold or other operating expenses. We have not provided information regarding costs and expenses because we do not regularly collect that data from franchisees and do not operate enough company-owned stores from which we could present reliable figures.

The financial performance representations in this Item 19 do not reflect the cost of sales, operating expenses, or other costs or expenses that must be deducted from the gross revenues figures to obtain your net income or profit. You will incur at least the following expenses, and possibly more: inventory, labor, occupancy costs, pre-opening expenses, depreciation and amortization, taxes, insurance, operating expenses, royalty fees to us, advertising fees to us, other fees to us in the Franchise Agreement, professional fees, bank charges, telephone, repairs. All of your expenses will affect the operating profit, net income and/or cash flow of your BAB Store and should be carefully considered and evaluated.

These financial performance representations do not necessarily reflect the actual Gross Revenues that you may experience. In addition, your results will vary depending on a number of factors which you should consider carefully in evaluating this information and in making any decision to purchase a franchise. These factors include: business skills, motivation, quality, effort, and effectiveness of the individual franchisee and of the franchisee's staff and management; the quality of your customer service; location of your Store; market conditions; weather and climate conditions; the effectiveness of your marketing efforts; the quality and effectiveness of your staff; income and demographic characteristics in your particular market area; the degree and quality of competition in your market area; number of years of operation; as well as conditions generally prevailing in the local and national economy, and, in particular, in your local market.

Prospective franchisees or sellers of franchises should be advised that no Certified Public Accountant has audited these figures or expressed his/her opinion with regard to their content of form. The amounts have not been audited or reviewed for reasonableness by independent auditors.

Some outlets have sold this amount. Your individual results may differ. There is no assurance that you'll sell as much.

You should conduct an independent investigation of the costs and expenses you will incur in operating your BAB Store. We encourage you to consult with your own accounting, business, and legal advisors to assist you to prepare your budgets and projections, and to assess the likely or potential financial per-formance of your BAB Store. We also encourage you to contact existing BAB Store operators to discuss their experiences with the system and their Store business. Existing franchisees are your best source of information.

Written substantiation of the data we used in preparing this statement will be made available upon reasonable request.

CHECKERS DRIVE-IN RESTAURANT

4300 W. Cypress St., # 600
Tampa, FL 33607
Tel: (888) 913-9135, (813) 283-7069
Fax: (813) 936-6201
Email: waibele@checkers.com
Website: www.checkersfranchising.com
Liz Waibel, Franchising Contract

Quick-service, fast-food restaurant (double drive-thru). Total below reflect ownership of both CHECKERS and RALLY'S brands.

BACKGROUND
IFA Member:	Yes
Established & First Franchised:	1986; 1991
Franchised Units:	455
Company-Owned Units:	322
Total Units:	777
Distribution:	US – 776; CAN – 0; O'seas – 1
North America:	40 States, 0 Provinces
Density:	152 in FL, 91 in GA, 32 in AL
Projected New Units (12 Months):	35

Qualifications:	5, 4, 5, 4, 4, 4

FINANCIAL/TERMS
Total Investment:	$240K – $1.235MM
Minimum Net Worth & Liquidity:	$750K; $250K
Fees (Franchise):	$30K
Fees (Royalty):	4%
Fees (Advertising):	3 – 5%
Term of Contract (Years):	20/Agrmt.
Average Number of Employees:	4 FT, 30 PT
Passive Ownership:	Allowed
Encourage Conversions:	Yes
Area Development Agreements:	Yes
Sub-Franchising Contracts:	No
Expand in Territory:	Yes
Space Needs:	15,000 – 25,000 SF

SUPPORT & TRAINING
Financial Assistance Provided:	No
Site Selection Assistance:	Yes
Lease Negotiation Assistance:	Yes
Co-operative Advertising:	Yes
Franchisee Association/Member:	Yes/Member
Size of Corporate Staff:	N/A
On-going Support:	A, B, C, D, E, F, G, H, I
Training:	5 Weeks FL

SPECIFIC EXPANSION PLANS
US:	All United States
Canada:	All Canada
Overseas:	All Countries

Statements of Average Net Sales of Checkers Restaurants for the 52-Week Period Ending January 2, 2012.

Company-owned Restaurants	$925,303
Franchisee-owned Restaurants	$881,218
Company and Franchisee-owned Restaurants	$897,568

Some Checkers Restaurants have sold this amount. Your individual results may differ. There is no assurance that you'll sell as well. A new franchisee's financial results are likely to differ from the results stated in the financial performance representation.

These financial performance representations do not reflect the costs of sales, operating expenses or other costs or expenses that must be deducted from the gross revenue or gross sales figures to obtain your net income or profit. You should conduct an independent investigation of the costs and expenses you will incur in operating your franchised business. Franchisees or former franchisees listed in this disclosure document may be one source of this information.

Information Regarding Statements of Average Net Sales.

The Average Net Sales statement consists of the averages of the reported annual Net Sales of the 168 Company-owned Restaurants and the 285 Franchisee-owned Restaurants that were open during the entire 52-week reporting period ending January 2, 2012. The Average Net Sales statement excludes the results from 6 Checkers Company-owned Restaurants, and 55 Franchisee-owned Restaurants, that were not open during the entire 52- week reporting period ending January

2, 2012. Of the 453 Checkers Restaurants used for calculating the Average Net Sales for the 52-week reporting period ending January 2, 2012, the 285 Franchisee-owned Restaurants had Net Sales ranging between $361,209 and $2,936,484 of which 129 Restaurants, or 45.3%, attained or surpassed $881,218 in Net Sales (the average Net Sales of Franchisee-owned Restaurants).

Written substantiation for the financial performance representation will be made available to the prospective franchisee upon reasonable request. However, we will not disclose the identity or sales data of any particular Checkers Restaurant without the consent of that owner, except to any applicable state registration authorities or except in connection with the sale of a particular existing Checkers Restaurants that we own.

The Net Sales of Franchisee-owned Restaurants were derived from unaudited financial reports submitted by Franchisees for the purpose of computing royalties. We compiled the Net Sales of Company-owned Restaurants on the basis of generally accepted accounting principles, consistently applied.

Sales To Investment Ratio

The following information discloses the average investment for the various types of Checkers building formats, based on the information provided in Item 7 (exclusive of real estate and related costs and transportation expenses, if applicable) and calculates an approximate sales to investment ratio based on the average Net Sales of Franchise-owned Restaurants disclosed above:

Building Format	Average Investment	Approximate Sales to Investment Ratio
Double Drive-Thru Modular Building	$585,950	1.5:1
Prototype Single Drive-Thru	$500,030	1.8:1
Conversion Free-Standing Restaurant	$399,900	2.2:1
End Cap Single Drive-Thru	$552,650	1.6:1
In-Line Restaurant	$418,837	2.1:1
Re-opened Checkers/Rally's Restaurant	$211,750	4.2:1

General

Other than the preceding financial performance representation, we do not make any financial performance representations. We also do not authorize our employees or representatives to make any such representations either orally or in writing. If you are purchasing an existing outlet, however, we

may provide you with the actual records of that outlet. If you receive any other financial performance information or projections of your future income, you should report it to the franchisor's management by contacting Brian Doster at 4300 West Cypress Street, Suite 600, Tampa, Florida 33607 or at (813) 283-7000, the Federal Trade Commission, and the appropriate state regulatory agencies.

CHURCH'S CHICKEN

980 Hammond Dr., Bldg. # 2, # 1100
Atlanta, GA 30328-6161
Tel: (800) 639-3495, (770) 350-3800
Fax: (770) 512-3924
Email: mkuzminsky@churchs.com
Website: www.churchsfranchising.com
Michael Kuzminsky, SVP Franchise Operations

Founded in San Antonio, Texas, in 1952, Church's Chicken® is a highly recognized brand name in the Quick Service Restaurant sector and is one of the largest quick service chicken concepts in the world. Church's serves up a rich tradition of gracious Southern hospitality and freshly prepared, high quality, authentic Southern-style fare, to help people provide affordable, complete meals for their families. Church's menu includes flavorful chicken both Original and Spicy, Tender Strips™ and chicken sandwiches with classic sides and handmade from scratch honey butter biscuits. The Church's system consists of more than 1,675 locations in 24 countries. For more information on Church's Chicken, visit www.churchs-franchising.com or www.churchs.com.

BACKGROUND

IFA Member:	Yes
Established & First Franchised:	1952; 1967
Franchised Units:	1,417
Company-Owned Units:	258
Total Units:	1,675

Distribution:	US – 1,321; CAN – 16; O'seas – 338
North America:	29 States, 2 Provinces
Density:	490 in TX, 86 in GA, 75 in CA
Projected New Units (12 Months):	120
Qualifications:	5, 5, 5, 3, 4, 5

FINANCIAL/TERMS

Cash Investment:	$650K
Total Investment:	$191.3K – $1.1MM
Minimum Net Worth:	$1.5M
Fees (Franchise):	$35K
Fees (Royalty):	5%
Fees (Advertising):	5%
Term of Contract (Years):	20/10
Average Number of Employees:	15 FT, 6 PT
Passive Ownership:	Discouraged
Encourage Conversions:	Yes
Area Development Agreements:	Yes
Sub-Franchising Contracts:	No
Expand in Territory:	Yes
Space Needs:	850 – 2,200 SF

SUPPORT & TRAINING

Financial Assistance Provided:	No
Site Selection Assistance:	Yes
Lease Negotiation Assistance:	No
Co-operative Advertising:	Yes
Franchisee Association/Member:	Yes/Member
Size of Corporate Staff:	163
On-going Support:	C, D, E, G, H, I
Training:	5 Weeks Regional

SPECIFIC EXPANSION PLANS

US:	All United States
Canada:	Selected Provinces
Overseas:	ME, Mexico, Brazil, Ecuador, Peru, Colombia, Panama, Carib., N. Africa, China, Thailand, E. Europe, AUS

The following four tables present information about the actual sales and expenses of domestic Church's restaurants in our 2011 fiscal year.

Table 1: 2011 Sales by Asset Type (Franchised Restaurants)

Below are average franchised restaurant sales for fiscal year 2011 by type of Church's Restaurant. 28 franchised Church's Restaurants that were not in operation for at least 48 weeks during fiscal year 2011 were excluded. Three franchised Church's Restaurants that were acquired by us during 2011 are included since a majority of their operating weeks were as franchised Church's Restaurants. The table includes only franchised restaurants in the continental United States, and does not include restaurants located in Puerto Rico and U.S. territories.

2011 Annual Sales	Free Standing With Drive Thru Tower Image	Free Standing With Drive Thru Image Other Than "Tower"	Free Standing Without Drive Thru	In-Line	C-Store	Co-branded	Other
Average – domestic franchise	$733,143	$708,805	$699,086	$520,427	$561,614	$197,639	$494,333
Top Quartile – domestic franchise	$838,409	$824,032	$787,170	$613,687	$665,243	$245,108	$578,860
Restaurant count	87	541	85	43	133	21	23
Franchise restaurants at or above domestic franchise average	39	236	41	17	52	9	9
% franchise restaurants at or above domestic franchise average	44.8%	43.6%	48.2%	39.5%	39.1%	42.9%	39.1%

Notes To Table 1: 2011 Sales By Asset Type (Franchise Restaurants)

1. "Free-Standing" and "In-Line" units are described in Item 7. "C-Store" means a unit attached to or part of a convenience store or travel plaza. "Co-branded" means a unit which shares operating space with another branded restaurant or business.

2. The Tower image reflects our 1,850 square foot prototype and is characterized by the use of a flat panel extending above the fascia mounted behind the building signs combined with the Tower color scheme.

Table 2: 2011 Sales by Asset Type (Company Restaurants)

Below are average company-owned restaurant sales for fiscal year 2011 by type of Church's Restaurant. Five company-owned Church's Restaurants that were not in operation for at least 48 weeks during fiscal year 2011 were excluded. Three Church's Restaurants that were acquired by us during 2011 are excluded since a majority of their operating weeks were as franchised Church's Restaurants. All company-owned Church's Restaurants in the table are currently operated by our wholly-owned subsidiary, Cajun Restaurants LLC.

2011 Annual Sales	Free Standing With Drive Thru Tower Image	Free Standing With Drive Thru Image Other Than "Tower"	Free Standing Without Drive Thru	In-Line	C-Store
Average - Co. Owned	$931,022	$872,995	$697,059	$493,395	$676,044
Top Quartile - Co. Owned	$1,045,815	$1,024,266	$772,590	$493,395	$735,207
Unit Count - Co.	57	164	27	1	2
Franchise Unit at or above Co. Owned Avg.	14	115	41	N/A	N/A
% Franchise at or above Co. Owned Avg.	16.1%	21.3%	48.2%	N/A	N/A

Table 3: 2011 Income Statement Summary (Company Restaurants Only)

Below is a summary based on Cajun Operating's unaudited income statement for fiscal year 2011 for restaurants that meet all of the following criteria: (1) owned by our wholly-owned subsidiary, Cajun Restaurants LLC, (2) free-standing "Tower" prototype, and (3) operated by our predecessor, Cajun Operating, for all of 2011. Table 3 excludes data related to 66 free-standing company-owned Church's restaurants that were not built under the "Tower" prototype.

We did not include data from franchisees in the following summary because financial statements provided by franchisees to us are not in a common format, and furthermore they are not independently verified by us. Franchisees will incur other costs in connection with the operation of Church's Restaurants including, without limitation, occupancy costs (such as rent or mortgage payments), utilities, royalties, advertising and promotional expenses, office expenses, legal and accounting expenses, insurance expenses, and various other general administrative expenses. Expenses in the operation of Restaurants will vary from franchisee to franchisee and from location to location, and are dependent upon seasonal, local and other factors beyond our control, such as the franchisee's efficiency in the utilization of products, the costs of transportation and the fluctuation in market prices for food and other products.

The operating costs information reflected in the following table is based on company financial statements (see Notes below).

	"TOWER" IMAGE %
Sales	100.0%
Food cost	34.3%
Labor - Management	5.7%
Labor - Shift Management	3.2%
Labor - Crew	12.6%
Labor - Other	4.0%
Labor - Total	25.5%
Gross Profit Margin	40.2%
Controllables	11.9%
Marketing	5.0%
Royalty	5.0%
Controllable Profit Margin	18.3%
Non-controllables	1.9%
Restaurant Operating Profit, pre-tax (EBITDAR)	**16.4%**
Unit Count	193

Notes To Table 3: 2011 Income Statement Summary (Company Restaurants Only)

1. Food costs include the delivered cost of food, beverages, paper and promotional items (i.e., limited-time offerings) to the restaurants. Delivered costs include distribution and freight costs. The calculation of food costs is primarily a function of the mix of products sold and the cost of commodities which compromise the products.

2. Labor costs include unit hourly labor, which is comprised of the average hourly rate and the number of hours worked (a direct correlation to sales volume). The cost of labor will vary from location to location and will be dependent upon factors beyond our control, including, without limitation, local minimum wage laws and local labor market conditions. Labor costs also include the salaries of general and assistant managers. Most company-owned restaurants employ one salaried general manager and one salaried assistant manager. The other components of labor expense are: payroll taxes, health insurance, vacation, wages, sick pay, bonuses and workers' compensation insurance. We make no warranties, representations, predictions, promises or guaranties with respect to the actual labor expenses likely to be experienced by individual franchisees. Also, with respect to labor costs, because a certain number of employees will be necessary to open and operate a restaurant irrespective of its Gross Sales, units that have lower than average Gross Sales probably will experience higher than average labor costs.

3. The Marketing fee is described as 5.0% because franchisees are required to pay up to 5% of gross income to the Advertising Fund. [See Item 6 and Item 11.] The percentage of income from company-owned restaurants which is spent on marketing may be higher or lower than 5.0%.

4. The Royalty fee is described as 5.0% because franchisees are required to pay 5% of gross income to Cajun. [See Item 6.] Company-owned restaurants do not pay a royalty fee.

5. Table 3 excludes occupancy costs, i.e. rent or mortgage payments

6. Table 3 excludes certain overhead and other expenses which are not classified as "store-level" for internal accounting purposes.

7. "Controllables" refers to miscellaneous store-level costs which are affected by or decided by management, such as the cost of maintenance and repair. "Non-controllables" refers to miscellaneous store-level costs where the owner has no decision-making ability regarding the expenditure, such as the cost of local operating permits.

8. "EBITDAR" is earnings before Interest, Taxes, Depreciation, Amortization and Real Estate.

Written substantiation for this financial performance representation will be made available to prospective franchisees upon reasonable request.

Other than the preceding financial performance representation, we do not make any financial performance representations. We also do not authorize our employees or representatives to make any such representations either orally or in writing. If you are purchasing an existing Restaurant, however, we may provide you with the actual records of that Restaurant. If you receive any other financial performance information or projections of your future income, you should report it to our management by contacting Kenneth A. Cutshaw, Cajun Global's Executive Vice President, Chief Legal Officer and Secretary at 980 Hammond Drive, Suite 1100, Atlanta, GA

30328, or 770-350-3800, the Federal Trade Commission and the appropriate state regulatory agencies.

Your individual financial results are likely to differ from results described in this Item 19. You should conduct an independent investigation of the costs and expenses you will incur in operating your Restaurant. Franchisees or former franchisees identified in this disclosure document may be one source of information.

DENNY'S

203 E. Main St.
Spartanburg, SC 29319
Tel: (800) 304-0222, (770) 777-0796
Fax: (864) 597-7708
Email: franchisedevelopment@dennys.com
Website: www.dennysfranchising.com

For 60 years, Denny's has been the trusted leader in family dining. Today, Denny's is a true icon, with brand awareness of almost 100%. Having grown to include almost 1,700 restaurants and system–wide sales of over $2.4 billion, Denny's is one of the largest and most recognized full-service family restaurant chains in the United States. We rank in the top 100 Chains in Food Service Sales in Nation's Restaurant News, Bond's Top 100 Franchises, and are ranked #1 in category by

Entrepreneur Magazine's Franchise 500®. If you are an experienced restaurateur or businessman, we invite you to contact us and learn more about growth opportunities within our great brand.

BACKGROUND
IFA Member:	Yes
Established & First Franchised:	1953; 1963
Franchised Units:	1,524
Company-Owned Units:	164
Total Units:	1,688
Distribution:	US – 1,590; CAN – 63; O'seas – 35
North America:	50 States, 5 Provinces
Density:	348 in CA, 168 in TX, 134 in FL
Projected New Units (12 Months):	35
Qualifications:	5, 5, 5, 3, 1, 5

FINANCIAL/TERMS
Cash Investment:	$350 – $400K
Total Investment:	$1.178 – $2.396MM
Minimum Net Worth:	$1M
Fees (Franchise):	$40K
Fees (Royalty):	4%
Fees (Advertising):	4%
Term of Contract (Years):	20/10 or 20

Average Number of Employees:	50 FT, 25 PT	Co-operative Advertising:	Yes
Passive Ownership:	Discouraged	Franchisee Association/Member:	Yes/Member
Encourage Conversions:	Yes	Size of Corporate Staff:	250
Area Development Agreements:	Yes	On-going Support:	C, D, e, G, I
Sub-Franchising Contracts:	No	Training:	10 – 13 weeks at the nearest
Expand in Territory:	Yes		certified training restaurant
Space Needs:	4,200 SF		

SUPPORT & TRAINING

SPECIFIC EXPANSION PLANS

US: All United States
Canada: All Canada
Overseas: Caribbean, C. America, Gulf States/Middle East, India, Indo, UK

Financial Assistance Provided:	Yes (I)
Site Selection Assistance:	Yes
Lease Negotiation Assistance:	No

The following financial schedule contains information relating to the performance of Denny's restaurants. The information is provided for the purposes of helping you evaluate the potential earnings capability of the Restaurant. The information presented does not represent the actual performance of any single resaurant. The notes following the schedule attempt to explain the information and provide the underlying assumptions.

The Net Sales, Gross Profits, and EBITDA are a compilation of the results of individual Denny's Resaurants, and should not be considered as the actual or probable Net Sales, Gross Profits, or EBITDA that will be realized by you. We do not represent that you can expect to attain any of the results reflected in the schedule. Actual results will vary from restaurant to restaurant and we cannot estimate or guaranty the results of

any specific restaurant.

In 2007, DI, our affiliate, began selling restaurants owned and operated bt DI in a strategic program to focus on higher volume restaurants in a smaller number of markets. The operating results for restaurants sold by DI do not appear in the following table. The operating performance of DI's remaining company restaurants which we present, and in particular average unit volumes and major expense categories, is unlike results in franchise operated units.

Actual sales and earnings of the restaurant are affected by many factors, including your own efforts, ability, and control of the restaurant, as well as factors over which you do not have any control. We do not represent that the restaurant will be profitable.

I. DI Restaurant Operating Performance
Denny's Company Restaurant Operating Performance

	Top Third		Middle Third		Bottom Third	
	$	%	$	%	$	%
Net Sales	2,575	100%	1,766	100%	1,397	100%
Food	566	22%	408	23%	326	23%
Crew Labor	548	21%	386	22%	309	22%
Management Labor	188	7%	149	8%	141	10%
Gross Profit	1,273	49%	833	47%	620	44%
Taxes/Fringe Benefits	207	8%	145	8%	120	9%
Utilities	99	4%	76	4%	71	5%
Repair & Maintenance	34	1%	31	2%	27	2%
Other Expense	134	5%	109	6%	91	7%

EBITDA before Royalties, Advertising Occupancy Cost, and Management Fees	$799	31%	$472	27%	$312	22%

EBITDA defined as Earnings Before Interest, Taxes, Depreciation, and Amortization without considering major capital expenditures. Above numbers reflect a total of 195 stores that were open the entire year - 65 units in each third. All dollar figures in thousands.

NOTES TO FINANCIAL SCHEDULE

A. The schedule presents the actual operating results with respect to sales and selected costs of 195 Denny's restaurants owned and operated by DI in the United States during the twelve month period beginning December 30, 2010, and ending December 28, 2011, excluding only those restaurants which were open for only part of such period. The three tiers are comprised of 65 Denny's restaurants in each tier. The schedule is based upon data received from DI's employees at each restaurant who, in the normal course of business, collect such data.

B. "Net Sales" reflected on the schedule represent all revenue derived from the restaurants, including all sales of food, goods, wares, merchandise, and all services made in, upon, or from the restaurants, including catering services, whether for cash, check, credit, or otherwise, without reserve or deduction for inability to collect same. Net Sales do not include rebates or refunds to customers or the amount of any sales taxes or other similar taxes that restaurants may be required to collect from customers to be paid to any federal, state, or local taxing authority.

C. We are not able to provide similar information relating to Denny's restaurants operated by our franchisees because we do not have reliable information relating to costs incurred by franchise operators. However, during the same period (a twelve month period beginning December 30, 2010, and ending December 28, 2011) the average Net Sales of all Denny's restaurants (including both franchised restaurants and restaurants owned and operated by DI) were $1,453,000. This figure excludes former company restaurants bought in 2011 and any restaurant that was open for only part of such period. See sales information below.

D. There are no material differences between the operations of the restaurants being franchised by us and the restaurants owned and operated by DI. Both groups of restaurants will operate under the same System, and with similar operating requirements.

E. The restaurants included in the schedule have been open for periods as short as one year and as long as 53 years. No restaurant has been open for less than twelve months.

F. The final line of the schedule reflects the restaurant profit before deducting expenses which differ among individual restaurants. These additional expenses, which are likely to be significant, will vary widely among restaurants, and may include, but not necessarily be limited to, the following:

• Royalty fees and advertising contributions
• Occupancy cost
• Management fees
• Interest or financing charges not included in lease payments
• Taxes
• Depreciation on property and equipment
• Any preopening or amortization of organization costs
• Accounting, legal fees, and general administrative expenses

We strongly encourage you to consult with your financial advisors in reviewing the schedule and, in particular, in estimating the categories and amount of additional expenses which you will incur in establishing and operating the Restaurant. The schedule contains only some of the categories in which you may incur expenses.

G. The schedule was prepared from the internal operating records of DI which, in turn, were prepared in accordance with generally accepted accounting principles. The schedule is unaudited. Substantiation for the data set forth in the schedule will be made available by us to all prospective franchisees upon reasonable request.

H. Except for the schedule set forth in this Item, and profit and loss statements which we may provide to you in circumstances in which we sell you a former company Restaurant (see the section titled, "Former Company Restaurant P&L's," below), we do not make information available to prospective franchisees in this state concerning actual, average, projected, or forecasted sales, costs, income, or profits. You should be aware that the financial performance of any particular restaurant may be affected by a number of factors, including, but not limited to the following:

1. The schedule does not reflect debt service costs. You will incur such costs to the extent you finance the initial fran-

chise fee and the development and construction cost of the Restaurant and the furniture, fixtures, and equipment, or to the extent you borrow funds to acquire the property and build the Restaurant.

2. The Restaurant may face competition from restaurants and food service outlets offering many different types of cuisine. The intensity of this competition will vary depending upon the location of the Restaurant. Further. the tastes of a community or community segment may not be accustomed to the type of products offered by the Restaurant. As such. appreciation for and acceptance of the products offered by the Restaurant may have to be developed to varying degrees depending upon the particular community.

3. You may not have comparable restaurant and food service experience and expertise as found in the Denny's restaurants owned and operated by DI. While we will provide certain assistance to you (see Item 11), you and the staff of the Restaurant will be primarily responsible for the daily operations of the Restaurant in accordance with the terms of the Franchise Agreement.

4. The quality and effectiveness of your managerial skills will affect, positively or negatively, the sales results of the Restaurant. Decisions with respect to location, additional advertising programs, employees, cost controls, and other factors may impact the results of the Restaurant.

5. Geographic and socio-economic variations from locality to locality may affect the results of the Restaurant, as well as factors bearing upon business cycles and performance of the national and world economy.

We recommend that you make your own independent investigation to determine whether or not the franchise may be profitable, and consult with an attorney and other advisors prior to executing any agreement.

We require all prospects who have never been Denny's franchisees, as a condition of being approved, to consult with an independent financial advisor and to review with that person operating statements for the restaurants to be acquired or developed and all other terms of the transaction. This review should include current and pro forma P&L's, as applicable. A prospective franchisee with financial expertise, or who has a person with such expertise on its staff, would be excused. Otherwise, the financial advisor would need to be a third party, and not affiliated with any other party to the transaction, including sellers, brokers, lenders or developers.

I. Except for the schedule set forth in this Item, and profit and loss statements which we may provide to you in circumstances in which we sell you a former company Restaurant (see the section titled, "Former Company Restaurant P&L's," below), we do not furnish, or authorize our salespersons to furnish, any oral or written information concerning the actual, average, projected, or forecasted sales, costs, income, or profits of a Denny's restaurant. Actual results vary from unit to unit, and we cannot estimate the results of any particular restaurant.

II. Sales of Denny's Restaurants

For 2011, 1,549 Denny's restaurants in the US and Canada were open the entire year. We operated 195 restaurants and 1,354 were franchised. Restaurants open less than one full year have been omitted, of which there were 9 Company-owned and 49 franchised, as well as 30 former company restaurants. These totals also exclude 11 Denny's Fresh Express (non-traditional) units and 2 Denny's Café units. The average sales of the franchised and Company-owned restaurants combined was $1,453,000. Franchised restaurants included in the analysis had average sales of $1,387,000. Company-owned restaurants included in the analysis had average sales of $1,909,000. The range was:

Franchised Restaurants

Sales Range	Number of Franchised Restaurants	Percentage of Franchised Restaurants
Over $2,000,000	97	7%
$1,387,000 to $2,000,000	463	34%
$1,000,000 to $1,387,000	611	45%
Under $1,000,000	183	14%
TOTAL	1354	100%

Company-Owned Restaurants

Sales Range	Number of Company-Owned Restaurants	Percentage of Company-Owned Restaurants
Over $2,000,000	58	30%
$1,363,000 to $2,000,000	106	54%
$1,000,000 to $1,363,000	28	14%
Under $1,000,000	3	2%
TOTAL	195	100%

NOTES AND ASSUMPTIONS

A. The size of the restaurants may vary significantly. Over the past few years we had several restaurant plans available, ranging from "Diner" concepts with 101 to 113 seats to classic buildings with 98 to 150 seats. Our "D Series" prototype has an average of 144 seats.

B. We compiled the figures provided above from our financial statements and from sales reports submitted to us by our franchise operators on a 52 week basis. The sales infor¬mation provided by our franchise operators has not been audited and has not necessarily been prepared on a basis consistent with generally accepted accounting principles.

C. The 30 former company restaurants open all of 2010 had an average volume in YE 2010 of $1,388,000.

III. Company Restaurant P&L's

If we sell to you a company restaurant, we will share with you information relating to the historical performance of the restaurant. Typically, this information consists of the profit and loss statement (the "P&L") for the restaurant, which is prepared in the normal course of busi¬ness by DI, the seller. The P&L is prepared in accordance with generally accepted accounting principles, but it is not audited. The P&L does not include royalty payments that you will be required to pay under your Franchise Agreement with us. P&L information will be shared with you only after we have come to some preliminary understandings regarding your purchase of the company restaurant, but before you make any binding commitment to purchase the company restaurant under the terms of a Purchase Agreement. The information will be subject to a confidentiality agreement. (See Exhibit H.)

In providing P&L's, we neither represent nor warrant that the level of sales achieved by DI will be the same as the sales which you may achieve. Moreover. various expenses incurred by DI in the operation of the company restaurant will likely differ from the expenses you incur. For example, to the extent you borrow funds to acquire the company restaurant, the P&L

figures will not reflect debt service costs which you will be required to pay. As a consequence, the results of your operation of the former company restaurant will not be the same as the results of operation by DI. Therefore, we strongly encourage you to consult with your financial advisors in reviewing P&L's for the company restaurant, in particular, in estimating the categories and amount of additional expenses which you will incur in establishing and operating the restaurant.

IV. New and Emerging Markets Incentive Program

The savings estimate of up to $1 million is based on the potential savings of developing, opening, and operating four Denny's restaurants under the New and Emerging Market Incentive Program, in comparison to developing, opening, and operating four Denny's restaurants without the incentive program. See Item 12 of this Disclosure Document for details of this program. The components of estimates regarding potential savings under the New and Emerging Market Program are as follows:

Initial Franchise Fee Potential Savings:

First Restaurant — pay $20,000	= savings of $20,000
Second Restaurant — pay $0	= savings of $40,000
Third Restaurant — pay $0	= savings of $40,000
Fourth Restaurant — pay $0	= savings of $40,000
	Total = $140,000

Royalty Payment Potential Savings (based on $1,387,000 average franchise restaurant sales volume):

1st year — pay 1% = 3% savings	= $41,610
2nd year — pay 2% = 2% savings	= $27,740
3rd year — pay 2% = 2% savings	= $27,740
4th year — pay 3% = 1% savings	= $13,870
5th year — pay 3% = 1% savings	= $13,870
Total	= $124,830
$124,830 x 4 restaurants	= $499,320

Pay 3% advertising = 1% savings for 5 years = $69,350 x 4 restaurants = $277,400

Broker market planning fee
(one time only incentive) -   up to $10,000
Store design plans (up to $30,000 x 4) -   up to $120,000
Free NRO training ($17,500 x4) -   up to $70,000
Free initial MGIP fee (one time only incentive) - $10,000
Total - $210,000

You will pay market planning and store design fees as incurred. We will credit your franchise account the lesser of the amount above or the actual expense once the restaurant opens.

Total Potential Savings = $1,126,720

We reserve the right to select the vendors, specifications, terms and conditions for these services.

DOC POPCORN

3200 Carbon Pl., #103
Boulder, CO 80301
Tel: (866) 559-9744, (720) 389-0649
Fax: (720) 961-0551
Email: getpopping@docpopcorn.com
Website: www.docpopcorn.com
Brent Dowling, Marketing Manager

Doc Popcorn (DP) is the first and only fresh popped branded all-natural popcorn franchise system. DP gives franchise owners the opportunity to provide a quality delicious product in high-traffic selling venues where few such options exist.

BACKGROUND

IFA Member:	No
Established & First Franchised:	2003; 2009
Franchised Units:	80
Company-Owned Units:	0
Total Units:	80
Distribution:	US – 80; CAN – 0; O'seas – 0
North America:	26 States, 0 Provinces
Density:	N/A

Projected New Units (12 Months):	30
Qualifications:	4, 2, 1, 3, 4, 5

FINANCIAL/TERMS

Cash Investment:	$72K
Total Investment:	$72 – $378K
Minimum Net Worth:	$250K
Fees (Franchise):	$37.5K
Fees (Royalty):	6%
Fees (Advertising):	0%
Term of Contract (Years):	10/10
Average Number of Employees:	0 FT, 2 – 3 PT
Passive Ownership:	Allowed
Encourage Conversions:	Yes
Area Development Agreements:	Yes
Sub-Franchising Contracts:	Yes
Expand in Territory:	Yes
Space Needs:	120 SF

SUPPORT & TRAINING

Financial Assistance Provided:	No
Site Selection Assistance:	Yes
Lease Negotiation Assistance:	Yes
Co-operative Advertising:	Yes
Franchisee Association/Member:	No
Size of Corporate Staff:	10
On-going Support:	A, B, C, D, E, H, I
Training:	5 Days Boulder, CO; 2 Days On-Site

SPECIFIC EXPANSION PLANS

US:	Yes
Canada:	Yes
Overseas:	Yes

The following is a chart of certain financial performance information for twelve Fixed Poperating Units and four Mobile Poperating Units, each of which has opened and been operating for a period of at least nine consecutive weeks during 2011. Financial information for our remaining thirteen Poperating Units opened and operating as of December 31, 2011 was unavailable, as such units had not been open and operating for a period of at least nine consecutive weeks as of such date. We also did not include financial information for our eight Poperating Units that operate in conjunction with an operating unit of Maui Wowi Franchising, Inc., which offers franchises to operate businesses that sell fresh Hawaiian beverages and related items including fresh fruit smoothies, bottled waters, Hawaiian coffee and related espresso beverages, a variety of Hawaiian products, and other products developed by or for Maui Wowi Franchising, Inc. under the trademark MAUI WOWI®. Doc Popcorn and Maui Wowi are not affiliated companies. Neither did we include financial information for the three Poperating Units owned by our Founder, as such units do not pay royalties, are permitted to sell other products and use other channels of distribution not available to you or other franchisees.

The following data should not be considered as the actual, potential or probable revenues that will be realized by you or any other franchisees. Actual results vary from location to location or event to event and we cannot estimate the results of any particular location or event. A particular location or event is always a determining factor in the success of a business, as are day-to-day management skill, business skill, and marketing, advertising and public relations initiatives of the franchisee. Your financial results are likely to differ from the figures presented.

Financial Performance Data for Poperating Units for the Calendar Year 2011

Unit Type	Average Annual Retail Sales
PopShop™	$388,899.90
PopKiosk™	$251,829
Mobile Poperating Unit	$82,175

Written substantiation for the financial performance representation will be made available to the prospective franchisee upon reasonable request. The accompanying explanatory notes are an integral part of this chart and should be read in their entirety for a full understanding of the information contained in the chart.

EXPLANATORY NOTES:

1. The Average Retail Sales by Type of Unit was determined for each type of Poperating Unit by adding the historic or projected 2011 annual retail sales of each Poperating Unit and dividing the total by the number of participating Poperating Units. For example, the projected 2011 annual retail sales of the four participating Mobile Poperating Units were added together and divided by four, the number of Units. The 2011 annual retail sales for each Poperating Unit, whether historic or projected, is based upon the data reported to us by our Franchisees for the number of weeks of operation during 2011. The PopShop™ Average Retail Sales is based upon 52 weeks of historical data provided to us by one Poperating Unit.

2. The PopKiosk™ and Mobile Poperating Unit Average Retail Sales is a projection based on historical data of 52 weeks or less from such Poperating Units. Nine of the eleven participating PopKiosk™ Poperating Units and the four participating Mobile Poperating Units reported retail sales in less than 52 weeks during 2011. Of these Poperating Units, five reported between 20 and 52 consecutive weeks during 2011 and eight reported between 9 and 19 consecutive weeks during 2011. The projected 2011 Annual Retail Sales for each such Poperating Unit was then determined by dividing the reported 2011 retail sales by the consecutive weeks of operation of such Poperating Unit during 2011 and multiplying such weekly average times 52 weeks. As a result, the projected 2011 Annual Retail Sales determined for a specific Poperating Unit is merely an estimate and may not reflect the actual retail sales of such Poperating Unit that may have occurred if it was open and operating during the entire 2011 calendar year.

3. Seven out of eleven PopKiosk™ Poperating Units had actual or projected 2011 Annual Retail Sales greater than the Average Annual Sales for such Poperating Unit type. One out of four Mobile Poperating Units had projected 2011 Annual Retail Sales greater than the Average Annual Retail Sales for such Poperating Unit type.

4. The financial performance figures(s) does (do) not reflect the costs of sales, operating expenses or other costs or expenses that must be deducted from the gross revenue or gross sales figures to obtain your net income or profit. You should conduct an independent investigation of the costs and expenses

you will incur in operating your DOC POPCORN Business. Franchisees or former franchisees, listed in Exhibit E to this Disclosure Document, may be one source of this information.

5. No franchise fees, royalties or margins in the cost of DOC POPCORN Products to franchisees are shown in this chart. See ITEMS 5, 6 and 7 for information regarding initial investment and other expense considerations. The initial investment and other expenses and costs will vary substantially for each franchisee, and are dependent on different factors particular to each franchisee. The above sales figures may not necessarily predict any given DOC POPCORN Business's profitability. You may sell DOC POPCORN Products at a price that may be higher or lower than the price range of the selected franchisees' operations. Sales prices vary between franchisees and may be impacted by competition, contractual requirements, geographical areas, demographics, etc. We recommend that you conduct your own evaluation of sales price or prices that would be acceptable in your own areas of operation.

6. Actual results may vary from franchise to franchise and depend on a variety of internal and external factors, many of which neither we nor any prospective franchisee can estimate, such as competition, economic climate, location, demographics, and changing consumer demands and tastes. A franchisee's ability to achieve any level of DOC POPCORN Products purchases, sales, revenues, or net income will depend on these factors and others, including the franchisee's level of expertise, none of which are within our control. Accordingly, we cannot, and do not, estimate the results of any particular franchise. There is no assurance that you will do as well as the units listed above. If you rely upon our figures, you must accept the risk of not doing as well.

7. Except for the information contained in this Item 19, we do not authorize our salespersons to furnish any oral or written information concerning the actual or potential sales, costs, income, or profits of a franchise. Actual results vary from franchise to franchise, as we cannot and do not estimate the results which any particular franchise may expect to achieve. NEW FRANCHISEE'S FINANCIAL RESULTS ARE LIKELY TO DIFFER FROM THE FINANCIAL INFORMATION CONTAINED IN THIS ITEM 19.

GREAT WRAPS

4 Executive Park E., # 315
Atlanta, GA 30329
Tel: (888) 489-7277, (404) 248-9900 x16
Fax: (404) 248-0180
Email: mkaplan@greatwraps.com
Website: www.greatwraps.com
Mark Kaplan, President

At GREAT WRAPS It's All About Flavor!, we use zesty, hot combinations of top-quality meats, real melted cheese, fresh produce, and hand-made sauces. GREAT WRAPS is already the number one Wrapped Sandwich and Hot Cheesesteak franchise, and we have taken our Brand and Operation to the next level. Our franchise opportunity is unique, proven, and provides tremendous growth potential. We just rolled out beautiful eye-catching new designs, a fresh Logo, and a revolutionary new hoodless cooking system that offers tons of operational efficiencies that you can not find anywhere else.

All three parts of our powerful menu are now prepared using only space-aged convection ovens. This means no vent hoods, no unhealthy fryers or oil, no grills, and no grease traps. It also means we can open in pretty much any type of location. The end product is fresher, tastier, and far more healthy than traditional fast food. Customers can choose from fresh salads to amazing hot cheesesteaks; it's hard to find this level of choice anywhere else. Our operation is extremely efficient, and literally push-button easy. Prior food experience is not necessary.

BACKGROUND
IFA Member:	Yes
Established & First Franchised:	1978; 1981
Franchised Units:	80
Company-Owned Units:	0
Total Units:	80
Distribution:	US – 80; CAN – 0; O'seas – 0
North America:	20 States, 0 Provinces
Density:	22 in GA, 18 in TX, 8 in FL
Projected New Units (12 Months):	15
Qualifications:	5, 3, 3, 3, 4, 4

FINANCIAL/TERMS
Cash Investment:	$100K
Total Investment:	$137 – $350K
Minimum Net Worth:	$250K

Fees (Franchise):	$17.5K
Fees (Royalty):	5.5%
Fees (Advertising):	0.5%
Term of Contract (Years):	15/10
Average Number of Employees:	5 FT, 6 PT
Passive Ownership:	Discouraged
Encourage Conversions:	Yes
Area Development Agreements:	Yes
Sub-Franchising Contracts:	Yes
Expand in Territory:	Yes
Space Needs:	350 – 2,000 SF

SUPPORT & TRAINING

Financial Assistance Provided:	Yes (I)
Site Selection Assistance:	Yes
Lease Negotiation Assistance:	Yes
Co-operative Advertising:	Yes
Franchisee Association/Member:	Yes/Member
Size of Corporate Staff:	11
On-going Support:	C, D, E, G, H
Training:	2 Weeks Atlanta, GA; 5-7 Days On-Site for Grand Opening

SPECIFIC EXPANSION PLANS

US:	MW, NE, SE, SW
Canada:	No
Overseas:	No

As of December 31, 2011 we had 61 units that had been open at least 12 months. Of those units, 49 are considered "Food Court" spaces which are generally located in enclosed office, shopping & entertainment malls and one airport. We anticipate the majority of future franchise sales being in Food Court locations which also will begin to include units in Food Courts on major universities and military bases. Our other locations are in strip shopping centers and tend to have lower sales volumes.

In 2011, our Average Gross Sales at all Food Court Units was $504,516, with 47% of those units exceeding the average. This figure reflects an average for forty nine (49) franchised that were open for more than 12 months as of December 31, 2011.

In 2011, our Average Gross Sales at the food court locations in Shopping & Entertainment Mall Food Courts was $601,522, with 48% of those units above the average. This figure reflects and average for twenty five (25) franchised units that were open for more than 12 months as of December 31, 2011. The averages in this paragraph do not include the Atlanta Airport unit, due to the significantly high volume that particular store achieves annually, which we did not feel was accurately representative of our "average" Mall & Entertainment Food Court store sales.

The average for the top 20% of all Shopping & Entertainment Mall Food Court units, not including the Atlanta Airport unit, was $727,633, with 50% of those units exceeding the average.

The figures shown above reflect gross sales only, and do not show profit levels. While your labor and food costs should be fairly predictable, you will also have rental, financing and other expenses. In addition, a new Franchisee's results may differ from the represented performance. There is no assurance that you will do as well and you must accept that risk. Written substantiation for the financial performance representation will be made available to the prospective franchisee upon reasonable request.

JACK IN THE BOX

9330 Balboa Ave.
San Diego, CA 92123-1516
Tel: (800) 955-5225, (858) 571-4044
Fax: (858) 694-1501
Email: franchising@jackinthebox.com
Website: www.jackinthebox.com/franchise
Grant Kreutzer, Dir. Franchise Licensing and Recruitment

Jack in the Box Inc. (NASDAQ: JACK), based in San Diego, is a restaurant company that operates and franchises Jack in the Box® restaurants, one of the nation's largest hamburger chains, with over 2,200 restaurants in 20 states. Additionally, through a wholly owned subsidiary, the company operates and franchises Qdoba Mexican Grill®, a leader in fast-casual dining, with over 600 restaurants in 42 states and the District of Columbia. Jack in the Box is known for its premium QSR menu items, offering a broad selection of distinctive, innovative products targeting fast-food lovers who want delicious, craveable, and affordable food that is served quickly by our friendly employees. The "breakfast all day" proposition is a major differentiator for the brand, and our breakfast menu is quite extensive. Complementing the broad selection of distinctive and innovative menu items is the new Mark 9 restaurant prototype, which maximizes kitchen efficiencies and operational execution while modernizing exterior/interior design elements to enhance the guest experience.

BACKGROUND

IFA Member:	No
Established & First Franchised:	1951; 1982
Franchised Units:	1,592
Company-Owned Units:	642
Total Units:	2,234
Distribution:	US – 2,234; CAN – 0; O'seas – 0
North America:	19 States, 0 Provinces
Density:	927 in CA, 615 in TX, 174 in AZ
Projected New Units (12 Months):	N/A
Qualifications:	N/A

FINANCIAL/TERMS

Cash Investment:	$750K
Total Investment:	$1.2 – $2.5MM
Minimum Net Worth:	$1.5MM
Fees (Franchise):	$50K
Fees (Royalty):	5%
Fees (Advertising):	5%
Term of Contract (Years):	N/A
Average Number of Employees:	10 FT, 10 PT
Passive Ownership:	Not Allowed
Encourage Conversions:	N/A
Area Development Agreements:	No
Sub-Franchising Contracts:	No
Expand in Territory:	No
Space Needs:	N/A

SUPPORT & TRAINING

Financial Assistance Provided:	No
Site Selection Assistance:	N/A
Lease Negotiation Assistance:	N/A
Co-operative Advertising:	No
Franchisee Association/Member:	No
Size of Corporate Staff:	0
On-going Support:	N/A
Training:	N/A

SPECIFIC EXPANSION PLANS

US:	No
Canada:	No
Overseas:	No

The following table represents the sales and operating figures of franchise-operated Jack in the Box restaurants in the continental United States (i.e., excluding Hawaii) that were in operation for more than 360 days within the twelve-month period ended September 30, 2011, and were operated by the same franchisee(s) for that entire period. The figures for two (2) of those restaurants were excluded because the franchisee did not submit complete financial information for that period. One thousand one hundred, ninety-seven (1,197) restaurants are represented in the table, comprising approximately 54% of all Jack in the Box restaurants and 75% of franchised Jack in the Box restaurants as of September 30, 2011.

The information in the table was prepared using financial information provided to us by franchisees. The franchisees' financial information is not audited, and may not have been prepared in accordance with generally accepted accounting practices. The footnotes to the table describe the primary types of items that we ask franchisees to include in each financial category, but we cannot guarantee that all franchisees used these categories in the manner we have requested. The data used in preparing this Item 19 will be made available to prospective franchisees upon reasonable request.

Various categories of costs have been excluded from the financial calculations in the table below. The excluded categories are as follows: occupancy costs, depreciation and amortization, interest, income taxes, general and administrative expenses, officer compensation and other income and expenses. Because any development fees paid to us under a development agreement, and the initial franchise fee and royalties paid to us under a franchise agreement, would normally appear in the excluded categories, those fees are not represented in the table.

You should consider that this information gives no weight to regional sales and cost variations. Sales and costs may differ widely from one geographic region to another. You must make your own investigation into the likely costs in your geographic area.

You should also consider that sales and expenses vary from restaurant to restaurant. Your restaurant's sales, costs and expenses will be directly affected by many factors, including but not limited to, the restaurant's size and geographic location; competition from other restaurants in the market; the presence of other Jack in the Box restaurants in the market; the quality of management and service at your restaurant; operating hours; contractual terms you have negotiated with vendors and lessors; the extent to which you finance the construction and operation of your restaurant; legal, accounting, real estate and other professional fees; federal, state and local income tax rates; and discretionary expenditures. Please also note that recessionary economic conditions, including higher levels of unemployment, lower levels of consumer confidence, and decreased consumer spending can reduce restaurant traffic and sales, and impose practical limits on pricing.

Written substantiation for the financial performance representation will be made available to you upon reasonable request.

THIS INFORMATION SHOULD NOT BE CONSIDERED AS THE ACTUAL OR POTENTIAL SALES, COSTS, OR OPERATING PROFITS THAT YOU WILL REALIZE. A FRANCHISEE'S INDIVIDUAL FINANCIAL RESULTS MAY DIFFER FROM THE RESULTS SHOWN IN THIS ITEM 19. THE COSTS IN THIS STATEMENT DO NOT REPRESENT ALL COSTS YOU WILL INCUR. WE DO NOT REPRESENT THAT ANY OPERATOR CAN EXPECT TO ATTAIN ANY PARTICULAR COSTS OR OPERATING PROFITS PRESENTED. WE DO NOT REPRESENT THAT YOU WILL DERIVE INCOME FROM YOUR RESTAURANT THAT EXCEEDS YOUR INVESTMENT IN YOUR RESTAURANT. IF YOU CHOOSE TO PURCHASE A FRANCHISE FROM US, YOU ACCEPT THE RISK THAT YOUR ACTUAL RESULTS MAY VARY GREATLY FROM THE RESULTS SHOWN HERE. WE URGE YOU TO CONSULT WITH APPROPRIATE FINANCIAL, BUSINESS AND LEGAL ADVISERS TO CONDUCT YOUR OWN ANALYSIS.

In the table on the following page, we have divided the restaurants into five ranges based on sales volume. We have calculated the average sales and certain expenses of restaurants in each of the five ranges.

Jack in the Box Inc. Average Sales and Costs of Franchise-Owned Restaurants in 5 Sales Ranges In the Continental U.S. (i.e., excluding Hawaii) for the 12-Month Period Ended September 30, 2011						
	Below $1,000,000	$1,000,000 to $1,250,000	$1,250,000 to $1,500,000	$1,500,000 to $1,750,000	$1,750,000 and above	Total/Average
Number of restaurants	263	340	309	182	103	1,197
	22%	28%	26%	15%	9%	100%
% by state						
CA	40%	48%	62%	69%	78%	56%
AZ	11%	11%	6%	7%	1%	8%
TX	40%	30%	23%	17%	13%	27%
Other	9%	11%	9%	7%	8%	9%
Sales (1)	860,680	1,125,914	1,368,398	1,618,440	1,983,268	1,278,895
	100.0%	100.0%	100.0%	100.0%	100.0%	100.0%
Cost of sales (2)	263,117	348,679	422,219	494,264	617,967	394,171
	30.6%	31.0%	30.9%	30.5%	31.2%	30.8%
Labor						
Production labor (3)	186,831	226,066	264,341	303,541	360,412	250,666
	21.7%	20.1%	19.3%	18.8%	18.2%	19.6%
Management comp. (4)	37,182	42,457	46,325	51,518	56,161	44,853
Payroll taxes/Ins. (5)	33,425	39,472	48,276	55,199	65,398	45,038
Total labor	257,437	307,995	358,943	410,257	481,971	340,557
	29.9%	27.4%	26.2%	25.3%	24.3%	26.6%

Gross profit	340,126	469,241	587,236	713,919	883,330	544,166
	39.5%	41.7%	42.9%	44.1%	44.5%	42.5%
Operating costs						
Advertising (6)	44,429	57,903	70,536	83,747	101,567	65,890
Utilities (7)	43,766	45,642	50,080	51,272	54,646	48,007
Other (8)	67,617	71,625	77,439	81,566	92,579	75,560
Total operating costs	155,812	175,171	198,055	216,585	248,792	189,457
	18.1%	15.6%	14.5%	13.4%	12.5%	14.8%
Operating margin before occupancy costs	184,314	294,070	390,181	497,334	634,538	354,710
	21.4%	26.1%	28.4%	30.7%	32.0%	27.7%

(1) Product sales and promotional sales

(2) Food and packaging costs, less supplier rebates

(3) Wages of hourly employees and team leaders, including overtime

(4) Wages and bonuses paid to restaurant and assistant restaurant managers

(5) Payroll taxes, paid time-off, workers' compensation and medical insurance

(6) Marketing fee, as described in the franchise agreement, and restaurant specific promotional programs

(7) Electricity, gas, water and sewer

(8) Maintenance and repairs, menu panels, uniforms, supplies, bank charges, and other services

Except for the information that the FTC Rule permits franchisors to provide, as outlined in the first paragraph of this Item 19, we do not furnish information about the actual or potential sales, costs, income or profits of Jack in the Box restaurants. We specifically instruct our employees and other agents that, other than by providing the written representations permitted by the FTC Rule, they are not authorized to make claims, estimates or other statements about the earnings, sales, profits, or prospects of success of Jack in the Box restaurants. If you receive any such unauthorized representations, whether oral or written, you should immediately notify us by contacting our General Counsel, Phillip H. Rudolph, 9330 Balboa Avenue, San Diego, California 92123, (858) 571-2435.

KOLACHE FACTORY
a history of good taste.

KOLACHE FACTORY

23240 Westheimer Pkwy., #A
Katy, TX 77494
Tel: (855) 565-2243, (281) 829-6188

Email: anielsen@kolfac.com
Website: www.kf-franchising.com
Aaron Neilsen, Franchise Sales Director

A quick-service bakery that specializes in making kolaches. Kolaches are ideal for breakfast, lunch, or as a snack, with over 25 different varieties to choose from, ranging from sausage to egg to fruit. Our delicious and satisfying meals are sure to please even the pickiest of eaters. Our kolaches have grown in popularity over the last 25 years, and business continues to grow. We take great pride in offering the freshest ingredients, and our dough is made fresh on-site daily at each one of our locations.

BACKGROUND

IFA Member:	No
Established & First Franchised:	1982; 2000
Franchised Units:	21
Company-Owned Units:	21
Total Units:	42
Distribution:	US – 42; CAN – 0; O'seas – 0
North America:	6 States, 0 Provinces
Density:	37 in TX, 1 in ID, 1 in MO
Projected New Units (12 Months):	10 – 20
Qualifications:	5, 4, 3, 3, 4, 4

FINANCIAL/TERMS

Cash Investment:	$30 – $50K
Total Investment:	$340 – $474K
Minimum Net Worth:	$500K
Fees (Franchise):	$35K
Fees (Royalty):	6%
Fees (Advertising):	3%
Term of Contract (Years):	10/5
Average Number of Employees:	5 – 7 FT, 1 PT

Passive Ownership:	Not Allowed
Encourage Conversions:	Yes
Area Development Agreements:	Yes
Sub-Franchising Contracts:	No
Expand in Territory:	Yes
Space Needs:	1,600 – 1,800 SF

SUPPORT & TRAINING

Financial Assistance Provided:	Yes (I)
Site Selection Assistance:	Yes
Lease Negotiation Assistance:	Yes
Co-operative Advertising:	Yes
Franchisee Association/Member:	No
Size of Corporate Staff:	14
On-going Support:	A, C, D, E, F, h, I
Training:	4 Weeks Houston, TX

SPECIFIC EXPANSION PLANS

US:	CA, CO, IN, KS, MO, TX, VA
Canada:	No
Overseas:	No

Characteristics of the Stores included in the Financial Performance Representations below may differ substantially from your Store depending on your previous experience, competition in the area, length of time that the included Stores have operated as compared to your Store, and the services or products sold at your Store as compared to the included Stores. Your individual financial results may differ substantially from the results stated in this financial performance representation. Written substantiation for this financial performance representation is available to you on reasonable request.

As of December 31, 2011, Kolache Factory, Inc. ("KFI") was operating 18 Stores in the Houston, Texas market, 2 additional stores in Texas outside of the Houston market and 1 store outside of the State of Texas (Indianapolis, Indiana). The following table presents sales and operating profit information (commonly called "EBITDA") for the KFI Stores in fiscal years

2010 and 2011. The "High" designation presents the average EBITDA of the four Stores that achieved the highest sales and operating profit during those two years. The "Middle" designation presents the average EBITDA of the four Stores that achieved the next highest sales and operating profit for those two years. The "Low" designation presents the average EBITDA of four KFI Stores. The Low group contains a store that is open only Monday through Friday.

The information in the table is derived from KFI's audited statements, but itself is unaudited. We will provide substantiation of the data we used in calculating the information upon receipt of a written request from you. You should conduct an independent investigation of the costs and expenses you will incur in operating your Store. Current franchisees or former franchisees listed in Exhibits F and G of this Disclosure Document may be one source of information.

	2011	2010	2011	2010	2011	2010
Sales	$756,039	$709,377	$634,401	$627,901	$572,306	$524,356
Food Cost	$205,425	$183,399	$172,161	$174,471	$163,917	$141,224
Gross Income	$550,614	$525,978	$457,240	$453,430	$848,389	$383,132
Operating Expenses:						
Wages/401(k) & Benefits*	$163,383	$149,211	$140,161	$142,347	$136,967	$129,000
Payroll Taxes	$12,429	$11,373	$10,660	$10,810	$10,439	$9,866

Rent	$59,519	$59,676	$54,542	$59,769	$49,732	$56,131
Utilities	$16,204	$16,457	$16,496	$13,756	$15,851	$15,269
Supplies	$8,917	$6,922	$6,751	$7,618	$5,943	$5,188
Phone	$2,169	$2,727	$3,135	3,054	$2,228	$2,466
Advertising	$17,598	$18,249	$18,373	$16,118	$24,912	$21,104
Insurance	$1,902	$1,883	$2,710	$3,110	$1,868	$1,182
Maintenance	$8,953	$5,089	$6,814	$8,639	$6,967	$6,136
Property Taxes	$56	$446	$260	$32	$329	$496
Professional Services	$2,104	$2,054	$2,327	$2,243	$2,106	$2,111
Auto	$0	$0	$0	$0	$0	$0
Credit Card Charges	$15,424	$12,881	$12,630	$11,101	$11,986	$10,324
Over/Short	$52	$41	$73	$92	$364	$244
Operating Expenses	$7,967	$4,447	$6,366	$6,724	$7,788	$5,951
Lease of Equipment	$0	$0	$0	$0	$0	$0
Total Operating Expenses	$316,068	$291,458	$284,298	$285,813	$277,480	$265,468
Earnings before Interest, Taxes, Depreciation and Amortization (EBITDA)	$234,546	$234,520	$175,942	$167,617	$130,909	$117,664

*KFI's average store manager expense, including employee tax contributions, averaged approximately $42,000 in 2010 and 2011. Each Store usually employs one management level employee and five hourly employees. If you serve as the manager, you will not incur this cost unless you pay yourself a salary.

As noted above, almost all of the Stores are located in strip centers in the Houston area. There is one Store in the low range located in Indianapolis, Indiana and one Store in the middle range that is located in a free-standing building in Houston, Texas. The ages of the Stores are from one year to 22 years. However, after the start-up phase, we do not consider age a significant factor in a Store's revenue or profit potential.

IF YOU BECOME A KOLACHE FACTORY FRANCHISEE, YOUR STORE'S FINANCIAL RESULTS ARE LIKELY TO DIFFER FROM THOSE OF OUR STORES. In determining how relevant the sales data of existing Stores may be to your situation, we caution you to keep the following points in mind. We also urge you to discuss and analyze this information with your own business, financial and legal advisers.

• KFI has operated Stores since 1981 and has accumulated vast experience in Store operations and management.

• Almost all of KFI's Stores are located in the Houston, Texas metropolitan area, which encompasses a population of several million people. We cannot predict how well a Store will perform in a less populous market.

• Kolaches are known and accepted in the Houston, Texas market to a degree that may not be true in your market.

• Almost all of KFI's Stores benefit from the mild winters that Houston, Texas experiences.

• KFI does not pay the 6% royalty on its sales that franchisees pay on theirs. If KFI had paid a 6% royalty, the average operating expenses of the Stores presented in the table would have increased as follows for 2011 and 2010: High – $45,362/$42,563; Middle – $38,064/$37,674; Low – $34,338/$31,462. Further, EBITDA for the 3 Stores would have decreased to the following amounts for 2011 and 2010: High – $189,184/$191,957; Middle – $137,878/$129,944; Low – $96,571/$86,202.

• KFI does not contribute 3% of Gross Sales to the Advertising Fund. However, KFI routinely spends more than 3% of Gross Sales on advertising. KFI also pays $25 monthly per Store for the Internet/website fee. Further, we cannot predict how much you will spend on local advertising in addition to your 3% Advertising Fund contribution. Consequently, the difference between KFI's advertising expense and yours cannot be readily ascertained.

- The information relates only to sales and operating expenses; you can draw no inferences with respect to any Store's interest expense, depreciation charges or after-tax profitability.

- There may be other costs and other expenses not identified. The costs and expenses of company owned locations may differ from franchisee owned Stores.

Except for the information presented above, we do not use or furnish statements of actual, average, projected or forecasted sales, costs, profits or earnings in marketing our franchises. We will not guarantee, nor do we represent, that you will or can expect to attain any specific amount or range of sales, profits or earnings from the operation of your Store. Actual results may vary from Store to Store, and we cannot estimate the results of any franchisee.

Except for the information presented above, we do not authorize any of our officers, employees or sales representatives to make any claims, statements, or representations regarding the sales, costs, profits or earnings, or the prospects or chances of success, that you can expect to achieve or that any other franchisee has achieved. We specifically instruct our representatives not to make these claims, statements or representations, and you are cautioned not to rely on any claims, statements or representations any person makes in disregard of these instructions. We accept no responsibility for, and will not be bound by, any unauthorized claims, statements or representations regarding your potential sales, costs, profits earnings, prospects, or chances of success.

If you receive any other financial performance information or projections of your future income other than the information above, you should report it to the franchisor's management by contacting Vicki Kozel in our franchise administration department at 23240 Westheimer Parkway, Suite A, Katy, Texas 77494 and (281) 829-6188, the Federal Trade Commission, and the appropriate state regulatory agencies.

MCDONALD'S

Campus Office Building, 2915 Jorie Blvd.
Oak Brook, IL 60523
Tel: (888) 800-7257, (630) 623-6196
Fax: (630) 623-5658
Email: bob.villa@us.mcd.com
Website: www.aboutmcdonalds.com
Bob Villa, National Franchise Manager

Quick-service restaurant.

BACKGROUND
IFA Member:	Yes
Established & First Franchised:	1955; 1955
Franchised Units:	27,970
Company-Owned Units:	6,595
Total Units:	34,565

Distribution:	US – 14,156; CAN – 1,405; O'seas – 19,004
North America:	50 States, 6 Provinces
Density:	1,339 in CA, 1,194 in TX, 868 in FL
Projected New Units (12 Months):	N/A
Qualifications:	3, 5, 3, 3, 4, 4

FINANCIAL/TERMS
Cash Investment:	$750K
Total Investment:	$1.1 – $2.1MM
Minimum Net Worth:	N/A
Fees (Franchise):	$45K
Fees (Royalty):	12%
Fees (Advertising):	4%
Term of Contract (Years):	20/20
Average Number of Employees:	50 PT
Passive Ownership:	Not Allowed
Encourage Conversions:	N/A
Area Development Agreements:	No
Sub-Franchising Contracts:	No
Expand in Territory:	Yes
Space Needs:	2,000 SF

SUPPORT & TRAINING
Financial Assistance Provided:	No

Site Selection Assistance:	N/A	Training:	N/A
Lease Negotiation Assistance:	N/A		
Co-operative Advertising:	Yes	SPECIFIC EXPANSION PLANS	
Franchisee Association/Member:	Yes/Member	US:	All United States
Size of Corporate Staff:	0	Canada:	All Canada
On-going Support:	C, D, E, G, H, I	Overseas:	All Countries

Of the approximately 12,073 domestic traditional McDonald's restaurants opened at least 1 year as of December 31, 2011, approximately 74% had annual sales volumes in excess of $2,100,000; approximately 63% had annual sales volumes in excess of $2,300,000; and approximately 51% had annual sales volumes in excess of $2,500,000 during 2011. The average annual sales volume of domestic traditional McDonald's restaurants open at least 1 year as of December 31, 2011, was $2,578,000 during 2011. The highest and lowest annual sales volume in 2011 for these domestic traditional McDonald's restaurants was $10,200,000 and $370,000, respectively.

The pro forma statements included below show annual sales volumes of $2,100,000, $2,300,000, and $2,500,000. These pro forma statements have been derived from independent franchisee traditional restaurant financial statements to provide information relevant to a prospective franchisee (see Note 1). Specific assumptions used in the presentation of these pro forma statements are indicated above and below each statement.

The pro forma statements are based upon a total of 8,713 independent franchisee traditional restaurants open and operated by a franchisee for at least 1 year. A FRANCHISEE'S INDIVIDUAL FINANCIAL RESULTS MAY DIFFER FROM THE RESULTS STATED IN THE PRO FORMA STATEMENTS FOR THE REASONS DESCRIBED IN THIS ITEM OR FOR OTHER REASONS. Substantiation of the data used in preparing the earnings claims, including computations of all actual or average profit or earnings, will be made available to prospective franchisees upon reasonable request.

It is anticipated that the information reported in these pro forma statements reflects the operating results before occupancy costs for independent franchisee restaurants open for at least 1 year. However, the operating income before occupancy cost figures appearing below should not be construed as the financial results or "profit" before occupancy costs which might be experienced by a franchisee with a similar sales volume or an indication that any particular sales volume will be obtained. An individual franchisee is likely to experience operating expense variations including, but not limited to, general insurance, legal and accounting fees, labor costs, and store management benefits (life and health insurance, etc.). Additionally, market conditions, operational and management methods employed by a franchisee, different geographic areas of the country, and menu price variations may significantly affect operating results. The nature of these variables makes it difficult to estimate the financial results for any particular franchisee or location.

PRODUCT SALES (see Note 2)	$2,100,000	100.0%	$2,300,000	100.0%	$2,500,000	100.0%
TOTAL COST OF SALES	650,000	31.0%	710,000	30.9%	770,000	30.8%
GROSS PROFIT	1,450,000	69.0%	1,590,000	69.1%	1,730,000	69.2%
OTHER OPERATING EXPENSES (excluding rent, service fees, depreciation and amortization (D&A), interest, and income taxes)*	903,000	43.0%	969,000	42.1%	1,036,000	41.4%
OPERATING INCOME BEFORE OCCUPANCY COSTS (excluding rent, service fees, D&A, interest, and income taxes) (see Note 3)**	547,000	26.0%	621,000	27.0%	694,000	27.8%

Of the 8,713 independent franchisee traditional restaurants included in the pro forma statements above, approximately 44% had operating income before occupancy costs greater than $547,000; approximately 32% had operating income before occupancy costs greater than $621,000; and approximately 22% had operating income before occupancy costs greater than $694,000.

* OTHER OPERATING EXPENSES — Includes, but is not limited to, the following costs: labor, franchisee's salary as manager, payroll taxes, advertising fee (as described in Item 6), promotion, outside services, linen, operating supplies, small equipment, maintenance and repair, utilities, office supplies, legal and accounting fees, insurance, real estate and personal property taxes, business operating licenses, and non-product income or expense. This is a combination of the Total Controllable Expenses and Other Operating Expenses excluding rent, service fees, D&A, and interest included in our typical store financial statements.

** OPERATING INCOME BEFORE OCCUPANCY COSTS — Represents Operating Income excluding rent, service fees, D&A, interest, and income taxes. The rent paid to McDonald's will vary based upon sales and McDonald's investment in land, site improvements, and building costs. Refer to Item 6 for information regarding franchise fees (including rent and service fees paid to McDonald's). D&A and interest will vary based upon the purchase price and required reinvestment of the specific restaurant acquired. Refer to Item 7 for a description of investment costs.

Additionally, organization overhead costs such as salaries and benefits of non-restaurant personnel (if any), cost of an automobile used in the business (if any), and other discretionary expenditures may significantly affect profits realized in any given operation. The nature of these variables makes it difficult to estimate the performance for any particular restaurant with sales of any given volume.

THESE SALES, PROFITS, OR EARNINGS ARE AVERAGES OF SPECIFIC RESTAURANTS AND SHOULD NOT BE CONSIDERED AS THE ACTUAL OR POTENTIAL SALES, PROFITS, OR EARNINGS THAT WILL BE REALIZED BY ANY OTHER FRANCHISEE. MCDONALD'S DOES NOT REPRESENT THAT ANY FRANCHISEE CAN EXPECT TO ATTAIN THESE SALES, PROFITS, OR EARNINGS.

Note 1 — Data for McOpCo company restaurants is not included in the pro forma statements because of certain expenses that are typically incurred by a McOpCo-operated restaurant that are not incurred by restaurants franchised to individuals. If data for McOpCo-operated restaurants open for at least 1 year were included along with franchised restaurants, the percent of total restaurants in each category would not be statistically different and the range of Operating Income Before Occupancy Costs would be $564,000 to $712,000.

Note 2 — The description of this line, "Product Sales," is to clarify that only product sales are included. Non-product sales and associated costs are included in Other Operating Expenses.

Note 3 — We are not presenting average occupancy costs in the above calculation because a wide variety of rent charts and ownership options exist. In addition, the effective rent paid by a franchisee may be more in any particular month than the stated percent rent indicated in the franchisee's lease because a portion of the rent may be fixed regardless of the sales level for a given month. The range of effective rent percentages in 2011 for franchised restaurants was 0% to 37%. Refer to Item 6 for a description of rents.

MOE'S SOUTHWEST GRILL

200 Glenridge Pt. Pkwy., #200
Atlanta, GA 30342
Tel: (800) 227-8353, (404) 255-3250
Fax: (404) 257-7073
Email: scorp@moes.com
Website: www.moes.com
Steven Corp, Vice President of Franchise Sales

BACKGROUND

IFA Member:	Yes
Established & First Franchised:	2000; 2001
Franchised Units:	500
Company-Owned Units:	4
Total Units:	504
Distribution:	US – 838; CAN – 27; O'seas – 33
North America:	48 States, 4 Provinces
Density:	71 in FL, 68 in TX, 49 in PA
Projected New Units (12 Months):	60
Qualifications:	4, 4, 1, 2, 3, 3

FINANCIAL/TERMS

Cash Investment:	N/A
Total Investment:	$453 – $788K
Minimum Net Worth:	$1.5MM
Fees (Franchise):	$30K
Fees (Royalty):	50%
Fees (Advertising):	2% for national
Term of Contract (Years):	20
Average Number of Employees:	1 FT, 5 PT
Passive Ownership:	Not Allowed

Encourage Conversions:	Yes
Area Development Agreements:	Yes
Sub-Franchising Contracts:	No
Expand in Territory:	No
Space Needs:	1,212 SF

SUPPORT & TRAINING

Financial Assistance Provided:	No
Site Selection Assistance:	Yes
Lease Negotiation Assistance:	Yes
Co-operative Advertising:	Yes
Franchisee Association/Member:	Yes/Not a Member
Size of Corporate Staff:	80
On-going Support:	C, D, E, f, G, h, I
Training:	On-Going Regional, Annual, On-Line; 5 Weeks On-Site; 3 Weeks Horsham, PA

SPECIFIC EXPANSION PLANS

US:	All United States
Canada:	All Canada
Overseas:	All Countries

Below is a profit and loss statement ("P&L Statement") for the calendar year 2011 (the "Period") for Restaurants that have been open continuously for 3 or more years ("Three-Year Group") and that provided us with complete financial information for the full Period.

PROFIT AND LOSS STATEMENT FOR THREE-YEAR GROUP OF RESTAURANTS		
During Period	Average	Percentage of Total Gross Sales during the Period
Total Gross Sales	$1,102,495	
Cost of Goods (i.e. food, beverages, paper)	$330,983	30.0%
Personnel Expenses (i.e. salaries and payroll, medical insurance, unemployment taxes)	$251,243	22.8%
Advertising (i.e. NAMF, co-op, local marketing, coupons)	$115,057	10.4%
Operating Expenses (i.e. royalties, maintenance, utilities, pest control, security, other controllable expenses)	$145,460	13.2%
Occupancy Expenses (i.e. rent, cam payments, equipment lease expense)	$89,350	8.1%
General and Administrative Expenses (i.e. credit card fees, bank service charges, general liability insurance, legal/accounting fees, business license& fees)	$19,427	1.8%
Earnings Before Interest, Taxes, Depreciation and Taxes, Depreciation and Amortization (EBITDA)	$150,975	13.7%

Bases

"Net Sales" has the same meaning shown in Item 6 that is used for purposes of calculating royalties due under the Franchise Agreement. There were 351 Restaurants there were in operation continuously for 3 years before the end of the Period. Of These 351 Restaurants, we received financial information for the full period from 148 Restaurants.

Of the 148 Restaurants represented in the Three-Year Group, 63 Restaurants (or 42.3% of the Three-Year Group) attained or exceeded the Average Total Gross Sales in the table above.

Two of the restaurants reflected in the table above had a Carvel Express Shoppe that operated in them for the period.

The Restaurants whose results are reflected in the table above were in operation continuously for the three-year period before the end of the Period. The table does not include results for Restaurants that (i) did not submit full and complete financial information for the entire Period or (ii) opened or closed during the Period or during the three-year period before the end of the Period. Two of the Restaurants reflected in the table above had a Carvel Express Shoppe that operated in them for part of the Period (one Carvel Express Shoppe opened in April 2010 and the other Carvel Express Shoppe opened in September 2010). The information in the P&L Statement includes the information for the operations of the two Carvel Express Shoppes discussed in the previous sentence.

The above data for the Three-Year Group has been taken from financial reports submitted by franchisees. We have not audited or verified these financial reports nor have we asked questions of the submitting franchisees to determine whether they are in fact accurate and complete, although we have no information or other reason to believe that they are unreliable. We did not use any reports that were incomplete or for which the information was presented in a manner that prohibited us from applying the information to one of the categories in the P&L Statements.

The data is for specific franchised Restaurants and should not be considered as the actual or potential sales, costs or profits that will be achieved by any other franchised Restaurant. Actual results vary from Restaurant to Restaurant and we cannot estimate the results of any specific Restaurant. A new franchisee's sales results are likely to be lower than the results shown above and expenses are likely to be higher that the results shown above. There may be other expenses in operating a Restaurant that are not identified in the P&L Statements. You should conduct an independent investigation of the expenses in operating a Restaurant, and franchisees and former franchisees listed in Exhibits E and F to this Disclosure Document may be one source for obtaining additional information on expenses in operating a Restaurant.

Assumptions

The data shown above is for Restaurants throughout the System, which includes various types of real estate locations (traditional and non-traditional venues) and formats. Sales, costs and profits for each format can vary widely. We suggest that you speak with franchisees of the same format type you intend to operate to better understand factors that may affect your potential sales, costs and profits.

Sales, costs and profits also can vary considerably due to a variety of other factors, such as demographics of the Restaurant's trade area; competition from other restaurants in the trade area; traffic flow, accessibility and visibility; economic conditions in the Restaurant's trade area; advertising and promotional activities; and the business abilities and efforts of the management of the Restaurant.

Increases in oil prices may increase food costs which could significantly increase the cost of goods.

Written substantiation for the financial performance representation will be made available to you on reasonable request.

Better Ingredients.
Better Pizza.

PAPA JOHN'S

2002 Papa John's Blvd.
Louisville, KY 40299
Tel: (502) 261-4825
Fax: (502) 261-4850
Email: stacy_bowling@papajohns.com
Website: www.papajohns.com
Stacy Bowling, Franchise Qualifications Specialist

Papa John's International, headquartered in Louisville, KY, is the world's third-largest pizza company, owning and franchising over 3,400 restaurants in all 50 U.S. states and in 29 countries. For nine out of the last ten years, consumers have rated Papa John's #1 in customer satisfaction among all national pizza chains and #1 seven out of the last ten years among all national Quick Service Restaurant (QSR) chains in the highly regarded American Customer Satisfaction Index (ACSI).

BACKGROUND

IFA Member:	No
Established & First Franchised:	1985; 1986
Franchised Units:	3,891
Company-Owned Units:	598
Total Units:	4,489
Distribution:	US – 3,250; CAN – 19; O'seas – 0
North America:	50 States, 7 Provinces
Density:	247 in FL, 211 in TX, 207 in CA
Projected New Units (12 Months):	120
Qualifications:	5, 5, 4, 3, 4, 5

FINANCIAL/TERMS

Cash Investment:	Varies
Total Investment:	$115.8 – $549.5K
Minimum Net Worth:	$250K – $2MM
Fees (Franchise):	$25K/Unit
Fees (Royalty):	5%
Fees (Advertising):	2.82%
Term of Contract (Years):	10/10
Average Number of Employees:	8 FT, 18 PT
Passive Ownership:	Allowed
Encourage Conversions:	N/A
Area Development Agreements:	Yes
Sub-Franchising Contracts:	No
Expand in Territory:	Yes
Space Needs:	1,000 – 1,400 SF

SUPPORT & TRAINING

Financial Assistance Provided:	No
Site Selection Assistance:	Yes
Lease Negotiation Assistance:	No
Co-operative Advertising:	Yes
Franchisee Association/Member:	Yes/Not a Member
Size of Corporate Staff:	13,990
On-going Support:	a, b, C, D, E, G, h, I
Training:	1 Week Papa John's University, Louisville, KY; Mentoring: Varied Location (Varies); 5 Weeks Mgmt. Training: Varied Locations

SPECIFIC EXPANSION PLANS

US:	All United States
Canada:	Yes
Overseas:	Yes

Presented below are average restaurant-level sales revenues of our domestic franchised and company-owned Papa John's restaurants for our fiscal year ended December 25, 2011, along with average restaurant-level cash expenses for company-owned Papa John's restaurants only. The following revenue and cash flow data is drawn from our financial books and records, which are kept on a basis consistent with Generally Accepted Accounting Principles ("GAAP") in the United States. All information is based on actual historical costs and results. Thus, there are no material assumptions associated with the data, other than the principles of GAAP. A number of factors may affect the comparability of the expense (or cash outflow) data, which is drawn solely from company-operated restaurants, to franchised restaurants and the data's effectiveness as a guide or template for potential operating results of a franchised restaurant. The most significant of these factors are discussed in the notes following the data. You should carefully consider these factors when reviewing, analyzing considering the data presented below.

Restaurant Revenues

Average Sales — Company-owned restaurants: $882,053

229 Company-owned restaurants, 43.1% of the total included in the data, achieved sales revenues of $882,053 or greater in 2011.

Average Sales — Franchised restaurants: $754,433

972 Franchised restaurants, 43.1% of the total included in the data, achieved sales revenues of $754,433 or greater in 2011.

Average Cash Flows (Company-owned restaurants only):

		Percent of Sales
Food Costs	$271,304	30.8%
Labor Costs and Taxes	177,384	20.1%
Manager's Labor and Taxes	42,986	4.9%
Mileage	39,767	4.5%
Advertising	84,580	9.6%
Controllables*	54,828	6.2%
Rent and Common Area Maintenance	31,397	3.6%
Other Non-Controllables**	40,006	4.5%
Training Costs	3,178	0.4%
Store Bonuses	14,044	1.6%
Pre-Tax Cash Flows	$122,579	13.9%

241 Company-owned restaurants, 45.4% of the total included in the data, achieved $122,579 or greater annual pre-tax cash flows in 2011.

*Controllables includes: cash over and short, smallwares, repairs and maintenance, commissions, telephone expenses, utilities, cleaning supplies, computer supplies, office supplies, laundry service, uniforms, equipment rental, postage, donations, dues and subscriptions, meals and entertainment, travel and lodging, employee incentives, professional fees, and special events.

**Other Non-Controllables includes: property taxes, management health insurance, general insurance, credit card charges, bank charges, business licenses, and worker's compensation insurance.

Notes and Comments

Historical Performance Data

The foregoing information is drawn from actual historical data from our domestic restaurants. Historical information may not be a reliable predictor of future results or experience. Future performance may be affected by many factors at variance from the conditions that yielded past results and experience, including without limitation: volatility of commodity costs (such as cheese, for example); inflation or rising costs in general, especially for labor and energy; general economic upturn or downturn; changing consumer tastes, preferences or sensibilities; and effectiveness of advertising or promotional campaigns. We do not make any guarantee of future sales, costs or profits.

Expense Data: Company-Owned Restaurants Only

Because we do not maintain or audit the accounting records of our franchisees, we would be unable to make any representation with respect to the reliability of the expense data of franchised restaurants. We are unable to determine, for example, whether franchisees' accounting and financial records are kept in a manner that would permit reporting of cost data in accordance with GAAP or whether the franchisees' bookkeeping and accounting systems, practices and controls are sufficiently robust to ensure that the data is reliable. As a result, we present only Company-owned restaurant data with respect to expense (or cash outflow) items.

Full Year Only

At the close of our fiscal year, there were 3,061 total domestic (United States) Papa John's restaurants, 598 of which were company-owned, including restaurants owned by franchisees in which we have a majority interest (a total of 128 restaurants). However, the foregoing data is drawn only from standard (or "traditional") restaurants that were open the entire year of 2011 because including results from Non-Traditional Restaurants and restaurants that were open only part of the year would skew the annual revenue and expense data. Therefore, the total number of restaurants included in the foregoing data is 2,784, comprising 2,253 franchised restaurants and 531 Company- owned restaurants.

Averages

The sales revenue data presented is based on averages for our domestic restaurants. Many restaurants have lower sales performance than the average for all restaurants. With a data base consisting of more than 2,500 restaurants, the lowest performing restaurants may have performance data that vary significantly from the average. Some restaurants have sold or earned as much as shown in the foregoing data. Your individual results may differ. We make no assurance that you will sell or earn as much. Similarly, the cash expense data for our Company-owned restaurants represents averages across a population of more than 500 restaurants. Thus, many Company-owned restaurants have costs that are higher than the system-wide average. Performance of a particular restaurant, in terms of both revenues and expenses, may be affected by many factors, including without limitation: location (whether the restaurant is in a free-standing building, in-line in a strip center or an end-cap in a strip center; whether the restaurant is in a high-visibility, high-traffic location); population density in the restaurant's trade area; business acumen and managerial skills of restaurant management personnel; prevailing wage rates and quality of the available labor pool; availability and cost of commercial rental property; the presence and aggressiveness of the competition; and utility costs.

Core Business Revenues

The revenue figures for both franchised and Company-owned restaurants include only sales of food and beverages arising in the ordinary course of retail operations. Non-recurring items, such as proceeds from the sale of used furniture or equipment, are not included.

Non-Cash Items

The cash flow data does not include depreciation expense or any other non-cash items. Over time, worn-out or obsolete restaurant equipment will have to be replaced and leasehold improvements, signage, computer systems and restaurant furnishings may have to be refurbished, remodeled, upgraded or replaced. The foregoing cash flow data does not include any reserves for funding any of these types of improvements or upgrades.

Royalty

Company-owned restaurants do not pay a royalty. The expenses incurred by a franchised restaurant will include our standard royalty.

Economies of Scale

Because we operate more than 500 company-owned restaurants, we are able to achieve certain economies of scale and operational efficiencies that may not be available to a franchisee operating one restaurant or a limited number of restaurants, as is the case for the typical franchisee. For example, we have a multi-tiered management hierarchy. At the higher levels of management, we are able to rely on the expertise of management executives with a wealth of experience in the restaurant and food service industries. You may not be able to achieve the same level of management expertise. You will be relying principally on your own business acumen and managerial skills and perhaps that of your Principal Operator. However, the income from our company-owned restaurants ultimately must bear the costs of our management team and other corporate office overhead. These costs are not reflected in the foregoing cash flow data, which reflect operational cash flows at the restaurant level, excluding the burden of corporate overhead.

Because of the size of our Company-owned operations, we are able to support a marketing department, with personnel dedicated to marketing functions, as well as dedicated cash management, payroll and other administrative functions. You and your Principal Operator will perform most of these functions, although some administrative functions may be out-sourced. Unless you are developing a significant number of restaurants, you may not be able to have experienced personnel dedicated to specific functions, such as marketing.

We are a publicly-traded company and have raised significant capital through our stock offerings. We typically do not require bank financing for construction or equipping of our restaurants or for capital improvements or for updating or replacement of worn-out or obsolete equipment in our restaurants. However, to the extent that we do require financing, we are able to draw on a significant line of credit from our primary bank. It is unlikely that these types of financing efficiencies will be available to you.

We are also able to obtain economies of scale in other areas, such as insurance, that may not be available to franchisees. Because of the size of our operations, insurance risks are spread over a greater number of restaurants, which enables us to bargain for lower group-rate insurance costs. We are also able to use the size of our operations to achieve volume discounts and other cost savings based on our purchasing power. These cost savings, in areas including telephone services and advertising, may not be available to franchisees operating on a smaller scale.

Restaurant and Market Maturity

Sales of a particular restaurant may be affected by how long the restaurant has been in operation and how successfully the surrounding market has been penetrated. Typically, sales "ramp up" as the restaurant and market develop. New restaurants (open for less than one year) typically do not operate as efficiently or as profitably as more mature restaurants. In particular, sales at restaurants open less than one year are typically lower than more mature restaurants, as it takes some time to establish consumer recognition and build a customer base in a new trade area. Greater penetration (the greater the number and concentration of restaurants) in a market also may affect performance. Clusters of restaurants may be able to pool resources to purchase advertising on local television or radio, which would be prohibitively expensive for a single restaurant, or even a small cluster of restaurants in a large media market. The foregoing Company-owned restaurant data represents averages for all of our domestic restaurants, some of which are long-established in their location and some of which are relatively new. Most of our Company-owned restaurants are in highly developed and highly penetrated markets.

Market Location

Our company-owned restaurants are typically clustered in and around major metropolitan areas, such as Atlanta, St. Louis and Nashville. Many franchised restaurants are operated in less densely populated areas, with more limited access to advertising media.

Traditional Restaurants Only

The foregoing data refers only to standard (or "traditional") Papa John's restaurants. Performance data for Non-Traditional Restaurants varies widely, depending upon the nature of the non-traditional location, number of events or sales dates and other widely varying factors. Thus, this Item 19 is applicable to traditional Papa John's restaurants only. We do not furnish or authorize our sales persons to furnish any oral or written information concerning the actual or potential sales, costs, income or profits of a Papa John's Non-Traditional Restaurant.

Other Data

Except as described below, we do not furnish or authorize the furnishing to prospective franchisees of any oral or written information other than the data provided above. We may provide to you the actual performance data of a particular restaurant that you are considering purchasing. Also, we may, but

we have no obligation to, provide to you supplemental data consisting of a segmentation or subset of the above data. For example, we may provide data for a particular region or individual state. If we do so, that supplemental data will be in writing and will be limited to the types of information set forth in the above data. We do not furnish and do not authorize anyone to furnish supplemental data that is outside the scope of the data provided above. If you obtain any other financial information concerning Papa John's restaurants, do not rely on it as a representation of Papa John's.

Your Own Due Diligence

You should construct your own pro forma cash flow statement and make your own projections concerning potential sales, operating costs, total capital investment requirements, operating cash requirements, debt, cash flow, and other financial aspects of operating a Papa John's restaurant. You should not rely solely on the information provided by us. You should conduct your own investigation of revenue and expense potential for your proposed Papa John's restaurant, including consultation with your own attorney, accountant or other adviser and other Papa John's franchisees.

CAUTION

AS A CONSEQUENCE OF THE FACTORS DISCUSSED ABOVE, AND OTHER VARIABLES THAT WE CANNOT ACCURATELY PREDICT, A NEW FRANCHISEE'S INDIVIDUAL FINANCIAL RESULTS ARE LIKELY TO DIFFER FROM THE RESULTS SHOWN IN THE DATA INCLUDED IN THIS ITEM 19.

Substantiation of Data

Substantiation of the data used in preparing the data set forth in this Item 19 will be available to prospective franchisees upon reasonable request.

PAPA MURHPY'S

8000 N.E. Parkway Dr., # 350
Vancouver, WA 98662
Tel: (800) 257-7272, (360) 260-7272
Fax: (360) 260-0500

Email: amy.stevens@papamurphys.com
Website: www.papamurphysfranchise.com
Amy Stevens, Franchise Development

Papa Murphy's is the largest take-and-bake pizza company in the world, with over 1,360 locations in the U.S. and Canada. The entire concept is built around the idea of take 'n' bake menu options. By baking Papa Murphy's pizzas at home, customers get to experience the home-baked aroma of a convenient, delicious meal that the brand is known for. To franchise owners, Papa Murphy's offers an opportunity that is attractive with a simplistic business model at a great investment price.

BACKGROUND		Encourage Conversions:	Yes
IFA Member:	Yes	Area Development Agreements:	Yes
Established & First Franchised:	1981; 1982	Sub-Franchising Contracts:	No
Franchised Units:	1,298	Expand in Territory:	Yes
Company-Owned Units:	62	Space Needs:	1,200 – 1,400 SF
Total Units:	1,360		
Distribution:	US – 1,343; CAN – 17; O'seas – 0		
North America:	37 States, 3 Provinces	SUPPORT & TRAINING	
Density:	150 in CA, 140 in WA, 95 in OR	Financial Assistance Provided:	Yes (I)
Projected New Units (12 Months):	100	Site Selection Assistance:	Yes
Qualifications:	4, 3, 2, 3, 2, 5	Lease Negotiation Assistance:	Yes
		Co-operative Advertising:	Yes
FINANCIAL/TERMS		Franchisee Association/Member:	Yes/Member
Cash Investment:	$80K	Size of Corporate Staff:	150
Total Investment:	$215.9 – $378.4K	On-going Support:	C, D, E, G, H, I
Minimum Net Worth:	$270K	Training:	23 Days Certified Train. Store; 5 Days
Fees (Franchise):	$25K		Owners Class at Corp.; 2 Days POS Train.
Fees (Royalty):	5%		
Fees (Advertising):	2%	SPECIFIC EXPANSION PLANS	
Term of Contract (Years):	10/5	US:	Central, Midwest, South
Average Number of Employees:	2 FT, 8 – 10 PT	Canada:	Yes
Passive Ownership:	Not Allowed	Overseas:	No

Under the three sections below, we have provided an unaudited statement of system store performance, benchmark costs, average annual Net Sales percentage increase, and new store performance. Information for franchise-owned stores has been taken from their respective self- reported weekly sales and profit and loss statements. We have not audited or verified these figures or reports nor have we asked questions of the submitting franchisees to determine whether they are in fact accurate and complete, although we have no information or other reason to believe that they are unreliable. We do not know whether the information was prepared consistent with generally accepted accounting principles.

The amount of sales realized and costs and expenses incurred will vary from store to store. The sales, costs and expenses of your Franchised Store will be directly affected by many factors, such as the Franchised Store's size, geographic location, menu mix, and competition in the marketplace; the presence of other Papa Murphy's stores; the quality of management and service at the Franchised Store; contractual relationships with lessors and vendors; the extent to which you finance the construction and operation of the Franchised Store; your legal, accounting, real estate and other professional fees; federal, state and local income, gross profits or other taxes; discretionary expenditures; and accounting methods used. You should, therefore, use this analysis only as a reference.

You are urged to consult with appropriate financial, business and legal advisors to conduct your own analysis of the information contained in this section.

System Store Performance:

All stores included in this System Store Performance section are traditional stores, in that the stores are not located within another retailer's space, such as a grocery or department store. As of January 2, 2012 (the end of our 2011 fiscal year) there were 1,283 stores open. Of the 1,283 stores open, 1,202 traditional stores were open and operating during the entire period of our fiscal year, and 81 stores were either non-traditional or were not open for the full fiscal year. The following statements are based on information reported by the 1,202 traditional stores, both franchise-owned and company-owned, in operation as of January 2, 2012. These stores represent 46 company-owned stores and 1,156 franchise-owned stores (collectively referred to herein as "System Stores"). The System Stores were divided into three groups with the same number of stores in each group, except for one less store in the Medium Group based on Net Sales results: top third ("High"), middle third ("Medium"), and lower third ("Low").

The average annual Net Sales of the System Stores was $559,495 ("System Store Average") per store. These System Stores offer substantially the same menu and product mix that your Franchised Store will offer. Of the 1,202 stores, 492 met or exceeded this average.

The High Group's average Net Sales are $828,296; the Medium Group's average Net Sales are $511,241; and the Low Group's average Net Sales are $338,829. The ranges of Net Sales and averages within the High, Medium and Low categories are listed below:

VOLUME	HIGH	MEDIUM	LOW
Number of Stores	401	400	401
Net Sales:			
Highest	$1,741,245	$606,304	$424,770
Lowest	$606,814	$425,114	$156,352
Average Net Sales by Category	$828,296	$511,241	$338,829
Number of Stores Exceeding Average Net Sales by Category	156	205	227
Total System Store Average Net Sales	$559,495		

Benchmark Costs:

On October 3, 2011, the end of our fiscal third quarter 2011, there were 1,154 franchise- owned stores which were open and operating for the trailing 53 weeks. Of those 1,154 stores, 634 submitted profit and loss statements in the correct format for the prior 53 weeks. The following benchmark is based on the sales and operating costs reflected in the profit and loss statements submitted by those 634 stores during that time period ("Benchmark Stores").

The average Net Sales for the Benchmark Stores over the trailing 53 weeks was $612,226. The range of Net Sales was between $207,399 and $1,778,370. These results have not been audited and though the numbers appear to accurately reflect the level of results expected, there is no guarantee that they are in whole or part correct.

VOLUME CATEGORY		HIGH	MEDIUM	LOW
Number of Stores		211	212	211
By Category:	Notes			
Average Gross Sales	1	$1,047,517	$656,689	$448,706
Average Discounts (on Gross Sales)	2	14.2%	14.9%	15.5%
Average Net Sales	3	$898,875	$559,052	$379,003
Number of Stores Exceeding Average Net Sales		82	102	118
Below are represented as a % of Net Sales				
Average COGS	4	37.1%	37.4%	38.4%
Average Employee Labor	5	14.6%	15.2%	17.2%
Average Management	6	4.2%	5.1%	5.6%
Average Payroll Taxes	7	2.3%	2.3%	2.5%
Average Advertising	8	6.9%	8.1%	8.8%
Average Rent and CAM	9	4.1%	6.1%	8.4%
Average Other Store Expenses	10	12.9%	14.1%	16.0%
Average Store Contribution	11	17.9%	11.7%	3.1%

The notes to the above table are an integral part of the bases and assumptions of this analysis. You should particularly note the following:

The table of Benchmark Stores' sales and average food and labor costs are based upon the self-reported profit and loss statements submitted by a portion of the System Stores. The average sales and average costs reflected in the analysis should not be considered as the actual or potential sales, costs, income or profits that you will realize. We do not represent that any franchisee can expect to attain the sales, costs, income or profits described in this section, or any particular level of sales, costs, income or profits. In addition, we do not represent that any franchisee will derive income that exceeds the initial payment for or investment in the Franchised Store. The individual financial results of any Franchised Store are likely to differ from the information described in this section, and your success will depend largely on your ability. Substantiation of the data used in preparing this analysis will be made available on reasonable request.

The analysis does not include any estimates of the federal income tax that would be payable on the net income from a store or state or local net income or gross profits taxes that may be applicable to the particular jurisdiction in which a store is located. Each franchisee is strongly urged to consult with its tax advisor regarding the impact that federal, state and local taxes will have on the amounts shown in the analysis.

Notes:

(1) Average Gross Sales. The gross sales figures set forth above represent all food and beverage sales before any coupons or other discounts are taken. It does not include sales taxes collected.

(2) Discount Percentages. The percentages included above include coupons and discounts offered on promotional items or offers. The percentage is calculated on gross sales.

(3) Average Net Sales. The sales figures set forth above represent all food and beverage sales, net of discounts. This is the amount on which you will calculate your royalty payments.

(4) Cost of Goods ("COGS"). Average COGS includes all food inventory and packaging delivered to the store and used in creating the product for sale, but excludes cleaning supplies and similar items. We negotiate contracts for quantity and price for both beverages and certain food products to take advantage of volume discounts. (See ITEM 8.)

(5) Employee Labor. Hourly wages, both regular and overtime (including crew, assistant managers, shift leaders), for food preparation and service. No corporate management personnel are included in labor costs. The amount of hourly labor necessary to operate a Franchised Store will vary from unit to unit, but should incrementally increase or decrease with the sales volume of the Franchised Store. Hourly wages may vary significantly by geographic location, the supply of and demand on the local labor pool, and state and federally mandated minimum wage laws. Labor includes wages only and does not include payroll taxes, medical or workers compensation insurance or 401(k) plan contributions.

(6) Management. Management costs include payroll expenses (salaries, bonuses for meeting performance objectives, and vacation) for the Franchised Store manager. The number of managers may vary based on sales volume and your requirements may differ from those of a Benchmark Store. In some cases, a franchise owner serves as the store manager and draws little or no salary.

(7) Payroll Taxes. Unemployment taxes (both federal and state), FICA, employee injury insurance or workers compensation where required.

(8) Advertising. This category is comprised of four types of expenditures: (a) local store marketing and merchandising, (b) contribution to the Advertising and Development Fund, (c) contribution to the Sales Building Print Plan, and (d) your Franchised Store's designated percentage contribution to your local advertising cooperative, which can be different for each designated marketing area.

(9) Rent and Common Area Maintenance ("CAM"). Rent and CAM includes rent and lease costs, common area maintenance expenses and tax and insurance due the landlord. Rent and lease costs include the base rent and any percentage rent. Common area maintenance costs typically include franchisee's pro rata charges for parking lot maintenance, lighting, real estate taxes, taxes on the common areas and costs of maintaining the common areas. Rental costs will vary as a result of space requirements and local market conditions.

(10) Other Store Expenses. Other store expenses include the cost of direct supervision, bank fees, accounting and payroll services, utilities, repairs and maintenance, telephone, employee benefits, insurance, janitorial, smallwares, taxes and licenses, broadband/internet, point-of-sale system costs, credit card processing charges, uniforms, laundry and supplies as well as royalty payments. Utilities include electricity, gas, water and telephone costs for the operation of the Franchised Store. The pro rata share of common area utility costs is included under rent and lease payments. (See Note 9.) These costs are subject to local market conditions and may vary depending on the geographic location of the Franchised Store. The Other category also includes personal property taxes, other real es-

tate taxes not included in rent and lease and other operating licenses required by state and local agencies. You should investigate property taxes in the area in which you plan to locate your Franchised Store.

(11) Store Contribution. The store contribution represents revenue less expenses described herein, and this figure does not reflect other costs which you may incur as a franchisee, which may include general and administrative costs, depreciation (consult with your tax advisor regarding depreciation and amortization schedules and the period over which the assets may be amortized or depreciated as well as the effect, if any, of recent and proposed tax legislation), and financing costs, if any. In addition, you will also pay local state and federal income taxes which are not reflected in the preceding table.

Average Annual Net Sales Percentage Increase:

This statement includes the average Net Sales percentage Increase for stores based on a comparison of Net Sales: (i) in 2006 and 2005 for stores that were in operation for the entire 52-week period ended January 1, 2007; (ii) in 2007 and 2006 for stores that were in operation for the entire 52-week period ended December 31, 2007; (iii) in 2008 and 2007 for stores that were in operation for the entire 52-week period ended December 29, 2008; (iv) in 2009 and 2008 for stores that were in operation for the entire 52-week period ended December 28, 2009; (v) in 2010 and 2009 for stores that were in operation for the entire 53-week period ended January 3, 2011; and (vi) in 2011 and 2010 for stores that were in operation for the entire 52-week period ended January 2, 2012. Only stores that were open all weeks in both years are compared.

Average Same Store Net Sales Percentage Increase			
Comparison Year	Stores	Percentage Increase	Number and Percentage of Stores Above Average
2006 v 2005	765	2.4%	408 (53%)
2007 v 2006	828	6.0%	398 (48%)
2008 v 2007	899	9.2%	461 (51%)
2009 v 2008	987	2.7%	489 (50%)
2010 v 2009	1,059	-2.9%	540 (51%)
2011 v 2010	1,113	5.8%	567 (51%)

Papa Murphy's had positive year-over-year comparable store sales performance for five out of the last six years.

New Store Performance:

Of the 65 new stores opened in fiscal year 2011, 48 stores had 12 or more full operating weeks as of the week ended January 2, 2012. The average weekly Net Sales for stores during the first 12 full operating weeks was $9,425. Of the 48 stores, 21 (44%) met or exceeded this average. The actual annual average Net Sales achieved may vary due to seasonality, location characteristics, owner involvement, marketing plans and competition, as well as other factors disclosed in this Disclosure Document.

Other than the preceding financial performance representation, we do not make any financial performance representations. We also do not authorize our employees or representatives to make any such representations either orally or in writing. If you are purchasing an existing outlet, however, we may provide you with the actual records of that outlet. If you receive any other financial performance information or projections of your future revenue and/or income, you should report it to the franchisor's management by contacting Victoria Blackwell, Papa Murphy's International LLC, at 8000 NE Parkway Drive, Suite 350, Vancouver, Washington 98662, (360) 449-4122, the Federal Trade Commission, and the appropriate state regulatory agencies.

PERKINS RESTAURANT & BAKERY

6075 Poplar Ave., #800
Memphis, TN 38119
Tel: (800) 877-7375, (901) 766-6400
Fax: (901) 766-6482
Email: bob.winters@prkmc.com
Website: www.perkinsrestaurants.com
Robert Winters, SVP of Franchise Development

Since 1958, Perkins Restaurant & Bakery has offered quality, tasty, affordable food for breakfast, lunch, and dinner. Our brand heritage and ability to adapt to trends make Perkins a leader in the family dining segment. We are seeking experienced restaurants operators to meet our expansion goals in key markets across the country. We provide professional support services in training, design and construction, marketing, operations, quality assurance, and R&D.

BACKGROUND
IFA Member:	Yes
Established & First Franchised:	1958; 1965
Franchised Units:	324
Company-Owned Units:	163
Total Units:	487
Distribution:	US – 460; CAN – 27; O'seas – 0
North America:	34 States, 0 Provinces
Density:	76 in MN, 59 in FL, 53 in PA

Projected New Units (12 Months):	N/A
Qualifications:	5, 4, 5, 3, 3, 5

FINANCIAL/TERMS
Cash Investment:	$500K
Total Investment:	$1.2 – $2.6K
Minimum Net Worth:	$1.5MM
Fees (Franchise):	N/A
Fees (Royalty):	4%
Fees (Advertising):	3%
Term of Contract (Years):	20/N/A
Average Number of Employees:	6 FT, 64 PT
Passive Ownership:	Discouraged
Encourage Conversions:	Yes
Area Development Agreements:	Yes
Sub-Franchising Contracts:	No
Expand in Territory:	Yes
Space Needs:	5,000 SF

SUPPORT & TRAINING
Financial Assistance Provided:	No
Site Selection Assistance:	Yes
Lease Negotiation Assistance:	Yes
Co-operative Advertising:	Yes
Franchisee Association/Member:	No
Size of Corporate Staff:	0
On-going Support:	C, D, E, F, h, I
Training:	Management Team Training Various Locations; University of Perkins Various Locations; New Product Roll-Out Training at Franchisee's Location

SPECIFIC EXPANSION PLANS
US:	All United States except AZ, CA, MA, ME, NM, NV, OR, RI, WA
Canada:	All Canada
Overseas:	No

The first table below of Average Annual Sales Volume (the "Average Sales Table") and the Schedule of Restaurant Financial Data (the "Schedule") discloses the average sales and selected costs of 130 Perkins restaurants owned and operated by PMC for the entire fiscal year ending December 25, 2011 (referred to as the "Restaurants").

AVERAGE ANNUAL SALES VOLUME - 2011

The following table groups the Restaurants into ranges (using three tiers) of annual sales volume and disclosing the number of Restaurants within each tier and further disclosing the average sales volume of each tier, the number of restaurants (of the 130) within each tier, the number of restaurants within a particular tier that met or exceeded the Average Annual Sales Volume for that tier, and the percentage of restaurants (out of the 130) that met or exceeded the Average Annual Sales Volume of the three tiers.

Average Restaurant Tier #	Average Annual Sales Volume	Sales Volume Range of Restaurants Included	# of Restaurants in Range	# of Restaurants Within Range that Met or Exceeded Average Annual Sales Volume	% of Restaurants (130) that Met or Exceeded Average Annual Sales Volume
1	$1,299,091	$1,020,000-$1,485,000	44	24	84.6%
2	$1,681,636	$1,485,000-$1,863,000	43	24	51.5%
3	$2,263,240	$1,863,000-$3,526,000	43	21	16.2%

The Restaurants are distributed throughout the north central and midwestern United States with the greatest concentrations in Minnesota, Wisconsin, Missouri, Iowa, and Florida. They are located predominantly in metropolitan areas on or near major traffic thoroughfares. The buildings housing the Restaurants are predominantly single-purpose, one story and free-standing, seating from 90 to 250 guests at one time, which are comparable to the restaurants expected to be operated pursuant to the License Agreement.

The location of the Restaurants used to compile the information disclosed in the Average Sales Table and Schedule are categorized by state, as follows:

Average Restaurant Tier 1 (44 locations): Colorado-4, Florida-10, Illinois-2, Iowa-4, Kansas-1, Minnesota-9, Missouri-4, Oklahoma- 1, Pennsylvania-2, Tennessee- 1 and Wisconsin-6.

Average Restaurant Tier 2 (43 locations): Florida-10, Illinois-3, Iowa-6, Kansas-1, Minnesota-16, Missouri-3, Oklahoma- 1 and Wisconsin-3.

Average Restaurant Tier 3 (43 locations): Florida-12, Iowa-6, Minnesota- II, Pennsylvania-3, Tennessee-I, North Dakota-4 and Wisconsin-6.

Substantially the same services were offered by PMC to the Restaurants as are provided to the franchisees; however, PMC did not and does not provide certain services to franchisees which are normally provided by the owner such as financing, accounting (unless the franchisee has entered into the Accounting Services Agreement), legal, personnel, management, financial and food and labor cost systems.

The Restaurants offered substantially the same products and services to the public as the restaurants to be operated pursuant to the License Agreement.

The following Schedule was prepared on a basis consistent with generally accepted accounting principles and the same accounting system was used for each Restaurant. The figures used in the Schedule are based on an annual performance.

Some restaurants have earned these amounts. Your individual results may differ. There is no assurance you'll earn as much.

Written substantiation of the data used in preparing the Schedule will be made available upon reasonable request.

THE INFORMATION PRESENTED BELOW HAS NOT BEEN AUDITED.

SCHEDULE OF RESTAURANT FINANCIAL DATA- 2011
(Dollars in Thousands)

	Average Restaurant Tier 1		Average Restaurant Tier 2		Average Restaurant Tier 3	
	Amount	Percentage of Sales	Amount	Percentage of Sales	Amount	Percentage of Sales
Net Food Sales	1,299	100.0	1,682	100.0	2,263	100.0
Food Cost	327	25.1	413	24.6	551	24.4
Gross Profit	972	74.9	1,269	75.4	1,712	75.6
Labor:						
Management	115	8.9	132	7.8	172	7.6
Hourly	271	20.9	356	21.1	454	20.1

Total	386	29.8	488	28.9	626	27.7
Benefits:						
Payroll Tax	49	3.8	62	3.7	81	3.6
Vacation/Sick	17	1.3	21	1.2	30	1.3
Workers Comp/Other	20	1.5	24	1.4	30	1.3
Employee Insurance	18	1.4	18	1.1	18	0.8
Total	104	8.0	125	7.4	159	7.0
Direct Operating Expenses:						
Supplies	40	3.1	50	3.0	63	2.8
Menus, guest checks, place-mats, toys	3	0.2	4	0.2	5	0.2
Uniforms, laundry	2	0.2	2	0.1	3	0.1
Smallwares, others	3	0.2	4	0.2	4	0.2
Total	48	3.7	60	3.6	75	3.3
Repairs & Maintenance	27	2.1	31	1.8	35	1.5
Outside Services	14	1.1	16	1.0	21	0.9
Utilities	78	6.0	84	5.0	99	4.4
Local Store Marketing	25	1.9	27	1.6	35	1.5
Administrative:						
Travel	1	0.1	0	0.0	0	0.0
Classified Advertising	0	0.0	0	0.0	0	0.0
Office Supplies	2	0.2	2	0.1	3	0.1
Legal, Bank fees, bad debt	21	1.6	27	1.6	36	1.6
Miscellaneous	1	0.1	2	0.1	2	0.1
Total	25	1.9	31	1.8	41	1.8
Total Operating Expenses	707	54.4	862	51.2	1,091	48.2
Total Controllable Income	265	20.4	407	24.2	621	27.4
Non-Controllable Expense:						
Advertising	39	3.0	50	3.0	68	3.0
Property insurance	7	0.5	9	0.5	13	0.6
Property taxes	26	2.0	30	1.8	34	1.5
CAM	3	0.2	1	0.1	2	0.1
Other	7	0.5	9	0.5	16	0.7
Total	82	6.3	99	5.9	133	5.9
Cash Flow from Operations	183	14.1	308	18.3	488	21.6

The average statements shown in the Schedule DO NOT include the following items of expense which have to be calculated and included separately for every restaurant:

a) Rent.

b) Royalty Fees consistent with current contractual requirements under the Franchise Agreement (see Item 22).

c) Depreciation of property and equipment.

d) Interest or other financing costs for land, buildings, equipment and inventory.

e) Initial license fee and organization costs (see Item 5).

f) Any accounting, legal or management fees.

g) Income taxes.

These excluded items affect the net income and/or cash flow of any restaurant and must be carefully considered and evaluated by any prospective franchisee. The actual performance of any restaurant will depend on a number of factors specific to the property including, but not limited to, the above factors.

The Restaurants and restaurants to be operated pursuant to the License Agreement have the following similarities:

a) Each Restaurant operates under the name "Perkins," including "Perkins Family Restaurant and Bakery" and "Perkins Restaurant and Bakery."

b) Each Restaurant generally offers the same selection of menu items and many are open 24 hours a day.

Sales and operating results of the Restaurants and the restaurants to be operated pursuant to the License Agreement are affected by the following:

a) Economic and weather conditions of various geographic areas.

b) Competition from a variety of other restaurants, including fast food businesses. Some restaurants have greater competition than others.

c) Different acquisition, development, construction and property costs.

d) Local property tax rates.

e) State laws affecting employee costs.

f) Different traffic counts, accessibility and visibility. The location of each restaurant may have a significant impact on sales and operating income.

g) Different benefits from advertising. Some Restaurants do not receive the benefits of television advertising. Some Restaurants are not grouped in such a way that local television or other media advertising can be efficiently obtained.

h) Although each Restaurant has seating and parking, the amount of seating and parking varies among the Restaurants.

i) All Restaurants have been in business for different periods of time and therefore have experienced varying periods of time to become established in their respective markets.

j) Each franchisee may set its own prices for menu items.

k) Each Restaurant may experience varying food costs due to geographic area and economies of scale due to the grouping of Restaurants in any single geographic area.

l) The quality and effectiveness of management of each Restaurant varies.

Licensed Restaurant Results

The following information is based on 299 licensed restaurants and does not include 2 licensed restaurants that opened and 16 that closed during 2011.

a) To PMC's knowledge, the number of the licensed restaurants described above that equaled or exceeded the Average Annual Sales Volumes shown in the Average Sales Volume Table are as follows: 34 (out of 103) for Average Restaurant Tier 1 (which is 11.4% of all 299 restaurants); 31 (out of 82) for Average Restaurant Tier 2 (which is 10.4% of all 299 restaurants); and 33 (out of 68) for Average Restaurant Tier 3 (which is 11.0% of all 299 restaurants) (and one exceeded the sales volume range of Average Restaurant Tier 3).

b) To PMC's knowledge, the number and approximate percentage of the 299 licensed restaurants described above that were in operation during the entire year ending December 25, 2011 with total sales that actually fell within the sales ranges shown in the Schedule were: 45 (15.1 %) were below the sales range of Average Restaurant Tier 1; 103 (34.4%) for the sales range of Average Restaurant Tier 1; 82 (27.4%) for the sales range of Average Restaurant Tier 2; and 68 (22.7%) for the sales range of Average Restaurant Tier 3.

c) To PMC's knowledge, one licensed restaurant during the same year actually surpassed the levels of income before royalties, advertising, occupancy costs and taxes as set forth in the Schedule.

d) Within a range of annual sales volumes from $1,020,000 to $3,526,000 for Restaurants owned and operated by PMC, to PMC's knowledge 84.6% of reporting licensed restaurants that were in operation during the entire year actually fell within such range of sales. Annual sales volumes of all reporting licensed restaurants for the year ending December 25, 2011 ranged from $538,000 to $3,903,000.

Written substantiation of the data used in preparing the above statement will be made available upon request. Because PMC does not require that existing licensed restaurants follow a particular accounting system, PMC cannot certify that the licensed restaurants follow generally accepted accounting principles. PMC will not disclose the identity of any specific franchisee whose data has been used to compile any information in this item except to the agency(ies) with which this filing is made.

Other than the preceding financial performance representation, PMC does not make any financial performance representations. We also do not authorize our employees or representatives to make any such representations either orally or in writing. If you are purchasing an existing outlet, however, we may provide you with the actual records of that outlet. If you receive any other financial performance information or projections of your future income, you should report it to the franchisor's management by contacting Bob Winters, 6075 Poplar Avenue, Suite 800, Memphis, TN 38119, 901-766-6400, the Federal Trade Commission, and the appropriate state regulatory agencies.

RITA'S ITALIAN ICE

1210 N. Brook Dr., # 310
Trevose, PA 19053
Tel: (800) 677-7482, (215) 876-9300
Fax: (866) 449-0974
Email: franchise_sales@ritascorp.com
Website: www.ritasice.com
Scott Schubiger, SVP Franchise Sales

Rita's is the largest Italian Ice chain in the nation. With a 28-year proven business model, Rita's offers a variety of frozen treats including its famous Italian Ice, Old Fashioned Frozen Custard, and layered Gelati as well as its signature Misto and Blendini creations.

BACKGROUND

IFA Member:	Yes
Established & First Franchised:	1984; 1989
Franchised Units:	552
Company-Owned Units:	0
Total Units:	552
Distribution:	US – 552; CAN – 0; O'seas – 0
North America:	20 States, 0 Provinces
Density:	196 in PA, 120 in NJ, 82 in MD
Projected New Units (12 Months):	40

Qualifications:	3, 3, 3, 3, 3, 5

FINANCIAL/TERMS

Cash Investment:	$100K
Total Investment:	$140.2 – $379.4K
Minimum Net Worth:	$300K
Fees (Franchise):	$30K
Fees (Royalty):	6.5%
Fees (Advertising):	3%
Term of Contract (Years):	10/10
Average Number of Employees:	2 FT, 15 PT
Passive Ownership:	Discouraged
Encourage Conversions:	No
Area Development Agreements:	Yes
Sub-Franchising Contracts:	No
Expand in Territory:	Yes
Space Needs:	800 – 1,200 SF

SUPPORT & TRAINING

Financial Assistance Provided:	Yes (I)
Site Selection Assistance:	Yes
Lease Negotiation Assistance:	Yes
Co-operative Advertising:	Yes
Franchisee Association/Member:	No
Size of Corporate Staff:	60
On-going Support:	C, D, E, F, G, H, I
Training:	4 Days On-Site; 5 Days Corporate Office

SPECIFIC EXPANSION PLANS

US:	All United States
Canada:	Yes
Overseas:	Yes

Included in this Item 19 are Rita's estimates of (1) 2011 average sales of Proprietary Products at franchised Shops ("Average Sales"), described in Section I, below, and (2) 2011 average food costs for ingredients for the Proprietary Products at franchised Shops ("Costs of Goods Sold"), described in Section II, below. No Financial Performing Representations are being made on the Fixed Satellite Unit, the Mobile Satellite Units or the Express Unit.

I. 2011 AVERAGE SALES OF PROPRIETARY PRODUCTS AT FRANCHISED SHOPS

The following chart represents our estimates of; the Average Sales of: franchised Shops for Italian ice, gelati, frozen custard, Misto shakes, and Blendini in 2011:

	Top Third	Middle Third	Bottom Third
Number of:Shops	166	166	166
Range of Sales:			
High	$760,996	$271,223	$200,731
Low	$271,289	$200,971	$46,400
Average	$342,645	$236,945	$153,659

Although Rita's obtained reports from Franchisees as to Gross Sales at franchised Shops for the 2011 season for marketing and research purposes, Rita's is not able to independently verify reported sales. In preparing the Average Sales gure for this Item 19, Rita's estimated Average Sales from franchised Shops. Reported sales were typically lower than estimated Average Sales. As stated in Item 6 of this disclosure document, Royalty Fees and Advertising Fees on Proprietary Products are based on estimated sales. Rita's describes below how Rita's estimated the Average Sales contained in this Item 19.

The sales estimates described in this Item 19 represent only the sales by Franchisees of Proprietary Products containing the proprietary Rita's Mixes. These Proprietary Products were Italian ice, gelati, frozen custard, Misto shakes, and Blendini. Not included in the sales calculations described in this Item 19 are any other products sold by Franchisees, such as pretzels and promotional items.

The information in the Chart above is based on Shops that have been open for at least 1 full season. Shops opened less than 1 full season are not included in the calculations. A full season is dened as 1 entire selling season for which Rita's requires operation and the Shop must be opened at least 5 days before spring. Florida franchised Shops may have been open for as many as 10 to 12 months. Where a Shop was open for a period longer than the selling season, all sales for such Shop were included in Rita's determination of Average Sales.

The Chart divides franchisees into three categories (Top Third, Middle Third, and Bottom Third), based on their sales as compared with the sales for the 498 total Shops considered in arriving at these gures. 60 franchisees (36% othe Shops in the Top Third) attained or surpassed the average sales for the Top Third; 87 franchisees (52% othe Shops in the Middle Third) attained or surpassed the average sales for the Middle Third; and 98 franchisees (59% othe Shops in the Bottom Third) attained or surpassed the average sales for the Bottom Third. The average sales represent the average sales for franchisees within each category. High sales and Low sales represent the Franchisee within each category that attained the highest and lowest sales.

As noted in Item 6 o this disclosure document, each Franchisee must pay to Rita's a Royalty Fee in the amount of 6 1/2% of the projected sales to be made by a Franchisee based on a Franchisee's purchase of Rita's proprietary Rita's Mixes. In calculating the Royalty Fee, Rita's estimates the projected sales that can be expected to be made from a Franchisee's purchase of Rita's Mixes, based on the amount of Rita's Mixes required for use in Rita's recipes for each product.

In calculating the Average Sales, Rita's estimated Franchisees' Average Sales based on the amount of Rita's Mixes purchased, Franchisees' prices, and the percentage of each type of Proprietary Product sold by Franchisees relative to all Proprietary Products sold (the "Product Percentages"). The historical data from which Rita's calculated the Product Percentages was provided to Rita's by each franchisee via weekly reporting oretail sales figures for each product during the 2011 season. Rita's knows the prices charged by each Franchisee because each Franchisee must notify Rita's of its prices so that Rita's may calculate the Royalty Fee to be paid by such Franchisee. The numbers in the chart above have been rounded to the nearest thousand.

Franchisee's Sales are generally lower during the first several years ooperation for franchised Shops. Therefore, franchised

Shops open for the first two to three years may be more likely than other franchised Shops to be in the Bottom Third in sales.

The Product Percentages for the 2011 season, as determined from Franchisees' franchised Shop register tapes (described in I, above) are described below. The Product Percentages vary based upon a Franchisee's location.

Proprietary Product	Percentage of All Proprietary Products Reported for Sale
ITALIAN ICE	35.7%
GELATI	26.5%
CUSTARD	20.0%
MISTO SHAKE	5.9%
BLENDINI	6.3%
MISCELLANEOUS	5.6%
TOTAL	100.00%

In calculating the Royalty Fee and Average Sales above Rita's assumed certain "usage" and "wastage" figures for franchisees. Rita's measures Franchisees' "usage" figures by comparing (1) the expected yield for Rita's Mixes that Rita's calculates and (2) the amount of Proprietary Products sold using such mixes. Rita's defines "wastage" as the Rita's Mix that will not be used in Proprietary Products that are sold (e.g. product that will be thrown away or given away in connection with promotions). Usage estimates vary among the franchisees' location. Such usage figures vary widely for some franchisees, and are much higher for some franchisees. Rita's believes that the reason for the variation is due to a variety of factors including certain Franchisees' reporting, give-away programs, over-portioning, internal theft, changes in product mix, the timing of the purchases, inexperience, and wastage. In calculating the Royalty Fee and Average Sales, Rita's assumed that some "wastage" would occur, as there is a certain amount of "wastage" that occurs in all sales of Proprietary Products that use the Rita's Mix. The Royalty Fee calculation for the 2011 season provided for 7% wastage. Accordingly, for purposes of the calculations above, when Rita's estimated projected sales on which a Franchisee owed Rita's a Royalty Fee, Rita's reduced its projections of sales expected to be made from a given amount of Rita's Mixes by 7%.

II. 2011 COSTS OF GOODS SOLD FOR PROPRIETARY PRODUCTS AT FRANCHISED SHOPS

Rita's estimates that Rita's Franchisees' Costs of Goods Sold represent 19% of Franchisees' revenue from sales of the products. Rita's has calculated the estimated Costs of Goods Sold of 19% based on (1) portions for ingredients reported in Rita's proprietary recipes, (2) 2011 prices for such ingredients, (3) the System-wide average selling price in 2011 for each Proprietary Product sold, (4) a weighted average of Proprietary

Products sold as determined by Franchisee reports of Product Percentages in 2011 (as defined in Section I, above), and (5) average cost of paper and packaging in 2011. Rita's calculation of Costs of Goods Sold assumes that proper recipes are followed, Franchisees adhere to proper serving sizes for Proprietary Products, and Franchisees maintain product wastage levels of 7%.

Rita's does not obtain reports from Franchisees as to Costs of Goods Sold at franchised Shops. Accordingly, to prepare the Costs of Goods Sold figures in this Item 19 it was necessary for Rita's to estimate the Costs of Goods Sold figures from franchised Shops. Rita's does not know what percentage of Franchisees incurred actual Costs of Goods Sold higher or lower than the estimated Costs of Goods Sold of 19%. Rita's describes below how it estimated the Costs of Goods Sold contained in this Item 19.

The calculation of Costs of Goods Sold contained in this Item 19 represents Costs of Goods Sold only for the products that Rita's requires each Franchisee to sell (i.e., kids, regular, large and quart Italian ice; regular and large gelati; kids, regular and large custard; regular and large Misto shakes; and Blendinis). As described in Section I, above, each franchisee provided its historical data to Rita's via weekly reporting of retail sales figures for each product during the 2011 season. Rita's used this data to estimate the Costs of Goods Sold in the 2011 season. Rita's can estimate the total cost of the ingredients for each Proprietary Product because the recipes for each Proprietary Product are prescribed by Rita's, Franchisees were required in 2011 to purchase the Rita's Mixes from Rita's, and Franchisees may also purchase the remaining ingredients from Rita's. Rita's has used the prices it charged in 2011 to Franchisees for ingredients. Rita's has determined the average selling price (not including sals tax) for each Proprietary Product during the 2011 season based on the prices submitted by Franchisees. In order to approximate the food costs resulting from wastage, in calculating Costs of Goods Sold for this Item 19, Rita's reduced the average selling price for each Proprietary Product by 7%. To determine the total pre tax sales represented by the register tapes, as adjusted to reflect wastage, Rita's multiplied the adjusted average selling price by the number of units of each Proprietary Product sold (as reflected on the register tapes). Rita's also estimated the total cost of ingredients necessary to produce the total sales represented by the register tapes by multiplying the total number of each Proprietary Product sold by the estimated total costs for the ingredients for each item. Rita's determined estimated total costs for all sales represented by the register tapes by adding the estimated total costs for each Proprietary Product. Rita's determined Costs of Goods Sold by dividing the estimated total costs by the pre-tax adjusted sales. From this calculation, Rita's determined Costs of Goods Sold to be 19% of Franchisees' sales of all Proprietary Products.

As described in Item 6, above, each Franchisee must pay to Rita's a Royalty Fee based upon the amount of Rita's Mixes purchased by the Franchisee. This Royalty Fee has not been included in the calculations to determine Costs of Goods Sold in this Item 19. As a Franchisee, payment of the Royalty Fee would be an additional cost.

The calculations in this Item 19 used in determining Costs of Goods Sold are made under the assumption that Franchisees adhere to Rita's proprietary recipes and serving sizes. Although Rita's has provided each Franchisee with training and support to assist each Franchisee in adhering to these recipes and serving sizes, Rita's Franchisees have indicated to Rita's that an indeterminate number of Franchisees may serve portions to guests larger than those Rita's specifies. However, Rita's strongly encourages Franchisees to adhere to Rita's standards, specifications and portion controls for purposes of System consistency.

Costs of Goods Sold vary depending on store location, menu, Product Percentages, seasonal variances in raw material prices, and Franchisees' ability to effectively control costs. The average new Franchisee generally finds the first year of operation of each franchised Shop to be the most challenging. During the first year of operation a new Franchisee typically experiences higher wastage levels due to sampling, couponing and other promotional programs designed to build brand and product acceptance and due to higher amounts of "throw-aways" resulting from inexperience in planning. Historical costs do not correspond to future costs because of factors such as inflation, changes in menu and market driven changes in raw material costs.

Rita's obtained reports from Franchisees as to Gross Sales at franchised Shops for the 2011 season for marketing and research purposes, but we have not relied on these reports in this Item 19 because we cannot independently verify reported sales. (Reported sales are typically less than estimated Average Sales.) Actual sales and food costs vary from franchise to franchise, and Rita's cannot estimate the sales or food costs for a particular franchise. As stated in Item 6 of this disclosure document, Royalty Fees and Advertising Fees are based on estimated sales. Rita's recommends that you make your own independent investigation to determine whether or not the franchise may be profitable, and consult with an attorney and other advisors before signing the Development Agreement or the Franchise Agreement.

Rita's will make available to you for inspection and review before your purchase of a franchise the data used in formulating the information contained in this Item 19 upon your reasonable request.

Some outlets have sold this amount. Your individual results may differ. There is no assurance that you'll sell as much.

Other than the preceding financial performance representation, Rita's does not make any financial performance representations. We also do not authorize our employees or representatives to make any such representations either orally or in writing. If you are purchasing an existing outlet, however, we may provide you with the actual records of that outlet. If you receive any other financial performance information or projections of your future income, you should report it to the franchisor's management by contacting Rita's Franchise Company, Franchise Department at 1210 Northbrook Drive, Suite 310, Trevose, PA 19053 and (800) 677-7482, the Federal Trade Commission, and the appropriate state regulatory agencies.

TOGO'S EATERY

18 N. San Pedro St.
San Jose, CA 95110-2413
Tel: (408) 280-6585, (714) 582-2236
Fax: (408) 280-5067
Email: lidia.larson@togos.com
Website: www.togosfranchise.com
Lidia Larson, Franchise Development Manager

Togo's was opened in Northern California in the early 1970s by a guy who did not have a business plan. He just made reasonably priced sandwiches the way he liked them—made-to-order in a deli-style format and stuffed with fresh, wholesome ingredients. Soon there were lines out the door, and Togo's was well on its way to becoming California's most loved sandwich shop. Now, nearly 40 years later, Togo's is still crafting the best sandwiches on the West Coast, with over 240 franchise restaurants serving over a million guests per month. Our bread is baked every day, especially for us, and we have added our own selection of hearty soups, fresh salads, and specialty wraps worthy of the Togo's name.

BACKGROUND

IFA Member:	Yes
Established & First Franchised:	1968; 1971
Franchised Units:	245
Company-Owned Units:	4
Total Units:	249

Distribution:	US – 246; CAN – 0; O'seas – 0
North America:	N/A
Density:	239 in CA
Projected New Units (12 Months):	10
Qualifications:	5, 5, 4, 4, 4, 5

FINANCIAL/TERMS

Cash Investment:	$150K
Total Investment:	$258 – $420K
Minimum Net Worth:	$300K
Fees (Franchise):	$40K for 20 yr, $25K for 10 yr
Fees (Royalty):	5%
Fees (Advertising):	2% currently, but can go up to 5%
Term of Contract (Years):	20
Average Number of Employees:	5 FT, 8 PT
Passive Ownership:	Discouraged
Encourage Conversions:	No
Area Development Agreements:	Yes
Sub-Franchising Contracts:	No
Expand in Territory:	Yes
Space Needs:	1,200 – 1,500 SF

SUPPORT & TRAINING

Financial Assistance Provided:	No
Site Selection Assistance:	Yes
Lease Negotiation Assistance:	Yes
Co-operative Advertising:	Yes
Franchisee Association/Member:	Yes/Member
Size of Corporate Staff:	24
On-going Support:	C, D, E, F, G, H, I
Training:	3 Weeks CA

SPECIFIC EXPANSION PLANS

US:	AZ, CA, NV, OR, WA
Canada:	No
Overseas:	No

Table 1 below represents the sales of franchisee-operated Togo's Restaurants that were in operation for more than 360 days within the 52 week period ended December 31, 2011. If a franchisee did not provide complete sales information for the stated period, then those figures were not included.

As of December 31, 2011, we had 241 restaurants open. These 241 restaurants were comprised of 174 "traditional" restaurants (full service, full menu, in 'line or freestanding), 61 "Combo" restaurants comprised of more than one brand operating in one location (typically a Baskin-Robbins Ice Cream Shop), and 6 "non-traditional" restaurants (limited service, limited menu, college or stadium location). Of the 174 traditional restaurants, 168 were operational for the full 52 week period ended December 31, 2011 and had submitted 52 weeks of sales reports. Table 1 below covers only those 168 traditional restaurants which submitted sales for the full 52-week period ended December 31, 2011. Tables 2 and 3 below include only those 153 restaurants which have submitted P&L Reports for part or all of the 52 week period ended December 31, 2011.

The information in the Tables below was prepared using financial information provided to us by the franchisees. The franchisees' financial information is not audited. The footnotes to the Tables describe the primary information used to create the information provided. You should consider that this information gives no weight to specific locations, types of operators, investment cost, or market conditions. Sales and costs may differ widely from one location to another, without respect to their geographic region. You must make your own investigation into the likely sales and costs in your specific location and region.

A prospective franchisee who is purchasing the assets of an existing restaurant should review the actual financial results of the restaurant(s) being purchased. Prospective franchisees for non traditional or Combo restaurants should not rely on these figures, since these type of restaurants may experience different results.

Table 1 contains the ranges of sales and averages with the High, Medium High, Medium Low and Low categories for 168 traditional restaurants which submitted sales for the full 52-week period ended December 31, 2011. Table 2 contains the average food and paper costs as a percentage of sales for 153 traditional restaurants that submitted P&L reports for part or all of the 52 weeks ended December 31, 2011. Table 3 contains the average direct labor costs as a percentage of sales for 153 traditional restaurants.

Average Restaurant Sales

TABLE 1

Average Restaurant Sales

168 Franchisee-owned Restaurants for the 52 Week Period Ended December 31, 2011

SALES	HIGH SALES QUARTILE	MEDIUM HIGH SALES QUARTILE	MEDIUM LOW SALES QUARTILE	LOW SALES QUARTILE
Number of Restaurants (1)	42	42	42	42
Number and % at or above Average Restaurant Sales	18 (42.9%)	20 (47.6%)	23 (54.8%)	22 (52.4%)
Range (in sales):				
HIGH	$1,342,919	$722,007	$584,247	$463,091
LOW	$731,337	$585,882	$464,774	$174,187
AVERAGE	$885,140	$644,827	$529,658	$355,411

AVERAGE UNIT VOLUME FOR ALL 168 RESTAURANTS IN TABLE 1 WAS $603,759. Seventy-three Restaurants (43.5%) met or exceeded the average unit volume.

Footnotes:

(1) The number of Restaurants represents traditional Togo's Restaurants open for the full 52 week period ended December 31, 2011. Only locations that have reported sales for this entire period are included.

TABLE2

Average Food and Paper Cost

153 Franchisee-owned Restaurants for the 52 Week Period Ended December 31, 2011

	NUMBER OF RESTAURANTS	TOTAL AVERAGE FOOD & PAPER COST (1) (2) (3)	# AND % AT OR BELOW AVERAGE FOOD & PAPER
Total:	153	35.69%	81 (52.9%)

(1) Food and paper costs can vary greatly depending on your ability to maintain portion controls and manage regular inventory counts.

(2) The average food and paper cost is shown as a percentage of gross sales.

(3) Food cost includes food cost, beverage cost and cost of paper products such as cups, napkins, sandwich wrap's and takeout packaging.

Footnotes:

(1) Labor cost is shown as a percentage of gross sales.

(2) Does not include manager salary, franchisee salary or draw, workers compensation insurance, payroll tax, medical insurance or any fringe benefits. Franchisee's who have a manager or who pay themselves a salary or draw will incur higher Direct Labor Costs.

Additional Notes:

The information set forth above reflects only a limited number of expenses associated with the ongoing operations of a Togo's Restaurant. You will incur many other types of expenses in operating a Togo's Restaurant, among them being: (1) royalty fee; (2) advertising fee; (3) occupancy costs (rent, common area maintenance, tax and insurance due to landlord); (4) debt service, interest, bank charges and other finance charges; (5) insurance; (6) professional fees (accounting, payroll & legal services); and (7) operating costs (kitchen supplies, utilities, repair and maintenance, smallwares, licenses & permits, credit card & gift card fees, laundry, telephone, office supplies and janitorial services).

Written substantiation for the financial performance representation will be made available to the prospective franchisee upon reasonable request.

WARNINGS:

A. YOU ARE LIKELY TO ACHIEVE RESULTS THAT ARE DIFFERENT, POSSIBLY SIGNIFICANTLY AND ADVERSELY, FROM THE RESULTS SHOWN ABOVE. MANY FACTORS, INCLUDING LOCATION OF THE BUSINESS, MANAGEMENT CAPABILITIES, LOCAL MARKET CONDITIONS, COMPETITION AND OTHER FACTORS, ARE UNIQUE TO EACH BUSINESS AND MAY SIGNIFICANTLY IMPACT THE FINANCIAL PERFORMANCE OF THE BUSINESS.

B. THE ACTUAL RESULTS INCLUDED IN THIS STATEMENT SHOULD NOT BE CONSIDERED AS THE ACTUAL OR PROBABLE PERFORMANCE RESULTS THAT YOU SHOULD EXPECT THROUGH THE OPERATION OF YOUR BUSINESS. WE DO NOT MAKE ANY PROMISES OR REPRESENTATIONS OF ANY KIND THAT YOU WILL ACHIEVE ANY PARTICULAR RESULTS OR LEVEL OF SALES OR PROFITABILITY.

C. YOU ARE RESPONSIBLE FOR DEVELOPING YOUR OWN BUSINESS PLAN FOR YOUR BUSINESS. WE ENCOURAGE YOU TO CONSULT WITH YOUR OWN ACCOUNTING, BUSINESS, AND LEGAL ADVISORS IN DOING SO. IN DEVELOPING THE BUSINESS PLAN, YOU ARE CAUTIONED TO MAKE NECESSARY ALLOWANCE FOR CHANGES IN FINANCIAL RESULTS TO INCOME, EXPENSES, OR BOTH, THAT MAY RESULT FROM OPERATION OF YOUR BUSINESS IN DIFFERENT GEOGRAPHIC AREAS OR NEW MARKET AREAS, OR DURING PERIODS OF, OR IN AREAS SUFFERING FROM, ECONOMIC DOWNTURNS, INFLATION, UNEMPLOYMENT, OR OTHER NEGATIVE ECONOMIC INFLUENCES.

Except as disclosed in this Item 19, we do not furnish or authorize our sales agents to furnish any oral or written information concerning the actual or potential sales, income or profits of a restaurant. Actual results vary from restaurant to restaurant, and we cannot estimate the results of any particular franchise. The extent to which your may succeed at any particular location cannot be predicted. If you receive any financial performance information or projections of your future income, you should report it to our management by contacting our Vice President of Finance, Susan Koch, c/o Togo's Franchisor, LLC, 18 North San Pedro Street, San Jose, CA 95110, (408) 280-6585, the Federal Trade Commission and the appropriate state regulatory agency.

TROPICAL SMOOTHIE CAFE

1117 Perimeter Center W., Suite W200
Atlanta, GA 30338
Tel: (770) 821-1900
Fax: (770) 821-1895
Email: info@tropicalsmoothie.com
Website: www.tropicalsmoothiefranchise.com
Charles Watson, Vice President of Franchise Development

Tropical Smoothie Café's business model is unique, as we offer both real fruit smoothies and a variety of fresh, flavorful food. We are two franchises in one! Our initial store development costs are lower because we do not utilize deep fryers, grills, or hooding systems (Making us healthier, too!), and our balanced business model of 50% Food Sales and 50% Smoothie sales allow us to drive higher gross sales and service all dayparts: breakfast, lunch, dinner, snack times and, dessert. In fact, for full year 2012, the top 50% of our Café's had average gross sales over $640,000*! Get the franchisee solutions, strength, and support you need at Tropical Smoothie Café. *Based on Calendar year 2012, 49 of 261 or 38% of the Café's gained or surpassed this sales level. Your results may differ. There is no assurance you will do as well. Offer made by prospectus only.

BACKGROUND
IFA Member: Yes
Established & First Franchised: 1997; 1998
Franchised Units: 340
Company-Owned Units: 0
Total Units: 340
Distribution: US – 340; CAN – 0; O'seas – 0
North America: 36 States, 0 Provinces
Density: 110 in FL, 75 in VA, 20 in NV
Projected New Units (12 Months): 55
Qualifications: 3, 1, 2, 4, 5, 5

FINANCIAL/TERMS
Cash Investment: $100 – $125K

Total Investment: $165 – $424K
Minimum Net Worth: $300K
Fees (Franchise): $25K
Fees (Royalty): 6%
Fees (Advertising): 3%
Term of Contract (Years): 15/10
Average Number of Employees: 1 FT, 10 – 12 PT
Passive Ownership: Discouraged
Encourage Conversions: Yes
Area Development Agreements: Yes
Sub-Franchising Contracts: Yes
Expand in Territory: Yes
Space Needs: 1,000 – 1,600 SF

SUPPORT & TRAINING
Financial Assistance Provided: Yes (D)
Site Selection Assistance: Yes
Lease Negotiation Assistance: Yes
Co-operative Advertising: Yes
Franchisee Association/Member: No
Size of Corporate Staff: 25
On-going Support: A, B, C, D, E, F, G, H, I
Training: 1 Week Corporate Office; 2 Weeks Local Stores; 1 Week Store Opening

SPECIFIC EXPANSION PLANS
US: All United States
Canada: Yes
Overseas: Yes

FINANCIAL PERFORMANCE REPRESENTATIONS: INDIVIDUAL UNIT TROPICAL SMOOTHIE CAFE FRANCHISES

The following tables provide historical sales information for Tropical Smoothi Cafe® franchised stores ("Stores") that were open at least one full year as of (a) the calendar year 2011 for 245 Stores (b) the calendar year 2010 for 262 Stores; and (c) the calendar year 2009 for 233 Stores. The tables do not include any financial performance information for any other types of franchises, such as non-traditional locations (i.e. college campus or other captive locations) or seasonal locations, and do not include any franchises of any type that had not been open for at least one year on December 31, 2011, December 31 2010 and December 31,2009, respectively. The information presented is not a forecast of future potential performance. The gross revenue figures are based on the same computation for computing royalties as required under the Franchise Agreement.

The tables provide the average gross revenues for the following categories of Stores in 2011, 2010, and 2009 on a category and cumulative basis: (a) our top 10% revenue producing Stores (meaning the average gross revenue for the number of Stores that were in the top 10% of gross revenues for that year); (b) our top 25% revenue producing Stores (which includes the Stores that are in the top 10%); (c) our top 50% revenue producing Stores (which includes the Stores that are in the top 10% and the top 25%); and (d) our top 75% revenue producing Stores. We present the average gross sales for the year in that category as well as the number and percentage achieving or surpassing the average gross sales in that category alone and cumulative for all Stores. For example, 24 of the 62 Stores in the top 25% for 2010 (or 39%), and 113 of the 250 total Stores for 2010 (or 45%) achieved or surpassed that average.

Average Gross Revenues in 2011

	Top 10%	Top 25%	Top 50%	Top 75%	Total
No. of Stores	25	61	122	184	245
Avg. Gross Revenues	$829,297	$710,319	$608,796	$540,516	$477,463
No. that Attained or Surpassed Stated Result in Category (Cumulative)	10/25	22/61	47/122	75/184	106/245
Percent that Attained or Surpassed Stated Result in Category (Cumulative)	40%	37%	39%	41%	43%

As of December 31, 2011 there were 301 franchised Stores and 4 company-owned Stores. Of the 301 franchised Stores 261 were franchised Stores that had been open for at least 12 months as of December 31, 2011. Of the 261 Stores: 16 Stores were excluded since they were non-traditional locations. Of the 245 Stores referenced in the above table all reported sufficient financial performance information to be included in this financial performance representation.

Average Gross Revenues in 2010

	Top 10%	Top 25%	Top 50%	Top 75%	Total
No. of Stores	25	62	125	188	250
Avg. Gross Revenues	$837,313	$712,346	$604,736	$529,639	$462,670
No. that Attained or Surpassed Stated Result in Category (Cumulative)	7/25	24/62	50/125	74/188	113/250
Percent that Attained or Surpassed Stated Result in Category (Cumulative)	28%	39%	40%	39%	45%

As of December 31, 2010, there were 289 franchised Stores and 2 company-owned Stores. 0f the 289 franchised Stores, 262 were franchised Stores that had been open for at least 12 months as of December 31, 2010. Of the 262 Stores, 12 Stores were excluded since they were non-traditional locations. Of the 250 Stores referenced in the above table, all reported sufficient financial performance information to be included in this financial performance representation.

Average Gross Revenues in 2009

	Top 10%	Top 25%	Top 50%	Top 75%	Total
No. of Stores	23	59	117	175	233
Avg. Gross Revenues	$752,752	$643,565	$545,822	$476,026	$415,026
No. that Attained or Surpassed Stated Result in Category (Cumulative)	7/23	26/59	45/117	74/175	105/233
Percent that Attained or Surpassed Stated Result in Category (Cumulative)	30%	44%	39%	42%	45%

As of December 31, 2009, there were 275 franchised Stores and 3 company-owned Stores. Of the 275 franchised Stores, 233 were franchised Stores that had been open for at least 12 months as of December 31, 2009. Of these 233 Stores, all reported sufficient financial performance information to be included in this financial performance representation.

As stated, the sales for each of the Stores presented are limited to the sales results for Stores that had been open for a full 12 months of operations as of December 31, 2011, December 31, 2010, and December 31, 2009, respectively. Sales during the first year of operations are likely to be significantly less than for those that have been open for a year or more.

All Tropical Smoothie Cafe® Stores offer substantially the same products and services to the public. None of the franchised Tropical Smoothie Cafe® Stores received any services not generally available to other franchisees and substantially the same services will be offered to new franchisees.

We obtained these historical financial results from the information submitted by our franchisees. Neither we nor an independent certified public accountant has independently audited or verified the information. Some Stores have sold the amounts shown in the tables. Your individual results may differ. There is no assurance you will sell as much.

YOUR INDIVIDUAL FINANCIAL RESULTS MAY DIFFER SUBSTANTIALLY FROM THE RESULTS DISCLOSED IN THIS ITEM 19.

The foregoing data relates to revenues only; we are not presenting any information on the costs and expenses of operating a Store. Operating a Store incurs a wide variety of expenses that will reduce the Store's income from the revenue levels shown. Examples of the types of these expenses include, without limitation, rent and occupancy expenses; food and beverage product and supply costs; salaries, wages and other personnel-related expenses; federal, state and local taxes and fees; utilities; financing costs (including on loans and leases); royalties and other amounts due us. See also Items 5, 6 and 7.

CHARACTERISTICS OF THE INCLUDED FRANCHISED STORES MAY DIFFER SUBSTANTIALLY FROM YOUR STORE DEPENDING ON YOUR PREVIOUS BUSINESS AND MANAGEMENT EXPERIENCE, COMPETITION IN YOUR AREA, LENGTH OF TIME THAT THE INCLUDED STORES HAVE OPERATED COMPARED TO YOUR STORE, AND THE SERVICES OR GOODS SOLD AT YOUR STORE COMPARED TO THE INCLUDED STORES. THE SALES, PROFITS AND EARNINGS OF AN INDIVIDUAL FRANCHISEE MAY VARY GREATLY DEPENDING ON THESE AND A WIDE VARIETY OF OTHER FACTORS, INCLUDING THE LOCATION OF THE STORE, POPULATION AND DEMOGRAPHICS IN YOUR MARKET AREA, ECONOMIC AND MARKET CONDITIONS, LABOR AND PRODUCT COSTS, ETC.

WE HAVE WRITTEN SUBSTANTIATION IN OUR POSSESSION TO SUPPORT THE INFORMATION APPEARING IN THIS FINANCIAL PERFORMANCE REPRESENTATION. WRITTEN SUBSTANTIATION WILL BE MADE AVAILABLE TO YOU ON REASONABLE REQUEST.

We recommend that you make your own independent investigation to determine whether or not the franchise may be profitable, and consult with an attorney and other advisors prior to executing the franchise agreement.

Other than the preceding financial performance representation, we do not make any financial performance representations about a franchisee's future financial performance or the past financial performance of company-owned or franchised outlets. We also do not authorize our employees or representatives to make any such representations either orally or in writing. If you receive any other financial performance information or projections of your future income, you should report it to our management by contacting Eric Jenrich, our President and CEO at 12598 U.S. Highway 98 West, Suite 200, Destin, Florida 32550 and (888) 292-2522, the Federal Trade Commission, and the appropriate state regulatory agencies.

Retail Franchises | 5

FRANCHISE OPPORTUNITIES

7-ELEVEN

1722 Routh St., #1000
Dallas, TX 75201
Tel: (800) 782-0711, (972) 828-7011
Fax: (972) 828-1046
Email: timothy.lankford@7-11.com
Website: www.Franchise.7-Eleven.com
Tim Lankford, Franchise Marketing & Recruiting Manager

7-ELEVEN stores were born from the simple concept of giving people "what they want, when and where they want it." This idea gave rise to the entire convenience store industry. While this formula still works today, customers' needs are changing at an accelerating pace. We are meeting this challenge with an infrastructure of daily distribution of fresh perishables, regional production of fresh foods and pastries, and an information system that greatly improves ordering and merchandising decisions.

BACKGROUND

IFA Member:	Yes
Established & First Franchised:	1927; 1964
Franchised Units:	48,757
Company-Owned Units:	1,755
Total Units:	50,512

Distribution:	US – 8,203; CAN – 479; O'seas – 41,830
North America:	32 States, 5 Provinces
Density:	1,587 in CA, 855 in FL, 727 in VA
Projected New Units (12 Months):	400
Qualifications:	4, 4, 4, 3, 5, 5

FINANCIAL/TERMS

Cash Investment:	Varies by Store
Total Investment:	Varies by Store
Minimum Net Worth:	$15K
Fees (Franchise):	Varies by Store
Fees (Royalty):	Gross Profit Split
Fees (Advertising):	N/A
Term of Contract (Years):	10/10
Average Number of Employees:	8 FT, 5 PT
Passive Ownership:	Not Allowed
Encourage Conversions:	Yes
Area Development Agreements:	No
Sub-Franchising Contracts:	No
Expand in Territory:	Yes
Space Needs:	2,400 SF

SUPPORT & TRAINING

Financial Assistance Provided:	Yes (D)
Site Selection Assistance:	N/A
Lease Negotiation Assistance:	N/A
Co-operative Advertising:	No
Franchisee Association/Member:	Yes/Member
Size of Corporate Staff:	1,000
On-going Support:	A, B, C, D, E, F, G, H, I
Training:	1 Week Dallas, TX; 5 – 8 Weeks Various Training Stores throughout US

SPECIFIC EXPANSION PLANS

US:	MW, NE, NW, SE, SW, Great Lakes
Canada:	All Canada
Overseas:	All Countries

We provide unaudited financial statements that show the most recently available annual averages of the actual sales, earnings and other financial performance (before applicable franchisee income taxes, if any) of franchised 7-Eleven stores in each Market Area in this state (excluding stores that the same franchisee did not operate for the full calendar year). The Unaudited Statements of Average Franchisee Sales and Earnings are attached as Exhibit H to this disclosure document.

THE FINANCIAL STATEMENTS ATTACHED AS EXHIBIT H CONTAIN HISTORICAL AVERAGES OF SPECIFIC FRANCHISES. YOU SHOULD NOT CONSIDER ANY OF THE NUMBERS TO BE THE ACTUAL OR POTENTIAL SALES, EARNINGS OR OTHER FINANCIAL PERFORMANCE THAT YOU WILL ATTAIN. WE DO NOT REPRESENT THAT ANY FRANCHISEE CAN EXPECT TO ATTAIN THESE SALES, EARNINGS OR OTHER FINANCIAL PERFORMANCE, AND YOUR INDIVIDUAL FINANCIAL RESULTS MAY DIFFER FROM THE RESULTS CONTAINED IN THE FINANCIAL PERFORMANCE REPRESENTATIONS.

As described in Item 11, we prepare bookkeeping records for our franchisees based on financial information they submit to us. We prepared the financial statements attached as Exhibit H using information from these bookkeeping records. The financial statements are only as accurate as the information submitted to us by our current franchisees. The financial statements are unaudited. The form and classification of the financial statements are consistent with the accounting provisions and definitions in the franchise agreement and are materially consistent with generally accepted accounting principles. We use the retail method of accounting to account for the stores' operations, in accordance with generally accepted accounting principles and the franchise agreement.

If a store you want to franchise has operated for at least the last 12 months, we will also give you a supplemental disclosure for that store. The supplemental disclosure, called "Here Are The Facts," shows the actual operating results of the store for the last 12 months. We will prepare the supplemental disclosure in the same manner, and using the same information, as the financial statements attached as Exhibit H. You should not use the supplemental disclosure to predict any results at a particular store you franchise.

Many factors will affect the actual sales and earnings of a store you franchise, including your own efforts, ability and control of the store, as well as factors over which you have no control. Therefore, you should not predict any future results of a store based on historical operating summaries for any particular store or averages for a group of stores that we may provide. Actual results vary from store to store, and we cannot estimate the results of any particular store. We will make available to you, upon reasonable request, substantiation of the data used to prepare the material in this Item 19.

EXHIBIT H: UNAUDITED STATEMENTS OF AVERAGE FRANCHISEE SALES AND EARNINGS FOR THE CALENDAR YEAR 2011

Editor's Note: 7-Eleven produces an exceptionally informative Exhibit H that is 110 pages in its entirety. What follows is an introductory section, as well as a sample of earnings data for two specific markets. If you would like to see the full 7-Eleven Exhibit H , you may purchase the enitre Item 19 document (Exhibit H included) at www.item19s.com.

See Item 19 for a complete explanation of this section.

NOTE: The average franchisee sales and earnings that follow are for the 2011 calendar year and are before applicable franchisee income taxes, if any.

The average franchisee sales and earnings that follow may include payments to franchisees under the Store Development Program, or other various programs we have offered in the past. These programs were based on various factors, including store location, franchisee performance, etc. Actual franchisee earnings were affected by the franchisee's eligibility for one or more of these programs. Some of these programs may not be available in your area.

The average franchisee sales and earnings that follow may include sales of Consigned Gasoline, although not all 7-Eleven Stores sell Consigned Gasoline. The results may include a one-time payment to certain franchisees related to our previous distribution of a non-contractual procedure for calculating commissions, on the sale of Consigned Gasoline, which payment would not be applicable to you. If a 7-Eleven Store does sell Consigned Gasoline, we may decide to discontinue the gasoline sales and remove the gasoline equipment from such store. The discontinuation of gasoline sales would affect actual franchisee earnings.

The average franchisee sales and earnings that follow may include a lower 7-Eleven Charge than you will be required to pay (see Item 6).

If there are less than 100 franchise outlets in the state where this Disclosure Document is presented, this Exhibit will also contain an additional list of franchise outlets (without financial information) from contiguous states until at least 100 franchise outlets are listed.

Letter codes in front of store numbers in the store lists refer
to the following:
A: Included in the Top Third
B: Included in the Middle Third

C: Included in the Bottom Third
D: Strip center location
E: Freestanding location
F: Payroll operating expense includes a salary paid to one or
more Franchisees

UNAUDITED STATEMENT OF AVERAGE FRANCHISEE SALES AND EARNINGS
FOR THE CALENDAR YEAR 2011
TRADITIONAL STORES
MARKET: 2111 - NORTH COUNTY MARKET

TOTAL SALES RANGE	BOTTOM THIRD	MIDDLE THIRD	TOP THIRD
NUMBER OF STORES IN AVERAGE	24	24	25
PERCENT OF FRANCHISED STORES IN THE 7-ELEVEN SYSTEM (OPERATED BY THE SAME FRANCHISEE FOR THE YEAR 2011) WHICH ACHIEVED OR EXCEEDED MEDIAN SALES AVERAGE WITHIN EACH RANGE	70.1%	40.6%	16.1%
TOTAL SALES (AVERAGE WITHIN EACH RANGE)	$1341,511	$1684,424	$2117,874
GROSS PROFIT	515,694	651,078	798,829
PERCENT OF SALES	38.4%	38.6%	37.7%
LESS 7-ELEVEN CHARGE	257,758	328,029	401,971
*GAS COMMISSION	1,810	3,421	5,075
OTHER INCOME	234	292	361
FRANCHISEE'S GROSS INCOME	$259,981	$326,762	$402,294
SELLING EXPENSES			
CASUAL & TEMPORARY LABOR	$12	$0	$0
PAYROLL (NOT INCL FRAN. DRAW)	119,292	143,703	177,824
STORE MANAGER PAYROLL	0	0	0
STORE MANAGER BONUS	0	0	0
STORE MANAGER BONUS TAXES	0	0	0
PAYROLL TAXES	12,437	14,896	17,732
PAPER BAGS	1,092	1,451	1,773
INVENTORY VARIATION	3,359	7,495	6,077
MONEY ORDER REPORTING VARIATION	0	0	0
COUPON VARIATION	0	0	0
LOTTERY TICKET INVENTORY VARIATION	693	409	507
LOTTO/LOTTERY REPORTING VARIATION	128-	359	71
LOTTO SALES REPORTING VARIATION	21-	5-	48-
SUPPLIES	2,886	3,263	4,205
TELEPHONE	1,673	1,547	2,623
CONTRACT MAINTENANCE EQUIPMENT	10,625	10,520	10,792
OTHER MAINTENANCE EQUIPMENT	919	808	888

BUILDING MAINTENANCE	455	438	872
OUTSIDE PREMISES MAINTENANCE	2,353	1,680	2,076
TAXES AND LICENSE	1,156	1,184	1,185
CASH VARIATION	1,636	1,637	2,212
RETURNED CHECKS	24	3	94
RUBBISH REMOVAL	1,955	2,188	3,321
JANITORIAL & LAUNDRY	1,465	1,667	2,298
BAD MERCHANDISE	0	0	0
SECURITY EXPENSE	391	598	1,161
MISCELLANEOUS EXPENSE	1,964	1,806	2,053
ADVERTISING FEES	7,568	9,731	11,982
ADVERTISING	78	86	171
MONEY ORDER LOSSES	0	0	0
WORKERS COMPENSATION	5,881	6,906	8,260
CRIME & CASUALTY LOSSES	278	4	127
EMPLOYEE GROUP INSURANCE	4,480	782	3,934
PRE-EMPLOYMENT EXPENSES	19	92	3
MISCELLANEOUS EMPLOYEE EXPENSES	1,766	1,288	1,299
CHECK CASHING EXPENSES	9	8	20
CREDIT CARD EXPENSES	8,356	10,344	13,259
INTEREST EXPENSE	1,298	1,131	1,398
TOTAL SELLING EXPENSES	$194,006	$226,050	$278,188
MERCHANDISE SALES FOR STORES USED IN THESE AVERAGE			
WERE A HIGH OF ...	1,565,581	1,774,269	2,622,626
AND A LOW OF ...	974,100	1,566,414	1,785,933
THERE MAY ALSO BE GENERAL & ADMINISTRATIVE EXPENSE RELATING TO THE OPERATION OF A 7-ELEVEN STORE. YOU MAY OR MAY NOT HAVE THESE EXPENSES. RANGE OF G&A EXPENSES, MINUS THE INTEREST EXPENSE:			
WERE A HIGH OF ...	17,533	84,173	59,501
AND A LOW OF ...	699	972	868

(EXAMPLES OF G&A EXPENSES ARE: OFFICER SALARY/BONUS, EMPLOYEE BONUS, PAYROLL TAXES, EQUIPMENT RENTAL, TRAVEL/ENTERTAINMENT, OUTSIDE INSURANCE COVERAGE, PROFESSIONAL SERVICE, MEMBER DUES, FINES/PENALTIES, MISC. G&A EXPENSES).

THE PAYROLL AND PAYROLL TAX NUMBERS MAY INCLUDE PAYROLL PAID TO AN INCORPORATED FRANCHISEE, OR PAYROLL PAID TO A SPOUSE OR OTHER FAMILY MEMBER OF THE FRANCHISEE. THE USE OF FAMILY MEMBERS AS EMPLOYEES, OR THE USE OF A CORPORATION AS THE FRANCHISEE, MAY IMPACT THE PAYROLL EXPENSES AT A PARTICULAR STORE

*GAS COMMISSION INCLUDES COMMISSION AMOUNTS PAID TO FRANCHISEES FOR THE SALE OF CONSIGNED GASOLINE UNDER A NON-CONTRACTUAL POLICY FOR CALCULATING GASOLINE COMMISSIONS. WE HAVE MADE VARIOUS CHANGES TO THIS POLICY AND ADDITIONAL CHANGES MAY BE MADE IN THE FUTURE WHICH COULD AFFECT THE ACTUAL FRANCHISEE EARNINGS AND THE AMOUNT OF GAS COMMISSION RECEIVED BY FRANCHISEES.

THE ABOVE UNAUDITED STATEMENT WAS PREPARED IN ACCORDANCE WITH THE ACCOUNTING PROVISIONS AND DEFINITIONS SPECIFIED IN THE FRANCHISE AGREEMENT AND IS CONSISTENT WITH GENERALLY ACCEPTED ACCOUNTING PRINCIPLES. THE INFORMATION INDICATES THE AVERAGE OF THOSE FRANCHISED 7-ELEVEN STORES IN THE ABOVE MARKET AREA WHICH WERE OPERATED THROUGHOUT THE CALENDAR YEAR BY THE SAME FRANCHISEE. THE OPERATING EXPENSES LINE SHOWN AS OTHER INCOME INCLUDES MISCELLANEOUS INCOME TO THE FRANCHISEE FROM COMMISSIONS (FOR THOSE STORES NOT INCLUDED IN TOTAL SALES) AND INCENTIVE AWARDS. THE AVERAGES SHOWN ARE NOT IN EXCESS OF THE AVERAGE OF SALES AND EARNINGS ACTUALLY ACHIEVED BY EXISTING FRANCHISEES. THE FRANCHISE OPERATIONS FROM WHICH THESE AVERAGES ARE TAKEN ARE SUBSTANTIALLY SIMILAR TO THE FRANCHISE OFFERED AND DID NOT RECEIVE ANY SERVICES NOT GENERALLY AVAILABLE TO OTHER FRANCHISEES.

THESE SALES OR EARNINGS ARE AVERAGES OF SPECIFIC FRANCHISES AND SHOULD NOT BE CONSIDERED AS THE ACTUAL OR POTENTIAL SALES OR EARNINGS THAT WILL BE REALIZED BY ANY OTHER FRANCHISEE. THE FRANCHISOR DOES NOT REPRESENT THAT ANY FRANCHISEE CAN EXPECT TO ATTAIN THESE SALES OR EARNINGS.

UNAUDITED STATEMENT OF AVERAGE FRANCHISEE SALES AND EARNINGS
FOR THE CALENDAR YEAR 2011
TRADITIONAL STORES
MARKET: 2112 - DESERT COAST MARKET

TOTAL SALES RANGE	BOTTOM THIRD	MIDDLE THIRD	TOP THIRD
NUMBER OF STORES IN AVERAGE	24	24	24
PERCENT OF FRANCHISED STORES IN THE 7-ELEVEN SYSTEM (OPERATED BY THE SAME FRANCHISEE FOR THE YEAR 2011) WHICH ACHIEVED OR EXCEEDED MEDIAN SALES AVERAGE WITHIN EACH RANGE	88.0%	56.9%	20.9%
TOTAL SALES (AVERAGE WITHIN EACH RANGE)	$1088,771	$1491,173	$1992,133
GROSS PROFIT	415,326	564,215	748,828
PERCENT OF SALES	38.1%	37.8%	37.5%
LESS 7-ELEVEN CHARGE	208,060	284,276	378,155
*GAS COMMISSION	4,534	6,952	8,057
OTHER INCOME	433	296	305
FRANCHISEE'S GROSS INCOME	$212,233	$287,187	$379,036
SELLING EXPENSES	$235	$640	$1,156
CASUAL & TEMPORARY LABOR	93,873	121,924	171,237
PAYROLL (NOT INCL FRAN. DRAW)			
STORE MANAGER PAYROLL	0	0	0
STORE MANAGER BONUS	0	0	0
STORE MANAGER BONUS TAXES	0	0	0
PAYROLL TAXES	9,991	12,658	17,502
PAPER BAGS	801	1,100	1,756
INVENTORY VARIATION	4,228	3,745	9,237
MONEY ORDER REPORTING VARIATION	0	0	0
COUPON VARIATION	0	0	0

LOTTERY TICKET INVENTORY VARIATION	727	901	240
LOTTO/LOTTERY REPORTING VARIATION	1,609	138	185
LOTTO SALES REPORTING VARIATION	58	14	9
SUPPLIES	2,471	3,960	4,300
TELEPHONE	1,823	1,952	2,637
CONTRACT MAINTENANCE EQUIPMENT	10,787	10,795	10,855
OTHER MAINTENANCE EQUIPMENT	511	622	716
BUILDING MAINTENANCE	767	896	577
OUTSIDE PREMISES MAINTENANCE	3,640	3,562	3,603
TAXES AND LICENSE	1,333	2,874	1,577
CASH VARIATION	1,733	3,034	2,754
RETURNED CHECKS	9	11	36
RUBBISH REMOVAL	2,006	2,454	3,241
JANITORIAL & LAUNDRY	1,893	1,953	4,077
BAD MERCHANDISE	0	0	0
SECURITY EXPENSE	191	855	994
MISCELLANEOUS EXPENSE	1,524	2,306	3,273
ADVERTISING FEES	5,787	7,989	11,232
ADVERTISING	33	102	220
MONEY ORDER LOSSES	0	0	0
WORKERS COMPENSATION	5,024	6,534	7,744
CRIME & CASUALTY LOSSES	71-	7	45
EMPLOYEE GROUP INSURANCE	571	1,570	4,163
PRE-EMPLOYMENT EXPENSES	37	3	44
MISCELLANEOUS EMPLOYEE EXPENSES	963	1,937	1,620
CHECK CASHING EXPENSES	0	0	0
CREDIT CARD EXPENSES	5,941	8,159	10,552
INTEREST EXPENSE	1,342	1,263	1,543
TOTAL SELLING EXPENSES	$159,850	$204,023	$277,324
MERCHANDISE SALES FOR STORES USED IN THESE AVERAGE			
WERE A HIGH OF ...	1,260,004	1,632,009	2,686,198
AND A LOW OF ...	679,674	1,298,430	1,632,371
THERE MAY ALSO BE GENERAL & ADMINISTRATIVE EXPENSE RELATING TO THE OPERATION OF A 7-ELEVEN STORE. YOU MAY OR MAY NOT HAVE THESE EXPENSES. RANGE OF G&A EXPENSES, MINUS THE INTEREST EXPENSE:			
WERE A HIGH OF ...	38,137	140,012	89,696
AND A LOW OF ...	377	1,171	965

(EXAMPLES OF G&A EXPENSES ARE: OFFICER SALARY/ BONUS, EMPLOYEE BONUS, PAYROLL TAXES, EQUIPMENT RENTAL, TRAVEL/ENTERTAINMENT, OUTSIDE INSURANCE COVERAGE, PROFESSIONAL SERVICE, MEMBER DUES, FINES/PENALTIES, MISC. G&A EXPENSES).

THE PAYROLL AND PAYROLL TAX NUMBERS MAY INCLUDE PAYROLL PAID TO AN INCORPORATED FRANCHISEE, OR PAYROLL PAID TO A SPOUSE OR OTHER FAMILY MEMBER OF THE FRANCHISEE. THE USE OF FAMILY MEMBERS AS EMPLOYEES, OR THE USE OF A CORPORATION AS THE FRANCHISEE, MAY IMPACT THE PAYROLL EXPENSES AT A PARTICULAR STORE

*GAS COMMISSION INCLUDES COMMISSION AMOUNTS PAID TO FRANCHISEES FOR THE SALE OF CONSIGNED GASOLINE UNDER A NON-CONTRACTUAL POLICY FOR CALCULATING GASOLINE COMMISSIONS. WE HAVE MADE VARIOUS CHANGES TO THIS POLICY AND ADDITIONAL CHANGES MAY BE MADE IN THE FUTURE WHICH COULD AFFECT THE ACTUAL FRANCHISEE EARNINGS AND THE AMOUNT OF GAS COMMISSION RECEIVED BY FRANCHISEES.

THE ABOVE UNAUDITED STATEMENT WAS PREPARED IN ACCORDANCE WITH THE ACCOUNTING PROVISIONS AND DEFINITIONS SPECIFIED IN THE FRANCHISE AGREEMENT AND IS CONSISTENT WITH GENERALLY ACCEPTED ACCOUNTING PRINCIPLES. THE INFORMATION INDICATES THE AVERAGE OF THOSE FRANCHISED 7-ELEVEN STORES IN THE ABOVE MARKET AREA WHICH WERE OPERATED THROUGHOUT THE CALENDAR YEAR BY THE SAME FRANCHISEE. THE OPERATING EXPENSES LINE SHOWN AS OTHER INCOME INCLUDES MISCELLANEOUS INCOME TO THE FRANCHISEE FROM COMMISSIONS (FOR THOSE STORES NOT INCLUDED IN TOTAL SALES) AND INCENTIVE AWARDS. THE AVERAGES SHOWN ARE NOT IN EXCESS OF THE AVERAGE OF SALES AND EARNINGS ACTUALLY ACHIEVED BY EXISTING FRANCHISEES. THE FRANCHISE OPERATIONS FROM WHICH THESE AVERAGES ARE TAKEN ARE SUBSTANTIALLY SIMILAR TO THE FRANCHISE OFFERED AND DID NOT RECEIVE ANY SERVICES NOT GENERALLY AVAILABLE TO OTHER FRANCHISEES.

THESE SALES OR EARNINGS ARE AVERAGES OF SPECIFIC FRANCHISES AND SHOULD NOT BE CONSIDERED AS THE ACTUAL OR POTENTIAL SALES OR EARNINGS THAT WILL BE REALIZED BY ANY OTHER FRANCHISEE. THE FRANCHISOR DOES NOT REPRESENT THAT ANY FRANCHISEE CAN EXPECT TO ATTAIN THESE SALES OR EARNINGS.

FLOOR COVERINGS *international*

FLOOR COVERINGS INTERNATIONAL

5250 Triangle Pkwy., # 100
Norcross, GA 30092
Tel: (800) 955-4324, (770) 874-7600
Fax: (770) 874-7605
Email: djames@floorcoveringsinternational.com
Website: www.floorcoveringsinternational.com
Denise James, Franchise Administrator

FLOOR COVERINGS INTERNATIONAL is the "Flooring Store at your Door." FCI is the first and leading mobile "shop at home" flooring store. Customers can select from over 3,000 styles and colors of flooring right in their own home! All the right ingredients are there to simplify a buying decision. We offer all the brand names you and your customers will be familiar with. We carry all types of flooring, as well as window blinds.

BACKGROUND

IFA Member:	Yes
Established & First Franchised:	1988; 1989
Franchised Units:	87
Company-Owned Units:	0
Total Units:	87
Distribution:	US – 80; CAN – 9; O'seas – 0
North America:	43 States, 5 Provinces
Density:	7 in CA, 7 in NC, 6 in MN
Projected New Units (12 Months):	35
Qualifications:	5, 5, 4, 3, 4, 4

FINANCIAL/TERMS		SUPPORT & TRAINING	
Cash Investment:	$150K	Financial Assistance Provided:	Yes (D)
Total Investment:	$133 – $305.5K	Site Selection Assistance:	Yes
Minimum Net Worth:	$50K	Lease Negotiation Assistance:	N/A
Fees (Franchise):	$45K	Co-operative Advertising:	No
Fees (Royalty):	5%	Franchisee Association/Member:	Yes/Member
Fees (Advertising):	2%	Size of Corporate Staff:	15
Term of Contract (Years):	10/10	On-going Support:	A, B, C, D, E, G, H, I
Average Number of Employees:	1 FT, 1 PT	Training:	1 Week Atlanta, GA
Passive Ownership:	Discouraged		
Encourage Conversions:	Yes	SPECIFIC EXPANSION PLANS	
Area Development Agreements:	Yes	US:	All United States
Sub-Franchising Contracts:	No	Canada:	All Canada
Expand in Territory:	Yes	Overseas:	No
Space Needs:	N/A		

This Item sets forth certain historical data submitted by our franchisees. Written substantiation of the data used in preparing this information will be made available upon reasonable request. We have not audited this information, nor independently verified this information. The information is for the period January 1, 2011 through December 31, 2011 (the "Measurement Period").

Importantly, the success of your franchise will depend largely upon your individual abilities and your market, and the financial results of your franchise are likely to differ, perhaps materially, from the results summarized in this item.

You should not use this information as an indication of how well your franchise will do. A number of factors will affect the success of your franchise. These factors include the current market conditions, the type of market in your franchise area, the location of your franchise area, the competition and your ability to operate the franchise.

Gross Sales

This Table presents the Gross Sales as reported to us by our 59 U.S. franchisees that were open and operating for more than 12-months as of December 31, 2011 and for whom we have complete sales data (the "Reporting Franchises"). This table excludes franchises who had not been open and operating for a full 12-months as of December 31, 2011, those for whom we do not have complete sales data and those that do not operate the franchise as a full time venture. The following table presents the high, low, average and median Gross Sales for the 59 Reporting U.S. Franchisees during the Measurement Period.

Gross Sales
For Calendar Year 2011

Years in Operation	Number of Reporting Franchises	High	Low	Average	Median	Number of Reporting Franchises Meeting or Exceeding the Average
Over 1 less than 2 Years	16	$598,021	$178,185	$344,183	$315,110	6
Over 2 Years	43	$2,044,034	$62,009	$634,539	$501,297	15

Notes:

1. Gross Sales is defined as a franchise's total sales invoices or other items or services billed to the customer for all "Completed Sales", less any discounts, cancellations or returns by FCI. Sales of products and services are deemed to be Completed Sales for purposes of reporting to FCI when the franchisee completes the final installation of all products and/or services sold to the customer.

2. The Average Gross Sales is defined as the sum of the Gross Sales of the Reporting Franchisees divided by

the number of Reporting Franchisees in each operating category.

3. The median means the amount that falls in the middle when all other amounts disclosed are arranged highest to lowest. In other words, half of the Reporting Franchisees exceeded the median value stated above and half did not in each operating category.

Average Job Size, Closing Rates and Slippage Rates

The following table presents the average job size, closing rate and slippage rates for the 33 franchisees open less than 2-years and 37 franchisees open and operating for more than 2- years as of December 31, 2011 which reported data in these categories to us. We excluded franchisees that did not report the number of jobs, closing rates and slippage rates to us.

Average Job Size, Closing Rate and Slippage Rates
For Calendar Year 2011

Years in Operation	Number of Franchises	Average Job Size	Closing Rate	Slippage Rate	Number of Reporting Franchisees Meeting or Exceeding the Average
Less than 2 Years	33	$3,186	35%	40%	Job Size: 16
					Closing Rate: 11
					Slippage Rate: 8
Over 2 Years	37	$3,971	50%	22%	Job Size: 16
					Closing Rate: 14
					Slippage Rate: 13

Notes:

1. Average Job Size is defined as the total Gross Sales of all jobs in each operating category divided by the number of jobs performed by franchisees in each operating category.

2. Average Closing Rate is the average percentage of jobs landed over the number of first proposals.

3. Average Slippage Rate is the average percentage of first proposals over the number of leads.

Assumptions

1. Your results may vary upon the location of your business. This analysis does not contain information concerning operating costs or expenses. Operating costs and expenses may vary substantially from business to business.

2. Expenses and costs, as well as the actual accounting and operational methods employed by a franchisee, may significantly impact profits realized in any particular operation.

CAUTION

There is no assurance you will do as well. If you rely upon our figures, you must accept the risk of not doing as well. Actual results vary from business to business, and we cannot estimate the result of a particular business. Gross Sales, revenues, expenses and Gross Margin on Sales may vary. In particular, the revenues and expenses of your Franchised Business will be directly affected by many factors, such as: (a) geographic location; (b) competition from other similar businesses in your area; (c) advertising effectiveness based on market saturation; (d) your product and service pricing; (e) vendor prices on materials, supplies and inventory; (f) labor costs (g) ability to generate customers; (h) customer loyalty; and (i) employment conditions in the market.

Importantly, you should not consider the Gross Sales presented above to be the actual potential revenues that you will realize. We do not represent that you can or will attain these revenues or any particular level of revenues or percentage of costs or expenses. We do not represent that you will generate income, which exceeds the initial payment of, or investment in, the franchise.

Therefore, we recommend that you make your own independent investigation to determine whether or not the franchise may be profitable to you. You should use the above information only as a reference in conducting your analysis and preparing your own projected income statements and cash flow statements. We suggest strongly that you consult your financial advisor or personal accountant concerning financial projections and federal, state and local income taxes and any other applicable taxes that you may incur in operating a Franchised Business.

Other than the preceding financial performance representation, Floorcoverings International, Ltd. does not make any financial performance representations. We also do not authorize our employees or representatives to make any such either orally or in writing. If you are purchasing an existing outlet, however, we may provide you with the actual records of that outlet. If you receive any other financial performance information or projections of your future income, you should report it to the franchisor's management by contacting Thomas Wood, Floorcoverings International, Ltd., 5250 Triangle Parkway, Suite 100, Norcross, Georgia 30092 and 800-955-4324, the Federal Trade Commission, and the appropriate state regulatory agencies.

FOOT SOLUTIONS

2359 Windy Hill Rd., # 400
Marietta, GA 30067
Tel: (866) 338-2597, (770) 955-0099
Fax: (770) 953-6270
Email: fscorp@footsolutions.com
Website: www.footsolutionsfranchise.com
Alison Strophus, Franchise Sales

Foot Solutions is the world's largest pedorthic footwear retail/mobile network, focusing on health and wellness, the baby boomer marketplace, and lifestyle shoes and inserts to change the way people live and feel. We also have a focus on cause-related marketing including affiliations with Susan G. Komen for the Cure, Arthritis Foundation, American Diabetes Association, International Council on Active Aging, to name a few.

BACKGROUND

IFA Member:	Yes
Established & First Franchised:	2000; 2000
Franchised Units:	159
Company-Owned Units:	1
Total Units:	160
Distribution:	US – 115; CAN – 17; O'seas – 28
North America:	23 States, 5 Provinces
Density:	12 in TX, 11 in CA, 11 in FL
Projected New Units (12 Months):	50

Qualifications:	3, 3, 1, 2, 3, 4

FINANCIAL/TERMS

Cash Investment:	Store Front – $40K
	Mobile Unit – $25K
Total Investment:	$200 – $225K
Minimum Net Worth:	Store Front – $300K
	Mobile Unit – $150K
Fees (Franchise):	Store Front – $32.5K
	Mobile Unit – $29.5K
Fees (Royalty):	5%
Fees (Advertising):	2%
Term of Contract (Years):	15/5/5
Average Number of Employees:	2 – 3 FT; 1 – 2 FT (Mobile Unit)
Passive Ownership:	Allowed
Encourage Conversions:	Yes
Area Development Agreements:	Yes
Sub-Franchising Contracts:	No
Expand in Territory:	Yes
Space Needs:	1,200 – 2,000 SF

SUPPORT & TRAINING

Financial Assistance Provided:	Yes (I)
Site Selection Assistance:	Yes
Lease Negotiation Assistance:	Yes
Co-operative Advertising:	Yes
Franchisee Association/Member:	Yes/Member
Size of Corporate Staff:	50
On-going Support:	C, D, E, G, H, I
Training:	1 Week Field; 3 Weeks Marietta, GA

SPECIFIC EXPANSION PLANS

US:	All United States
Canada:	All Canada
Overseas:	All Countries

The following financial performance representation contains information relating to franchised Foot Solutions Stores that were open and continuously operating and located within the State of Arizona for at least 12 months as of December 31, 2011. 8 franchised Stores were open and continuously operating for at least 12 months in the State of Arizona as of December 31, 2011.

The financial performance representation includes actual sales information for the 9 franchised Stores reported for the 2011 calendar year, i.e. the period from January 1, 2011 through December 31, 2011. Pricing of products we have in a range of footwear products and custom orthotics that retail at $80.00 to $450.00. We have chosen to report financial performance information for the 8 Stores located in Arizona only. These 8 Stores are located in markets of varying sizes with varying demographics from small towns to a major city (Phoenix). The 8 Stores included in this financial performance representation are owned by franchisees with varying degrees of experience operating Foot Solutions Stores. The length of time that the Stores included in this financial performance representation were open and operating as of December 31, 2011 ranges from two years to nine years.

The financial performance representation figures do not reflect the costs of sales, operating expenses or other costs or expenses that must be deducted from the "Net Sales" figures to obtain your net income or profit. You should conduct an independent investigation of the costs and expenses you will incur in operating your (franchised business). Franchisees or former franchisees, listed in the disclosure document, may be one source of this information. However, the average cost of goods sold for products purchased through Shu Re Nu Equipment, Inc., an approved FS supplier and orthotics lab, is 40%.

Substantiation of the data contained in this financial performance representation will be made available to you upon reasonable request.

"Net Sales", as the term is used in this financial performance representation, means the gross receipts from the sale of all products and services at the Store, minus sales and use taxes. Net Sales includes sales covered by Medicare and insurance and sales transacted using credit or debit cards, even if payment has not yet been received by the franchisee from such third party payers.

"Average Ticket Amount" means the average amount spent by customers of the franchisees, per transaction. The calculation was done by taking the average transaction amounts reported by (11) eleven stores in the study during the year January 1 through December 31, 2010.

NET SALES AND AVERAGE TICKET AMOUNT OF FRANCHISED FOOT SOLUTIONS STORES FOR 8 STORES LOCATED IN ARIZONA

TOTAL NET SALES (9 STORES)	$3,884,310
AVERAGE NET SALES	$,485,538
HIGHEST INDIVIDUAL STORE NET SALES	$951,206
LOWEST INDIVIDUAL STORE NET SALES	$292,738

This financial performance representation includes information only from the 8 Foot Solutions Stores that have been open and operating within the State of Arizona continuously for at least 12 months as of December 31, 2011. Foot Solutions Stores outside the State of Arizona may not have performed as well as the Stores in Arizona during 2011 and the national average for Net Sales of Foot Solutions Stores may have been lower than the average Net Sales and Average Ticket Amount reported above. We caution you that these statements relate to historical performance and are not guarantees of future results. We do not claim or expect that you will or can expect to achieve the same Net Sales as shown above. We cannot predict, much less guarantee, the results of any individual franchise, and you are likely to achieve results that are different, possibly significantly and adversely, from the results shown above.

Customer Profile Analysis

Based on feedback from customer survey, demographics have a direct impact on our average customer spend,

Household Income is $125,000 and above	Average Spend is $200
Household Income is Between $75,000 and $125,000	Average Spend is $160
Household Income is $75,000 and lower	Average Spend is $125

This customer spend is based on averages and will be impacted by a number of variables in each individual marketplace. However, we feel this information is important for you to properly investigate any potential business opportunity.

These numbers are based on a professional survey conducted in January 2010 by an outside consultant using a population of approximately 80,000 Foot Solutions customers' addresses and a random selection process of every fourth entry was used to insure the population was random in nature. A response rate of six percent (6%) which is substantial providing a ninety-five percent (95%) confidence level for the research with a margin of error of+/- 5% was obtained.

The average cost of sales from all FS purchases through Shu Re Nu Distribution Company is forty percent (40%). This is based on suggested retail prices against actual discounted wholesale prices for Foot Solutions franchisees including Foot Solutions lines as well as Foot Solutions Technology products and custom arch supports. The Shu Re Nu average cost is based on the full range of products that are offered to franchisees through the Shu Re Nu distribution company for all orders received following initial store opening.

Other than the preceding financial performance representation, Foot Solutions, Inc. does not make any financial performance representations. We also do not authorize our employees or representatives to make any representations either orally or in writing. If you are purchasing an existing outlet, however, we may provide you with the actual records of that outlet. If you receive any other financial performance information or projections of your future income, you should report it to the franchisor's management by contacting Ray Margiano, CEO or Donna English, Supervisor: Legal Department, in writing, at Foot Solutions, Inc., 2359 Windy Hill Rd., Suite 400, Marietta, GA 30067, Phone: 770-916-5969, the Federal Trade Commission, and the appropriate state regulatory agencies.

MAC TOOLS

505 N. Cleveland Ave., #200
Westerville, OH 43082
Tel: (800) 622-8665, (330) 929-4949
Fax: (800) 294-1888
Email: ddc@sbdinc.com
Website: www.mactools.com
Theresa Petruzzell, U.S. Media International

With Mac Tools, you benefit from our 70+ years in the automotive equipment industry, with over 100,000 products, including hand tools, tool boxes, and specialty items, as well as a full range of power tools, electronics, and shop equipment. Our tool boxes are manufactured in Georgetown, OH, and the majority of our sockets, wrenches, and ratchets are made in Dallas, TX. Because we are a division of Stanley Black & Decker, Inc. our franchisees have access to well-known product lines such as DEWALT®, Stanley® and Vidmar®.

BACKGROUND

IFA Member:	No
Established & First Franchised:	1938; 2011
Franchised Units:	52
Company-Owned Units:	4
Total Units:	56
Distribution:	US – 51; CAN – 5; O'seas – 0
North America:	21 States, 4 Provinces
Density:	6 in FL, 5 in OH, 3 in TX

Projected New Units (12 Months):	150
Qualifications:	3, 5, 4, 2, 1, 5

FINANCIAL/TERMS

Cash Investment:	N/A
Total Investment:	$87.7 – $206.2K
Minimum Net Worth:	$18K
Fees (Franchise):	$3K
Fees (Royalty):	$82.50/month
Fees (Advertising):	0.0%
Term of Contract (Years):	5/5
Average Number of Employees:	1 FT, 0 PT
Passive Ownership:	Allowed
Encourage Conversions:	Yes
Area Development Agreements:	No
Sub-Franchising Contracts:	No
Expand in Territory:	Yes
Space Needs:	N/A

SUPPORT & TRAINING

Financial Assistance Provided:	Yes (I)
Site Selection Assistance:	Yes
Lease Negotiation Assistance:	N/A
Co-operative Advertising:	No
Franchisee Association/Member:	No
Size of Corporate Staff:	175
On-going Support:	A, B, C, D, E, F, G, H, I
Training:	5 Days Mentor Ride (Various Locations); 5 Days Westerville, OH (Class Time); 10 Days Initial District Manager Field Training

SPECIFIC EXPANSION PLANS

US:	All United States
Canada:	All Canada
Overseas:	No

Those Mac Tools Businesses which were in operation for all of calendar year 2011 had total purchases from Mac Tools during calendar year 2011 in the amounts noted below. The amounts of purchases noted below represent the prices paid by franchisees and distributors to Mac Tools for product inventory. Mac Tools sells products to its franchisees and distributors at discounts from the recommended prices at which sales products to customers are made. Franchisees and distributors set the prices at which they sell products to their customers. The information presented below includes information for distributors within the United States generally and for franchisees located within Kentucky. No information regarding Mac Tools employee distributors is included below.

Total Purchases of Products from Mac Tools during 2011	Number of Franchisees and Distributors Reporting Total Purchases Within This Category	Percentage of all Franchisees and Distributors
Less than $50,000.00	57	6.53%
$50,000.00 to $74,9999.99	76	8.71%
$75,000.00 to $99,999.99	110	12.60%
$100,000.00 to $124,999.99	117	13.10%
$125,000.00 to $149,999.99	107	12.26%
$150,000.00 to $174,999.99	97	11.11%
$175,000.00 to $199,999.99	90	10,31%
$200,000.00 to $224,999.99	69	7.90%
$225,000.00 to $249,999.99	58	6.64%
$250,000.00 to $274,999.99	28	3.21%
$275,000.00 to $299,999.99	29	3.32%
$300,000.00 to $324,999.99	11	1.26%
$325,000.00 to $349,999.99	9	1.03%
$350,000.00 to $374,999.99	4	0.46%
$375,000.00 to $399,999.99	5	0.57%
$400,000.00 to $424,999.99	1	0.11%
$425,000.00 to $449,999.99	0	0.00%
$450,000.00 to $474,999.99	0	0.00%
$475,000.00 to $499,999.99	1	0.11%
$500,000.00 to $524,999.99	2	0.23%
$525,000.00 to $549,999.99	0	0.00%
$550,000.00 to $574,999.99	1	0.11%
$575,000.00 to $599,999.99	0	0.00%
Greater than $600,000.00	1	0.11%
Total	873	100.00%

These actual product purchase totals are of all Mac Tools distributors and franchisees who were in business during all of calendar year 2011. They should not be considered as the actual or probable total product purchases that will be made by you. Some Mac Tools Businesses have purchased this amount. Your individual results may differ. There is no assurance that you'll purchase as much product inventory, and Mac Tools does not represent that you can expect to attain these amounts of purchases.

Other than the preceding financial performance representation, Mac Tools does not make any financial performance representations. We also do not authorize our employees or representatives to make any such representations either orally or in writing. If you are purchasing an existing outlet, however, we may provide you with the actual records of that outlet. If you receive any other financial performance information or projections of your future income, you should report it to the franchisor's management by contacting Mac Tools, Attn: On-

Boarding Manager, 505 North Cleveland Avenue, Westerville, Ohio 43082, the Federal Trade Commission, and the appropriate state regulatory agencies.

Written substantiation for the financial performance representation included in this Item 19 will be made available to you upon reasonable request. Mac Tools substantiation of this information will be done in a manner that does not require disclosure of the identity of a specific franchisee distributor, or require the release of franchisee-specific or distributor-specific data without the consent of the franchisee or distributor.

WIRELESS ZONE

34 Industrial Park Place
Middletown, CT 06457
Tel: (866) 994-3577, (860) 632-9494
Fax: (860) 632-0703
Email: clayn@wirelesszone.com
Website: www.wirelesszone.com
Clay Neff, Executive Director of Franchise Development

WIRELESS ZONE stores are primarily retail, with strong emphasis on local ownership, networking, and community involvement. Franchise provides local field support staff, centralized advertising and purchasing, initial and on-going training, and strong commissions and residual income from Verizon Wireless phones, service, accessories, wireless email, etc. Join a winning team!

BACKGROUND

IFA Member:	Yes
Established & First Franchised:	1988; 1989
Franchised Units:	452
Company-Owned Units:	23
Total Units:	475
Distribution:	US – 475; CAN – 0; O'seas – 0
North America:	13 States, 0 Provinces
Density:	46 in CT, 38 in PA, 23 in NY

Projected New Units (12 Months):	65
Qualifications:	2, 4, 3, 2, 1, 5

FINANCIAL/TERMS

Cash Investment:	$100 – $150K
Total Investment:	$65.3 – $228.5K
Minimum Net Worth:	N/A
Fees (Franchise):	$30K
Fees (Royalty):	10%
Fees (Advertising):	$800/Mo.
Term of Contract (Years):	7/7
Average Number of Employees:	2 FT, 1 PT
Passive Ownership:	Discouraged
Encourage Conversions:	Yes
Area Development Agreements:	No
Sub-Franchising Contracts:	Yes
Expand in Territory:	Yes
Space Needs:	1,000 SF

SUPPORT & TRAINING

Financial Assistance Provided:	Yes (D)
Site Selection Assistance:	Yes
Lease Negotiation Assistance:	Yes
Co-operative Advertising:	No
Franchisee Association/Member:	Yes/Member
Size of Corporate Staff:	64
On-going Support:	B, C, D, E, G, H
Training:	2 Days Third Party Trainer New Store; Up to 1 Week Executive Trainer

SPECIFIC EXPANSION PLANS

US:	FL and VA to ME
Canada:	No
Overseas:	No

Below are tables containing financial performance representations based on Providers' postpay activations and upgrades data (unaudited) of all franchised Stores for the calendar year 2011, as provided to us by Providers. Providers report postpay activations and upgrades data to us using a consistent reporting system applicable to all of the Stores. We have not audited these figures. The average number of postpay activation and upgrade transactions in the tables are net of any deactivations. We offered substantially the same services to all of the Stores whose data is reported in the tables below. The Stores offer substantially the same products and services to consumers.

Wireless Zone® Franchised Stores
January 1, 2011 – December 31, 2011

The following tables do not reflect any dollar revenue of the Stores, including commission revenue, monthly residuals, or other revenue for sales of accessories or other related items.

All Franchised Stores Open At Any Time During 2011 (463 Stores)

		Number of Stores that Attained or Surpassed the Average
Average Number of Postpay Activations Per Store Per Month	29	(168 of 463 Stores or 36%)
Average Number of Upgrades Per Store Per Month	100	(168 of 463 Stores or 36%)
Average Number of Combined Transactions Per Store Per Month (Postpay Activations & Upgrades Combined)	128	(172 of 463 Stores or 37%)

Franchised Stores Open 12 Full Months In 2011 (370 Stores)

		Number of Stores that Attained or Surpassed the Average
Average Number of Postpay Activations Per Store Per Month	30	(135 of 370 Stores or 36%)
Average Number of Upgrades Per Store Per Month	105	(146 of 370 Stores or 39%)
Average Number of Combined Transactions Per Store Per Month (Postpay Activations & Upgrades Combined)	135	(144 of 370 Stores or 39%)

Top 10% of Franchised Stores Open 12 Full Months In 2011 (37 Stores)

		Number of Stores that Attained or Surpassed the Average
Average Number of Postpay Activations Per Store Per Month	66	(16 of 37 Stores or 43%)
Average Number of Upgrades Per Store Per Month	261	(12 of 37 Stores or 32%)
Average Number of Combined Transactions Per Store Per Month (Postpay Activations & Upgrades Combined)	327	(12 of 37 Stores or 32%)

Bottom 10% of Franchised Stores Open 12 Full Months In 201 1 (37 Stores)

		Number of Stores that Attained or Surpassed the Average
Average Number of Postpay Activations Per Store Per Month	12	(14 of 37 Stores or 38%)
Average Number of Upgrades Per Store Per Month	28	(20 of 37 Stores or 54%)
Average Number of Combined Transactions Per Store Per Month (Postpay Activations & Upgrades Combined)	39	(21 of 37 Stores or 57%)

New Franchised Stores Opened In 2011(Omitting 1st Month) (48 Stores)

		Number of Stores that Attained or Surpassed the Average
Average Number of Postpay Activations Per Store Per Month	35	(17 of 48 Stores or 35%)
Average Number of Upgrades Per Store Per Month	92	(17 of 48 Stores or 35%)
Average Number of Combined Transactions Per Store Per Month (Postpay Activations & Upgrades Combined)	126	(18 of 48 Stores or 38%)

The first table above reports data for all 463 Stores that were open at any time as a franchised Store for a full month during 2011. There were 408 franchised Stores open on January 1, 2011 and during the year, 52 franchised Stores opened and four company-owned outlets were purchased by franchisees and became franchised Stores, totaling 464 franchised Stores that were technically open at any time during 2011. One franchised Store did not do any business in 2011 and was treated as closed on January 1, 2011 for purposes of the table.

The second table reports data for all 370 Stores that were open as franchised Stores during the entire calendar year 2011. A total of 372 franchised Stores open as of January 1, 2011 remained continuously open during the entire calendar year 2011, of which two were continuously open but were converted from franchised Stores to company-Stores during the year. These two company-owned Stores are excluded from the second table. Additionally, three Stores which were company-owned Stores as of January 1, 2011 were continuously opened but were converted from company-owned Stores to franchised Stores during the year and are also excluded from the second table. The third table reports data for the top 10% of the 370 franchised Stores that were open during the entire calendar year 2011, and the fourth table reports data for the bottom 10% of these 370 franchised Stores. The rankings of the top 10% and bottom 10% of these 370 franchised Stores were based on the total number of transactions per Store per month, postpay activations and upgrades combined.

Finally, the last table above reports data for all franchised Stores that opened during 2011 and had at least one full month of data. A total of 52 franchised Stores opened in 2011, four of which opened in December 2011, and four company-owned outlets were purchased by franchisees and became franchised Stores. Because we omitted data for the month in which each of these 52 franchised Stores opened, since using only a partial month's data would understate the number of transactions occurring per month, there is no data to report for these four franchised Stores that opened in December 2011. We also excluded the four converted company-owned outlets because they did not first open for business in 2011.

Other than the preceding financial performance representation, Automotive Technologies, Inc. does not make any financial performance representations. We also do not authorize our employees or representatives to make any such representations either orally or in writing. If you are purchasing an existing outlet, however, we may provide you with the actual records of that outlet. If you receive any other financial performance information or projections of your future income, you should report it to the franchisor's management by contacting Susan E. Suhr, 34 Industrial Park Place, Middletown, Connecticut 06457, telephone number 860/632-9494 extension 1800, the Federal Trade Commission, and the appropriate state regulatory agencies.

The financial performance representation figures do not reflect the costs of sales, operating expenses, royalties or other costs or expenses that must be deducted from the gross revenue or gross sales figures to obtain your net income or profit. You should conduct an independent investigation of the costs and expenses you will incur in operating your Wireless Zone® Store. Franchisees or former franchisees, listed in this disclosure document, may be one source of this information.

The data reported in the above tables are averages and could vary greatly by geographic region, the length of time the Store has been in business, the length of time Provider has been operating in the area, your particular Provider, the terms of our contract with Provider, the service plan selected by the Store customer and customer usage. Results also vary from Store to Store.

Actual results may vary from franchise to franchise, and we cannot estimate the results of any particular franchise.

Some Stores have realized the number of transactions listed in the charts. Your individual results may differ. There is no assurance that you will realize as many transactions.

Written substantiation for the financial performance representation will be made available to the prospective franchisee upon reasonable request.

Service-Based Franchises | 6

AAMCO TRANSMISSIONS

201 Gibraltar Rd., # 150
Horsham, PA 19044
Tel: (800) 292-8500, (610) 668-2900
Fax: (215) 956-0340
Email: franchise@aamco.com
Website: www.aamcofranchises.com
Eric Meyer, VP Franchise Sales & Development

AAMCO TRANSMISSIONS is the world's largest chain of transmission specialists and one of the leaders in total car care services. AAMCO has approximately 900 automotive centers throughout the United States, Canada, and Puerto Rico. Established in 1962, AAMCO is proud to have served more than 35 million drivers.

BACKGROUND

IFA Member:	Yes
Established & First Franchised:	1963; 1963
Franchised Units:	900
Company-Owned Units:	12
Total Units:	912
Distribution:	US – 838; CAN – 27; O'seas – 33
North America:	48 States, 4 Provinces
Density:	71 in FL, 68 in TX, 49 in PA

Projected New Units (12 Months):	40
Qualifications:	4, 4, 1, 2, 3, 3

FINANCIAL/TERMS

Cash Investment:	$60 – $100K
Total Investment:	$224 – $299K
Minimum Net Worth:	$50 – $182K
Fees (Franchise):	$39.5K
Fees (Royalty):	7.50%
Fees (Advertising):	Varies, $150/month for national
Term of Contract (Years):	15/15
Average Number of Employees:	4 FT, 0 PT
Passive Ownership:	Not Allowed
Encourage Conversions:	Yes
Area Development Agreements:	Yes
Sub-Franchising Contracts:	No
Expand in Territory:	No
Space Needs:	1,212 SF

SUPPORT & TRAINING

Financial Assistance Provided:	Yes (I)
Site Selection Assistance:	Yes
Lease Negotiation Assistance:	Yes
Co-operative Advertising:	Yes
Franchisee Association/Member:	Yes/Not a Member
Size of Corporate Staff:	120
On-going Support:	C, D, E, f, G, h, I
Training:	On-Going Regional, Annual, On-Line; 5 Weeks On-Site; 3 Weeks Horsham, PA

SPECIFIC EXPANSION PLANS

US:	All United States
Canada:	All Canada
Overseas:	All Countries

We make three (3) different financial performance representations in this Item 19. We disclose: (i) the average gross sales in 2011 of U.S. AAMCO Centers that were open by the same franchisee for two years or more as of 12/31/2011 segmented by the number of service bays in the respective Centers; (ii) the average gross sales In 2011 of U.S. AAMCO Centers that were open by the same franchisee for five years or more as of 12/31/2011 segmented by quartiles; and (iii) the average gross sales In 2011 of U.S. AAMCO Centers that were open by the same franchisee for five years or more as of 12/31/2011 segmented by the number of service bays In the respective Centers, with this latter category being further segmented by quartiles. Approximately 98.38% of the average gross sales data was compiled from Weekly Business Reports prepared and submitted to AAMCO by franchisees owning such Centers; and, approximately 1.2% of the average gross sales data was compiled from the data contained In the Weekly Business Reports being verbally communicated to AAMCO by franchisees owning such Centers. We have not audited this data; and therefore cannot make representations or warranties as to the accuracy of this franchisee-reported information.

YOUR INDIVIDUAL FINANCIAL RESULTS MAY DIFFER FROM THE INFORMATION THAT WE PRESENT IN THIS ITEM 19. WE URGE YOU TO CONSULT WITH YOUR OWN FINANCIAL, BUSINESS, AND LEGAL ADVISORS TO CONDUCT YOUR OWN ANALYSIS OF THE INFORMATION CONTAINED IN THIS SECTION OF ITEM 19 AND IN THIS ENTIRE FRANCHISE DISCLOSURE DOCUMENT. GROSS SALES RESULTS NOT ONLY DEPEND ON THE SCOPE OF SERVICES WHICH A CENTER OFFERS, BUT ON THE QUALITY OF A CENTER'S MANAGEMENT TEAM, THE CENTER'S OPERATING HOURS, THE ENERGY AND DEDICATION OF A CENTER'S OWNER, AND THE QUALITY OF THE SERVICES WHICH THE CENTER PERFORMS. YOUR RESULTS MAY DIFFER.

Bay Count	Number of centers open for 2 or more years as of 12/31/2011	Average sales for fiscal year 2011	Number of Centers that attained or surpassed the average sales amount	Percent of Centers that attained or surpassed the average sales amount
9+ Bays	36	$829,238	16	41.4%
8 Bays	58	$747,803	26	44.8%
7 Bays and Less	512	$596,615	220	43.0%
Total Centers / Average Sales	606	$624,904	262	43.2%

Sales Quartiles	Number of centers open for 5 or more years as of 12/31/2011	Average sales for fiscal year 2011	Number of Centers that attained or surpassed the average sales amount	Percent of Centers that attained or surpassed the average sales amount
Top Quartile	110	$1,003,843	40	36.4%
2nd Quartile	110	$681,395	50	45.5%
3rd Quartile	110	$522,669	60	54.5%
Bottom Quartile	111	$336,424	67	60.1%
Total Centers / Average Sales	441	$635,403	217	49.2%

Bay Count	Number of centers open for 5 or more years as of 12/31/2011	Average sales for fiscal year 2011	Number of Centers that attained or surpassed the average sales amount	Percent of Centers that attained or surpassed the average sales amount
9+ Bays	31	$781,179	16	51.6%
8 Bays	53	$765,681	24	45.3%
7 Bays and Less	357	$603,404	151	42.3%

	441	$635,403	191	43.3%
Total Centers / Average Sales				

Bay Count of Top Sales Quartile	Number of centers open for 5 or more Year as of 12/31/2011	Average sales for fiscal year 2011	Number of Centers that attained or surpassed the average sales amount	Percent of Centers that attained or surpassed the average sales amount
9+ Bays	15	$1,037,069	5	33.3%
8 Bays	22	$1,049,800	6	27.3%
7 Bays and Less	73	$983,165	30	41.1%
Total Centers / Average Sales	110	$1,003,843	41	37.3%

For the second quartile, the average annual gross sales in 2011 for U.S. AAMCO Centers that were open for five years or more with the same owner is: $719,259 for 9 or more bays, which such group included 9 Centers, of which 5 Centers (or 55.6%) attained or surpassed the average; $672,875 for 8 bays, which such group included 13 Centers, of which 5 Centers (or 38.5%) attained or surpassed the average; $678,781 for 7 bays or less, which such group included 88 Centers, of which 39 Centers (or 44.3%) attained or surpassed the average; and $681,395 for all 110 centers on average, of which 49 Centers (or 44.5%) attained or surpassed the average. For the third quartile, the average annual gross sales in 2011 for U.S. AAMCO Centers that were open for five years or more with the same owner is: n/a for 9 or more bays, which such group included 0 Centers, of which 0 Centers (or n/a%) attained or surpassed the average; $530,377, for 8 bays, which such group included 13 Centers, of which 7 Centers (or 53.8%) attained or surpassed the average; $521,636 for 7 bays or less, which such group included 97 Centers, of which 52 Centers (or 53.6%) attained or surpassed the average; and $522,669 for all 110 centers on average, of which 59 Centers (or 53.6%) attained or surpassed the average. For the bottom quartile, the average annual gross sales in 2011 for U.S. AAMCO Centers that were open for five

years or more with the same owner is: $312,452 for 9 or more bays, which such group included 7 Centers, of which 4 Centers (or 57.1%) attained or surpassed the average; $368,652 for 8 bays, which such group included 5 Centers, of which 3 Centers (or 60%) attained or surpassed the average; $336,491 for 7 bays or less, which such group included 99 Centers, of which 60 Centers (or 60.6%) attained or surpassed the average; and $336,424 for all 110 centers on average, of which 67 Centers (or 60.4%) attained or surpassed the average.

Other than the preceding financial performance representation, AAMCO does not make any financial performance representations. We also do not authorize our employees or representatives to make any such representations either orally or in writing. If you are purchasing an existing outlet however, we, or the current franchisee, may provide you with the actual records of that outlet. If you receive any other financial performance information or projections of your future income, you should report it to the franchisor's management by contacting Matthew Wright at 201 Gibraltar Road, Horsham, PA 19044 or 610-668-2900 ext 212, the Federal Trade Commission, and the appropriate state regulatory agencies.

ADVICOACH®

900 Main St. S., Bldg. #2
Southbury, CT 06488
Tel: (203) 405-2164
Fax: (203) 264-3516
Email: sstilwell@franchisesource.com
Website: www.advicoach.com
Susan Stilwell, Franchise Development

With over 25 years of experience, our unique ADVICOACH® business model is designed to empower business owners to increase the productivity and value of their businesses. We keep our clients focused on driving results though our coaching methodology, not by selling mass market solutions. ADVICOACH® franchisees help business owner's increase the value of their businesses by indentifying business weaknesses, educating them on business solutions, and holding them accountable to implement appropriate "Rapid Impact Strategies" through weekly coaching sessions.

BACKGROUND

IFA Member:	Yes
Established & First Franchised:	2002; 2003
Franchised Units:	51
Company-Owned Units:	0
Total Units:	51
Distribution:	US – 51; CAN – 0; O'seas – 0
North America:	24 States, 0 Provinces
Density:	6 in NC, 5 in VA
Projected New Units (12 Months):	39
Qualifications:	4, 4, 1, 3, 4, 4

FINANCIAL/TERMS

Cash Investment:	$67K
Total Investment:	$73 – $83K
Minimum Net Worth:	$199K

Fees (Franchise):	$45K
Fees (Royalty):	5 – 15%
Fees (Advertising):	$400/month
Term of Contract (Years):	10/10
Average Number of Employees:	1 FT, 0 PT
Passive Ownership:	Allowed
Encourage Conversions:	Yes
Area Development Agreements:	Yes
Sub-Franchising Contracts:	No
Expand in Territory:	Yes
Space Needs:	N/A

SUPPORT & TRAINING

Financial Assistance Provided:	No
Site Selection Assistance:	N/A
Lease Negotiation Assistance:	N/A
Co-operative Advertising:	No
Franchisee Association/Member:	No
Size of Corporate Staff:	35
On-going Support:	b, C, D, G, h, I
Training:	24 weeks Virtual; 5 days Southbury, CT

SPECIFIC EXPANSION PLANS

US:	All United Stated
Canada:	All Canada
Overseas:	All Countries

Statement of Franchisee Annual Projected Revenues

The following are statements of annual projected revenues for AdviCoach Franchised Businesses. We have calculated these numbers based on our average suggested monthly billing per client, industry average length of engagements, and the experience of our business coaches.

There are three projections based on a set number of clients serviced each month. The charts reflect five years of projected revenue. The first chart below reflects a coach who services one new client each month from month 2 through 12 up to a total of 11, then services 15 clients per month each month through the end of the five year period. The second chart below reflects a coach who services one new client each month from month 2 through 12 up to a total of 11, then services 12 clients per month each month through the end of the five year period. The third chart below reflects a coach who services one new client each month from month 2 through 10 up to a total of 9, then services 10 clients per month each month through the end of the five year period.

We calculated the numbers in accordance with the low end of the average business coaching revenue range within the industry for each given year of operation. We subtract the Royalties paid to achieve a Gross Profit amount and Gross Profit percentage. We then identify expenses based on our experience and knowledge of current economic conditions, communications with franchisees regarding their expenses, and review of current costs for products necessary in the operation of the franchised business. We subtract the expenses from the Gross Profit amount to identify the Net Profit and Net Profit Percentage. If a franchisee chooses to operate from an office location outside of the home, the projected expenses will be higher and the Net Profit and Net Profit percentage will be reduced. We do not require nor anticipate that any franchisee will operate from an office location outside the home.

The assumptions we made in compiling these projections are shown following the projections. Any changes in these assumptions would require material alterations to the projections.

Chart 1:

	Year 1	Year 2	Year 3	Year 4	Year 5	5 Year Total
Total Revenues:	$66,000	$270,000	$360,000	$450,000	$540,000	$1,686,000
Royalty	$9,900	$33,849	$39,999	$44,499	$48,999	$177,246
Gross Profit:	$56,100	$236,151	$320,001	$405,501	$491,001	$1,508,754
Gross Profit %:	85%	87%	89%	90%	91%	90%
Expenses:						
Equipment	$500	$500	$500	$500	$500	$2,500
Professional Svcs	$2,000	$2,000	$2,000	$2,000	$2,000	$10,000
Phone/Internet	$840	$840	$840	$840	$840	$4,200
Marketing	$8,100	$18,300	$22,800	$27,300	$31,800	$108,300
Office Supplies	$600	$600	$600	$600	$600	$3,000
Insurance	$400	$400	$400	$400	$400	$2,000
Misc.	$6,000	$6,000	$6,000	$6,000	$6,000	$30,000
Total Expenses:	$18,440	$28,640	$33,140	$37,640	$42,140	$160,000
Net Profit:	$37,660	$207,511	$286,861	$367,861	$448,861	$1,348,754
Net Profit %:	57%	77%	80%	82%	83%	80%

Chart 2:

	Year 1	Year 2	Year 3	Year 4	Year 5	5 Year Total
Total Revenues:	$66,000	$				
Royalty	$9,900					
Gross Profit:	$56,100					
Gross Profit %:	85%					
Expenses:						
Equipment	$500	$500	$500	$500	$500	$2,500
Professional Svcs	$2,000	$2,000	$2,000	$2,000	$2,000	$10,000
Phone/Internet	$840	$840	$840	$840	$840	$4,200
Marketing	$8,100					
Office Supplies	$600	$600	$600	$600	$600	$3,000
Insurance	$400	$400	$400	$400	$400	$2,000
Misc.	$6,000	$6,000	$6,000	$6,000	$6,000	$30,000
Total Expenses:	$18,440					
Net Profit:	$37,660					
Net Profit %:	57%					

One new client per month:

	Year 1	Year 2	Year 3	Year 4	Year 5	5 Year Total
Total Revenues:	$33,750	$153,250	$277,000	$351,000	$423,000	$1,238,000
Royalty	$5,063	$22,140	$34,409	$39,549	$43,149	$144,310
Gross Profit:	$28,688	$131,110	$242,591	$311,451	$379,851	$1,093,690
Gross Profit %:	85%	86%	88%	89%	90%	88%
Expenses:						
Equipment[1]	$500	$500	$500	$500	$500	$2,500
Professional Svcs[2]	$2,000	$2,000	$2,000	$2,000	$2,000	$10,000
Phone/Internet[3]	$840	$840	$840	$840	$840	$4,200
Marketing[4]	$2,700	$12,260	$22,160	$28,080	$33,840	$99,040
Office Supplies[5]	$600	$600	$600	$600	$600	$3,000
Insurance[6]	$400	$400	$400	$400	$400	$2,000
Misc.[7]	$6,000	$6,000	$6,000	$6,000	$6,000	$30,000
Total Expenses:	$13,040	$22,600	$32,500	$38,420	$44,180	$150,740
Net Profit:	$15,648	$108,510	$210,091	$273,031	$335,671	$949,950
Net Profit %:	46%	71%	76%	78%	79%	76%

Being engaged by more or less clients in any given month will cause your individual results to differ. Charging clients at a rate other than those proposed will cause your individual results to differ. There is no assurance that you will earn the same amount as reflected in the projections.

These figures were prepared without an audit. Prospective franchisees should be advised that no certified public accountant has audited these figures or expressed an opinion with regard to the content or form.

The following assumptions were made regarding expenses:

1. Equipment. This figure assumes the need for replacing existing equipment. It does not include the equipment necessary to begin a Franchised Business as identified in Item 7 of this disclosure document, and is amortized over the term of the franchise agreement.

2. Professional Services. This figure assumes that you will hire a professional accountant to prepare your taxes and consult with you on various accounting matters throughout the year, as well as hiring an attorney to do any necessary business filings and registrations.

3. Phone and Internet. This figure assumes an annual contract for a separate telephone line and dial up connection for the internet. If you purchase multiple phone lines or other premium services, this figure may be higher.

4. Marketing. This figure assumes you will expend 8% of your gross revenue on Marketing efforts. We have not decreased this percentage in Years 2-5 despite decreasing the number of clients. This number will increase or decrease depending upon your client development activities.

5. Office Supplies. This figure assumes an expenditure of $50 per month for office supplies.

6. Insurance. This figure assumes that you will obtain insurance in accordance with the terms of the Franchise Agreement. If you purchase additional insurance above that which is required, this figure may be higher.

7. Miscellaneous. This figure assumes miscellaneous expenses to operate your franchised business, including costs for the annual conference, conference room rentals, and technology fees.

Additional Assumptions:

These projections assume that you will be the Principal Operator of the Franchised Business and that you do not receive an additional salary. They assume that you do not hire any other employees.

We have not provided any allowance for corporate or personal income taxes, nor have we included expenses for depreciation, amortization, interest or debt repayment. Each franchisee funds their purchase of the Franchised Business differently and we cannot project how you will account for those items.

These projections are based on economic conditions as of March 2012 and we have made no adjustments in any category to account for inflation.

These projections assume that you follow our guidelines for suggested pricing and that you operate your Franchised Business in strict accordance with our licensing standards and System. If you do not, your results will likely vary dramatically from the projections we have provided.

Other than the preceding financial performance representation, AdviCoach Franchising, LLC does not make any financial performance representations. We also do not authorize our employees or representatives to make any such representations either orally or in writing. If you are purchasing an existing outlet, however, we may provide you with the actual records of that outlet. If you receive any other financial performance information or projections of your future income, you should report it to the franchisor's management by contacting Lorinda Church, 900 Main Street South, Building 2, Southbury, CT 06488, 203-405-2171, the Federal Trade Commission, and the appropriate state regulatory agencies.

Written substantiation for the projections will be made available to the prospective franchisee upon reasonable request.

ALADDIN DOORS

2255 Lois Dr., #6
Rolling Meadows, IL 60008
Tel: (800) DOOR-247, (847) 310-3515
Fax: (847) 310-3518
Email: franchising@aladdindoors.com
Website: www.aladdindoors.com
Al Abdelaal, President/CEO

ALADDIN DOORS has been the number one choice for all garage door needs in Chicago, IL, Minneapolis, MN and surrounding areas with over 45 years of experience. Our family-owned company has a long-lasting reputation of excellence with regard to garage door installation, garage door repair, and any other garage door situation that needs to be addressed. Our vision is to be known as the worldwide leader in quick, high-quality, and comprehensive overhead garage door services, delivering exceptional services and products to each customer. We will continue to grow the ALADDIN brand through people, innovation, and technology, resulting in unsurpassed loyalty from our customers and a solid business model for our company-owned locations. Our mission is to grant our customers' wishes by providing a hassle-free experience for all their garage door needs while exceeding their expectations. As the owner of an ALADDIN DOORS franchise, you can expect to receive first-rate support from our management team.

BACKGROUND
IFA Member:	Yes
Established & First Franchised:	2004; 2013
Franchised Units:	0
Company-Owned Units:	2
Total Units:	2
Distribution:	US – 2; CAN – 0; O'seas – 0
North America:	2 States, 0 Provinces
Density:	1 in IL, 1 in MN
Projected New Units (12 Months):	6
Qualifications:	4, 3, 1, 4, 4, 5

FINANCIAL/TERMS
Cash Investment:	$30K
Total Investment:	$29.9 – $99.95K
Minimum Net Worth:	$100K
Fees (Franchise):	$10 – $35K
Fees (Royalty):	7%
Fees (Advertising):	3%
Term of Contract (Years):	5/5
Average Number of Employees:	1 FT, 1 PT
Passive Ownership:	Discouraged
Encourage Conversions:	Yes
Area Development Agreements:	No
Sub-Franchising Contracts:	No
Expand in Territory:	No
Space Needs:	800 SF

SUPPORT & TRAINING
Financial Assistance Provided:	Yes (I)
Site Selection Assistance:	N/A
Lease Negotiation Assistance:	N/A
Co-operative Advertising:	Yes
Franchisee Association/Member:	No
Size of Corporate Staff:	15

On-going Support:	a, d, i
Training:	3 Days within First 60 Days of Operation
	Franchisee Location; 12 Days Rolling Meadows, IL

SPECIFIC EXPANSION PLANS
US:	IL, MN
Canada:	No
Overseas:	No

The following statement is based on historical financial data of our affiliate, Action Doors, Inc. Action Doors, Inc. has been operating a garage door installation and repair service business since February 2004. While the services and products offered and sold by Action Doors, Inc. are substantially similar to those that will be offered and sold by Aladdin Doors franchise businesses, the company operations differ in that they have operated throughout the Chicago metropolitan area, an area much larger than any territory that will be granted to an Aladdin Doors franchisee. Action Doors, Inc. has operated in this large territory by maintaining a number of trained technicians who deliver the services to customers.

During the initial operation of the business, it is expected that the franchise owner will be acting as the technician for the Aladdin Doors business and performing all of the installation and repair services with the possibility of hiring one part-time helper during the initial period of operation.

The following statement is of the actual annual gross revenue, cost of goods sold and gross profit realized by Action Doors, Inc. as a result of the services conducted by three of its trained technicians during the calendar year 2011. The average of the figures for the 3 technicians is presented in the second table. During 2011, services to customers were performed by Action Doors, Inc. through a total of 13 technicians. The following statement is based on the services provided by a subset of 3 of the 13 technicians. These 3 technicians were the only technicians of the total of 13 who worked on a full-time basis for Action Doors, Inc. and who worked with Action Doors, Inc. for the full period of January 1, 2011 through December 31, 2011. Technician A has been a technician of Action Doors, Inc. since April 2008, Technician B has been a technician of Action Doors, Inc. since January 2009, and Technician C has been a technician of Action Doors, Inc. since November 2007. None of the technicians had previous experience in providing garage door installation and repair services and were trained by Action Doors, Inc. These technicians did not rely solely on their own marketing and sales skills in procuring customers. The securing of customers for the worked they performed was done predominantly by Action Doors, Inc.

The figures were below were compiled internally sales receipts, supplier invoices and other internal recordkeeping of our Action Doors, Inc. The data has not been audited.

The following actual annual Gross Revenue, Cost of Goods Sold and Gross Profit reflects the experience of 3 technicians of our affiliate, and should not be considered as the actual or probable Gross Revenue or Gross Profit that will be realized by any given franchise. A new franchisee's individual financial results may differ from the results stated in the financial performance representation. The following data is from our affiliate which had been in business for almost 7 years as of January 1, 2011.

ACTUAL ANNUAL GROSS REVENUE, COST OF GOODS SOLD AND GROSS PROFIT
OF 3 TECHNICIANS OF AFFILIATE FOR 2011

	Technician A			Technician B			Technician C		
	Repairs	Doors	Total	Repairs	Doors	Total	Repairs	Doors	Total
Gross Revenue	$195,806	$18,706	$214,512	$101,374	$68,000	$169,374	$145,742	$56,486	$202,228
Cost of Goods Sold	$29,927	$8,828	$38,755	$16,784	$31,960	$48,744	$24,924	$28,355	$53,279
Gross Profit	$165,879	$9,878	$175,757	$84,590	$36,040	$120,630	$120,818	$28,131	$148,949

AVERAGE ACTUAL ANNUAL GROSS REVENUE, COST OF GOODS SOLD AND GROSS PROFIT
OF 3 TECHNICIANS OF AFFILIATE FOR 2011

	Repairs	Doors	Total
Gross Revenue	$147,641	$47,731	$195,372
Cost of Good Sold	$23,878	$23,048	$46,926
Gross Profit	$123,763	$24,683	$148,446

2 of the 3 technicians exceeded the average annual total Gross Revenue of $195,372.
2 of the 3 technicians exceeded the average annual Gross Profit of $148,446.

Notes to tables:

1. Gross Revenue is the total of all money received for the services rendered to a customer, whether for installation of garage doors and openers or for providing repair services.

2. Repair Revenue includes revenue received from garage door and opener repairs and replacements of springs, cable, garage door openers, sections, rollers, hinges, drums, brackets, bottom rubber, weather stripping, gears, sprockets, capacitors, remotes, keypads, tracks and other parts related to garage doors and garage door openers.

3. Doors Revenue include the installation of a new garage doors and the installation of a new garage door opener in connection with the installation of the new doors.

4. To the extent that any installation or repair services performed for a customer were performed by more than one technician, Action Doors, Inc. internally allocated a percentage of the revenue and cost of goods to each technician involved in performing the installation or the repair services and that share is included in the revenue figures provided.

5. Cost of Goods Sold means the total amount paid to suppliers for the garage doors, openers and replacement parts used in the installation or repair service, including shipping charges and applicable sales taxes.

6. Gross Profit means Gross Revenue minus Cost of Goods Sold.

EXPLANATORY NOTES AND ASSUMPTIONS:

The following should be considered in reviewing and determining whether to rely on these figures:

Your results may vary as a start-up business. Action Doors, Inc. has been in operation for over 8 years and has developed brand awareness within the geographic area where it operates.

Your results may vary with a newly trained technician providing the installation and repair services. The technicians included in the above statement had a minimum of 2 years of experience as a technician by the beginning of the period covered by the statement.

During the initial operation of the business, it is expected that the franchise owner will be acting as the technician and performing all of the installation and repair services with the possibility of hiring one part-time helper during the initial period of operation. During the initial period, it is expected that the new franchise owner will also be responsible for marketing, advertising and promoting the business.

This actual statement of total Gross Revenues and Gross Profit does not include information concerning net profits that may be realized in the operation of an Aladdin Doors business. Net profits in the operation of an Aladdin Doors business will vary from franchisee to franchisee and from location to location and are dependent upon the total gross revenues you achieve and upon your ability to minimize expenses as well as numerous other factors beyond your control. We make no representations in this Item 19 with respect to the net profits likely to be experienced by an Aladdin Doors business.

You will incur numerous costs and expenses in connection with the operation of an Aladdin Doors business in addition to the Cost of Goods Sold, including other labor costs; occupancy costs (such as office rent and utilities); cost of equipment, materials and supplies needed to perform services; transportation expenses, including gasoline and maintenance of the van; advertising and promotional expenses; royalties and advertising contributions paid to us; legal and accounting expenses; insurance expenses; taxes; various other general and administrative expenses and debt service. This is not an all-inclusive list of expenses.

Factors which may cause material differences in the gross revenue and gross profits of technicians for an Aladdin Doors franchise business from the gross revenue and gross profit of technicians of our affiliate include:

- Management and business experience and the amount of time the franchise owner spends working in the business
- Quality of customer service
- Prices charged to customers
- Marketing and promotional efforts and related skills of the franchise owner
- Demographic factors, including geographic size, number of non-multi-unit housing units, income levels and economic conditions in the franchise territory
- Local competition in the franchise territory
- Weather and climate of the franchise territory.

The above list is not an all-inclusive list of factors. You should carefully consider these and other factors in evaluating this information and in making any decision to purchase a franchise.

The information in this statement is provided for reference only. You should make your own independent investigation on the revenues and profit potential of the franchise business. You should seek the advice of legal, business and financial advisors before making a determination concerning the revenues and profit potential of the Aladdin Doors franchise business.

Written substantiation of the data used in preparing this statement will be made available to prospective franchisees on reasonable request.

Other than the above financial performance representations, we do not make any representations about a franchisee's future financial performance or the past financial performance of company-owned or franchised outlets. We also do not authorize our employees or representatives to make any such representations either orally or in writing. If you are purchasing an existing outlet, however, we may provide you with the actual records of that outlet. If you receive any other financial performance information or projections of your future income, you should report it to the franchisor's management by contacting Alaa Kareem Abdelaal, 2255 Lois Drive Unit 6, Rolling Meadows, Illinois 60008 (888) 325-2334, or the Federal Trade Commission, and the appropriate state regulatory agencies.

We do not make any representations about a franchisee's future financial performance or the past financial performance of company-owned or franchised outlets. We also do not authorize our employees or representatives to make any such representations either orally or in writing. If you are purchasing an existing outlet, however, we may provide you with the actual records of that outlet. If you receive any other financial performance information or projections of your future income, you should report it to the franchisor's management by contacting Alaa Kareem Abdelaal, 2255 Lois Drive Unit 6, Rolling Meadows, Illinois 60008 (888) 325-2334, or the Federal Trade Commission, and the appropriate state regulatory agencies.

ALWAYS BEST CARE SENIOR SERVICES

1406 Blue Oaks Rd.
Roseville, CA 95747
Tel: (888) 430-2273 (916) 759-1825
Fax: (916) 722-8780
Email: franchisesales@abc-seniors.com
Website: www.alwaysbestcare.com
Barry Parish, Director of Franchising

ALWAYS BEST CARE SENIOR SERVICES is the only senior care franchise system to offer three revenue streams: Assisted Living Placement, In-Home Care, and Skilled Home Health Care. We have been in business since 1996, and have contracts with communities representing more than 2,000 assisted-living units. We provide the following: an exclusive insurance program, two weeks of one-on-one training in addition to 90 days of training modules, an exclusive care provider retention and recruitment program, national contracts for our franchisees, a 24/7 call center so franchisees never miss a lead, and a virtual office (all-in-one web-based software system).

BACKGROUND

IFA Member	Yes
Established & First Franchised:	1996; 2007
Franchised Units:	175
Company-Owned Units:	0
Total Units:	175
Dist.:	US – 169; CAN – 6; O'seas – 0
North America:	34 States, 1 Province
Density:	3 in OH, 9 in CA
Projected New Units (12 Months):	75
Qualifications:	5, 5, 3, 2, 3, 4

FINANCIAL/TERMS

Cash Investment:	$39.5 – $90.7K
Total Investment	$50.7 – $150K
Minimum Net Worth:	$50K
Fees (Franchise):	$39.5K
Fees (Royalty):	6%
Fees (Advertising):	2%
Term of Contract (Years):	10/5
Avg. # of Employees:	3 FT, 0 PT
Passive Ownership:	Discouraged
Encourage Conversions:	Yes
Area Develop. Agreements:	Yes
Sub-Franchising Contracts:	No
Expand in Territory:	Yes
Space Needs:	N/A

SUPPORT & TRAINING

Financial Assistance Provided:	Yes (I)
Site Selection Assistance:	N/A
Lease Negotiation Assistance:	N/A
Co-operative Advertising:	Yes
Franchisee Assoc./Member:	No
Size of Corporate Staff:	17
On-going Support:	D,G,H,I
Training:	Per and post training modules about 90 days one-on-one with sales trainer; 1 week Corporate; 1 week On-Site

SPECIFIC EXPANSION PLANS

US:	All US
Canada:	Yes, N/A
Overseas:	Australia, Chile, Germany, UK

The table presented below contains certain information related to Net Billings realized by Franchisees'Businesses for the period beginning January 1, 2011 and ending December 31, 2011, and compares it with Net Billings during 2010.

Net Billings Information for Franchise's Business Locations Open At Least One Year

Time in Business	Total Franchises	Average Net Billings	Highest Franchise Net Billings	Lowest Franchise Net Billings	Average Percent Increaase Over 2009	Percentage of Franchisees that Achieved the Average Net Billings
37 Months or Greater	6	$1,021,615.78	$2,076,745.59	$123,655.27	15.88%	50%
25 Months to 36 Months	11	$287,238.08	$579,594.54	$27,328.80	74.51%	55%
13 Months to 24 Months	39	$248,013.99	$825,749.00	$14,083.13	445.70%	38%

1. The information in the "Time in Business" column is based upon results of all unit franchisees which had billed Clients for services for at least a full calendar year as of December 31, 2011 and each of the preceding 2 years. The numbers are not related to when franchisees signed franchise agreements. The numbers do not include results from 5 franchises which were terminated in 2011.

2. "Net Billings" means the total of all revenues from the operation of each franchisee's business whether received in cash, in services in kind, from barter and/or exchange, on credit (whether or not payment is received therefore) or otherwise. Net Billings does not include the amount of all sales tax receipts or similar tax receipts which, by law, are chargeable to clients, if these taxes are separately stated when the client is charged and if these taxes are paid to the appropriate taxing authority. In addition, Net Billings does not include the amount of any documented refunds, charge backs, credits and

allowances given in good faith to clients by a franchisee.

3. "Average Net Billings"is the "mean"billings, calculated by adding the Net Billings of each of the franchisees and dividing the total by the number of franchisees in the category.

4. A Franchisee's Business may contain between 1 and 4 Assigned Areas.

5. The information in the table is based upon all franchisees of the franchisor which met the "Time in Business"criterion as of December 31, 2011. It does not include franchises terminated in 2011.

6. The "Average Percent Increase" was calculated by dividing the Total Net Billings for 2010 for all Franchisee's Business and comparing them against Total Net Billings for all Franchisee's Businesses for 2011.

If you become an ABCSP franchisee, your financial results may differ from the results presented in this Item 19.

Written substantiation of the information set out in this Item 19 will be provided to prospective franchisees on reasonable request.

Other than the preceding financial performance representation, ABCSP Inc. does not make any financial performance representations. We also do not authorize our employees or representatives to make any such representations either orally or in writing. If you are purchasing an existing outlet, however, we may provide you with the actual records of that outlet. If you receive any other financial performance information or projections of your future income, you should report it to the franchisor's management by contacting, Michael Newman, 1406 Blue Oaks Blvd, Roseville, California 95747, 1-888-430-CARE, the Federal Trade commission, and the appropriate state regulatory authorities.

ANYTIME FITNESS

12181 Margo Ave. S. #100
Hastings, MN 55033
Tel: (800) 704-5004, (651) 438-5000
Fax: (651) 438-5099
Email: info@anytimefitness.com
Website: www.anytimefitness.com
Mark Daly, National Media Director

ANYTIME FITNESS is the #1 co-ed fitness club chain in the world. We have boiled our business model down to the core essentials that members expect. Our loyal family of preferred vendors supply our franchisees with quality products at the best available prices. Financial and real estate support are available. More than half of our franchisees own multiple clubs. Enjoy the freedom of spending time with your friends and family, and the knowledge that you're making your community a better place to live.

BACKGROUND
IFA Member:	Yes
Established & First Franchised:	2002; 2002
Franchised Units:	2,015
Company-Owned Units:	25

Total Units:	2,040
Distribution:	US – 1,682; CAN – 59; O'seas – 274
North America:	49 States, 4 Provinces
Density:	156 in TX, 119 in MN, 112 in LA
Projected New Units (12 Months):	400
Qualifications:	3, 2, 2, 2, 3, 4

FINANCIAL/TERMS
Cash Investment:	$80K
Total Investment:	$78.6 – $345.5K
Minimum Net Worth:	$250K
Fees (Franchise):	$29.9K
Fees (Royalty):	$499/month
Fees (Advertising):	$300/month
Term of Contract (Years):	5/5
Average Number of Employees:	1 FT, 2 PT
Passive Ownership:	Allowed
Encourage Conversions:	Yes
Area Development Agreements:	Yes
Sub-Franchising Contracts:	Yes
Expand in Territory:	Yes
Space Needs:	4,000 SF

SUPPORT & TRAINING
Financial Assistance Provided:	Yes (D)
Site Selection Assistance:	Yes
Lease Negotiation Assistance:	Yes
Co-operative Advertising:	Yes
Franchisee Association/Member:	Yes/Member
Size of Corporate Staff:	162
On-going Support:	A, B, C, D, E, F, G, H, I

Training:	1 week Hastings, MN	Overseas:	Australia, England, Grand Cayman, India, Japan, Mexico, the Netherlands, New Zealand, Poland, Scotland, Spain, Qatar
SPECIFIC EXPANSION PLANS			
US:	All United States		
Canada:	All Canadia		

AVERAGE MEMBER NUMBERS

We had 1,361 Anytime Fitness clubs open for at least 12 months as of February 29, 2012. The average number of members at these clubs as of that date was 769. 571 of the 1,361 clubs that were open for at least 12 months as of February 29, 2012 (42%) had 769 or more members, and 790 (58%) had less than 769 members. This is an increase from an average of 737 members as of February 28, 2011.

We also had 46 Anytime Fitness Express clubs open for at least 12 months as of February 29, 2012. The average number of members at these clubs was 523. 19 of the 46 clubs that were open for at least 12 months as of February 29, 2012 (41.3%) had 523 or more members, and 27 (58.7%) had less than 523 members.

STATEMENT OF ANNUAL PROJECTED REVENUES AND EARNINGS FOR AN ANYTIME FITNESS CENTER

The following are statements of projected annual revenues and earnings for a franchised Anytime Fitness center. These projections are for a second year of operation. They assume that at the end of the first year you have a fixed number of memberships, and, even though most of our clubs continue to increase their memberships after the first year, that you remain at that level for the entire year, adding as many new members as the number of members that leave. (During the first year, it will take you time to build your member base.) We have listed below three projections, one based on a center having 500 members, one based on 769 members, and one based on 950 members. They are based on revenue information provided to us by our designated billing processor for our franchisees in 2011, and on the 6 Anytime Fitness centers that we or our affiliates operated during all of 2011.

The first example, for a 500-member club, is intended to give you an idea of the revenues, expenses and projected income of a club that performs well below our average, but is still profitable. Of the 1,361 Anytime Fitness clubs open for at least 12 months as of February 29, 2012, 1,083 (79.6%) had over 500 members as of February 29, 2012. The 769-member example will give you an idea of the revenues, expenses and income of a club that is able to maintain throughout the year the same number of members as the average number of members we had in our clubs that were open for at least 12 months as of February 29, 2012 (a relatively strong time of year for club memberships). Of the 1,361 Anytime Fitness clubs open for at least 12 months as of February 29, 2012, 571 (42%) had over 769 members as of February 29, 2012. The 950-member example gives you an idea of the revenues, expenses and profitability of a high achieving club. Of the 1,361 Anytime Fitness clubs open for at least 12 months as of February 29, 2012, 331 (24.3%) had over 950 members as of February 29, 2012.

The assumptions we made in compiling these projections are detailed following the projections. Any change in these assumptions would require material alterations to the projections.

Revenues[1]	500 Members	769 Members	950 Members
Enrollment Fee[2]	$11,000	$17,000	$20,900
Membership Fees[3]	$186,500	$286,900	$354,400
Vending Revenues[5]	$1,500	$2,300	$2,900
Personal Training[6]	$40,000	$61,500	$76,000
Total Revenues[7]	$239,000	$367,700	$454,200
Operating Expenses[1]			
Rent[8]	$83,600	$83,600	$83,600
Equipment Lease[9]	$45,600	$45,600	$45,600
Royalties	$6,000	$6,000	$6,000

Processing/Credit Card Fees[10]	$9,300	$14,300	$17,700
Bad Debt[11]	$6,700	$10,300	$12,800
Utilities[12]	$15,750	$15,750	$15,750
Insurance	$2,500	$2,500	$2,500
Proximity Cards[2,3]	$1,100	$1,600	$2,000
Advertising Funds[13]	$3,600	$3,600	$3,600
Local Advertising[14]	$6,000	$8,200	$9,200
Anytime Health Fees[15]	$2,700	$2,700	$2,700
Vending Products[5]	$500	$700	$900
Maintenance	$6,500	$10,000	$12,400
Software/Web Hosting[16]	$2,400	$2,400	$2,400
Bodyworkz Fees[17]	$1,900	$1,900	$1,900
Annual Training Fee	$350	$350	$350
Miscellaneous[18]	$12,000	$15,000	$17,500
Total Operating Expenses	$206,500	$224,500	$236,900
Income Before Salaries, Depreciation, Interest, Taxes and Debt Expense[19]	$32,500	$143,200	$216,900
Manager Salary and Payroll Costs[19]		$30,000	$40,000
Personal Training Commissions[6]	$20,000	$30,750	$38,000
Income Before Depreciation, Interest, Taxes and Debt Expense[19]	$12.500	$82,450	$138,900

NOTES AND ASSUMPTIONS

1. We rounded most revenues and expenses to the nearest $100.

2. In projecting enrollment fee revenues and the cost of proximity cards, we assumed that 45% of your members would be replaced through attrition, and that the average enrollment fee you charge is $49. The 45% attrition rate is an average in the industry.

3. In projecting membership revenues, we had to make certain assumptions regarding the types of memberships you will sell in your center and the prices you will charge for each type of membership. Based on reports we received from our designated billing processor, the average Anytime Fitness franchisee for whom they processed memberships fees in 2011 had 75% as many membership agreements in effect as members. In other words, if you have 500 members, on average, you could expect to have 375 memberships, with approximately 75% of those memberships being individual memberships, and 25% of those memberships being couples (or family or multiple)

memberships. Some of these memberships will be for fitness only, while others will include tanning memberships. It is up to you to set your own prices for each type of membership you sell (subject to minimum and maximum amounts we may specify). Based on the report from our designated processor, the average monthly membership fees paid under each membership agreement to our Anytime Fitness franchisees for whom they processed billings in 2011 was $41.45. (Individual memberships would typically pay lower fees, couples memberships would pay fees higher than the average, and those with tanning would pay higher fees than those without tanning.) We used this average in compiling the membership fee projection. However, membership rates will vary significantly between clubs, depending upon what you elect to charge, how your rates are affected by competition, the number of members you have who add tanning memberships, the number of couples memberships you sell, and the number of memberships you sell that receive corporate discounts.

4. Under the 2010 Affordable (Health) Care Act, you are required to collect sales taxes on tanning services, and remit those taxes to the Internal Revenue Service. We assumed that you will collect the tax and pay it to the taxing authorities, which has no effect on your bottom line, and that tanning sales will not be impacted by this new tax.)

5. It is up to you to determine whether you offer vending machines in your center, the products you place in those machines and the vending prices. The amounts we have projected for vending revenue reflect the per membership revenues we receive from vending. We also do not tell you the sources from which you can purchase vending products. We assumed you would purchase your vending products from a warehouse seller such as Sam's Club, and that you pick up these items. If you go to other sources, or have these products delivered, your expenses will likely be higher.

6. Most of our clubs hire personal trainers to provide personal training services to their members. Members pay the trainers, and our franchisees typically collect a percentage of what the trainers receive. (In some cases, franchisees charge trainers a monthly rental, and allow them to keep all or a greater share of the training revenues they receive.) We have projected training revenues equal to $80 per member per year. The training fees will vary by trainer, but the average training fee is $40 an hour. Thus, the training revenues assume you have between 2 and 4 members per day, 5 days per week, taking training. We believe that this is consistent with the average for all our franchisees, but many franchisees do not report their training revenues to us. Near the bottom of each column, we projected that you pay one-half of these revenues to your trainer. If you perform all or a portion of the training services yourself, this would increase your income from operating your center.

7. There are other revenue sources we have not included. For example, we have recommended that our clubs charge members $1 a month for membership in Anytime Health ($2 for a couples or family membership). While we included in expenses the fees you pay us for each member (which we cap at $225 a month), since the majority of our clubs have elected not to separately charge their members for these memberships, we did not include them in revenues. Likewise, we recommend that our franchisees charge members a club enhancement fee of $20-$25 per year that can be used to purchase new equipment and upgrade their club. While more than a third of our clubs are charging these fees, and most of our newer clubs are charging them, we have not included these fees in revenues because we also did not include in your expenses the cost of purchasing new equipment or upgrading your facilities. Thus, if you are charging these fees, your cash flow would increase.

8. Your rent can vary significantly depending on the size and location of your center. However, in our experience, the number of members you have does not necessarily correlate to the size of your center. Our projections therefore assumed that the center had 4,500 square feet, and that the gross rent paid was $18.57 per square foot per year. If you have a larger center, or you pay more for rent, your rent expense could increase significantly.

9. This amount assumes you enter into a 3 year lease purchase agreement for your equipment, paying approximately 15% down, and financing the balance. For a center with 4,500 square feet, we estimated that the balance was $110,500. (Larger centers will typically have more equipment. See Item 7 for additional information about the range of initial investment for equipment and improvements.) Our projection assumes an interest rate of 10% per annum. We also assumed you are required to pay sales tax of 6 5/8% on these lease payments. These numbers will likely be different for each franchisee, as you may decide to make more of a down payment (which would lower your payments), you may decide to finance your equipment over a longer period of time (which will also lower your payments), you may have to pay a higher interest rate (which would increase your payments), and your sales tax may be higher or lower than 6 5/8%. In our company-owned centers, we typically purchase these assets without leasing.

10. Processing and credit card fees will vary depending on how many members prepay their membership fees, how many pay by credit card, and the credit card they use. In our experience, costs for these services generally average about 5% of your membership fees.

11. We assumed you would have 3.6% bad debt on your membership fees. This is consistent with the bad debt experience for our franchisees in 2011 as reported to us by our designated billing processor.

12. This amount includes gas, electric, water, cable, Internet and telephone. It assumes utilities average $3.50 per square foot.

13. This amount is based on our current requirement that you contribute $150 per month to our General Advertising Fund and $150 per month to our Local Marketing Fund.

14. We expect you to spend at least $6,000 per year for advertising. Our projection assumes your spending or local advertising increases more as you have more members.

15. As noted in footnote 7, you will be selling Anytime Health memberships for us, and you keep everything you charge for those memberships above $0.50 for individual members, and $1.00 for couples or family memberships. However, the maximum amount you must pay us each month for these memberships is $225 (and $675 if you own 3 or more centers).

16. In some states, you will also be required to pay sales tax on these fees. We have not included those sales taxes because they are payable in only a handful of states.

17. You are not required to use the Bodyworkz Training Program, but our revenue projection assumes that you do so. Thus, we have also assumed expenses of $160 per month for using this program. (If you have more than 2 centers, the fee is actually reduced to $135 per month for the second and any subsequent center.)

18. Miscellaneous includes janitorial services, legal and accounting fees, cell phone, supplies, licenses, and other similar items. Many of these costs can vary significantly depending on the location of your center and the time you spend looking for the best possible cost on these items. The projections are consistent with the experience of our company owned centers.

19. The low projection assumes you act as manager of your center and do not receive a separate salary. As your business grows, you may wish to hire a manager to oversee the club operations. We are assuming you would pay that manager $1,800 per month, plus commissions and limited benefits, so that with payroll costs, the total cost for a manager will be $30,000 a year. This is consistent with what we understand to be the average compensation our franchisees pay their managers. In the 950 member projection, we assumed the manager would receive a salary closer to $2,500 per month, plus additional commissions as the club continues to grow. Except as noted in footnote 6, the projections assume you do not hire any other employees to help you. (Because our centers are designed to operate 24 hours a day, without the necessity of having staff on premises, you should not need any other employees. However, some states or municipalities may require you have an employee on premises whenever your center is open. If you are an absentee-owner, or you operate in a location that requires the center to be staffed at all times, your expenses will increase significantly because you will have to pay salaries and benefits to employees. In our company-owned centers, we do pay a manager, or a management fee, to somebody to oversee the centers for us. Thus, we had additional expenses for wages or management fees.)

We gave you information above about the number of all our centers that were open for at least 12 months as of February 29, 2012. We or our affiliates operated 6 of those centers. All 6 (100%) had 500 or more members, al16 (100%) had 769 or more members, and 3 (50%) had over 950 members, as of February 29, 2012. 5 of those 6 centers (83.3%) exceeded the revenue and income projections in the first (500 members) column, 3 (50%) exceeded the revenue and income projections in the second (769 members) column, and 1 (16.7%) exceeded the revenues and income projections in the third (950 members) column. Because our franchisees are not required to give us this level of detail as to their revenues and expenses, we cannot tell you how many of our franchisees exceeded the projected revenues or projected profits.

STATEMENT OF ANNUAL PROJECTED REVENUES AND EARNINGS FOR AN ANYTIME FITNESS EXPRESS® CENTER

The following are statements of projected annual revenues and earnings for a franchised Anytime Fitness Express® center. These projections are for a second year of operation. They assume that at the end of the first year you have a fixed number of memberships, and, even though most of our clubs continue to increase their memberships after the first year, that you remain at that level for the entire year, adding as many new members as the number of members that leave. (During the first year, it will take you time to build your member base.) We have listed below three projections, one based on a center having 350 members, one based on 523 members, and one based on 650 members. They are based on revenue information provided to us by our designated billing processor for our 46 Anytime Fitness Express franchisees that operated during all of the 12 months ended February 29, 2012, and our expense experience operating Anytime Fitness centers.

The first example, for a 350-member club, is intended to give you an idea of the revenues, expenses and projected income of a club that performs well below our average, but is still profitable. Of the 46 Anytime Fitness Express clubs open for at least 12 months as of ended February 29, 2012, 36 (78.3%) had over 350 members as of February 29, 2012. The 523-member example will give you an idea of the revenues, expenses and income of a club that is an above average club, and is able to maintain throughout the year the same number of members as the average number of members at those of our clubs that were open for at least 12 months as of February 29, 2012. Of the 46 Anytime Fitness Express clubs that were open for at least 12 months as of February 29, 2012, 19 (41.3%) had 523 or more members as of February 29, 2012. The third example gives you an idea of the revenues, expenses and profitability of a high-achieving club with 650 members. Of the 46 Anytime Fitness Express clubs that were open for at least 12 months as of February 29, 2012, 12 (26.1%) had 650 or more members as of February 29, 2012.

Revenues[1]	350 Members	523 Members	650 Members
Enrollment Fee[2]	$7,700	$11,500	$14,300
Membership Fees [3,4]	$132,900	$198,600	$246,800
Vending Revenues[5]	$1,100	$1,600	$2,000
Total Revenues[6]	$141,700	$211,700	$263,100
Operating Expenses[1]			
Rent[7]	$39,900	$39,900	$39,900
Equipment Lease[8]	$35,100	$35,100	$35,100
Royalties	$5,400	$5,400	$5,400
Processing/Credit Card Fees[9]	$6,600	$9,900	$12,300
Bad Debt[10]	$4,800	$7,100	$8,900
Utilities[11]	$10,200	$10,200	$10,200
Insurance	$1,900	$1,900	$1,900
Proxomity Cards [2,3]	$700	$1,100	$1,400
Advertising Fund[12]	$3,600	$3,600	$3,600
Local Advertising[13]	$4,000	$5,600	$6,300
Anytime Health Fees[14]	$2,700	$2,700	$2,700
Vending Products[5]	$500	$700	$900
Maintenance	$4,600	$6,800	$8,500
Software/Web Hosting[15]	$2,400	$2,400	$2,400
Annual Training Fee	$350	$350	$350
Miscellaneous[16]	$10,000	$12,000	$14,000
Total Operating Expenses	$132,750	$144,750	$153,850
Income Before Salaries, Depreciation, Interest, Taxes, and Debt Expenses[17]	$8,950	$66,950	$109,250

THESE PROJECTIONS OF SALES, INCOME, GROSS OR NET PROFITS ARE MERELY ESTIMATES AND SHOULD NOT BE CONSTRUED AS THE ACTUAL OR PROBABLE SALES, INCOME, GROSS OR NET PROFITS THAT WILL BE REALIZED BY ANY FRANCHISEE. WE DO NOT REPRESENT THAT ANY FRANCHISEE CAN EXPECT TO ATTAIN SUCH SALES, INCOME, GROSS OR NET PROFITS. THE FINANCIAL RESULTS FOR A NEW FRANCHISEE ARE LIKELY TO DIFFER FROM THE RESULTS STATED IN THESE PROJECTIONS.

THESE FIGURES WERE PREPARED WITHOUT AN AUDIT. PROSPECTNE FRANCHISEES OR SELLERS OF FRANCHISES SHOULD BE ADVISED THAT NO CERTIFIED PUBLIC AC- COUNTANT HAS AUDITED THESE FIGURES OR EXPRESSED HIS/HER OPINION WITH REGARD TO THE CONTENT OR FORM.

NOTES AND ASSUMPTIONS

1. We rounded most revenues and expenses to the nearest $100.

2. In projecting enrollment fee revenues and the cost of proximity cards, we assumed that 45% of your members would be replaced through attrition, and that the average enrollment fee you charge is $49. The 45% attrition rate is an average in the industry.

3. In projecting membership revenues, we had to make certain assumptions regarding the types of memberships you will sell in your center and the prices you will charge for each type of membership. Based on reports we received from our designated billing processor, the average Anytime Fitness franchisee for whom they processed memberships fees in 2011 had 75% as many membership agreements in effect as members. In other words, if you have 350 members, on average, you could expect to have 262 memberships, with approximately 75% of those memberships being individual memberships, and 25% of those memberships being couples (or family or multiple) memberships. Some of these memberships will be for fitness only, while others will include tanning memberships. It is up to you to set your own prices for each type of membership you sell (subject to minimum and maximum amounts we may specify). Based on the report from our designated processor, the average monthly membership fees paid under each membership agreement to our Anytime Fitness Express franchisees for whom they processed billings in 2011 was $42.19. (Individual memberships would typically pay lower fees, couples memberships would pay fees higher than the average, and those with tanning would pay higher fees than those without tanning.) We used this average in compiling the membership fee projection. However, membership rates will vary significantly between clubs, depending upon what you elect to charge, how your rates are affected by competition, the number of members you have who add tanning memberships, the number of couples memberships you sell, and the number of memberships you sell that receive corporate discounts.

4. Under the 2010 Affordable (Health) Care Act, you are required to collect sales taxes on tanning services, and remit those taxes to the Internal Revenue Service. We assumed that you will collect the tax and pay it to the taxing authorities, which has no effect on your bottom line, and that tanning sales will not be impacted by this new tax.)

5. It is up to you to determine whether you offer vending machines in your center, the products you place in those machines and the vending prices. The amounts we have projected for vending revenue reflect the per membership revenues we receive from vending. We also do not tell you the sources from which you can purchase vending products. We assumed you would purchase your vending products from a warehouse seller such as Sam's Club, and that you pick up these items. If you go to other sources, or have these products delivered, your expenses will likely be higher.

6. There are other revenue sources we have not included. For example, we have recommended that our clubs charge members $1 a month for membership in Anytime Health ($2 for a couples or family membership). While we included in expenses the fees you pay us for each member (which we cap at $225 a month), since the majority of our clubs have elected not to separately charge their members for these memberships, we did not include them in revenues. Likewise, we recommend that our franchisees charge members a club enhancement fee of $20-25 per year that can be used to purchase new equipment and upgrade their club. While more than a third of our clubs are charging these fees, and most of our newer clubs are charging them, we have not included these fees in revenues because we also did not include in your expenses the cost of purchasing new equipment or upgrading your facilities. Thus, if you are charging these fees, your cash flow would increase.

7. Your rent can vary significantly depending on the size and location of your center. However, in our experience, the number of members you have does not necessarily correlate to the size of your center. Our projections therefore assumed that the center had 2,900 square feet, and that the gross rent paid was $13.75 per square foot per year. If you have a larger center, or you pay more for rent, your rent expense could increase significantly.

8. This amount assumes you enter into a 3 year lease purchase agreement for your equipment, paying approximately 15% down, and financing the balance. For a center with 2,900 square feet, we estimated that the balance was $85,000. (Larger centers will typically have more equipment. See Item 7 for additional information about the range of initial investment for equipment and improvements.) Our projection assumes an interest rate of 10% per annum. We also assumed you are required to pay sales tax of 6 5/8% on these lease payments. These numbers will likely be different for each franchisee, as you may decide to make more of a down payment (which would lower your payments), you may decide to finance your equipment over a longer period of time (which will also lower your payments), you may have to pay a higher interest rate (which would increase your payments), and your sales tax may be higher or lower than 6 5/8%. In our company-owned centers, we typically purchase these assets without leasing.

9. Processing and credit card fees will vary depending on how many members prepay their membership fees, how many pay by credit card, and the credit card they use. In our experience, costs for these services generally average about 5% of your membership fees.

10. We assumed you would have 3.6% bad debt on your membership fees. This is consistent with the bad debt experience for our franchisees in 2011 as reported to us by our designated billing processor.

11. This amount includes gas, electric, water, cable, Internet and telephone. It assumes utilities average $3.50 per square foot.

12. This amount is based on our current requirement that you

contribute $150 per month to our General Advertising Fund and $150 per month to our Local Marketing Fund.

13. We expect you to spend at least $4,000 per year for advertising. Our projection assumes your spending on local advertising increases as you have more members.

14. As noted in footnote 7, you will be selling Anytime Health memberships for us, and you keep everything you charge for those memberships above $0.50 for individual members, and $1.00 for couples or family memberships. However, the maximum amount you must pay us each month for these memberships is $225 (or $675 if you own 3 or more centers).

15. In some states, you will also be required to pay sales tax on these fees. We have not included those sales taxes because they are payable in only a handful of states.

16. Miscellaneous includes janitorial services, legal and accounting fees, cell phone, supplies, licenses, and other similar items. Many of these costs can vary significantly depending on the location of your center and the time you spend looking for the best possible cost on these items. The projections are consistent with the experience of our company owned centers.

17. The projection assumes you act as manager of your center and do not receive a separate salary. We therefore have not included any additional expense for salary. The projections assume you do not hire any other employees to help you. Because our centers are designed to operate 24 hours a day, without the necessity of having staff on premises, you should not need any other employees. However, some states or municipalities may require you have an employee on premises whenever your center is open. If you are an absentee-owner, or you operate in a location that requires the center to be staffed at all times, your expenses will increase significantly because you will have to pay salaries and benefits to employees. In our company-owned centers, we do pay a manager, or a management fee, to somebody to oversee the centers for us. Thus, we had additional expenses for wages or management fees.

ADDITIONAL ASSUMPTIONS APPLICABLE TO BOTH ANYTIME FITNESS CENTERS AND ANYTIME FITNESS EXPRESS CENTERS:

A. We did not provide any allowance for corporate or personal income taxes.

B. While we did include expenses for a lease/purchase of your equipment, we did not include any other expenses for depreciation, amortization, interest, or the repayment of debt. We anticipate every franchisee will fund its initial investment differently, and we therefore cannot project how you would account for these items.

C. The projections are based on economic conditions that existed in March 2011, with no consideration in any category for inflation related adjustments or further weaknesses in general economic conditions.

D. The projections assume you follow our guidelines in terms of the products and services you offer and the way you operate your business. If you do not, your results will likely vary dramatically from the results we have projected.

Written substantiation for the financial performance representations made in this Item 19 will be made available to you upon reasonable request.

We recommend you use QuickBooks Pro, the desktop version, as your accounting system. Most of the centers we used in compiling these projections used the accounting system we and our affiliates use in centers we operate. That system is consistent with generally accepted accounting principles.

We provided substantially the same services to those centers as we will offer to you. All of these centers offered substantially the same products and services as you are expected to offer.

We do not furnish or authorize our salespersons to furnish any other oral or written information concerning the actual, average or potential sales, costs, income or profits of an Anytime Fitness or Anytime Fitness Express business. If you receive any other oral or written information concerning the actual, average or potential sales, income or profits of an Anytime Fitness or Anytime Fitness Express center from any of our representatives, or from a person claiming to act on our behalf, you should immediately report that incident to us, as we have not authorized that information. You should not rely on any oral or written estimate or projection of sales, income or profits, or statement of actual, average, estimated or potential sales, income or profits of an existing or future Anytime Fitness or Anytime Fitness Express center, because reliance on that information would not be reasonable in light of the fact that we have not authorized that information to be provided to you or to any other prospective franchisee.

archadeck | outdoor living

Better Building *by* Design

ARCHADECK

2924 Emerywood Pkwy., #101
Richmond, VA 23794
Tel: (800) 722-4668, (804) 353-6999 x102
Fax: (804) 358-1878
Email: spucel@outdoorlivingbrands.com
Website: www.archadeck.com
Shemar Pucel, Franchise Recruitment Consultant

ARCHADECK, founded in 1980, started the nation's first network specializing in custom-designed and built decks, porches, and other outdoor products. Because construction experience is not required, our franchisees come from a variety of professional backgrounds.

BACKGROUND

IFA Member:	No
Established & First Franchised:	1980; 1984
Franchised Units:	56
Company-Owned Units:	0
Total Units:	56
Distribution:	US – 55; CAN – 1; O'seas – 0
North America:	20 States, 1 Province
Density:	6 in NC, 6 in SC
Projected New Units (12 Months):	25
Qualifications:	5, 5, 1, 3, 4, 5

FINANCIAL/TERMS

Cash Investment:	$80 – $100K
Total Investment:	$80 – $100K
Minimum Net Worth:	$250K
Fees (Franchise):	$49.5K
Fees (Royalty):	2.5 – 5.5%
Fees (Advertising):	1%
Fees (Guarantee Fund):	0.5% (initial year); 0.25% (subsequent years)
Term of Contract (Years):	8/8
Average Number of Employees:	1 FT, 1 PT
Passive Ownership:	Discouraged
Encourage Conversions:	Yes
Area Development Agreements:	Yes
Sub-Franchising Contracts:	No
Expand in Territory:	Yes
Space Needs:	N/A

SUPPORT & TRAINING

Financial Assistance Provided:	Yes (D)
Site Selection Assistance:	N/A
Lease Negotiation Assistance:	N/A
Co-operative Advertising:	Yes
Franchisee Association/Member:	Yes/Member
Size of Corporate Staff:	35
On-going Support:	C, D, G, H, I
Training:	20 Business Days Richmond, VA; 9 Days On-Site

SPECIFIC EXPANSION PLANS

US:	All United States
Canada:	All Canada
Overseas:	Europe

Actual results will vary from franchise to franchise, territory to territory and market to market, and USS cannot estimate the results for any particular franchise. Except as provided by applicable law, USS will not be bound by allegations of any unauthorized representation as to sales, income, profits, or prospects or chances for success, and you will be required to acknowledge that you have not relied on any such representation in purchasing your franchise.

Written substantiation of the data used in preparing the financial performance representations included in this Item 19 will be made available to you upon reasonable request.

A. Average Gross Sales for ARCHADECK Franchisees for the 12 Months Ending December 31, 2011

The following table presents the average annual gross sales re-alized by certain ARCHADECK franchisees in 2011. USS has provided this information to help you to make a more informed decision regarding USS' franchise system. You should not use this information as an indication of how your specific franchise business may perform. The success of your franchise will depend largely on your individual abilities and your market. The actual numbers you experience will be influenced by a wide variety of factors including your management, market size and demographics and competition. You should conduct your own independent research and due diligence to assist you in preparing your own projections.

The information provided in the table below was compiled from 50 of USS' franchise owners that were operational for the entire 12 month period ending December 31, 2011. The data excludes franchisees that either began operations, ceased active operations, or temporality ceased operations during this period.

Sales Volume	# of Franchisees	Sales in Dollars			% of Franchisees	Years in Business		
		Minimum	Average	Maximum		Minimum	Average	Maximum
Greater than $600K	16	626,203	1,317,939	5,924,665	32.0%	3.8	13.9	23.9
Between $300K-$600K	15	304,431	402,187	589,497	30.0%	6.7	15.0	32.0
Less than $300K	19	89,575	173,031	274,213	38.0%	2.1	9.9	21.9
Franchisees	50		608,148		100.0%		12.7	

Four of the 16 franchisees (25%) reporting sales in excess of $600,000 generated sales in excess of the $1,317,939 average for this subset of the 50 reporting franchises shown in the table above. This represents 8.0% of the 50 reporting franchises. Six of the 15 franchisees (40%) reporting sales between $300,000 to $600,000 generated sales in excess of the $402,187 average for this subset of the 50 reporting franchises. This represents 12.0% of the 50 reporting franchises. Ten of the 19 franchisees (53%) reporting sales less than $300,000 generated sales in excess of the $173,031 average for this subset of the 50 reporting franchises. This represents 20.0% of the 50 reporting franchises.

Some ARCHADECK franchisees have earned this amount. Your individual results may differ. There is no assurance that you will earn as much.

The Gross Sales figures presented above represent the total dollar value of customer contracts sold by the 50 franchises listed above in the reported period. ARCHADECK contracts are for construction services and can be long term in nature. Gross Sales should not be construed as a measure of revenue or cash collections, which can vary substantially from Gross Sales dependent on several factors, including franchisees' backlog of projects, size of projects or contract terms. The fi-

nancial performance representations above do not reflect the costs of sales, royalties or operating expenses that must be deducted from the gross sales figures to obtain a net income or owner's profit number. The best source of cost and expense data may be from current or former franchisees as listed in this disclosure document.

B. Average 2011 Contract Price for ARCHADECK Franchisees

The following table presents data regarding the average project size for the entire ARCHADECK franchise system for the 12 months ending December 31, 2011. The information provided was compiled from every ARCHADECK franchisee that sold at least one project during that period. USS has provided this information to help you to make a more informed decision regarding its franchise system. You should not use this information as an indication of how your specific franchise business may perform. The success of your franchise will depend largely on your individual abilities and your market. The actual numbers you experience will be influenced by a wide variety of factors including your management, market size and demographics and competition. You should conduct your own independent research and due diligence to assist you in preparing your own projections.

	Contract Sales Price	# of Projects	# of Projects at or Above Average	% of Projects at or Above Average
Average Residential Project	17,349	1,705	635	37.24%
Average Builder Projects	2,020	456	201	44.08%
Average Overall Project	14,114	2,1617	793	36.70%

Some ARCHADECK franchisees have achieved the averages shown in the table above. Your individual results may differ. There is no assurance that you will achieve the averages shown in the table above.

The financial performance representations above do not reflect the costs of sales, royalties or operating expenses that must be deducted from revenues to obtain a net income or owner's profit. The best source of cost and expense data may be from current or former franchisees as listed in this disclosure document.

C. Gross Margin Benchmarking Study for ARCHADECK Franchisees for the 12 Months Ending December 31, 2010

USS does not provide prospective franchisees with projections of income, profits or earnings. There is no guarantee that you, as a new ARCHADECK franchisee, will attain the same level of sales or profits that have been attained by USS' existing franchisees. The success of your franchise will depend largely on your individual abilities and your market. However, USS does provide prospective franchisees with information from a financial benchmarking study (the "Benchmarking Study") conducted for the ARCHADECK franchise system by Profit Planning Group ("PPG"), an independent third party financial benchmarking organization serving trade associations and franchise networks across the country.

In 2011, PPG conducted an independent financial Benchmarking Study for ARCHADECK franchisees. The Benchmarking Study was conducted solely on a voluntary basis. Interested franchisees were required to submit their income statements

for the year ending December 31, 2010, to PPG. PPG then calculated certain financial metrics to allow participants to compare their financial performance against their peer group of ARCHADECK franchisees. 40 out of 57 (70.2%) ARCHADECK franchisees participated in the Benchmarking Study. USS has reviewed the composition of franchise participants and believes it contains a random, representative sampling of ARCHADECK franchisees based on level of sales, years in the business and geography.

As defined in the Benchmarking Study, Gross Profit Margin measures profitability after material, construction labor and other direct construction costs are subtracted from gross revenue. It is calculated by dividing gross profit dollars by gross revenues. While Gross Profit Margin measures profitability after material, construction labor and other direct costs are subtracted from gross revenue, it excludes royalties, any commissions and other operating expenses.

The Gross Profit Margin figure provided by the Benchmarking Study is the median. The median for any variable is the middle number of all values reported arrayed from lowest to highest. Unlike the mean (or average), the median is not influenced by any extremely high or low variables reported. Therefore, the Benchmarking Study reports the median as the preferred statistic for its analysis.

As reported in the Benchmarking Study, the Gross Profit Margin of the participating ARCHADECK franchisee is 36.6%. The table below provides a further breakdown of Gross Profit Margins among the ARCHADECK franchisees participating in the Benchmarking Study.

	Participating ARCHADECK Franchise	Sales Under $400,000	Sales Over $400,000	Less than 8 Years in Business	More than 8 Years in Business
Number and % of Participating Franchisees Reporting	40/100%	20/50.0%	20/50.0%	17/42.5%	23/57.5%
Gross Profit Margin (Median)	36.6%	38.7%	34.7%	35.7%	37.3%

The above results taken from the Benchmarking Study are provided to prospective franchisees in evaluating the experience of existing ARCHADECK franchisees who participated in the study and not as a projection or forecast of what a new ARCHADECK franchisee may experience. A new franchisee's financial results are likely to differ from the results provided above.

Some ARCHADECK franchisees have achieved the results

shown in the table above. Your individual results may differ. There is no assurance that you will perform as well.

This financial information utilized in the benchmarking study was based entirely upon information voluntarily reported by the 40 ARCHADECK franchisees, none of which information was audited or otherwise reviewed or investigated by USS or by any independent accountant or auditing firm, and no one has audited, reviewed or otherwise evaluated this information for accuracy or expressed his/her opinion with regard to its content or form.

In preparing any pro forma financial projections, you and other prospective franchisees must keep in mind that each individual franchisee's experience is unique and results may vary, depending on a number of factors. These factors include general economic conditions of the franchise territory, demographics, competition, effectiveness of the franchisee in the management of the franchise business and the use of the ARCHADECK operating systems, scope of investment and the overall efficiency of the franchise operation.

Notes That Apply To Subsections A, B and C Above:

A. You are likely to achieve results that are different, possibly significantly and adversely, from the results shown above. Many factors, including those described in the preceding paragraph, are unique to each ARCHADECK franchise and may significantly impact the financial performance of your ARCHADECK franchise.

B. The actual results included above relate to results for the reporting ARCHADECK franchises and should not be considered as the actual or probable performance results that you should expect through the operation of your ARCHADECK franchise. There is no assurance that you or any other ARCHADECK franchisee will do as well. If you rely on these figures in preparing your own pro forma financial statements or otherwise, you must accept the risk of not doing as well. USS does not make any promises or representations of any kind that you will achieve any particular results or level of sales or profitability or even achieve break-even results in any particular year of operation.

C. As with other businesses, USS anticipates that a new AR-CHADECK franchise will not achieve sales volumes or maintain expenses similar to a ARCHADECK franchise that has been operating for a number of years.

D. You are responsible for developing your own business plan for your ARCHADECK franchise, including capital budgets, financial statements, projections, pro forma financial statements and other elements appropriate to your particular circumstances. In preparing your business plan, USS encourages you to consult with your own accounting, business and legal advisors to assist you to identify the expenses you likely will incur in connection with your ARCHADECK franchise, to prepare your budgets, and to assess the likely or potential financial performance of your ARCHADECK franchise.

E. In developing the business plan for your ARCHADECK franchise, you are cautioned to make necessary allowance for changes in financial results to income, expenses or both that may result from operation of your ARCHADECK franchise during periods of, or in geographic areas suffering from, economic downturns, inflation, unemployment, or other negative economic influences.

Other than the preceding financial performance representations, USS does not make any financial performance representations. USS also does not authorize its employees or representatives to make any such representations either orally or in writing. If you are purchasing an existing outlet, however, USS may provide you with the actual records of that outlet. If you receive any other financial performance information or projections of your future income, you should report it to the franchisor's management by contacting Chris Grandpre, U.S. Structures, Inc., 2924 Emerywood Parkway, Suite 101, Richmond, Virginia 23294, (804) 353-6999, the Federal Trade Commission, and the appropriate state regulatory agencies.

CMIT SOLUTIONS

500 N. Capital of TX HWY, Bldg. 6, #200
Austin, TX 78746
Tel: (800) 710-2648, (512) 879-4512
Fax: (512) 692-3711

Email: svandermause@cmitsolutions.com
Website: www.cmitsolutions.com
Sheri Vandermaus, VP Franchise Development

CMIT SOLUTIONS offers IT managed services and computer support to small businesses. Franchises can be home-based, as we service the clients remotely or at their place of business.

BACKGROUND
IFA Member: Yes
Established & First Franchised: 1996; 1996

Franchised Units:	135	
Company-Owned Units:	0	
Total Units:	135	
Distribution:	US – 135; CAN – 0; O'seas – 0	
North America:	32 States, 0 Provinces	
Projected New Units (12 Months):	20	
Qualifications:	2, 3, 4, 2, 4, 4	

FINANCIAL/TERMS

Cash Investment:	$45 – $74.2K
Total Investment:	$125 – $150K
Minimum Net Worth:	$300K
Fees (Franchise):	$49.5K
Fees (Royalty):	6 – 0%
Fees (Advertising):	2%
Term of Contract (Years):	10/10
Average Number of Employees:	1 – 2 FT, 1 – 2 PT
Passive Ownership:	Not Allowed
Encourage Conversions:	Yes
Area Development Agreements:	Yes

Sub-Franchising Contracts:	No
Expand in Territory:	No
Space Needs:	N/A

SUPPORT & TRAINING

Financial Assistance Provided:	No
Site Selection Assistance:	N/A
Lease Negotiation Assistance:	N/A
Co-operative Advertising:	No
Franchisee Association/Member:	No
Size of Corporate Staff:	17
On-going Support:	A, B, C, d, G, H, I
Training:	2 Weeks Austin, TX; 2 Weeks Jump Start

SPECIFIC EXPANSION PLANS

US:	All United States
Canada:	No
Overseas:	No

The following survey of CMIT franchisees was conducted during February and March 2012. In the survey only 10 questions were asked. The survey is a measure of 10, and only 10, aspects of the historic financial performance of those existing franchisees who responded to the survey. The "Response Average" column in the table below shows averages of the individual responses received to each survey question. In the two columns labeled "Highest Response" and "Lowest Response" we show the highest and lowest responses received to each question, we list the number of responses received in "Number Responding to Question," and in the final column to the far right under "% Who Exceeded the Average" we show the percentage of respondents who exceeded the average response to each question.

The figures in this table represent responses to a survey of CMIT Solutions franchisees who had been in operation for one-and-a-half years or more. At the time of the survey there were a total of 123 franchisees in the CMIT System operating 134 territories, and, of these, 63 franchisees, or 51%, had been in operation for one-and-a-half years or more. The number of responses varied for each question asked, as not all CMIT Solutions franchisees surveyed offer all of the products or services in the survey. These figures are based on responses received voluntarily from 63 CMIT Solutions franchisees.

Responding franchisees represent 50% of all CMIT Solutions franchisees; and 100% of franchisees who had been in operation for one-and-a-half years or more. We have not audited this information to confirm that it is correct, and have relied on the information provided directly by responding franchisees. There are no material differences between the businesses operated by the respondents to this survey and the franchise offering described in this franchise disclosure document.

Survey Question	Average Response	Highest Response	Lowest Response	Number Responding to Question	% Who Exceeded the Average
How many different business establishments did you derive revenue from in 2011?	54	546	5	63	30%
What percentage of the above businesses do you have on managed services contracts of 1 year or more?	38%	92%	5%	63	48%

How much per month do you charge a client with 8 PCs and 1 server for:					
Marathon Performance?	$346	$720	$125	52	53%
Marathon Performance Plus?	$565	$890	$125	50	58%
Marathon Ultra?	$939	$1324	$600	53	70%
How much per month do you charge a client with 30 PCs and 3 servers for:					
Marathon Performance?	$1142	$2675	$675	45	44%
Marathon Performance Plus?	$2025	$3600	$1230	44	56%
Marathon Ultra?	$3083	$4720	$2250	50	50%
How much per month do you charge a client with 1–3 servers and up to #500 gigabytes of off-site storage for CMIT Guardian?	$485	$1125	$165	52	58%
What hourly rate do you charge a client for project, professional services or break fix work?	$120	$150	$90	62	59%
What hourly rate do you pay your technicians for project, professional services, or break fix work?	$31.80	$150	$12	60	40%

The difference between the amount charged for the specific services cited in the survey and the amount paid to employee technicians for the services illustrates a narrow measure of net revenue and does not reflect other expenses that may be directly or indirectly paid from that revenue, such as office and equipment overhead, taxes, franchise royalties, and employee wages and benefits.

The rates charged to clients and paid to employee technicians in your market will be affected by a number of factors, including the strength of the market in your area for computer services, employee payment rate levels, and the existence of competition for computer services and qualified computer technicians in your market.

These figures do not reflect the costs of sales, operating expenses, or other costs or expenses that must be deducted from the gross revenue or gross sales figures to obtain your net income or profit. You should conduct an independent investigation of the costs and expenses you will incur in operating your CMIT Solutions business. Franchisees or former franchisees, listed in this franchise disclosure document, may be one source of this information.

Some of our franchisees have earned and charged these amounts. Your individual results may differ. There is no assurance that you will earn or charge as much. If you rely on our figures, you must accept the risk of not doing as well.

We have written substantiation to support the representations presented in this Item 19. Written substantiation of the data used in preparing this statement will be made available to you on reasonable request.

Other than the preceding financial performance representation, CMIT Solutions does not make any financial performance representations. We also do not authorize our employees or representatives to make such representations either orally or in writing. If you are purchasing an existing outlet, however, we may provide you with the actual records of that outlet. If you receive any other financial performance information or projections of your future income, you should report it to our management by contacting Sheri Vandermause at 500 N. Capital of Texas Hwy., Bldg 6 Ste 200, Austin TX 78746, telephone number (800) 710-2648, the Federal Trade Commission, and the appropriate state regulatory agencies.

Specialists in **COLOR RESTORATION & REPAIR**

COLOR GLO INTERNATIONAL

7111-7115 Ohms Ln.
Minneapolis, MN 55439
Tel: (800) 333-8523, (952) 835-1338
Fax: (952) 835-1395
Email: scott@colorglo.com
Website: www.colorglo.com
Scott L. Smith, CFO Sales Marketing Director

COLOR GLO is the leader in the leather and fabric restoration and repair industry. From automotive to marine to aircraft to all-leather furniture, COLOR GLO leads the way with innovative products and protected application techniques. We serve all US and foreign car manufacturers.

BACKGROUND

IFA Member:	Yes
Established & First Franchised:	1976; 1984
Franchised Units:	125
Company-Owned Units:	0
Total Units:	125
Distribution:	US – 90; CAN – 1; O'seas – 32
North America:	30 States, 1 Province
Density:	12 in FL, 8 in WA, 7 in OR
Projected New Units (12 Months):	12

Qualifications:	4, 4, 3, 4, 3, 3

FINANCIAL/TERMS

Cash Investment:	$44.9K
Total Investment:	$44.9 – $50K
Minimum Net Worth:	$50K
Fees (Franchise):	$25K
Fees (Royalty):	4% or $300 monthly
Fees (Advertising):	0%
Term of Contract (Years):	10/10
Average Number of Employees:	1 FT, 0 PT
Passive Ownership:	Allowed
Encourage Conversions:	N/A
Area Development Agreements:	Yes
Sub-Franchising Contracts:	Yes
Expand in Territory:	Yes
Space Needs:	N/A

SUPPORT & TRAINING

Financial Assistance Provided:	Yes (D)
Site Selection Assistance:	Yes
Lease Negotiation Assistance:	N/A
Co-operative Advertising:	No
Franchisee Association/Member:	Yes/Member
Size of Corporate Staff:	15
On-going Support:	B, C, D, G, H, I
Training:	2 weeks Headquarters, MN; 1 week Franchisee's territory

SPECIFIC EXPANSION PLANS

US:	All United States
Canada:	All Canada
Overseas:	All Countries

You and your accountant should make an independent evaluation and build a business plan for the opportunity you are pursuing taking into account such independent information as may be available at the time. While we are not able to review and comment on your plan, the plan should help you in making your investment decision, and in getting under way if you enter the Color Glo system. The average new franchisee generally finds the first 12 months of operation to be the most challenging. There are numerous factors that may affect sales and costs. Below are notes regarding some of the factors. There may be some factors not listed below.

We encourage you to discuss our business with existing franchisees and to retain a competent attorney and accountant to assist you in evaluating our franchise.

A New franchisee's financial results are likely to differ from the results stated.

The sales and cost information provided is not intended as a representation of the level that you are likely to achieve in the future. The figures stated relate to sales and certain costs only and not profits. Sales and the costs provided are not necessarily indicative of profits.

Substantiation of the data used in preparing these sales and cost claims are available in Minneapolis, MN upon reasonable request and notice.

Annualized sales data for the period January 1, 2011 to December 30, 2011:

The following Calculation of Potential Gross Profit includes estimates of gross profit at seven different sales volumes. During the calendar year individual gross sales of existing Color Glo franchisees ranged from $20,000 to $300,000. The Calculation does not include any estimate of a franchisee's overhead expenses (such as office, vehicle, insurance) or advertising or legal and accounting. Some franchisees have earned this amount. Your-individual results may differ. There is no assurance you'll earn as much.

Written substantiation for the financial performance representation will be made available to the prospective franchisee upon reasonable request.

1) Gross Sales. During the calendar year, the individual gross sales of existing Color Glo franchisees ranged from $16,700.00 to $285,500.00. Gross sales are the results of the number of services performed times the price charged to the customer for the service. The existing franchisees of Color Glo will charge differently for the type of service performed. Following is an example of charges for repair and or re-dye of leather seats. The pricing will range from $30.00 on the low side to $250.00 on the high side with $80.00 being on the medium side. Thus using the $30,000.00 figure for gross sales, the franchisee would need to repair and or re-dye 375 leather seats per year at an average price of $80.00.

2) Cost of Product. Color Glo's existing franchisees cost of product ranges from 8% to 13% of gross sales. The variance depends primarily upon the efficiency in the use of products by the franchisee as well as the size of the services performed and the number of services performed. Experience usually results in a more efficient use of the products. The $2,500.00 product cost is shown for the example using zero gross sales due to the minimum purchase requirement contained in the franchise agreement. The cost of product figures includes the proprietary Color Glo products.

3) Maintenance Fee. The maintenance fee is calculated at 4% of gross sales.

4) Gross profit. Gross profit is calculated by subtracting product cost and royalty from gross sales. The estimated gross profit in the above examples ranges from 83% to 88% of gross sales.

5) Net Profit. To calculate net profit, the franchisee will need to deduct from gross profit expenses incurred for advertising and promotion, insurance, office overhead, transportation, telephone, legal and accounting and miscellaneous. Except for insurance and telephone costs, these expenses can vary dramatically depending upon the franchisees personal choices such as existing vehicle or purchasing or leasing a new vehicle. Many Color Glo franchisees have elected to work from their homes to reduce office expenses. Other miscellaneous expenses such as interest payments to lenders will vary depending upon the franchisees' own method of raising capital and decisions regarding financing the business.

Unaudited calculation of Potential Annual Gross profit

Gross Sales(1)	$20,000	$50,000	$100,000	$150,000	$200,000	$250,000	$300,000
Product (2)	$2,500	$2,500	$2,500	$2,500	$2,500	$2,500	$2,500
Maintenance Fee (3)	$800	$2,000	$4,000	$6,000	$8,000	$10,000	$12,000
Gross Profit(4)	$16,700	$45,500	$93,500	$141,500	$184,500	$237,500	$285,500

Percentage of franchises in operation for the entire calendar year that achieved above Gross Sales and Gross Profit Level:

1 (1.61%)	2 (3.23%)	4 (6.45%)	9 (14.52%)	40 (35.48%)	14 (22.58%)	9 (14.52%)	1 (1.61%)

COMFORCARE SENIOR SERVICES

2510 Telegraph Rd., # 100
Bloomfield Hills, MI 48302
Tel: (800) 886-4044, (248) 745-9700
Fax: (248) 745-9763
Email: info@comforcare.com
Website: www.comforcarefranchise.com
Phil LeBlanc, Vice President of Franchise Development

COMFORCARE SENIOR SERVICES franchise members provide non-medical home care (assistance with the activities of daily living via companion and personal care services) and skilled nursing services to all members of the community, but primarily to the exploding market of those over the age of 65. COMFORCARE franchise members provide the increasingly-needed services that support individuals' independence, dignity, and quality of life.

BACKGROUND
IFA Member:	Yes
Established & First Franchised:	1996; 2001
Franchised Units:	171
Company-Owned Units:	0
Total Units:	171
Distribution:	US – 167; CAN – 3; O'seas – 1
North America:	29 States, 1 Provinces

Density:	26 in CA, 19 in NJ, 12 in MI
Projected New Units (12 Months):	40
Qualifications:	5, 5, 2, 4, 3, 5

FINANCIAL/TERMS
Cash Investment:	$50 – $75K
Total Investment:	$77.8 – $141.8K
Minimum Net Worth:	$300K
Fees (Franchise):	$42K
Fees (Royalty):	5 – 3% (Decl.)
Fees (Advertising):	0%
Term of Contract (Years):	10/10
Average Number of Employees:	2 FT, 18 PT
Passive Ownership:	Not Allowed
Encourage Conversions:	Yes
Area Development Agreements:	Yes
Sub-Franchising Contracts:	No
Expand in Territory:	Yes
Space Needs:	250 – 450 SF

SUPPORT & TRAINING
Financial Assistance Provided:	Yes (I)
Site Selection Assistance:	Yes
Lease Negotiation Assistance:	Yes
Co-operative Advertising:	No
Franchisee Association/Member:	No
Size of Corporate Staff:	24
On-going Support:	A, B, C, D, E, G, H, I
Training:	1 Week Home; 2 Weeks Bloomfield Hills, MI;1 Week Franchise Location

SPECIFIC EXPANSION PLANS
US:	All United States
Canada:	All Canada
Overseas:	All Countries

Other than the preceding financial performance representation, ComForcare does not make any financial performance representations. We also do not authorize our employees or representatives to make any such representations either orally or in writing. If you are purchasing an existing outlet, however, we may provide you with the actual records of that outlet. If you receive any other financial performance information or projections of your future income, you should report it to the franchisor's management by contacting ComForcare Health Care Holdings, Inc., 2510 S. Telegraph Road, Bloomfield Hills, MI 48302, 248-745-9700, the Federal Trade Commission and the appropriate state regulatory agencies.

This Item 19 contains certain historical financial performance data as provided by our franchisees; and thus we have a reasonable basis and written substantiation for the representation set forth below. Written substantiation of the data used in preparing this information and for the financial performance representation made in this Item 19 will be made available to you upon reasonable request. The representations made in this Item 19 are based upon the franchise system's outlets existing for the period of time indicated below unless otherwise specifically excluded, as discussed below.

Importantly, the success of your franchise will depend largely upon your personal abilities, your use of those abilities and your market. Some franchisees have generated gross sales in these amounts. Your individual results may differ. There is no assurance you will achieve gross sales in these amounts.

The data in the table below contains certain information related to gross sales realized by our franchisees open for the period January 1, 2011 through December 31, 2011 and does not include any sales taxes. We consider an office to be open once they have completed their training, their assigned door opening tasks and are able to provide, at least, unlicensed homemaker/companionship services within their exclusive area.

The gross sales amounts presented in the table below are based upon information reported to us by ComForcare franchisees whose offices have been open for at least 24-months for the period ending December 31, 2011, and only for those offices that have reported a full 12 months of gross sales data in each of the last two years. We have found that first and second year performance is not indicative of the franchise system as a whole. The gross sales amounts presented in the table below do not include:

(1) data for territories purchased and not yet opened by franchise owners,

(2) data for territories held by owners for resale that have been idled pending location of a buyer, and

(3) data for territories transferred to new owners during the current year. In some instances ComForcare franchise owners have purchased more than one franchise territory and report franchise sales and royalty information as a single unit for all territories they own. We have included this sales data in the table below, as reported.

The information has been extracted from royalty reports reported to ComForcare. We have not audited this information, nor have we independently verified this information. These figures are only estimates of what we think your gross sales may be. Your individual results may differ. There is no assurance that you will achieve the same results.

In addition, in conjunction with the services provided to seniors, the population size, density of seniors and number of people over the age of 65 in the exclusive territories for the franchise owners represented in the table below may not be similar to, or representative of, the exclusive area you may purchase.

TABLE OF GROSS SALES INFORMATION FOR FRANCHISEES OPERATING AT LEAST TWO FULL YEARS

Franchisee Time in Business	Total Owners	Average Owner's Gross Sales	Number/ Percent Attained or Exceeded Average	Median Owner's Gross Sales	Number/ Percent Attained or Exceeded Median	Highest and Second Highest Owner's Gross Sales	Lowest and Second Lowest Owner's Gross Sales
Franchisees – 85 months and greater	23	$1,254,327	7 (30%)	$1,082,496	12 (52%)	$4,631,517 $4,524,606	$222,759 $318,919
Franchisees – 73-84 months	11	$1,054,679	4 (36%)	$861,605	6 (55%)	$2,202,929 $1,905,442	$209,299 $264,746
Franchisees – 49-72 months	20	$743,325	6 (30%)	$661,444	10 (50%)	$1,962,745 $1,768,789	$117,451 $320,813
Franchisees – 25-48 months	39	$495,089	13 (33%)	$390,033	20 (51%)	$1,284,435 $1,170,103	$124,886 $142,682
Total/Average	93	$802,429	33 (35%)	$583,258	47 (51%)	n/a	n/a

Table Notes

(a) The 23 franchisees operating for 85 months and greater as listed in this table includes the gross sales totaling $4,631,517 for the 12 months ended December 31, 2011 for the first franchisee who originally began operations on May 1, 1996, which is a sister company to ComForcare and who is affiliated through a common owner.

(b) The 93 owner's data listed in the table and corresponding sales information includes the results of 8 additional franchise territories that were purchased by franchise owners who report sales and royalty information as a single unit for all territories owned. We have included this data in the table, as reported by franchise owners, although this results in higher average reported revenue results.

(c) This table includes offices opening in each year from 1996 through December 31, 2009 with the distribution of start dates as follows: 2009 – 29; 2008 – 10; 2007 – 7; 2006 – 13;

2005 – 11; 2004 – 8; 2003 - 10 ; 2002 – 4 and 1996 – 1. We consider an office to be open once they have completed their training, their assigned door opening tasks and are able to provide, at least, unlicensed homemaker/companionship services within their exclusive area.

These disclosure figures do not reflect the cost of sales, operating expenses, or other costs or expenses that must be deducted from the gross revenue or gross sales figures to obtain your net income or profit. You should conduct an independent investigation of costs and expenses you will incur in operating your franchise business. Current franchisees or former franchisees listed in the disclosure document may be one source of this information.

Based on all of the matters mentioned in this Item 19, we recommend that you make your own independent investigation to determine whether or not the franchise may be profitable to you and worth the risk. We suggest strongly that you consult your financial advisor or personal accountant concerning financial projections and federal, provincial and local income taxes and any other applicable taxes that you may incur in owning and operating a franchised business.

ComForcare will provide written substantiation for the financial performance representation to any prospective franchisee upon written, reasonable request.

COMFORT KEEPERS

6640 Poe Ave., # 200
Dayton, OH 45414-2600
Tel: (888) 836-7488, (937) 665-1320
Fax: (937) 665-1360
Email: larryfrance@comfortkeepers.com
Website: www.comfortkeepersfranchise.com
Larry France, Manager of Franchise Development

COMFORT KEEPERS is the service leader with 95% client satisfaction. We provide in-home care, such as companionship, meal preparation, light housekeeping, grocery and clothing shopping, grooming, and assistance with recreational activities for the elderly and others who need assistance in daily living.

BACKGROUND
IFA Member:	Yes
Established & First Franchised:	1998; 1999
Franchised Units:	650
Company-Owned Units:	15
Total Units:	665
Distribution:	US – 665; CAN – 51; O'seas – 34
North America:	47 States, 5 Provinces
Density:	85 in CA, 59 in FL, 46 in OH

Projected New Units (12 Months):	32
Qualifications:	5, 5, 2, 3, 3, 4

FINANCIAL/TERMS
Cash Investment:	$66K
Total Investment:	$66 – $99.4K
Minimum Net Worth:	$200K
Fees (Franchise):	$45K
Fees (Royalty):	5/4/3%
Fees (Advertising):	2%
Term of Contract (Years):	10/10
Average Number of Employees:	2 FT, 4 – 5 PT
Passive Ownership:	Not Allowed
Encourage Conversions:	Yes
Area Development Agreements:	No
Sub-Franchising Contracts:	No
Expand in Territory:	Yes
Space Needs:	400 – 700 SF

SUPPORT & TRAINING
Financial Assistance Provided:	Yes (D)
Site Selection Assistance:	No
Lease Negotiation Assistance:	No
Co-operative Advertising:	Yes
Franchisee Association/Member:	Yes/Member
Size of Corporate Staff:	50
On-going Support:	C, D, G, h, I
Training:	4 Weeks & Ongoing Dayton, OH

SPECIFIC EXPANSION PLANS
US:	All United States
Canada:	Yes
Overseas:	Yes

Table A and Tables PMG 1 through 3 are historical financial performance representations, based on revenue and, as applicable, expense experience reported by franchisees. For purposes of all of the tables in this Item 19, "net revenue" means that revenue on which a franchisee pays royalty fees (but which is, in the Franchise Agreement, called "Gross Revenue"), that is, the total amount of money the franchisee and its owners receive for all goods sold and services rendered in connection with the Marks, and all other income of any kind derived directly or indirectly in connection with the operation of a Franchised Business, including client deposits and payments for mileage charges but excluding sales tax and client refunds.

Table A, following, shows information relating to all Franchised Businesses operating at September 30, 2011 that had been operating for at least one year and reported revenue for every month during the period October 1, 2010 through September 30, 2011 (the "Reporting Period"). Table A shows net revenue achieved during the Reporting Period by Franchised Businesses that had been operating the specified number of months. The last line in the table shows information relating to net revenue for the Reporting Period for all of the Franchised Businesses included above in the table.

We used the Start Date for a Franchised Business as the date its operations began. Under a Startup Agreement, the Start Date is the end of the month after the franchisee completes initial training. Under an Expansion Agreement executed before January 1, 2007, the Start Date is the date of execution of the Expansion Agreement; under an Expansion Agreement executed January 1, 2007 or after, the Start Date is 60 days after the date of execution of the Expansion Agreement.

For purposes of the net revenue shown in Table A, we used the Gross Revenue figures from the royalty reports the franchisees filed with us; these revenues are reported on a cash basis. While we have not audited this information or independently confirmed the royalty reports, we have no reason to believe that any franchisee would overstate its revenues to us.

TABLE A

Number of Months in Operation (1)	Total # of Franchised Businesses (2)	Average Net Revenue	Number and Percentage of Franchised Businesses Meeting or Exceeding Average	Median Net Revenue	Highest Franchised Business Net Revenue	Lowest Franchised Business Net Revenue
73 or more	390	$719,496.57	157/40%	$579,948.61	$4,688,818.39	$15,983.53
61 to 72	42	$441,767.10	14/33%	$312,417.38	$2,443,869.69	$43,313.67
49 to 60	37	$534,405.40	11/30%	$293,730.75	$2,775,888.84	$61,765.25
37 to 48	29	$343,191.05	10/34%	$252,118.87	$803,887.68	$71,425.28
25 to 36	24	$258,727.77	14/58%	$271,586.65	$566,484.43	$66,024.15
12 to 24	29	$195,704.79	15/52%	$172,688.22	$780,396.18	$13,329.41
All Franchised Businesses Open One Year or More Ending September 30, 2011	551	$618,454.31	205/37%	$440,069.91	$4,688,818.39	$13,329.41

Notes to Table A:

(1) Franchised Businesses operating 73 or more months had Start Dates between March 1, 1998 and September 30, 2005. Franchised Businesses operating 61 to 72 months had Start Dates between October 19, 2005 and September 30, 2006. Franchised Businesses in each subsequent descending tier of months shown in this table had Start Dates one year later than those in the preceding tier.

(2) The total number of Franchised Businesses that had been operating at least 12 months at September 30, 2011 is 551; we have no company-owned Units. The number in this column represents all Franchised Businesses that reported revenue for every month during the Reporting Period and that had been operating for at least 12 months at September 30, 2011. The table excludes 19 Franchised Businesses that closed during the Reporting Period and 33 Franchised Businesses that reported no revenue or did not file a royalty report for one or more months during the Reporting Period. Each of the Franchised Businesses included in the table provided the homemaker/companionship services and personal care services that you must provide under the Franchise Agreement and most provided Personal Technology Services and Equipment under the SafetyChoice® program.

The following three tables are historical financial performance representations for the 12 months ended September 30, 2011, for a limited group of franchisees (the "PMG Group"). The PMG Group consists of smaller groups of franchisees ("performance management groups") who have voluntarily come together to improve the performance of their Franchised Businesses. These franchisees meet periodically in person or by telephone to discuss their performance goals and their actual outcomes. In order to participate in the performance management groups, the franchisees must own one or more units that have been in operation for at least a year, they must agree to a uniform system of revenue and expense reporting, and they must provide CKFI with financial reports based on that uniform system of revenue and expense reporting. CKFI provides no additional instruction or business guidance to the PMG Group. All 62 members of the PMG Group, representing 153 Franchised Businesses, provided data presented in Tables PMG 1 and 2. 15 of the Franchised Businesses are held by single unit franchisees; the remainder of the Franchised Businesses are held by 47 multi-unit franchisees. 20 franchisees held 2 Franchised Businesses each; 14 franchisees

held 3 each; 6 franchisees held 4 each; 6 franchisees held 5 each; and 1 franchisee held 7. The Franchised Businesses in the PMG Group are located throughout the country, in 25 different states. All of the Franchised Businesses in the PMG Group had been operating at least one year as of September 30, 2011. The Franchised Businesses in the PMG Group offer the homemaker/companionship and personal care services that you must offer under the Franchise Agreement; all but 4 also offer Personal Technology Services and Equipment, which you must offer under the Franchise Agreement.

Table PMG-1 on the next page represents the average net revenues of the Franchised Businesses in the PMG Group for the twelve months ending September 30, 2011, based on length of time in operation (using the Start Date as the commencement of operations). We used the Gross Revenue figures from the royalty reports that PMG Group members filed with us, which reflect revenues reported on a cash basis. While we have not audited this information or independently confirmed the royalty reports, we have no reason to believe that any franchisee would overstate its revenues to us.

TABLE PMG-I

Time in Operation (Years)	No. of Franchised Businesses	Average Net Revenue	No. and Percentage Meeting/Exceeding Average	Median Net Revenue	Highest Net Revenue	Lowest Net Revenue
10 or more	37	$918,932	15/40.5%	$834,789	$2,928,430	$143,744
8 to 10	50	$710,524	22/44.0%	$591,226	$3,062,769	$15,984
5 to 8	34	$895,507	15/44.1%	$741,751	$3,993,365	$23,425
2 to 5	28	$554,869	9/32/1%	$346,610	$2,775,889	$61,765
More than 1 but less than 2	4	$104,387	2/50%	$92,966	$215,261	$16,354
Total	153	$757,698	63/41.2%	$626,661	$3,993,265	$15,984

Table PMG-2, following, is a statement of the average performance of the PMG Group as a whole, based on the costs listed and then measured against their Net Revenue for the twelve months ending September 30, 2011. As indicated above, the members of the PMG Group have agreed to a uniform methodology for reporting revenue and expenses and the revenue and expense information shown comes from the reports provided by the PMG Group members to CKFI. The information in Table PMG-2 reflects reporting of both revenues and expenses on an accrual basis by members of the PMG Group; accordingly, the average net revenue figure is different from that shown in Table PMG-1, which reflects net revenue reported, on a cash basis, on the franchisees' royalty reports to CKFI. While we have not audited this information or independently confirmed the expense information or the information on the sub-categories of revenue, because a fran-

chisee's financial performance does not affect its obligations to us and because of the specific commitment of PMG Members to accurate and uniform financial reporting, we have no reason to believe that any franchisee would misrepresent its revenue and expense information.

PMG Group members who own more than one Franchised Business report expenses on an aggregated basis for all of their Franchised Businesses; typically, due to the nature of the business (services-based, rather than a location-based retail operation), multi-unit franchisees operate and manage their Franchised Businesses as a whole. The averages shown in Table PMG-2 represent the revenues and expenses reported (on a single unit or aggregated basis) divided by 153, the number of Franchised Businesses held by franchisees in the PMG Group. Thus, the average shown does not take into account that a multi-unit franchisee may have one or more of its Franchised Businesses that are performing well below the "average" shown. For the 15 single unit franchisees in the PMG Group, we have indicated in the applicable note to Table PMG-2 the number and percentage of their Franchised Businesses that met or exceeded the average shown for certain line items.

TABLE PMG-2

Revenue	AVERAGE for all PMG Group Members	As percent of Total Revenue
In-home Care Service Revenue[1]	$713,790	98.7%
Personal Technology Services[2]	$3,955	0.5%
All Other Revenue[3]	$5,687	0.8%
Total Revenue[4]	$723,432	100.0%
Cost of Sales		
Caregiver (CG) Payroll[5]	$361,527	50.0%
CG Payroll Taxes and Benefits[6]	$46,802	6.5%
CG Workers' Compensation Insurance[7]	$16,521	2.3%
Cost of Personal Technology Equipment[8]	$2,369	0.3%
Direct Revenue Incentive Compensation[9]	$1,248	0.2%
Franchise Royalty[10]	$28,359	3.9%
Direct Costs for All Other Revenue[11]	$5,371	0.7%
Total Cost of Sales[12]	$462,197	63.9%
Gross Profit[13]	$261,235	36.1%

Notes to Table PMG-2:

(1) This represents revenue received from providing homemaker/companionship and personal care services. Each franchisee sets its own rates; typically, franchisees will charge different rates for different types of services and may charge more or less depending on the number of hours of service a client needs and whether live-in care is required. Of the 15 single unit franchisees, 11, or 73.3%, met or exceeded the average shown.

(2) This represents revenue received from the sale or lease of Personal Technology Services and Equipment under the SafetyChoice® program. 2 franchisees, owning 4 Franchised Businesses, did not have revenue from the SafetyChoice®

program; all single unit franchisees did. Of the 15 single unit franchisees, 11, or 73.3%, met or exceeded the average shown.

(3) This represents income from ancillary services that CKFI has approved but does not require, such as private duty nursing services (being offered by a limited number of franchisees under a pilot program) and reimbursements for transportation services, grocery purchases, and similar items. Of the 15 single unit franchisees, 8, or 53.3%, met or exceeded the average shown.

(4) Of the 15 single unit franchisees, 12, or 80%, met or exceeded the average shown.

(5) This represents wage expense for caregivers. Hourly wages will vary depending on the economic conditions in a given area. Typically, where hourly wages are higher, rates for services are higher.

(6) This represents payroll taxes and benefits (for example, health and/or life insurance) associated with caregivers. Payroll taxes vary significantly by state, but typically where payroll taxes are higher, rates for services are higher.

(7) This represents workers compensation insurance coverage for caregivers. CKFI requires that you carry workers compensation with Part Two (employer's liability) policy limits at state minimum or $1,000,000, whichever is greater. Workers compensation rates vary significantly by state.

(8) This represents the cost paid to CKFI for SafetyChoice® equipment and services that were then sold or leased to clients.

(9) This represents the bonuses and other incentives that the franchisees paid to employees.

(10) This represents the royalty fees paid to CKFI. Franchisees under older franchise agreements generally pay royalty fees based on lower royalty tier breakpoints.

(11) This represents costs such as mileage reimbursement costs paid to caregivers and, for those franchisees participating in a pilot program for private duty nursing, private duty nurse wages (and related payroll expenses).

(12) The expenses that are included in the Cost of Sales calculation do not include all of the expenses associated with operating a Franchised Business.

(13) Gross Margin means Total Revenue less Total Cost of Sales. Of the 15 single unit franchisees, 5, or 33%, met or exceeded the average shown.

Table PMG-3 is a statement of the actual performance of the

highest-performing single unit owner and the lowest-performing single unit owner in the PMG Group for the twelve

months ending September 30, 2011. Revenue and expenses included in the table were reported on an accrual basis.

TABLE PMG-3

Revenue	Highest-Performing Single Unit		Lowest Performing Single Unit	
	Actual	As percent of Total Revenue	Actual	As percent of Total Revenue
In-home Care Service Revenue[1]	$2,907,315	100.25%	$336,191	95.28%
Personal Technology Services[2]	$6,157	0.21%	$5,592	1.58%
All Other Revenue[3]	($13,433)	-0.46%	$11,071	3.14%
Total Revenue	$2,900,039	100.00%	$352,854	100.00%
Cost of Sales				
Caregiver (CG) Payroll[4]	$1,562,418	53.88%	$164,562	46.64%
CG Payroll Taxes and Benefits[5]	$128,648	4.44%	$22,337	6.33%
CG Workers' Compensation Insurance[6]	$28,498	0.98%	$17,939	5.08%
Cost of Personal Technology Equipment[7]	$3,109	0.11%	$2,626	0.74%
Direct Revenue Incentive Compensation[8]	$0	0.00%	$0	0.00%
Franchise Royalty[9]	$96,422	3.32%	$17,948	5.09%
Direct Costs for All Other Revenue[10]	$4,754	0.16%	$0	0.00%
Total Cost of Sales[11]	$1,823,849	62.89%	$225,413	63.88%
Gross Profit[12]	$1,076,190	37.11%	$127,441	36.12%

Notes to Table PMG-3:

(1) This represents revenue received from providing homemaker/companionship and personal care services. Each franchisee sets its own rates; typically, franchisees will charge different rates for different types of services and may charge more or less depending on the number of hours of service a client needs and whether live-in care is required. The percent of total revenue is shown as greater than 100% because of the negative figure for "All Other Revenue" in the third line of the table.

(2) This represents revenue received from the sale or lease of Personal Technology Services and Equipment under the SafetyChoice® program.

(3) This represents income from reimbursements for transportation services, grocery purchases, and similar items. For the highest performing single unit, the figure is negative; this most likely represents refunds due clients.

(4) This represents wage expense for caregivers. Hourly wages will vary depending on the economic conditions in a given area. Typically, where hourly wages are higher, rates for services are higher.

(5) This represents payroll taxes and benefits (for example, health and/or life insurance) associated with caregivers. Payroll taxes vary significantly by state, but typically where payroll taxes are higher, rates for services are higher.

(6) This represents workers compensation insurance coverage for caregivers. CKFI requires that you carry workers compensation with Part Two (employer's liability) policy limits at state minimum or $1,000,000, whichever is greater. Workers compensation rates vary significantly by state.

(7) This represents the cost paid to CKFI for SafetyChoice® equipment and services that were then sold or leased to clients.

(8) This represents the bonuses and other incentives that the franchisees paid to employees.

(9) This represents the royalty fees paid to CKFI; the figure shown for the lowest performing single unit is slightly higher than the top royalty rate of 5% because of timing differences caused by accrual reporting. Franchisees under older franchise agreements generally pay royalty fees based on lower royalty tier breakpoints.

(10) This represents costs associated with mileage reimbursements to caregivers.

(11) The expenses that are included in the Cost of Sales calculation do not include all of the expenses associated with operating a Franchised Business.

(12) Gross Margin means Total Revenue less Total Cost of Sales.

We will make available to you upon reasonable request written substantiation of the information contained in the tables above.

The financial performance representations in Table A do not reflect the costs of sales, and none of the financial performance representations in any of the tables reflects all of the operating expenses, or other costs or expenses that must be deducted from the gross revenue or gross sales figures to obtain your net income or profit. The net revenue and net profit of your Franchised Business will depend on many factors, including the prices you charge for services and products, labor costs and general economic conditions in your area, your ability to network and generate clients, and competition from other similar businesses in your area. There is no assurance that your Fran-

chised Business will do as well as the Franchised Businesses in the tables above. You should conduct an independent investigation of the costs and expenses you will incur in operating your Franchised Business. Franchisees or former franchisees listed in the disclosure document may be one source of this information.

THE RESULTS GIVEN IN THESE TABLES ARE HISTORIC REPRESENTATIONS OF FINANCIAL RESULTS ACHIEVED BY CERTAIN COMFORT KEEPERS® FRANCHISED BUSINESSES. A NEW FRANCHISEE'S RESULTS ARE LIKELY TO DIFFER FROM THE RESULTS STATED IN THE TABLES. ACTUAL RESULTS VARY FROM FRANCHISED BUSINESS TO FRANCHISED BUSINESS, AND THE SUCCESS OF YOUR FRANCHISED BUSINESS WILL DEPEND IN LARGE PART UPON YOUR SKILLS AND ABILITIES, COMPETITION FROM OTHER BUSINESSES, AND OTHER ECONOMIC AND BUSINESS FACTORS. WE MAKE NO REPRESENTATION OR WARRANTY THAT YOU WILL, OR ARE LIKELY TO, ACHIEVE THE RESULTS SHOWN IN THE TABLES.

Other than the preceding financial performance representations, CKFI does not make any financial performance representations. We also do not authorize our employees or representatives to make any such representations either orally or in writing. If you are purchasing an existing outlet, however, we may provide you with the actual records of that outlet. If you receive any other financial performance information or projections of your future income, you should report it to the franchisor's management by contacting Jim Brown, Vice President of Franchise Development, 6640 Poe Avenue, Suite 200, Dayton, OH 45414, 937-665-1300, the Federal Trade Commission, and the appropriate state regulatory agencies.

COVERALL HEALTH-BASED CLEANING SYSTEM

350 SW 12th Ave.
Deerfield, FL 33442
Tel: (800) 537-3371, (561) 922-2500
Fax: (561) 922-2423
Email: diane.emo@coverall.com
Website: www.coverall.com

Diane Emo, Vice President of Marketing

The COVERALL® brand represents a better way to clean. As a COVERALL® Franchised Business Owner, you will be fully trained and certified in the Health-Based Cleaning System® Program, and prepared to help your customers improve the cleanliness, health, and wellness of their facilities. COVERALL is recognized as a leading brand in the commercial cleaning industry. The COVERALL® Program removes the maximum amount of dirt as quickly as possible, kills germs that can cause illness, and improves air quality. For over 28 years we have helped thousands of entrepreneurs build commercial cleaning franchised businesses by implementing our program. Are you ready to start your business today?

BACKGROUND				
IFA Member:		Yes		

BACKGROUND	
IFA Member:	Yes
Established & First Franchised:	1985; 1985
Franchised Units:	9,202
Company-Owned Units:	0
Total Units:	9,202
Distribution:	US – 8,094; CAN – 390; O'seas – 718
North America:	40 States, 3 Provinces
Density:	1,107 in CA, 1,020 in FL, 709 in OH
Projected New Units (12 Months):	1,090
Qualifications:	3, 3, 2, 2, 3, 5

FINANCIAL/TERMS	
Cash Investment:	$3.9 – $21.9K
Total Investment:	$12.2 – $44.2K
Minimum Net Worth:	$12.2K
Fees (Franchise):	$10.6 – $37K
Fees (Royalty):	5%
Fees (Advertising):	0%
Term of Contract (Years):	20/20
Average Number of Employees:	1 – 2 FT, 2 – 3 PT
Passive Ownership:	Allowed

Encourage Conversions:	Yes
Area Development Agreements:	No
Sub-Franchising Contracts:	Yes
Expand in Territory:	Yes
Space Needs:	N/A

SUPPORT & TRAINING	
Financial Assistance Provided:	Yes (D)
Site Selection Assistance:	N/A
Lease Negotiation Assistance:	N/A
Co-operative Advertising:	No
Franchisee Association/Member:	No
Size of Corporate Staff:	62
On-going Support:	A, B, D, G, H, I
Training:	32 – 48 Hours Local Regional Support Center

SPECIFIC EXPANSION PLANS	
US:	All United States
Canada:	No
Overseas:	No

We do not make any representations about a franchisee's future financial performance or the past financial performance of company-owned or franchised outlets. We also do not authorize our employees or representatives to make any such representations either orally or in writing. If you are purchasing an existing outlet, however, we may provide you with the actual records of that outlet. If you receive any other financial performance information or projections of your future income, you should report it to the franchisor's management by contacting the Compliance Director in the Legal Department at the Global Support Center located at located at 350 SW 12th Avenue, Deerfield Beach, Florida 33442 (561-922-2534); the Federal Trade Commission, and the appropriate state regulatory agencies.

We sell our franchises as packages. The Franchise Package is described as a specified amount of Initial Business, which we must offer to you within a certain amount of time. For convenience and to be consistent with business practices in the janitorial franchise industry, we describe these Franchise Packages in terms of monthly Gross Dollar Volume (i.e., a P-1500 Franchise Package means $1,500.00 in monthly Gross Dollar Volume). In addition, under the Franchise Agreement, we will guarantee your Initial Business for up to a maximum of 12 months, subject to the conditions described in Item 11 above. The Franchise Package purchased is not a guarantee that you will earn an equivalent amount of Gross Dollar Volume each month; neither does it mean that we are obligated at any time

to replace lost customers to enable you to maintain that level of Gross Dollar Volume.

If we do not offer the Initial Business within the specified time, you may request a refund of a portion of the initial franchisee fee, as described in Item 5, above.

The monthly Gross Dollar Volume of the Initial Business that you purchase should not be considered as the actual or potential income or profit, you will realize. The total monthly Gross Dollar Volume you achieve are affected by many factors such as: the Initial Business may be offered in stages during the specified time period; you may decline a customer; you may lose a customer for poor service; the customer may cancel through no fault of your own and you did not perform the required inspections to earn the extended guarantee; and you may lose a customer through no fault of your own and there is a time lag before the replacement customer is offered.

Other factors affecting your Gross Dollar Volume are the quality and efficiency of your cleaning services; the degree to which you finance the purchase and operation of the franchise; and business expenses associated with operating your business, many of which expenses you control, such as wages to employees.

We make no disclosure as to when, or if, you will recover your investment in your franchise business. There are too many variables to permit a reliable estimate. Commercial cleaning customers can be lost for any number of reasons, including but not limited to, poor service, the customer chooses a lower priced provider, the customer goes out of business or files for bankruptcy protection, economic circumstances cause the customer to terminate outside vendors. In 2011, average customer attrition rate was 2.51% per month. You can expect to lose customers, and that is a risk of doing business. In 2011, the average life of a customer was forty (40) months, which is not an assurance that you will retain your customers for a similar period of time.

COVERALL'S FULFILLMENT OF FRANCHISE PACKAGES

We analyzed our compliance with the Franchise Agreement concerning the amount, timeliness, and refund requirements for Initial Business provided to our franchisees. We reviewed all franchise sales made during our fiscal year, and determined whether or not as of December 31, 2011 the Initial Business had been offered in compliance with the Franchise Agreement.

During our fiscal year January 1, 2011 to December 31, 2011, we sold 516 franchises. Of those sold, as of the close of the fiscal year: (a) franchisees either had their packages timely filled or have accepted our performance in 273 cases; or 53%; (b) we and the franchisee made a mutually acceptable adjustment to the franchise package, such as by our recalculation of the franchise fee or an extension of time to provide customers, in 83 cases; or 16%; (c) the time for us to provide initial customers under franchise packages had not expired in 160 cases, or 31%; and (d) it is undetermined whether the package has been filled in 0 cases, or 0%.

Therefoer, we complied with the amount, timelines, and recalculation requirements for the Initial Business provided to our franchisees in 100% of the cases. Our compliance could not be determined in less than one percent of the sales. Substantiation of the data used in preparing these statistics will be made available upon request.

The basis for our claim about Initial Business is Paragraph 13 of the Franchise Agreement.

CRESTCOM INTERNATIONAL

6900 E. Belleview Ave., #300
Greenwood Village, CO 80111
Tel: (888) 273-7826, (303) 515-3925
Fax: (303) 267-8207
Email: charles.parsons@crestcom.com
Website: www.crestcomfranchise.com
Charles Parsons, VP Franchise Development

For more than 25 years, CRESTCOM INTERNATIONAL franchisees have trained business people across the globe in the areas of management and leadership. Today, CRESTCOM has grown to become one of the training industry's most successful and widely-used management and leadership programs among Fortune magazine's Top 100 Companies. Each month,

thousands of business professionals across six continents participate in the CRESTCOM Bullet Proof® Manager training. CRESTCOM's proprietary training is improving the way businesses motivate, communicate, and help managers succeed. Businesses turn to CRESTCOM to help transform managers into leaders and generate real business results. CRESTCOM's training program accommodates organizations of all sizes, from small to mid-sized businesses, to global multi-national organizations. Crestcom has met the needs of some of the most successful businesses and brands around the world. CRESTCOM currently has franchise owners in over 62 countries, and the Bullet Proof® Manager training program is available in 25 languages.

BACKGROUND

IFA Member:	Yes
Established & First Franchised:	1987; 1992
Franchised Units:	192
Company-Owned Units:	0
Total Units:	192
Distribution:	US – 31; CAN – 14; O'seas – 147
North America:	25 States, 4 Provinces
Density:	N/A

Projected New Units (12 Months):	30	Space Needs:	N/A
Qualifications:	3, 3, 4, 4, 5, 3	SUPPORT & TRAINING	
FINANCIAL/TERMS		Financial Assistance Provided:	Yes (D)
Cash Investment:	$69.5K	Site Selection Assistance:	N/A
Total Investment:	$85.3 – $104K	Lease Negotiation Assistance:	N/A
Minimum Net Worth:	N/A	Co-operative Advertising:	No
Fees (Franchise):	$69.5K	Franchisee Association/Member:	Yes/Member
Fees (Royalty):	1.5%	Size of Corporate Staff:	15
Fees (Advertising):	N/A	On-going Support:	C, D, G, H
Term of Contract (Years):	7/7/7	Training:	7 Days US
Average Number of Employees:	0 – 2 FT, 0 PT		
Passive Ownership:	Discouraged	SPECIFIC EXPANSION PLANS	
Encourage Conversions:	N/A	US:	All United States
Area Development Agreements:	Yes	Canada:	All Canada
Sub-Franchising Contracts:	No	Overseas:	All Countries
Expand in Territory:	Yes		

Below are charts showing our estimate of gross revenue margins before expenses related to the sale or marketing of Materials and the average sales and Gross Revenues from those U.S. franchisees who were active during calendar year 2011. See Item 6 for a discussion of what constitutes Gross Revenues. These financial performance representations have not been prepared in accordance with the statement on Standards for Accountant's Services on Prospective Financial Information.

CHART NO. 1

ESTIMATE OF GROSS REVENUE MARGINS BEFORE EXPENSES[1]-[18]

GROSS MARGIN PER PARTICIPANT ATTENDING THE BULLET PROOF MANAGER PROGRAM[1][2][9]						
Materials (per participant)	Recommended Retail Price[4]	Cost of Materials as % of Recommended Retail[5][6][9]	Fees as % of Recommended Retail[7]	Est. Shipping as % of Recommended Retail[8]	Total % of Recommended Retail	Gross Revenue Margin (%/$s) [2][3][7]
BPM Materials	$4,320	2.13%	35.5%	.5%	38.13%	61.87% $2,672.78

CHART NO. 2

CALENDAR YEAR 2011 AVERAGE FRANCHISEE GROSS REVENUES BEFORE EXPENSES
ON SALE OF MATERIALS[9][10][14][15][16][17][18]

2011

Franchisees[11][12][13]	Average Sales[14][15][18]	% Increase or Decrease from 2010[19]	Estimated Gross Margin %[2][17]	Average Gross Revenues[2][3][10][14][16]
Top 1/3- U.S. Franchisees	$279,028	36.58%	61.87%	$172,635
Middle 1/3- U.S. Franchisees	$103,964	16.74%	61.87%	$ 64,964
Lower 113 -U.S. Franchisees	$ 36,481	-5.69%	61.87%	$ 22,794
Combined Average -U.S. Franchisees Meeting the Established Criteria	$139,824	28.42%	61.87%	$86,509

THE ACCOMPANYING FOOTNOTES ARE AN INTEGRAL PART OF THESE CHARTS AND SHOULD BE READ IN THEIR ENTIRETY FOR A FULL UNDERSTANDING OF THE INFORMATION CONTAINED IN THESE CHARTS. ALL OF THE FOOTNOTES SHALL BE READ TO APPLY TO ALL OF THE ITEMS IN THE ABOVE CHARTS, WHETHER OR NOT A PARTICULAR ITEM IN THE CHART SPECIFICALLY REFERENCES THE FOOTNOTE.

FOOTNOTES:

(1) The estimated gross revenue margins reflected in Chart No. 1 above relate only to franchisees' sales of Materials for and enrollments of participants in The BULLET PROOF® Manager programs (the "BPM Programs"), and exclude sales of other Materials or enrollments in other programs franchisees can offer. We offer other programs and Materials that may have greater or lesser margins. We estimate that more than 95 percent of all sales revenues are derived from the BPM Programs.

(2) The term "Gross Revenue Margin" as used in Chart No. 1 and "Estimated Gross Margin %"used in Chart 2 refer to the amount or percentage, as indicated, of the applicable gross revenues that remain after deduction of only those costs specifically identified in Chart No. 1.

(3) In presenting this data, we do not estimate the length of time it will take for any particular franchisee to sell the Materials acquired by it in order to realize any of the gross revenue margins presented. A franchisee's ability to sell the Materials is a major factor in determining its profitability and is dependent upon its sales ability and efforts, its sales and marketing staff, competition within its market, the economy and other market factors. YOU ARE CAUTIONED THAT YOU MAY NEVER REALIZE THE GROSS REVENUE MARGINS PRESENTED IN THIS DATA IF YOU ARE UNABLE TO ENROLL BPM PROGRAMS PARTICIPANTS OR OTHERWISE MARKET THE MATERIALS PURCHASED OR ACQUIRED BY YOU.

(4) The recommended retail price for each of calendar year 2011 was $4,320 per participant. In prior years, the recommended retail price may have been lower. Franchisees may charge a fee that is higher or lower than our recommended retail price. They sometimes will reduce the per participant fee they charge for clients who enroll multiple managers to attend the BPM Programs. Market conditions, such as competition, market recognition, quality of a franchisee's training skills and location may affect a franchisee's actual retail pricing.

(5) The costs shown in the charts are based on the costs in effect as of the date of this Disclosure Document and are subject to change. These charts show certain costs incurred in market-ing the Materials and conducting BPM Programs only. They do not include all of the expenses a franchisee will incur during the term of its franchise agreement, including the initial investment in the franchise, start-up costs, overhead, and certain operating expenses. Operating expenses vary substantially and are based on particular factors relevant to each franchisee. A franchisee may incur operating expenses for a computer, DVD player, iPad, tablet computer, projector, or other equipment, automobile, telephone and voice mail system or service, marketing and advertising, direct mail, special incentive offers, Facilitator's or other instructional items or materials, amounts paid to Facilitators for those franchisees who do not conduct their own Live Instruction programs, amounts paid to telemarketers for those franchisees who elect to employ telemarketers, New Materials introductory surcharge (discussed below), and other isolated and/or recurring expenses. It also does not include amounts representing the franchisee's (and its authorized representatives') time or effort, or account for interest expense, appreciation or depreciation of assets, capital expenses and carrying costs which will vary from franchisee to franchisee. Franchisees may operate from an office location, in which case there may be office lease and other related expenses, although most of our franchisees operate out of their homes. You should refer to Items 5, 6 and 7 for a discussion of other initial franchise fees, other fees and expenses, and initial investment considerations.

(6) The actual cost of the Materials for participants in the BPM Programs or other programs we offer varies. Depending on the number of participants a client enrolls, the mix of Materials the client receives is different. Further, many franchisees provide additional Materials to cash purchasers as a bonus for early payment. Some franchisees also offer free or "scholarship" enrollments as a bonus for clients who enroll a specified number of their managers in the BPM Programs. The expenses shown in the first chart assumes these incentive Materials come from the franchisee's own inventory and the costs of any free enrollments or bonus Materials are not reflected in the chart. Franchisees are not required to offer free enrollments or give bonus Materials. Based on our estimates, the average expense for required Materials for one participant in a BPM Program, including the payment of the Video Media Access Fee owed to us for any video media materials that we grant you the right to access and market, such as CDs or DVDs, if applicable, is approximately $92 or 2.13 percent ofthe current recommended retail price of$4,320.

(7) The aggregate fees paid to us when a franchisee sells the Materials total 35.5 percent of the retail price. This is comprised of a Distribution Fee of 34 percent and a Royalty Fee of 1.5 percent. The fees due us are paid as a franchisee receives the proceeds from BPM Programs, which may not always be at the time of the sale. We recommend that franchisees require enrollment fees and other amounts paid by a client be paid on

a cash basis or on a basis of 25 percent down, with the balance payable in 30, 60, and 90 days. You may agree to other terms. The gross revenue margins shown on the charts assume that all amounts owed by clients are collected at the time of the sale, and that all Distribution Fees, Royalty Fees, and any other fees or amounts owed to us by franchisees are paid at the time of the sale.

(8) We estimate shipping costs at 0.5 percent of the retail price of the Materials. This may be higher depending on the location of a franchisee and other factors, particularly for shipments of small quantities of Materials.

(9) We periodically introduce New Materials or programs to our inventory of Materials available to franchises. There is a one-time introductory surcharge to offset our production costs of these Materials at the earlier of (i) the first order of any video media unit of the New Materials; or (ii) six months from the date the New Materials become available. The current introductory surcharge is $400 per new training program video media unit. Franchisees are required to acquire the rights to access and market any New Materials within six months of their availability. Since the introductory surcharge is a one-time charge, we have not included it in these charts as the percentage effect would constantly vary as rights to more of these New Materials are acquired over the life of a franchise.

(10) Chart No.2 reflects the sales of Materials per U. S. franchisee during calendar year 2011. In computing these figures, we took the yearly average of the total sales of our franchisees who were active on a full-time basis to obtain this information. We also took the yearly average of the sales of those franchisees that fell into the top 1/3, middle 113, lower 1/3 in sales.

(11) Only U.S. franchisees that were active on a full-time basis during a particular year have their sales included in the computations used in the second chart. For purposes of this chart, a U.S. franchisee is deemed "active on a full-time basis" if it conducted at least one monthly BPM Program training seminar each month during the applicable year and actively marketed our programs each month ofthe year. During the calendar year 2011, we had 30 U.S. franchisees that met this definition. Franchisees that did not qualify as active on a full-time basis are not shown. Non-qualifying franchisees include new franchisees that did not commence operations by the beginning of a particular year, franchisees that ceased operations during a particular year, franchisees that were otherwise inactive for a portion of a particular year due to sickness, health issues, or other personal reasons. In the case of one franchisee whose numbers were included in the chart, sales were combined with an independent sales agent who jointly marketed the programs with that franchisee. Also, some franchisees own more than one franchise. In computing the numbers in Chart 2, we combined the sales of each of these franchisees as if they were operating under one franchise and counted the sales results as one franchisee in this chart. The total number of individual franchises in the U.S. at the end of calendar year 2011, including franchisees who joined the system during course of the year, was 43.

(12) Data has been compiled based on the experience of our U.S. Franchisees only. Our system is comprised of franchisees operating within the United States and franchisees and distributors operating in other countries. Our foreign franchise/ distributorship programs operate in a manner similar to our franchise system within the United States as it relates to the information contained in these charts, although retail prices for the Materials distributed internationally may differ from the recommended retail price presented in Chart No. 1 and are often subject to customs and duty expenses as well as higher shipping costs. International prices are also subject to change with exchange rate fluctuations. The results of our foreign franchise/distributorship programs are not included in this data. Also, at different times we have promoted other franchise programs in additional to our Executive Franchise program. These programs generally had lower initial franchise fees and higher Distribution Fees and Royalty Fees. We currently do not offer any of these programs. We currently do not have any U.S. franchisee participating in any of these programs. Also, a franchisee is permitted to employ up to two salespersons, in addition to him or herself, to market the Materials. This chart only includes the sales made by one person in each franchise except for the one franchisee noted in footnote 11 above.

(13) In 2008, we began offering an area developer franchise program in the United States. Currently in the United States, all of our area developers are Executive Franchisees who acquire the right to market our programs to prospective franchises. We pay our area developers a commission on sales made by franchisees located in their development areas, including their own sales, which effectively reduces the Distribution Fee and Royalty Fee they pay us on their sales. For purposes of the information in Chart No.2, however, we have assumed that all of our franchisees, including those who also serve as our area developers, paid Distribution Fees and Royalty Fees of 35.5 percent.

(14) No attempt is made to estimate potential profits, income or earnings. We cannot accurately determine expenses because some of our franchisees have other business investment holdings or interests in addition to their CRESTCOM Business.

(15) Our franchisees must participate in our Multiple Area Sales ("MAS") program. Under the MAS program, if a franchisee acquires a client whose employees attend training sessions in Assigned Area(s) of other franchisee(s), the "selling" franchisee pays the franchisee(s) who conduct the training

sessions a fee of $620, plus material costs, for each participant attending training in the other Assigned Area(s). We have not included MAS revenues or expenses in calculating the sales and gross margins results of the franchisees, because, on average, the net increase in expenses by a "selling" franchisee would be offset by the increased revenues of those franchisees who conduct the training.

(16) The information in Chart No. 2 was compiled based on actual sales of BPM Programs and other programs by our existing franchisees during calendar year 2011 based on sales reports provided by the franchisees to us. We have not audited these sales reports and we cannot guarantee their accuracy. We do not require our franchisees to provide us with financial statements. Some of our franchisees provide other services to their clients in addition to the management, sales and personnel development training programs we offer. Those revenues are not included in the sales numbers shown in the charts.

(17) For purposes of Chart 2, we have estimated a gross margin percentage of 61.87 percent as shown in the preceding chart.

(18) There is a large variation in the range of sales generated by our franchisees during calendar year 2011. Generally speaking, those franchisees with more experience in utilizing our sales and training techniques are the higher producers. In 2011, there were 10 franchisees in the top 1/3, ofwhich 4, (40.0%) exceed the average sales volume ofthat group with one additional franchisee within approximately $800 of exceeding the average of that group, 10 franchisees in the middle 1/3, of which 4 (40.0%) exceed the average sales volume of that group, and 10 in the lower 1/3, of which 5 (50%) exceed the average sales volume of that group.

(19) The third column of Chart No. 2 shows the percentage increase or decrease, by group and in total, in annual sales by the franchisees who were active on a full-time basis during calendar year 2011 as compared to those franchisees who were active on a full-time basis in calendar year 2010.

CAUTION: YOUR ACTUAL FINANCIAL RESULTS ARE LIKELY TO DIFFER FROM THE FIGURES PRESENTED. WE DO NOT REPRESENT THAT YOU CAN EXPECT TO ATTAIN THE GROSS REVENUE MARGINS CONTAINED IN THIS ITEM. SOME OF OUR FRANCHISEES HAVE ATTAINED THE GROSS REVENUE MARGINS SHOWN IN THIS DOCUMENT. THERE IS NO ASSURANCE THAT YOU WILL DO AS WELL. IF YOU RELY ON OUR FIGURES, YOU MUST ACCEPT THE RISK OF NOT DOING AS WELL. YOUR ABILITY TO ACHIEVE ANY LEVEL OF NET INCOME WILL DEPEND UPON FACTORS NOT WITHIN OUR CONTROL, INCLUDING THE OCCURRENCE OF CERTAIN START UP AND OPERATING EXPENSES AND THE AMOUNT OF THOSE EXPENSES, AND YOUR LEVEL OF EXPERTISE. IF POSSIBLE, SHOW THESE FIGURES TO SOMEONE WHO CAN ADVISE YOU, LIKE A LAWYER OR ACCOUNTANT.

YOU SHOULD NOTE THAT THE INFORMATION CONTAINED IN THIS ITEM IS NOT INTENDED TO EXPRESS OR INFER AN ESTIMATE, PROJECTION OR FORECAST OF INCOME, SALES, PROFITS OR EARNINGS TO BE DERIVED IN CONNECTION WITH ANY PARTICULAR FRANCHISE. THE INFORMATION PRESENTED IN CHART NO.1 IS LIMITED TO AN ESTIMATE OF GROSS REVENUE MARGINS BEFORE OPERATING EXPENSES THAT COULD BE DERIVED BY A FRANCHISEE FROM THE ENROLLMENT OF ONE BULLET PROOF MANAGER PARTICIPANT AT OUR CURRENT RECOMMENDED RETAIL PRICE. THE INFORMATION PRESENTED IN THE CHART NO.2 IS LIMITED TO AVERAGES OF CERTAIN RESULTS REPORTED TO US BY U.S. FRANCHISEES THAT OPERATED ON AN ACTIVE FULL-TIME BASIS DURING CALENDAR YEAR 2011. WE MAKE NO REPRESENTATION AS TO WHETHER YOU WILL EVER BE ABLE TO SELL ANY OF THE MATERIALS, HOW MANY PARTICIPANTS YOU MAY BE ABLE TO ENROLL, OR THE LENGTH OF TIME IT WILL TAKE YOU TO ENROLL ONE OR MORE PARTICIPANTS OR REALIZE ANY GROSS REVENUES.

The financial performance representation figures in the preceding charts reflect the estimated costs of materials, estimated costs of shipping, and estimated Distribution Fees and Royalty Fees related to the enrollment of Bullet Proof Manager participants. The financial performance representation figures in the charts do not reflect the cost of any other sales, marketing, operating or other costs or expenses that must be deducted from the gross revenues or gross sales figures to obtain your net income or profit. You should conduct an independent investigation of the costs and expenses you will incur in operating your CRESTCOM Business. Franchisees or former franchisees listed in Attachments G and H may be one source of this information.

Written substantiation for the financial performance representation will be made available to you at our Greenwood Village office upon reasonable request.

Other than the preceding charts, we do not make any financial performance representations. We also do not authorize our employees or representatives to make any such representations either orally or in writing. If you are purchasing an existing CRESTCOM Business, however, we may provide you with the actual records of that CRESTCOM Business outlet. If you receive any other financial performance information or projections of your future income, you should report it to the franchisor's management by contacting George Godfrey at 6900 East Belleview Avenue, Suite 300, Greenwood Village, Colorado 80111 and (303) 267-8200, the Federal Trade Commission, and the appropriate state regulatory agencies.

DISCOVERY MAP INTERNATIONAL

5197 Main St., #8, P.O. Box 726
Waitsfield, VT 05673
Tel: (877) 820-7827, (802) 496-6277
Fax: (360) 466-2710
Email: charlie@discoverymap.com
Website: www.discoverymap.com
Charlie Capp, Franchise Facilitator

Headquartered in the Green Mountains of Vermont, DISCOVERY MAP INTERNATIONAL, INC. (DMI) has been creating and publishing beautifully illustrated, hand-drawn alternative-advertising maps for over 30 years. In 1993 we were predominantly a Northeastern operation, but due to increasing demand and success, DMI (at that time called Resort Maps) expanded its reach by developing a franchise model for individual ownership and distribution of its maps of resort towns, vacation destinations and, cities all over the US and beyond. Today, that network of franchises has grown to 126 Discovery Map® maps in publication in the US, the UK, Puerto Rico, and Costa Rica, with several more in the process of being published. Nearly 25 million Discovery Map® maps will be printed and distributed in 2012, and these figures continue to grow.

BACKGROUND

IFA Member:	Yes
Established & First Franchised:	1981; 1993
Franchised Units:	126
Company-Owned Units:	0

Total Units:	126
Distribution:	US – 122; CAN – 1; O'seas – 3
North America:	21 States, 1 Province
Density:	12 in VT, 10 in CO, 10 in MA
Projected New Units (12 Months):	N/A
Qualifications:	4, 3, 3, 3, 3, 4

FINANCIAL/TERMS

Cash Investment:	$40K
Total Investment:	$35 – $45K
Minimum Net Worth:	$100K
Fees (Franchise):	$25K
Fees (Royalty):	10%
Fees (Advertising):	1%
Term of Contract (Years):	10/5/5
Average Number of Employees:	N/A
Passive Ownership:	Not Allowed
Encourage Conversions:	N/A
Area Development Agreements:	Yes
Sub-Franchising Contracts:	No
Expand in Territory:	Yes
Space Needs:	N/A

SUPPORT & TRAINING

Financial Assistance Provided:	No
Site Selection Assistance:	N/A
Lease Negotiation Assistance:	N/A
Co-operative Advertising:	No
Franchisee Association/Member:	Yes/Not a Member
Size of Corporate Staff:	10
On-going Support:	C, D, F, G, H, I
Training:	Franchise Owner's Home Varies; 4 Days Waitsfield, VT; Field Training Varies

SPECIFIC EXPANSION PLANS

US:	All United States
Canada:	All Canada
Overseas:	Yes

Along with awarding franchises to others, our officers and employees own and operate 3 franchises similar to the franchise business opportunity described in this Disclosure Document. Because business maturation can take up to two years, we are reporting only on those businesses open two years or more. All franchised units operate in a defined territory that has within its borders a population of approximately 400 small business establishments and typically publish one Map per year. Each Map generates gross sales by selling space advertising to local businesses whose ads border the Map. Maps are two sided and are currently published in three sizes: 17 inches by 11, inches 17 inches by 22 inches and 17 inches by 25 inches. We publish only four 17 inch by 11 inch maps and do not offer franchises for new maps this size. There are no other key demographic elements necessary in defining a territory.

Based upon the performance of the franchises which were in operation for a minimum of two years and completed the selling cycle within the reported fiscal year, we are providing the following disclosure of the actual Gross Sales which includes both unrelated and affiliate owned franchises.

The Average Map's Unit sales for Fiscal Year ending September 30, 2011 is as follows:

Map Size		October 1, 2010 to September 30, 2011
17 in. x 22 in.	Average Sales per map	$47,563.54
	Number of Units	49
		47% of these franchises attained or surpassed this result.
17 in. x 25 in.		
	Average Sales per map	$67,641.29
	Number of Units	17
		53 % of these franchises attained or surpassed this result.

Out of the 113 units that were in operation as of September 30, 2011 we are reporting on 66 units which comply with the two year maturation requirement and are not 17 inch by 11 inch maps.

The above figures, which reflect Gross Sales not profits, were calculated based upon information reported to us by our franchisees in their month]y reports. The above figures have not been audited by us. The figures do not reflect the costs of sales, operating expenses or other costs and expenses that must be deducted from the Gross Sales figures to obtain your net income or profit. You should conduct an independent investigation of the costs and expenses you will incur in operating your DISCOVERY MAP Franchised Business.

The Gross Sales and financial results of your DISCOVERY MAP Franchised Business are likely to differ from the figures stated above, and there is no assurance that you will do as well. The average Franchised Business included in the above calculations is a mature business a minimum of two years old; accordingly, a new franchisee's individual Gross Sales and financial results are likely to differ from the results stated above. Further, your Gross Sales and your financial results will depend upon, among other things, factors including local and national economic conditions; how much you follow our methods and procedures; your sales skills; your management skill, experience and business acumen; whether you personally manage your Franchised Business or hire a manager; the region in which your Franchised Business is located; the competition in your local market; the prevailing wage rate; and the sales level reached during the initial period.

Your analysis of a DISCOVERY MAP Franchised Business should include estimates of expenses for all applicable items, including printing, royalties, a home-based office or if you choose to rent office space, staff salaries or commissions, your own salary, phone/fax charges, postage and courier charges, travel, auto expense, insurance, and the costs of marketing materials. All of these items are based largely on factors within your control, for which you can obtain information through your own research. Since these amounts are to a great degree a matter of personal preference, w have included no estimates for these items, and you should make appropriate assumptions. However, you should also be aware that the expense items listed above are by no means exhaustive. There are likely to be additional expenses that we have not listed, some of which may be unique to your market or situation. Written substantiation of the data used in preparing the earnings claim will be made available to you upon reasonable request.

"Your success is our only business"

THE ENTREPRENEUR'S SOURCE

900 Main St. S., Bldg. # 2
Southbury, CT 06488
Tel: (203) 405-2131
Fax: (203) 264-3516
Email: lchurch@franchisesource.com
Website: www.theesource.com
Lorinda Church, Franchise Development

THE ENTREPRENEUR'S SOURCE® is an all-inclusive, one-source resource for entrepreneurship. With over 25 years of experience and 33% of the market, E-SOURCE dominates the coaching industry. E-SOURCE coaches provide education, coaching, and resources to individuals who desire to achieve their dreams of becoming self-sufficient through business ownership. This allows our clients to explore alternate career options that meet their goals, needs, and expectations utilizing our Possibilities Passport Discovery process. Our coaches also work with existing franchise business owners to help them grow revenues and increase the value of their business.

BACKGROUND

IFA Member:	Yes
Established & First Franchised:	1984; 1997
Franchised Units:	160
Company-Owned Units:	0

Total Units:	160
Distribution:	US – 160; CAN – 5; O'seas – 0
North America:	40 States, 1 Province
Density:	33, in CA, 17 in MI, 17 in NC
Projected New Units (12 Months):	30
Qualifications:	4, 4, 1, 1, 2, 5

FINANCIAL/TERMS

Cash Investment:	$67K
Total Investment:	$66.2 – $77.4K
Minimum Net Worth:	$199K
Fees (Franchise):	$45K
Fees (Royalty):	25%/5 – 15%
Fees (Advertising):	$750/month
Term of Contract (Years):	10/10
Average Number of Employees:	1 FT, 0 PT
Passive Ownership:	Allowed
Encourage Conversions:	Yes
Area Development Agreements:	Yes
Sub-Franchising Contracts:	No
Expand in Territory:	Yes
Space Needs:	N/A

SUPPORT & TRAINING

Financial Assistance Provided:	No
Site Selection Assistance:	N/A
Lease Negotiation Assistance:	N/A
Co-operative Advertising:	No
Franchisee Association/Member:	No
Size of Corporate Staff:	35
On-going Support:	D, H, I
Training:	6 Weeks Virtual; 5 Days Southbury, CT

SPECIFIC EXPANSION PLANS

US:	All United States
Canada:	All Canada
Overseas:	Most Countries

Statement of Franchisee Annual Projected Revenues

The following are statements of annual projected revenues for TES Franchised Businesses. These projections have been calculated based on the experience of TES in the business and placement coaching industry, including the experience of our franchisees and staff, as well as industry standards.

There are three projections based on a set number of clients engaged by one coach in each month for business coaching and the number of placement fees received by one coach for franchise placement coaching. In our experience in the fran-chise placement and business coaching industry, we believe that the calculations reasonably reflect attainable levels of revenue. We have created projections that reflect varying degrees of client development activity and increasing experience in the industry. The charts below reflect five years of projected revenue. An explanation of the calculations for each chart is cited about the chart.

We have calculated these numbers based on the low end of our suggested monthly business coaching billing rate range and the industry average length of coaching engagements for business coaches. We have factored longer terms for coaching engagements as the coach develops greater confidence and experience. For placement coaching clients, we have applied TES's Average Gross Placement Fee to Year 5 and decreased the Average Gross Placement Fee each previous year 4 through 1. All calculations for placement coaching are at or below the average placement fee rate.

Following the calculations for revenue, we subtract the Royalties paid on business coaching and placement coaching to achieve a Gross Profit amount and Gross Profit percentage. We then identify expenses based on our experience and knowledge of current economic conditions, communications with franchisees regarding their expenses, and review of current costs for products necessary in the operation of the franchised business. We subtract the expenses from the Gross Profit amount to identify the Net Profit and Net Profit Percentage. If a franchisee chooses to operate from an office location outside of the home, the projected expenses will be higher and the Net Profit and Net Profit percentage will be reduced.

We do not require nor anticipate that any franchisee will operate from an office location outside the home.

The assumptions we made in compiling these projections are shown following the projections. Any changes in these assumptions would require material alterations to the projections.

Chart 1:

We have calculated this chart based on the client development for both business coaching and placement coaching. This chart reflects one business coaching client per month for Years 1-3 and two business coaching clients per month for Years 4-5. The chart reflects one paid placement fee per month in Years 1-2, one and one half paid placement fees per month in Years 3 and 4, and two paid placement fees per month in Year 5.

	Year 1	Year 2	Year 3	Year 4	Year 5	5 Year Total
Total Revenue:	$122,000	$150,000	$168,000	$294,000	$408,000	$1,142,000
Royalty:						
Business Coaching:	$1,800	$2,700	$3,600	$9,000	$10,800	$27,900
Placement Coaching:	$27,500	$33,000	$36,000	$58,500	$84,000	$239,000
Gross Profit:	$92,700	$114,300	$128,400	$226,500	$313,200	$875,100
Gross Profit %:	76%	76%	76%	77%	77%	77%
Expenses:						
Equipment[1]	$500	$500	$500	$500	$500	$2,500
Prof. Services[2]	$2,000	$2,000	$2,000	$2,000	$2,000	$10,000
Phone/Internet[3]	$840	$840	$840	$840	$840	$4,200
Marketing[4]	$15,100	$16,500	$17,400	$23,700	$29,400	$102,100
Office Supplies[5]	$600	$600	$600	$600	$600	$3,000
Insurance[6]	$400	$400	$400	$400	$400	$2,000
Misc.[7]	$6,000	$6,000	$6,000	$6,000	$6,000	$30,000
Total Expenses:	$25,440	$26,840	$27,740	$34,040	$39,740	$153,800
Net Profit:	$67,260	$87,460	$100,660	$192,460	$273,460	$721,300
Net Profit %:	55%	58%	60%	65%	67%	63%

Chart 2:

We have calculated this chart based on the client development for both business coaching and placement coaching. This chart reflects one business coaching client per month for Years 1-3

and two business coaching clients per month for Years 4-5. The chart reflects one paid placement fee per month in Years 1-2, one and one half paid placement fees per month in Years 3-5.

	Year 1	Year 2	Year 3	Year 4	Year 5	5 Year Total
Total Revenue:	$122,000	$150,000	$168,000	$294,000	$324,000	$1,058,000
Royalty:						
Business Coaching:	$1,800	$2,700	$3,600	$9,000	$10,800	$27,900
Placement Coaching:	$27,500	$33,000	$36,000	$58,500	$63,000	$218,000
Gross Profit:	$92,700	$114,300	$128,400	$226,500	$250,200	$812,100
Gross Profit %:	76%	76%	76%	77%	77%	77%
Expenses:						
Equipment[1]	$500	$500	$500	$500	$500	$2,500
Prof. Services[2]	$2,000	$2,000	$2,000	$2,000	$2,000	$10,000
Phone/Internet[3]	$840	$840	$840	$840	$840	$4,200
Marketing[4]	$15,100	$16,500	$17,400	$23,700	$25,200	$97,900
Office Supplies[5]	$600	$600	$600	$600	$600	$3,000
Insurance[6]	$400	$400	$400	$400	$400	$2,000
Misc.[7]	$6,000	$6,000	$6,000	$6,000	$6,000	$30,000
Total Expenses:	$25,440	$26,840	$27,740	$34,040	$35,540	$149,600
Net Profit:	$67,260	$87,460	$100,660	$192,460	$214,660	$662,500
Net Profit %:	55%	58%	63%	65%	66%	62%

Chart 3:

We have calculated this chart based on the client development for both business coaching and placement coaching. This chart reflects one business coaching for the five year period. The chart reflects one paid placement fee per month for the five year period.

	Year 1	Year 2	Year 3	Year 4	Year 5	5 Year Total
Total Revenue:	$122,000	$150,000	$174,000	$192,500	$218,000	$856,500
Royalty:						
Business Coaching:	$1,800	$2,700	$3,600	$4,500	$5,400	$18,000
Placement Coaching:	$27,500	$33,000	$37,500	$40,625	$50,900	$184,125
Gross Profit:	$92,700	$114,300	$132,900	$147,375	$167,100	$654,375
Gross Profit %:	76%	76%	76%	77%	77%	76%
Expenses:						
Equipment[1]	$500	$500	$500	$500	$500	$2,500
Prof. Services[2]	$2,000	$2,000	$2,000	$2,000	$2,000	$10,000
Phone/Internet[3]	$840	$840	$840	$840	$840	$4,200
Marketing[4]	$15,100	$16,500	$17,700	$18,625	$19,900	$87,825
Office Supplies[5]	$600	$600	$600	$600	$600	$3,000
Insurance[6]	$400	$400	$400	$400	$400	$2,000
Misc.[7]	$6,000	$6,000	$6,000	$6,000	$6,000	$30,000
Total Expenses:	$25,440	$26,840	$28,040	$28,965	$30,240	$139,525
Net Profit:	$67,260	$87,460	$104,860	$118,410	$136,860	$514,850
Net Profit %:	55%	58%	60%	62%	63%	60%

Being engaged by more or less clients in any given month will cause your individual results to differ. Charging clients at a rate other than those suggested by us will cause your individual results to differ. There is no assurance that you will earn the same amount as reflected in the projections.

These figures were prepared without an audit. Prospective franchisees should be advised that no certified public accountant has audited these figures or expressed an opinion with regard to the content or form.

The following assumptions were made regarding expenses:

1. Equipment. This figure assumes the need for replacing existing equipment. It does not include the equipment necessary to begin a Franchised Business as identified in Item 7 of this disclosure document, and is amortized over the term of the franchise agreement.

2. Professional Services. This figure assumes that you will hire a professional accountant to prepare your taxes and consult with you on various accounting matters throughout the year, as well as hiring an attorney to do any necessary business filings and registrations.

3. Phone and Internet. This figure assumes an annual contract for a separate telephone line and dial up connection for the internet. If you purchase multiple phone lines or other premium services, this figure may be higher.

4. Marketing. This figure represents your annual Brand Building Fund fee contributions, plus 5% local marketing expenses. You are not required to expend any funds for local marketing but we recommend that you do so.

5. Office Supplies. This figure assumes an expenditure of $50 per month for office supplies.

6. Insurance. This figure assumes that you will obtain insurance in accordance with the terms of the Franchise Agreement. If you purchase additional insurance above that which is required, this figure may be higher.

7. Miscellaneous. This figure assumes miscellaneous expenses to operate your franchised business, including costs for the annual conference, conference room rentals, and technology fees and E-Myth fees.

Additional Assumptions:

These projections assume that you will be the Principal Operator of the Franchised Business and that you do not receive an additional salary. They assume that you do not hire any other employees.

We have not provided any allowance for corporate or personal income taxes, nor have we included expenses for depreciation, amortization, interest or debt repayment. Each franchisee funds their purchase of the Franchised Business differently and we cannot project how you will account for those items. These projections are based on economic conditions as of March 2012 and we have made no adjustments in any category to account for inflation.

These projections assume that you follow our guidelines for suggested pricing and that you operate your Franchised Business in strict accordance with our licensing standards and System. If you do not, your results will likely vary dramatically from the projections we have provided.

Other than the preceding financial performance representation, TES Franchising, LLC does not make any financial performance representations. We also do not authorize our employees or representatives to make any such representations either orally or in writing. If you are purchasing an existing outlet, however, we may provide you with the actual records of that outlet. If you receive any other financial performance information or projections of your future income, you should report it to the franchisor's management by contacting Lorinda Church, 900 Main Street South, Building 2, Southbury, CT 06488, 203-405-2171, the Federal Trade Commission, and the appropriate state regulatory agencies.

Written substantiation for the projections will be made available to the prospective franchisee upon reasonable request.

ESTRELLA INSURANCE

3750 W. Flagler St.
Miami, FL 33134
Tel: (888) 511-7722, (305) 443-2829
Fax: (305) 444-2933
Email: franchise@estrellainsurance.com
Website: www.estrellainsurance.com
Jose Merille, President

Since 1980, ESTRELLA INSURANCE has built its foundation on values and excellent customer service. By continuing to exceed our customers' expectations with outstanding service and competitive rates, ESTRELLA INSURANCE continues to be the #1 choice for all insurance needs. We offer auto, home-owners, and commercial insurance. We can also insure your business, boat, motorcycle or recreational vehicle. Our loyal customers keep recommending Estrella Insurance to friends and other family members so that they, too, can receive the same friendly dedication and expertise they've come to expect from all Estrella agents.

BACKGROUND

IFA Member:	Yes
Established & First Franchised:	1980; 2008
Franchised Units:	60
Company-Owned Units:	0

Total Units:	60
Distribution:	US – 60; CAN – 0; O'seas – 0
North America:	1 State, 0 Provinces
Density:	60 in FL
Projected New Units (12 Months):	10
Qualifications:	5, 4, 4, 3, 3, 5

FINANCIAL/TERMS

Cash Investment:	$50K
Total Investment:	$50K
Minimum Net Worth:	$100K
Fees (Franchise):	$25K
Fees (Royalty):	1 – 1.5%
Fees (Advertising):	0.50 – 0.75%
Term of Contract (Years):	10/10/10
Average Number of Employees:	2 FT, 1 PT
Passive Ownership:	Not Allowed
Encourage Conversions:	Yes
Area Development Agreements:	Yes
Sub-Franchising Contracts:	No
Expand in Territory:	Yes
Space Needs:	800 – 1,200 SF

SUPPORT & TRAINING

Financial Assistance Provided:	Yes
Site Selection Assistance:	Yes
Lease Negotiation Assistance:	Yes
Co-operative Advertising:	Yes
Franchisee Association/Member:	Yes
Size of Corporate Staff:	6
On-going Support:	a, B, C, D, E, G, H, I
Training:	8 Weeks On-Site

SPECIFIC EXPANSION PLANS

US:	FL, TX
Canada:	No
Overseas:	No

Except for the Gross Revenue levels set forth below, we do not make information available to prospective franchisees concerning actual, average, projected, or forecasted sales, profits, or earnings. We do not furnish or authorize our sales personnel to furnish any other oral or written information concerning the actual, average, projected, forecasted, or potential sales, costs, income or profits of a franchise. We specifically instruct sales personnel, agents, employees and officers that, other than as set forth in this Item 19, they are not permitted to make any claims, or statements as to the earnings, sales, or profits, or prospects or chances of success, nor are they authorized to represent or estimate dollar figures as to a franchisee's operation. We will not be bound by any unauthorized representations as to earnings, sales, profits, or prospects or chances for success. Actual results will vary from franchise to franchise and will be dependent on a variety of internal and external factors, some of which neither we nor a prospective franchisee can estimate, such as competition, general economic climate, demographics, and the changing regulatory environment. Accordingly, we cannot estimate the results of a particular franchise. We recommend that prospective franchisees make their own independent investigation to determine whether or not the franchise may be profitable, and consult with an attorney and other advisors of their own choosing prior to executing any agreement.

THE GROSS REVENUES REFLECTED SHOULD NOT BE CON-SIDERED AS THE ACTUAL OR POTENTIAL LEVELS OF GROSS REVENUES THAT WILL BE REALIZED BY ANY FRAN-CHISEE. WE DO NOT REPRESENT THAT ANY FRANCHISEE CAN EXPECT TO ATTAIN SUCH LEVELS, OR ANY PARTICU-LAR LEVEL. IN ADDITION, WE DO NOT REPRESENT THAT ANY FRANCHISEE WILL DERIVE INCOME THAT EXCEEDS THE INITIAL PAYMENT FOR OR INVESTMENT IN THE ESTRELLA INSURANCE FRANCHISE. THE SUCCESS OF A FRANCHISEE LARGELY WILL DEPEND UPON THE ABIL-ITY OF THE FRANCHISEE, AND THE INDIVIDUAL FINAN-CIAL RESULTS OF A FRANCHISEE ARE LIKELY TO DIFFER FROM THE INFORMATION DESCRIBED HEREIN. SUBSTAN-TIATION OF THE DATA USED WILL BE MADE AVAILABLE UPON REASONABLE REQUEST, AT OUR OFFICES.

BASES AND ASSUMPTIONS

The agencies reviewed in connection with the preparation of the statement were located either in a shopping center, with a strong, local anchor tenant or a neighborhood "strip" center. The typical customer is a low to middle income automobile owner and/or licensed driver, needing a full line of automobile insurance coverages.

The agencies reviewed were all located in Miami-Dade and Broward County, Florida. Florida has a mandatory automobile insurance requirement of personal injury protection with a limit of $10,000 per person and property damage liability with a limit of $20,000. These requirements are considered to be lenient, when contrasted with those of other states.

THE STATEMENT AND THE INFORMATION UPON WHICH IT IS BASED HAVE NOT BEEN AUDITED OR REVIEWED BY ANY INDEPENDENT CERTIFIED PUBLIC ACCOUNTANT. NO SUCH ACCOUNTANT ASSUMES ANY RESPONSIBILITY FOR THEM.

In 2011, of the franchised agencies open at least two years as of December 31, 2011, approximately 89% had annual sales in excess of $1,500,000; approximately 41% had annual sales in excess of $2,000,000; approximately 23% had annual sales volumes in excess of $2,500,000; approximately 16% had annual sales volumes in excess of $3,000,000 and approximately 5% had annual sales in excess of $6,000,000. Note: The percentages exceed 100% as the categories are cumulative.

In 2011, the average sales volumes of the franchised agencies open at least two years, was $2,163,600. The highest and lowest annual sales volumes in 2011 of agencies operated by franchisees were $7,183,527 and $785,882.

	HIGH	AVERAGE	LOW
SALES	$6,019,316	$2,332,255	$1,394,667
PREMIUMS	($5,194,670)	($1,987,080)	($1,181,283)
TOTAL COMMISIONS	$824,646	$345,175	$213,384
COMMISIONS ADJUSTMENTS	($151,233)	($84,116)	($36,658)
NET COMMISIONS	$673,413	$261,059	$176,726

THE ABOVE SHOULD NOT BE CONSIDERED AS THE ACTUAL OR POTENTIAL AMOUNTS THAT WILL BE REALIZED BY ANY FRANCHISEE. THE FRANCHISOR DOES NOT REPRESENT THAT ANY FRANCHISE CAN EXPECT TO ATTAIN THESE LEVELS.

Statement of Gross Revenues - Notes

Sales: Total amount of gross premiums sold. (This is equivalent to Gross Revenues under the Franchise Agreement.)

Premiums: The cost associated with policies sold to insureds.

Commission adjustments: Adjustments as a result of refunds and/or credits to insureds for insurance cancellations or overpayments. It is reported net of any unearned premium received from either the insurance company, MGAs or the premium finance company, and fees which are additional revenues collected from the insured for preparation of the corresponding insurance application.

Other than the preceding financial performance representation, Estrella Franchising Corp. does not make any financial performance representations. We also do not authorize our employees or representatives to make any such representations either orally or in writing. If you are purchasing an existing outlet, however, we may provide you with the actual records of that outlet. If you receive any other financial performance information or projections of your future income, you should report it to the franchisor's management by contacting Jose Merille, Estrella Franchising Corp., 3750 West Flagler Street, Miami, Florida 33134, 305-443-2829, the Federal Trade Commission, and the appropriate state regulatory agencies.

EXPRESS OIL CHANGE

1880 Southpark Dr.
Birmingham, AL 35244
Tel: (888) 945-1771 x114, (205) 945-1771 x114
Fax: (205) 943-5779
Email: dlarose@expressoil.com
Website: www.expressoil.com
Donald R. LaRose, SVP Franchise Development

We are among the top ten fast oil change chains in the world. Per unit, sales out-pace our competitors by over 40%. Attractive, state-of-the-art facilities offer expanded, highly profitable services in addition to our ten minute oil change. We also provide transmission service, air conditioning service, brake repair, tire rotation and balancing and miscellaneous light repairs. Most extensive training and franchise support in the industry.

BACKGROUND
IFA Member:	Yes
Established & First Franchised:	1979; 1984
Franchised Units:	111
Company-Owned Units:	84
Total Units:	195
Distribution:	US – 195; CAN – 0; O'seas – 0
North America:	14 States, 0 Provinces

Density:	90 in AL, 35 in GA, 20 in TN
Projected New Units (12 Months):	12
Qualifications:	5, 5, 1, 3, 3, 5

FINANCIAL/TERMS
Cash Investment:	$300 – $350K
Total Investment:	$1,300 – $1,600K
Minimum Net Worth:	$450K
Fees (Franchise):	$35K
Fees (Royalty):	5%
Fees (Advertising):	0
Term of Contract (Years):	10/10
Average Number of Employees:	7 FT, 0 PT
Passive Ownership:	Not Allowed
Encourage Conversions:	Yes
Area Development Agreements:	Yes
Sub-Franchising Contracts:	No
Expand in Territory:	Yes
Space Needs:	22,000 SF

SUPPORT & TRAINING
Financial Assistance Provided:	Yes (I)
Site Selection Assistance:	Yes
Lease Negotiation Assistance:	Yes
Co-operative Advertising:	Yes
Franchisee Association/Member:	Yes/Member
Size of Corporate Staff:	44
On-going Support:	A, B, C, D, E, F, G, H, I
Training:	Closest Training Center Birmingham, AL; On-Site; Post-Opening Training; Continuous Training

SPECIFIC EXPANSION PLANS
US:	South
Canada:	No
Overseas:	No

Except for the historical data relating to certain average sales & expenses set forth in Exhibit I, we do not make any financial performance representations.

Most EOC Centers offer substantially the same products and services to the public. None of the franchised EOC Centers have customarily received services not generally available to other franchisees and substantially the same services will be available to you.

Your EOC franchised Center average may vary from averages of Company-operated and other franchised centers. The results of the first 6-18 months of operation will vary greatly depending on your involvement, advertising, location, size of market, awareness in the market and other factors. Results also differ greatly between conforming and non-conforming markets. We feel you should anticipate a negative cash flow for a minimum of 6 months.

These results are averages of specific express oil change centers and should not be considered as the actual or probable results that will be realized by you. Some Centers have sold and earned the amounts set forth in Exhibit I. Your individual results may differ. There is no assurance that you will sell or earn as much. You are urged to consult with appropriate financial, business and legal advisors in connection with this historical information. Substantiation of data used in preparing this item 19 will be made available to you upon reasonable request.

However, we will not disclose the identity or sales data of any particular center without the consent of that franchisee, except to any applicable state registration authorities or except in connection with the sale of a company-owned center.

None of our officers or employees is authorized to make any other claims or statements as to the financial performance, sales or profits or prospects or chances of success that you can expect or that have been experienced by present or past Centers. We have specifically instructed our officers and employees that they are not permitted to make other claims or statements as to the financial performance, sales or profits or the prospects or chances of success, nor are they authorized to represent or estimate dollar figures as to any particular Center or any particular site for a Center. You should not rely on any unauthorized representations as to financial performance, sales, profits or prospects or chances of success. If you receive any other financial performance information or projections of your future income you should report it to the Company's management by contacting our Chief Executive Officer, Richard A. Brooks at 1880 Southpark Drive, Birmingham, Alabama 35244, (205) 945-1771, the Federal Trade Commission and the appropriate state regulatory agencies.

EXHIBIT I

EXPRESS OIL CHANGE, L.L.C.

HISTORICAL FINANCIAL INFORMATION

Average Per Store Sales

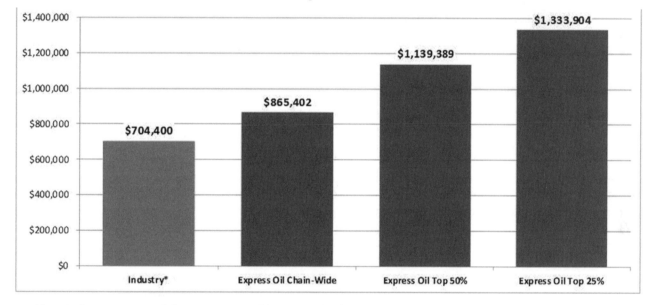

- Note: Industry average of chains as reported by National Oil & Lube News. Express Oil Change average of all locations open at least 12 months.

First Full Year Sales*

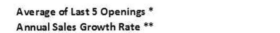

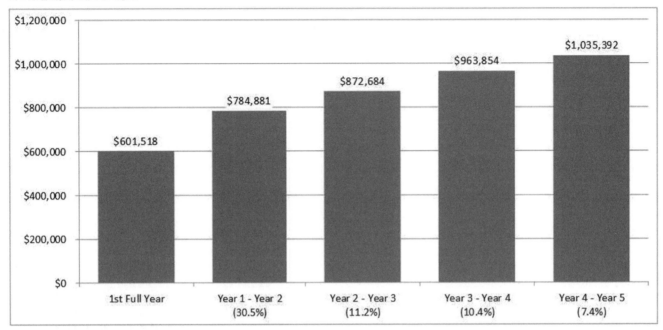

* Average sales for first full 12 months for the five most recent openings.

** Average percentage sales increase of most recent 30 stores completing the corresponding year of operation, excluding conversions.

Note: These results should not be considered as the actual or probable results that will be realized by you. Your own financial results are likely to differ from these results. You are urged to consult with appropriate financial, business and legal advisors in connection with this historical information. Substantiation of data used in preparing this analysis will be made available to you upon reasonable request.

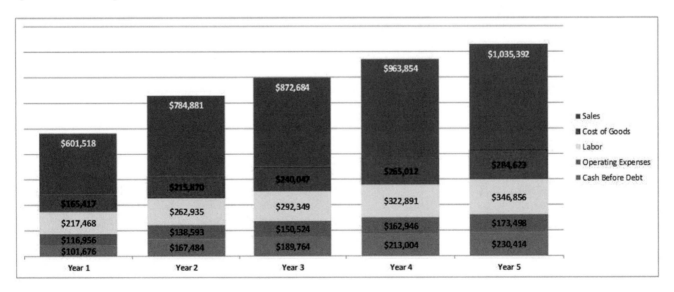

1. Average sales for first full 12 months for the 5 most recent openings. Average percentages sales increase of most recent 30 stores completing the corresponding year of operation, excluding conversions.

2. Cost of Goods estimated at 27.5% of sales, may decrease or increase depending on pricing in your market, business mix and operational management.

3. It is recommended that you invest in your labor to build early sales. A typical location will spending $16,00 to$20,000 per month including a 15% burden in labor costs. Once sales reach approximately $50,000 per month, labor should move as a percentage of sales with a target of 32% to 35%. We strongly recommend use of a third- party payroll service, with an estimated annual cost of $4,200 to $7,200 for a six person crew, which has been included in operating expenses below. In the illustration above, labor has been calculated at $18,000 per month or 33.5% of sales, whichever is greater.

4. We divide operating expenses into two categories:
A) Variable Costs—are items directly related to store sales, which include: royalty fee at 5%, advertising at 3%, credit card fees at 1.4% and shop supplies at 0.9%.
A) Non-Variable Costs—Although these costs are not truly fixed, they do have a controlled aspect, and include accounting, insurance, bank fees, computer expense, dues and subscriptions, office supplies, repair and maintenance, small tools, uniforms, utilities, miscellaneous items and the use of a payroll service. We estimate non-variable costs to be in the range of $50,000 to $60,000 with a marginal annual increase. In the illustration above we have estimated these expenses at $55,000 per year with a 5% increase per year to account for sales volume increases. This estimate does not include property tax. Please check with local authorities for estimated cost.

Note: These expenses should not be considered as the actual or probable results that will be realized by you. Your own financial results are likely to differ from these results. You are urged to consult with appropriate financial, business and legal advisors in connection with this historical information. Substantiation of data used in preparing this analysis will be made available to you upon reasonable request.

Quarterly Same Store Sales Growth

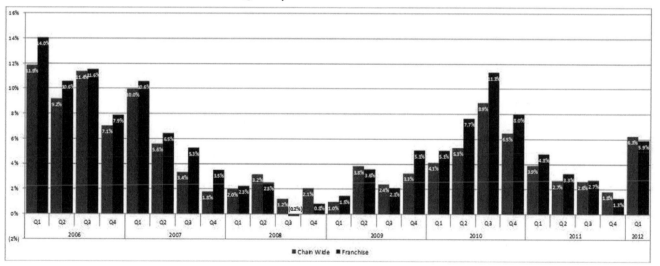

* Note: Same Store Sales (SSS) defined as aggregate revenue for all stores open at least 13 months at the end of indicated quarter. Percent change represents growth/decline over the same quarter for the previous year

Store Count by Revenue Brackets

2011 Total Revenue		
Range	# of Stores	% of Total
Minimum: $325,477		
$300k - $500k	20	11.7%
$500k - $700k	47	27.5%
$700k - $900k	36	21.1%
$900k- $1.1M	25	14.6%
$1.1M- $1.3M	25	14.6%
>$1.3M	18	10.5%
Maximum: $2,006,842		
TOTAL	171	100.0%

* Note: 2011 Total Revenue for all stores open at least one year as of 12/31/11.

Start-Up Cost Summary

	Typical
Land[1]	$550,000
Building & Site[1]	$575,000
Equipment, Signs, Furnishings[1]	$180,000
Organization, Professional Fees	$35,000
Loan Origination	$35,000
Sub-Total	**$1,375,000**
Soft Costs	
Franchise Fee* [2]	$35,000
Pre-Opening[3]	$33,500
Opening Inventory	$27,500
Opening Advertising[4]	$10,000
Working Capital[5]	$70,000
Sub-Total	**$176,000**
Total	**$1,551,000**

[1] The amounts set forth above for land, building and site work, and equipment include the cost of purchasing a 20,000 to 30,000 square foot site in a commercial or retail area and constructing a 6 to 8 bay facility on property which has all utilities to the site and does not require any excessive site preparation. The actual costs will vary materially depending on location, size and condition of lot, size of building and other factors. Many existing buildings (former service stations, automotive service centers, etc.) have been successfully converted at lower costs. To view a range of these costs, see Item 7 of this FDD.

[2] The initial franchise fee is $35,000 for your first unit, and $17,500 for any additional unit. Initial Franchise Fee is payable in a lump sum due at signing and is uniform to all franchisees currently purchasing a franchise.

[3] Amounts set forth above for pre-opening include (a) the manager's and assistant manager's salaries during pre-opening; (b) payroll costs of the crew for pre-opening training; and (c) costs of transportation, lodging, and meals during the training at the franchisor's headquarters. Also includes amounts for change fund, utility deposits, uniforms and other discretionary purchases.

[4] Amount set forth covers the requirement under the franchise agreement for grand opening promotions.

[5] Amounts set forth above are for working capital and normal early operating losses.

* There are no other direct or indirect payments in connection with the purchase of the franchise.

There are a variety of options available to pursue for financing the costs of starting the business, from conventional loans to Small Business Administration (SBA) financing. The example below is for an SBA 7-A loan for the hard and soft costs.

Hard Costs		Soft Costs	
Debt Structure	**SBA 504**	**Debt Structure**	**SBA 7-A**
Land	$550,000	Franchise Fee	$35,000
Building	$575,00	Inventory	$27,500
Equipment	$180,000	Working Capital	$113,500
Origination	$35,000		
Professional Fees	$35,000		
Total Hard Costs	$1,375,000	Total Soft Costs	$176,000
Loan to Value[1]	80%	Loan to Value[1]	90%
Financed Amount	$1,240,800	Financed Amount	$158,400
Cash Injection	**$310,200**	**Cash Injection**	**$17,600**
Loan Term	25 Years	Loan Term	10 Years
Interest Rate[2]	6%	Interest Rate[2]	6%
Monthly Payment	$7,955	Monthly Payment	$1,759
Annual Payment	$95,457	Annual Payment	$21,103

Total Cash Injection for above example: $310,200.

* The actual interest rate, terms of amortization and other costs of financing may vary from these assumptions. Interest rates and lease rates are typically related to the Federal Reserve Board's Prime Rate.

[1] Loans to project cost will be determined by SBA and supporting lending institution. This percentage will differ based on applicant's experience, credit-worthiness and financial portfolio. The typical range is 75% to 90%.

[2] Interest rates are a blend of both the SBA and supporting lender rates. These rates will vary depending on applicant's experience, credit-worthiness and financial portfolio. We have estimated at the average of 6%.

EXPRESS EMPLOYMENT PROFESSIONALS

8516 NW Expressway
Oklahoma City, OK 73162
Tel: (877) 652-6400, (405) 840-5000
Fax: (405) 717-5665
Email: rachel.rudisill@expresspros.com
Website: www.expressfranchising.com
Rachel Rudisill, Marketing Specialist

The U.S. staffing industry hit a record $114 billion in 2012, with more than $121 billion projected in North America for 2013. EXPRESS EMPLOYMENT PROFESSIONALS is a growing franchise with 600 franchises, ranked No. 1 in the Staffing Industry category and No. 66 overall in the Entrepreneur 500 in 2013. In 2011, EXPRESS franchisees generated on average of more than $4.5 million in sales per territory, with over $2 million in growth per territory since 2009. In 2013, EXPRESS is celebrating its 30th anniversary by giving the first 30 new franchisees $30,000 in working capital.

BACKGROUND

IFA Member:	Yes
Established & First Franchised:	1983; 1985
Franchised Units:	564
Company-Owned Units:	1
Total Units:	565
Distribution:	US – 523; CAN – 27; O'seas – 15
North America:	49 States, 3 Provinces

Density:	55 in TX, 49 in CA, 34 in OK
Projected New Units (12 Months):	50
Qualifications:	4, 4, 3, 4, 4, 4

FINANCIAL/TERMS

Cash Investment:	$50K
Total Investment:	$100.5 – $193K
Minimum Net Worth:	$200K
Fees (Franchise):	$35K
Fees (Royalty):	8%
Fees (Advertising):	0.6%
Term of Contract (Years):	5/5
Average Number of Employees:	3 FT, 0 PT
Passive Ownership:	Not Allowed
Encourage Conversions:	Yes
Area Development Agreements:	Yes
Sub-Franchising Contracts:	No
Expand in Territory:	Yes
Space Needs:	1,000 – 1,200 SF

SUPPORT & TRAINING

Financial Assistance Provided:	No
Site Selection Assistance:	Yes
Lease Negotiation Assistance:	Yes
Co-operative Advertising:	Yes
Franchisee Association/Member:	No
Size of Corporate Staff:	200
On-going Support:	A, C, D, E, G, H, I
Training:	2 Weeks Oklahoma City, OK; 1 Week Certified Training Office (In Field)

SPECIFIC EXPANSION PLANS

US:	All United States
Canada:	All Canada except Quebec
Overseas:	Australia and South Africa

Set forth below is information showing Gross Margins of certain Express Employment Professionals Businesses during Our fiscal years 2011, 2010, and 2009.

Table 1

All Units (Territories) Open	FY 2011	FY 2010	FY 2009
Average Annual Sales	$4,500,709	$3,692,279	$2,495,112
Average Annual Gross Margin	$825,706	$700,549	$483,605
Average Annual Gross Receipts	$39,791	$30,367	$23,298
Average Annual Franchisee Share of Gross Margin and Gross Receipts (AAGM)	$558,797	$476,073	$330,883
Number of Units in Survey	462	467	473
Number of Units Equaling or Exceeding AAGM	165	165	162

% of Units Equaling or Exceeding AAGM	35.7%	35.3%	34.2%
Average Royalty Paid Percent of AAGM	34.9%	34.3%	34.4%
Average Royalty Paid Percent of Annual Sales	6.7%	6.8%	7.0%

Table 2

Circle of Excellence Award Results Based on Annual Gross Margin Dollars and Gross Receipts Generated	FY 2011		FY 2010		FY 2009	
	# Units	% to Total Units	# Units	% to Total Units	# Units	% to Total Units
$825,000 to $1,125,000 - Circle of Excellence	71	13.63%	56	11.11%	38	6.95%
$1,125,000 to $1,700,000 - Bronze	74	14.20%	65	12.90%	33	6.04%
$1,700,000 to $2,200,000 – Silver	26	4.99%	13	2.58%	6	1.10%
$2,200,000 to $3,400,000 - Gold	18	3.45%	14	2.78%	3	0.55%
$3,400,000 to $4,500,000 – Platinum	3	0.58%	2	0.40%	1	0.18%
$4,500,000 to $5,600,000 - Sapphire	0	0.00%	0	0.00%	1	0.18%
$5,600,000 and Above - Diamond	1	0.19%	1	0.20%	0	0.00%
Totals	193	37.04%	151	29.96%	82	15.02%

Table 3 – Monthly Averages for Units Opened between 07-01-09 and 12-31-11

24 Month of Operation	Sales	Gross Margin	Gross Receipts	Number of Units	Units Equaling or Exceeding Average Gross Margin	
					Number	Percent
1	$17,964.74	$2,681.80	$0.00	30	5	16.67%
2	$35,295.55	$5,733.79	$1,341.67	30	7	23.33%
3	$54,697.98	$10,837.28	$337.19	29	11	35.48%
4	$74,752.64	$11,498.12	$1,536.00	27	8	29.63%
5	$64,774.88	$11,137.05	$3,463.31	25	10	40.00%
6	$76,400.35	$13,088.68	$4,096.75	24	9	37.50%
7	$86,663.30	$14,550.77	$2,186.56	20	9	45.00%
8	$96,707.85	$16,517.81	$268.78	19	8	42.11%
9	$107,751.45	$18,427.28	$507.80	18	7	38.89%
10	$109,858.06	$19,474.43	$1,345.15	17	9	52.94%
11	$104,552.06	$18,232.92	$5,934.82	17	8	47.06%
12	$135,937.37	$24,431.99	$4,089.93	16	8	50.00%
13	$133,419.94	$23,446.29	$2,160.91	13	6	46.15%
14	$194,238.36	$35,889.68	$1,271.43	12	4	33.33%
15	$185,330.57	$32,968.57	$80.00	12	6	50.00%
16	$183,601.65	$33,339.35	$1,438.33	12	4	33.33%
17	$215,132.14	$37,560.69	$1,759.41	12	4	33.33%
18	$201,052.82	$35,311.91	$4,124.67	12	5	41.67%
19	$215,313.06	$37,818.04	$850.83	12	5	41.67%

20	$207,690.64	$38,348.28	$3,462.50	8	4	50.00%
21	$224,665.53	$42,126.01	$7,542.86	7	2	28.57%
22	$238,326.93	$42,305.46	$5,120.00	7	3	42.86%
23	$267,306.87	$48,817.90	$4,957.14	7	2	28.57%
24	$249,228.86	$45,397.12	$2,990.38	7	2	28.57%

Notes:

1. Circle of Excellence is based on performance, participation and compliance criteria. Franchisees reach Circle of Excellence after generating $825,000 in gross margin and gross receipts. Six additional levels of Circle can be attained. To qualify for the 2012 Circle of Excellence Award, a franchisee must:

• Reach a minimum of $825,000 in temporary/contract staffing and HR services gross margin as well as direct hire fees collected.
• Invoice all fees through Q3 or Q4.
• Comply with all Express specifications and standardization practices as outlined and covered in the Franchise Agreement.
• Personally attend International Leadership Conference and one other international headquarters-sponsored training session.

Gross-margin associated with any bad debt will be deducted from the current year's production.

Franchise territories, as defined by the individual Franchise Agreements, may not be combined for qualification purposes.

2. "Gross Margin" means adjusted billings, less: (a) wages earned by associates based upon the work hours reported; (b) all credits and taxes measured by sales or gross receipts; (c) the employer's share of Federal Social Security taxes, federal and state unemployment tax contributions, workers' compensation insurance premiums, disability insurance premiums where required by local law, taxes on union health and welfare payments; (d) premiums on comprehensive liability, fidelity bonding insurance, errors and omissions insurance, and professional liability insurance premiums, if applicable; and (e) any other direct payroll taxes and insurance premiums based upon sales or payrolls which may be levied (all of which are collectively referred to as direct payroll costs).

3. "Gross Receipts" means the total of all money and other things of value received on Your Career Placement business conducted in accordance with the Franchise Agreement at the location specified; the term "Gross Receipts" shall not include bona fide discounts for promotional programs recommended by Us, refunds, or any amount collected and paid to any federal, state, municipal or governmental authorities

under the provisions of any sales tax act or similar act of governmental authorities.

4. The units reported in Charts 1 and 2 above include both domestic and international territories. All dollar amounts are reported in U.S. dollars. In FY 11, We had a total of 45 international units (Canada – 29; South Africa – 14). In FY10, We had a total of 43 international units (Canada – 28; South Africa – 14; Australia – 1). In FY09, We had a total of 43 international units (Canada – 28; South Africa – 14; Australia – 1). Some Express Employment Professionals Businesses also have "branch offices." The charts above reflect the combined Gross Margins and Gross Receipts of the branch offices together with their "main offices." In FY11, 47 or 10.2% of the units had branch offices. In FY10, 45 or 8.9% of the units had branch offices. In FY09, 46 or 8.4% of the units had branch offices.

5. The units reported in Chart 3 above were new domestic franchise territories that opened their offices between July 1, 2009 and December 31, 2011. There were a total of 30 units included in the survey. 12 units were opened at various intervals in FY 2009; 8 units were opened at various intervals in FY 2010; and 10 units were opened at various intervals in FY 2011. Chart 3 excludes "branch offices" and units added to the system through Our Conversion Program as described in Item 1 above.

6. Gross Margin and Gross Receipts do not reflect Your profits or net income, because We will take deductions from both Gross Margin and Gross Receipts before sending monies to You. Your portion of the Gross Margin will be 60%, and is subject to further deductions and adjustments authorized by the Franchise Agreement and Manual. Your portion of the Gross Receipts will be 90%. Please also refer to Item 6 for more details about additional deductions and adjustments.

7. In addition to deductions and adjustments made by Us as described in Note 6 above, You will incur other expenses that will reduce Your profits or net income, such as land, building and/or equipment rent, labor, debt service, depreciation and amortization, advertising, administrative expenses such as accounting or legal expenses, taxes, licenses, insurance, and others. These expenses vary from unit to unit.

8. The information set forth in the Charts reflect the actual

results of existing Express Employment Professionals Businesses, and should not be considered as the actual or probable results that will be realized by any franchisee. A new franchisee's individual financial results are likely to be lower.

9. Substantiation for the data set forth in these tables will be made available to You upon reasonable request.

10. Actual results vary from franchise to franchise and are dependent on a variety of internal and external factors, some of which We cannot estimate or forecast, such as competition, taxes, and the general economic climate. Accordingly, We cannot and do not estimate the results of a particular franchise.

11. We recommend that You make Your own independent investigation to determine whether or not the franchise may be profitable, and consult with your financial, legal and other advisors prior to executing any agreement.

12. Other than the preceding financial performance representation, We do not make any financial performance representations. We also do not authorize our employees or representatives to make any such representations either orally or in writing. If You are purchasing an existing outlet, however, We may provide you with the actual records of that outlet. If You receive any other financial performance information or projections of Your future income, You should report it to the franchisor's management by contacting Diane Carter, 8516 NW Expressway, Oklahoma City, Oklahoma 73162, 800-652-6400 ext. 4380, the Federal Trade Commission, and the appropriate state regulatory agencies.

FAST-FIX JEWELRY AND WATCH REPAIRS

1300 NW 17th Ave., # 170
Delray Beach, FL 33445-2554
Tel: (800) 359-0407, (561) 330-6060
Fax: (561) 330-6062
Email: franchise@fastfix.com
Website: www.fastfixfranchise.com
George Lambro, Director of Franchise Development

With a 27-year track record, FAST-FIX JEWELRY AND WATCH REPAIRS is the #1 national chain of dedicated jewelry and watch repair stores, with more than 160 franchised locations operating in the United States and Canada. FAST-FIX stores operate only in major regional malls that afford customers "while-they-shop" jewelry and watch repair service. Prior jewelry experience is not necessary. Our full training program at FAST-FIX University, along with our support system that includes national conventions and regional marketing meetings, will motivate you and prepare you to operate your FAST-FIX store.

BACKGROUND
IFA Member:	Yes
Established & First Franchised:	1984; 1987
Franchised Units:	163
Company-Owned Units:	0
Total Units:	163
Distribution:	US – 161; CAN – 2; O'seas – 3
North America:	27 States, 2 Provinces
Density:	39 in CA, 24 in FL, 17 in TX
Projected New Units (12 Months):	15
Qualifications:	4, 5, 2, 2, 2, 5

FINANCIAL/TERMS
Cash Investment:	$100K
Total Investment:	$166 – $308K
Minimum Net Worth:	$250K
Fees (Franchise):	$40K
Fees (Royalty):	6%
Fees (Advertising):	2%
Term of Contract (Years):	10/10
Average Number of Employees:	3 FT, 2 PT
Passive Ownership:	Discouraged
Encourage Conversions:	No
Area Development Agreements:	Yes
Sub-Franchising Contracts:	Yes
Expand in Territory:	Yes
Space Needs:	250 – 850 SF

<table>
<tr><td colspan="2">SUPPORT & TRAINING</td><td>Training:</td><td>5 Days On-Site; 10 Days National</td></tr>
<tr><td>Financial Assistance Provided:</td><td>Yes (I)</td><td></td><td>Training Center in Delray Beach, FL</td></tr>
<tr><td>Site Selection Assistance:</td><td>Yes</td><td></td><td></td></tr>
<tr><td>Lease Negotiation Assistance:</td><td>Yes</td><td>SPECIFIC EXPANSION PLANS</td><td></td></tr>
<tr><td>Co-operative Advertising:</td><td>No</td><td>US:</td><td>All United States</td></tr>
<tr><td>Franchisee Association/Member:</td><td>Yes/Member</td><td>Canada:</td><td>All Canada</td></tr>
<tr><td>Size of Corporate Staff:</td><td>18</td><td>Overseas:</td><td>All Countries</td></tr>
<tr><td>On-going Support:</td><td>C, D, E, G, H, I</td><td></td><td></td></tr>
</table>

To help you to evaluate our franchise, we have summarized selected historical sales information for our fiscal year ending December 31, 2011. We have compiled the information for each type of franchise we offer, based upon what franchisees have reported to us in the ordinary course of business through our monthly sales reporting system. We assume that the information submitted is accurate, complete and contains no material misrepresentations or omissions.

We have included within this data information from franchisees whose franchised businesses were in operation as of December 31, 2011 and had been in uninterrupted operation for at least 24 months. The claim does not include information about businesses that began or discontinued their affiliation with us during 2010 or 2011. The averages and ranges would differ had the results of new and former franchises been included.

The data presented does not reflect the cost of sales, operating expenses or other costs or expenses that must be deducted from the gross sales figures to obtain net income or profit. You should conduct an independent investigation of the costs and expenses you will incur in operating your franchised business. Franchisees or former franchisees listed in the disclosure document may be one source of this information.

The sales information is presented for periods during which economic conditions may be substantively different from future economic conditions. Competitors may enter or leave the market over time. Brand recognition and awareness and consumer goodwill may vary by market. Market potential and consumer demand may change over time. Each franchisee's managerial skill, experience and resources will differ. Accordingly, you are urged to consult with appropriate financial, business and legal counsel to conduct your own independent analysis of the information presented.

Written substantiation for the financial performance representation will be made available to the prospective franchisee upon reasonable request.

	No. of Stores	Average Sales	Range	
			High	low
Kiosk/Wall Store[2]	32	$287,736	$561,623	$113,786
In-Line Store[3]	106	$473,752	$136,995	$171,817
All Stores[4]	138	$430,618		

(1) The percentage of stores having attained or surpassed these average results (Kiosk/Wall Store 47%; In Line Store 44%; and All Stores 41%).

(2) Free-standing self contained retail fixture typically located within the exposed aisles (approx. 150-180 sq. ft.).

(3) In-line store built out within a traditional retail store front setting (approx. 300-800 sq. ft).

(4) 138 represent the total number of outlets measured. The total number of outlets in the system as of December 31, 2011 was 148.

Other than the preceding financial performance representations, Jewelry Repair does not make any financial performance representations. We also do not authorize our employees or representatives to make any such representations either orally or in writing. If you are purchasing an existing outlet, however, we may provide you with the actual records of that outlet. If you receive any other financial performance information or projections of your future income, you should report it to the franchisor's management by contacting Kenneth A. Marks at 1300 NW 17'h Avenue, Suite 170 Delray Beach, Florida 33445, (561) 330-6060, the Federal Trade Commission, and the appropriate state regulatory agencies.

FASTSIGNS

2542 Highlander Wy.
Carrollton, TX 75006
Tel: (800) 827-7446 x5679, (214) 346-5679
Fax: (866) 422-4927
Email: mark.jameson@fastsigns.com
Website: www.fastsigns.com
Mark L. Jameson, SVP, Franchise Support & Development

Signage has never been more important. Right now, businesses are looking for new and better ways to compete. Industries are revamping to meet compliance standards. Advertisers are expanding their reach into new media, like digital signage, QR codes, and mobile websites. Join the franchise that's leading the next generation of business communication. Now more than ever, businesses look to FASTSIGNS® for innovative ways to connect with customers in a highly competitive marketplace. Our high standards for quality and customer service have made FASTSIGNS the most recognized brand in the industry, driving significantly more traffic to the Web than any other sign company. We also lead in these important areas: #1 Sign Franchise in Entrepreneur magazine Franchise 500, 2011; Franchise Business Review Best in Category 2006-2010; World Class Franchisee Satisfaction Recognition, 2011 Franchise Research Institute; Franchisees' Choice Designation, 2011 Canadian Franchise Association. FASTSIGNS is one of only a handful of franchises approved for the Franchise America Finance Program, with 6 million dollars in financing for approved franchise owners.

BACKGROUND

IFA Member:	Yes
Established & First Franchised:	1985; 1986
Franchised Units:	529

Company-Owned Units:	0
Total Units:	529
Distribution:	US – 451; CAN – 22; O'seas – 56
North America:	45 States, 6 Provinces
Density:	58 in TX, 45 in CA, 35 in FL
Projected New Units (12 Months):	25
Qualifications:	5, 5, 1, 3, 4, 5

FINANCIAL/TERMS

Cash Investment:	$75K
Total Investment:	$176 – $292.5K
Minimum Net Worth:	$250K
Fees (Franchise):	$34.5K
Fees (Royalty):	6%
Fees (Advertising):	2%
Term of Contract (Years):	20/10
Average Number of Employees:	2 – 3 FT, 0 PT
Passive Ownership:	Allowed
Encourage Conversions:	Yes
Area Development Agreements:	Yes
Sub-Franchising Contracts:	No
Expand in Territory:	Yes
Space Needs:	1,200 – 1,500 SF

SUPPORT & TRAINING

Financial Assistance Provided:	Yes (I)
Site Selection Assistance:	Yes
Lease Negotiation Assistance:	Yes
Co-operative Advertising:	No
Franchisee Association/Member:	Yes/Member
Size of Corporate Staff:	100
On-going Support:	C, D, E, G, H, I
Training:	2 Weeks Dallas, TX; 1 Week On-Site

SPECIFIC EXPANSION PLANS

US:	All United States
Canada:	All Canada except Quebec
Overseas:	Australia, New Zealand, UK

2011 FINANCIAL PERFORMANCE REPRESENTATION

On December 31, 2011, there were 523 FASTSIGNS Centers open and in operation of which 72 were international. 443 Centers were open and in continuous operation in the US during the entire calendar year ending December 31, 2011. The analysis set forth below is based solely on the average yearly gross sales for those 443 Centers for 2011.

Based on gross sales reported by the 443 Centers, the average gross sales for such Centers for the year ended December 31,

2011 was $579,403. For purposes of this analysis, gross sales includes cash and credit sales as well as any goods or services received by the franchisee in exchange for goods and services sold at the Center. Gross sales do not include sales or use taxes.

Of the 443 Centers included in this analysis, 161 or 36% of the Centers reported gross sales above the average, ranging from $582,465 to $5,051,550 and 282 or 64% of the Centers reported gross sales below the average, ranging from $62,363 to $579,204. These figures include "Satellite" Centers, which are typically smaller Centers without full production capabilities. The Centers in the top quartile (111 Centers) had average gross sales of $1,037,393 in 2011. Overall, the Centers included in this analysis reported gross sales in the following ranges for the year:

2011 SALES ENDING DECEMBER 31

2011 Sales	# of Centers
$0 - $300,000	85
$300,001 - $600,000	204
$600,001 - $1,000,000	108
$1,000,001 - $1,500,000	37
$1,500,001 - $2,000,000	6
$2,000,001 - $3,000,000	1
$3,000,001- $4,000,000	1
Over $5,000,000	1
Total Centers	443
Average Sales	$579,403
Median Sales	$492,401

2011 Sales	1st Year Centers[1]	2nd Year Centers[2]	3rd Year Centers[3]
$0 - $300,000	9	3	11
$300,001 - $600,000	7	6	5
$600,001 - $1,000,000	0	1	3
Total Centers	16	10	19

[1] Centers opened during calendar year 2010 averaged $297,945 (or $24,829/month) during calendar year 2011
[2] Centers opened in calendar year 2009
[3] Centers opened in calendar year 2008

Gross Sales of Top 25 FASTSIGNS Centers

The average annual gross sales for the top 25 FASTSIGNS Centers in the United States were $1,617,453 for 2011. To be included in the top 25, a Center had to have reported its gross sales for each of the 12 months in the calendar year. We had a total of 451 Centers in the United States as of December 31, 2011.

Gross Sales Study – Centers with Outside Sales Representatives

It has been our experience that having a full time outside sales representative is an essential part of a successful marketing program. The average gross sales of FASTSIGNS Centers in the US during the twelve month period from January 1, 2011 to December 31, 2011 was $890,764 for franchise owners who (1) were in business for at least two years prior to January 1, 2011; (2) reported gross sales for each of the 12 months in 2011 and (3) advised us that they employed a full-time outside representative during this period who was not one of the owners of the Center. The number of Centers who met this criteria in 2011, and were used in this study, was 73 which represented 16.5% of the FASTSIGNS open and operational in the US for the full year in 2011. The number of these Centers whose sales attained or surpassed the system average gross sales number for the US was 44 or 60.3%.

Of the 161 Centers reporting gross sales above the average, 41 Centers are located in the Southwest Region of the United States, 31 in the West Region, 25 in the Northeast Region, 34 in the Southeast Region and 30 in the Midwest Region. Of the 282 Centers reporting gross sales below the average, 49 are located in the Southwest Region, 58 in the West Region, 63 in the Northeast Region, 51 in the Southeast Region and 61 in the Midwest Region.

For purposes of this analysis, the Southwest Region consists of Arkansas, Colorado, Louisiana, New Mexico, Oklahoma and Texas; the West Region consists of Alaska, Arizona, California, Hawaii, Idaho, Montana, Nevada, Oregon, Utah, Washington and Wyoming; the Northeast Region consists of Connecticut, Delaware, Maine, Maryland, Massachusetts, New Hampshire, New Jersey, New York, Pennsylvania, Rhode Island, Vermont, Virginia, Washington, D.C. and West Virginia; the Southeast Region consists of Alabama, Florida, Georgia, Mississippi, North Carolina, South Carolina and Tennessee; and the Midwest Region consists of Illinois, Indiana, Iowa, Kansas, Kentucky, Ohio, Michigan, Minnesota, Missouri, Nebraska, North Dakota, South Dakota and Wisconsin.

We offer substantially the same services to all franchisees. Additionally, advertising and promotional materials developed by the NAC are available to all Franchisees. (See Item 11.) An individual Franchisee is not limited in the amount or type of advertising that it may conduct; provided, however, that all advertising materials developed by Franchisee must be approved in advance by us. (See Item 16.) Consequently, Franchisee's gross sales may be directly affected by the amount, type and effectiveness of advertising conducted by Franchisee.

The Franchise Agreement provides that Franchisees must offer and sell at the Center products and services required by us and may offer and sell such additional products and services approved by us. (See Item 16.) Franchisees offer substantially the same products and services to the public. In certain states, as noted in Item 1, Franchisees may be required to have a contractor's license to perform certain types of sign installation work. In those states, if you do not have, or meet the requirements to obtain a license, then you may not be able to offer those installation services requiring a license. Additionally, Franchisees may offer and sell products and services at varying prices. As a result, the products and services offered and the prices at which such products and services are offered to the public at the Centers included in this analysis may vary.

The average gross sales figures included in this analysis are based on sales reports submitted to us by each Franchisee. The figures in the sales reports have not been audited and we have not undertaken to otherwise independently verify (i) the accuracy of such information or (ii) whether such information was prepared in accordance with generally accepted accounting principles.

In addition to the average gross sales analysis, certain expenses, expressed as a percentage of Gross Revenues, have been provided based on the experience of certain of the foregoing FASTSIGNS Centers described below. The expense figures were extracted from the 2011 financial statements submitted by the FASTSIGNS Franchisees included in the 2011 analysis described above. As of the date of this DISCLOSURE DOCUMENT, we have not been provided with expense data from 200 of the 443 Centers open and in continuous operation during 2011. This was primarily due to the close proximity of year-end to the time of compilation of these numbers and such 200 Centers were not included in the expense figures provided herein. You should note that with respect to the 243 FASTSIGNS Centers included in the compilation of the expense figures, the expense data relates to operations conducted during the one-year period ended 2011. Of the 243 Centers reporting expenses 1 was opened in 1985, 1 was opened in 1986, 2 was opened in 1987, 7 were opened in 1988, 17 were opened in 1989, 28 were opened in 1990, 12 were opened in 1991, 15 were opened in 1992, 8 were opened in 1993, 12 were opened in 1994, 14 were opened in 1995, 17 were opened in

1996, 13 were opened in 1997, 13 were opened in 1998, 6 were opened in 1999, 5 were opened in 2000, 5 were opened in 2001, 3 were opened in 2002, 4 were opened in 2003, 8 were opened in 2004, 9 were opened in 2005, 6 were opened in 2006, 11 were opened in 2007, 8 were opened in 2008, 7 were opened in 2009, 8 was opened in 2010 and 3 were opened in 2011. These Centers are located in the following regions; 46 in the Southwest region of the United States, 48 in the West region, 42 in the Northeast region, 55 in the Southeast region and 50 in the Midwest region. The information relating to the operations expenses provided by the FASTSIGNS Centers and used by the us in determining the numerical values provided have not been audited and such information has not necessarily been prepared on a basis consistent with generally accepted accounting principles. In particular, we are unable to verify whether the expense data submitted by each FASTSIGNS Center for each separately provided expense item appropriately reflects the types of expenses which are ordinarily incurred by FASTSIGNS Centers and which should be included in the item according to generally acceptable accounting principles.

Each percentage given on this analysis reflects the mean average of the total percentages for the applicable expense item provided by the reporting FASTSIGNS Center (i.e., the aggregate sum of the expense percentages of all reporting FASTSIGNS Centers divided by the number of reporting Centers). The expense percentages for the various expense items provided by each reporting FASTSIGNS Center reflects that Center's expenses as a percentage of its Gross Revenues. No percentage given on this analysis is the actual expenses percentage experienced by any one FASTSIGNS Center and the actual expense percentages for the reporting FASTSIGNS Centers on any particular expense item may vary significantly. The following expenses represent the major expense items for a FASTSIGNS Center and should not be considered the only expenses that a FASTSIGNS Center will incur:

2011 Year-End Average P&L

	Company Average (243 Centers Reporting)		Top 25% Based on Profitability (61 Centers)	
	Annual	% of Sales	Annual	% of Sales
SALES	$657,077.95	100.0%	$815,272.42	100.0%
COST OF GOODS	$187,807.87	28.6%	$208,927.73	25.6%
LABOR EXPENSES (Including Owner)	$222,831.76	33.9%	$250,604.51	30.7%
ADVERTISING EXPENSES	$20,516.41	3.1%	$25,159.33	3.1%
AUTO EXPENSES	$10,385.04	1.6%	$10,399.35	1.3%
FACILITY EXPENSES	$48,230.02	7.3%	$49,291.37	6.0%

EQUIPMENT EXPENSES	$5,359.86	.8%	$6,908.32	.8%
GENERAL AND ADMINISTRATIVE EXPENSES	$92,969.91	14.1%	$100,326.81	12.3%
EBITDA	$68,977.08	10.5%	$163,655.00	20.1%
Owner's Salary from Labor Expenses	$37,758.49	5.7%	$67,902.73	8.3%
Total Owner Benefit	$106,735.57	16.2%	$231,557.73	28.4%

The franchisor is unable to verify the accuracy of the expense information provided by FASTSIGNS franchisees and makes no representations or warranties regarding the same.

The average gross sales for all Centers included in the above study were $657,078. The amount of gross sales realized and expenses incurred will vary from unit to unit. In particular, gross sales and expenses at Franchisee's Center will be directly affected by many additional factors not noted above, including, without limitation, the Center's geographic location, competition in the market, the presence of other FASTSIGNS Centers, the quality of management, the effectiveness of sales and marketing and the prices charged for products and services sold at the Center. Further, the franchise agreement to which each franchisee included in this analysis is subject is different from the Franchise Agreement attached to this DISCLOSURE DOCUMENT as Exhibit B. Among other terms, the Franchise Agreement attached to this DISCLOSURE DOCUMENT requires an initial franchise fee of $34,500 and a continuing Service Fee of 6%. Further, Franchisee may be required to participate in an Advertising Cooperative. This analysis, therefore, should only be used as a reference for Franchisee to use in conducting its own analysis.

Finally, Franchisee should particularly note the following:

Each franchisee is urged to consult with appropriate financial, business and legal advisors in connection with the information set forth in this analysis.

The average sales and major expenses reflected in this analysis should not be considered as the actual or potential sales that will be realized by any franchisee. We do not represent that any franchisee can expect to attain such sales. In addition, we do not represent that any franchisee will derive income that exceeds the initial payment for or investment in a FASTSIGNS franchise. No inference as to expenses, cost of goods sold or profits relating to existing or future centers should be drawn from the sales information reflected in this analysis. The success of franchisee will depend largely upon the ability of franchisee, and the individual financial results of a franchisee are likely to differ from the information set forth herein. Substan-

tiation of the data used in preparing this analysis will be made available upon reasonable request.

Other than the preceding financial performance representation, FASTSIGNS International, Inc. does not make any financial performance representations. We also do not authorize our employees, representatives or the National Advertising Council, Inc. to make any such representations either orally or in writing. If you are purchasing an existing outlet, however, we may provide you with the actual records of that outlet. If you receive any other financial performance information or projections of your future income, you should report it to the our management by contacting Catherine Monson, CEO, FASTSIGNS International, Inc., 2542 Highlander Way, Carrollton, Texas 75006, 214-346-5774, the Federal Trade Commission, and the appropriate state regulatory agencies.

2010 FINANCIAL PERFORMANCE REPRESENTATION

On December 31, 2010, there were 529 FASTSIGNS Centers open and in operation of which 77 were international. 437 Centers were open and in continuous operation in the United States during the entire calendar year ending December 31, 2010. The analysis set forth below is based solely on the average yearly gross sales for those 437 Centers for 2010.

Based on gross sales reported by the 437 Centers, the average gross sales for such Centers for the year ended December 31, 2010 was $540,137. For purposes of this analysis, gross sales includes cash and credit sales as well as any goods or services received by the franchisee in exchange for goods and services sold at the Center. Gross sales do not include sales or use taxes.

Of the 437 Centers included in this analysis, 167 or 38% of the Centers reported gross sales above the average, ranging from $540,350 to $4,932,193 and 270 or 62% of the Centers reported gross sales below the average, ranging from $102,462 to $539,428. These figures include "Satellite" Centers, which are typically smaller Centers without full production capabilities. The Centers in the top quartile (109 Centers) had average gross sales of $978,427 in 2010. Overall, the Centers included in this analysis reported gross sales in the following ranges for the year:

2010 SALES ENDING DECEMBER 31

2010 Sales	# of Centers
$0 – $300,000	90
$300,001 – $600,000	212
$600,001 – $1,000,000	100
$1,000,001 – $1,500,000	30
$1,500,001 – $2,000,000	1
$2,000,001 – $3,000,000	3
Over $4,000,000	1
Total Centers	437
Average Sales	$540,137
Median Sales	$468,061

2010 Sales	1st Year Centers[1]	2nd Year Centers[2]	3rd Year Centers[3]
$0 – $300,000	5	14	5
$300,001 – $600,000	6	6	10
$600,001 – $1,000,000	0	0	3
Total Centers	11	20	18

* Centers opened during calendar year 2009 averaged $295,648 (or $24,637/month) during calendar year 2010
**Centers opened in calendar year 2008
***Centers opened in calendar year 2007

Of the 167 Centers reporting gross sales above the average, 44 Centers are located in the Southwest Region of the United States, 32 in the West Region, 24 in the Northeast Region, 38 in the Southeast Region and 29 in the Midwest Region. Of the 270 Centers reporting gross sales below the average, 46 are located in the Southwest Region, 54 in the West Region, 61 in the Northeast Region, 46 in the Southeast Region and 63 in the Midwest Region.

For purposes of this analysis, the Southwest Region consists of Arkansas, Colorado, Louisiana, New Mexico, Oklahoma and Texas; the West Region consists of Alaska, Arizona, California, Hawaii, Idaho, Montana, Nevada, Oregon, Utah, Washington and Wyoming; the Northeast Region consists of Connecticut, Delaware, Maine, Maryland, Massachusetts, New Hampshire, New Jersey, New York, Pennsylvania, Rhode Island, Vermont, Virginia, Washington, D.C. and West Virginia; the Southeast Region consists of Alabama, Florida, Georgia, Mississippi, North Carolina, South Carolina and Tennessee; and the Mid-

west Region consists of Illinois, Indiana, Iowa, Kansas, Kentucky, Ohio, Michigan, Minnesota, Missouri, Nebraska, North Dakota, South Dakota and Wisconsin.

We offer substantially the same services to all Franchisees. Additionally, advertising and promotional materials developed by the National Advertising Council, Inc. are available to all Franchisees. (See Item 11.) An individual Franchisee is not limited in the amount or type of advertising that it may conduct; provided, however, that all advertising materials developed by Franchisee must be approved in advance by us. (See Item 16.) Consequently, Franchisee's gross sales may be directly affected by the amount, type and effectiveness of advertising conducted by Franchisee.

The Franchise Agreement provides that Franchisees must offer and sell at the Center products and services required by us and may offer and sell such additional products and services approved by us. (See Item 16.) Franchisees offer substantially the same products and services to the public. In certain states, as noted in Item 1, Franchisees may be required to have a contractor's license to perform certain types of sign installation work. In those states, if you do not have, or meet the requirements to obtain a license, then you may not be able to offer those installation services requiring a license. Additionally, Franchisees may offer and sell products and services at varying prices. As a result, the products and services offered and the prices at which such products and services are offered to the public at the Centers included in this analysis may vary.

The average gross sales figures included in this analysis are based on sales reports submitted to us by each Franchisee. The figures in the sales reports have not been audited and we have not undertaken to otherwise independently verify (i) the accuracy of such information or (ii) whether such information was prepared in accordance with generally accepted accounting principles.

In addition to the average gross sales analysis, certain expenses, expressed as a percentage of Gross Revenues, have been provided based on the experience of certain of the foregoing FASTSIGNS Centers described below. The expense figures were extracted from the 2010 financial statements submitted by the FASTSIGNS Franchisees included in the 2010 analysis described above. As of the date of this DISCLOSURE DOCUMENT, we have not been provided with expense data from 202 of the 437 Centers open and in continuous operation during 2010. This was primarily due to the close proximity of year-end to the time of compilation of these numbers and such 202 Centers were not included in the expense figures provided herein. You should note that with respect to the 235 FASTSIGNS Centers included in the compilation of the expense figures, the expense data relates to operations conducted during the one-year period ended 2010. Of the 235 Centers reporting expenses 1 was opened in 1985, 1 was opened in 1986, 1 was opened in 1987, 3 were opened in 1988, 12 were opened in 1989, 30 were opened in 1990, 15 were opened in 1991, 16 were opened in 1992, 12 were opened in 1993, 12 were opened in 1994, 15 were opened in 1995, 14 were opened in 1996, 14 were opened in 1997, 10 were opened in 1998, 8 were opened in 1999, 4 were opened in 2000, 4 were opened in 2001, 3 were opened in 2002, 4 were opened in 2003, 8 were opened in 2004, 9 were opened in 2005, 8 were opened in 2006, 11 were opened in 2007, 13 were opened in 2008, 6 were opened in 2009 and 1 was opened in 2010. These Centers are located in the following regions; 45 in the Southwest region of the United States, 46 in the West region, 40 in the Northeast region, 46 in the Southeast region and 58 in the Midwest region. The information relating to the operations expenses provided by the FASTSIGNS Centers and used by the us in determining the numerical values provided have not been audited and such information has not necessarily been prepared on a basis consistent with generally accepted accounting principles. In particular, we are unable to verify whether the expense data submitted by each FASTSIGNS Center for each separately pro-

vided expense item appropriately reflects the types of expenses which are ordinarily incurred by FASTSIGNS Centers and which should be included in the item according to generally acceptable accounting principles.

Each percentage given on this analysis reflects the mean average of the total percentages for the applicable expense item provided by the reporting FASTSIGNS Center (i.e., the aggregate sum of the expense percentages of all reporting FASTSIGNS Centers divided by the number of reporting Centers). The expense percentages for the various expense items provided by each reporting FASTSIGNS Center reflects that Center's expenses as a percentage of its Gross Revenues. No percentage given on this analysis is the actual expenses percentage experienced by any one FASTSIGNS Center and the actual expense percentages for the reporting FASTSIGNS Centers on any particular expense item may vary significantly. The following expenses represent the major expense items for a FASTSIGNS Center and should not be considered the only expenses that a FASTSIGNS Center will incur:

2010 Year-End Average P&L

	Company Average (235 Centers Reporting)		Top 25% Based on Profitability (59 Centers)	
	Annual	% of Sales	Annual	% of Sales
SALES	$601,891.31	100.0%	$771,172.50	100.0%
COST OF GOODS	$164,180.32	27.3%	$199,628.35	25.9%
LABOR EXPENSES (Including Owner)	$203,657.86	33.8%	$248,125.68	32.2%
ADVERTISING EXPENSES	$22,126.91	3.7%	$28,567.62	4.0%
AUTO EXPENSES	$9,164.91	1.5%	$9,043.08	1.2%
FACILITY EXPENSES	$50,453.08	8.4%	$50,723.03	6.6%
EQUIPMENT EXPENSES	$7,607.21	1.3%	$7,775.15	1.0%
GENERAL AND ADMINISTRATIVE EXPENSES	$86,442.79	14.4%	$97,230.80	12.6%
EBITDA	$58,258.23	9.7%	$132,407.40	17.2%
Owner's Salary from Labor Expenses	$35,456.10	5.9%	$67,799.00	8.8%
Total Owner Benefit	$93,714.34	15.6%	$200,206.39	26.0%

Franchisor is unable to verify the accuracy of the expense information provided by FASTSIGNS Franchisees and makes no representations or warranties regarding the same.

The average gross sales for all Centers included in the above study were $601,891. The amount of gross sales realized and

expenses incurred will vary from unit to unit. In particular, gross sales and expenses at Franchisee's Center will be directly affected by many additional factors not noted above, including, without limitation, the Center's geographic location, competition in the market, the presence of other FASTSIGNS Centers, the quality of management, the effectiveness of sales and marketing and the prices charged for products and services sold at the Center. Further, the Franchise Agreement to which each franchisee included in this analysis is subject is different from the Franchise Agreement attached to this DISCLOSURE DOCUMENT as Exhibit B. Among other terms, the Franchise Agreement attached to this DISCLOSURE DOCUMENT requires an initial franchise fee of $34,500 and a Service Fee of 6%. Further, Franchisee may be required to participate in an Advertising Cooperative. This analysis, therefore, should only be used as a reference for Franchisee to use in conducting its own analysis.

Finally, Franchisee should particularly note the following:

Each Franchisee is urged to consult with appropriate financial, business and legal advisors in connection with the information set forth in this analysis.

The average sales and major expenses reflected in this analysis should not be considered as the actual or potential sales that will be realized by any Franchisee. We do not represent that any Franchisee can expect to attain such sales. In addition, we do not represent that any Franchisee will derive income that exceeds the initial payment for or investment in a FASTSIGNS franchise. No inference as to expenses, cost of goods sold or profits relating to existing or future Centers should be drawn from the sales information reflected in this analysis. The success of each Franchisee will depend largely upon the ability of Franchisee, and the individual financial results of a Franchisee are likely to differ from the information set forth herein. Substantiation of the data used in preparing this analysis will be made available upon reasonable request.

Other than the preceding financial performance representation, FASTSIGNS International, Inc. does not make any financial performance representations. We also do not authorize our employees, representatives or the National Advertising Council, Inc. to make any such representations either orally or in writing. If you are purchasing an existing outlet, however, we may provide you with the actual records of that outlet. If you receive any other financial performance information or projections of your future income, you should report it to the our management by contacting Catherine Monson, CEO, FASTSIGNS International, Inc., 2542 Highlander Way, Carrollton, Texas 75006, 214-346-5774, the Federal Trade Commission, and the appropriate state regulatory agencies.

FIBRENEW

Box 117
Black Diamond, AB T0L 0HO Canada
Tel: (800) 345-2951, (403) 278-7818
Fax: (403) 278-1434
Email: topdog@fibrenew.com
Website: www.fibrenew.com
Denele Shelby, Vice President of Franchising

FIBRENEW is a "niche market" business, refurbishing and re-dyeing all leather and plastic, offering clients a "green" environmental and cost-saving alternative to replacing or recovering damaged pieces. FIBRENEW supports men and women worldwide in owning and operating a successful home-based mobile service business. FIBRENEW accomplishes this by encouraging cooperation between our franchises to share their knowledge and experience. We promote education through seminars, workshops, and self-directed business and personal studies. FIBRENEW strives to be environmentally responsible. Our services prevent thousands of tons of used leathers, plastics, and vinyl from filling our landfills annually.

BACKGROUND

IFA Member:	No
Established & First Franchised:	1985; 1987
Franchised Units:	198
Company-Owned Units:	0
Total Units:	198
Distribution:	US – 105; CAN – 72; O'seas – 21
North America:	32 States, 10 Provinces
Density:	25 in ON, 15 in CA, 14 in BC
Projected New Units (12 Months):	20
Qualifications:	5, 3, 1, 1, 2, 3

FINANCIAL/TERMS	
Cash Investment:	$70K
Total Investment:	$82 – $105K
Minimum Net Worth:	$150K
Fees (Franchise):	$67K
Fees (Royalty):	$550/mo.
Fees (Advertising):	N/A
Term of Contract (Years):	7/7
Average Number of Employees:	1 FT, 0 PT
Passive Ownership:	Not Allowed
Encourage Conversions:	N/A
Area Development Agreements:	No
Sub-Franchising Contracts:	No
Expand in Territory:	Yes
Space Needs:	N/A

SUPPORT & TRAINING	
Financial Assistance Provided:	Yes (I)
Site Selection Assistance:	N/A
Lease Negotiation Assistance:	N/A
Co-operative Advertising:	No
Franchisee Association/Member:	No
Size of Corporate Staff:	7
On-going Support:	B, C, D, G, h, I
Training:	2 Weeks in Calgary, AB Canada

SPECIFIC EXPANSION PLANS

US:	All United States except HI, ND, SD
Canada:	AB, BC, NS, ON, QC, SK
Overseas:	Australia

We do not require our franchisees to report financial information to us. However, in 2011 we conducted a survey of all of our franchisees to determine the relative range of their fixed and variable costs of operating a Franchised Business. The survey asked our franchisees to report their fixed and variable costs by selecting the survey answer stating the range that their costs fell into. We have averaged the survey results from the franchisees who responded.

1. Average monthly fixed costs were reported by our franchisees to be in the range between $2,500 and $3,000 per month. For purposes of the survey, monthly fixed costs were defined as the total of only the cost of ongoing fees paid to us, office supplies, phone/fax, meals & entertainment, insurance, legal & accounting, advertising, computer, and tools. The survey requested the franchisees not to include any other fixed costs (such as debt service costs) in determining their responses.

2. Average variable costs as a percentage of gross revenues were reported by our franchisees to be in the range of 10% of gross revenues. For purposes of the survey, variable costs were defined as only the cost of gasoline and repair product costs.

Explanatory Notes:

1. Participation Rate. Of our 102 franchisees at the time, 11 (or 11 %) responded to the survey. Responding franchisees included those who had been in business for only a few months, as well as those who have been Fibrenew franchisees for many years. The average survey results do not reflect any information from the franchisees who did not respond to the survey. A greater participation rate by our franchisees could have an impact on the average survey results.

2. No Independent Verification. Based on the previous experience by current Fibrenew management who have operated their own Fibrenew franchise, we believe that the average survey results accurately depict the average range of fixed and variable costs. However, we have not independently verified the information provided by our franchisees. Surveys, by their nature, may not always be completely accurate. For example, some respondents may interpret and answer questions differently than others.

3. Vehicle. Many of our franchisees start operating the Franchised Business with vehicles they already own. The fixed costs reported do not include the additional costs associated with purchasing a vehicle and amortizing that cost over time.

4. Marketing. There is wide variation in the amounts that our franchisees spend on marketing and advertising. Before 2012, we did not require our franchisee to participate or pay for any Google Adwords marketing. Starting in 2012, we require each franchisee to make a minimum monthly expenditure of $100 for Google Adwords marketing.

5. Insurance. The survey specified that the cost of insurance included in the fixed costs was only for the insurance required under the franchise agreement. Some franchisees may have additional fixed costs for insurance, such as for health insurance (which we do not require).

6. Operators. Many of our franchisees are owner-operators. However, some of our franchisees have contracted with or hired additional operators and may have additional costs relating to the additional operators. While a franchisee's fixed costs and gross revenues should increase with additional operators, the franchisee's variable costs should generally remain the same.

7. Full-Time Operation. There is a wide variation in revenues generated and expenses incurred by our franchisees who operate the Franchised Business on a full- time basis compared to those who operate on a part-time basis.

8. Other Costs. The survey did not ask our franchisees to report costs and expenses associated with corporate or personal income taxes, depreciation, amortization, interest or debt repayment. Each franchisee funds their purchase of the Franchised Business differently and we cannot project how you will account for those items.

THE INFORMATION IN THE ITEM 19 ARE MERELY SURVEY RESULTS FOR OUR EXISTING FRANCHISEES WHO RESPONDED TO A VOLUNTARY SURVEY WE CONDUCTED, AND SHOULD NOT BE CONSTRUED AS THE ACTUAL OR PROBABLE REVENUE OR EXPENSES THAT WILL BE REALIZED BY ANY FRANCHISEE. WE DO NOT REPRESENT THAT ANY FRANCHISEE CAN EXPECT TO ATTAIN SUCH REVENUE OR LIMIT EXPENSES TO THOSE NUMBERS REPORTED.

Other than the preceding financial performance representation, Fibrenew U.S.A. Ltd. does not make any financial performance representations. We also do not authorize our employees or representatives to make any such representations either orally or in writing. If you are purchasing an existing outlet, however, we may provide you with the actual records of that outlet. If you receive any other financial performance information or projections of your future income, you should report it to the franchisor's management by contacting our president, Michael Wilson, Comp 33, Site 16, RR 8, Calgary, Alberta, Canada T2J 2T9, telephone (800) 345-2951, the Federal Trade Commission, and the appropriate state regulatory agencies.

FIESTA AUTO INSURANCE AND TAX SERVICE

16162 Beach Blvd., #100
Huntington Beach, CA 92647
Tel: (877) 905-3437, (714) 842-5420 x1210
Fax: (714) 842-5401
Email: rcampos@fiestainsurance.com
Website: www.fiestafranchise.com
Robert Campos, Director of Franchise Sales

FIESTA INSURANCE FRANCHISE CORPORATION is an authorized franchisor rapidly growing throughout the US. With a FIESTA AUTO INSURANCE & TAX SERVICE franchise, you gain immediate access to many personal lines, insurance programs, and the ability to process every kind of income tax return, as well as offer bank products. Additional revenue from services such as accounting and bookkeeping, travel, money transfers, motor vehicle registrations, and notary public are available in some states. FIESTA INSURANCE FRANCHISE CORPORATION will provide you with the necessary structure and training to run a successful insurance and tax preparation business.

BACKGROUND
IFA Member:	No
Established & First Franchised:	1999; 2007
Franchised Units:	150
Company-Owned Units:	3
Total Units:	153
Distribution:	US – 153; CAN – 0; O'seas – 0
North America:	13 States, 0 Provinces
Density:	50 in CA, 22 in TX, 13 in NY
Projected New Units (12 Months):	150
Qualifications:	4, 4, 1, 3, 3, 5

FINANCIAL/TERMS
Cash Investment:	$25 – $35K
Total Investment:	$35 – $55K
Minimum Net Worth:	N/A
Fees (Franchise):	$10K
Fees (Royalty):	10 – 25%
Fees (Advertising):	0%
Term of Contract (Years):	5/5
Average Number of Employees:	1 FT, 1 PT
Passive Ownership:	Discouraged
Encourage Conversions:	Yes
Area Development Agreements:	Yes
Sub-Franchising Contracts:	No
Expand in Territory:	Yes

Space Needs:	700 – 1,200 SF	Size of Corporate Staff:	25
		On-going Support:	A, B, C, D, E, G, H, I
		Training:	1 Week Huntington Beach, CA
SUPPORT & TRAINING			
Financial Assistance Provided:	Yes (I)		
Site Selection Assistance:	Yes	SPECIFIC EXPANSION PLANS	
Lease Negotiation Assistance:	Yes	US:	All United States
Co-operative Advertising:	Yes	Canada:	No
Franchisee Association/Member:	No	Overseas:	No

The following is actual historical unaudited information we have accumulated for 100% of our current Fiesta franchisees who were operating businesses similar to the franchise offered in this Disclosure Document on a full time basis within the Fiesta Insurance system during the period May 1, 2011 through April 30, 2012.

	FRANCHISED LOCATIONS IN OPERATION FOR 13-24 MONTHS ON APRIL 30, 2012	FRANCHISED LOCATIONS IN OPERATION FOR 25-36 MONTHS ON APRIL 30, 2012	FRANCHISED LOCATIONS IN OPERATION FOR 37-48 MONTHS ON APRIL 30, 2012	FRANCHISED LOCATIONS IN OPERATION FOR 49-60 MONTHS ON APRIL 30, 2012	FRANCHISED LOCATIONS IN OPERATION FOR 61-72 MONTHS ON APRIL 30, 2012
Average Gross Revenue**	$84,337.34	$198,676.09	$233,975.71	$367,707.77	$654,502.99
Number of Franchised Businesses Included in Calculation of Average Gross Revenue	22	14	7	1	3

** "Average Gross Revenue" means the Gross Revenue in each twelve month period divided by the total number of Franchised Businesses in operation for the stated periods.

THIS TABLE DOES NOT INCLUDE ANY EXPENSES RELATED TO THE OPERATION OF A FRANCHISED BUSINESS. THE EXPENSES RELATED TO THE OPERATION OF A FRANCHISED BUSINESS WILL AFFECT THE PROFITABILITY OF A FRANCHISED BUSINESS. YOU SHOULD CONSIDER THEM AND EVALUATE THEIR IMPACT. THE ACTUAL PERFORMANCE OF YOUR FRANCHISED BUSINESS WILL DEPEND ON A NUMBER OF FACTORS SPECIFIC TO YOU, INCLUDING THE EXPENSES RELATED TO THE OPERATION OF A FRANCHISED BUSINESS.

Before signing any documents or making any investment, you must make your own independent investigation regarding the purchase of a franchise including independent market and industry reviews and comparisons and talking to current and former franchisees. You must consult with your own independent advisors, such as attorneys and accountants, to assist in determining the suitability of this investment for you.

Other than the preceding financial performance representation, we do not make any financial representations about a franchisee's future financial performance or the past financial performance of company-owned or franchised outlets. We also do not authorize our employees or representatives to make any such representations either orally or in writing. If you are purchasing an existing outlet, however, we may provide you with the actual records of that outlet. If you receive any other financial performance information or projections of your future income, you should report it to the franchisor's management by contacting John Rost, President and Chief Executive Officer, 16162 Beach Boulevard, Suite 100, Huntington Beach, California 92647; (714) 842-5420, the Federal Trade Commission, and the appropriate state regulatory agencies.

YOUR REVENUES MAY DIFFER SUBSTANTIALLY FROM THE DATA PRESENTED IN THE TABLE ABOVE DUE TO A VARIETY OF FACTORS, SUCH AS REGIONAL MARKET VARIATIONS, SEASONALITY, COMPETITION, THE DEMOGRAPHICS OF AN AREA, LIFESTYLES OF CUSTOMERS IN THE MARKET AREA, LOCATION OF YOUR FRANCHISED BUSINESS AND OTHER MARKET CHARACTERISTICS AS WELL AS YOUR BUSINESS ABILITIES AND EFFORTS. YOU SHOULD CONSULT OTHER SOURCES, YOUR FINANCIAL ADVISORS, AND FRANCHISEES OF EXISTING FRANCHISED BUSINESSES IN ORDER TO COMPARE REVENUE AND EXPENSES AND TO OBTAIN ADDITIONAL INFORMATION NECESSARY TO DEVELOP ESTIMATES OF REVENUE AND EXPENSES OF A FRANCHISED BUSINESS. YOUR INDIVIDUAL RESULTS MAY

DIFFER. THERE IS NO ASSURANCE THAT YOU WILL OB-TAIN THE SAME RESULTS.

EXCEPT AS OTHERWISE PROVIDED IN THIS ITEM 19, THE PRESENTATION OF INFORMATION REGARDING THE REVENUE AND EXPENSES OF A FRANCHISED BUSINESS IN CONNECTION WITH THIS FRANCHISE OFFERING IS AB-SOLUTELY PROHIBITED. Any representations to the contrary and any projections or predictions, written or oral, direct or indirect, as to the amount of attainment of any potential sales, costs, and expenses, profits or earnings which may arise from the operation of a Franchised business, if given or made, MUST NOT BE RELIED UPON as having been authorized by us for use in connection with the sale of this franchise. Written substantiation of the data used in preparing this financial performance representation will be available to you on reasonable request.

FIRSTLIGHT HOMECARE

9435 Waterstone Blvd., #190
Cincinnati, OH 45249
Tel: (877) 570-0002, (513) 766-8402
Fax: (513) 830-5003
Email: bmcpherson@firstlighthomecare.com
Website: www.firstlighthomecare.com
Bill McPherson, Executive Director of Franchise Development

FIRSTLIGHT HOMECARE offers comprehensive, in-home, non-medical, and personal care services to seniors, new mothers, adults with disabilities, and others needing assistance. Based in Cincinnati, OH, FIRSTLIGHT's founders bring more than 130 years of franchising experience and over 82 years of health-care and senior services experience, creating the core of FIRSTLIGHT's foundation. FIRSTLIGHT franchisees are passionate and caring, and strive to provide exceptional service. FIRSTLIGHT creates both a personal avenue to help others as well as a professional opportunity for strong growth potential with corporate support to build a rewarding career path. If you want to make a difference in people's lives while building a powerful business, this is the opportunity for you. Owning a FIRSTLIGHT franchise offers the benefits of traditional business ownership with less risk and provides an established business system along with other advantages. Business owners in the home healthcare industry have bright futures. The demand for services in the senior care industry continues to increase each year. In 2011, more than 8,000 people will turn 65 every day and, by the end of that year, the senior population in America will reach nearly 49 million. By 2025, it will grow to nearly 72 million. (Source: The Department of Health and Human Services and the State Department). FIRSTLIGHT's value-driven approach touches every aspect of the business, including groundbreaking, industry-leading tools for clients and their families. If you are interested in providing exceptional care and making a difference in the lives of others while establishing a rewarding career, we want to hear from you. Please contact FIRSTLIGHT HOMECARE today!

BACKGROUND:
IFA Member:	Yes
Established & First Franchised:	2009; 2010
Franchised Units:	106
Company-Owned Units:	0
Total Units:	106
Dist.:	US-106; CAN-0; O'seas-0
North America:	25 States
Density:	11 in OH, 3 in FL, 3 in GA
Projected New Units (12 Months):	40
Qualifications:	5, 5, 1, 3, 4, 5

FINANCIAL/TERMS:
Cash Investment:	$50K
Total Investment:	$71.6 – $99.8K
Minimum Net Worth:	$150K
Fees (Franchise):	$33.5K
Fees (Royalty):	5%
Fees (Advertising):	0%
Term of Contract (Years):	10/10
Avg. # of Employees:	2 FT, 6-50+ PT
Passive Ownership:	Discouraged
Encourage Conversions:	Yes
Area Develop. Agreements:	Yes
Sub-Franchising Contracts:	No
Expand in Territory:	Yes
Space Needs:	N/A

177

SUPPORT & TRAINING:	On-going Support: C,D,E,H,I
Financial Assistance Provided: Yes (I)	Training: 1 Week and Ongoing Cincinnati, OH
Site Selection Assistance: No	
Lease Negotiation Assistance: N/A	SPECIFIC EXPANSION PLANS:
Co-operative Advertising: Yes	US: All United States
Franchisee Assoc./Member: Yes	Canada: Yes
Size of Corporate Staff: 10	Overseas: No

The table below describes the "net revenue" of 11 franchised FirstLight HomeCare businesses (the "Item 19 Businesses"), as reported to us by the businesses, for the 12-month period ended February 1, 2012 (the "Reporting Period"). There were a total of 31 FirstLight HomeCare businesses in operation as of December 31, 2011. The Item 19 Businesses consist of all franchised FirstLight HomeCare businesses that were in operation during the entire Reporting Period. We have not audited the figures below, although we believe them to be reliable.

For purposes of the table below, "net revenue" means that revenue on which a franchisee pays royalty fees, which is referred to as "gross revenue" in the Franchise Agreement. This is the total amount of money the franchisee and its' owners receive for all goods and services rendered in connection with the Marks, and all other income of any kind derived directly or indirectly in connection with the operation of Item 19 Business.

# Months Operating (1)	Average Net Revenue (2)	Median Net Revenue (3)	Highest Net Revenue (4)	Lowest Net Revenue (5)
12 to 16	$205,830	$257,095	$387,888	$24,413

(1) The Item 19 Businesses began operation as FirstLight HomeCare businesses between August 2010 and February 2011.

(2) 6 Item 19 Businesses (or 55%) reported net revenue equal to or in excess of this amount.

(3) 6 Item 19 Businesses (or 55%) reported net revenue equal to or in excess of this amount.

(4) 1 Item 19 Business (or 9 %) reported net revenue equal to or in excess of this amount.

(5) 11 Item 19 Businesses (or 100 %) reported net revenue equal to or in excess of this amount.

NOT ALL FRANCHISED FIRSTLIGHT HOMECARE BUIS-NESSES ACHIEVED THE ABOVE RESULTS. THERE IS NO ASSURANCE THAT YOU WILL DO AS WELL. IF YOU RELY UPON OUR FIGURES, YOU MUST ACCEPT THE RISK OF NOT DOING AS WELL.

Written substantiation of the above figures will be made available to you on reasonable request.

Except as described above, we do not make any representations about a franchisee's future financial performance or the past financial performance of company-owned or franchised outlets. We also do not authorize our employees or representatives to make any such representations either orally or in writing. If you are purchasing an existing outlet, however, we may provide you with the actual records of that outlet. If you receive any other financial performance information or projections of your future income, you should report it to the franchisor's management by contacting Jeff Bevis, President & CEO, FirstLight HomeCare Franchising, LLC, One Waterstone Place, 9435 Waterstone Boulevard, Suite 190, Cincinnati, Ohio 45249.

GRANITE TRANSFORMATIONS

10306 USA Today Way
Miramar, FL 33025
Tel: (800) 685-5300, (954) 435-5538
Fax: (954) 435-5579
Email: markj@granitetransformations.com
Website: www.granitetransformations.com
Mark Johnson, Chief Executive Officer

GRANITE TRANSFORMATIONS is a franchise organization that provides an important and compelling service to homeowners, allowing them to transform kitchen and baths with our gorgeous trend stone, trend glass, and trend mosaic surfaces. Trend Stone is engineered to outperform ordinary granite. It is heat, scratch, and stain resistant, and it is the only surface engineered to fit right over existing countertop surfaces. That means no costly demolition, no mess, and fast and easy installation, usually in about a day!

BACKGROUND

IFA Member:	Yes
Established & First Franchised:	2001; 2001
Franchised Units:	160
Company-Owned Units:	3
Total Units:	163
Distribution:	US – 67; CAN – 15; O'seas – 80
North America:	32 States, 3 Provinces
Density:	11 in CA, 7 in ON, 6 in FL
Projected New Units (12 Months):	12
Qualifications:	4, 5, 2, 2, 4, 5

FINANCIAL/TERMS

Cash Investment:	$50 – $100K
Total Investment:	$141.5 – $346K
Minimum Net Worth:	$100K
Fees (Franchise):	$35 – $75K
Fees (Royalty):	2%
Fees (Advertising):	1%
Term of Contract (Years):	10/10
Average Number of Employees:	7 FT, 2 PT
Passive Ownership:	Not Allowed
Encourage Conversions:	N/A
Area Development Agreements:	No
Sub-Franchising Contracts:	No
Expand in Territory:	No
Space Needs:	N/A

SUPPORT & TRAINING

Financial Assistance Provided:	No
Site Selection Assistance:	Yes
Lease Negotiation Assistance:	No
Co-operative Advertising:	No
Franchisee Association/Member:	No
Size of Corporate Staff:	25
On-going Support:	C, D, E, F, G, h, I
Training:	5 Days at Corporate Office; 10 Days On-Site

SPECIFIC EXPANSION PLANS

US:	All United States
Canada:	All Canada
Overseas:	UK

This Item sets forth certain historical data provided by our franchised Businesses which are substantially similar to those being offered through this Franchise Disclosure Document that (a) were in operation as of December 31, 2011 and (b) which have fully reported their Gross Sales to us.

We have not audited this information, nor independently verified this information. The information is for the period January 1, 2011 through December 31, 2011 (the "2011 Fiscal Year"). Written substantiation of the data used in preparing this information will be made available upon reasonable request.

Importantly, the success of your franchise will depend largely upon your individual abilities and your market, and the financial results of your franchise are likely to differ, perhaps materially, from the results summarized in this item.

You should not use this information as an indication of how well your franchise will do. A number of factors will affect the success of your franchise. These factors include the current market conditions, the type of market in your franchise area, the location of your franchise area, the competition and your ability to operate the franchise.

Gross Sales: January 1, 2011 through December 31, 2011

The follow tables presents the Gross Sales as reported to us by 70 U.S. franchisees that were open and operating as of December 31, 2011 and for whom we have complete sales data (the "Reporting Businesses"). Excluded from this Item 19 are 11 Businesses located in Canada, as well as 4 Businesses located in the United States that report gross sales to us.

Table 1 profiles the one Reporting Business that only offered granite resurfacing products and services during the 2011 Fiscal Year. Table 2 profiles the 6 Reporting Businesses that offered Door and Cabinet refacing products and services along with granite resurfacing products and services during the 2011 Fiscal Year. Table 3 profiles.the 2 Reporting Businesses that offered tile and mosaic products and services, along with granite refadng products and services during the 2011 Fiscal Year. Table 4 profiles the 21 Reporting Businesses that offered granite resurfacing products and services, door and cabinet refacing products and services, and tile and mosaic products and services during the 2011 Fiscal Year. Table 5 profiles the 40 Reporting Businesses that offered granite resurfacing products and services, door and cabinet refacing products and services, tile and mosaic products and services and acrylic bath and shower insert services during the 2011 Fiscal Year.

Table 1
Granite Resurfacing Services

The information listed below sets forth the Gross Sales of the one Reporting Business that only offered granite resurfacing products and services during the 2011 Fiscal Year. The Reporting Business represented in Table 1 did not participate in the Door and Cabinet Re-facing Program, the Tile and Mosaic Program or the Acrylic Bath and Shower Insert Program.

Gross Sales	$634,334.00

Table 2
Granite Resurfacing and Door and Cabinet Re-facing Program

The information listed below sets forth the Gross Sales of the 6 Reporting Businesses which, in addition to offering granite resurfacing products and services, also participated in our Door and Cabinet Re-facing Program during the 2011 Fiscal Year. The Reporting Businesses represented in Table 2 did not participate in our Tile and Mosaic Program or the Acrylic Bath and Shower Insert Program.

Average Gross Sales	$943,496.26
Number of Businesses Above/Below Average	3/3
Percentage of Businesses the Met or Exceeded Average	50%
Median	916,758.78

Number of Businesses Above/Below Median	3/3
High	$1,762,542.00
Low	$270,890.00

Table 3
Granite Resurfacing and Tile and Mosaic Program

The information listed below sets forth the Gross Sales of the 2 Reporting Businesses which, in addition to offering granite resurfacing products and services, also participated in our Tile and Mosaic Program during the 2011 Fiscal Year. The Reporting Businesses represented in Table 3 did not participate in our Door and Cabinet Refacing Program or the Acrylic Bath and Shower Insert Program.

Gross Sales- Reporting Business One	$880,292.00
Gross Sales - Reporting Business Two	$270,890.00

Table 4
Granite Resurfacing, Door and Cabinet Re-facing Program and Tile and Mosaic Program .

The information listed below sets forth the Gross Sales of the 21 Reporting Businesses which, in addition to offering granite resurfacing products and services, also participated in our Door and Cabinet Refacing Program and our Tile and Mosaic Program during the 2011 Fiscal Year. The Reporting Businesses represented in Table 4 did not participate in the Acrylic Bath and Shower Insert Program.

Average Gross Sales	$914,807.90
Number of Businesses Above/Below Average	11110
Percentage of Businesses the Met or Exceeded Average	52%
Median	$943,089.00
Number of Businesses Above/Below Median	10/11
High	$1,749,639.00
Low	137,258.00

Table 5
Granite Resurfacing. Door and Cabinet Re-facing Program. Tile and Mosaic Program and Acrylic Bath and Shower Insert Program

The information listed below sets forth the Gross Sales of the

40 Reporting Businesses which, in addition to offering granite resurfacing products and services, also participated in our Door and Cabinet Refacing Program, our Tile and Mosaic Program, and our Acrylic Bath and Shower Insert Program in during the 2011 Fiscal Year.

Average Gross Sales	$1,727,947.83
Number of Businesses Above/Below Average	14/26
Percentage of Businesses the Met or Exceeded Average	35%
Median	$1,527,426.00
Number of Businesses Above/Below Median	26/14.
High	4;817,222.75
Low	364,025.00

Notes:

1. Gross Sales is defined as all sums or things of value received by a Reporting Businesses as a result of the sale of services, goods and products whether for cash, check, credit, barter or otherwise without reserve for deduction for inability or failure to collect. Gross Sales do not include refunds to customers or the amount of any sales taxes or any similar taxes collected from customers to be paid to any federal or local taxing authority.

2. The average was determined by dividing the sum of the Reporting Businesses' Gross Sales by the number of Reporting Businesses included in each table.

3. The median is the number in which an equal number of Reporting Businesses' Gross Sales fall above and below.

4. The high number represents the highest Gross Sales achieved by a Reporting Business during the 2011 Fiscal Year and the low number represents the lowest Gross Sales achieved by a Reporting Business during the 2011 Fiscal Year.

5. All currency is in U.S. dollars.

General Notes to Item 19:

1. Your results may vary upon the location of your Business. This analysis does not contain information concerning operating osts or expenses. There may be costs and other expenses not identified above. Operating costs and expenses may vary substantially from Business to Business, as well as the actual accounting and operational methods employed by a Business, may significantly impact profits realized in any particular operation:

2. The above figures exclude royalties, advertising and marketing fees and costs, inventory costs, administrative payroll, payroll taxes, owner compensation/salary, healthcare, employee benefits, uniforms, office supplies, postage, travel and entertainment expenses, utilities and telephone charges, late fees, training costs and expenses and other fees and expenses which you may incur as a franchisee.

3. The above figures exclude tax liabilities that you will be responsible for.

4. The above figures exclude professional fees or other administrative expenses that you may incur, including legal and accounting fees.

5. The above figures exclude finance charges and depreciation. Interest expense, interest income, depreciation, amortization and other income or expenses will vary substantially from Business to Business, depending on the amount and kind of financing you obtain to establish your Business. You should consult with your tax advisor regarding depreciation and amortization schedules and the period over which assets of your Business may be amortized or depreciated, as well as the effect, if any, of any recent or proposed tax legislation.

6. Some Businesses have earned this amount. Your individual results may differ. There is no assurance that you will earn as much. In particular, the revenues listed above will be directly affected by many factors, such as: (a) geographic location; (b) competition from other similar businesses in your area; (c) advertising effectiveness based on market saturation; (d) your product and service pricing; (e) vendor prices on materials, supplies and inventory; (f) labor costs; (g) health and other fringe benefits you provide; (h) ability to generate customers; (i) customer loyalty; and G) employment conditions in the market. Because of these factors, results vary from business to business. Therefore, we recommend that you make your own independent investigation to determine whether or not the franchise may be profitable to you. You should use the above information only as a reference in conducting your analysis and preparing your own projected income statements and cash flow statements. We strongly suggest that you consult with your financial advisor or personnel accountant concerning financial projections and federal, state and local income taxes and any other applicable taxes that you may incur in operating a franchised business.

7. Other than the preceding financial performance representation, Rocksolid Granit (USA), Inc. does not make any financial performance representations. We also do not authorize our employees or representatives to make any such either orally or in writing. If you are purchasing an existing outlet, however, we may provide you with the actual records of that outlet. If you receive any other financial performance informa-

tion or projections of your future income, you should report it to the franchisor's management by contacting Mark Johnson, our Chief Executive Officer and Senior Vice President, Rock-solid Granit (USA) Inc., 10306 USA Today Way, Miramar, FL 33025, (954) 435-5538, the Federal Trade Commission, and the appropriate state regulatory agencies.

GRISWOLD HOME CARE

717 Bethlehem Pk., # 300
Erdenheim, PA 19038
Tel: (888) 777-7630 x2, (215) 402-0200 x116
Fax: (215) 402-0202
Email: tom@griswoldhomecare.com
Website: www.griswoldhomecare.com
Tom Monaghan, President

GRISWOLD HOME CARE is dedicated to providing "Extraordinary Home Care at Affordable Rates." We refer caregivers for older adults, people recovering from illness or surgery, and people with long-term disabilities. Caregiver services include personal care, homemaking, companionship, incidental transportation, and other services to clients wishing to remain safe and independent. We operate a model that is completely unique in the industry. We also offer the largest protected territories and lowest on-going fees.

BACKGROUND
IFA Member:	Yes
Established & First Franchised:	1982; 1984
Franchised Units:	237
Company-Owned Units:	9
Total Units:	177
Distribution:	US – 246; CAN – 0; O'seas – 0
North America:	32 States, 0 Provinces
Density:	22 in PA, 19 in NJ, 15 in CA

Projected New Units (12 Months):	56
Qualifications:	5, 4, 2, 3, 4, 5

FINANCIAL/TERMS
Cash Investment:	$75K
Total Investment:	$94 – $116K
Minimum Net Worth:	$275K
Fees (Franchise):	$45K
Fees (Royalty):	3.5%
Fees (Advertising):	$200 gross billings/month** NTE
Term of Contract (Years):	10/5
Average Number of Employees:	3 – 5 FT (in office) FT
Passive Ownership:	Allowed
Encourage Conversions:	No
Area Development Agreements:	No
Sub-Franchising Contracts:	No
Expand in Territory:	Yes
Space Needs:	Minimum 150 SF

SUPPORT & TRAINING
Financial Assistance Provided:	No
Site Selection Assistance:	Yes
Lease Negotiation Assistance:	N/A
Co-operative Advertising:	Yes
Franchisee Association/Member:	No
Size of Corporate Staff:	30
On-going Support:	C, D, G, H, I
Training:	10 Days Corporate Office; 1 – 2 Days On-Site

SPECIFIC EXPANSION PLANS
US:	Yes
Canada:	Yes
Overseas:	No

Background

This Item sets forth certain historical data relating to Office Fees provided by our franchisees and company-owned outlets. The outlets included in this Item operate businesses substantially similar to the business being offered in this Disclosure Document. Except as otherwise stated in this Item 19, each outlet included in this Item 19 operates in a single territory. Some of the outlets included in this Item 19 operate in territories that are larger or smaller than the territory you will be granted under the Franchise Agreement. "Office Fees" are payments made by franchises or company-owned offices to GHC for Services performed for Clients, net of Caregiver wages.

Written substantiation of the data used in preparing this information will be made available upon reasonable request. We have not audited this information, nor independently verified this information.

Importantly, the success of your franchise will depend largely upon your individual abilities and your market, and the financial results of your franchise are likely to differ, perhaps materially, from the results summarized in this item.

You should not use this information as an indication of how well your franchise will do. A number of factors will affect the success of your franchise. These factors include the current market conditions, the type of market in your franchise area, the location of your franchise area, the competition and your ability to operate the franchise.

Top Performing Units Office Fees Earned

Table A below sets forth the Office Fees earned by our franchisee and company-owned outlets for the twelve month period January through December for each of the last three calendar years as well as the average total office fees generated by our top 25% performing offices as of December 31, 2011 including franchisee and company-owned outlets that had been in operation for more than twelve months.

TABLE A
Office Fees
Calendar Years 2009, 2010 and 2011

	Highest	Average of Top 25%	System-wide Average
Jan - Dec 2011 - OFFICE FEES	$1,643,611	$806,887	$352,453
# of outlets	1	30	112
Jan - Dec 2010 - OFFICE FEES	$1,487,536	$799,782	$357,051
# of outlets	1	24	97
Jan - Dec 2009 - OFFICE FEES	$1,282,428	$795,832	$363,932
# of outlets	1	23	90

Notes:

1. "Office Fees" are payments presented by franchises or company-owned offices to GHC for Services performed for Clients, net of Caregiver wages. The averages were determined by totaling each Outlet's (individual territory) annual Office Fees for each calendar year and dividing by the number of offices in each subset presented.

2. The Top 25% results presented in Table A include three company-owned outlets. For each calendar year presented, the highest Office Fee was achieved by a franchised outlet.

3. In 2011, 50% of the Top 25% outlets met or exceeded the Average Office Fees for the group and 38% of all offices met or exceeded the system wide Average Office Fees. In 2010, 41% of Top 25% outlets met or exceeded the Average Office Fees for the group and 33% of all offices met or exceeded the system-wide Average Office Fees. In 2009, 44% of Top 25% met or exceeded the Average Office Fees for the group and 33% of all offices met or exceeded the system-wide Average Office Fees.

4. All of the outlets profiled in Table A conducted business under the "Griswold Special Care" trademark.

Financial Performance for Company Owned Outlets

Table B below sets forth the Gross Revenue and certain costs and expenses for calendar year 2011 for our company owned units.

TABLE B
Financial Performance for Company Owned Outlets
January 1, 2011 through December 31, 2011

CH Office	Jan	Feb	Mar	Apr	May	Jun	Jul	Aug	Sep	Oct	Nov	Dec	Year to Date	% of Revenue
Office Fees	$79,411	$89,843	$97,637	$83,371	$90,970	$72,846	$96,210	$75,840	$104,020	$85,399	$82,414	$78,064	$1,036,025	100%
Operating Expenses														
Payroll	$26,983	$25,621	$24,216	$20,769	$20,485	$20,457	$20,468	$21,073	$20,411	$21,505	$18,666	$14,507	$255,160	25%
Insurance	$3,390	$2,416	$2,022	$4,010	$3,378	$3,034	$2,263	$1,995	$2,524	$1,533	$2,098	$3,168	$31,830	3%
Occupancy	$4,278	$4,003	$4,526	$4,699	$4,072	$4,215	$4,030	$4,095	$5,786	$4,073	$3,782	$4,340	$51,897	5%
Marketing & Other	$6,228	$3,122	$2,708	$4,104	$2,420	$2,003	$2,579	$2,075	$1,508	$2,378	$1,801	$2,867	$33,793	3%
Total Operating Expenses	$40,879	$35,162	$33,472	$33,582	$30,355	$29,709	$29,339	$29,238	$30,228	$29,488	$26,347	$24,882	$372,681	36%
Net Income	$38,532	$54,681	$64,165	$49,789	$60,615	$43,137	$66,871	$46,602	$73,793	$55,911	$56,068	$53,182	$663,344	64%
Gross Profit Margin	49%	61%	66%	60%	67%	59%	70%	61%	71%	65%	68%	68%	64%	
Total Client Count														127

LV Office	Jan	Feb	Mar	Apr	May	Jun	Jul	Aug	Sep	Oct	Nov	Dec	Year to Date	% of Revenue
Office Fees	$71,899	$65,122	$56,087	$59,322	$48,922	$80,768	$62,801	$87,053	$82,003	$69,892	$91,392	$74,958	$850,219	100%
Operating Expenses														
Payroll	$15,988	$22,398	$18,402	$19,506	$14,481	$20,895	$17,205	$22,859	$22,795	$20,957	$16,512	$21,260	$233,257	27%
Insurance	$1,215	$2,345	$2,388	$1,780	$1,805	$959	$199	$199	$199	$926	$1,05	$2,026	$15,078	2%
Occupancy	$1,152	$1,152	$1,152	$1,152	$1,152	$1,152	$1,152	$1,152	$1,152	$1,152	$1,152	$1,152	$13,824	2%
Marketing & Other	$2,923	$30,095	$25,557	$25,537	$20,419	$26,440	$22,353	$29,261	$27,841	$26,401	$21,514	$28,056	$304,753	36%
Net Income	$50,620	$35,027	$30,531	$33,785	$28,503	$54,328	$40,448	$57,792	$54,162	$43,490	$69,879	$46,902	$545,466	64%
Gross Profit Margine	70%	54%	54%	57%	58%	67%	64%	66%	66%	62%	76%	63%	64%	
Client Count														118

B&H Offices	Jan	Feb	Mar	Apr	May	Jun	Jul	Aug	Sep	Oct	Nov	Dec	Year to Date	% of Revenue
Office Fees	$35,475	$50,872	$38,681	$41,490	$39,540	$40,952	$46,546	$53,260	$45,384	$45,197	$57,545	$63,899	$558,842	100%
Ooperating Expenses														
Payroll	$15,256	$16,423	$19,234	$12,394	$14,367	$18,674	$18,355	$15,605	$15,412	$13,532	$12,442	$12,439	$184,131	33%
Insurance	$4,941	$4,941	$4,915	$5,108	$$3,926	$6,197	$4,433	$4,340	$4,316	$17,327	$5,016	$5,073	$70,532	13%
Occupancy	$1,565	$1,699	$1,477	$1,633	$1,597	$1,676	$1,497	$1,681	$1,691	$1,595	$1,476	$1,522	$19,109	3%
Marketing & Other	$1,773	$2,959	$1,144	$1,747	$2,500	$2,870	$2,640	$2,825	$2,585	$1,736	$1,433	$2,316	$26,528	5%
Total Operating Expenses	$23,534	$26,021	$26,769	$20,881	$22,389	$29,418	$26,925	$24,451	$24,004	$34,190	$20,367	$21,350	$300,300	54%
Net Income	$11,941	$24,852	$11,912	$20,608	$17,150	$11,535	$19,621	$28,809	$21,380	$11,007	$37,178	$42,549	$258,542	46%

ML Office	Jan	Feb	Mar	Apr	May	Jun	Jul	Aug	Sep	Oct	Nov	Dec	Year to Date	% of Revenue
Gross Profit Margin	34%	49%	31%	50%	43%	28%	42%	54%	47%	24%	65%	67%	46%	
Client Count													77	
Office Fees	$44,343	$45,313	$54,256	$52,665	$50,404	$55,332	$55,589	$62,552	$60,511	$62,596	$74,010	$69,004	$686,575	100%
Operating Expenses														
Payroll	$17,750	$16,136	$16,405	$16,057	$14,423	$14,404	$14,745	$14,734	$14,469	$14,525	$14,441	14,447	$182,537	27%
Insurance	$1,835	$2,004	$1,927	$2,068	$2,694	$1,141	$1,267	$1,140	$1,140	$1,152	$1,127	$1,819	$19,315	3%
Occupancy	$1,801	$1,847	$1,793	$1,897	$1,780	$1,846	$5,464	$1,921	$1,866	$1,825	$1,825	$1,670	$25,533	4%
Marketing & Other	$1,954	$1,408	$2,389	$1,597	$1,907	$1,619	$2,865	$2,204	$2,409	$1,833	$2,697	$2,579	$25,463	4%
Total Operating Expenses	$23,341	$21,395	$22,514	$21,621	$20,804	$19,010	$24,341	$19,998	$19,884	$19,335	$20,090	$20,516	$252,848	37%
Net Income	$21,002	$23,918	$31,743	$31,044	$29,600	$36,322	$31,248	$42,554	$40,627	$43,260	$53,920	$48,489	$433,727	63%

LVNE Office	Jan	Feb	Mar	Apr	May	Jun	Jul	Aug	Sep	Oct	Nov	Dec	Year to Date	% of Revenue
Gross Profit Margin	47%	53%	59%	59%	59%	66%	56%	68%	67%	69%	73%	70%	63%	
Client Count													95	
Office Fees	$34,164	$27,377	$32,522	$33,759	$34,111	$30,718	$36,826	$41,011	$44,590	$42,598	$45,967	$41,358	$445,002	100%
Operating Expenses														
Payroll	$10,408	$8,140	$6,787	$6,992	$7,720	$1,661	$4,783	$2,093	$2,348	$2,201	$6,621	$2,297	$62,053	14%
Insurance	$1,081	$1,081	$633	$148	$630	$722	$671	$208	$689	$208	$180	$435	$6,687	2%
Occupancy	$1,005	$1,031	$1,004	$876	$912	$799	$941	$934	$880	$849	$817	$843	$10,890	2%
Marketing & Other	$747	$1,257	$1,297	$1,309	$1,326	$1,125	$1,324	$1,122	$1,216	$1,010	$1,828	$1,122	$14,68	3%
Total Operating Expenses	$13,241	$11,509	$9,721	$9,326	$10,588	$4,308	$7,720	$4,356	$5,133	$4,267	$9,446	$4,697	$94,313	21%
Net Income	$20,923	$15,868	$22,802	$24,433	$23,523	$26,410	$29,107	$36,655	$39,456	$38,331	$36,521	$36,661	$350,688	79%

DC Office	Jan	Feb	Mar	Apr	May	Jun	Jul	Aug	Sep	Oct	Nov	Dec	Year to Date	% of Revenue
Gross Profit Margin	61%	58%	70%	72%	69%	86%	79%	89%	88%	90%	79%	89%	79%	
Client Count													59	
Office Fees	$26,985	$35,174	$33,655	$37,542	$29,579	$26,113	$31,535	$24,173	$23,519	$26,831	$34,111	$28,775	$357,993	100%
Operating Expenses														
Payroll	$9,560	$8,884	$10,266	$11,686	$13,155	$12,673	$12,623	$12,620	$12,620	$10,477	$8,581	$8,588	$131,734	37%
Insurance	$1,602	$1,672	$1,755	$504	$1,172	$1,042	$1,128	$2,222	$2,248	$1,491	$839	$1,049	$16,725	5%
Occupancy	$1,490	$1,479	$1,304	$1,534	$1,468	$1,481	$1,560	$1,486	$1,419	$1,471	$2,323	$1,430	$18,445	5%
Marketing & Other	$983	$1,397	$876	$1,496	$989	$1,684	$1,573	$1,602	$1,327	$1,130	$1,678	$5,943	$20,562	6%
Total Operating Expenses	$13,635	$13,433	$14,201	$15,194	$16,783	$16,880	$16,885	$17,931	$17,615	$14,569	$13,420	$17,009	$187,555	52%

	Jan	Feb	Mar	Apr	May	Jun	Jul	Aug	Sep	Oct	Nov	Dec	Year to Date	% of Revenue
Net Income	$13,350	$21,741	$19,454	$22,348	$12,796	$9,233	$14,650	$6,242	$5,905	$12,262	$20,690	$11,766	$170,438	48%
Gross Profit Margin	49%	62%	64%	58%	52%	63%	51%	67%	59%	57%	59%	51%	58%	
Client Count													43	
WB Office	Jan	Feb	Mar	Apr	May	Jun	Jul	Aug	Sep	Oct	Nov	Dec	Year to Date	% of Revenue
Office Fees	$27,952	$27,369	$28,029	$28,943	$24,969	$25,593	$24,667	$37,393	$33,070	$30,346	$32,500	$26,020	$346,850	100%
Operating Expenses														
Payroll	$9,799	$7,874	$7,885	$9,468	$9,088	$7,536	$9,223	$9,172	$9,224	$8,788	$9,350	$8,761	$106,167	31%
Insurance	$733	$733	$733	$733	$733	$68	$672	$651	$651	$651	$651	$651	$8,,440	2%
Occupancy	$1,395	$1,404	$1,407	$1,353	$1,384	$1,289	$1,372	$1,425	$1,426	$1,379	$1,354	$1,373	$16,560	5%
Marketing & Other	$1,007	$448	$203	$503	$851	$26	$759	$1,269	$2,128	$2,104	$2,100	$1,839	$13,237	4%
Total Operating Expenses	$12,934	$10,460	$10,228	$12,057	$12,056	$9,498	$12,026	$12,517	$13,429	$12,922	$13,454	$12,824	$144,404	42%
Net Income	$15,018	$16,910	$17,801	$16,886	$12,913	$16,095	$12,641	$24,876	$19,642	$17,424	$19,046	$13,196	$202,446	58%
Gross Profit Margin	54%	62%	64%	58%	52%	63%	51%	67%	59%	57%	59%	51%	58%	
Client Count													43	
BB Office	Jan	Feb	Mar	Apr	May	Jun	Jul	Aug	Sep	Oct	Nov	Dec	Year to Date	% of Revenue
Office Fees	$24,205	$24,800	$25,177	$24,492	$19,219	$23,030	$22,582	$25,356	$29,505	$23,482	$30,409	$20,942	$293,200	100%
Operating Expenses														
Payroll	$8,810	$8,653	$8,672	$10,596	$10,561	$9,974	$9,976	$8,621	$9,646	$9,779	$10,112	$10,272	$115,673	39%
Insurance	$1,110	$1,110	$1,083	$1,283	$1,287	$1,932	$1,019	$373	$456	$940	$994	$1,348	$12,936	4%
Occupancy	$1,401	$1,465	$1,384	$1,339	$1,348	$1,042	$1,562	$1,451	$1,427	$1,368	$1,267	$1,297	$16,701	6%
Marketing & Other	$998	$510	$1,026	$1,398	$1,042	$1,601	$2,064	$2,700	$1,295	$2,374	$1,986	$1,227	$18,221	6%
Total Operating Expenses	$12,319	$11,739	$12,165	$14,616	$1,238	$14,910	$14,622	$13,145	$12,824	$14,462	$14,349	$14,143	$163,531	56%
Net Income	$11,886	$13,062	$13,011	$9,876	$4,981	$8,121	$7,960	$12,212	$16,681	$9,020	$16,060	$6,799	$129,669	44%
Gross Profit Margin	49%	53%	52%	40%	26%	35%	35%	48%	57%	38%	53%	32%	44%	
Client Count													46	
9 Territories Consolidated	Jan	Feb	Mar	Apr	May	Jun	Jul	Aug	Sep	Oct	Nov	Dec	Year to Date	% of Revenue
Office Fees	$344,433	$365,871	$366,045	$361,583	$337,713	$355,353	$376,758	$406,638	$422,603	$386,340	$448,348	$403,020	$4,574,705	100%
Operating Expenses														
Payroll	$114,554	$114,128	$111,867	$107,68	$104,282	$106,275	$107,379	$106,776	$106,925	$101,763	$96,724	$92,570	$1,270,710	28%
Insurance	$15,907	$16,303	$15,456	$15,635	$15,625	$15,676	$11,653	$11,127	$12,223	$24,228	$11,941	$15,770	$181,543	4%
Occupancy	$14,086	$14,079	$14,046	$14,484	$13,710	$13,860	$17,578	$14,145	$15,646	$13,711	$13,985	$13,627	$172,959	4%
Marketing & Other	$16,161	$15,302	$13,258	$15,227	$14,015	$14,362	$17,601	$18,849	$16,164	$15,932	$16,338	$21,512	$195,173	4%

Total Operating Expenses	$161,161	$159,813	$154,626	$152,814	$147,632	$150,173	$154,212	$150,896	$150,957	$155,634	$138,987	$143,478	$1,820,384	40%
Net Income	$183,273	$206,059	$211,418	$208,769	$190,081	$205,180	$222,546	$255,741	$271,646	$230,706	$309,361	$259,542	$2,754,321	60%
Gross Profit Margin	53%	56%	58%	58%	56%	58%	59%	63%	64%	60%	69%	64%	60%	
Total Client Count													616	

9 Territories Consolidated	Office Fees	Payroll	Insurance	Occupancy	Marketing & Other	Total Operating Expenses	Net Income	Gross Profit Margin	Total Client Count	Avg. Hrs/ Week/Client
2011 Avg. (9)	$508,301	$141,190	$20,171	$19,218	$21,686	$202,265	$306,036	60%	68	54

Notes:

1. Gross Revenue is defined as the total "Office Fees" generated by the Outlet for calendar year 2011.

2. Payroll includes gross wages and payroll taxes for the employees at that location – typically includes a Manager, Care Coordinator and Marketer. Company Owned Units pay out an annual bonus in December. Typically, the Owner/Operator of a Franchise would replace the equivalent Manager position (at Company Owned Units) resulting in a lower payroll expense. The average Manager annual total compensation at Company Owned Units is $84,528.

3. Insurance includes expenses associated with health, life, dental, professional, general liability, workers compensation, and long-term disability. Typically, the Owner/Operator of a Franchise would replace the equivalent Manager position (at Company Owned Units) resulting in a lower insurance expense. The average Manager insurance expense at Company Owned Units is $6,366 per year.

4. Occupancy includes expenses for rent, utility, telephone (land-line and mobile), and janitorial services.

5. Marketing/Other includes expenses associated with advertising, trade shows, and print/reproduction. Also other expenses is defined as office supplies, dues/subscriptions, computer supplies, software, internet, criminal background checks, office expenses, professional fees, postage/delivery, travel/entertainment, and information/technology.

6. Net Income is defined as Gross Revenue less Total Operating Expenses as set forth in Table B.

7. The B/H office services two territories.

General Notes to Item 19:

1. Your results may vary upon the location of your franchised business. Your results may also vary as start-up business.

2. This analysis does not contain complete information concerning the operating costs and expenses that you will incur in operating your franchised business. Operating costs and expenses may vary substantially from business to business.

3. The above figures exclude royalties, advertising and marketing fees which you will incur as a franchisee.

4. The above figures exclude tax liabilities that you will be responsible for.

5. Interest expense, interest income, depreciation, amortization and other income or expenses will vary substantially from business to business, depending on the amount and kind of financing you obtain to establish your franchised business. You should consult with your tax advisor regarding depreciation and amortization schedules and the period over which assets of your franchised business may be amortized or depreciated, as well as the effect, if any, of any recent or proposed tax legislation.

6. Expenses and costs, as well as the actual accounting and operational methods employed by a franchisee, may significantly impact profits realized in any particular operation.

7. Some system businesses have earned this amount. Your individual results may differ. There is no assurance that you will earn as much. In particular, the revenues, costs and expenses of your franchised business will be directly affected by many factors, such as: (a) current market conditions, (b) the type of market in your franchise area, (c) the geographic location, square mileage, and population density of your franchise area, (c) the competition from other similar services in the market (d) your personal ability to operate the franchise, (e) marketing, public relations and advertising effectiveness based on market saturation; (f) whether you continue to operate the franchise after the first 3 years or hire a manager; (g) your pricing; (g) vendor selections and prices on materials, supplies

and inventory; (h) salaries and benefits to employees and other personnel; (i) business personnel benefits (life and health insurance, etc.); (j) weather conditions; (k) employment and economic conditions in the market, (l) your individual efforts, choices and abilities. Because of these factors, results vary from business to business. Therefore, we recommend that you make your own independent investigation to determine whether or not the franchise may be profitable to you. You should use the above information only as a reference in conducting your analysis and preparing your own projected income statements and cash flow statements. We suggest strongly that you consult your financial advisor or personal accountant concerning financial projections and federal, state and local income taxes and any other applicable taxes that you may incur in operating a franchised business.

8. Other than the preceding financial performance representation, we do not make any financial performance representations. We also do not authorize our employees or representatives to make any such representations either orally or in writing. If you are purchasing an existing outlet, however, we may provide you with the actual records of that outlet. If you receive any other financial performance information or projections of your future income, you should report it to the franchisor's management by contacting Graham Weihmiller, President and CEO, Griswold International, LLC, Suite 300, 717Bethlehem Pike, Suite 300, Erdenheim, Pennsylvania 19038-8101, t: 215-402-0200, the Federal Trade Commission, and the appropriate state regulatory agencies.

HOUSEMASTER HOME INSPECTIONS

426 Vosseller Ave.
Bound Brook, NJ 08805
Tel: (800) 526-3939, (732) 469-6565
Fax: (802) 419-3434
Email: kim.fanus@housemaster.com
Website: www.franchise.housemaster.com
Kim Fanus, Franchise Development Manager

HOUSEMASTER has been helping entrepreneurs from all educational and business backgrounds realize their dreams for the past 33 years, and has collectively performed over 2 million inspections. It is our motto to go above and beyond in supporting our franchisees; providing training, comprehensive business planning, solid marketing programs, operations support, resources, and coaching in all areas of the business. Franchisee and customer satisfaction alike, along with the highest level of quality service available are why HOUSEMASTER continues to be the recognized authority on everything home inspection.

BACKGROUND

IFA Member	Yes
Established & First Franchised:	1971;1979
Franchised Units:	365
Company-Owned Units:	0
Total Units:	365
Dist.:	US-331; CAN-34; O'seas-0
North America:	45 States, 8 Provinces

Density:	23 in NJ, 20 in NY, 18 in FL
Projected New Units (12 Months):	20
Qualifications:	3, 3, 2, 2, 5, 5

FINANCIAL/TERMS

Cash Investment:	$18 – $40K
Total Investment	$59.2 – $89.2K
Minimum Net Worth:	$80K
Fees (Franchise):	$42.5K
Fees (Royalty):	7.5%
Fees (Advertising):	2.5%
Term of Contract (Years):	10/10
Avg. # of Employees:	Varies FT, 0 PT
Passive Ownership:	Not Allowed
Encourage Conversions:	N/A
Area Develop. Agreements:	Yes
Sub-Franchising Contracts:	No
Expand in Territory:	Yes
Space Needs:	N/A

SUPPORT & TRAINING

Financial Assistance Provided:	Yes (I)
Site Selection Assistance:	N/A
Lease Negotiation Assistance:	N/A
Co-operative Advertising:	Yes
Franchisee Assoc./Member:	Yes/Member
Size of Corporate Staff:	12
On-going Support:	A, B, C, D, E, G,h,I
Training:	2 Weeks Medford, NJ

SPECIFIC EXPANSION PLANS

US:	All United States
Canada:	All Canada
Overseas:	Australia, UK

Other than the financial performance representations contained in this Item 19, we do not make any financial performance representations. We also do not authorize our employees or representatives to make any such representations either orally or in writing. If you are purchasing an existing outlet, however, we may provide you with the actual records of that outlet. If you receive any financial performance information or projections of your future income, you should report it to the franchisor's management by contacting Lenny Rankin, 426 Vosseller Avenue, Bound Brook, New Jersey 08805, (800) 526-3939, the Federal Trade Commission, and the appropriate state regulatory agencies.

STATEMENT OF AVERAGE GROSS SALES OF U.S. FRANCHISEES FOR THE 12 MONTHS ENDING DECEMBER 31, 2011

The following is a statement of average annual gross sales for the calendar year 2011 for 4 different subsets of U.S. HouseMaster franchisees based on number of Owner-Occupied Homes (OOH) in the territory (or combined territories if they own multiple licenses) granted to the franchisee. This information was compiled from monthly gross sales reports submitted to us by the franchisees. This statement has not been audited and we are relying solely on the information submitted to us by the franchisees.

The number of OOH in each franchisee's territory varies and is based on the size of territory each franchisee decided to purchase. The range of OOH for the franchisees included in each subset is disclosed in notes below the chart. The information on OOH has been taken from US census figures for each franchisee and is not necessarily the same as of the date of signing of the franchise agreement by the franchisee and us. Information on OOH in the charts includes OOH of existing franchisees that have a license for a Limited Area as well as franchisees in a Reciprocal Opportunity Franchise Territory (see Item 12).

The averages do not include revenue from (a) any franchisees operating less than two years, whether (i) the franchisee began operations after January 1, 2010 and, therefore, did not operate for the full two year period, or (ii) the franchisee's franchise was terminated, expired or transferred prior to December 31, 2011 and therefore the franchisee did not operate for the full two year period and (b) any franchisees from whom we did not receive monthly sales reports for all of the 24 months up through December 31, 2011.

The following averages reflect the actual annual gross sales of specific franchisees, and should not be considered as the actual or probable figures that will be realized by any given franchisees. We do not represent, warrant, promise or guarantee that any given franchisee can expect to attain such annual gross sales.

A new franchisee's financial results are likely to differ from the results stated in this statement. There is no assurance that you will earn as much. If you rely upon these figures, you must accept the risk of not doing as well.

Average Annual Gross Sales of U.S. HouseMaster Franchisees
For The Twelve Months Ending December 31, 2011

US Franchisees	Total Franchisees	Average Gross Sales (US$)	# of Franchisees at or above Average	% of Franchisees at or above Average
Franchisees with less than 75,000 OOH (Note 1)	33	$ 101,437	16	48%
Franchisees with more than 75,000 OOH and less than 300,000 OOH (Note 2)	57	136,611	25	44%
Franchisees with more than 300,000 OOH (Note 3)	15	369,696	5	33%
All Franchisees (Note 4)	105	$ 158,854	46	44%

Note 1: 33 franchisees were included in computing this average. 3 franchisees were excluded (for one of the reasons listed above) in computing the average. The number of OOH in the territories of these 32 franchisees ranges from 24,372 to 74,773.

Note 2: 57 franchisees were included in computing this average. 30 franchisees were excluded (for one of the reasons listed above) in computing the average. The number of OOH in the territories of these 57 franchisees ranges from 76,354 to 287,722.

Note 3: 15 franchisees were included in computing this average. 1 franchisee was excluded (for one of the reasons listed above) in computing the average. The number of OOH in the territories of these 15 franchisees ranges from 345,723 to 1,820,330.

Note 4: 105 franchisees were included in computing this average. 34 franchisees were excluded (for one of the reasons listed above) in computing the average. The number of OOH in the territories of these 105 franchisees ranges from 24,372 to 1,820,330.

Annual gross sales will vary from franchise operation to franchise operation, and we do not represent that the annual gross sales of franchisees for 2011 reported in this financial performance representation will accurately predict the future results of those outlets or for any prospective franchisee. Factors that may affect the annual gross revenues of a HouseMaster franchise include but are not necessarily limited to:

- Business skills, motivation and effort of the individual franchisee
- Sales and marketing skills of the individual franchisee and sales staff
- Franchisee's local marketing and promotional efforts
- How closely a Franchisee follows the HouseMaster Method and HouseMaster Marketing
- Strategy in operating and promoting the franchise
- Number of OOH in the franchise territory
- Location of the franchise territory
- Current market for home sales in franchise territory
- Local economic conditions
- Demographics of the franchise territory
- Competition
- Franchisee's pricing policies
- Number of years in operation

- Applicable regulations of home inspection and real estate industries
- Service options offered/available.

STATEMENT OF AVERAGE INSPECTION FEES OF U.S. FRANCHISEES FOR THE 12 MONTHS ENDING DECEMBER 31, 2011

The following is a statement of average inspection fees charged during the calendar year 2011 for 4 different subsets of U.S. HouseMaster franchisees based on the region in which the franchisee's territory is located. This information was compiled from monthly gross sales reports submitted to us by the franchisees. This statement has not been audited and we are relying solely on the information submitted to us by the franchisees.

The same franchisees that were included in the Statement of Average Gross Sales above were included in this Statement of Average Inspection Fees, and the same franchisees that were excluded in the Statement of Average Gross Sales were excluded in this Statement of Average Inspection Fees for the same reason.

The following averages reflect the actual average inspection fees charged of specific franchisees, and should not be considered as the actual or probable fees that will be realized by any given franchisees. We do not represent, warrant, promise or guarantee that any given franchisee can expect to receive such fees.

A new franchisee's financial results are likely to differ from the results stated in this statement. There is no assurance that you will earn as much. If you rely upon these figures, you must accept the risk of not doing as well.

Average Inspection Fee of HouseMaster Franchisees
For The Twelve Months Ending December 31, 2011

Region	Total Franchisees	Average Inspection Fee (US$)	Number (#) of Franchisees at or above Average	Percentage (%) of Franchisees at or above Average
Northeast (see Note 5)	32	$532	8	25%
Midwest (see Note 6)	21	376	8	38%
West (see Note 7)	22	402	8	36%
South (see Note 8)	30	366	14	47%
Total (see Note 9)	105	$425	38	36%

Note 5: 32 franchisees were included in computing this average. 6 franchisees were excluded (for one of the reasons listed above) in computing the average. The States included in this region are: Connecticut, Delaware, District of Columbia, Maine, Maryland, Massachusetts, New Hampshire, New Jersey, New York, Pennsylvania, Rhode Island, Vermont, Virginia, and West Virginia.

Note 6: 21 franchisees were included in computing this average. 7 franchisees were excluded (for one of the reasons listed above) in computing the average. The States included in this region are: Illinois, Indiana, Iowa, Kansas, Kentucky, Michigan, Minnesota, Missouri, Nebraska, North Dakota, Ohio, South Dakota, and Wisconsin.

Note 7: 22 franchisees were included in computing this average. 8 franchisees were excluded (for one of the reasons listed above) in computing the average. The States included in this region are: Alaska, Arizona, California, Colorado, Hawaii, Idaho, Montana, Nevada, New Mexico, Oklahoma, Oregon, Utah, Washington and Wyoming.

Note 8: 30 franchisees were included in computing this average. 13 franchisees were excluded (for one of the reasons listed above) in computing the average. The States included in this region are: Alabama, Arkansas, Florida, Georgia, Louisiana, Mississippi, North Carolina, South Carolina, Tennessee and Texas.

Note 9: 105 franchisees were included in computing this average. 34 franchisees were excluded (for one of the reasons listed above) in computing the average. All States and Provinces were included in this group.

Inspection fees charged and received will vary from franchise operation to franchise operation, and we do not represent that the average inspection fees of franchisees for 2011 reported in this financial performance representation will accurately predict the future results of those outlets or for any prospective franchisee. Factors that may affect the annual gross revenues of a HouseMaster franchise include but are not necessarily limited to:

- Business skills, motivation and effort of the individual franchisee
- Sales and marketing skills of the individual franchisee and sales staff
- Franchisee's local marketing and promotional efforts
- How closely a Franchisee follows the HouseMaster Method and HouseMaster Marketing Strategy in operating and promoting the franchise
- Location of the franchise territory
- Current market for home sales in franchise territory
- Local economic conditions

- Demographics of the franchise territory
- Competition
- Franchisee's pricing policies
- Number of years in operation
- Applicable regulations of home inspection and real estate industries
- Service options offered/available.

This financial performance representation does not provide information on the net profits of franchises. This financial performance representation does not include information concerning expenses or profits that may be realized in the operation of a HouseMaster business. Profits in the operation of a HouseMaster business will vary from franchisee to franchisee and from territory to territory and are dependent upon numerous factors beyond our control. We make no warranties, representations, predictions, promises or guarantees with respect to the profits likely to be experienced by individual franchisees.

You should carefully consider these and other factors in evaluating this information and in making any decision to purchase a franchise. Further, we urge you to consult with appropriate financial, business and legal advisors in connection with the use of any of the information contained in this financial performance representation and in estimating potential revenue from a HOUSEMASTER franchise business.

Substantiation of the data presented above will be made available to a prospective franchisee on reasonable request made in writing.

HUNTINGTON LEARNING CENTER

496 Kinderkamack Rd.
Oradell, NJ 07649-1512
Tel: (800) 653-8400, (201) 261-8400
Fax: (800) 361-9728
Email: franchise@hlcmail.com
Website: www.huntingtonfranchise.com
Laura Gehringer, Executive Director of Marketing & Advertising

HUNTINGTON offers tutoring to 5 – 19 year-olds in reading, writing, language development study skills, and mathematics, as well as programs to prepare for standardized entrance exams. Instruction is offered in a tutorial setting and is predominately remedial in nature.

BACKGROUND

IFA Member:	Yes
Established & First Franchised:	1977; 1985
Franchised Units:	240
Company-Owned Units:	32
Total Units:	272
Distribution:	US – 272; CAN – 0; O'seas – 0
North America:	41 States, 0 Provinces
Density:	30 in CA, 26 in FL, 26 in NY
Projected New Units (12 Months):	60
Qualifications:	5, 3, 1, 3, 1, 5

FINANCIAL/TERMS

Cash Investment:	$50K
Total Investment:	$121.4 – $255.6K
Minimum Net Worth:	$150K
Fees (Franchise):	$14.5K
Fees (Royalty):	9.5%
Fees (Advertising):	2%/$500 Min.
Term of Contract (Years):	10/10
Average Number of Employees:	2 – 4 FT, 12 – 20 PT
Passive Ownership:	Not Allowed
Encourage Conversions:	Yes
Area Development Agreements:	Yes
Sub-Franchising Contracts:	No
Expand in Territory:	No
Space Needs:	1,200 – 1,600 SF

SUPPORT & TRAINING

Financial Assistance Provided:	Yes (I)
Site Selection Assistance:	Yes
Lease Negotiation Assistance:	Yes
Co-operative Advertising:	Yes
Franchisee Association/Member:	No
Size of Corporate Staff:	100
On-going Support:	C, D, E, F, G, h, I
Training:	On-Going Regional; 1 Week Oradell, NJ (Corp. HQ); 2 Weeks Online

SPECIFIC EXPANSION PLANS

US:	Contiguous US
Canada:	No
Overseas:	No

This Item 19 presents 2011 financial performance about franchised and corporate-owned Huntington Learning Centers®.

Franchise Centers. In 2011, the average annual sales of the 234 franchised Centers in operation for the entire year were $417,393. Of these, 98 or 42% achieved sales greater than the average.

Corporate-owned Centers. In 2011, the average annual sales of the 30 corporate-owned Centers in operation for the entire year were $913,450. Of these, 13 or 43% achieved sales greater than the average.

CAUTIONARY NOTES: Not all Huntington Learning Centers® achieved these average sales. There is no assurance you will do as well. If you rely upon our figures, you must accept the risk of not doing as well. Sales likely will be lower for newer franchisees.

Your individual financial results may, and likely will, differ from the result stated above. Many factors influence the revenue at a Huntington Learning Center®, including the way the manager operates the business, the number of inquiries, conversion of these inquiries to enrolled students, program duration, and tuition rates, as well as factors outside the business, like foot and car traffic, road structure, and demographic factors, including the number of school-age children located near the Center. Operation of the Center may be affected by factors like the curriculum used in the schools attended by students in the area, and the length of the school day and the length of the school year. The presence of direct and indirect competitors, including other Huntington Learning Centers®, may affect your revenue. Factors that determine expenses at a Center include debt service; the number of teachers and other staff hired and their length of employment; the amount of compensation you pay yourself, as well as staff; and the benefits offered. Other factors include premises rent and marketing expenditures. Many franchisees spend substantially more on marketing than required under the Franchise Agreement. In addition, your Advertising Cooperative Association can require money for cooperative advertising.

Franchised Centers differ from each other in many important ways, including their market area and geographic location and the number of children and population contained thereabout and the economic and financial circumstances of this population. Centers also differ from each other in their physical, marketing, employee, and manager's characteristics and in many other factors that may or may not exist or be similar to the factors that exist in any other location or geographic area or market area that you or any prospective franchisee may consider. Actual sales, expenses, profits, and earnings vary from one Center to another by significant amounts, and we cannot and do not estimate or forecast the sales, expenses, profits, or earnings that you may achieve.

You should conduct an independent investigation of the costs and expenses you will incur in operating the Franchised Business. Current franchisees and former franchisees listed in Exhibits M and N, respectively, may be a source of this information. You should consult with financial, business and legal advisors about this Item 19.

Written substantiation for the financial performance representation will be made available to the prospective franchisee upon reasonable request.

We do not authorize anyone, including our officers or sales personnel, to furnish you with any oral or written information about actual or potential sales, expenses, profits, or earnings of Huntington Learning Centers®, other than the information in this Item 19.

If you receive any oral or written information about actual or potential sales, expenses, profits, or earnings of Huntington Learning Centers®, other than the specific information contained in this Item 19, please notify the Chairman of Huntington Learning Centers, Inc. immediately in writing.

How we calculated average actual sales

Franchised and corporate-owned Huntington Learning Centers® in operation all of 2011 reported the gross revenues ("sales") in this item. We compiled the data for franchised Centers from the monthly income statements our franchisees submitted to us, which they prepare according to a standardized method described in the Operating Manual. We believe these statements are accurate as to sales, because each franchisee must pay us Continuing Royalty and Advertising Fees that are calculated as a percentage of sales. We have not audited nor in any other manner substantiated the truthfulness, accuracy, or completeness of any information supplied by our franchisees. We compiled the data for corporate-owned Centers according to a standardized method described in the Operating Manual.

In 2011, Huntington Learning Corporation operated Centers in New Jersey, New York, and Connecticut. The following table lists the states in which franchised Centers operated during 2011:

States in which Franchised Huntington Learning Centers® Were in Operation during all of 2011			
AL	IA	MS	OK
AR	ID	MT	OR
AZ	IL	NC	PA
CA	IN	NE	SC
CO	KY	NH	TN
CT	LA	NJ	TX
DC	MA	NM	UT
DE	MD	NV	VA
FL	MI	NY	WA
GA	MN	OH	WI

Expense Items on a Franchise Huntington Learning Centers® End-of-Year P&L Statement

The following table presents certain expense items listed on the End-of-Year Profit and Loss Statement franchisees must submit to us. Your profit and loss statement may contain additional or different expense items.

Expenses Listed on the End-of-Year P&L Statement that Franchisees Must Submit to Us
Gross payroll for franchisee, center director, assistant director
Other full-time staff (like a regional director)
Gross payroll for part-time teachers
Gross payroll for any other part-time staff
Payroll taxes (Employer's portion of FICA, FUTA, etc.)
Advertising center services, including broadcast TV and radio, cable TV, daily and weekly newspaper, magazine, direct mail, free standing insert, yellow pages, Internet, school programs, and marketing
Advertising payment to your Advertising Cooperative Association
Building, including rent, utilities, janitor, and maintenance
Repairs and maintenance of equipment
Supplies - office and administrative
Call Center fees
Conference Services fees
Supplies - educational
Professional fees (accounting, legal, etc.)
Telephone
Travel and entertainment
Continuing Royalty
Advertising Fee
Insurance (property, liability, health, etc.)
Depreciation and amortization
Debt service
Training (travel, food, lodging, etc.)
Employee benefits
Other expenses
Taxes, other than payroll

IKOR

511 Schoolhouse Lane, # 600
Kennett Square, PA 19348
Tel: (877) 456-7872, (610) 444-1454
Fax: (610) 444-9001
Email: cgartman@ikorusa.com
Website: www.ikorusa.com
Cynthia Gartman, President

IKOR provides advocacy directed to the life issue facing the elderly/disabled and their families—the missing element in eldercare. IKOR provides RN assessment, strategic planning, implementation, and ongoing quality assurance, enabling families to address the day-to-day concerns. IKOR also provides basic bill-pay services and financial support. IKOR meets the needs of persons with no family, family at a distance, or when family is in conflict in making the decisions. In addition to core advocacy services, IKOR also provides professional guardianship of person/estate by the court appointment.

BACKGROUND

IFA Member:	Yes
Established & First Franchised:	1998; 2010
Franchised Units:	20
Company-Owned Units:	1
Total Units:	21

Distribution:	US – 21; CAN – 0; O'seas – 0
North America:	12 States, 0 Provinces
Density:	5 in PA
Projected New Units (12 Months):	20
Qualifications:	3, 5, 3, 5, 4, 5

FINANCIAL/TERMS

Cash Investment:	$76 – $110K
Total Investment:	$78 – $109K
Minimum Net Worth:	$87K
Fees (Franchise):	$39.9K
Fees (Royalty):	8%
Fees (Advertising):	N/A
Term of Contract (Years):	10/5 (3 renewal terms)
Average Number of Employees:	3 FT, 2 PT
Passive Ownership:	Allowed
Encourage Conversions:	No
Area Development Agreements:	Yes

Sub-Franchising Contracts:	No
Expand in Territory:	No
Space Needs:	500 SF

SUPPORT & TRAINING

Financial Assistance Provided:	No
Site Selection Assistance:	Yes
Lease Negotiation Assistance:	Yes
Co-operative Advertising:	No
Franchisee Association/Member:	No
Size of Corporate Staff:	8
On-going Support:	A, B, C, D, E, G, h, I
Training:	3 Days Local; 12-16 Days Kennett Square, PA

SPECIFIC EXPANSION PLANS

US:	Yes
Canada:	No
Overseas:	No

Background

This Item sets forth certain historical income and operating expense information for our affiliate, IKOR, Inc., for its fiscal year ended December 31, 2011. IKOR, Inc. has been operating a substantially similar business to that being offered through this Disclosure Document in Kennett, Square, Pennsylvania since 1998. We believe that the following financial data has been compiled using generally accepted accounting principles, but the data is unaudited and no assurance can be offered that the data does not contain inaccuracies that an audit might disclose. Written substantiation of the data used in preparing this information will be made available upon reasonable request.

You should not use this information as an indication of how well your Franchised Business will do. A number of factors will affect the success of your Franchise Business. These factors include the current market conditions, the type of market in your territory, the location of your territory, the competition and your ability to operate the Franchised Business.

IKOR, Inc. has earned this amount. Your individual results may differ. There is no assurance that you will earn as much.

Affiliate Gross Receipts, Certain Expenses and Net Income

The table below presents our affiliate's: (i) Gross Receipts1; (ii) certain expenses; and (iii) and Net Income (before income taxes and depreciation), for its fiscal year ended December 31 2011.

January 1 through December 31 2011

Gross Receipts[1]	
Healthcare Advocacy	$501,669.80
Personal Needs Advocacy	$49,464.52
Personal Guardianship Services	$48,915.55
Estate Guardianship Services	$52,623.73
Total Operating Revenue	$652,673.60
Expenses	
Payroll[2]	$219,138.24
Transportation[3]	$22,332.22
Marketing [4]	$5,330.11
Insurance[5]	$12,484.31
Financing Expenses[6]	$12,478.88
Utilities[7]	$14,393.36
Operating Expenses[8]	$35,593.25
Total Select Expenses[9]	$321,750.37
Net Income (Before Income Taxes And Depreciation)[10]	$330,923.24

Notes:

Note 1. Gross Receipts are defined as all revenue earned by our affiliate IKOR, Inc. from the provision of healthcare advocacy and personal care advocacy and personal and estate guardianship services.

Note 2. Payroll includes salaries and wages for one Personal Needs Coordinator and 2-3 RN Patient Advocates.

Note 3. Transportation includes the cost of travel expenses and automotive expenses.

Note 4. Marketing is defined as the total expenditures on marketing made by our affiliate within its market, including marketing materials and dues and subscriptions among other items.

Note 5. Insurance includes our affiliate's cost to maintain auto insurance, worker's compensation insurance, general business coverage, and liability insurance, including errors and omissions insurance.

Note 6. Financing expenses include bank fees and interest.

Note 7. Utilities include the cost of telephone and internet services. This figure also includes computer support costs.

Note 8. Operating Expenses include office expenses, collections assistance, accounting expenses, legal and professional fees, the cost of independent contractors, and bad debt expenses.

Note 9. Total Select Expenses includes the sum of Payroll, Transportation, Marketing, Insurance, Financing, Utilities, and Miscellaneous Operating Expenses.

Note 10. The Net Income is equal to Gross Receipts less the Total Select Expenses, before income taxes and depreciation.

Note 11. Your expenses will vary depending upon the location of your business. This analysis may not contain complete information concerning your potential operating costs. Operating costs may vary substantially from business to business.

Note 12. The above figures exclude rent, royalty fees, brand development contributions, insurance expenses relating to including us as an additional insured, start-up costs, and living expenses which you will incur as a franchisee.

Note 13. The above figures exclude finance charges. Interest expense, interest income, depreciation, amortization and other income or expenses will vary substantially from business to business, depending on the amount and kind of financing you obtain to establish the Business. You should consult with your tax advisor regarding depreciation and amortization schedules and the period over which the assets of the Business may be amortized or depreciated, as well as the effect, if any, of recent or proposed tax legislation.

Note 14. The revenues and expenses list above will be directly affected by many factors, such as: (a) geographic location; (b) competition from other similar businesses in your area; (c) marketing effectiveness; (d) whether you operate the business personally or hire a general manager; (e) service pricing; (f) vendor prices on materials supplies and inventory; (g) employee salaries and benefits (life and health insurance, etc.); (h) insurance costs; (i) the size of your office space, if any, and real estate costs in your territory; (j) your ability to generate and retain Customers and Clients; and (k) employment conditions in the market. As a result, we cannot represent that you will obtain a particular level of revenues or expense, or generate income which will exceed the initial payment of, or investment in the franchise.

Note 15. Other than the preceding financial performance representation, we do not make any financial performance representations. We also do not authorize our employees or representatives to make any such representations either orally or in writing. If you are purchasing an existing outlet, however, we may provide you with the actual records of that outlet. If you receive any other financial performance information or projections of your future income, you should report it to our management by contacting Cynthia Gartman at 415 McFarlan Road, Suite 200, Kennett Square, PA 19348, telephone numbers (610) 444-1454 or (877) IKOR USA; the Federal Trade Commission; and the appropriate state regulatory agencies.

California residents, see the California Addendum to this disclosure document for additional disclosures required by California law.

INTELLIGENT OFFICE

1515 Wynkoop St., #360
Boulder, CO 80302
Tel: (800) 800-4987, (303) 417-2100
Fax: (303) 448-8880
Email: scochran@intelligentoffice.com
Website: www.intelligentoffice.com
Sean Cochran, Director of Franchise Development

This highly evolved alternative to the traditional office provides a prestigious address, anywhere communications, and a live receptionist for businesses, corporate executives, and professionals, releasing them from the limitations and expense of a traditional or home office. INTELLIGENT OFFICE offers private offices, conference rooms, and professional office services on an as-needed basis and at only a fraction of the cost of a traditional office.

BACKGROUND

IFA Member:	Yes
Established & First Franchised:	1995; 1999
Franchised Units:	49
Company-Owned Units:	5
Total Units:	54
Distribution:	US – 38; CAN – 16; O'seas – 0
North America:	16 States, 1 Province
Density:	11 in ON, 7 in DC, 4 in VA
Projected New Units (12 Months):	18
Qualifications:	5, 1, 1, 1, 1, 5

FINANCIAL/TERMS

Cash Investment:	$100K
Total Investment:	$316 – $496.5K
Minimum Net Worth:	$750K
Fees (Franchise):	$54K
Fees (Royalty):	5%
Fees (Advertising):	$1,500/Mo.
Term of Contract (Years):	20/20
Average Number of Employees:	2 FT, 1 PT
Passive Ownership:	Not Allowed
Encourage Conversions:	No
Area Development Agreements:	Yes
Sub-Franchising Contracts:	No
Expand in Territory:	No
Space Needs:	3,000 – 4,000 SF

SUPPORT & TRAINING

Financial Assistance Provided:	No
Site Selection Assistance:	Yes
Lease Negotiation Assistance:	Yes
Co-operative Advertising:	Yes
Franchisee Association/Member:	Yes/Member
Size of Corporate Staff:	10
On-going Support:	A, B, C, D, E, G, H, I
Training:	1 Week Denver, CO; 1 Week On-Site; 2 weeks online

SPECIFIC EXPANSION PLANS

US:	All United States
Canada:	All Canada
Overseas:	All Countries

To help you evaluate our franchise, we have summarized selected historical sales information for our fiscal year ending December 31, 2011. Table 1 below provides the average monthly gross sales of both the top 25% and top 50% (measured by average monthly gross sales) of outlets whose franchised businesses were located in North America, were in operation as of December 31, 2011, and had been in uninterrupted operation for at least 12 months. Table 1 does not include information about franchised businesses that began or discontinued their affiliation with us during 2011. Table 1 also does not include

information about company-owned locations.

The information in Table 1 is not a forecast of your future financial performance. We have compiled the information based upon what franchisees have reported to us in the ordinary course of business through our sales reporting system. We assume that the information submitted is accurate, complete and contains no material misrepresentations or omissions.

Table 1- Statement of 2011 Average Gross Sales Information by Month[1]

	Average Sales	High	Low
Top 25%	$73,834[2]	$129,877	$58,729
Top 50%	$61,277[3]	$129,877	$42,528

(1) The total number of outlets whose franchised businesses were located in North America, were in operation as of December 31, 2011, had been in uninterrupted operation for at least 12 months, and were not company-owned, was 36. The total number of outlets (including company-owned outlets) in North America as of December 31, 2011 was 47.

(2) The total number of outlets in the top 25% was nine. This is the set of outlets used to calculate the stated average. Two of these outlets (or 22%) had average monthly sales volume above the stated average.

(3) The total number of outlets in the top 50% was 18. This is the set of outlets used to calculate the stated average. Eight of these outlets (or 44%) had average monthly sales volume above the stated average.

The information presented in Table 1 does not reflect the cost of sales, operating expenses or other costs or expenses that must be deducted from the gross sales figures to obtain net income or profit. You should conduct an independent investigation of the costs and expenses you will incur in operating your franchised business. Franchisees or former franchisees listed in the disclosure document may be one source of this information.

The information in Table 1 is presented for periods during which economic conditions may be substantively different from future economic conditions. Competitors may enter or leave the market over time. Brand recognition and awareness and consumer goodwill may vary by market. Market potential and consumer demand may change over time. Each franchisee's managerial skill, experience and resources will differ. Accordingly, you are urged to consult with appropriate financial, business and legal counsel to conduct your own independent analysis of the information presented.

We have written substantiation of the information used to compile the preceding financial performance representations. We will make this written substantiation available to you upon written request.

Other than the preceding historical financial performance representations, we do not make any representations about a franchisee's future financial performance or the past financial performance of company-owned or franchised outlets. We also do not authorize our employees or representatives to make any such representations either orally or in writing. If you are purchasing an existing outlet, however, we may provide you with the actual records of that outlet. If you receive any other financial performance information or projections of your future income, you should report it to the franchisor's management by contacting Chief Operating Officer, 4450 Arapahoe Avenue, Boulder, Colorado, (303) 417-2100, the Federal Trade Commission, and the appropriate state regulatory agencies.

JANI-KING

16885 Dallas Pkwy.
Addison, TX 75001
Tel: (800) 526-4546, (972) 991-0900

Fax: (972) 764-3950
Email: tlooney@janiking.com
Website: www.janiking.com
Ted Looney, Vice President of Franchising

JANI-KING INTERNATIONAL is the world's largest commercial cleaning franchisor, with locations in 19 countries and over 125 regions in the US and abroad. Our franchise opportunity includes initial customer contracts, training, continuous local support, administrative and accounting assistance, an equipment leasing program, and national advertising. If you are searching for a flexible business opportunity, look no further.

BACKGROUND

IFA Member:	Yes
Established & First Franchised:	1969; 1974
Franchised Units:	11,000
Company-Owned Units:	22
Total Units:	11,022
Distribution:	US – 10,143; CAN – 351; O'seas – 528
North America:	39 States, 7 Provinces
Density:	900 in CA, 900 in FL, 500 in TX
Projected New Units (12 Months):	1,000
Qualifications:	2, 2, 1, 2, 2, 3

FINANCIAL/TERMS

Cash Investment:	$2.9 – $33K
Total Investment:	$8.2 – $74K
Minimum Net Worth:	$2.9 – $33K
Fees (Franchise):	$8 – $33K
Fees (Royalty):	10%
Fees (Advertising):	1%
Term of Contract (Years):	20/20
Average Number of Employees:	0 PT

Passive Ownership:	Allowed
Encourage Conversions:	N/A
Area Development Agreements:	Yes
Sub-Franchising Contracts:	Yes
Expand in Territory:	Yes
Space Needs:	N/A

SUPPORT & TRAINING

Financial Assistance Provided:	No
Site Selection Assistance:	N/A
Lease Negotiation Assistance:	N/A
Co-operative Advertising:	No
Franchisee Association/Member:	Yes/Member
Size of Corporate Staff:	65
On-going Support:	A, B, C, D, G, H, I
Training:	2+ Weeks Local Regional Office

SPECIFIC EXPANSION PLANS

US:	All United States
Canada:	All Canada
Overseas:	All Countries

ANALYSIS OF ACTUAL INITIAL BUSINESS OFFERING EXPERIENCE

This analysis sets forth information about our performance of the obligation to provide Initial Business for certain Jani-King franchises.

The analysis is based on data as of December 31, 2011, reported for 1,115 franchisees that either purchased their franchise between January 1, 2011 and December 31, 2011 or they purchased their franchise prior to 2011 and their offering period ended in 2011.

Under the terms of the Franchise Agreement, we agree to se-cure and offer you the opportunity to service signed commercial cleaning and/or maintenance contracts that in total would provide a minimum in gross monthly billings in an amount defined as the "INITIAL BUSINESS". These contracts will be secured and offered within the number of days identified in the Franchise Summary of the Franchise Agreement as the "INITIAL OFFERING PERIOD", such time period beginning on the date all required equipment and supplies listed in the "Supply and Equipment Package" and "Additional Electric Equipment" have been obtained and the Acknowledgment of Completion of Training is signed, or a later date as discussed later in this item. The schedule below is a sample of Plan E-4 and plans Plan E-10 through Plan E-25, other plans with more Initial Business are available:

PLAN	INITIAL BUSINESS ($)	INITIAL OFFERING PERIOD (Days)
E-25	25,000*	780**
E-24	24,000	750
E-23	23,000	720
E-22	22,000	690
E-21	21,000	660
E-20	20,000	630
E-19	19,000	600
E-18	18,000	570
E-17	17,000	540

E-16	16,000	510
E-15	15,000	480
E-14	14,000	450
E-13	13,000	420
E-12	12,000	390
E-11	11,000	360
E-10	10,000	330
E-4	4,000	150
	*An Additional $1,000 for each higher level of the "E" Plan	**Plus An Additional 30 Days for each level higher of the "E" Plan

Under Plan E-4, the Initial Offering Period is 150 days. Under each level of Plan E-10 or higher, the Initial Offering Period is calculated as the total of: 330 days, plus an additional 30 days for each higher level of the "E" Plan.

Example:
E-10   = 330 days
E-11   [330 + 30 (2nd level)]   = 360 days
E-12   [330 + 60 (3rd level)]   = 390 days, etc.

The franchises reported in this analysis are listed by ranges of Initial Business obligated to be offered in order to provide a more meaningful presentation of the relevant information about the offering of accounts for Initial Business by JANI-KING. The time period in which the Initial Business is contractually required to be offered is the Initial Offering Period stated in the Franchise Agreement, while the average time period within which the Initial Business was offered represents the actual number of days within which JANI-KING had secured and offered cleaning contracts with gross monthly billings that equal or exceed the total obligation required under each Franchise Agreement for the specified range.

You should particularly note the following:

THE INFORMATION CONCERNING FRANCHISEE INITIAL CONTRACT BUSINESS SHOULD NOT BE CONSIDERED AS THE ACTUAL OR POTENTIAL SALES, COSTS, INCOME OR PROFITS THAT YOU WILL REALIZE. YOUR SUCCESS WILL DEPEND LARGELY UPON YOUR OWN ABILITY, AND THE INDIVIDUAL FINANCIAL RESULTS ACHIEVED BY YOU MAY DIFFER FROM THE FRANCHISEE INFORMATION STATED IN THIS DISCLOSURE DOCUMENT. THEREFORE WE DO NOT REPRESENT THAT ALL FRANCHISEES CAN EXPECT TO ACHIEVE THESE GROSS BILLINGS, OR ANY PARTICULAR LEVEL OF SALES, COSTS, INCOME OR PROFITS, OR ANY INCOME THAT EXCEEDS THE INITIAL PAYMENT FOR, OR INVESTMENT IN, THE FRANCHISED BUSINESS.

WE HAVE WRITTEN SUBSTANTIATION IN OUR POSSESSION TO SUPPORT THE INFORMATION APPEARING IN THIS ITEM 19 AND SUCH SUBSTANTIATION WILL BE MADE AVAILABLE TO YOU ON REASONABLE REQUEST.

THE TOTAL REVENUE, AND THE TOTAL GROSS BILLING FOR ANY SPECIFIC MONTH, REALIZED BY YOU MAY NOT BE DIRECTLY RELATED TO OUR PERFORMANCE OF OUR OBLIGATION TO OFFER THE INITIAL BUSINESS REQUIRED BY THE FRANCHISE AGREEMENT. THE AMOUNT OF REVENUE IS AFFECTED BY MANY FACTORS, SUCH AS (1) THE INITIAL BUSINESS MAY BE OFFERED IN STAGES DURING THE INITIAL OFFERING PERIOD; (2) YOU MAY NOT ACCEPT ALL OF THE ACCOUNTS OFFERED; (3) ACCOUNTS MAY CANCEL THE CONTRACT OR REQUEST A CHANGE OF FRANCHISEES DUE TO POOR PERFORMANCE BY YOU; OR (4) THE ACCOUNT MAY GO OUT OF BUSINESS BEFORE THE END OF THE CONTRACT PERIOD.

Other factors that affect the amount of revenue you realize include the quality of management and service, the rate of cleaning production you achieve; the extent to which you finance the acquisition and/or operation of the franchise; your legal, accounting and other professional fees; federal state and local income, gross profits or other taxes; discretionary expenditures; and accounting methods used.

We will make a good faith effort to secure and offer accounts to you as soon as possible, but we will have the total period to offer the Initial Business under each plan, and we are not obligated to offer any portion of the Initial Business before the end of that time. We calculate the Initial Offering Period from the date you sign the Acknowledgment of Completion of Training and you obtain all required equipment and supplies.

The actual time to secure and offer the Initial Business to you may, at our sole discretion, be automatically extended under certain conditions. Item 11 of this disclosure document has a detailed explanation of those conditions, but they are summarized as follows:

- Upon your written request

- You are in default of the Franchise Agreement

- Upon a transfer or cancellation due to non-performance of an account accepted by you as Initial Business.

- You fail to comply with policies or procedures

All accounts offered will apply toward the minimum amount of business as specified in your Franchise Agreement, whether the offered business is accepted or declined by you. Our obligation is to secure and offer those accounts to you within the specified time. However, you might choose not to accept some of the accounts offered. That is why the Franchise Agreement says that we will secure and "offer" those accounts to you. We can only make a good faith effort to offer the amount of business for the plan specified, and you must choose to accept or decline the "offer." Under a situation where you either decline an offer of an account or an account cancels at no fault of you, we are relieved of our obligation regarding the Initial Offering Period for that amount of gross monthly billings, however, we will provide you finder's fee credit equal to the difference be-

tween your Initial Business Obligation and the total amount of gross monthly billings of the accounts that you accepted and serviced for a full 12 months.

If an account cancels or is transferred from you due to non-performance, theft, your failure to service the account properly, customer relations problems caused by you or your failure to comply with Jani-King Policies and Procedures, the account will not be replaced. If an account cancels at no fault of you before you service the account for 12 full months, the full gross monthly billing value of that account will be replaced within a reasonable period of time by another account until a cumulative total of 12 full months of billing between both the original account and any replacement account occur (See Item 11: Transfers Or Cancellation Of Initial Business). There is no other obligation for us to replace the contracts if the contracts are canceled before the full term.

If we are unable to secure and offer you the full amount of Initial Business within the time frame allocated for the Initial Offering Period in the plan you purchase, an amount equal to three times the amount of Initial Business not offered to you may be refunded. Any refund will be first applied to any outstanding balance owed to us or LEASING, with the remaining sum, if any, paid to you. A refund under this provision will fulfill our obligation to offer any remaining portion of the Initial Business.

INFORMATION CONCERNING FRANCHISEE INITIAL BUSINESS FOR JANI-KING OF MIAMI, INC.'S FRANCHISEES – 2011

Range of Monthly Initial Business Purchased ($)	500	1,000	2,000	3,000	4,000 to 8,000	9,000 to 15,000	TOTAL
Time Period (days) in which Initial Business contractually required to be offered[1]	120	120	120	120	150 to 270	300 to 480	N/A
Average time period (days) in which Initial Business was actually offered[1]	49	131	N/A	46	74	N/A	N/A
Number of franchisees purchasing within range during 2011	0	1	0	1	2	1	5
Number of franchisees purchased prior to 2011 and their offering period ended in 2011	2	0	0	1	0	0	3
Percentage[3] of franchisees in which Initial Business was offered[1] within required period	100	100	N/A	100	100	N/A	100
Number of franchises whose initial offering period expired in 2011 and Initial Business was offered[1] within required period	2	1	0	2	1	0	6
Number of franchises whose offering period has ended in 2011	2	1	0	2	1	0	6

Number of franchises in which time period for Initial Business was extended pursuant to franchise agreement	1	1	1	1	3	0	7

Percentage[2] of Franchisees For All U.S. Regions In Which Initial Business Was Offered[1] Within Required Period

REGION	%	REGION	%
Alexandria	N/A	Macon	100
Atlanta	100	Madison	100
Augusta	100	Memphis	100
Austin	100	Miami	100
Baltimore	100	Milwaukee	100
Baton Rouge	100	Minneapolis	100
Birmingham	95	Mississippi Coast	N/A
Boston	50	Mobile	N/A
Buffalo	N/A	Monroe	N/A
Charleston	100	Montgomery	100
Charlotte	100	Myrtle Beach	100
Chattanooga	N/A	Nashville	100
Chicago	100	New Jersey	89
Cincinnati	100	New Mexico	100
Cleveland	100	New Orleans	93
Columbia, MO	100	New York	100
Columbia, SC	89	Oklahoma City	100
Columbus	100	Omaha	100
Dallas	100	Orlando	100
Dayton	100	Pensacola	100
Denver	83	Philadelphia	100
Detroit	87	Phoenix	100
Dothan	100	Pittsburgh	N/A
Eugene/Salem	100	Portland	80
Ft. Myers	100	Raleigh/Durham	58
Ft. Worth	100	Reno	100
Greater Rhode Island	100	Richmond	100
Greensboro	86	Roanoke/Lynchburg	100
Greenville/Spartanburg	100	St. Louis	89
Hampton Roads	69	Sacramento	100
Hartford	100	Salt Lake City	86
Hawaii	100	San Antonio	100
Houston	100	San Diego	100
Huntsville	100	San Francisco/Oakland	100
Indianapolis	100	Savannah	89

Jackson	100	Seattle	100
Jacksonville	94	Shreveport	N/A
Kansas City	100	South East Mississippi	100
Knoxville	100	Springfield	100
Lafayette/Lake Charles	100	Tampa Bay	100
Las Vegas	100	Tri-Cities	N/A
Lexington	100	Tucson	100
Little Rock	100	Tulsa	100
Los Angeles/Colton	95	Washington D.C.	100
Louisville	100	Wichita	100

[1] Offered means the accounts totally fulfilling the Initial Business were offered to the franchisee. Initial Business Packages not shown indicates that no plans were sold in those ranges for which the Initial Offering Period expired in 2011.

[2] Percentage calculated as number of franchises whose Initial Offering Period had expired in 2011 and whose total Initial Business was offered within required time period, divided by the total number of franchises sold during 2011 or prior to 2011 and whose Initial Offering Period had expired in 2011.

Other than the preceding financial performance representation, JANI-KING OF MIAMI, INC. does not make any financial performance representations. We also do not authorize our employees or representatives to make any such representations either orally or in writing. If you are purchasing an existing outlet, however, we may provide you with the actual records of that outlet. If you receive any other financial performance information or projections of your future income, you should report it to the franchisor's management by contacting Jani-King of Miami, Inc., 16885 Dallas Parkway, Addison, Texas (972) 991-0900 Attn: Legal Department, the Federal Trade Commission, and the appropriate state regulatory agencies.

JAN-PRO CLEANING SYSTEMS

2520 Northwinds Pkwy., #375
Alpharetta, GA 30004
Tel: (866) 355-1064, (678) 336-1780
Fax: (678) 336-1782
Email: brad.smith@jan-pro.com
Website: www.jan-pro.com
Brad Smith, Vice President of Franchise Licensing

JAN-PRO provides one of today's exceptional business opportunities, allowing you to enter one of the fastest-growing industries by safely becoming your own boss through the guidance and support of an established franchise organization.

BACKGROUND

IFA Member:	Yes
Established & First Franchised:	1991; 1992
Franchised Units:	10,100
Company-Owned Units:	2
Total Units:	10,102
Distribution:	US – 9,235; CAN – 793; O'seas – 64
North America:	39 States, 5 Provinces
Density:	1,316 in CA, 858 in GA, 695 in FL
Projected New Units (12 Months):	12 Masters and over 2,000 units
Qualifications:	3, 2, 1, 1, 1,1

FINANCIAL/TERMS

Cash Investment:	$1 – $30K
Total Investment:	$2.8 – $44K
Minimum Net Worth:	$50K
Fees (Franchise):	$1 – $30K
Fees (Royalty):	10%
Fees (Advertising):	0%
Term of Contract (Years):	5/5

Average Number of Employees:	0 FT; 0 PT	Lease Negotiation Assistance:	Yes
Passive Ownership:	Discouraged	Co-operative Advertising:	No
Encourage Conversions:	Yes	Franchisee Association/Member:	Yes/Not a Member
Area Development Agreements:	Yes	Size of Corporate Staff:	15
Sub-Franchising Contracts:	Yes	On-going Support:	A, B, C, D, E, F, G, H, I
Expand in Territory:	Yes	Training:	5 Weeks Regional and Local
Space Needs:	0		

SUPPORT & TRAINING

SPECIFIC EXPANSION PLANS

		US:	All United States
Financial Assistance Provided:	Yes (D)	Canada:	All Canada
Site Selection Assistance:	Yes	Overseas:	All Countries except England and Ireland

Your Initial Franchise Fee is based on the Initial Plan you want. The Initial Plan consists of a stated number of Accounts for customers located in our Territory. These accounts are estimated to generate a stated amount of Account Gross Billings. For example, a FP-17 Initial Plan means $17,000 in Account Gross Billings.

The Account Gross Billings that you want for your Franchised Business should not, however, be considered as the actual income or profit you will realize. We do not represent, warrant, or guaranty that any Accounts will be profitable or that the Account Gross Billings that Accounts are initially estimated to generate will be the actual Gross Billings that you realize from those Accounts. The total annual Gross Billings you actually achieve are affected by many factors such as: the Account Gross Billings being offered in installments during the specified time period; your rejecting or losing an Account; and the interval of time before any required replacement Account is offered. The quality of the services you perform and the efficiency with which you perform them may also affect your actual Gross Billings. Another factor affecting your actual Gross Billings is the quality and efficiency of your cleaning services.

OUR FULFILLMENT OF FRANCHISE PLAN

We reviewed our compliance with Unit Franchise Agreements concerning the amount, timeliness, and refund requirements for Account Gross Billings provided to our unit franchisees. We reviewed all Franchise sales made during our last completed fiscal year, and determined whether or not, as of December 31, 2011, Account Gross Billings had been offered in compliance with the Unit Franchise Agreement.

During our last fiscal year, namely, January 1, 2011 to December 31, 2011, we sold 4 unit franchises. Of those sold, as of the close of the fiscal year: (a) unit franchisees either had their Initial Plans timely filled or had accepted our performance in 4 cases; (b) we and the unit franchisee made a mutually ac-

ceptable adjustment to the Initial Plans, such as by our recalculation of the Initial Franchise Fee or an extension of time to provide Accounts or replacement Accounts, in 0 cases; (c) the time for us to provide initial Accounts under Initial Plans had not expired in 0 cases; and d) our obligations to fulfill the Initial Plans terminated in 0 cases because the Unit Franchise Agreement was terminated.

Therefore, we complied with the amount, timeliness, and account substitution requirements for Account Gross Billings provided to our unit franchisees in 100% of the cases. Substantiation of the data used in preparing these statistics will be made available upon request.

Other than the preceding financial performance representations, we do not make any financial performance representations. We also do not authorize our employees or representatives to make any such representations either orally or in writing. If you are purchasing an existing outlet, however, we may provide you with the actual records of that outlet. If you receive any other financial performance information or projections of your future income, you should report it to the franchisor's management by contacting Michael Cendro, 1355 Halyard Drive, Suite 150, West Sacramento, CA 95691, (916) 376-8977 the Federal Trade Commission, and the appropriate state regulatory agencies.

Community Begins Here.®

KIDDIE ACADEMY

CHILD CARE LEARNING CENTERS

KIDDIE ACADEMY

3415 Box Hill Corporate Center Dr.
Abingdon, MD 21009
Tel: (800) 554-3343, (410) 515-0788 x245
Fax: (410) 569-2729
Email: sales@kiddieacademy.com
Website: www.kiddieacademy.com
Susan Hilger, VP of Franchise Development

We offer comprehensive training and support without additional cost. KIDDIE ACADEMY's step-by-step program assists with staff recruitment, training, accounting support, site selection, marketing, advertising, and curriculum. A true turn-key opportunity that provides on-going support so you can focus on running a successful business.

BACKGROUND

IFA Member:	Yes
Established & First Franchised:	1981; 1992
Franchised Units:	106
Company-Owned Units:	2
Total Units:	108
Distribution:	US – 108; CAN – 0; O'seas – 0
North America:	22 States, 0 Provinces

Density:	18 in NY, 14 in NJ, 13 in PA
Projected New Units (12 Months):	17
Qualifications:	4, 4, 2, 3, 2, 4

FINANCIAL/TERMS

Cash Investment:	$150K
Total Investment:	$355.7 – $657K
Minimum Net Worth:	$400K
Fees (Franchise):	$20K
Fees (Royalty):	7%
Fees (Advertising):	2%
Term of Contract (Years):	15/15
Average Number of Employees:	10 –12 FT, 10 – 12 PT
Passive Ownership:	Discouraged
Encourage Conversions:	Yes
Area Development Agreements:	No
Sub-Franchising Contracts:	No
Expand in Territory:	Yes
Space Needs:	7,000 – 10,000 SF

SUPPORT & TRAINING

Financial Assistance Provided:	Yes (D)
Site Selection Assistance:	Yes
Lease Negotiation Assistance:	Yes
Co-operative Advertising:	Yes
Franchisee Association/Member:	Yes/Not a Member
Size of Corporate Staff:	45
On-going Support:	a, B, C, D, E, G, H, I
Training:	Ongoing Staff Train.; 1 week Director Train., Corp. HQ; 2 weeks Owner Train., Corp. HQ

SPECIFIC EXPANSION PLANS

US:	All United States
Canada:	No
Overseas:	No

The information in this Item 19 represents an actual historic financial performance representation. Franchised Academies that have been open and operational for less than 18 months are called "ramping academies." Franchised Academies that have been open and operational for more than 18 months are called "mature academies." We have excluded the ramping academies from the historic financial performance representation below because mature academy revenues and expenses more accurately reflect revenues and expenses achieved at existing academies in that they include only stabilized, full year revenues and expenses actually achieved over time. Of the mature academies in our system 64 reported all of the required expense information for the calendar year ending December 31, 2010 pursuant to their contractual reporting requirements (See Item 9 of this Franchise Disclosure Document). Accord-

ingly, operating information is presented for those 64 fully reporting mature academies in the tables below. We have not conducted an independent investigation or an audit to verify the figures presented; the information presented was provided to us by our franchisees.

Financial performance information about our mature academies includes gross revenues, payroll, occupancy and miscellaneous expenses. All units offer substantially the same services and products to the public. However, the actual sales and expenses of any franchised unit may vary substantially. The results presented in the tables below represent the Gross Profit, which equals the gross revenue minus the listed operating expenses. More detailed descriptions of these expense items are presented in the notes provided below. In addition to the individual academy performance information supplied in the tables, the average performance information for the reporting locations is also presented. The time periods expressed in the chart below are not meant to be an indication as to when or if a unit will reach maturity. The performance of each academy and its growth rate (if any) will vary by location, competitive environment, the region and market area in which the unit is located, labor costs, programs and the individual franchisee's marketing efforts and management skills. Accordingly, the information presented should only be used as a reference guide in conducting an independent analysis of the proposed business. We have in our possession written substantiation to support the information appearing in this Item 19. Written substantiation of the data used in preparing these financial performance representations will be made available to prospective franchisees upon reasonable request.

The data presented in this Item 19 was prepared without an audit. Prospective franchisees should be advised that no certified public accountant has audited these figures or expressed his or her opinion with regard to their content or form. We do not make any representations about a prospective franchisee's future financial performance, including, without limitation, actual, average, projected or forecasted sales, expenses, profits,

cash flow or earnings. We also do not authorize our employees or representatives to make any such representations orally or in writing. If you are purchasing an existing unit, however, we may provide you with actual records of that outlet. If you receive any other financial performance information or projections of your future income, you should immediately report it to the franchisor's management by contacting Gregory Helwig, 3415 Box Hill Corporate Center Drive, Abingdon, Maryland, 21009, (410) 515-0788, the Federal Trade Commission and the appropriate state regulatory agencies.

Not all franchised academies achieved this level of average revenues and/or average gross profits. There is no assurance that you will do as well and you must accept the risk of not doing as well. You should conduct and independent investigation of the costs and expenses you will incur in operating a franchised academy. The figures presented below are for mature academies that have been in operation, on average, for a number of years. A new franchisee's financial results are likely to differ from the results stated in this financial performance representation. Accordingly, you must accept the risk that in the initial stages of your operation of your academy your revenue figures will be substantially below, and your expense figures may be substantially higher than, what is presented below.

FOR CALENDAR YEAR ENDED DECEMBER 31, 2010

Number of locations reporting	64
Average # of months open	90.33
*Average Revenue	$1,062,150
Average Labor Expense	451,510
Average Occupancy Expense	216,989
Average Miscellaneous Expense	129,624
*Average Gross Profit	$264,027

Notes:

*28 Academies or 44% of the 64 mature academies reporting operated at or above the Average Revenue figure presented above. 28 Academies or 44% of the 64 mature academies reporting operated at or above the Average Gross Profit figure presented above.

Revenue – Gross sales based on actual operating results as reported weekly by franchisees to Kiddie Academy, representing registration fees, tuition, and other amounts paid by families to the franchisee.

Labor – Employee-related expenses including: wages, salaries, bonus, commission, payroll taxes, insurance benefits, and

worker's compensation expenses (where applicable) as reported monthly by franchisees to Kiddie Academy. This also includes the cost of an Academy Director(s).

Occupancy – Includes rent, common area maintenance, real estate taxes and percentage rent (if any). This includes other lease related charges, such as: maintenance, security, trash removal, association dues and shopping center marketing expenses as reported monthly by franchisees to Kiddie Academy, if applicable.

Miscellaneous – Includes other (discretionary) variable expenses related to the operation of the business, including but not limited to: royalties and brand building fund fees, telephone, advertising, utilities, cleaning services, postage and training as reported monthly by franchisees to Kiddie Academy.

Gross Profit – Revenue minus Labor, Occupancy and Miscellaneous Expenses. Other (non- listed) expenses may impact net profit (or net loss).

INDIVIDUAL ACADEMY PERFORMANCE FOR CALENDAR YEAR ENDING DECEMBER 31, 2010

Location#	Revenue	Labor Expense	Occupancy Expense	Misc. Expense	Gross Profit
1	$1,157,553	$483,332	$209,441	$179,255	$285,525
2	$1,063,297	$467,795	$229,176	$129,319	$237,006
3	$564,282	$324,717	$117,751	$72,711	$49,104
4	$1,355,248	$757,337	$153,486	$154,399	$290,026
5	$503,501	$255,025	$16,969	$78,169	$153,338
6	$755,277	$334,678	$203,487	$67,007	$150,105
7	$754,505	$353,941	$233,760	$99,727	$67,078
8	$1,174,521	$504,554	$299,396	$136,654	$233,917
9	$790,542	$386,751	$144,229	$45,723	$213,839
10	$630,699	$259,497	$152,383	$103,195	$115,624
11	$627,019	$185,002	$107,606	$44,738	$289,673
12	$1,196,243	$602,847	$205,171	$121,135	$267,090
13	$1,451,140	$750,683	$240,457	$157,168	$302,832
14	$1,100,883	$492,752	$179,151	$149,771	$279,210
15	$1,008,333	$497,192	$238,348	$106,915	$165,878
16	$881,874	$307,768	$303,307	$122,017	$148,782
17	$1,677,963	$687,033	$189,049	$188,278	$613,603
18	$838,362	$333,436	$217,516	$110,450	$176,960
19	$1,092,545	$400,583	$328,967	$160,623	$202,372
20	$1,493,010	$472,668	$309,342	$196,685	$514,315
21	$1,817,693	$858,396	$355,700	$190,691	$412,906
22	$852,795	$442,900	$120,473	$51,110	$238,312
23	$648,751	$295,147	$143,569	$75,376	$134,659
24	$1,432,509	$520,588	$265,416	$191,511	$454,995
25	$1,044,139	$440,780	$261,918	$313,239	$210,202
26	$1,360,068	$607,532	$338,263	$151,798	$262,475
27	$966,206	$466,386	$186,497	$134,981	$178,342
28	$1,431,922	$553,876	$357,192	$196,697	$324,158
29	$780,155	$383,087	$212,401	$99,183	$85,484
30	$912,050	$407,833	$92,591	$97,447	$314,179
31	$1,888,345	$557,096	$439,356	$269,837	$622,056
32	$1,862,398	$625,439	$290,997	$207,845	$738,118
33	$1,004,917	$466,860	$173,766	$79,313	$284,978
34	$1,160,758	$405,324	$310,890	$131,316	$313,227
35	$493,381	$282,051	$139,653	$79,321	$(7,644)
36	$668,851	$164,540	$141,198	$64,671	$298,442

37	$1,162,262	$401,095	$204,075	$107,506	$449,586
38	$545,041	$249,555	$255,063	$75,743	($35,320)
39	$752,926	$331,248	$201,438	$99,279	$120,961
40	$1,120,002	$504,925	$241,250	$140,828	$232,999
41	$860,429	$388,931	$234,838	$115,824	$120,835
42	$916,137	$419,875	$181,613	$87,149	$227,500
43	$1,643,927	$721,280	$206,445	$208,371	$507,831
44	$1,092,348	$420,971	$208,276	$148,914	$314,186
45	$2,649,492	$794,025	$430,631	$308,497	$1,116,339
46	$1,011,253	$426,535	$206,196	$120,021	$258,502
47	$1,236,124	$467,747	$319,823	$192,676	$255,879
48	$1,070,827	$496,252	$242,332	$104,890	$227,353
49	$1,059,557	$408,077	$169,089	$157,518	$324,873
50	$658,957	$328,237	$63,393	$103,890	$163,436
51	$818,677	$318,605	$309,517	$97,143	$93,411
52	$644,545	$300,740	$164,826	$81,242	$97,736
53	$994,426	$311,511	$185,892	$137,749	$359,274
54	$521,082	$264,188	$189,870	$80,772	($13,748)
55	$1,312,888	$568,954	$245,720	$151,648	$346,566
56	$1,164,095	$532,139	$173,695	$130,524	$327,737
57	$1,259,078	$570,620	$211,029	$171,734	$305,694
58	$632,357	$280,609	$131,827	$96,016	$123,905
59	$862,543	$536,409	$272,086	$128,323	($74,275)
60	$2,005,477	$760,946	$240,429	$196,053	$808,049
61	$1,157,515	$666,244	$189,528	$174,646	$127,097
62	$869,509	$347,499	$164,342	$83,333	$274,334
63	$698,910	$359,814	$140,799	$108,224	$90,073
64	$815,460	$384,154	$194,400	$111,160	$125,746

THE REVENUES, EXPENSES AND GROSS PROFIT FIGURES CONTAINED IN THE BOXES ABOVE ARE REVENUES, EXPENSES AND GROSS PROFITS OF THE EXISTING MATURE FRANCHISED LOCATIONS DESCRIBED, AS PROVIDED BY THE INDIVIDUAL REPORTING FRANCHISEES, AND SHOULD NOT BE CONSIDERED AS THE ACTUAL OR PROBABLE REVENUES, EXPENSES OR GROSS PROFITS THAT WILL BE REALIZED OR INCURRED BY ANY PROSPECTIVE FRANCHISEE. WE DO NOT REPRESENT THAT ANY FRANCHISEE CAN EXPECT TO ATTAIN SUCH REVENUES OR GROSS PROFITS OR WILL INCUR SUCH EXPENSES. NONE OF THIS INFORMATION IS INTENDED AS A REPRESENTATION OF WHAT REVENUES AND GROSS PROFITS YOU CAN EXPECT TO ACHIEVE OR EXPENSES YOU CAN EXPECT TO INCUR AT ANY PARTICULAR FRANCHISED KIDDIE ACADEMY LOCATION.

KUM♦N℠

MATH. READING. SUCCESS.

KUMON NORTH AMERICA

300 Frank W. Burr Blvd., #6
Teaneck, NJ 07666-67
Tel: (800) 633-0740, (201) 928-0444
Fax: (201) 692-3130
Email: tkuczek@kumon.com
Website: www.kumonfranchise.com
Thomas Kuczek, Franchise Recruitment Manager

Premiere supplemental education franchise where you will find success, one child at a time.

BACKGROUND

IFA Member:	Yes
Established & First Franchised:	1958; 1958
Franchised Units:	1,975
Company-Owned Units:	25
Total Units:	2,000
Distribution:	US – 1,425; CAN – 328; O'seas – 23,580
North America:	50 States, 9 Provinces
Density:	241 in CA, 110 in TX, 93 in NY
Projected New Units (12 Months):	120
Qualifications:	3, 3, 3, 5, 4, 4

FINANCIAL/TERMS

Cash Investment:	$70K
Total Investment:	$65.5 – $139.6K
Minimum Net Worth:	$150K
Fees (Franchise):	$1K, Materials:$1K
Fees (Royalty):	$32 – $36/subj./month
Fees (Advertising):	N/A
Term of Contract (Years):	5
Average Number of Employees:	1 FT, 1 – 3 PT
Passive Ownership:	Not Allowed
Encourage Conversions:	N/A
Area Development Agreements:	No
Sub-Franchising Contracts:	No
Expand in Territory:	No
Space Needs:	1,000 SF

SUPPORT & TRAINING

Financial Assistance Provided:	No
Site Selection Assistance:	Yes
Lease Negotiation Assistance:	No
Co-operative Advertising:	Yes
Franchisee Association/Member:	Yes/Member
Size of Corporate Staff:	400
On-going Support:	C, D, E, F, G, H, I
Training:	Kumon University Teaneck, NJ and local region; 13 – 16 Days Total Start-Up

SPECIFIC EXPANSION PLANS

US:	All United States
Canada:	All Canada
Overseas:	All Countries

The following chart represents information on the enrollments for Kumon centers after 12 and 24 months of operation. All numbers are as of December 31, 2011.

Year Center Opened	Average Number of Enrollments After 12 Reporting Months For Centers Opened in Year Indicated*	Average Number of Enrollments After 24 Reporting Months For Centers Opened In Year Indicated*	Average Number of Enrollments After 12 Reporting Months For Top 25 % Performing Centers by Year Opened*	Average Number of Enrollments After 24 Reporting Months For Top 25% Performing Centers by Year Opened*
2010	98	N/A	157	N/A
2009	86	126	149	221
2008	103	143	174	226
2007	90	120	137	191
2006	71	95	118	157
2005	80	111	135	178

The average enrollment for mature Centers as of December 31, 2011 was 201. We define a mature Center as a Center that has been open for 3 years or more. It does not include Centers that have closed.

*This information is for new centers. It excludes transfer Centers and Centers that have closed. Enrollments are subject-students that are reported to Kumon by franchisees. For example, one student may enroll in Math and Reading subjects. This student would count as two enrolled subject-students. You charge tuition, and correspondingly pay a royalty to Kumon, for each subject-student.

The average enrollment numbers set forth above are based upon numbers supplied to us by our franchisees. While we have no reason to doubt their accuracy, we have not conducted any audits or otherwise independently verified the numbers submitted to us by franchisees.

The information contained in this Item 19 should not be considered to be the actual or probable enrollment that you will realize. Your results will likely differ from the results contained in this Item 19. Performance varies from Center to Center and the above information cannot be used to make estimates related to future performance of any particular Center. Written substantiation of the information used in preparing the statements contained in this Item 19 will be made available to you upon reasonable request. However, we will not disclose the identity, enrollment or other information about any particular Center.

Other than the preceding financial performance representation, we do not make any financial performance representations. We also do not authorize employees or representatives to make any such representations either orally or in writing. If you are purchasing an existing outlet, however, we may provide you with the actual records of that outlet. If you receive any other financial performance information or projections of your future income, you should report it to the franchisor's management by contacting Robert Lichtenstein, Corporate Counsel, 300 Frank W. Burr Boulevard, Teaneck, New Jersey 07666, (201) 928-0444, the Federal Trade Commission, and the appropriate state regulatory agency.

LEARNINGRX

5085 List Dr., # 200
Colorado Springs, CO 80919
Tel: (866) 679-1569, (719) 955-6708
Fax: (719) 218-9944
Email: tanya@learningrx.com
Website: www.learningrx-franchise.com
Tanya Mitchell, VP of Franchise Development

LearningRx is a personal one on one Brain Training franchise leading the Brain Training industry with unmatched training results. LearningRx improves skills like memory, attention, and processing speed and has programs that can help people of all ages with ADHD, autism, dyslexia, brain injury, etc. Studies show that 88% of learning/processing problems are caused by one or more weak cognitive skills, and LearningRx is the expert in assessing and improving these skills. One on one brain training and our proprietary methodology make LearningRx the answer to remediation and enhancement for all ages.

BACKGROUND

IFA Member:	Yes
Established & First Franchised:	1986; 2003
Franchised Units:	85
Company-Owned Units:	2
Total Units:	87
Distribution:	US – 87; CAN – 0; O'seas – 0
North America:	28 States, 0 Provinces
Density:	16 in TX, 7 in MN, 7 in VA
Projected New Units (12 Months):	20
Qualifications:	3, 3, 3, 3, 4, 4

FINANCIAL/TERMS

Cash Investment:	$65 – $75K
Total Investment:	$109 – $209K
Minimum Net Worth:	$250K
Fees (Franchise):	$25 – $35K
Fees (Royalty):	10%
Fees (Advertising):	2.5%
Term of Contract (Years):	10/10
Average Number of Employees:	3 FT, 20 PT
Passive Ownership:	Discouraged

Encourage Conversions:	N/A	Co-operative Advertising:	No
Area Development Agreements:	Yes	Franchisee Association/Member:	No
Sub-Franchising Contracts:	No	Size of Corporate Staff:	20
Expand in Territory:	Yes	On-going Support:	A, C, G, H
Space Needs:	1,200 – 1,800 SF	Training:	2 Weeks+ On-Site

SUPPORT & TRAINING

SPECIFIC EXPANSION PLANS

Financial Assistance Provided:	No	US:	Yes
Site Selection Assistance:	Yes	Canada:	No
Lease Negotiation Assistance:	No	Overseas:	No

We have based the claims upon the business records and financial statements prepared by our franchisees and have compiled the claims to the extent possible in a manner consistent with generally accepted accounting principles consistently applied. Written substantiation for the financial performance representation will be made available to you upon reasonable request. The products and services offered by each franchisee, although essentially the same, may vary slightly based on market conditions, demand for specific products, the learning requirements of customers, and the sales skills utilized by the owners and employees of each individual center.

The gross revenue attained by each center will depend on a wide range of factors including, but not limited to, geographic differences, competition within the immediate market area, the quality of the service provided to customers by the franchisee and its employees, consumer demand for our products, and the marketing skills and sales efforts employed by each franchisee. The profitability of individual franchisees will depend on a number of factors which may vary due to the individual characteristics of each center. Factors affecting the net profits may include, but are not limited to, the costs of labor, insurance, supplies, and compliance with state and local laws regulating the provision of educational training services, including any state-specific licensing requirements.

Other than the information provided on the following pages, we do not furnish or authorize our salespersons to furnish any oral or written information concerning the actual or potential sales, income or profits of a LearningRx Brain Training Center[SM].

The net revenue, expense numbers and ratios, average marketing expenditures by category, average marketing cost per prospect by category, percentage of prospects by marketing category, sales conversion rates, and percentage of revenue by service type, represent historical operating figures for all LearningRx franchisee-owned Centers open during the full fiscal year October 1, 2010 through September 30, 2011. Each chart reflects the performance experienced by the average of all LearningRx franchisee-owned Centers by revenue who operated a Center during the full fiscal year 2010 - 2011. As of September 30, 2011, out of 73 franchisee-owned Centers, 52 Centers operated during the full fiscal year ending September 30 2011, and are represented below. Forty One (41) out of the Fifty Two (52) Centers, or 79%, attained or surpassed the stated results.

Some outlets have earned this amount. Your individual results may differ. There is no assurance that you'll earn as much.

The numbers reflected in the charts below should not be considered as potential revenues, expenses or conversion ratios that may be realized by you. If you rely on these figures, you must accept the risk that your franchise will not perform as well.

Oct 2010 through Sept 2011	Avg. of top 1/3	Avg. of middle 1/3	Avg. of bottom 1/3	Avg. all Centers
Total Revenue Charged (1)	$610,375	$360,403	$167,561	$375,372
Total Expenses (2)	$489,602	$306,933	$161,073	$316,162
Net Operating Income	$120,774	$53,470	$6,488	$59,210
Profit % (Non-adjusted)	20%	15%	4%	16%
Profit (Adjusted for 35% Payroll) (6)	$143,985	$72,385	$18,009	$76,970
Profit % (Adjusted)	24%	20%	11%	21%
Average Case Size	$6,896	$6,081	$5,400	$6,112

Program Results				
Avg Percentile Gains/Core Tests (7)	20	20	22	21
Word Attack (ReadRx) Percentile Gains (7)	18	16	20	18
% of Final Surveys Completed	95%	88%	75%	86%
Average Client Satisfaction Rating (out of 10)	9.5	9.4	7.9	8.9
Revenue By Program				
Assessment Charges	$19,558	$14,597	$7,695	$13,830
Einstein Charges	$110,793	$30,407	$12,407	$50,456
LiftOff Charges	$29,148	$17,788	$7,928	$18,089
MathRx Charges	$46,963	$19,877	$9,193	$25,034
Max Charges	$1,540	$1,575	$1,515	$1,543
Miscellaneous Charges	-$4,036	$4,046	$1,915	$666
ReadRx Charges	$227,283	$155,318	$63,941	$147,215
ThinkRx Charges	$179,126	$116,794	$62,967	$118,539
Total Revenue Charged	$610,375	$360,403	$167,561	$375,372
Revenue Collected	$552,496	$340,494	$154,020	$345,253
% Revenue by Program				
% Assessment Charges	3%	4%	5%	4%
% Einstein Charges	18%	8%	7%	13%
% LiftOff Charges	5%	5%	5%	5%
% MathRx Charges	8%	6%	5%	7%
% Max Charges	0%	0%	1%	0%
% Miscellaneous Charges	-1%	1%	1%	0%
% ReadRx Charges	37%	43%	38%	39%
% ThinkRx Charges	29%	32%	38%	32%
Expenses				
Total Marketing Expenses	$75,430	$43,758	$32,072	$50,067
Bank & Credit Card Fees	$8,324	$3,389	$2,140	$4,570
Facilities (3)	$55,847	$45,326	$27,900	$42,734
Insurance	$3,064	$2,691	$1,968	$2,563
Miscellaneous	$2,523	$7,513	$1,092	$3,659
Outside Services	$15,424	$5,429	$2,422	$7,656
Pay Admin (4)	$102,684	$62,995	$34,930	$66,256
Pay Trainers	$134,159	$82,062	$35,238	$82,885
Royalty LearningRx (5)	$51,448	$31,733	$12,880	$31,652
Supplies	$28,994	$14,092	$7,728	$16,761
Taxes (Non-payroll)	$4,334	$2,118	$253	$2,197
Travel & Entertainment	$7,372	$5,828	$2,448	$5,163
Total Expenses	$489,602	$306,933	$161,073	$316,162

% Expense				
Advertising	12%	12%	19%	13%
Bank & Credit Card Fees	1%	1%	1%	1%
Facilities	9%	13%	17%	11%
Insurance	1%	1%	1%	1%
Miscellaneous	0%	2%	1%	1%
Outside Services	3%	2%	1%	2%
Pay Admin	17%	17%	21%	18%
Pay Trainers	22%	23%	21%	22%
Royalty LearningRx (5)	8%	9%	8%	8%
Supplies	5%	4%	5%	4%
Taxes (Non-payroll)	1%	1%	0%	1%
Travel & Entertainment	1%	2%	1%	1%
Status counts				
Prospect	290	198	143	209
Assessments	206	141	97	147
Consultations	171	108	58	111
Students started	90	62	31	61
Sale Conversion Rates				
% Assessment/Prospect	71%	71%	68%	70%
% Consultation/Assessment	83%	76%	60%	76%
% Student/Consultation	53%	57%	54%	55%
% Student/Assessment	44%	44%	32%	41%
% Student/Prospect	31%	31%	22%	29%
Marketing Cost/Prospect	$260	$221	$225	$240
Marketing Cost/Student	$836	$705	$1,027	$827
Prospect Marketing Type Counts				
DM Direct Mail	18	11	8	12
OA Other Advertising	163	103	81	115
PA Print Ads	20	15	11	16
PPC Pay-Per-Click	57	110	66	78
RD Radio	33	8	4	15
TV Television	6	5	9	7
WB Web	123	123	93	113
YP Yellow Pages	2	1	1	1
Marketing Student Count By Type				
DM Direct Mail	7	4	2	4
OA Other Advertising	47	33	16	32
PA Print Ads	5	4	2	4
PPC Pay-Per-Click	1	1	0	1

RD Radio	9	2	1	4
TV Television	1	1	1	1
WB Web	14	11	5	10
YP Yellow Pages	0	0	0	0
Marketing Cost/Prospect By Type				
DM Direct Mail	$368	$456	$514	$426
OA Other Advertising	$118	$118	$128	$120
PA Print Ads	$650	$578	$615	$618
PPC Pay-Per-Click	$46	$20	$25	$28
RD Radio	$374	$425	$490	$395
TV Television	$374	$445	$251	$334
WB Web (incl local + 50% of MDF)	$86	$40	$28	$53
YP Yellow Pages	$531	$413	$164	$398
Marketing Cost/Student By Type				
DM Direct Mail	$1,005	$1,203	$1,702	$1,198
OA Other Advertising - Networking	$405	$366	$637	$433
PA Print Ads	$2,694	$2,014	$2,960	$2,498
PPC Pay-Per-Click	$3,753	$2,692	$5,920	$3,623
RD Radio	$1,371	$1,575	$2,177	$1,478
TV Television	$1,673	$1,970	$1,854	$1,833
WB Web (incl local + 50% of MDF)	$737	$456	$525	$600
YP Yellow Pages	$3,716	$1,487	$557	$1,791
Marketing Expense by Type				
DM Direct Mail	$6,623	$4,884	$3,971	$5,136
OA Other Advertising	$19,117	$12,135	$10,403	$13,818
PA Print Ads	$13,314	$8,768	$6,906	$9,609
PPC Pay-Per-Click	$2,649	$2,217	$1,644	$2,160
RD Radio	$12,260	$3,428	$2,177	$5,882
TV Television	$2,066	$2,433	$2,370	$2,291
WB Web	$2,705	$530	$749	$1,317
YP Yellow Pages	$874	$437	$155	$482
Total Local Marketing Exp.	$59,609	$34,832	$28,375	$40,697
MDF Marketing Dev. Fund	$15,821	$8,926	$3,697	$9,370
Marketing ROI (incl MDF)	$8.09	$8.24	$5.22	$7.50
ROI by Marketing Type (8)(9)				
DM Direct Mail	6.9	5.1	3.2	5.1
OA Other Advertising	17.0	16.6	8.5	14.1
PA Print Ads	2.6	3.0	1.8	2.4

PPC Pay-Per-Click	1.8	2.3	0.9	1.7
RD Radio	5.0	3.9	2.5	4.1
TV Television	4.1	3.1	2.9	3.3
WB Web (incl local + 50% of MDF)	9.4	13.3	10.3	10.2
YP Yellow Pages	1.9	4.1	9.7	3.4

Notes for the charts displayed above:

(1) Net Revenue is based on the accrual basis. These numbers reflect amounts billed to clients during the fiscal year October 1, 2010 through September 30, 2011, but do not reflect actual collections during that period. The numbers in this category reflect the average net revenue achieved by all 52 franchisee-owned Centers which were in operation for the entire fiscal year of 2010/2011.

(2) All expenses reflect actual expenses paid during the fiscal year October 1, 2010 through September 30, 2011.

(3) Facilities expense includes rent, utilities, telephone and Internet service.

(4) Administration compensation includes some amount of trainer compensation.

(5) The Royalty numbers reported in this chart are based on Revenues collected by franchisees during the fiscal year October 1, 2010 through September 30, 2011.

(6) This may not include all expenses you will incur in operating a Center. Examples of excluded expenses include insurance, basic business supplies, interest, travel, and other expenses.

(7) Profit adjusted for Salary and Draws set Trainer and Admin pay adjusted at 35% of revenue and then either increases or decreases profit. This is reported because Franchisees differ in how they pay themselves.

(8) Percentile: the change in ranking among 100 students.

(9) ROI = (average case size)*(students by marketing type)/ (marketing expense by type).

(10) WB Web includes 50% of MDF (Marketing Development Funds) whereas the other marketing types don't include any MDF.

LIBERTY TAX SERVICE

1716 Corporate Landing Pkwy.
Virginia Beach, VA 23454
Tel: (800) 790-3863, (757) 493-8855
Fax: (800) 880-6432
Email: sales@libtax.com
Website: www.libertytaxfranchise.com
David Tarr, Director of Franchsie Development

LIBERTY TAX SERVICE is the fastest-growing international tax service ever, and has been ranked on Entrepreneur magazine's annual "Franchise 500" every year since 1998. Any given year, there is a ready market of taxpayers, and as the tax laws change frequently, many taxpayers are turning to professional preparers to complete that annual task. LIBERTY's growth is fueled by a proven operating system that has been fine-tuned by the leadership and field support staff's more than 600 total years of experience. As a result, no prior tax experience is required to put this system to work. Founder/CEO John Hewitt has worked 44 tax seasons, including 12 years with H&R Block. Accounting Today magazine has named Hewitt one of the accounting profession's Top 100 Most Influential People – 11 times! The International Franchise Association has honored Hewitt as its "Entrepreneur of the Year."

BACKGROUND

IFA Member:	Yes
Established & First Franchised:	1997; 1997
Franchised Units:	4,028
Company-Owned Units:	234
Total Units:	4,262
Distribution:	US – 4,262; CAN – 258; O'seas – 0
North America:	50 States, 10 Provinces
Density:	N/A
Projected New Units (12 Months):	400 – 500
Qualifications:	2, 4, 2, 1, 3, 5

FINANCIAL/TERMS

Cash Investment:	$56.8 – $69.9K
Total Investment:	$56.8 – $69.9K
Minimum Net Worth:	No net worth requirement
Fees (Franchise):	$40K
Fees (Royalty):	14%
Fees (Advertising):	5%
Term of Contract (Years):	5/5
Average Number of Employees:	4 – 6 FT, 2 PT
Passive Ownership:	Allowed

Encourage Conversions:	No
Area Development Agreements:	Yes
Sub-Franchising Contracts:	No
Expand in Territory:	Yes
Space Needs:	400+ SF

SUPPORT & TRAINING

Financial Assistance Provided:	Yes (I)
Site Selection Assistance:	Yes
Lease Negotiation Assistance:	Yes
Co-operative Advertising:	No
Franchisee Association/Member:	No
Size of Corporate Staff:	520
On-going Support:	A, B, C, D, E, F, G, H, I
Training:	5 Days Virginia Beach, VA – Initial, Intermediate, Advanced; 3 Days Various Cities – Intermediate, Advanced

SPECIFIC EXPANSION PLANS

US:	All United States
Canada:	Yes
Overseas:	No

For our Financial Performance Representation, we set forth five sample Profit Loss Statements from our franchisees. The universe from which the Profit Loss Statements were selected is as follows: third year or older Liberty franchised offices of franchisees who operated one storefront office or one storefront and kiosk during the time period May 1, 2010 - April 30, 2011.

During this May 1, 2010 to April 30, 2011 time period we had 629 outlets in the United States who met the characteristics of the selected universe. As to these five sample Profit and Loss Statements, the number and percent of those ti•anchisees in the universe who attained or surpassed the stated results is set forth as follows:

Tax Return Count	Number of franchisees who met or exceeded results	% of franchisees who met or exceeded results
315	526	83.62%
500	345	54.85%
700	184	29.25%
1001	58	9.22%
1899	5	.79%

A kiosk location refers to a temporary location embedded within another retailer, such as a desk at an Ace check cashing store or a booth at a Kmart location. Excluded from this data are offices owned by franchisees with multiple storefront offices in operation, and company operated outlets. The data presented is based upon inf01mation received from independent franchise owners, and has not been audited or otherwise veritled by us. Immediately following the Financial Performance Representations is additional information that you should carefully consider in order to understand this performance information in the appropriate context.

Financial Performance Representation #1: P&L 315 Tax Returns Prepared:

TOTAL # RETURNS INCLUDING # FREE RETURNS	315
# FREE RETURNS	54
AVERAGE FEES (NET)	$296

INCOME

TAX PREP FEES (GROSS FEES)	$109,396
DISCOUNTS	15,861
DISCOUNTS FOR FREE RETURNS	16,169
CASH IN A FLASH	50
TOTAL NET FEES	77,316
TAX SCHOOL INCOME	0
TOTAL INCOME	77,316

EXPENSE

MANAGER'S WAGE	0
WAGES	10,406
GUERILLA MARKETING WAGES	4,393
PAYROLL TAXES	1,773
RENT	28,614
UTILITIES (INCLUDE INTERNET FEES)	4,337
TELEPHONE	2,221
LEASEHOLD IMPROVEMENT/ REPAIRS	284
EQUIPMENT LEASE	0
OFFICE SUPPLIES	987
POSTAGE	0
TAX SCHOOL EXPENSE	0
REFUNDS	583
SEND A FRIEND/CASH IN A FLASH	200
IRS/ST PENALTY & INTEREST	0
INSURANCE	625
PERMITS/LICENSES	185
ZEE PAID ADVERTISING	1,985
GUERILLA MARKETING SUPPLIES	1,332
ADVERTISING ROYALTIES (5%)	3,803

TRAVEL/ENTERTAINMENT/TRAINING	709
BANKING/PROFESSIONAL FEES	586
ROYALTIES	11,000
MISCELLANEOUS	600
TOTAL EXPENSES	74,623
NET INCOME	$2,693

Financial Performance Representation #2: P&L 500 Tax Returns Prepared:

TOTAL # RETURNS INCLUDING # FREE RETURNS	500
# FREE RETURNS	102
AVERAGE FEES (NET)	$308

INCOME

TAX PREP FEES (GROSS FEES)	$279,895
DISCOUNTS	128,913
DISCOUNTS FOR FREE RETURNS	28,167
CASH IN A FLASH	200
TOTAL NET FEES	122,615
TAX SCHOOL INCOME	0
TOTAL INCOME	122,615

EXPENSE

MANAGER'S WAGE	3,750
WAGES	29,469
GUERILLA MARKETING WAGES	300
PAYROLL TAXES	2,929
RENT	15,000
UTILITIES (INCLUDE INTERNET FEES)	4,648
TELEPHONE	5,914
LEASEHOLD IMPROVEMENT/ REPAIRS	876
EQUIPMENT LEASE	0
OFFICE SUPPLIES	5,316
POSTAGE	220
TAX SCHOOL EXPENSE	184
REFUNDS	599

SEND A FRIEND/CASH IN A FLASH	0
IRS/ST PENALTY & INTEREST	30
INSURANCE	711
PERMITS/LICENSE	1,105
ZEE PAID ADVERTISING	0
GUERILLA MARKETING SUPPLIES	0
ADVERTISING ROYALTIES (5%)	6,073
TRAVEL/ENTERTAINMENT/ TRAINING	2,199
BANKING/PROFESSIONAL FEES	556
ROYALTIES	16,576
MISCELLANEOUS	112
TOTAL EXPENSES	96,567
NET INCOME	$26,048

Financial Performance Representation #3: P&L 700 Tax Returns Prepared:

TOTAL # RETURNS INCLUDING # FREE RETURNS	700
# FREE RETURNS	78
AVERAGE FEES (NET)	$224

INCOME

TAX PREP FEES (GROSS FEES)	$181,591
DISCOUNTS	29,080
DISCOUNTS FOR FREE RETURNS	13,118
CASH IN A FLASH	300
TOTAL NET FEES	139,093
TAX SCHOOL INCOME	0
TOTAL INCOME	139,093

EXPENSE

MANAGER'S WAGE	0
WAGES	12,000
GUERILLA MARKETING WAGES	5,000
PAYROLL TAXES	4,000
RENT	12,000
UTILITIES (INCLUDE INTERNET FEES)	3,600

TELEPHONE	1,200
LEASEHOLD IMPROVEMENT/ REPAIRS	0
EQUIPMENT LEASE	0
OFFICE SUPPLIES	500
POSTAGE	100
TAX SCHOOL EXPENSE	500
REFUNDS	299
SEND A FRIEND/CASH IN A FLASH	0
IRS/ST PENALTY & INTEREST	0
INSURANCE	100
PERMITS/LICENSES	0
ZEE PALD ADVERTLSLNG	1,000
GUERILLA MARKETING SUPPLIES	500
ADVERTISING ROYALTIES (5%)	6,885
TRAVEUENTERTAINMENT/ TRAINING	100
BANKING/PROFESSIONAL FEES	100
ROYALTIES	19,277
MISCELLANEOUS	100
TOTAL EXPENSES	67,261
NET INCOME	$71,832

Financial Performance Representation #4: P&L 1,001 Tax Returns Prepared:

TOTAL # RETURNS INCLUDING # FREE RETURNS	1,001
# FREE RETURNS	187
AVERAGE FEES (NET)	$235

INCOME

TAX PREP FEES (GROSS FEES)	$350,872
DISCOUNTS	93,318
DISCOUNTS FOR FREE RETURNS	55,700
CASH IN A FLASH	10,550
TOTAL NET FEES	191,304
TAX SCHOOL INCOME	0
TOTAL INCOME	191,304

EXPENSE	
MANAGER'S WAGE	0
WAGES	20,220
GUERILLA MARKETING WAGES	12,410
PAYROLL TAXES	3,210
RENT	8,000
UTILITIES (INCLUDE INTERNET FEES)	3,300
TELEPHONE	0
LEASEHOLD IMPROVEMENT/ REPAIRS	750
EQUIPMENT LEASE	0
OFFICE SUPPLIES	4,250
POSTAGE	240
TAX SCHOOL EXPENSE	500
REFUNDS	1,297
SEND A FRIEND/CASH IN A FLASH	600
IRS/ST PENALTY & INTEREST	0
INSURANCE	1,200
PERMITS/LICENSES	620
ZEE PAID ADVERTISING	240
GUERILLA MARKETING SUPPLIES	6,440
ADVERTISING ROYALTIES (5%)	9,335
TRAVEL/ENTERTAINMENT/ TRAINING	1,240
BANKING/PROFESSIONAL FEES	440
ROYALTIES	24,404
MISCELLANEOUS	3,240
TOTAL EXPENSES	101,936
NET INCOME	$89,368

Financial Performance Representation #5:
P&L 1,899 Tax Returns Prepared:

TOTAL # RETURNS INCLUDING # FREE RETURNS	1,899
# FREE RETURNS	164
AVERAGE FEES (NET)	$261

INCOME	
TAX PREP FEES (GROSS FEES)	$209,286
DISCOUNTS	23,271
DISCOUNTS FOR FREE RETURNS	33,224
CASH IN A FLASH	0
TOTAL NET FEES	452,791
TAX SCHOOL INCOME	0
TOTAL INCOME	452,791

EXPENSE	
MANAGER'S WAGE	41,721
WAGES	56,300
GUERILLA MARKETING WAGES	12,120
PAYROLL TAXES	13,217
RENT	23,762
UTILITIES (INCLUDE INTERNET FEES)	4,799
TELEPHONE	2,467
LEASEHOLD IMPROVEMENT/ REPAIRS	2,700
EQUIPMENT LEASE	3,229
OFFICE SUPPLIES	10,316
POSTAGE	268
TAX SCHOOL EXPENSE	3,600
REFUNDS	1,765
SEND A FRIEND/CASH IN A FLASH	1,940
IRS/ST PENALTY & INTEREST	178
INSURANCE	1,540
PERMITS/LICENSES	50
ZEE PAID ADVERTISING	18,237
GUERILLA MARKETING SUPPLIES	9,437
ADVERTISING ROYALTIES (5%)	215LL
TRAVEL/ENTERTAINMENT/ TRAINING	5,411
BANKING/PROFESSIONAL FEES	2,214
ROYALTIES	53,627
MISCELLANEOUS	969
TOTAL EXPENSES	$291,378
NET INCOME	$161,413

Additional information applicable to all three Financial Performance Representations:

A number of factors will directly affect the performance of your office. These include, but are not limited to, the general market for preparer provided tax preparation in your area, competitive factors from other tax preparers in your market, and the success of your efforts to obtain quality sites, provide recommended tax courses, hire a sufficient number of trained personnel, engage in successful marketing, offer high customer service, and generally follow the Manual and Liberty system. Your individual financial results may differ substantially from the results stated in this financial performance representation. Written substantiation for this financial performance representation is available to you upon reasonable request. We will not disclose the performance data of a specific office without the owner's consent.

LIQUID CAPITAL

5525 N. MacArthur Blvd., # 535
Irving, TX 75038
Tel: (877) 228-0800x226, (416) 342-8199
Fax: (866) 611-8886
Email: birnbaum@liquidcapitalcorp.com
Website: www.liquidcapitalcorp.com
Brian Birnbaum, President

Factoring is the funding of B2B receivables. It is a $2 trillion global industry. The LIQUID CAPITAL competitive advantage is the relationship a client enjoys with the franchisee. Typically a franchisee has 10 - 15 clients, who generally will factor their receivables for 2 to 3 years. LIQUID CAPITAL is a low overhead, high return, home based business that provides a franchisee with a great life style and high earning potential. LIQUID CAPITAL will loan its franchisees up to 6 times their investment.

BACKGROUND
IFA Member:	Yes
Established & First Franchised:	1999; 2000
Franchised Units:	65
Company-Owned Units:	2
Total Units:	67
Distribution:	US – 37; CAN – 28; O'seas – 1
North America:	32 States, 6 Provinces

Density:	7 in AB, 5 in FL, 3 in IL
Projected New Units (12 Months):	12
Qualifications:	5, 5, 2, 4, 2, 3

FINANCIAL/TERMS
Cash Investment:	$200K – $1M
Total Investment:	$200K – $1M
Minimum Net Worth:	$250K
Fees (Franchise):	$50K
Fees (Royalty):	8%
Fees (Advertising):	$500/Mo.
Term of Contract (Years):	10/10
Average Number of Employees:	1 FT, 0 PT
Passive Ownership:	Not Allowed
Encourage Conversions:	N/A
Area Development Agreements:	No
Sub-Franchising Contracts:	No
Expand in Territory:	No
Space Needs:	N/A

SUPPORT & TRAINING
Financial Assistance Provided:	Yes (D)
Site Selection Assistance:	N/A
Lease Negotiation Assistance:	N/A
Co-operative Advertising:	Yes
Franchisee Association/Member:	Yes/Member
Size of Corporate Staff:	8
On-going Support:	N/A
Training:	5 Days Toronto, Canada

SPECIFIC EXPANSION PLANS
US:	All United States
Canada:	All Canada
Overseas:	Yes

This Financial Performance Representation presents various illustrations of the money flow associated with a Liquid Capital Funding Transaction (as defined below). The information provided in this item is hypothetical and is not derived from existing territories. It is, however, an accurate illustration of the mechanics of Liquid Capital Funding Transactions. Your results are likely to differ from the results of the figures contained in this item. There are no assurances that you will do as well as the illustrations contained in this item and by becoming a franchisee you will accept the risk of not doing as well.

The information disclosed is not intended as any guarantee of results that you are likely to achieve. We are providing information based on hypothetical illustrations only. The information provided in this disclosure is not necessarily indicative of profits.

We possess written substantiation for all illustrations contained in this item. Upon written request and reasonable notice, the information and substantiation of the information used in preparing this item is available for inspection by you at our headquarters. Your individual financial results may differ from the results stated in this item.

The following definitions are related to the illustrations that appear below.

DEFINITIONS

The following defined terms apply to all illustrations:

"Account" means a right to payment of a monetary obligation, whether or not earned by performance, and includes any "Account" as defined in Article 9 of the UCC.

"Accounts (45 days)" means that the client's customer's Accounts are, for the purposes of illustration only, assumed to be outstanding for 45 days. Because Scheduled Invoices are assumed to be $100,000 and Accounts are assumed to be collected only after 45 days, at any point in time the amount of Accounts outstanding is assumed to be $150,000.

"Advance" means the amount of money that you and other participating Liquid Capital franchisees pay the client for the Accounts at the time of funding. Liquid Capital franchisees only pay the client a portion of the total Accounts. We recommend that our franchisees hold back 20% of the value of the Accounts for a reserve, as well as the amount of the initial discount fee (assumed to be 3%). As a result, for the purposes of illustration only, the Advance is assumed to be 77%.

"Back Office Services Fee" means the fee you must pay for Back Office Support Services (as defined in the Franchise Agreement). For full factoring, this fee is currently set at the greater of a percentage (not to exceed 0.75%) of the Accounts represented by the Scheduled Invoices. The Back Office Services Fee for Spot Factoring is calculated differently. (See ITEM 6).

"Exchange Fee" means the fee you pay the Service Provider to identify Participants for a Funding Transaction and to process their share of the Advance. This fee is currently set at 0.25% of the Accounts represented by the Scheduled Invoices and processed through the Service Provider. It is paid only when there is more than one franchisee funding a transaction.

"Financing Cost" means the cost of securing financing for the Advance through Exchange. Exchange may loan Liquid Capital franchisees who are Qualified Borrowers (defined in ITEM 10) up to the lesser of 56.25% of eligible Accounts or 75% of outstanding Advances in its discretion if a Qualified Borrower satisfies Exchange's then-current financing criteria. Exchange charges a fee equal to the greater of 16% per annum or Bank of America prime plus 10% for the loan, calculated on a daily basis. (See ITEM 10). For purposes of illustration, we have assumed 16% applies.

"Funding Transaction" means the delivery of funds by the Participants for the purchase by Exchange of those Accounts that are the subject of the Funding Transaction. For full factoring arrangements, the invoices underlying the Accounts are those listed on each Schedule of Accounts issued by the client under the purchase and sale agreement. These are referred to in this ITEM 19 as the "Scheduled Invoices". In each Funding Transaction, Participants provide funds for the purchase of the Accounts in an amount equal to their proportionate share of the total Advance.

"Gross Revenue" has the meaning given to it in the Franchise Agreement. (See ITEM 6). "Initial Discount Fee" means the fee you charge the client for the first 30 days the client's customer's Accounts are outstanding. For purposes of illustration only, a 3% initial discount fee is assumed.

"Loan to franchisee" means the total amount Exchange may loan a Qualified Borrower meeting its financing criteria. For the purposes of illustration only, in Case 1(b) below, Exchange is loaning the maximum allowable amount (56.25% of eligible Accounts).

"Managing Participant" means the Liquid Capital franchisee who is responsible for managing the ongoing relationship with the client whose Accounts are being factored.

"Management Fee" means the fee the Managing Participant earns for managing the ongoing relationship with the client. This fee is paid by the Originating Franchisee (if the Originating Franchisee is not also acting as the Managing Participant) and the other Participants. This fee is currently 0.5% of the Accounts represented by the Scheduled Invoices.

"Originating Franchisee" means the Liquid Capital franchisee who identifies and processes the client whose Accounts are being factored.

"Originating Franchisee Fee" means the fee the Originating Franchisee earns as a result of identifying and processing the client. This fee is paid by the Managing Participant (if the Originating Franchisee is not also acting as the Managing Participant) and the other Participants. This fee is currently 12% of the gross revenue earned by the non-originating Participants in a Funding Transaction.

"Participant" means a Liquid Capital franchisee who is funding at least a portion of the client's Accounts, but is neither the Originating Franchisee nor the Managing Participant.

"Required Franchisee Capital" means the amount of your own money you advance to the client.

"Royalty" means the royalty you must pay to us. This fee is currently set at 8% of total Gross Revenue of the Franchised Business (as defined in the Franchise Agreement).

"Schedule of Accounts" means each list of invoices representing the Accounts to be purchased under the purchase and sale agreement and that are the subject of a Funding Transaction. For purposes of illustration only, we have assumed Scheduled Invoices representing $100,000 in Accounts. When more than one franchisee is funding the Accounts, the assumed $100,000 of Scheduled Invoices is divided among those franchisees participating in the Funding Transaction based on the amount each is factoring.

"Subsequent Daily Discount Fee" means the fee you charge the client for each additional day the client's customer's Accounts are outstanding after the first 30 days. For the purposes of illustration only, a 0.1% subsequent daily discount fee is assumed.

"Total Advance to Client" means the total amount of money you have advanced to the client in exchange for the client's Accounts. For illustration purposes only, because Accounts are outstanding for 45 days, the Advances represent the value of 45 days worth of Accounts ($150,000) minus the recommended 20% reserve and Initial and Subsequent Daily Discount Fees.

Illustrations

In order to illustrate the nature and allocation of money-related transactional costs, as the basis for all cases we have used an illustrative Funding Transaction with Scheduled Invoices of $100,000. $100,000 is an arbitrary number and should not be viewed as indicative of what you may expect to do in a Funding Transaction. These cases are not a representation of an actual Funding Transaction or of actual or potential fees or costs. These cases do, however, illustrate an accurate overview of the money flow components of a Liquid Capital funding transaction.

Illustration Case 1a: In this illustration, you have found the client on your own, are managing the relationship, and are funding the client's financing needs without the help of any other franchisees and without financing from Exchange.

SMALL FULL FACTORING EXAMPLE: TYPICAL CLIENT			
			CASE 1
Licensee Revenue			Baseline
			No Participation
	Borrow		no
	Originates		yes
	Participate %		100%
	Manage		yes
MONTHLY SALES			$100,000
ACCOUNTS RECEIVABLE	45 DAYS		$150,000
ADVANCE	77%		$115,500
GROSS REVENUE	3.00% for first 30 days		$3,000
	0.1000% for each additional day: 15 additional days		$1,500

Originating Fee (earned)	12.00% of gross revenue earned by other participates	$0
Management fee (earned)	0.50% of the monthly sales of the other participates	$0
TOTAL GROSS REVENUE		$4,500
COST		
PROCESSING FEE	0.75% of sales	$750
ROYALTY	8% Total gross revenue	$360
Originating Fee (paid)	12% Of the gross revenue earned	$0
Management Fee (paid)	0.40% Of the participates sales	$0
Exchange Fee	0.25% Of the Monthly Sales	
		$1,110
NET REVENUE	PRE FINANCING	$3,390
ANNUALIZED		$40,680
FINANCING COST	16% Annualized based on 75% of ADVANCED	$-
NET REVENUE	POST FINANCING	$3,390
ANNUALIZED		$40,680
TOTAL ADVANCE TO CLIENT		$115,500
LOAN TO LICENSEE	56.25% of A/R	$-
REQUIRED LICENSEE CAPITAL		$115,500

Notes:

(1) We recommend you reserve 20% of eligible Accounts, as well as the Initial Discount Fee, thus advancing the client 77% of the Accounts (45 days).

(2) The client is charged an Initial Discount Fee for the first 30 days the Accounts are outstanding. After the first 30 days, the client is charged a Subsequent Daily Discount Fee, for total discount fees of $4,500 (3% x $100,000) + (0.1% x $100,000 x 15 days).

(3) On the cost side, you would pay Exchange a Back Office Services Fee of 0.75% of the Scheduled Invoices or $750 (0.75% x $100,000), and you would pay us a Royalty of 8% of

Gross Revenue or $360 (8% x $4,500). These figures are all based on the assumption that the transaction requires 40 days to complete. The numbers will vary based on a larger or shorter transaction time frame.

(4) Net Fees in this Funding Transaction would be $3,390 ($4,500- $1,100).

(5) For purposes of this exhibit, we assumed an interest rate of 16% per annum. For the financing program offered through Exchange, interest rates vary from 10% to 16%. We chose the highest interest rate to make the most conservative projection. Your interest rate may be lower, and therefore your returns may be higher.

Illustration Case 1b: This illustration is the same as Case 1a, except that you secure the maximum financing from Exchange to fund the Advance.

SMALL FULL FACTORING EXAMPLE: SAMPLE CLIENT		
		CASE 1b
Franchisee Revenue		Baseline with funding
		No Participation
	Borrow	yes
	Originates	yes
	Participate %	100%

	Manage	yes
MONTHLY SALES		$100,000
ACCOUNTS RECEIVABLE	45 DAYS	$150,000
ADVANCE	77%	$115,500
GROSS REVENUE		
Initial discount rate	3.00% For first 30 days	$3,000
Subsequent daily discount rate	0.1000% for each additional day: 15 additional days	$1,500
Originating Fee (earned)	12.00% Of the gross discount revenue	$0
Management Fee (earned)	0.50% of the monthly sales of the other participants	$0
TOTAL GROSS REVENUE (40 DAYS)		$4,500
COST		
PROCESSING FEE	0.75% of sales	$750
ROYALTY	8% of total gross revenue	$360
Originating Fee (paid)	12% Of the gross discount revenue	$0
Management Fee (paid)	0.40% Of the participant's sales	$0
Exchange Fee	0.50% Of the Monthly Sales	
FINANCING COST	16% Annualized based on 75% of ADVANCED	$1,110
		$2,220
NET REVENUE	POST FINANCING	$2,280
NET REVENUE	ANNUALIZED	$27,365
TOTAL ADVANCE TO CLIENT		$115,500
LOAN TO FRANCHISEE	56.25% of A/R	$64,375
REQUIRED FRANCHISEE CAPITAL		$31,125

Notes:

(1) On the cost side, you would still pay a Back Office Services Support Fee of $375 and a Royalty of $360; but in addition, you would pay a financing cost of 16% annualized (calculated daily) of the amount advanced by Exchange or $1,100 (16% x 30/365 x $84,375). This reflects the financing available from Exchange (the lower of 56.25% of $150,000 in eligible Accounts ($84,375) or 75% of $115,500 in outstanding advances ($86,625). These calculations assume that fees will be paid at the conclusion of a Funding Transaction. Some service providers, including Exchange, require fees to be paid up-front. The up-front payment of fees does not materially modify our calculations. For example, on Scheduled Invoices of $100,000, the timing difference would result in a $14.00 difference in fees if you secure the financing from Exchange; otherwise, there would be no difference in fees due to the timing difference.

(2) Net Fees would be $3,390 ($4,500- $2,220 = $2,280).

(3) In this case, Exchange is loaning $84,375 and the amount of capital you invest is $31,125 ($115,500- $84,375).

(4) For purposes of this exhibit, we assumed a leverage rate of 3 to 1. For the financing program offered through Exchange, leverage ratios vary from 56.25% (3:1) to 65% (6:1). We chose the lowest ratio to make the most conservative projection. Your leverage ratio may be higher, and therefore your returns may be higher.

(5) For purposes of this Illustration Case 1b, we assumed an interest rate of 16% per annum. For the financing program offered through Exchange, interest rates vary from 8% to 16%. We chose the highest interest rate to make the most conservative projection. Your interest rate may be lower, and therefore your returns may be higher.

Illustration Case 2: This case illustrates the use of Exchange and the allocation of various fees among the Participants. You originate the client and participate at a 20% level in funding the client's financing needs, but do not manage the client relationship. Another franchisee is the Managing Participant and also participates in funding the client's needs at a 20% level. A third franchisee participates in funding the client's needs at a 60% level. All Participants use their own funds.

SMALL FULL FACTORING EXAMPLE SAMPLE CLIENT			
		CASE 3	
Franchisee Revenue		MANAGER & ORIGINATOR	PARTICI-PANT
	Borrow	no	no
	Originates	yes	no
	Participate %	20%	80%
	Manage	yes	no
MONTHLY SALES		$20,000.00	$80,000
ACCOUNTS RECEIVABLE	45 DAYS	$30,000.00	$120,000
ADVANCE	77%	$23,100.00	$92,400
GROSS REVENUE			
Initial discount rate	3.00% for first 30 days	$600.00	$ 2,400
Subsequent daily discount rate	0.1000% for each additional day: 15 additional days	$300.00	$1,200
Originating Fee (earned)	12.00% Of the gross discount revenue	$432.00	$0
Management Fee (earned)	0.50% of the monthly sales of the other participants	$400.00	
TOTAL GROSS REVENUE (45 DAYS)		$1,732.00	$3,600
COST			
PROCESSING FEE	0.75% of sales	$150.00	$600
ROYALTY	8% Total gross revenue	$139.00	$255
Originating Fee (paid)	12% Of the gross discount revenue	$-	$432
Management Fee (paid)	0.50% Of the participant's sales	$-	$400
Exchange Fee	0.25% Of the Monthly Sales	$50.00	$200
FINANCING COST	16% Annualized based on 75% of ADVANCED	$-	$-
		$339.00	$1,920
NET REVENUE	PRE FINANCING	$1,393.00	$1,680
NET REVENUE	ANNUALIZED	$16,721.00	$20,160
TOTAL ADVANCE TO CLIENT		$23,100	$92,400
LOAN TO FRANCHISEE	56.25% of A/R	$-	$-
REQUIRED FRANCHISEE CAPITAL		$23,100	$92,400

Notes:

(1) The Participants' total Advance to the client is $115,000 or 77% of the value of the Accounts (45 days). The Originating Franchisee and the Managing Participant each advance 20% of the total or $23,100. The other Participant advances 60% of the total or $69,300.

(2) The total discount fees payable by the client are $4,500 [(3% x $100,000) + (0.1% x $100,000).] Based on their respective participating interests in the funding, the Originating Franchisee and Managing Participant each receive 20% of these fees ($900 each) and the other Participant receives 60% ($2,700). In addition to its share of the total discount fees payable by the client, the Originating Franchisee receives an Originating Franchisee Fee of $324, which is 12% of the gross

discount fee revenue earned by the Managing Participant and the other Participant (12% x $900 + $2,700). The Managing Participant receives a Management Fee of $400, which is .5% of the Scheduled Invoices.

(3) On the cost side,

- Each Participant pays its share of the total Back Office Services Support Fee and Exchange Fee, based on its respective participation interest in the funding. The total Back Office Services Support Fee is $750 (.75% x $100,000), of which the Originating Franchisee and Managing Participant each pay $150 (20%) and the other Participant pays $450 (60%). The total Exchange Fee is $250 (.25% x $100,000), of which the Originating Franchisee and Managing Participant each pay $50 (20%) and the other Participant pays $150 (60%).

- The Originating Franchisee and the other Participant each pay their share of the total Management Fee based on their participation interest in the funding. The total Management Fee is $400 (.5% x $80,000), of which the Originating Franchisee pays $100 and the other Participant pays $300.

- The Managing Participant and the other Participant each pay an Originating Franchisee Fee based on the total discount fees they each received. In this case, the Managing Participant received discount fees of $450 and pays an Originating Franchisee Fee of $108 (12% x $900). The other Participant received discount fees of $2,700 and pays an Originating Franchisee Fee of $324 (12% x $2,700).

- Each of the Participants pay us a Royalty of 8% of their respective Gross Revenue, including discount fees and all other fees received. In this case, the Originating Franchisee would pay a Royalty of $107 (8% x $1,332); the Managing Participant would pay a Royalty of $104 (8% x $1,300); and the other Participant would pay a Royalty of $216 (8% x $2,700).

Illustration Case 3: In this case you originate the client, manage the client relationship, and participate in funding the client's financing needs at a 20% level. Through Exchange, one or more other franchisees participate at an 80% level in funding the cliens financing needs. All Participants use their own funds.

SMALL FULL FACTORING EXAMPLE: SAMPLE CLIENT				
			CASE 3	
Franchisee Revenue		ORIGI-NATOR	MAN-AGER	PARTIC-IPANT
	Borrow	no	no	no
	Originates	yes	no	no
	Participate %	23%	20%	60%
	Manage	no	yes	no
MONTHLY SALES		$20,000	$20,000	$60,000
ACCOUNTS RECEIVABLE	45 DAYS	$30,000	$30,000	$90,000
ADVANCE	77%	$23,100	$23,100	$59,200
GROSS REVENUE				
Initial discount rate	3.00% For first 30 days	$600	$600	$1,600
Subsequent daily discount rate	0.1000% for each additional day 15 Additional days	$300	$300	$500
Originating Fee (earned)	12.00% Of the gross discount revenue	$432	$0	$0
Management Fee (earned)	0.50% of the monthly sales of the other participants		$400	
TOTAL GROSS REVENUE (45 DAYS)		$1,332	$1,300	$2,700
COST				
PROCESSING FEE	0.75% of Sales	$150	$150	$450
ROYALTY	8% Total gross revenue	$107	$104	$216
Originating Fee (paid)	12% of the gross discount revenue	$0	$103	$324

Management Fee (paid)	0.50% Of the participant's sales	$100	$-	$300
Exchange Fee	0.25% Of the Monthly Sales	$50	$50	$150
FINANCING COST	16% Annualized based on 75% of ADVANCED	$-	$-	$-
NET REVENUE	PRE FINANCING	$925	$655	$1,260
NET REVENUE	ANNUALIZED	$11,105	$10,656	$15,120
TOTAL ADVANCE TO CLIENT		$23,100	$23,100	$69,300
LOAN TO FRANCHISEE	56.25% of A/R	$-	$-	$-
REQUIRED FRANCHISEE CAPITAL		$23,100	$23,100	$69,300

THE LITTLE GYM

7001 N. Scottsdale Rd., # 1050
Scottsdale, AZ 85253
Tel: (888) 228-2878, (480) 948-2878
Fax: (480) 948-2765
Email: info@thelittlegym.com
Website: www.thelittlegymfranchise.com
Ruk Adams, Senior Vice President

THE LITTLE GYM helps children ages 4 months through 12 years build the confidence and skills needed at each stage of childhood. Our trained instructors nurture happy, confident kids through a range of programs including parent/child classes, gymnastics, karate, dance, and sports skills development, plus enjoyable extras like camps, Parents' Survival Nights, and Awesome Birthday Bashes. Each week, progressively structured classes and a positive learning environment create opportunities for children to try new things and build self-confidence, all with a grin that stretches from ear to ear.

BACKGROUND
IFA Member: Yes
Established & First Franchised: 1976; 1992
Franchised Units: 271
Company-Owned Units: 0
Total Units: 271
Distribution: US – 203; CAN – 11; O'seas – 57
  North America: 37 States, 6 Provinces

Density: 27 in TX, 16 in NJ, 15 in CA
Projected New Units (12 Months): 15
Qualifications: 4, 4, 1, 3, 4, 5

FINANCIAL/TERMS
Cash Investment: $75 – $100K
Total Investment: $157.5 – $294K
Minimum Net Worth: $150 – $200K
Fees (Franchise): $49.5 – $69.5K
Fees (Royalty): 8%
Fees (Advertising): 1%
Term of Contract (Years): 10/10
Average Number of Employees: 2 – 3 FT, 4 – 8 PT
Passive Ownership: Not Allowed
Encourage Conversions: N/A
Area Development Agreements: Yes
Sub-Franchising Contracts: Yes
Expand in Territory: No
Space Needs: 2,500 – 3,600 SF

SUPPORT & TRAINING
Financial Assistance Provided: Yes (I)
Site Selection Assistance: Yes
Lease Negotiation Assistance: Yes
Co-operative Advertising: No
Franchisee Association/Member: No
Size of Corporate Staff: 32
On-going Support: C, D, E, h
Training: 7 Days Various Locations; 14 Days Scottsdale, AZ

SPECIFIC EXPANSION PLANS
US: All United States except SD
Canada: All Canada
Overseas: All Countries

Shown below are unaudited annual gross revenues as reported to us by our U.S. and Puerto Rican franchisees for the year ended December 31, 2011. All franchise locations that opened before January 1, 2011 are included.

YOUR INDIVIDUAL FINANCIAL RESULTS ARE LIKELY TO DIFFER FROM THE RESULTS STATED BELOW. IT WILL TAKE APPROXIMATELY TWO TO THREE YEARS FOR YOU TO ACHIEVE YOUR INCOME POTENTIAL.

Written substantiation of the data used in preparing this item 19 will be made available to you on reasonable request. The financial performance representation figures do not reflect the costs of sales or operating expenses that must be deducted from the gross revenue or gross sales figures to obtain your net income or profit. The best source of cost and expense data may be from franchisees and former franchisees, some of whom may be listed in Exhibit D.

ACTUAL RESULTS VARY FROM UNIT TO UNIT. THE GYMS LISTED BELOW HAVE EARNED THE STATED AMOUNTS. YOUR INDIVIDUAL RESULTS MAY DIFFER FROM THOSE STATED BELOW AND THERE IS NO ASSURANCE YOU WILL EARN AS MUCH. WE CANNOT ESTIMATE THE RESULTS OF ANY PARTICULAR FRANCHISE.

Other than this financial performance representation, we do not make any financial performance representations. We also do not authorize our employees or representatives to make any such representations either orally or in writing. If you are purchasing an existing outlet, however, we may provide you with the actual records of that outlet. If you receive any other financial performance information or projections of your future income, you should report it to our management by contacting J. Ruskin ("Ruk") Adams at 7001 N. Scottsdale Road, Suite 1050, Scottsdale, Arizona 85253, phone (480) 948-2878; the Federal Trade Commission; and the appropriate state regulatory agencies.

Notes:

[1] 11 months reported
[2] 10 months reported
[3] 8 months reported
[4] 7 months reported (Temp Closed)
[5] 8 months reported (Temp Closed)

Annual Gross Revenues year ended Dec. 31, 2011 as reported by US & Puerto Rican Franchisees (Unaudited) Opened Full Year 2011, listed by year opened from 2007 – 2010, highest to lowest US and Puerto Rican Franchisees Reported in US Dollars

Opened 2010	Opened 2009	Opened 2008	Opened 2007
236,056	136,407	317,100	290,710
229,051	291,899	533,223	1,070,653
470,389	813,673	359,221	438,236
358,994	224,327	266,503	252,084
291,682	249,206	253,485	535,687
177,765	353,002	259,083	327,960
191,286	454,694	60,413	395,700
259,557	326,182	142,856	196,565
582,269		255,563	322,581
		334,755	338,013
		211,758	487,118
		210,462	176,779[1]
		186,491	239,297
		265,947	303,150
		227,827	323,832
		470,427	251,912
		441,751	393,674
		259,244	220,477
		548,070[1]	193,072[1]
			248,091
			424,623
			177,478
			900,033
			305,919
			252,018
			278,659
			279,896

Annual Gross Revenues year ended Dec. 31, 2011 as
reported by US & Puerto Rican Franchisees (Unaudited)
Pre-2007 Franchises Opened Full Year 2011,
highest to lowest
US and Puerto Rican Franchisees Reported in US Dollars

390,276	245,216	313,670	261,934	493,180
382,633	280,609	434,664	330,338	600,772
384,651	637,386	210,809	564,546	185,834
335,762	127,546	1,029,498	229,046	182,098
359,408	306,290	337,055	364,921	381,784
470,447	276,688	644,832	331,795	660,681
363,493	352,687	332,343	266,077	302,852
225,768	279,826	308,439	282,281	308,187[3]
336,549	289,717	178,906	354,674	128,543[2]
680,549	334,975	341,528	352,387	190,971
156,879	233,927	311,658	202,691	282,554
409,316	290,754	243,000	400,406	227,229
337,311	248,542	438,887	468,013	400,002
238,246	151,479	706,560	400,392	213,508
466,124	499,217	472,103	932,202	881,118
327,390	349,813	270,099	388,531	236,372
104,575[5]	306,913	202,745	544,463	243,105
360,735	316,895	298,449	585,340	193,870
399,005	369,682	328,260	226,683	215,308
473,046	535,032	292,802	197,458	217,528
229,154[2]	346,533	335,366	299,722	
358,048	482,479	372,311	343,728	
340,732	361,318	475,098	294,948	
78,876[4]	251,507[1]	401,459	303,107	
166,122	397,643	354,947	370,810	
387,096	805,892	186,432	372,618	
466,680	646,106[1]	402,750[1]	511,588	
443,429	324,150	406,662	585,270	
523,299	560,746	249,618	214,893[1]	
607,507	307,103	407,881	172,186	

THE MAIDS

9394 W. Dodge Rd., #140
Omaha, NE 68114
Tel: (800) 843-6243, (402) 558-5555
Fax: (402) 558-4112
Email: rcordova@maids.com
Website: www.themaidsfranchise.com
Ronn Cordova, Vice President of Franchise Development

Distinguished as the number one residential cleaning franchise in 2007, 2008, 2009, 2011, and 2012, and the Fastest Growing residential cleaning franchise four years running by Entrepreneur magazine, THE MAIDS is the quality leader in the industry. THE MAIDS was founded in 1979 and began franchising in 1980. We currently have 165 Franchise Partners operating over 1,000 territories in the US and Canada. Franchise partners benefit from a time-tested cleaning system and business model based on leading-edge technology. THE MAIDS provides the most comprehensive package of training, support, and exclusive territory in the industry. We provide extensive training, including seven weeks of pre-training and nine days of classroom and field training. We are in touch and involved with the new franchisee a minimum of 195 days within the first year. With THE MAIDS, you can build a great business and achieve the lifestyle you desire, all with nights, weekends, and holidays off. THE MAIDS is looking for individuals to join its franchise system. We are looking for people who want an executive experience. With THE MAIDS you are working ON the business, not IN the business. Our franchise partners are not cleaning homes, and are building their business Monday through Friday; no nights, no weekends, and no holidays. THE MAIDS's ideal franchise candidate will have good management and business skills, and most importantly, great people skills.

BACKGROUND

IFA Member:	Yes
Established & First Franchised:	1979; 1980
Franchised Units:	1,075
Company-Owned Units:	23
Total Units:	1,098
Distribution:	US – 1,066; CAN – 32; O'seas – 0
North America:	39 States, 4 Provinces
Density:	103 in CA, 88 in TX, 81 in MA
Projected New Units (12 Months):	80
Qualifications:	5, 5, 1, 2, 1, 5

FINANCIAL/TERMS

Cash Investment:	$56 – $60K
Total Investment:	$95 – $123K
Minimum Net Worth:	$250K
Fees (Franchise):	$10K + $0.95 per QHH
Fees (Royalty):	3.9 – 6.9%
Fees (Advertising):	2%
Term of Contract (Years):	20/20
Average Number of Employees:	2 FT, 6 to start (maids) PT
Passive Ownership:	Discouraged
Encourage Conversions:	Yes
Area Development Agreements:	Yes
Sub-Franchising Contracts:	No
Expand in Territory:	Yes
Space Needs:	1,000 – 1,200 SF

SUPPORT & TRAINING

Financial Assistance Provided:	No
Site Selection Assistance:	Yes
Lease Negotiation Assistance:	No
Co-operative Advertising:	Yes
Franchisee Association/Member:	No
Size of Corporate Staff:	35
On-going Support:	A, B, C, D, E, F, G, h, I
Training:	9 days Corporate Training Omaha, NE; 2 – 3 days Power Training On-Site; 7 weeks Foundation Training (Pre-Training)

SPECIFIC EXPANSION PLANS

US:	All United States
Canada:	All except Saskatchewan and Quebec
Overseas:	No

Below is certain historic financial information regarding The Maids® businesses operated by franchisees ("Franchise Owners") or our affiliates ("Affiliate Owners") that operated within in the United States and Canada from October 1, 2010, through September 30, 2011. Canadian Franchise Owners submitted information in Canadian Dollars and we converted that information to U.S. Dollars using the exchange rate in place at the time the information was submitted. Your individual financial results may differ from the information provided below.

We have not presented any information for Franchise Owners

which were not in operation for the full period. You should be aware that some of the Franchise Owners whose results were used to prepare this information have been in business for a long time, have had a greater opportunity to achieve these results than a new office operated by a new Franchise Owner and it's unlikely that a new Franchise Owner will achieve results like those reported.

As of September 30, 2011, there were a total of 1,098 franchised and company-owned Territories. A total of 150 franchisees licensed and operated 1,072 of the 1,098 Territories. We operated the remaining 26 Territories. A The Maids® territory generally consists of approximately 10,000 potential customers, although some territories may be larger. The information presented in this report does not distinguish between Franchise Owners that purchased a large number of territories and those who did not purchase a large number of territories.

The basis for the Franchise Owner information presented is weekly reports submitted to us by our Franchise Owners and affiliates operating throughout the periods represented that form the basis for royalty payments. We calculated the averages and percentages presented in this Item 19 using exclusively the actual results reported to us by Franchise Owners and Affiliate Owners. Of the 9,366 total weekly reports required from Franchise Owners, 2% or 201 were not received in time for the preparation of this statement and, therefore, could not be included in calculating the information presented. If we had received in time the missing weekly reports, the information presented in this statement may have increased or decreased depending on the information contained in the missing reports. We have assumed that the Franchise Owner's information submitted by Franchise Owners (and which forms in substantial part the basis for the information presented in this document) is accurate, complete and contains no material misrepresentations or omissions. The information

presented is, so far as we know, based on actual experience. We have not audited or verified these reports.

The basis for the information from our Affiliate Owners is our internal books and records, which have been maintained as far as reasonable possible in accordance with U.S. GAAP.

I. STATEMENT OF AVERAGE REVENUE PER CLEAN, AVERAGE REVENUE PER CUSTOMERS, PERCENTAGE OF CLEAN BY SERVICE AND LABOR PERCENTAGES BY OFFICE AND TERRITORY

The following statements are based on information reported by Franchise Owners and Affiliate Owners that were in operation for the 12 month period from October 1, 2010, until September 30, 2011. The statements in this Section I are based on information by offices and territories, and not by Franchise Owner or Affiliate Owner. Most Franchise Owners operate one office, although several Franchise Owners operate two or more offices. There were 180 offices operated by Franchise Owners in 1,072 territories and 3 offices operated by 3 Affiliate Owners in 26 territories as of September 30, 2011. Of those offices operated by Franchise Owners, 178 offices and 1,053 territories were in operation for the entire 12 month period ended September 30, 2011, and all 3 offices operated by Affiliate Owners were in operation for the entire 12 month period ended September 30, 2011. We did not include information for the 2 offices operated by 2 Franchise Owners and 4 Franchise Owners who had not yet opened an office, who collectively are in 19 territories who were not in operation for the entire 12 month period ending September 30, 2011, or for the 11 offices operated by Franchise Owners in 60 territories who did not submit complete reports. The statement includes the average revenue per clean, the average annual revenue per customer, the percentage of total cleans by service and the labor percentage by a regular maid service or a special project.

	Average Revenue Per Clean[(1)]	Average Annual Revenue per Customer[(2)]	Average Percentage of Cleans by Type of Service[(3)]	Average Labor Percentages[(4)]
Regular Maid Service	$138.37	$3,637.81	88.63%	34.92%
Total Number of Offices/ Territories included	170 Offices/1,019 Territories	170 Offices/1,019 Territories	170 Offices/1,019 Territories	170 Offices/1,019 Territories
Number of Offices/Territories Who Met or Exceeded Averages	93 Offices/616 Territories	81 Offices/511 Territories	88 Offices/542 Territories	77 Offices/454 Territories
Percentage (%) of Offices/ Territories Who Met or Exceeded Average	54.71% of Offices/ 60.45% of Territories	47.65% of Offices/ 50.15% of Territories	51.76% of Offices/ 53.19% of Territories	45.29% of Offices/ 44.55% of Territories
Special Project[(5)]	$236.23	$236.23	11.37%	31.30%
Total Number of Offices/ Territories included	170 Offices/1,019 Territories	170 Offices/1,019 Territories	170 Offices/1,019 Territories	170 Offices/1,019 Territories

Number of Offices/Territories Who Met or Exceeded Averages	79 Offices/508 Territories	79 Offices/508 Territories	82 Offices/477 Territories	79 Offices/527 Territories
Percentage (%) of Offices/Territories Who Met or Exceeded Average	46.47% of Offices/ 49.85% of Territories	46.47% of Offices/ 49.85% of Territories	48.24% of Offices/ 46.81% of Territories	46.47% of Offices/ 51.72% of Territories

1. "Average Revenue per Clean" means the average revenue received from a customer from one cleaning project (a "Clean"). It is calculated by dividing the total reported revenue by the total reported number of Cleans.

2. "Average Annual Revenue per Customer" means the total reported revenue that each classification of customer would generate in one year. It is calculated by multiplying the Average Revenue per Clean by the total number of Cleans per year in each classification (Regular Maid Service includes 52 for Weekly, 26 for Every Other Week, and 12 for Monthly, Special project includes a single clean per year).

3. "Percentage of Cleans by Type of Service" means the percentage of total reported number of cleans derived from regular customers and Special Project customers. It is calculated by dividing the total reported number of cleans for each category by total reported number of cleans and multiplying by 100%.

4. "Labor Percentage" means the portion of total reported revenue that is expensed for direct labor costs for each type of Clean and for labor to drive to the Clean location. It is calculated by dividing the labor cost by the total reported revenue and multiplying by 100%.

5. "Special Projects" are one-time projects and are not regularly scheduled cleanings.

II. STATEMENT OF HIGH REVENUE, LOW REVENUE AND AVERAGE REVENUE BY NUMBER OF MONTHS IN OPERATION BY FRANCHISE OWNER AND TERRITORY

The following statements are based on information reported by Franchise Owners and Affiliate Owners that were in operation for the 12 month period from October 1, 2010, until September 30, 2011. There were 150 Franchise Owners operating in 1,072 territories and 3 Affiliate Owners operating in 26 territories as of September 30, 2011. Of those Franchise Owners, 144 operating in 1,053 territories were in operation for the entire 12 month period ended September 30, 2011, and all 3 Affiliate Owners were in operation for the entire 12 month period ended September 30, 2011. We did not include information for the 6 Franchise Owner operating in 19 territories who was not in operation for the entire 12 month period ending September 30, 2011, or for the 11 Franchise Owners operating in 60 territories who did not submit complete reports. The statement includes the high revenue, low revenue and average revenue for the 12 month period from October 1, 2010, until September 30, 2011 for Franchise Owners and Affiliate Owners and territories based upon the number of month in operation.

Months In Operation	High Revenue	Low Revenue	Average Revenue (Including percentage and number of franchisees that met or exceeded the average)
12-24 Months (Out of _0 Owners/0 Territories)	$0	$0	$0 0% of Owners/0% of Territories (0 Owners/0 Territories)
25-36 Months (Out of 2 Owners/10 Territories)	$343,520	$332,008	$337,764 50% Owners/60% of Territories (1 Owners/6 Territories)
37-48 Months (Out of 9 Owners/60 Territories)	$526,596	$163,712	$353,570 44% of Owners/53% of Territories (4 Owners/32 Territories)
Greater than 48 Months (Out of 125 Owners/949 Territories)	$4,634,141	$125,352	$930,164 34% of Owners/53% of Territories (43 Owners/505 Territories)
Entire The Maids® System (Out of 136 Owners/1,019 Territories)	$4,634,141	$125,352	$883,295 32% of Owners/50% of Territories (44 Owners/509 Territories)

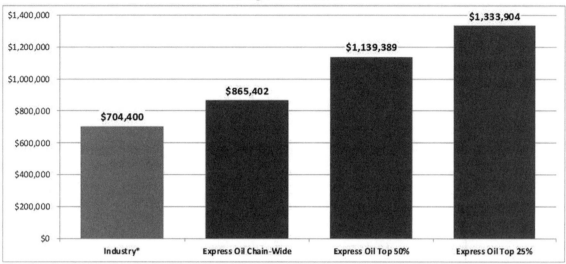

Average Per Store Sales

III. STATEMENT OF REVENUE AND EXPENSE INFORMATION FOR AFFILIATE OWNERS

The following statements are based on information reported by all Affiliate Owners in the United States that were in operation for the 12 month period from October 1, 2010, until September 30, 2011. The statement includes the total revenue, expense information and net income for each Affiliate Owner's The Maids® Business, the average total revenue, expense information and net income for all Affiliate Owner's The Maids® Businesses and the average percentage of revenue of expenses and net income for all Affiliate Owners' The Maids® Businesses. Affiliate Owners operate under franchise agreements with us, pay us the same ongoing fees and have the same local advertising requirements as Franchise Owners. However, Affiliate Owners may pay a lower percentage of Gross Revenue as a Continuing Free than you because Affiliate Owners' weekly Gross Revenues allow Affiliate Owners to pay a lower percentage of Gross Revenue as a Continuing Fee based on the Continuing Fee scale described in Item 6. In addition, all Affiliate Owners have been in operation for over 5 years. As a result, the Affiliate Owners' results may differ materially from your results.

	Affiliate Owner #1 (5 Territories)	Affiliate Owner #2 (7 Territories)	Affiliate Owner #3 (14 Territories)	Average of Affiliate Owners	Average Percentage of Revenue
TOTAL REVENUE	$1,097,813	$1,487,207	$1,711,266	$1,432,095	100.00%
OPERATING EXPENSES					
LICENSING FEE	40,801	55,620	62,231	158,651	11.08%
ADVERTISING FUNDS FEE	22,084	27,012	33,576	27,557	1.92%
ADVERTISING	85,277	132,367	121,451	113,031	7.89%
DIRECT LABOR	425,058	550,002	660,658	545,239	38.07%
OUTSIDE SERVICE	0	552	0	184	0.01%
EMPLOYEE BENEFITS - MAIDS	33,158	27,497	43,865	34,840	2.43%
CLEANING SUPPLIES & UNIFORMS	27,943	21,441	31,815	27,067	1.89%

RENT & UTILITIES	22,490	38,680	42,755	34,642	2.42%
AUTO	39,235	71,914	62,840	57,997	4.05%
AUTO DEPRECIATION	4,198	9,453	16,393	10,015	0.70%
AUTO LEASE PAYMENTS	0	0	1,405	468	0.03%
PAYROLL TAXES	39,276	51,138	59,449	49,954	3.49%
CUSTOMER DAMAGE	3,697	3,687	3,549	3,644	0.25%
TELEPHONE	10,905	16,447	15,901	14,418	1.01%
INSURANCE - W/C & PDBI	33,781	40,826	106,038	60,215	4.20%
EMPLOYEE RECRUITING	1,773	1,738	590	1,367	0.10%
EQUIPMENT RENT & REPAIR	2,180	2,058	3,470	2,569	0.18%
OTHER EXPENSE	1,491	26,384	(298)	9,192	0.64%
TOTAL OPERATING EXPENSES:	793,348	1,076,815	1,265,689	1,045,284	72.99%
NON-MANAGEMENT GENERAL & ADMINISTRATIVE EXPENSES					
OPERATIONS SALARIES	71,345	50,598	84,341	68,761	4.80%
CLERICAL SALARIES	45,719	34,088	39,881	39,896	2.79%
SALES SALARIES		53,401	0	17,800	1.24%
CALL CENTER COSTS	14,362	14,960	22,539	17,287	1.21%
DEPRECIATION EXPENSE	2,070	1,204	2,802	2,025	0.14%
OUTSIDE SERVICES-PROFESSIONAL	14,206	11,156	17,090	14,151	0.99%
BANK CHARGES	20,069	25,200	38,004	27,758	1.94%
OFFICE SUPPLIES	3,267	3,902	6,618	4,596	0.32%
INTEREST EXPENSE	10	816	1,600	809	0.06%
TRAVEL & ENTERTAINMENT	7,753	698	2,138	3,530	0.25%
EMPLOYEE BENEFITS-MGMNT & OFFICE	5,289	9,775	10,007	8,357	0.58%
EMPLOYEE BENEFITS - 401K	5,206	3,637	1,326	3,390	0.24%
OTHER ADMINISTRATIVE	295		(2,894)	(866)	-0.06%
TOTAL NON-MANAGEMENT GENERAL & ADMINISTRATIVE EXPENSES	189,593	209,435	223,451	207,493	14.49%
MANAGEMENT GENERAL & ADMINISTRATIVE EXPENSES					
MANAGEMENT SALARIES	40,984	0	79,373	40,119	2.80%
MANAGEMENT BONUS	8	4,391	5,000	3,133	0.22%

PAYROLL TAXES - OFFICE	12,184	11,483	13,066	12,244	0.85%
AUTO EXPENSE - MGMNT & OFFICE	0	0	4,800	1,600	0.11%
TOTAL MANAGEMENT GENERAL & ADMINISTRATIVE EXPENSES	53,177	15,874	102,239	57,097	3.99%
TOTAL EXPENSES	1,036,118	1,302,124	1,591,379	1,309,874	91.47%
NET INCOME	$61,696	$185,084	$119,886	$122,222	8.53%

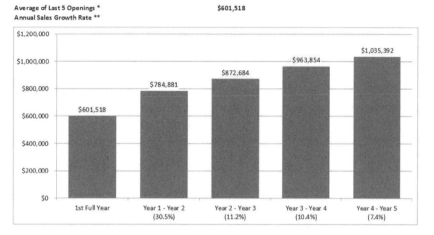

Although The Maids® Franchise Owners are located in many different areas, location can be an important factor affecting results, particularly with respect to demographics, general economic influence and your prospective area may differ from the typical area for a The Maids® franchise. Many of the Franchise Owners whose results are reported are located in major metropolitan areas or other territories with relatively favorable characteristics. You should independently verify whether such factors and conditions in your intended area of operation are comparable to those in existing The Maids® franchise areas.

Prospective Franchise Owners should, before making any investment decision, research the need in their proposed area of operation for, and the ability of potential customers to pay for, services of the type offered by The Maids® Franchise Owners, including actual and potential competition and the so-cioeconomic and demographic background of their area. In this regard, we strongly encourage you to research your area, speak with existing The Maids® Franchise Owners and make an independent judgment as to whether their experience may or may not be transferable to your proposed area of operation.

You should consult with appropriate financial, business and legal advisors in evaluating the information in this document and the accompanying charts and notes.

Some outlets have earned this amount. Your individual results may differ. There is no assurance that you'll earn as much.

We will be glad to provide you with written substantiation of the data used to prepare the information presented in this document on reasonable request.

Other than the preceding financial performance representation, we do not make any financial performance representations. We also do not authorize our employees or representatives to make any such representations either orally or in writing. If you are purchasing an existing outlet, however, we may provide you with the actual records of that outlet. If you receive any other financial performance information or projections of your future income, you should report it to the franchisor's management by contacting Franchise Development, The Maids International, Inc., 9394 West Dodge Road, Suite 140, Omaha, NE 68114, (402) 558-5555, the Federal Trade Commission, and the appropriate state regulatory agencies.

MATHNASIUM

5120 W. Goldleaf Circle, #130
Los Angeles, CA 90056
Tel: (877) 531-MATH, (323) 421-8000
Fax: (310) 943-2111
Email: dan.huntington@mathnasium.com
Website: www.mathnasium.com
Dan Huntington, VP Franchise Development

MATHNASIUM Learning Centers is an excellent blend of a rewarding business opportunity and making a difference in children's lives. We help kids make sense of math, giving them the tools to catch up, maintain, and get ahead.

BACKGROUND

IFA Member:	Yes
Established & First Franchised:	2002; 2003
Franchised Units:	387
Company-Owned Units:	2
Total Units:	389
Distribution:	US – 387; CAN – 0; O'seas – 0
North America:	37 States, 0 Provinces

FINANCIAL/TERMS

Cash Investment:	$50 – $107.5K
Total Investment:	$78.3 – $107.5K
Minimum Net Worth:	$0K
Fees (Franchise):	$37K
Fees (Royalty):	10%
Fees (Advertising):	2%
Term of Contract (Years):	5/5
Average Number of Employees:	N/A
Passive Ownership:	Not Allowed
Encourage Conversions:	N/A
Area Development Agreements:	No
Sub-Franchising Contracts:	No
Expand in Territory:	No
Space Needs:	N/A

SUPPORT & TRAINING

Financial Assistance Provided:	No
Site Selection Assistance:	N/A
Lease Negotiation Assistance:	N/A
Co-operative Advertising:	No
Franchisee Association/Member:	No
Size of Corporate Staff:	0
On-going Support:	N/A
Training:	N/A

SPECIFIC EXPANSION PLANS

US:	No
Canada:	No
Overseas:	No

The following is a historic financial performance representation for the period from January 1, 2011 through December 31, 2011, and for the period from January 1, 2010 through December 31, 2010. It includes average Gross Receipts of Mathnasium's existing centers that had been open for 12 months or longer as of December 31, 2011 or December 31, 2010, respectively, broken down by quartiles. "Gross Receipts" means your monthly gross receipts from all sources in your operation of the Center, including student tuition, registration and testing fees, sales of learning materials, hourly per student private tutoring, and any other approved services. "Gross Receipts" excludes only sales tax receipts that you must by law collect from customers and that you pay to the government, any customer refunds actually paid, and coupons or promotional discounts approved by us.

As of December 31, 2011, we had 284 Mathnasium Centers in operation. Of the 284 Mathnasium Centers, 71 were not included in this financial performance representation because they had not been open for 12 months or longer as of December 31, 2011. In addition, an additional 19 Mathnasium Centers who had been open for at least 12 months were not included because they had not reported their Gross Receipts to us for the full 12 month period.

As of December 31, 2010, we had 226 Mathnasium Centers in operation. Of the 226 Mathnasium Centers, 63 were not included in the comparative financial performance representation because they had not been open for 12 months or longer as of December 31, 2010. In addition, an additional 5 Mathnasium Centers who had been open for at least 12 months were not included because they had not reported their Gross Receipts to us for the full 12 month period.

Mathnasium Centers may not mature until they are at least 24 to 36 months old. As of December 31, 2011, 47% of Mathnasium Centers had been open 24 or fewer months. As of December 31, 2010, 53% of Mathnasium Centers had been open 24 or fewer months.

2011
AVERAGE GROSS RECEIPTS
FOR MATHNASIUM CENTERS OPERATING
12 MONTHS OR MORE BY QUARTILE

TOP 25% OF CENTERS BY GROSS RECEIPTS	MID-UPPER 25% OF CENTERS BY GROSS RECEIPTS	MID-LOWER 25% OF CENTERS BY GROSS RECEIPTS	BOTTOM 25% OF CENTERS BY GROSS RECEIPTS
CATEGORY AVERAGE GROSS RECEIPTS			
$268,684	$155,088	$103,578	$57,952
NUMBER OF CENTERS MEETING OR EXCEEDING AVERAGE FOR CATEGORY			
18 or 38% of 48 Centers in Top 25%	24 or 50% of 48 Centers in Mid-Upper 25%	23 or 48% of 48 Centers in Mid-Lower 25%	31 or 62% of 50 Centers in Bottom 25%
GROSS RECEIPTS OF TOP 10 CENTERS IN CATEGORY			
$477,908	$182,474	$129,231	$77,874
432,771	181,680	128,140	77,663
414,339	181,154	128,055	77,071
406,791	178,719	127,620	76,292
406,394	177,145	126,682	75,896
381,113	176,231	125,983	75,848
375,832	174,358	125,951	74,938
366,220	173,851	125,502	74,799
350,980	171,847	125,233	74,518
344,211	171,594	121,894	74,331

2010
AVERAGE GROSS RECEIPTS
FOR MATHNASIUM CENTERS OPERATING
12 MONTHS OR MORE BY QUARTILE

TOP 25% OF CENTERS BY GROSS RECEIPTS	MID-UPPER 25% OF CENTERS BY GROSS RECEIPTS	MID-LOWER 25% OF CENTERS BY GROSS RECEIPTS	BOTTOM 25% OF CENTERS BY GROSS RECEIPTS
CATEGORY AVERAGE GROSS RECEIPTS			
$232,573	$131,226	$87,680	$46,949
NUMBER OF CENTERS MEETING OR EXCEEDING AVERAGE FOR CATEGORY			
13 or 33% of 39 Centers in Top 25%	21 or 54% of 39 Centers in Mid-Upper 25%	20 or 51% of 39 Centers in Mid-Lower 25%	18 or 44% of 41 Centers in Bottom 25%
GROSS RECEIPTS OF TOP 10 CENTERS IN CATEGORY			
$461,254	$156,002	$103,258	$72,902
416,426	155,255	103,095	72,168
394,502	152,521	101,974	72,132
365,119	151,426	100,285	70,985
362,674	150,646	100,220	69,787
340,322	150,303	100,100	69,263
276,843	146,953	98,174	66,895
275,720	144,966	96,982	65,931
270,383	144,616	94,554	64,828
270,329	142,377	94,041	62,690

2011 AVERAGE GROSS RECEIPTS FOR MATHNASIUM CENTERS OPERATING 12 MONTHS OR MORE BY TOP HALF AND BOTTOM HALF	
TOP 50% OF CENTERS BY GROSS RECEIPTS	$211,886
Number of centers in top 50% meeting or exceeding the average of the top 50%	31 or 32% of 96 Centers included in average
BOTTOM 50% OF CENTERS BY GROSS RECEIPTS	$80,300
Number of centers in bottom 50% meeting or exceeding the average of the bottom 50%	44 or 45% of 98 Centers included in average

2010 AVERAGE GROSS RECEIPTS FOR MATHNASIUM CENTERS OPERATING 12 MONTHS OR MORE BY TOP HALF AND BOTTOM HALF	
TOP 50% OF CENTERS BY GROSS RECEIPTS	$181,900
Number of centers in top 50% meeting or exceeding the average of the top 50%	27 or 34.6% of 78 Centers included in average
BOTTOM 50% OF CENTERS BY GROSS RECEIPTS	$67,315
Number of centers in bottom 50% meeting or exceeding the average of the bottom 50%	45 or 57.6% of 78 Centers included in average

The above averages of Gross Receipts for franchised Mathnasium Centers open at least 12 months and reporting throughout the year shown was calculated by us based on reports on Gross Receipts furnished to Mathnasium by its franchisees. It is important to note that neither the submitting franchisees nor Mathnasium audited this information.

As a new franchisee, your financial results will likely differ from the results described above and those differences may be material. Your results may also vary significantly from those shown above depending on a number of other factors, including the location of your center; the nature and extent of your competition; whether your geographic area has a greater or lesser demand for Mathnasium services; the skill, experience and business acumen of your management and staff; local eco-nomic conditions; and how long you have operated your center. Centers may not mature until their 24th to 36th month of operation or later.

The financial information in the above tables shows only historic gross receipts of franchised Mathnasium centers. The financial information above does not reflect the costs of sales, operating expenses or other costs or expenses that you will incur and that must be deducted from the gross receipts to obtain your net income or profit.

Mathnasium will make written substantiation of the data used in preparing the information above available to you upon reasonable request.

MEINEKE

440 S. Church St.
Charlotte, NC 28202
Tel: (800) 275-5200, (704) 377-8855
Fax: (704) 377-9904
Email: dave.schaefers@meineke.com

Website: www.meinekefranchise.com
Dave Schaefers, VP Driven Brands Franchise Development

MEINEKE has been offering superior automotive repair services at discount prices for over 30 years. We are a nationally-recognized brand with a proven system. Brand recognition, comprehensive training, and on-going technical and operational support are some of the benefits enjoyed by MEINEKE franchisees.

BACKGROUND
IFA Member:	Yes
Established & First Franchised:	1972; 1972
Franchised Units:	935
Company-Owned Units:	15

Total Units:	940
Distribution:	US – 862; CAN – 35; O'seas – 43
North America:	27 States, 6 Provinces
Density:	19 in ON, 6 in AB, 3 in BC
Projected New Units (12 Months):	45
Qualifications:	4, 4, 1, 2, 3, 4

FINANCIAL/TERMS

Cash Investment:	$100K
Total Investment:	$160 – $400K
Minimum Net Worth:	$250K
Fees (Franchise):	$30K
Fees (Royalty):	9%
Fees (Advertising):	8%
Term of Contract (Years):	15/15
Average Number of Employees:	6 – 10 FT, 0 PT
Passive Ownership:	Allowed
Encourage Conversions:	Yes
Area Development Agreements:	Yes

Sub-Franchising Contracts:	No
Expand in Territory:	Yes
Space Needs:	8,000 SF

SUPPORT & TRAINING

Financial Assistance Provided:	Yes (I)
Site Selection Assistance:	Yes
Lease Negotiation Assistance:	Yes
Co-operative Advertising:	No
Franchisee Association/Member:	Yes/Member
Size of Corporate Staff:	110
On-going Support:	A, B, C, D, E, G, H, I
Training:	4 Weeks Charlotte, NC

SPECIFIC EXPANSION PLANS

US:	All United States
Canada:	All Canada
Overseas:	All Countries

MEINEKE CENTER AVERAGE BY SERVICE BAY GROSS SALES FOR FISCAL YEAR END
JUNE 25, 2011 FOR CENTERS OPENED FOR MORE THAN 2 YEARS

Number of Bays	Number of Centers open for more than 2 years as of June 25, 2011	Average sales for fiscal year end June 25, 2011 for centers open more than 2 years
5 Bays	87	$638,754
6 Bays	108	$632,543
7 Bays	35	$638,234
8 Bays	28	$818,919
+8 Bays	6	$1,001,331
Total Centers/Average Sales	264	$675,652

THIS CHART REFLECTS THE AVERAGE GROSS SALES BY SERVICE BAY FOR THE 264 MEINEKE CENTERS IN THE UNITED STATES OPEN AS OF FISCAL YEAR END JUNE 25, 2011 UNDER THE FOLLOWING CRITERIA: HAS AT LEAST 5 BAYS, HAS A 3 STAR RATING OR HIGHER, AND HAS BEEN OPEN FOR AT LEAST 2 YEARS PRIOR TO JUNE 25, 2011. AS OF JUNE 25, 2011, THERE ARE 768 FRANCHISEES CURRENTLY OPERATING IN THE MEINEKE CHAIN. THE RESULTS IN THIS CHART SHOULD NOT BE CONSIDERED AS THE ACTUAL OR PROBABLE RESULTS THAT WILL BE REALIZED BY YOU OR ANY OTHER FRANCHISEE. WE DO NOT REPRESENT THAT ANY FRANCHISEE CAN EXPECT TO ATTAIN THESE RESULTS. A NEW FRANCHISEE'S RESULTS ARE LIKELY TO DIFFER FROM THESE RESULTS. THESE RESULTS DO NOT REFLECT THE RESULTS OF ANY CO-BRANDED MEINEKE LOCATION, WHICH ARE NOT RELEVANT TO THE OPERATION OF YOUR CENTER.

The chart for the Average Gross Sales by number of service bay for fiscal year end June 25, 2011 statement ("Average Gross Sales Statement") reflects the average gross sales for fiscal year end June 25, 2011 reported by 264 franchised Meineke Centers, all of which are located in the United States, and which had been open and operating for more than 2 years as of June 25, 2011 under the same owner, operated a center with at least 5 bays, and had a star rating of 3 or better. The Average Sales Statement is based on weekly sales reports submitted by Meineke franchisees and our company owned centers for the purpose of computing royalty fees. These reports have not been audited by certified public accountants nor have we sought to independently verify their accuracy for purposes of the Average Sales Statement.

The 5 Star Rating program was implemented by the Company in the fall of 2008. Each Meineke center is given a score of one to five stars, based on a set of established criteria each calendar quarter. For complete detail of the 5 Star scoring metrics, refer to Exhibit X. We consider a 3 Star rating to represent an average performing center.

As of June 25, 2011, there were 849 U.S. Meineke franchises. Of those, 768 centers were already opened, 14 had locations and were awaiting opening, 3 had approved locations that had not yet been secured, and 63 had not yet identified locations. There were 5 company franchise outlets and 2 joint ventures, which are not included in this statement. Of the open centers, 77 have been open less than one year, 65 have been open more than one year but less than two years, and 626 have been open more than two years under the current owner.

The Average Gross Sales Charts that we have included above omit all centers with less than 5 bays, as this is the recommended model for Meineke franchises. Currently you are required to open a center that has a minimum of 4 service bays. We do still have locations in the system that only have 3 service bays; however these are franchised locations that were developed before we changed the required minimum number of service bays for a Meineke center. $510,535 represents the average sales as reported for the fiscal year ending June 25, 2011 for the 25 3 bay centers with a star rating of 3 or higher that were open and operating under the same owner for at least 2 years as of June 25, 2011. $568,551 represents the average sales as reported for the fiscal year ending June 25, 2011 for the 85 4 bay centers with a star rating of 3 or higher that were open and operating under the same owner for at least 2 years as of June 25, 2011. These sales figures have not been audited by certified public accountants nor have sought to independently verify their accuracy.

$520,397 represents the average unaudited gross sales figures as reported to Meineke Car Care Centers, Inc., from June 26, 2010, to June 25, 2011, for the 40 centers, regardless of the number of operating bays at their location, that were rated a 3 star or higher that were open for more than one but less than two years under the same owner as of fiscal year end June 25, 2011.

$631,691 represents the average unaudited gross sales figures as reported to Meineke Car Care Centers, Inc., from June 26, 2010, to June 25, 2011 for the 374 centers, regardless of the number of operating bays at their location that were rated a 3 star or higher that were open for more than two years under the same owner as of fiscal year end June 25, 2011.

Exhibit O-1, Part 1 to this document is a list of the franchises together with their geographic locations from which Meineke compiled these figures. All of these franchises, whether or not their results appear in the chart above, are not substantially similar to the co branded location that you will operate pursuant to the terms of the co branded Addendum.

Attached below is a summary of certain customary and typical expenses of our business shown as a percentage of sales. The number of service bays you use in the operation of your center likely will be a material component in calculating the amount of expenses that you incur in your center operations. The listing of expenses is not all-inclusive. Our Meineke franchisees more than likely will incur additional expenses in the operation of their Meineke Centers that do not appear on this listing. The amount of your expenses also will be dictated by the geographic region your Meineke store is located.

We obtained the expense and sales information for these stand alone Meineke centers listed in the following charts from profit and loss statements and tax returns for the calendar year 2010 submitted to us by our franchisees in the ordinary course of business. Most of the reports have not been audited by certified public accountants nor have we sought to independently verify their accuracy. Not all franchisees supplied us with their profit and loss statements.

Note that sales and expenses vary for Meineke Centers depending on many factors, including local and regional variations in real estate values or rental rates, construction costs and building specifications (including the number of bays), financing terms which the franchisee was able to obtain, local and regional variations in utility and telephone rates (including the number of telephone lines in the center), insurance rates, local and state taxes and wage rates, degree of skilled labor employed and the availability of such labor, cost of parts and supplies used, services offered and the efficiency and managerial skills of the franchisee, local economic factors, the density of vehicle ownership, the number of other automotive aftermarket outlets in a particular market area and the proximity of such competition to the Meineke center, length of time the center has been in operation and the length of time operating at its current location, type of area (including number of traffic lanes and the type of traffic flow) in which the center is located, and whether the center is managed by the owner or an employee manager.

Substantiation of the data used in preparing the Average Sales Statement and the following charts will be made available to you on reasonable request, provided we will not disclose data that identifies specific locations. Our sales representatives are prohibited from providing you with any further information about actual, average or potential sales, or operating expenses, income, profits or earnings, and are prohibited from commenting on the likelihood of success of any Meineke Center or the business potential of any territory. Any such unauthorized information is inherently unreliable, and you should not rely on it.

THE EXPENSES LISTED IN THE CHARTS ON THE FOLLOWING PAGE ARE BASED ON PROFIT AND LOSS STATEMENTS PROVIDED BY MEINEKE FRANCHISEES AND YOU SHOULD NOT CONSIDER THESE AS THE ACTUAL OR POTENTIAL OPERATING EXPENSES THAT WILL BE REALIZED BY YOU OR ANY OTHER FRANCHISEE. MOREVOVER, THESE EXPENSES ARE FROM STAND ALONE MEINEKE CENTERS ONLY. WE DO NOT REPRESENT THAT ANY FRANCHISEE CAN EXPECT TO ATTAIN THESE RESULTS. THE RESULTS FOR A CENTER THAT IS YET TO REACH MATURITY (A NEW CENTER) ARE LIKELY TO DIFFER FROM THOSE CONTAINED IN THE FOLLOWING CHARTS.

AVERAGE EXPENSE INFORMATION
FOR CENTERS REPORTING FOR CALENDAR YEAR 2010

	EBITDA Quartile [1]			
	Top	2nd	3rd	4th
	102	103	103	103
Avg. COGS %	23.6%	26.1%	25.7%	26.9%
Direct Technician Labor	14.7%	16.6%	18.4%	20.5%
Other Center Variables[2]	1.4%	1.4%	1.4%	1.5%
Fixed Expenses[3]	18.7%	22.1%	25.8%	33.5%
EBITDA[1]	41.6%	33.8%	28.7%	17.6%

		Bay Size				
	All Centers	5	6	7	8	>8
No. of Centers	411	100	113	33	21	4
Avg. COGS %	25.3%	25.5%	25.0%	25.3%	26.1%	31.3%
Direct Technician Labor	17.0%	16.7%	17.3%	18.8%	17.8%	21.2%
Other Center Variables[2]	1.4%	1.4%	1.4%	1.5%	1.5%	1.8%
Fixed Expenses[3]	23.7%	23.6%	23.9%	23.2%	21.5%	15.3%
EBITDA[1]	32.6%	32.8%	32.4%	31.2%	33.1%	30.4%

(1) EBITDA is defined as earnings before interest, taxes, depreciation, and amortization. What this means is that subtracted from your earnings will be the costs of any interest you pay to finance your business as well any taxes you will be required to pay to the federal, state, or local government related to the operation of your Meineke business. Expenses for those centers that provided us with their financial statements for calendar year 2010 are included in this chart.

In these charts, EBITDA % does not include the impact of franchise fees or advertising fees (National and local). It also assumes that the franchisee will run the center and hence excludes any salaries for managers.

(2) Other center variables include credit card processing costs.

(3) Fixed expenses include payroll taxes, employee benefits, rent, taxes and licenses, supplies, insurance, utilities, telephone, trash, laundry and uniforms, bank charges, center repairs, IT support, and accounting, legal and miscellaneous expenses.

Average royalties and MAF contributions for centers included in this analysis are 5.2% and 7.6%, respectively. Some centers choose to charge the costs of a vehicle to their business; these expenses have not been included in our analysis. Equipment lease expenses have also been excluded from our analysis as it will only apply to a limited number of new owners. Finally, it is assumed that the franchisee will operate the center. THESE AMOUNTS WOULD BE SUBTRACTED FROM THE EBITDA LISTED ABOVE.

EXCEPT AS PROVIDED ABOVE, WE DO NOT FURNISH OR AUTHORIZE OUR SALESPERSONS TO FURNISH ANY ORAL OR WRITTEN INFORMATION CONCERNING ACTUAL, PRO-JECTED OR POTENTIAL SALES, COSTS, EXPENSES, INCOME OR PROFITS OF A PROPOSED FACILITY.

MONEY MAILER

12131 Western Ave.
Garden Grove, CA 92841
Tel: (800) 418-3030, (714) 889-4698
Fax: (800) 819-4322
Email: jpatinella@moneymailer.com
Website: www.moneymailer.com
John Patinella, SVP Franchise Operations

MONEY MAILER is the franchise for the sales entrepreneur ready to run his/her own local marketing consulting company. Franchisees help businesses succeed with cutting-edge marketing solutions including direct mail, online, mobile, and interactive. This is a B2B, home-office based model with fast startup, high repeat business, and multiple revenue streams. Franchisees do the consulting, MONEY MAILER does the rest. Once a campaign is finalized, the order is sent to MONEY MAILER for printing, inserting, mailing, and Internet placement. MONEY MAILER's accelerator financing and launch package reduces the initial investment to a low $7,500 and provides $20,000 in first-year production credits to put franchisees on the profitability fast track. Named "one of the Top 10 businesses for a recession" as coupon redemption continues at record pace and ranked #1 in Category by Entrepreneur Magazine 7 years in a row. This is a highly consultative, relationship-driven business that can be rapidly scaled.

BACKGROUND

IFA Member	Yes
Established & First Franchised:	1979;1980
Franchised Units:	194

Company-Owned Units:	44
Total Units:	238
Dist.:	US-256; CAN-6; O'seas-0
North America:	0 States, 0 Province
Density:	44 in CA, 25 in IL, 21 in NJ
Projected New Units (12 Months):	37
Qualifications:	2, 2, 4, 2, 5, 5

FINANCIAL/TERMS

Cash Investment:	$27.5K
Total Investment	$42.6 – $69.5K
Minimum Net Worth:	$75K
Fees (Franchise):	$37.5K
Fees (Royalty):	$200/10,000 mailed households
Fees (Advertising):	$3/ad sold, matched 60% by MM
Term of Contract (Years):	10/10
Avg. # of Employees:	Owner/operator first year FT
Passive Ownership:	Not Allowed
Encourage Conversions:	No
Area Develop. Agreements:	No
Sub-Franchising Contracts:	No
Expand in Territory:	Yes
Space Needs:	Standard Home Office

SUPPORT & TRAINING

Financial Assistance Provided:	Yes (I)
Site Selection Assistance:	N/A
Lease Negotiation Assistance:	N/A
Co-operative Advertising:	Yes
Franchisee Assoc./Member:	Yes/Member
Size of Corporate Staff:	425
On-going Support:	A, B, C, D, G,H,I
Training:	1 Week Corp. HQ; 11 Days Field Training in Territory

SPECIFIC EXPANSION PLANS

US:	All United States
Canada:	No
Overseas:	No

We will make written substantiation for the following financial performance representations available to you upon your reasonable request.

Historical Financial Performance Representations for Calendar Year 2011
Relating to Certain Existing Money Mailer Franchised Outlets

Franchisee Groups (Note 1)	Average Total Revenue (Note 5)	Average Total Franchisor Credits (Note 6)		Average Total Cost of Goods Sold (Note 7)		Average Gross Profit (Note 8)
		Per Agreement	Promotional	Fixed Costs	Variable Costs	
Group 1 (111 Outlets) (Note 2)	$401,654	$7,994	$17,457	$131,357	$199,412	$96,336
Group 2 (21 Outlets) (Note 3)	$967,072	$21,971	$42,578	$281,230	$462,190	$288,201
Group 3 (5 Outlets) (Note 4)	$1,824,571	$65,537	$192,300	$711,004	$800,242	$571,162

Some franchisees have earned this amount. Your individual results may differ. There is no assurance that you'll earn as much.

Notes to Chart:

1. The above chart provides certain average financial statistics for three subsets of our franchised outlets that conducted shared mailings for the entire calendar year 2011. We have separated the franchised outlets into three groups to account for the wide range in territory sizes of the outlets. The specific characteristics of each group are described in Notes 2 – 4 below. The three groups' size categories are substantially similar to the size categories we use for initial franchise fees (see Item 5 above) and initial training (see Item 11 above).

For each group, we included only those franchisees in each size category that had provided complete sales and revenue data through our AdBooks order entry program. Such information is self-reported by our franchisees. We are not able to verify and, thus, have not verified the accuracy of this or any other information entered into AdBooks by franchisees.

We did not include results from our 44 company-owned outlets as they are operated very differently from franchised outlets. The majority of our company-owned outlets (referred to as "transitional" outlets) are not staffed with dedicated salespeople and are only maintained for the purpose of re-licensing to new franchisees. Accordingly, revenues are artificially low for these transitional outlets. For the company-owned outlets that we actively manage, they do not receive the same credits or incur the same costs as franchised outlets (e.g., fixed cost credits, royalties, etc.).

2. Group 1 consists of 111 of 180 franchised outlets with territories of 4 but less than 8 zones. This group conducted an average of 9.5 shared mailings for calendar year 2011, mailing an average of 50.0 duplicated zones. They sold an average of 30.57 spots per zone. No data from the non-measured outlets

(see Note 1 above) was included in any of the calculations. The average length of time that group 1 outlets have been in operation at the end of 2011 was eight years. Finally, 48 franchised outlets in group 1 (43% of the measured group 1 outlets) surpassed the average gross profit for the group.

3. Group 2 consists of 22 of 34 franchised outlets with territories of 8 but less than 16 zones. On average, each member of this group conducted 9.8 shared mailings in 2011, mailing 111.7 duplicated zones. This group sold an average of 33.97 spots per zone. No data from the non-measured outlets (see Note 1 above) was included in any of the calculations. The average length of time that group 2 outlets have been in operation at the end of 2011 was 12 years. Finally, 9 franchised outlets in group 2 (40.9% of the measured group 2 outlets) surpassed the average gross profit for the group.

4. Group 3 consists of 5 of 14 franchised outlets with territories consisting of 16 or more zones. This group conducted an average of 11.0 shared mailings during 2011, mailing an average of 304.4 duplicated zones. These 5 outlets sold an average of 23.29 spots per zone. No data from the non-measured outlets (see Note 1 above) was included in any of the calculations. The average length of time that group 3 outlets have been in operation at the end of 2011 was 13 years. Finally, 2 franchised outlets in group 3 (40% of the measured group 3 outlets) surpassed the average gross profit for the group.

5. Some of the 2011 revenue information (including cross sale information) for the franchised outlets in each group was obtained from reports provided by franchisees and placed in our AdBooks order entry system. This is self-reported information. We are not able to verify, and have not verified, such information. Other 2011 revenue information for such outlets (for cross sales we place in our franchisees' envelopes) was provided by our unaudited production records.

6. Franchisor credits in 2011 were of two types. First, some

credits are mandated by the franchise agreement if a franchisee meets the required criteria: national insert revenue sharing (which is accounted for in the cross sales), fixed costs credits and remnant insert bonus. We did not include any credits related to the high piece count bonus, as we have not included any accrued credits. While this credit was earned by some franchisees in 2011, it will not be paid out until the end of March 2012. We have not included any accrued credits. We also did not include any credits for the precursor to the remnant insert bonus, known as the "regional insert bonus". While we paid a total of $363,952.50 in regional insert bonus credits in early 2011, these related to 2010 operations under our old form of franchise agreement. Second, some credits are optional; we occasionally provide these credits for short-term promotional purposes. We have been providing many of these promotions for many years, such as our frequency and zone expansion programs) but we are not obligated to continue providing them in the future. For 2011, promotional credits included: convention credits, early payment discounts, expansion credits, food and long run promotional credits, frequency credits, print discounts and 10% December discounts. The data source for the 2011 franchisor credits is our unaudited accounting books and records.

7. Information regarding the cost of goods sold in 2011 also was derived from our unaudited accounting books and records. This cost information includes data for average fixed costs (royalties, postage, freight, envelopes, address lists, inserting costs and inkjet costs) and average variable costs (printing, cross sales fees, back of envelope fees, other production charges such as folding and perforating, and marketing fees). Some costs are not included in these calculations because they depend on local characteristics (state and local sales taxes) or they are optional (sample print ads, sample envelopes, in-store point-of-purchase displays for clients, banner ads, interactive ads (mobile phone and online), one to one ads, trade show booths, cancellation charges and NSF check charges). AdEase fees (for the use of our online art creation system) are considered fixed costs, while fees for custom art work by independent artists and our corporate art center are considered variable costs. These specific costs were not included in the cost of goods sold because, while we have data on AdEase fees paid and custom artwork fees for art we produced, we do not have data on custom artwork fees charged by independent artists. The average cost for the use of AdEase and purchase of our artwork services by our franchisees in 2011 was $4.44 per spot.

8. Average gross profit per outlet was determined by adding average revenue with average franchisor credits and then subtracting average fixed and variable costs of goods sold. This formula only produces a rough estimate since the statistics added and subtracted are themselves the result of "average" calculations.

9. The above financial performance representations do not cover overhead expenses, such as office rent, office staff salaries (including any salespeople you may hire), your own salary, phone/fax charges, office postage and courier charges, travel, bad debt expenses, auto expenses, insurance costs, advertising expenses and the costs of your marketing materials. These items are based largely on factors in your control (for example, you may operate from a home office). See Items 6 and 7 (and Item 10 if you obtain any financing from us) for a description of certain other expense items that you are likely to incur in acquiring and operating a Money Mailer franchise. There are likely to be additional expenses that we have not listed, some of which may be unique to your market or situation.

10. The above information is presented to assist you in conducting your own investigation for the purpose of evaluating the purchase of a Money Mailer franchise. It is your sole responsibility to do your own research before purchasing a Money Mailer franchise. We cannot provide you with all of the financial information concerning the operation of a Money Mailer franchise because the results often will vary significantly between franchisees and many of the expense items you should consider are unknown to us and frequently within your control.

11. We recommend that you contact a number of Money Mailer franchisees to discuss other operational and financial information and to compare their experience with the information that we provide. Except as otherwise described in the franchise agreement regarding the setting of maximum pricing, franchisees have the right to set their own sales prices. Accordingly, sales prices vary widely by market. In talking to franchisees about sales prices for advertising, be sure to distinguish between their asking price (also referred to as their "rate card") and their actual selling price for advertising, and to ask what kinds of discounts they provide for volume purchases or annual contracts with advertisers.

12. The performance of franchisees varies dramatically between markets for a variety of reasons, including, for example, differences in sales and management abilities, demographics, financing availability and sources, the economic and business environment in a particular market, the history of a particular franchise and the strength of competing advertisers in a given market. You cannot assume that the information provided to you by a Money Mailer franchisee is necessarily relevant to your market. If you are buying an existing Money Mailer franchise, it is your responsibility to verify the seller's historical financial information. We do not review franchisees' financial statements and we have no responsibility for the accuracy or completeness of the same.

13. You should also research the prices charged by competing advertisers in your prospective market to determine the degree

of price competition you will face. Even if a selling franchisee has historically sold advertising at above-average prices in his or her market, it is not safe to assume that you will be able to charge those same prices in the future, especially if major competitors are providing significant price competition.

14. Finally, the information above does not address many of the variables that can affect your revenue, expenses or cash flow. It is intended merely as a starting place for your analysis. Reviewing this limited amount of information cannot substitute for thorough research on your part and a careful evaluation of this franchise opportunity with professional financial and legal advisors.

Other than the preceding financial performance representations, we do not make any representations about a franchisee's future financial performance or the past financial performance of company-owned or franchised outlets. We also do not authorize our employees or representatives to make any such representations either orally or in writing. If you are purchasing an existing outlet, however, we may provide you with the actual records of that outlet. If you receive any other financial performance information or projections of your future income, you should report it to the franchisor's management by contacting Joseph Craciun, Vice President and General Counsel, Money Mailer Franchise Corp., 12131 Western Avenue, Garden Grove, California 92841, Telephone: (714) 889-3822

MOSQUITO SQUAD

2924 Emerywood Pkwy., #101
Richmond, VA 23294
Tel: (800) 722-4668, (804) 353-6999
Fax: (804) 358-1878
Email: dbuchel@outdoorlivingbrands.com
Website: www.mosquitosquadfranchise.com
David Buchel, Franchise Recruiting

MOSQUITO SQUAD is North America's fastest growing outdoor living franchise concept with an incredible, high-margin recurring revenue stream. Since joining the Outdoor Living Brands' franchise lineup in 2009, MOSQUITO SQUAD has been experiencing explosive franchise unit and consumer sales growth. Clients want to take back their backyards by combating annoying insect bites and protecting their families and pets from the dangerous diseases such as Lyme Disease, Encephalitis, and West Nile Virus.

BACKGROUND

IFA Member:	Yes
Established & First Franchised:	2004; 2005
Franchised Units:	131
Company-Owned Units:	0
Total Units:	131
Distribution:	US – 131; CAN – 0; O'seas – 0

North America:	26 States, 0 Provinces
Density:	9 in IL, 9 in VA, 8 in NC
Projected New Units (12 Months):	30
Qualifications:	5, 5, 1, 3, 3, 4

FINANCIAL/TERMS

Cash Investment:	$35K
Total Investment:	$35 – $75K
Minimum Net Worth:	$75K
Fees (Franchise):	$25K
Fees (Royalty):	$400 – $1,900 monthly
Fees (Advertising):	$100 – $400 monthly
Term of Contract (Years):	7/7
Average Number of Employees:	1 FT, 2 PT
Passive Ownership:	Allowed
Encourage Conversions:	Yes
Area Development Agreements:	Yes
Sub-Franchising Contracts:	No
Expand in Territory:	Yes
Space Needs:	N/A

SUPPORT & TRAINING

Financial Assistance Provided:	Yes (D)
Site Selection Assistance:	N/A
Lease Negotiation Assistance:	N/A
Co-operative Advertising:	No
Franchisee Association/Member:	No
Size of Corporate Staff:	30
On-going Support:	b, C, D, E, F, G, h, I
Training: 4-5 Days (depending on class size) Richmond, VA	

SPECIFIC EXPANSION PLANS

US:	All United States
Canada:	All Canada
Overseas:	No

Actual results will vary from franchise to franchise, territory to territory and market to market, and we cannot estimate the results for any particular franchise. Except as provided by applicable law, we will not be bound by allegations of any unauthorized representation as to sales, income, profits, or prospects or chances for success, and you will be required to acknowledge that you have not relied on any such representation in purchasing your franchise. We have provided this information to help you to make a more informed decision regarding our franchise system. You should not use this information as an indication of how your specific franchise business may perform. The success of your franchise will depend largely on your individual abilities and your market. The actual numbers you experience will be influenced by a wide variety of factors including your management, market size and demographics and competition. You should conduct your own independent research and due diligence to assist you in preparing your own projections.

Written substantiation of the data used in preparing the financial performance representations included in this Item 19 will be made available to you upon reasonable request.

A. Average Gross Revenues for MOSQUITO SQUAD Franchisees for the 12 Months Ending December 31, 2011

The following table presents the average annual Gross Revenues realized by certain MOSQUITO SQUAD franchisees in 2011. "Total Gross Revenues" mean the total "Gross Revenues" (as defined in the Franchise Agreement) received by the reporting franchisees in 2011, as reported by the franchisees.

Each MOSQUITO SQUAD franchisee's operating season will vary depending on the location of their Territory. As used in this Item 19, "Operating Season" refers to a calendar year beginning on January 1st and ending on December 31st.

As of December 31, 2011, there were 90 MOSQUITO SQUAD franchisees. The information provided in the table below was compiled from the 63 MOSQUITO SQUAD franchisees that were operational for all of the 2011 Operating Season. The data excludes 27 MOSQUITO SQUAD franchisees that either signed franchise agreements and began operations during the 2011 Operating Season or did not collect any Gross Revenues during the 2011 Operating Season, or any franchisees that ceased operations during the 2011 Operating Season.

While all of the 63 MOSQUITO SQUAD businesses were operational for all of the 2011 Operating Season, the length of their spraying season varied depending on the region of the country in which they are located. Although the table below only contains information for the 63 of the 90 MOSQUITO SQUAD franchisees as of December 31, 2011, the Total Gross Revenues of the 63 franchisees for the 2011 Operating Season represents 99.7% of the Total Gross Revenues reported to us by all MOSQUITO SQUAD franchisees for the 2011 Operating Season. The table below presents minimum, average and maximum Total Gross Revenues for the 2011 Operating Season for the MOSQUITO SQUAD franchisees in operation for the full 2011 Operating Season by their number of Operating Seasons in business.

	Number of Franchisees	Gross Revenue in Dollars			% of Franchisees In Subset	# of Franchises Above the Average
		Minimum	Average	Maximum		
3 or more Full Operating Seasons	11	21,190	355,122	1,002,022	17.5%	3
At least 2 Full Operating Seasons	29	10,629	82,997	307,800	46.0%	9
At least 1 Full Operating Season	23	9,265	58,423	139,046	36.5%	8
Franchisees	63				100.0%	

Three of the 11 franchisees (27%) that have been operational for 3 or more full Operating Seasons met or exceeded the average Gross Revenues of $355,122 for this subset. Nine of the 29 franchisees (31%) that have been operational for at least 2 full Operating Season (but less than 3 full Operating Seasons) met or exceeded the average Gross Revenues of $182,997 for this subset. Eight of the 23 franchisees (35%) that were operational for at least one full Operation Season (but less than 2 full Operating Seasons) met or exceeded the average Gross Revenues of $58,423 for this subset.

The Gross Revenue figures presented above represent the Total Gross Revenues of outdoor pest control services sold by the 63 franchises listed above in the 2011 Operating Season. The financial performance representations above do not reflect the costs of sales, brand licensing fees or operating expenses that must be deducted from the sales figures to obtain a net income or owner's profit number. The best source of cost and expense data may be from current or former franchisees as listed in this disclosure document.

B. Revenue per Spray and Sprays Per Customer Study for Certain MOSQUITO SQUAD Franchisees for Operating Season Ending December 31, 2011

The information provided in the table below is based on information reported to us from 58 of the 63 total MOSQUITO SQUAD franchisees ("Reporting Franchisees") whose MOSQUITO SQUAD businesses were operational for all of the 2011 Operating Season. While all of the Reporting Franchisees' MOSQUITO SQUAD businesses were operational for all of the 2011 Operating Season, the length of their spraying season may have varied depending on the region of the country in which they are located.

The other 5 MOSQUITO SQUAD franchisees who were operational for all of the 2011 Operating Season are not included on the table below because they failed to report to us all of the information we needed in order to include them. The table also excludes 27 MOSQUITO SQUAD franchisees that either signed franchise agreements and began operations during the 2011 Operating Season or did not collect any Gross Revenues during the 2011 Operating Season, or ceased active operations during the 2011 Operating Season. Although the table below only contains information for the 58 Reporting Franchisees out of the 90 total MOSQUITO SQUAD franchisees as of December 31, 2011, the Total Gross Revenues (as defined above in Section A) of the Reporting Franchisees for the 2011 Operating Season represent 96.27% of the Total Gross Revenues reported to us by all MOSQUITO SQUAD franchisees for the 2011 Operating Season.

The table below presents average Revenue per Spray and the average Sprays per Customer for the Reporting Franchisees during the 2011 Operating Season. The table also categorizes the information as to how many Operating Seasons each Reporting Franchisee has been in operation.

	Number of Franchisees	Gross Revenue per Spray			# of Franchisees Above the Avg.	Sprays per Customer			# of Franchisees Above the Avg.
		Minimum	Average	Maximum		Minimum	Average	Maximum	
3 or more Full Operating Seasons	11	$58.11	$93.97	$167.14	5	3.3	6.0	10.2	5
At least 2 Full Operating Seasons	28	$32.34	$64.00	$119.81	13	3.3	4.5	7.4	11
At least 1 Full Operating Season	19	$51.47	$85.11	$119.81	9	2.6	3.7	4.9	9
Total Franchisees	58								

Five of the 11 franchisees (45%) that have been operational for 3 or more full Operating Seasons met or exceeded the average Revenue per Spray of $93.97 for this subset. Five of the 11 franchisees (45%) that have been operational for 3 or more full Operating Seasons met or exceeded the average Sprays per Customer of 6.0 for this subset.

Thirteen of the 28 franchisees (46%) that have been operational for at least 2 full Operating Seasons (but less than 3 full Operating Seasons) met or exceeded the average Revenue per Spray of $64.00 for this subset. Eleven of the 28 franchisees (39%) that have been operational for at least 2 full Operating Seasons (but less than 3 full Operating Seasons) met or exceeded the average Sprays per Customer of 4.5 for this subset.

Nine of the 19 franchisees (47%) that have been operational for at least 1 full Operating Season (but less than 2 full Operating Seasons) met or exceeded the average Revenue per Spray of $85.11 for this subset. Nine of the 19 franchisees (47%) that have been operational for at least 1 full Operating Season (but less than 2 full Operating Seasons) met or exceeded the average Sprays per Customer of 3.74 for this subset.

C. Gross Margin Study for Certain MOSQUITO SQUAD Franchisees for the Operating Season ending December 31, 2010

We do not provide prospective franchisees with projections of income, profits or earnings. There is no guarantee that you, as a new MOSQUITO SQUAD franchisee, will attain the same level of sales or profits that have been attained by our existing franchisees. The success of your franchise will depend largely on your individual abilities and your market. However, we do provide prospective franchisees with information from a financial benchmarking study (the "Benchmarking Study") conducted for the MOSQUITO SQUAD franchise system by Profit Planning Group ("PPG"), an independent third party financial benchmarking organization serving trade associations and franchise networks across the country.

In 2011, PPG conducted an independent financial Benchmarking Study for MOSQUITO SQUAD franchisees. PPG asked all 64 MOSQUITO SQUAD franchisees operating as of December 31, 2010, to submit their income statements for the year ending December 31, 2010, to PPG. PPG then calculated certain financial metrics to allow participants to compare their financial performance against their peer group of MOSQUITO SQUAD franchisees. 35 out of 64 (55%) MOSQUITO SQUAD franchisees participated in the Benchmarking Study. The other 29 MOSQUITO SQUAD FRANCHISEES either did not participate in the Benchmarking program or did not operate for the complete 2010 Operating Season. Although the table below only contains information for the 35 participating Franchisees out of the 64 total MOSQUITO SQUAD franchisees as of December 31, 2010, the Total Gross Revenues (as defined above in Section A) of the participating Franchisees for the

2010 Operating Season represent 77.6% of the Total Gross Revenues reported to us by all MOSQUITO SQUAD franchisees for the 2010 Operating Season. We have reviewed the composition of franchise participants and believes it contains a random, representative sampling of MOSQUITO SQUAD franchisees based on level of sales, years in the business and geography.

As defined in the Benchmarking Study, Gross Profit Margin measures profitability after material and direct labor to provide each barrier spray application are subtracted from gross revenue to calculate gross profit dollars. Gross Profit Margin is then calculated by dividing gross profit dollars by gross revenues. While Gross Profit Dollars measures profitability after material, direct labor are subtracted from gross revenue, it excludes brand licensing fees, vehicle and fuel expenses, and any other operating expenses.

The table below presents average Gross Profit Margin for the participating franchisees during the 2010 Operating Season. The table also categorizes the information as to how many Operating Seasons each participating franchisee has been in operation.

	Number of Franchisees	Gross Profit Margin Percentage			% of Franchisees In Subset	# of Franchises Above the Average
		Minimum	Average	Maximum		
2 or more Full Operating Seasons	9	45.30%	58.86%	81.30%	25.7%	4
At least 1 Full Operating Season	26	32.30%	58.94%	88.60%	74.3%	13
Franchisees	35				100.0%	

Four of the 9 franchisees (44%) that have been operational for 2 or more full Operating Seasons met or exceeded the average Gross Profit Margin of 58.86% for this subset. Thirteen of the 26 franchisees (50%) that have been operational for at least one full Operating (but not 2 or more Operating Seasons) met or exceeded the average Gross Profit Margin of 58.94% for this subset.

D. Client Renewal Rates for Certain MOSQUITO SQUAD Franchisees for the Operating Season ending December 31, 2011

The information provided in the table below is based on information reported to us from 43 of the 47 MOSQUITO SQUAD franchisees whose MOSQUITO SQUAD businesses were operational for the entire 2010 and 2011 Operating Seasons (the "Qualifying Franchisees"). The other 4 MOSQUITO SQUAD

franchisees who were operational for the complete 2010 and 2011 Operating Seasons are not included on the table below because they failed to report to us all of the information we needed in order to include them. The table also excludes 43 current MOSQUITO SQUAD franchisees as of December 31, 2011, who were not active for the entire 2010 Operating Season because they (i) signed franchise agreements or began operations after the start of the 2010 Operating Season, and only operated for a partial season in 2010; (ii) signed franchise agreements in 2011 and were not operational during the 2010 Operating Season; or (iii) ceased active operations during the 2010 or 2011 Operating Seasons.

Although the table below only contains information for the 43 Qualifying Franchisees, we have reviewed the composition of Qualifying Franchisees and believes it contains a random, representative sampling of MOSQUITO SQUAD franchisees based on level of sales, years in the business and geography. In addition, although the table below only contains information for the 43 Qualifying Franchisees out of the 90 total MOSQUITO SQUAD franchisees as of December 31, 2011, the Total Gross Revenues (as defined above in Section A) of the Qualifying Franchisees for the 2011 Operating Season represent 81.8% of the Total Gross Revenues reported to us by all MOSQUITO SQUAD franchisees for the 2011 Operating Season.

We have calculated the number of customers that purchased MOSQUITO SQUAD services for the entire 2010 Operating

Season and then subsequently renewed their service for the entire 2011 Operating Season ("Renewal Customers"). The "Customer Renewal Rate" is calculated by dividing the number of Renewal Customers by the total number of full season customers for the 2010 Operating System. Only customers that had contracted for an entire year of service in 2010 and 2011 were included in the calculation of the Customer Renewal Rates. We did not include customers who initially contracted for only a portion of the 2010 Operating Season then subsequently renewed for the entire 2011 Operating Season.

MOSQUITO SQUAD Customer Renewal Rates from the 2010 Operating Season to the 2011 Operating Season						
Number of Franchisees	Median Customer Renewal Rates	Number of Franchisees At or Above the Median	Percent of Franchisees Above the Median	Average Customer Renewal Rates	Number of Franchisees At or Above the Average	Percent of Franchisees Above the Average
43	72.0%	22	51.2%	71.8%	22	51.2%

(1) Twenty-two of the 43 Qualifying Franchisees (51.2%) met or exceeded the median Customer Renewal Rate of 72.0%.

(2) Twenty-two of the 43 Qualifying Franchisees (51.2%) met or exceeded the average Customer Renewal Rate of 71.8%.

The above results are provided to prospective franchisees in evaluating the experience of certain existing MOSQUITO SQUAD franchises and not as a projection or forecast of what a new MOSQUITO SQUAD franchisee may experience. A new franchisee's financial results are likely to differ from the results provided above.

Some MOSQUITO SQUAD franchisees have experienced the above results. Your individual results may differ. There is no assurance that you will perform as well.

The financial information we utilized in preparing the preceding financial performance representations was based entirely upon information reported to us by MOSQUITO SQUAD franchisees. None of this information was audited or otherwise reviewed or investigated by us or by any independent accountant or auditing firm, and no one has audited, reviewed or otherwise evaluated this information for accuracy or expressed his/her opinion with regard to its content or form.

The figures in the tables above do not reflect other fixed and variable costs and expenses associated with operating a MOSQUITO SQUAD franchise, including officer's salaries, administrative salaries, automobile expenses, insurance costs and advertising and marketing expenses, which must be deducted from the Gross Revenues to obtain your net income or profit.

You should conduct an independent investigation of your potential Gross Revenues and the costs and expenses you will incur in operating your MOSQUITO SQUAD business. Franchisees or former franchisees, listed in this disclosure document, may be valuable source of this information.

In preparing any pro forma financial projections, you and other prospective franchisees must keep in mind that each individual franchisee's experience is unique and results may vary, depending on a number of factors. These factors include general economic conditions of the franchisee's territory, length of the franchisee's spraying season, demographics, competition, and effectiveness of the franchisee in the management of the franchised business and the use of the MOSQUITO SQUAD operating systems, scope of investment and the overall efficiency of the franchise operation.

You are responsible for developing your own business plan for your MOSQUITO SQUAD franchise, including capital budgets, financial statements, projections, pro forma financial statements and other elements appropriate to your particular circumstances. In preparing your business plan, we encourage you to consult with your own accounting, business and legal advisors to assist you to identify the expenses you likely will incur in connection with your MOSQUITO SQUAD franchise, to prepare your budgets, and to assess the likely or potential financial performance of your MOSQUITO SQUAD franchise.

In developing the business plan for your MOSQUITO SQUAD franchise, you are cautioned to make necessary allowance for changes in financial results to income, expenses or both that may result from operation of your MOSQUITO SQUAD franchise during periods of, or in geographic areas suffering from, economic downturns, inflation, unemployment, or other negative economic influences.

Other than the preceding financial performance representations, we do not make any financial performance representations. We also do not authorize our employees or representatives to make any such representations either orally or in writing. If you are purchasing an existing outlet, however, we may provide you with the actual records of that outlet. If you receive any other financial performance information or projections of your future income, you should report it to the franchisor's management by contacting Chris Grandpre, Mosquito Squad Franchising Corporation, 2924 Emerywood Parkway, Suite 101, Richmond, Virginia 23294, (804) 353-6999, the Federal Trade Commission, and the appropriate state regulatory agencies.

OUTDOORLIGHTING
PERSPECTIVES ®

OUTDOOR LIGHTING PERSPECTIVES

2924 Emerywood Pkwy., #101
Richmond, VA 23294
Tel: (800) 772-4668, (804) 353-6999 x102
Fax: (804) 358-1878
Email: spucel@outdoorlivingbrands.com
Website: www.outdoorlightingfranchise.com
Shemar Pucel, Franchise Recruitment Consultant

BACKGROUND

IFA Member:	Yes
Established & First Franchised:	1995; 1998
Franchised Units:	45
Company-Owned Units:	0
Total Units:	45
Distribution:	US – 42; CAN – 1; O'seas – 2
North America:	24 States, 1 Province
Density:	4 in FL, a in NC
Projected New Units (12 Months):	39
Qualifications:	4, 4, 1, 3, 4, 4

FINANCIAL/TERMS

Cash Investment:	$75K
Total Investment:	$70 – $100K
Minimum Net Worth:	$200K
Fees (Franchise):	$39.5K
Fees (Royalty):	7%
Fees (Advertising):	1.5% or $300 (min)/month
Term of Contract (Years):	7/7
Average Number of Employees:	1 FT, 0 PT
Passive Ownership:	Allowed
Encourage Conversions:	Yes
Area Development Agreements:	Yes
Sub-Franchising Contracts:	No
Expand in Territory:	Yes
Space Needs:	N/A

SUPPORT & TRAINING

Financial Assistance Provided:	Yes
Site Selection Assistance:	N/A
Lease Negotiation Assistance:	N/A
Co-operative Advertising:	No
Franchisee Association/Member:	Yes
Size of Corporate Staff:	35
On-going Support:	B, C, D, G, H, I
Training:	1 Week Classroom/In-Field; Annual Holiday Training (August) Richmond, VA; On-going Training and On-Site Visits for all Franchisees

SPECIFIC EXPANSION PLANS

US:	All United Stated
Canada:	All Canada
Overseas:	All Countries

Written substantiation of the data used in preparing the financial performance representations included in this ITEM 19 will be made available to you upon reasonable request.

A. Average Gross Sales for Outdoor Lighting Businesses for the 12 Months Ending December 31, 2011

The following table presents the Average Gross Sales realized by certain Outdoor Lighting franchisees in during the period between January 1, 2011 and December 31, 2011 ("Reporting Period"). We have provided this information to help you to make a more informed decision regarding the Outdoor Lighting System. You should not use this information as an indication of how your specific Outdoor Lighting Business may perform. The success of your Outdoor Lighting Business will depend largely on your individual abilities and your market. The actual numbers you experience will be influenced by a wide variety of factors including your management, market size, demographics, competition, and the general state of the economy in your Territory. You should conduct your own independent research and due diligence to assist you in preparing your own projections.

The information provided in the table below was compiled from 41 Outdoor Lighting franchisees that were operational during the Reporting Period, including all Outdoor Lighting franchisees operating in the United States and internationally. The data excludes franchisees that either began operations or ceased active operations during the Reporting Period.

| Sales Volume | # of Franchisees | Sales in Dollars | | | | Years in Business | | |
		Minimum	Average	Maximum	% of Franchisees	Minimum	Average	Maximum
Greater than $400,000	10	$439,186	$690,600	$1,004,015	24.4%	2.0	8.0	10.2
Between $200,000-$400,000	17	$211,546	$316,084	$391,473	41.5%	1.8	8.3	13.0
Less than $200,000	14	$23,356	$123,206	$196,043	34.1%	2.0	6.4	10.7
Franchisees	41		$341,569		100.0%		7.6	

Two of the 10 franchisees reporting sales in excess of $400,000 generated sales in excess of the $690,600 average for this subset of the 41 reporting franchisees shown in the table above. Seven of the 17 franchisees reporting sales between $200,000 and $400,000 generated sales in excess of the $316,084 average for this subset of the 41 reporting franchises. Seven of the 14 franchisees reporting sales less than $200,000 generated sales in excess of the $123,206 average for this subset of the 41 reporting franchisees.

There is no assurance that you or any other Outdoor Lighting Business will perform as well as the 41 Outdoor Lighting Businesses used in preparing the averages shown in the table above.

The Average Gross Sales figures presented above represent the total dollar value of customer installation contracts and ongoing maintenance services sold during the Reporting Period by the 41 Outdoor Lighting franchisees identified above. Average Gross Sales should not be construed as a measure of revenue or cash collections, which can vary substantially from Average Gross Sales depending on several factors, including franchisees' backlog of projects, size of projects or contract terms. The financial performance representations above do not reflect the costs of sales, royalties or operating expenses that must be deducted from the gross sales figures to obtain a net income or owner's profit number. The best source of cost and expense data may be from current or former franchisees as listed in this disclosure document.

B. Gross Margin Benchmarking Study for Outdoor Lighting Businesses for the 12 Months Ending December 31, 2010

We do not provide prospective franchisees with projections of income, profits or earnings. There is no guarantee that you, as a new Outdoor Lighting Business, will attain the same level of sales or profits that have been attained by our existing franchisees. The success of your franchise will depend largely on your individual abilities and your market. However, we do provide prospective franchisees with information from a financial benchmarking study ("Benchmarking Study") conducted for the Outdoor Lighting System by Profit Planning Group ("PPG"), an independent third party financial benchmarking organization serving trade associations and franchise networks across the country.

In 2011, PPG conducted an independent financial Benchmarking Study for Outdoor Lighting franchisees. The Benchmarking Study was conducted solely on a voluntary basis and was offered only to franchisees who had been operating their Outdoor Lighting Businesses at least twelve months at the time of the Benchmarking Study. As a result, one franchisee who joined the system in 2010 was ineligible to participate in the Benchmarking Study. Interested franchisees were required to submit their income statements for the year ending December 31, 2010 ("Benchmarking Reporting Period") to PPG. PPG then calculated certain financial metrics to allow participants to compare their financial performance against their peer group of Outdoor Lighting franchisees. 17 out of 39 (43.6%) Outdoor Lighting Businesses as of December 31, 2011, participated in the Benchmarking Study. We have reviewed the composition of franchise participants and believes it contains a random, representative sampling of Outdoor Lighting franchisees based on level of sales, years in the business and geography.

The Benchmarking Study examined a number of key performance metrics, and we have determined that Gross Profit Margin is helpful to prospective franchisees looking to acquire the rights to operate one or more Outdoor Lighting Businesses. For purposes of the Benchmarking Study, Gross Profit Margin measures profitability after material, installation labor and other direct installation costs are subtracted from gross revenue. It is calculated by dividing gross profit dollars by gross revenues. While Gross Profit Margin measures profitability after material, installation labor and other direct costs are subtracted from gross revenue, it excludes royalties, any commissions and other operating expenses.

The Gross Profit Margin figures provided by the Benchmarking Study are the median. The median for any variable is the middle number of all values reported arrayed from lowest to highest. Unlike the mean (or average), the median is not influenced by any extremely high or low variables reported. Therefore, the Benchmarking Study reports the median as the preferred statistic for its analysis.

The table below provides a further breakdown of median Gross Profit Margins among the Outdoor Lighting franchisees participating in the Benchmarking Study.

	Participating Outdoor Lighting Perspectives Franchise	Sales Under $300,000	Sales Over $300,000	Less than 7 Years in Business	More than 7 Years in Business
Number of Franchisees Reporting	17	10	7	10	7
Gross Profit Margin (Median)	55.5%	51.7%	56.7%	51.7%	56.7%

The above results taken from the Benchmarking Study are provided to prospective franchisees in evaluating the experience of existing Outdoor Lighting Businesses who participated in the study and not as a projection or forecast of what a new Outdoor Lighting Business may experience. A new franchisee's financial results are likely to differ from the results provided above.

The financial information utilized in the benchmarking study was based entirely upon information voluntarily reported by the 17 Outdoor Lighting franchisees who participated in the benchmarking study, and none of this information has been audited or otherwise reviewed or investigated by us or by any independent accountant or auditing firm, and no one has audited, reviewed or otherwise evaluated this information for accuracy or expressed his/her opinion with regard to its content or form.

In preparing any pro forma financial projections, you and other prospective franchisees must keep in mind that each individual franchisee's experience is unique and results may vary, depending on a number of factors. These factors include general economic conditions of the franchise territory, demographics, competition, effectiveness of the franchisee in the management of the Outdoor Lighting Business, the general state of the economy in your Territory, and the use of the Outdoor Lighting System, scope of investment and the overall efficiency of the franchise operation.

NOTES THAT APPLY TO SUBSECTIONS A AND B ABOVE:

A. Many factors, including those described in the preceding paragraph, are unique to each Outdoor Lighting Business and may significantly impact the financial performance of your outdoor lighting business.

B. There is no assurance that you or any other Outdoor Lighting Business will do as well.

C. As with other businesses, we anticipate that a new Outdoor Lighting Business will not achieve sales volumes or maintain expenses similar to an Outdoor Lighting Business that has been operating for a number of years.

D. You are responsible for developing your own business plan for your Outdoor Lighting Business, including capital budgets, financial statements, projections, pro forma financial statements and other elements appropriate to your particular circumstances. In preparing your business plan, we encourage you to consult with your own accounting, business and legal advisors to assist you to identify the expenses you likely will incur in connection with your Outdoor Lighting Business, to prepare your budgets, and to assess the likely or potential financial performance of your Outdoor Lighting Business.

E. In developing the business plan for your Outdoor Lighting Business, you are cautioned to make necessary allowance for changes in financial results to income, expenses or both that may result from operation of your Outdoor Lighting Business during periods of, or in geographic areas suffering from, economic downturns, inflation, unemployment, or other negative economic influences.

Some Outdoor Lighting Businesses sold this amount. Your individual results may differ. There is no assurance that you'll sell as much.

C. Median Retail Price Per Fixture, Number of Fixtures Installed, and Retail Price Per Project for New Lighting System Installations for OUTDOOR LIGHTING PERSPECTIVES Franchisees the Last Twelve Months Ending June 30, 2011.

The following table presents the median "Retail Price Per Fixture" for new OUTDOOR LIGHTING PERSPECTIVE installation projects by certain Outdoor Lighting Businesses in the twelve month period ending June 30, 2011 ("Reporting Period"). Retail Price Per Fixture is calculated by taking the total dollar sale for a particular new OUTDOOR LIGHTING PERSPECTIVE installation project, divided by the number of lighting fixtures installed on that particular project.

The information provided in the table below was compiled by examining 1,116 new OUTDOOR LIGHTING PERSPECTIVE installation projects identified from the all of the monthly statements of Gross Revenues provided by all Outdoor Lighting Businesses during the Reporting Period. Examination of the monthly statements of Gross Revenues clearly identified 1,116 new Outdoor Lighting installation projects, the total dollar sale for each project and the number of lighting fixtures installed for each project.

These 1,116 new OUTDOOR LIGHTING PERSPECTIVE installation projects generated a total of $5,001,070 in retail sales, which represents 57.1% of all the retail sales performed by all Outdoor Lighting Businesses during the twelve month period ending June 30, 2011. The data in the table excludes: (i) revenues from new OUTDOOR LIGHTING PERSPECTIVE instal-

lation projects where the number of lighting fixtures installed were not reported; (ii) revenue from installations of additional OUTDOOR LIGHTING PERSPECTIVE fixtures that are being added to an existing OUTDOOR LIGHTING PERSPECTIVE system, otherwise known as an "add-on sale"; (iii) revenues derived from maintenance and service work on previously installed OUTDOOR LIGHTING PERSPECTIVE systems; (iv) revenues derived from holiday decorative lighting systems; and (v) revenues derived from commercial lighting projects. Our management team has reviewed the composition of the franchisees that completed the 1,116 new lighting system installation projects was reviewed and determined that the set of lighting installation projects is comprised of a random, representative sampling of Outdoor Lighting Businesses based on level of sales, years in the business, and geographic location.

For the entire sample of 1,116 new OUTDOOR LIGHTING PERSPECTIVE installations, the median Retail Price Per Fixture during the Reporting Period, was $251.08 per fixture. The median number of fixtures installed ("Number of Fixtures Installed") per new OUTDOOR LIGHTING PERSPECTIVE system installation project was 13 and the median retail price per project ("Retail Price Per Project") for a new OUTDOOR LIGHTING PERSPECTIVE system installation was $3,310. The median for any variable is the middle number of all values reported arrayed from lowest to highest. Unlike the mean (or average), the median is not influenced by any extremely high or low variables reported. The table below provides a further break down of Retail Price Per Fixture, Number of Fixtures Installed, and Retail Price Per Project for new OUTDOOR LIGHTING PERSPECTIVE system installations during the Reporting Period.

OUTDOOR LIVING PERSPECTIVES – New Lighting System Installations During the Twelve Months Ending June 30, 2011

Retail Price per Fixture	# of Projects	% of all Projects	Median Price per Fixture	# of Projects Above Median	Median Number of Fixtures per Project	Maximum Number of Fixtures per Project	Minimum Number of Fixtures per Project	Median Retail Sales per Project	Maximum Retail Sales per Project	Minimum Retail Sales per Project
$401 or more	76	6.8%	$503.65	38	7	81	2	$4,235	$33,175	$831
$351-$400	78	7.0%	$369.96	39	11	98	2	$3,935	$36,020	$750
$301-$350	146	13.1%	$323.51	73	13	112	1	$4,279	$36,845	$345
$251-$300	262	23.5%	$272.00	131	15	124	1	$4,021	$36,335	$255
$201-$250	334	29.9%	$228.44	167	14	114	2	$3,088	$26,190	$405
$151-$200	185	16.6%	$187.50	93	11	89	1	$2,100	$15,000	$195
$150 or less	35	3.1%	$130.65	18	17	45	2	$2,120	$5,210	$170
Total Projects	1,116	100.0%	$251.08	558	13	124	1	$3,310	$2,280	$170

The figures in the table above reflect only the revenues from the Retail Price Per Fixture and the Retail Price Per Project; they do not reflect the direct variable costs of a new OUTDOOR LIGHTING PERSPECTIVE system installation project which would include the direct cost of the lighting fixture, the cost of wire, the cost of a transformer, the cost of other normal lighting installation materials and the direct cost of labor to install the new outdoor lighting system.

Additionally, other fixed and variable costs and expenses associated with operating an Outdoor Lighting Business, including franchisee's salary, administrative salaries, sales expenses, automobile expenses, insurance costs and advertising and marketing expenses are not considered in the measurement of Retail Price Per Fixture and Retail Price Per Project. You should conduct an independent investigation of the potential costs and expenses you will incur in operating your Outdoor Lighting Business.

The above results are provided to prospective franchisees in evaluating the experience of certain existing Outdoor Lighting Businesses and not as a projection or forecast of what a new Outdoor Lighting Business may experience. A new franchisee's financial results are likely to differ from the results provided above.

Some Outdoor Lighting Businesses have experienced the above results. Your individual results may differ. There is no assurance that you will perform as well.

The financial information we utilized in preparing the preceding financial performance representations was based entirely upon information reported to us by Outdoor Lighting Businesses. None of this information was audited or otherwise reviewed or investigated by us or by any independent accountant or auditing firm, and no one has audited, reviewed or otherwise evaluated this information for accuracy or expressed his/her opinion with regard to its content or form.

In preparing any pro forma financial projections, you and other prospective franchisees must keep in mind that each individual franchisee's experience is unique and results may vary, depending on a number of factors. These factors include general economic conditions of the franchisee's territory, demographics, competition, and effectiveness of the franchisee in the management of the franchised business and the use of the Outdoor Lighting System, scope of investment and the overall efficiency of the franchise operation.

You are responsible for developing your own business plan for your Outdoor Lighting Business, including capital budgets, financial statements, projections, pro forma financial statements and other elements appropriate to your particular circumstances. In preparing your business plan, we encourage you to consult with your own accounting, business and legal advisors to assist you to identify the expenses you likely will incur in connection with your Outdoor Lighting Business to prepare your budgets, and to assess the likely or potential financial performance of your Outdoor Lighting Business.

In developing the business plan for your Outdoor Lighting Business, you are cautioned to make necessary allowance for changes in financial results to income; expenses or both that may result from operation of your Outdoor Lighting Business during periods of, or in geographic areas suffering from, economic downturns, inflation, unemployment, or other negative economic influences.

Other than the preceding financial performance representa-

tions, we do not make any financial performance representations. We also do not authorize our employees or representatives to make any such representations either orally or in writing. If you are purchasing an existing outlet, however, we may provide you with the actual records of that outlet. If you receive any other financial performance information or projections of your future income, you should report it to the franchisor's management by contacting Chris Grandpre, Outdoor Lighting Perspectives Franchising, Inc., 2924 Emerywood Parkway, Suite 101, Richmond, Virginia 23294, (804) 353-6999, the Federal Trade Commission, and the appropriate state regulatory agencies.

PADGETT BUSINESS SERVICES

400 Blue Hill Dr., #201
Westwood, MA 02090
Tel: (877) 729-8725 x290, (781) 251-9410
Fax: (781) 251-9520
Email: cclark@smallbizpros.com
Website: www.smallbizpros.com
Carol Clark, Franchise Development

America's top-rated and fastest-growing tax and accounting franchise, serving the fastest-growing segment of the economy: America's small business owners. Initial training. Specialized software. On-going support.

BACKGROUND
IFA Member:	Yes
Established & First Franchised:	1966; 1975
Franchised Units:	429
Company-Owned Units:	0
Total Units:	429
Distribution:	US – 305; CAN – 124; O'seas – 0
North America:	44 States, 7 Provinces
Density:	67 in ON, 38 in QC, 26 in GA
Projected New Units (12 Months):	50

Qualifications:	3, 3, 4, 4, 2, 4

FINANCIAL/TERMS
Cash Investment:	$100K
Total Investment:	$106K
Minimum Net Worth:	$100K
Fees (Franchise):	$38K + $18K Training
Fees (Royalty):	9 – 4.5%
Fees (Advertising):	0%
Term of Contract (Years):	10/10
Average Number of Employees:	1 FT, 2 PT
Passive Ownership:	Not Allowed
Encourage Conversions:	Yes
Area Development Agreements:	No
Sub-Franchising Contracts:	No
Expand in Territory:	Yes
Space Needs:	200 – 400 SF

SUPPORT & TRAINING
Financial Assistance Provided:	No
Site Selection Assistance:	Yes
Lease Negotiation Assistance:	N/A
Co-operative Advertising:	No
Franchisee Association/Member:	Yes/Member
Size of Corporate Staff:	40
On-going Support:	A, C, D, G, H, I
Training: 3 (2.5 Day) On-Site Visits; 2.5 Weeks Athens, GA	

SPECIFIC EXPANSION PLANS
US:	All United States
Canada:	All Canada
Overseas:	No

As of May 31, 2012, PADGETT had 297 franchised locations operated by 289 franchisees in the U.S. subject to revenue reporting requirements. Twenty of these franchisees had not been open for business a full year and the operating results of those locations are not included in the franchisee financial summary information that follows. PADGETT franchisees who file extensions may file their income tax returns either September 15th or October 15th depending on their entity status, which is after the date we prepare this document for FTC filing. As of the filing date of this document, 230 of PADGETT's franchisees had submitted complete financial information to PADGETT, which was used to determine the franchisee profit information within this section. The revenue information, including average client fees, was based on all franchisees' operating results. The Financial Performance Representations do not include any profit information for franchisees who operated for only a part of FY2011 if he/she closed during that year. The revenues shown on the Report are the revenues upon which franchisees' monthly royalty fees were calculated.

PADGETT offered substantially the same services to all of the businesses included in the Report and substantially all the businesses offered the same business services. Some factors or variables affect the gross revenues of the franchised businesses, including:

- the amount and effectiveness of advertising or marketing effort
- being fully engaged in the business
- willingness and ability to promote and operate the business

Your PADGETT business will likely be affected by one or more of these factors, some to a greater extent than others.

Overall Franchisee revenues and profits:

Franchisee revenues are primarily derived from monthly fees (for write-up and consultation services), tax preparation fees and year-end fees (to prepare W-2, 1099, etc. documents for clients). In addition, franchisees also have additional revenue from payroll processing and certain one-time fees (such as set-up fees and backwork fees) and other additional fees (such as representation fees).

As of May 31, 2012, the average monthly fee paid by Padgett clients was $204. This is compared to $198 and $191 respectively as of May 31, 2011 and May 31, 2010. In addition, tax preparation fees represent approximately thirty percent (30%) of ongoing client fees. This relationship of monthly fees and tax preparation fees has remained consistent during the same three-year period. Based on these two components of the PADGETT fee structure, as of May 31, 2012, the average on- going annual revenue from a client is $3,497.

Franchisee profitability was also analyzed for franchisees' fiscal years that ended during PADGETT's fiscal year ending May 31, 2012. We adjusted the profit figures by eliminating depreciation, interest and franchisees' own expenses that vary considerably among franchisees, including owners' salaries and discretionary owners' expenses. These adjustments have the effect of increasing the profits reported. In reviewing this information, you will need to account for those variable expenses that you will incur in operating your business. Your fixed and variable expenses will vary from those presented based on the operating structure that you establish. As a result, even if your gross revenues fall within the reported range of revenues experienced by our franchisees, your profitability may vary. The data received from reporting businesses was accumulated using a uniform method that included direct reports to PADGETT by the franchisees. PADGETT has not independently verified the figures given by the franchised businesses. PADGETT does not require its franchisees to utilize a uniform accounting method and therefore cannot confirm whether their revenue figures were compiled in accordance with generally accepted accounting principles. PADGETT franchisees primarily use a cash basis of accounting.

With regard to the profit information compiled, PADGETT reports that adjusted profits as a percent of revenues were as follows:

Franchisee Revenues	Adjusted Profit Percent			
	Average	High	Mean	Low
$500,000 +	43.1%	64.2%	40.9%	20.1%
$350,000 - $499,999	42.0%	65.2%	44.3%	19.0%
$150,000 - $349,999	40.7%	78.4%	42.6%	4.9%
$100,000 - $149,999	43.3%	80.4%	44.6%	8.7%
Sub-Total $100,000 +	41.7%			
< $100,000	24.2%	83.4%	25.5%	-100+%
Total	39.2%			

Although we do not estimate the average "break-even" sales volume of the reporting franchisees, franchisees with revenues greater than $100,000 reported profits and, conversely, all franchisees who reported losses had revenues of less than $100,000.

A new franchisee's financial results are likely to differ from the results stated in the financial performance representation.

We will provide you with written substantiation of the data used in preparing this Report upon your reasonable request; however, this does not require us to disclose the identity of any specific licensee or require us to release data without the consent of any specific franchisee.

Recommended expenditures for the first three years:

The following table is a forecast as opposed to a summary of actual data reported by Franchisees. Padgett assists new Franchisees with a three-year forecast to develop the franchised business. The following chart shows the three-year expense forecast recommended for a "fully engaged" franchise owner. "Fully engaged" refers to Franchisees who employ all five steps of the Padgett Comprehensive Marketing Program, as described in the Operations Manual, and attend at least one Padgett seminar each year. As mentioned above, marketing costs vary depending on the Franchisee's background and involvement. The marketing expenses in this forecast represent the costs of a marketing plan in which more outside services are employed as compared to a marketing plan in which Franchisee or Franchisee's employee(s) are performing the same tasks. The expense forecast excludes royalty expense, which is explained in Item 6 – Other Fees, above.

YEAR I EXPENSE FORECAST													
Month	1	2	3	4	5	6	7	8	9	10	11	12	YEAR ONE TOTAL
Expense													
Payroll - Operations													
Payroll - Marketing							1,080	1,080	1,080	1,080	1,080	1,080	6,480
Payroll - Tax Preperation													
Employer Taxes							137	137	137	137	137	137	820
Tax Processing													
Marketing Fees	2,400	2,400	2,400	2,400	2,400	2,400							14,400
Marketing Materials/Postage	725	725	725	725	725	725	725	725	745	745	745	745	8,780
Rent							400	400	400	400	400	400	2,400
PAS Software License Fee	3,000												3,000
Office Supplies	350	150	150	150	150	150	150	150	150	150	150	150	2,000
Telephone/Data	75	75	75	75	75	75	75	75	75	75	75	75	900
Postage	25	25	25	25	25	25	25	25	25	25	25	25	300
Insurance	800												800
Travel	125	125	125	125	1,000	125	125	125	125	125	125	125	2,375
Utilities													
Misc expenses	100	100	100	100	100	100	100	100	100	100	100	100	1,200
Total Expenses	7,600	3,600	3,600	3,600	3,600	4,475	2,817	2,817	2,837	2,837	2,837	2,837	43,455
Operating Profit/(Loss) -$ Operating Profit/(Loss) -%	(7,600)	(3,600)	(3,600)	(3,600)	(3,600)	(4,475)	(2,817)	(2,817)	(2,837)	(2,837)	(2,837)	(2,837)	(43,455)
Start-Up Costs													
Application Fee	1,000												1,000
Initial License Fee	37,000												37,000
Training Fee	18,000												18,000

Training Expense	2,000												2,000
Initial Computer for Office	1,000												1,000
Other Fixtures & Equipment	3,500												3,500
Total Start-Up Costs	62,500												62,500
Cash Increase/Decrease - Period	(70,100)	(3,600)	(3,600)	(3,600)	(3,600)	(4,475)	(2,817)	(2,817)	(2,837)	(2,837)	(2,837)	(2,837)	(105,955)

YEAR 2 EXPENSE FORECAST													
Month	13	14	15	16	17	18	19	20	21	22	23	24	YEAR TWO TOTAL
Expense													
Payroll - Operations	2,600	2,600	2,600	2,600	2,600	2,600	2,600	4,000	4,000	4,000	4,000	4,000	38,200
Payroll - Marketing	2,600	2,600	2,600	2,600	2,600	2,600	2,600	2,600	2,600	2,600	2,600	2,600	31,200
Payroll - Tax Pre-peration											6,000	6,000	12,000
Employer Taxes	720	720	720	720	720	720	720	914	914	914	1,745	1,745	11,274
Tax Processing													
Marketing Fees													
Marketing Materials/Postage	900	900	900	900	900	900	900	900	900	900	900	900	10,800
Rent	750	750	750	750	750	750	750	750	750	750	750	750	9,000
PAS Software License Fee												3,000	3,000
Office Supplies	200	200	200	200	200	200	200	200	200	200	200	200	2,400
Telephone/Data	100	100	100	100	100	100	100	100	100	100	100	100	1,200
Postage	25	25	25	25	25	25	25	25	25	25	25	25	300
Insurance	1,000												1,000
Travel	125	1,000	125	125	125	1,000	125	125	125	125	125	125	3,250
Utilities	150	150	150	150	150	150	150	150	150	150	150	150	1,800
Misc expenses	200	200	200	200	200	200	200	200	200	200	200	200	2,400
Total Expenses	9,370	9,245	8,370	8,370	8,370	9,245	8,370	9,964	9,964	9,964	16,795	19,795	127,824
Operating Profit/(Loss) -$ Operating Profit/(Loss) -%	(9,370)	(9,245)	(8,370)	(8,370)	(8,370)	(9,245)	(8,370)	(9,964)	(9,964)	(9,964)	(16,795)	(19,795)	(127,824)

YEAR 3 EXPENSE FORECAST													
Month	25	26	27	28	29	30	31	32	33	34	35	36	YEAR THREE TOTAL
Expense													
Payroll - Operations	5,000	5,000	5,000	5,000	5,000	5,000	6,000	6,000	6,000	6,000	6,000	6,000	66,000
Payroll - Marketing	5,000	5,000	5,000	5,000	5,000	5,000	5,000	6,000	6,000	6,000	6,000	6,000	65,000
Payroll - Tax Preperation											6,000	6,000	12,000
Employer Taxes	1,385	1,385	1,385	1,385	1,385	1,385	1,524	1,662	1,662	1,662	2,493	2,493	19,806
Tax Processing													
Marketing Fees													
Marketing Materials/ Postage	1,000	1,000	1,000	1,000	1,000	1,000	1,000	1,000	1,000	1,000	1,000	1,000	12,000
Rent	750	750	750	750	750	750	750	750	750	750	750	750	9,000
PAS Software License Fee												3,000	3,000
Office Supplies	200	200	200	200	200	200	200	200	200	200	200	200	2,400
Telephone/ Data	125	125	125	125	125	125	125	125	125	125	125	125	1,500
Postage	25	25	25	25	25	25	25	25	25	25	25	25	300
Insurance	1,200												1,200
Travel	125	1,000	125	125	125	1,000	125	125	125	125	125	125	3,250
Utilities	175	175	175	175	175	175	175	175	175	175	175	175	2,100
Misc expenses	200	200	200	200	200	200	200	200	200	200	200	200	2,400
Total Expenses	15,185	14,860	13,985	13,985	13,985	14,860	15,124	16,262	16,262	16,262	23,093	26,093	199,956
Operating Profit/ (Loss) -$ Operating Profit/ (Loss) -%	(15,185)	(14,860)	(13,985)	(13,985)	(13,985)	(14,860)	(15,124)	(16,262)	(16,262)	(16,262)	(23,093)	(26,093)	(199,956)

"Trusted Locksmith" ®

POP-A-LOCK

1018 Harding St., #101
Lafayette, LA 70503
Tel: (877) 233-6211, (337) 233-6211 x224
Fax: (337) 233-6655
Email: michaelkleimeyer@systemforward.com
Website: www.popalock.com
Michael Kleimeyer, Director of Franchise Development

POP-A-LOCK is America's largest locksmith, car door unlocking, and roadside assistance service. We provide fast, professional, guaranteed service using our proprietary tools and opening techniques. We offer an outstanding community service through our industry.

BACKGROUND

IFA Member:	Yes
Established & First Franchised:	1991; 1994
Franchised Units:	269
Company-Owned Units:	0
Total Units:	269
Distribution:	US – 225; CAN – 2; O'seas – 16
North America:	40 States, 0 Provinces
Density:	22 in TX, 17 in FL, 14 in LA
Projected New Units (12 Months):	38
Qualifications:	4, 5, 1, 3, 3, 4

FINANCIAL/TERMS

Cash Investment:	$120+K
Total Investment:	$101 – $134K + $15.5K/add. franchise
Minimum Net Worth:	$250 – $400K
Fees (Franchise):	$62K Min.
Fees (Royalty):	6%
Fees (Advertising):	1%
Term of Contract (Years):	10/10
Average Number of Employees:	2 FT, 1 PT
Passive Ownership:	Allowed
Encourage Conversions:	N/A
Area Development Agreements:	Yes
Sub-Franchising Contracts:	No
Expand in Territory:	Yes
Space Needs:	N/A

SUPPORT & TRAINING

Financial Assistance Provided:	No
Site Selection Assistance:	N/A
Lease Negotiation Assistance:	N/A
Co-operative Advertising:	No
Franchisee Association/Member:	Yes/Member
Size of Corporate Staff:	15
On-going Support:	A, b, C, D, e, F, G, h, I
Training:	5-15 Days + additional local Lafayette, LA

SPECIFIC EXPANSION PLANS

US:	All United States
Canada:	Toronto/GTA
Overseas:	China, Ireland, UK

1. The top 30% of our Franchisees' net annual income ranges from $743,000.00 to $1,388,000.00 per year.
   a. Based on royalty reports – historical performance
   b. Franchisees have multiple franchise territories, contiguous major markets and/or non-contiguous mid-size markets.
   c. Service areas population range from 1.2 million to 4 million.
   d. Franchises have been operating from seven to sixteen years.

2. Franchise transfers (re-sales) have averaged 4.6 times earnings over the last six years.
   a. Low number of re-sales necessitates this time frame for relevant average.

3. Franchisee failures over the last 12 months: Three.
   a. 3% of the total system (101 franchisees)

Other than stated above, we do not make any representations about a franchisee's future financial performance of company-owned or franchised outlets. We also do not authorize our employees or representatives to make any such representations either orally or in writing. If you are purchasing an existing outlet, however, we may provide you with the actual records of that outlet. If you receive any other financial performance information or projections of your future income, you should report it to the franchisor's management by contacting Donald Marks, CEO at 1018 Harding Street, Suite 101, Lafayette, Louisiana 70503 and (337) 233-6211, the Federal Trade Commission, and the appropriate state regulatory agencies.

PRONTO INSURANCE

805 Media Luna Rd., # 400
Brownsville, TX 78520
Tel: (888) 338-6523, (956) 574-9787
Fax: (956) 574-9076
Email: jorge.garcia@prontoinsurance.com
Website: www.prontoinsurance.com
Jorge Garcia, Franchise Director

PRONTO INSURANCE franchise is a full-service retail office dedicated to providing low cost insurance products and income tax services. PRONTO prides itself in providing fast and efficient services. "Pronto. It's our name and our promise," speaks for itself. The company has enjoyed stunning growth, more than quadrupling its size in the last three years. We have 100+ locations and our own in-house claims and underwriting departments. Through aggressive marketing, brand awareness, and highly competitive pricing, we have quickly become an industry leader in Texas.

BACKGROUND

IFA Member:	Yes
Established & First Franchised:	1997; 2009
Franchised Units:	26
Company-Owned Units:	98
Total Units:	124
Distribution:	US – 115; CAN – 0; O'seas – 0
North America:	1 State, 0 Provinces
Density:	115 in TX
Projected New Units (12 Months):	40
Qualifications:	3, 5, 1, 2, 3, 5

FINANCIAL/TERMS

Cash Investment:	$50 – $60K
Total Investment:	$60 – $100K
Minimum Net Worth:	$200K
Fees (Franchise):	$20K
Fees (Royalty):	0%
Fees (Advertising):	$500 or 1% of sales
Term of Contract (Years):	5/5
Average Number of Employees:	4 FT, 0 PT
Passive Ownership:	Allowed
Encourage Conversions:	Yes
Area Development Agreements:	Yes
Sub-Franchising Contracts:	No
Expand in Territory:	Yes
Space Needs:	1,200 SF

SUPPORT & TRAINING

Financial Assistance Provided:	Yes (I)
Site Selection Assistance:	Yes
Lease Negotiation Assistance:	Yes
Co-operative Advertising:	Yes
Franchisee Association/Member:	Yes
Size of Corporate Staff:	300
On-going Support:	A, B, C, D, E, G, H, I
Training:	2 Weeks San Antonio, TX; or 2 Weeks Brownsville, TX; or 2 Weeks Houston, TX

SPECIFIC EXPANSION PLANS

US:	TX
Canada:	No
Overseas:	No

The following table represents the average Insurance Premium Revenue achieved by: (i) the 71 affiliate-owned Pronto Businesses; (ii) the 7 Pronto Businesses which are owned by our principals; and (iii) the 11 franchisee-owned Pronto Businesses. Each Pronto Business included in the following table was opened for the entire fifteen (15) month period from January 1, 2011 through March 31, 2012. Pronto Businesses not opened for this entire period were excluded. Insurance Premium Revenue means all premium revenue received resulting from all insurance policies sold, excluding related fees such as set up fees, application fees or administrative fees. We are not representing that you can expect to achieve these revenue figures at any time during the term of your Franchise Agreement. Your Insurance Premium Revenue may vary significantly depending on a number of factors, including the location of your Franchised Business and how you operate your business. If you rely upon our figures, you must accept the risk of not doing as well. The figures below do not reflect other revenue sources such as Tax Preparation Fee Revenue or related fees such as set up fees, application fees or administrative fees, nor do the figures include operating expenses, or other costs or expenses, including related interest, depreciation, amortization, and income taxes, that must be deducted from gross revenue figures to obtain your net income or profit. You should conduct an independent investigation of the costs and expenses you will incur in operating your Pronto Business. Franchisees or former franchisees, listed in this Disclosure Document, may be one source of this information.

We have compiled the following information from the internal, unaudited financial statements of our affiliate, Pronto General Agency, Ltd., for the fifteen (15) month period from January 1, 2011 through March 31, 2012. You are advised that no Certified Public Accountant has audited the data or expressed an opinion with regard to the content or form of such data. Further, the financial information was not prepared in accordance with Generally Accepted Accounting Principles (GAAP), but is believed to be reliable. Substantiation of the data used in preparing the below figures will be made available to you upon reasonable request. The affiliate-owned and principal-owned Pronto Businesses offer substantially the same products and services as you will as a franchisee operating a franchised Pronto Business.

Pronto Businesses	Average Insurance Premium Revenue	Number of Businesses Above Average/ Number of Businesses Below Average
Affiliate-Owned (71 Businesses)	$44,863	28 / 43
Principal-Owned (7 Businesses)	$108,913	3 / 4
Franchisee-Owned (11 Businesses)	$34,132	3 / 8

THE REVENUE FIGURES ABOVE ARE OF SPECIFIC UNITS REFERENCED ABOVE, AND SHOULD NOT BE CONSIDERED AS THE ACTUAL OR PROBABLE REVENUE THAT WILL BE REALIZED BY ANY FRANCHISE OWNER. WE DO NOT REPRESENT THAT ANY FRANCHISE OWNER CAN EXPECT TO ATTAIN SUCH REVENUE. YOUR RESULTS WILL VARY AND SUCH VARIANCES MAY BE MATERIAL AND ADVERSE TO THE REVENUES SHOWN HERE. YOU SHOULD USE THE ABOVE INFORMATION ONLY AS A REFERENCE IN CONDUCTING YOUR OWN ANALYSIS. WE STRONGLY URGE YOU TO CONSULT WITH YOUR FINANCIAL ADVISOR OR PERSONAL ACCOUNTANT CONCERNING THE FINANCIAL ANALYSIS THAT YOU SHOULD MAKE IN DETERMINING WHETHER OR NOT TO PURCHASE A PRONTO BUSINESS FRANCHISE. WE SPECIFICALLY INSTRUCT OUR SALES PERSONNEL, AGENTS, EMPLOYEES, MEMBERS, MANAGERS AND OFFICERS THAT THEY MAY NOT MAKE ANY REPRESENTATIONS OR STATEMENTS AS TO EARNINGS, SALES OR PROFITS, OR PROSPECTS OR CHANCES OF SUCCESS OF A PRONTO BUSINESS OTHER THAN WHAT IS STATED IN THIS ITEM 19. THEY ARE NOT AUTHORIZED TO REPRESENT OR ESTIMATE DOLLAR FIGURES AS TO A UNIT'S OPERATION OTHER THAN WHAT IS SHOWN ABOVE. EXCEPT AS PROVIDED BY APPLICABLE LAW, WE WILL NOT BE BOUND BY ALLEGATIONS OF ANY UNAUTHORIZED REPRESENTATION AS TO EARNINGS, SALES, PROFITS, OR PROSPECTS OR CHANCES FOR SUCCESS, AND YOU WILL BE REQUIRED TO ACKNOWLEDGE THAT YOU HAVE NOT RELIED ON ANY SUCH REPRESENTATION IN PURCHASING YOUR PRONTO BUSINESS FRANCHISE.

RENAISSANCE EXECUTIVE FORUMS

7855 Ivanhoe Ave., # 300
La Jolla, CA 92037-4500
Tel: (858) 551-6600
Fax: (858) 551-8777
Email: shawna@executiveforums.com

Website: www.executiveforums.com
Shawna Bergstrom, Director of Franchise Development

RENAISSANCE EXECUTIVE FORUMS bring together top executives from similarly-sized, non-competing companies into an advisory board process in which thousands of chief executives throughout the world participate. These CEOs, presidents, and owners meet once a month in small groups of approximately eight to fourteen individuals. The meetings provide an environment designed to address the opportunities and challenges they face as individuals and leaders of their respective organizations.

BACKGROUND			
IFA Member:	Yes	Passive Ownership:	Not Allowed
Established & First Franchised:	1994; 1994	Encourage Conversions:	N/A
Franchised Units:	50	Area Development Agreements:	No
Company-Owned Units:	0	Sub-Franchising Contracts:	No
Total Units:	50	Expand in Territory:	Yes
Distribution:	US – 45; CAN – 1; O'seas – 11	Space Needs:	N/A
North America:	20 States, 1 Provinces		
Density:	7 in CA, 4 in IL, 3 in FL	SUPPORT & TRAINING	
Projected New Units (12 Months):	10	Financial Assistance Provided:	No
Qualifications:	5, 5, 4, 4, 4, 5	Site Selection Assistance:	No
		Lease Negotiation Assistance:	No
		Co-operative Advertising:	No
FINANCIAL/TERMS		Franchisee Association/Member:	Yes/Member
Cash Investment:	$55.4 – $73.3K	Size of Corporate Staff:	15
Total Investment:	$75.5 – $110K	On-going Support:	A, B, C, D, G, H
Minimum Net Worth:	$500K	Training:	8 Days La Jolla, CA
Fees (Franchise):	$39.5K		
Fees (Royalty):	20%	SPECIFIC EXPANSION PLANS	
Fees (Advertising):	0%	US:	All United States
Term of Contract (Years):	10/10	Canada:	All Canada
Average Number of Employees:	1 FT, 0 PT	Overseas:	All Countries

Average Occupancy Rate, Average Daily Room Rate and Average RevPAR

As of December 31, 2011, there were 82 North American (U.S. and Canada) open and operating managed and franchised Renaissance Hotels; of these, 43 were franchised. There were 40 North American franchised hotels for which Smith Travel Research, Inc. ("Smith Travel") data was available and which were open and operating at least one year as of January 1, 2011 (see "Basis and Assumptions" below). For the one-year period ending December 31,2011, those franchised hotels achieved an average occupancy rate of 68.0%, an average daily room rate of $126.73, and an average revenue per available room ("RevPAR") of $86.22. The occupancy rate for the 40 franchised hotels ranged from a high of 89.1% to a low of 47.2%. Twenty-five of the franchised hotels (63%) achieved an average occupancy

rate equal to or greater than 68.0%. The average daily room rate ranged from a high of $181.09 to a low of $88.09. Twenty of the franchised hotels (50%) achieved an average daily room rate equal to or greater than $126.73. The RevPAR ranged from a high of $130.17 to a low of $54.85. Eighteen of these hotels (54%) achieved or exceeded the average RevPAR of$86.22.

The "average occupancy rate" is the total occupied rooms reported divided by total available rooms for the entire period. The "average daily room rate" is the gross room sales divided by total occupied rooms. The "average RevPAR" is the gross room sales divided by total available rooms.

Yield Index

The 40 North American franchised Renaissance Hotels that had been open for at least one year as of January 1, 2011, based on Smith Travel data, achieved an average yield index of 114.7% for the one year period ending December 31, 2011. The total yield index ranged from a high of 194.0% to a low of 86.4% for the hotels during that period. Twenty-two North American franchised hotels (55%) achieved a total yield index equal to or greater than 114.7%.

Yield-index measures the fair share of the amount of available revenue a hotel (or hotel brand) receives relative to its competitive set (as defined by each hotel or brand) within a given market.

Reservations

During 2011, based on inquiries received for Renaissance Hotels through our domestic and international reservations numbers ("Voice Reservations"), 1,215,973 gross room nights were booked for all Renaissance Hotels worldwide and out of that number, 951,717 gross room nights were booked for all North American (U.S. and Canada) Renaissance Hotels. In addition, 3,423,509 gross room nights were generated through Marriott.com for all Renaissance Hotels worldwide and out of that number, 2,523,182 gross room nights were booked for all North American Renaissance Hotels. Global distribution systems ("GDS") generated 1,862,948 gross room nights for all Renaissance Hotels worldwide and out of that number,

1,107,002 gross room nights were booked for all North American Renaissance Hotels. Certain online distribution channels such as Orbitz, Travelocity, and Expedia ("eChannels") generated 982,299 gross room nights for all Renaissance Hotels worldwide and out of that number, 598,273 gross room nights were booked for all North American Renaissance Hotels. In the aggregate, a total of 7,484,729 gross room nights were booked for all Renaissance Hotels worldwide and out of that number, a total of 5,180,174 gross room nights were booked for all North American Renaissance Hotels through Voice Reservations, marriott.com, GDS, and eChannels (collectively, the "Marriott Channels"). The Marriott Channels do not include group business and other room nights booked directly at the property or through area or regional sales offices, which are treated as "on-property" reservations.

During 2011, the average number of gross room nights booked through the Marriott Channels was 50,975 for the 41 North American franchised Renaissance Hotels that had been open for at least one year as of January 1, 2011 that were tracked in Marriott's internal databases (see "Basis and Assumptions" below): Gross room nights per Renaissance franchised hotel ranged from 12,363 for a small Renaissance Hotel with fewer than 150 rooms to 136,647 for a hotel with more than 500 rooms. Nineteen franchised Renaissance Hotels (46%) had more than 450,975 gross room nights. As a percentage of gross room nights per hotel, the percentage generated by the Marriott Channels for such 41
North American franchised Renaissance Hotels in 2011 ranged from 35.5% to 82.3%, and the average percentage was 53.2%. Twenty-two franchised Renaissance Hotels (54%) had more than 53.2% of their gross room nights booked through the Marriott Channels.

During 2011, the total number of gross room nights booked for Renaissance Hotels worldwide through the Marriott Channels were generated approximately: 16% from Voice Reservations, 46% from Marriott.com, 25% from GDS, and 13% from eChannels. During 2011, the total number of gross room nights booked for Renaissance Hotels in North America through the Marriott Channels were generated approximately: 18% from Voice Reservations, 49% from Marriott.com, 21% from GDS, and 12% from eChannels. During 2011, the 41 North American franchised Renaissance Hotels that had been open for at least one year as of January 1, 2011, had an average room night contribution mix of the following percentages: 17% from Voice Reservations, 47% from Marriott.com, 25% from GDS, and 11% from eChannels. Sixteen of such franchised Renaissance Hotels (39%) booked 17% of their gross room nights or more through Voice Reservations. Sixteen of such franchised Renaissance Hotels (39%) booked 47% of their gross room nights or more through Marriott.com online reservations. Twenty-three of such franchised Renaissance Hotels (56%) booked 25% of their gross room nights or

more through GDS. Twenty of such franchised Renaissance Hotels (49%) booked 11% of their gross room nights or more through eChannels. In 2011, as a percentage of gross room nights per hotel, the percentage generated by all 41 North American franchised Renaissance Hotels from: (1) Voice Reservations ranged from 7.8% to 42.6%; (2) Marriott.com ranged from 26.6% to 74.0%; (3) GDS ranged from 3.2% to 52.4%; and (4) eChannels ranged from 1.8% to 22.9%.

There are per-reservation, per-transaction, and other charges for participating in the reservation system, as described in Item 6 of this disclosure document. Your cost for each reservation will vary substantially, depending on the mix of reservations, occupancy, and rates you charge for your hotel.

The number of room nights booked through the Marriott Channels will vary from hotel to hotel and will depend upon many variables and factors, including size, location, seasonality, competition, general economic conditions, the length of time your hotel has been open or affiliated with us, the condition and attractiveness of the hotel, the perception of your hotel by customers utilizing our distribution channels, the reputation for quality of service at the hotel, and how effectively you participate in our programs and market your affiliation with us.

Marriott Rewards

All references to Marriott Rewards include both The Ritz-Carlton Rewards and the Marriott Rewards programs. Marriott Rewards has approximately 38 million members worldwide, and over 3,600 hotels and resorts in 68 countries participate in Marriott Rewards. Marriott's Consumer Marketing Department tracked the 41 North American franchised Renaissance Hotels that had been open and operating for one year as of January 1, 2011. For those hotels, for the one-year period ending December 31, 2011, Renaissance Hotel guests who were members of Marriott Rewards generated Marriott Rewards eligible revenue that is approximately 56% of the total room night revenue with an average daily spend of $155. The total of all Marriott Rewards room nights for such 41 North American franchised Renaissance Hotels was 1,314,000, generating approximately $203,673,000 in room revenue, not including taxes and tips. For such 41 hotels, Marriott Rewards members paid for an average of 32,100 room nights. The Marriott Rewards hotel room nights ranged from 9,800 to 66,900 and 15 North American franchised Renaissance Hotels (37%) achieved or exceeded the average of 32,100 paid Marriott Rewards room nights.

Renaissance ClubSport

The first franchised Renaissance ClubSport opened in November 2002 in Walnut Creek, California. For the one-year period ending December 31, 2011, the hotel had an occupancy rate of 73.5%, an average daily room rate of $129.90, an average RevPAR of $95.46, and a yield index of 140.1%. At year-end 2011, the hotel had total club memberships of 4,788 and average monthly membership dues of $172.96.

The second franchised Renaissance ClubSport opened in July 2008 in Aliso Viejo, California. For the one-year period ending December 31, 2011, the hotel had an occupancy rate of 74.14%, an average daily room rate of $143.28, an average RevPAR of $106.19, and a yield index of 115.94%. At year-end 2011, the hotel had total club memberships of 3,027 and average monthly membership dues of $154.91.

YOUR RESULTS ARE LIKELY TO DIFFER SUBSTANTIALLY FROM THE DATA AND RESULTS INDICATED ABOVE.

Basis and Assumptions

Smith Travel, an independent research firm servicing the travel industry, compiles average occupancy rate, average daily room rate, average RevPAR, yield index, and other relevant information concerning the lodging industry and is used by substantially all of the major lodging companies for tracking this data. The information in this Item 19 regarding average occupancy rate, average daily room rate, average RevPAR, and yield index, including the number of North American franchised hotels that were open and operating for more than two full years, was compiled and reported by Smith Travel, and such information has not been audited or otherwise confirmed by us. The data in this Item 19 regarding reservations and Marriott Rewards was not provided by Smith Travel, but instead was drawn from Marriott's internal databases. Because of Smith Travel's minimum competitive set reporting requirements, some hotels that were actually open and operating for more than two years and are reflected in Marriott's internal databases are not included in the Smith Travel data.

These statements relate to historical performance of franchised North American Renaissance Hotels and are not guarantees of future performance. The figures above were based on hotels with at least two years of operating results. Hotels typically achieve lower results in their first year of operation. We do not claim or expect that you can or will expect to achieve the same average occupancy rate, average daily room rate, average RevPAR, reservations, Marriott Rewards room nights or yield index, as these figures will vary from hotel to hotel and will depend upon many variables and factors, including size, location, seasonality, competition, the length of time your hotel has been open or affiliated with us, the condition of the hotel, the quality of service at the hotel, and the efficiency with which you operate your hotel. Operating results are subject to numerous risks and uncertainties, including the duration and severity of economic conditions, public reaction to terrorist attacks and political unrest, supply and demand changes for hotel rooms, competitive conditions in the hospitality industry, relationships with customers and property owners, and the availability of capital.

We will provide you with written substantiation of the data used in preparing this Item 19 upon your request. The information described above that was provided to us by third parties has not been audited or otherwise verified by us. We are under no specific obligation to disclose specific information for a particular hotel in the system.

BACKGROUND		Passive Ownership:	Discouraged
IFA Member:	Yes	Encourage Conversions:	Yes
Established & First Franchised:	2001; 2008	Area Development Agreements:	No
Franchised Units:	93	Sub-Franchising Contracts:	No
Company-Owned Units:	12	Expand in Territory:	No
Total Units:	105	Space Needs:	N/A
Distribution:	US – 105; CAN – 0; O'seas – 0		
North America:	26 States, 0 Provinces	SUPPORT & TRAINING	
Density:	16 in TX, 12 in FL, 7 in CA	Financial Assistance Provided:	Yes (I)
Projected New Units (12 Months):	25	Site Selection Assistance:	No
Qualifications:	3, 3, 1, 3, 4, 5	Lease Negotiation Assistance:	No
		Co-operative Advertising:	Yes
FINANCIAL/TERMS		Franchisee Association/Member:	No
Cash Investment:	$80 – $128K	Size of Corporate Staff:	24
Total Investment:	$80 – $128K	On-going Support:	C, D, E, F, G, H
Minimum Net Worth:	$50K	Training:	8 Days Atlanta, GA
Fees (Franchise):	$45K		
Fees (Royalty):	4%	SPECIFIC EXPANSION PLANS	
Fees (Advertising):	2%	US:	All United States
Term of Contract (Years):	5/5	Canada:	All Canada
Average Number of Employees:	0 FT, 4 PT	Overseas:	No

The following tables present information regarding the average order, and closed order rates for the System in 2009, 2010 and 2011 and current estimated cost of goods as of the date of this Disclosure Document. The data has been generated using sales and order information submitted by franchisees and our affiliates. We have not audited or verified the sales and order information nor have we asked questions of the submitting franchisees to determine whether they are in fact accurate and complete, although we have no information or other reason to believe that they are unreliable. For purposes of this Item 19, (i) the "2009 Summary Period" means the 12-month period from January 1, 2009 to December 31, 2009, (ii) the "2010 Summary Period" means the 12-month period from January 1, 2010 to December 31, 2010, and (iii) the "2011 Summary Period" means the 12-month period from January 1, 2011 to December 31, 2011.

AVERAGE ORDER FOR THE SYSTEM DURING 2009 SUMMARY PERIOD	
Average Order for the System (not including Excluded Orders)	Total Number of Orders for the System that achieved or surpassed Average Order for the System (not including Excluded Orders)
$1,824.25	619 (39%)

AVERAGE ORDER FOR THE SYSTEM DURING 2010 SUMMARY PERIOD	
Average Order for the System (not including Excluded Orders)	Total Number of Orders for the System that achieved or surpassed Average Order for the System (not including Excluded Orders)
$2,003.37	1,555 (39%)

AVERAGE ORDER DURING 2011 SUMMARY PERIOD			
Group	Number of SHELFGENIE Businesses in the Group	Average Order (not including Excluded Orders)	Total Number of Orders for the System that achieved or surpassedverage Order for the System (not including Excluded Orders)
All SHELFGENIE Businesses operating under the System in 2011 that had orders that were not Excluded Orders	51	$2,232.18	2,218 (39%)
1st Quintile[5]	10	$2,733.46	
2nd Quintile[5]	10	$2,426.01	
3rd Quintile[5]	11	$2,173.02	
4th Quintile[5]	10	$1,983.99	
5th Quintile[5]	10	$1,629.56	

1. "Average Order for the System" was calculated by dividing the total amount of System sales reported by franchisees and affiliate-owned SHELFGENIE Businesses by the total number of orders for the System during the summary period. In calculating the Average Order for the System, we excluded all orders (i) where the order involved a discount of 80% or more off the franchisee's suggested retail price, and (ii) where the order was placed by a SHELFGENIE franchisee in their first 6 months of operations ("Excluded Orders"). An order having a discount of 80% or more off the franchisee's suggested retail price indicates (a) the order was a reorder of products, (b) the order was for personal or display usage, and/or (c) the order was not an arms-length sales transactions. Average Order for the System does not include any sales taxes that were collected or paid in connection with orders.

2. The orders included in each Summary Period are for sales orders placed during the Summary Period.

3. For repeat customers, each order for a project placed by a customer is treated as a separate order.

4. The information is based on data reported by franchisees and affiliate-owned SHELFGENIE Businesses.

5. "Quintile" refers to the relative performance of the SHELFGENIE Business. Therefore, the 1st Quintile refers to the top 20% performing SHELFGENIE Businesses, based on Average Order, the 2nd Quintile refers to the next highest 20% performing SHELFGENIE Businesses, and so on.

PERCENTAGE OF APPOINTMENTS THAT RESULTED IN A CLOSED ORDER FOR THE SYSTEM DURING 2009 SUMMARY PERIOD		
Percentage of Appointments Resulting in a Closed Order for the System (not including Excluded Orders)	Total Number of Appointments for the System (not including Excluded Orders)	Total Number of Closed Orders for the System Resulting from Appointments (not including Excluded Orders)
36%	4,503	1,623

PERCENTAGE OF APPOINTMENTS THAT RESULTED IN A CLOSED ORDER FOR THE SYSTEM DURING 2010 SUMMARY PERIOD		
Percentage of Appointments Resulting in a Closed Order for the System (not including Excluded Orders)	Total Number of Appointments for the System (not including Excluded Orders)	Total Number of Closed Orders for the System Resulting from Appointments (not including Excluded Orders)
44%	9,153	4,038

PERCENTAGE OF APPOINTMENTS THAT RESULTED IN A CLOSED ORDER DURING 2011 SUMMARY PERIOD				
Group	Number of SHELFGENIE Businesses in the Group	Percentage of Appointments Resulting in a Closed Order (not including Excluded Orders)	Total Number of Appointments for the System (not including Excluded Orders)	Total Number of Closed Orders for the System Resulting from Appointments (not including Excluded Orders)
All SHELFGENIE Businesses operating under the System in 2011 that had orders that were not Excluded Orders	51	46%	12,963	5,916
1st Quintile[7]	10	59%		
2nd Quintile[7]	10	49%		
3rd Quintile[7]	10	44%		
4th Quintile[7]	11	42%		
5th Quintile[7]	10	32%		

1. The "Percentage of Appointments Resulting in a Closed Order" was calculated by dividing the total number of Closed Orders for the System during the Summary Period by the total number of Appointments for the System (whether or not the Appointment was booked by the Business Center) and multiplying the result by 100. In calculating the Percentage of Appointments Resulting in a Closed Orders, we did not include Excluded Orders.

2. The Appointments included in each Summary Period are for sales orders placed during or after the Summary Period. The Closed Order information reflects orders information as of March 15, 2012.

3. An "Appointment" is viewed as an initial meeting at a customer's home or business where the work will be performed. A "Closed Order" is an order where a franchisee or an affiliate-owned SHELFGENIE Business reported a sale to a customer. A Closed Order may involve more than one meeting with the same customer to close the sale.

4. In the event of a new order by a customer, the new order is treated as an additional Closed Order with an additional Appointment.

5. The information is based on data reported by franchisees and affiliate-owned SHELFGENIE Businesses.

6. We do not have access to data related to any referral appointments or self-generated appointments ("Referral Leads") that do not result in a Closed Order. We do not require franchisees to track Referral Leads or provide to us information on Referral Leads that do not result in Closed Orders.

7. "Quintile" refers to the relative performance of the SHELFGENIE Business. Therefore, the 1st Quintile refers to the top 20% performing SHELFGENIE Businesses, based on the Percentage of Appointments leading to a Closed Order, the 2nd Quintile refers to the next highest 20% performing SHELFGENIE Businesses, and so on.

WEIGHTED AVERAGE COST OF GOODS SOLD
25.6%[2]

1. Cost of Goods Sold ("COGS") means the cost of goods sold. COGS is a figure which reflects the cost of Core Products you will order from G-O to install for your customers. COGS does not include (i) miscellaneous items like strip mounts, clips, spacers and other supplies that may be necessary to install the Core Products, (ii) insurance, shipping, freight, and delivery charges for the Core Products, and (iii) any sales tax, use tax or other taxes that may be due in connection with your purchases of Core Products. "Franchisee Pricing" means Manufacturing's wholesale price for Core Products as of February 7, 2012, minus a 10% discount for franchisees under the System. "Suggested Retail Pricing" means the prices that we suggest to franchisees for Core Products sold in SHELFGENIE Businesses as of February 7, 2012. Suggested Retail Pricing does not include any taxes that you may be required to charge or pay. The "Weighted Average Cost of Goods Sold" was calculated by taking the sum of the cost, using Franchisee Pricing, of all Core Products ordered by our franchisees in 2011, divided by

the sum of the Suggested Retail Pricing for all Core Products ordered by our franchisees in 2011.

2. COGS does not include any additional manufacturing rebates that G-O may offer.

3. The information in the above chart is based on data from 52 franchised SHELFGENIE Businesses and 9 SHELFGENIE Businesses owned by our affiliates. We do not represent that you can obtain the level of COGS. Your actual operations results will be based on (i) the mix of Core Products you purchase, (ii) Franchising Pricing, and (iii) the actual prices your customers pay you. You must accept the risk of not doing as well as the average shown above.

This Item 19 should not be considered to be the actual or probable results that you will experience. We do not represent that you can expect to obtain the results provided in this Item 19. Actual results vary from franchisee to franchisee, and we cannot estimate the results of any particular franchisee. Sales, revenues, costs and profits also can vary considerably due to a variety of other factors, such as the length of time the SHELFG-ENIE Business has been open; location, demographics of the SHELFGENIE Business; competition from other businesses in the area; economic conditions in the SHELFGENIE Business's area; advertising and promotional activities; your owners' active involvement in the management of the SHELFGENIE Business; the business abilities and efforts of the management of the SHELFGENIE Business; and other factors.

You are responsible for developing your own business plan for your SHELFGENIE Business, including capital budgets, financial statements, projections and other appropriate factors, and you are encouraged to consult with your own accounting, business and legal advisors in doing so. The business plan should make necessary allowances for economic downturns, periods of inflation and unemployment, and other negative economic influences.

This Item 19 consists of historical performance figures for the System. Historical order information may not correspond to future order information due to a variety of factors. AS WITH MOST BUSINESSES, THE INITIAL FINANCIAL PERFORMANCE OF YOUR SHELFGENIE BUSINESS IS LIKELY TO BE LESS FAVORABLE THAN THOSE REPRESENTED IN THIS ITEM 19.

SNAP-ON

2801 80th St., P.O. Box 1410
Kenosha, WI 53141
Tel: (800) 786-6600, (877) 476-2766
Fax: (262) 656-5635
Email: thomas.j.kasbohm@snapon.com
Website: www.snaponfranchise.com
Tom Kasbohm, Director of Franchising

The premier solutions provider to the vehicle service industry. Premium quality products, delivered and sold with premium service. We are proud of our heritage and are boldly addressing the future needs of our customers with improved efficiency, creating products and services from hand tools to data and management systems. Contact us today for discussion.

BACKGROUND

IFA Member:	Yes
Established & First Franchised:	1920; 1991

Franchised Units:	4,534
Company-Owned Units:	246
Total Units:	4,780
Distribution:	US – 3,456; CAN – 351; O'seas – 973
North America:	50 States, 12 Provinces
Density:	364 in CA, 243 in TX, 196 in NY
Projected New Units (12 Months):	N/A
Qualifications:	3, 4, 2, 2, 3, 5
FINANCIAL/TERMS	
Cash Investment:	$30.1 – $79.3K
Total Investment:	$143.7 – $307.7K
Minimum Net Worth:	$30K
Fees (Franchise):	$7.5 – $15K
Fees (Royalty):	$107/month
Fees (Advertising):	0%
Term of Contract (Years):	10/5
Average Number of Employees:	1 FT, 0 PT
Passive Ownership:	Not Allowed
Encourage Conversions:	Yes
Area Development Agreements:	No
Sub-Franchising Contracts:	No
Expand in Territory:	Yes
Space Needs:	N/A

SUPPORT & TRAINING
Financial Assistance Provided: Yes (D)
Site Selection Assistance: N/A
Lease Negotiation Assistance: N/A
Co-operative Advertising: No
Franchisee Association/Member: No
Size of Corporate Staff: 0
On-going Support: A, B, C, D, E, F, G, h, I

Training: 6 Days National Training Facility;
Minimum 3 Weeks On-Site

SPECIFIC EXPANSION PLANS
US: All United States
Canada: All Canada
Overseas: Australia, Benelux, Germany, Japan, New
Zealand, S. Africa, UK

The following Statement of "Paid Sales" ("Statement") illustrates the various levels of sales reported by numerous franchisees in the Snap-on system for sales activity during the 2011 reporting period. "Paid Sales" are presented in $25,000 increments. This information reflects a number of assumptions and limitations noted after the Statement, and which you should read together with the Statement.

THE NOTES THAT FOLLOW THIS STATEMENT ARE AN INTEGRAL PART OF THE STATEMENT.

REPORTED PAID SALES FOR 2011	Number of Franchisees Reporting	%
Less than $50,000	5	0.2%
$50,000 to $74,999	4	0.1%
$75,000 to $99,999	4	0.1%
$100,000 to $124,999	13	0.4%
$125,000 to $149,999	14	0.5%
$150,000 to $174,999	28	0.9%
$175,000 to $199,999	46	1.5%
$200,000 to $224,999	54	1.8%
$225,000 to $249,999	95	3.1%
$250,000 to $274,999	106	3.5%
$275,000 to $299,999	137	4.5%
$300,000 to $324,999	193	6.3%
$325,000 to $349,999	201	6.6%
$350,000 to $374,999	223	7.3%
$375,000 to $399,999	230	7.5%
$400,000 to $424,999	205	6.7%
$425,000 to $449,999	240	7.8%
$450,000 to $474,999	192	6.3%
$475,000 to $499,999	196	6.4%
$500,000 to $524,999	153	5.0%
$525,000 to $549,999	135	4.4%
$550,000 to $574,999	108	3.5%
$575,000 to $599,999	102	3.3%
Over $600,000	374	12.2%
TOTAL	3058	100.0%

THE PAID SALES FIGURES USED IN THIS STATEMENT ARE REPORTED BY SPECIFIC FRANCHISEES AND SHOULD NOT BE CONSIDERED THE ACTUAL OR PROBABLE PAID SALES THAT MAY BE REALIZED BY ANY FRANCHISEE. YOUR PAID SALES MAY BE AFFECTED BY A NUMBER OF COMMERCIAL VARIABLES AND COMPETITIVE MARKET CONDITIONS. SNAP-ON DOES NOT REPRESENT THAT YOU OR ANY FRANCHISEE CAN EXPECT TO ATTAIN ANY PARTICULAR LEVEL OF PAID SALES.

NOTES:
I. Franchisee Information Included in the Statement.

We compiled the Statement from information reported to us by Snap-on franchisees. We did not verify these reports.

Since the franchisees reporting Paid Sales have, for the most part, operated under a Standard Franchise Agreement the Paid Sales information presented may not be as meaningful to a prospective Gateway Franchisee.

The Statement includes only information received from franchisees who operated for all 12 months of the 2011 reporting period and for which we have received Paid Sales information for the full period. Accordingly, franchisees who began or ended operations during calendar year 2011 are not included in the Statement nor are franchisees who failed to submit all Paid Sales information for all of 2011. Some franchisees included in the Statement may have operated part of the year as a Gateway Franchisee and part of the year as a Standard Franchisee, but to be included, they must have operated during the entire calendar year as a Gateway Franchisee or a Standard Franchisee or a combination thereof. We have not attempted to verify the information received from franchisees and have no knowledge whether franchisees prepared the information submitted to us in accordance with generally accepted accounting principles.

If a franchisee operated an additional van under a Franchise Agreement, the Paid Sales of that additional van are not included in this Statement, either as sales under the franchise under which that additional van operates or as a separate franchise. If a franchisee operated an additional franchise, that additional franchise is reported as a separate "franchise" on the Statement.

The Statement does not include information on Paid Sales for Snap-on employees who sell tools and equipment to customers that are similar to a franchisee's customers or Paid Sales of Independents.

II. Definition of "Paid Sales".

Snap-on franchisees do not have to report their total revenue to us. A franchisee's Paid Sales (defined below) should approximate "total revenues," except that a franchisee's sales of tools and equipment purchased from a source other than Snap-on (which is permitted in older contracts) and the value of tools and equipment accepted by a franchisee as a trade-in may not be included in the Paid Sales figure reported to us.

The Statement does not include information about franchisee expenses, or profits and losses; it sets forth Paid Sales only, and a prospective franchisee should discuss the significance of the numbers with an advisor of his choice.

A franchisee's Paid Sales means the sum of: (1) all of the franchisee's cash sales and revolving account collections; (2) all open account and extended credit sales assigned to Snap-on or Snap-on Credit by the franchisee; and (3) all leases assigned to Snap-on or Snap-on Credit by the franchisee. To the extent sales taxes are reported to Snap-on by franchisee, they are included in Paid Sales (each of these terms is defined below). All franchisees included in the Statement were requested to use the same definition of Paid Sales in the reports submitted to Snap-on.

Cash Sales – Those sales for which a franchisee receives a cash payment at the time of the sale and any cash down payment received on an extended credit sale or a lease.

Revolving Account Collections – As described in Item 7, Revolving Account sales are credit sales between a franchisee and a franchisee's customer where a franchisee extends personal credit, usually at no interest, to finance the customer's purchase of tools and equipment. Revolving account collections are the collections made by a franchisee on revolving account financing extended by the franchisee.

Open Account Sales – Open account sales are short term credit sales made by a franchisee to businesses which the franchisee assigns to Snap-on and for which Snap-on gives the franchisee immediate credit as if the franchisee's customer had paid in cash (See Item 10). Included in Paid Sales is the dollar amount of the credit (which excludes any down payment and trade-in allowance) given to a franchisee when Snap-on accepted assignment of an open account.

Extended Credit Sales – For certain customer purchases a franchisee may assign to Snap-on Credit with Snap-on Credit's consent the purchase money security agreements (also referred to as the "Extended Credit Contracts") for customer purchases (See Item 10). Snap-on Credit credits a franchisee the net sales price (which excludes any down payment and trade-in allowance) for the tools or equipment being sold. This credit is included in Paid Sales.

Leases – For certain tools and equipment, Snap-on Credit has offered in the past and may in the future offer certain customers the opportunity to lease the Products. Such a lease with a customer of a franchisee may be assigned to Snap-on Credit. Once Snap-on Credit accepts the assignment, the franchisee receives a credit calculated in the same manner as for an Extended Credit contract. This credit is included in Paid Sales.

Sales Tax – Most states require that a franchisee collect and pay sales tax on purchases made by franchisee's customers. To the extent sales taxes are reported to Snap-on by franchisee they are included in Paid Sales.

III. Other Notes and Assumptions.

Percentage totals may not equal 100% due to rounding.

Reported Paid Sales are based on franchisee reports submitted weekly and do not correspond exactly with the calendar year. Some weekly reports cover Paid Sales beginning a few days before the start of the calendar year; others end a few days after. In all cases Paid Sales figures in this Appendix reflect no more than one year's Paid Sales.

The Statement reflects the various levels of Paid Sales in all parts of the United States and the prospective franchisee should not assume that the level of sales shown will be reflected in his particular area or in his particular franchise.

Substantiation of the data used in preparing this Statement will be made available to a prospective franchisee upon reasonable request; however, no information that relates to any specific franchise will be made available.

Except for the financial performance representations above, we do not furnish or authorize our employees to furnish any oral or written information concerning the potential sales, costs, income or profits of a Snap-on franchise. You will be asked to sign the Claims Representation Form attached as Appendix N as confirmation that you have not received any financial performance representations other than as provided in this Item 19. Please carefully consider this, and accurately complete this form.

Results vary, and we cannot estimate the results of any particular franchisee.

SPHERION

2015 South Park Place
Atlanta, GA 30339
Tel: (800) 903-0082, (404) 964-5508
Fax: (770) 303-6846
Email: sandymazur@spherion.com
Website: www.spherion.com
Sandy Mazur, Senior Vice President

SPHERION franchise opportunities provide individuals a chance to join an exciting and rewarding industry: temporary staffing. We placed millions of workers in flexible and full-time jobs during our nearly 60 years in business. Continuous innovation and decades of growth have helped SPHERION become an industry leader. Entrepreneur Magazine ranked SPHERION Best Staffing Service for five straight years. Our franchisees contribute their talent, commitment, and passion to building our brand.

BACKGROUND

IFA Member:	Yes
Established & First Franchised:	1946; 1956
Franchised Units:	153
Company-Owned Units:	0
Total Units:	153
Distribution:	US – 153; CAN – 0; O'seas – 0
North America:	46 States, 0 Provinces
Density:	29 in CA, 29 in FL, 27 in OH
Projected New Units (12 Months):	10
Qualifications:	5, 4, 1, 3, 4, 4

FINANCIAL/TERMS

Cash Investment:	$100 – $170K
Total Investment:	$98 – $164K
Minimum Net Worth:	$100K
Fees (Franchise):	$25K
Fees (Royalty):	3 – 6%/25%
Fees (Advertising):	0.25%
Term of Contract (Years):	10/5
Average Number of Employees:	3 FT, 0 PT
Passive Ownership:	Not Allowed
Encourage Conversions:	Yes
Area Development Agreements:	No

Sub-Franchising Contracts:	No	Size of Corporate Staff:	525
Expand in Territory:	Yes	On-going Support:	A, B, C, D, E, G, H, I
Space Needs:	1,500 SF	Training:	Over 112 Hours In-Office Instruction; Additional Self-Paced Instruction

SUPPORT & TRAINING

Financial Assistance Provided:	No	**SPECIFIC EXPANSION PLANS**	
Site Selection Assistance:	Yes	US:	Targeted Cities in US
Lease Negotiation Assistance:	Yes	Canada:	No
Co-operative Advertising:	Yes	Overseas:	No
Franchisee Association/Member:	No		

Spherion believes it will be helpful for a prospective franchisee to know the average Gross Profit percentage, the average per Franchise Agreement annual Sales, and the average per franchise agreement annual Gross Profit of its franchises for FY 2011. "Gross Profit" and "Sales" have the meanings given them in the Franchise Agreement.

The average Gross Profit percentage of our franchises for FY 2011 was 17.7%. The average annual Sales per Franchise Agreement of our franchises for FY 2011 were $4,454,351, and the average annual Gross Profit per Franchise Agreement of our franchises for FY the same period was $744,307.

The information for the average Gross Profit percentage, annual Gross Profit, and annual Sales is only for our franchises in operation for all of FY 2011. The information for Sales and Gross Profit is for franchises on a per Franchise Agreement basis. That is, if a franchisee has more than one Franchise Agreement with us, then the numbers achieved under each Franchise Agreement are considered separately. If a franchisee has more than one office under the same Franchise Agreement, these offices are aggregated to determine the average number for agreements. For this performance representation, however, the results of two tenured franchisees with multiple offices under the same agreement are divided into separate markets and included in the average Sales and Gross Profit numbers as under multiple agreements. We believe breaking out the information in this manner for these tenured franchises provides a more accurate picture for future agreements.

In FY 2011, the franchises under twenty-nine of the sixty-seven Franchise Agreements attained or surpassed the average Gross Profit percentage stated above. Those under twenty-five of the Agreements attained or surpassed the average annual Sales stated above, and the franchises under twenty-five of the Agreements attained or surpassed the average annual Gross Profit stated above.

This information is that of mature franchises. We had only four franchisees start up a new office under a new Franchise Agreement in Fiscal Years 2009-2011. Other new franchisees in that period bought existing offices, either from us or from a franchisee, as opposed to starting a new office. The information is for all of our franchised operations (other than Today's franchised offices), including Spherion branded franchised offices operating under the Norrell agreement. The information does not include the area based program franchises (refer to Item 1), which operate under a fundamentally different agreement.

Your results will likely differ from the results presented above, depending on your efforts and those of your staff, your particular market size and makeup, and the competition. Other factors that could impact your numbers include, but are not limited to local, regional, national, and international general economic conditions, your business mix (temporary staffing vs. permanent placement, clerical vs. light industrial, and the amount of professional staffing you have, if you receive the right to offer professional staffing services), etc.

Gross Profit calculations are fundamental to our business. We have prepared the following to assist you in understanding a Gross Profit calculation.

The following would be the detailed line items normally involved:

Revenue		
Payroll		
Burden		
WC –Base Rates		
(mod-.1.00)		
WC-Risk Factor		
SUI		
FICA		
FUI		
Other Insurance		

Total Burden		
Gross Profit		
GP % of Revenue		

To determine what you would charge a client to achieve a certain Gross Profit (GP) percentage, you would do the following calculation:

Pay rate (PR) = x
Burden cost = y
Total cost = TC
(TC) divided by (1- desired GP%) = Bill Rate (BR)

Example:
Pay rate = $10.00
Burden cost = $ 1.40(14%)
Total cost = $11.40
($11.40) divided by (1-20.4%) = Bill Rate
$11.40 divided by .796 = $14.32

The Gross Profit amount here would be:

$14.32 BR
-$11.40 TC
$ 2.92 GP

Note that we have used example numbers based on our average Gross Profit as stated above. Your burden numbers will vary depending on what state you are in. The Workers' Compensation Risk Factor will vary depending on the type of job you are filling, and the payrate will vary depending on the job you are filling and the comparable payrates in your market. The purpose of this example is only to show you how the basic Gross Profit calculation is done in our industry.

The financial performance representations above do not reflect the costs of sales, operating expenses, or other costs or expenses that must be deducted from the gross revenues or gross sales figures to obtain your net income or profit. As stated below, you should conduct an independent investigation of the costs and expenses you will incur in operating your franchised business. Franchisees or former franchisees listed in the disclosure document may be one source of information. To help you analyze what your expenses might be on a monthly basis, we have listed below what we believe to be your normal monthly expense items.

- Salaries and Wages
- Commission/bonus accrual
- Employee Benefits (including payroll taxes and health, life and disability insurance)
- Franchise Data Processing Allocation (MISTEF fee-para-

graph 8 of the Franchise Agreement)
- Insurance (for example, see the required insurances in paragraph 7(q) of the Franchise Agreement)
- National Advertising
- Local Advertising
- Classified and yellow page advertising Meetings/seminars/courses/conventions Office supplies
- Equipment/software repair/maintenance
- Bank/credit card fees
- Rent (premises lease)
- Rent (equipment)
- Repairs and maintenance
- Depreciation and amortization expense
- Utilities
- Interest Expense (includes interest on AR over 60 days charged by Spherion)
- Professional fees
- Telecommunications
- Automobile & parking
- Other Travel
- Customer relations/development
- Bad debt expense
- Taxes & franchises
- Miscellaneous

This expense listing may not be a complete listing for you, and we do not make any representations to you as to what the actual expenses in each category will be. The answers to those questions will depend on your market and how you set up your business. You should consult with your financial advisor, as well as discuss the list and the expenses involved with our other franchisees, and former franchisees, which are listed in an exhibit to this disclosure document.

Substantiation of the data used in the preparation of this Item 19 will be made available to you upon reasonable request.

IT'S GOOD TO BE A GUY

SPORT CLIPS

P.O. Box 3000-266, 110 Briarwood
Georgetown, TX 78628
Tel: (800) 872-4247 x240, (512) 869-1201
Fax: (512) 864-2522
Email: franchise@sportclips.com
Website: www.sportclips.com
Beth Boecker, Director of Franchising

Our fun, sports-themed, men's and boys's haircutting concept is so unique, it has made us the fastest-growing haircutting franchise in the country. This is a great recession-resistant business that is all cash, no receivables, and no industry experience is necessary. Better yet, you keep your current job, while building your SPORT CLIPS business for the future.

BACKGROUND

IFA Member:	Yes
Established & First Franchised:	1993; 1995
Franchised Units:	1,029
Company-Owned Units:	28
Total Units:	1,057
Distribution:	US – 1,056; CAN – 1; O'seas – 0
North America:	44 States, 1 Province
Density:	187 in TX, 96 in CA, 73 in IL
Projected New Units (12 Months):	225

Qualifications:	4, 5, 1, 1, 3, 5

FINANCIAL/TERMS

Cash Investment:	$100K
Total Investment:	$158.3 – $306.5K
Minimum Net Worth:	$300K
Fees (Franchise):	$10 – $49.5K
Fees (Royalty):	6%
Fees (Advertising):	$300/week
Term of Contract (Years):	5/5
Average Number of Employees:	6 – 8 FT, 0 PT
Passive Ownership:	Allowed
Encourage Conversions:	No
Area Development Agreements:	Yes
Sub-Franchising Contracts:	No
Expand in Territory:	Yes
Space Needs:	1,200 SF

SUPPORT & TRAINING

Financial Assistance Provided:	Yes (D)
Site Selection Assistance:	Yes
Lease Negotiation Assistance:	Yes
Co-operative Advertising:	Yes
Franchisee Association/Member:	No
Size of Corporate Staff:	93
On-going Support:	C, D, E, F, G, H, I
Training:	1 Week Locally for Manager; 1 Week Locally; 5 Days Georgetown, TX for Franchisee

SPECIFIC EXPANSION PLANS

US:	All United States
Canada:	Yes
Overseas:	No

At the end of calendar year 2011, there were 819 franchised Sport Clips stores. The two Statements of Gross Sales below do not include four stores in Rochester, New York, which are not typical Sport Clips stores and operate under a special limited services license agreement that is not offered to new franchisees. Although we do not have complete sales data for the stores in Rochester, New York, we know that their gross sales are, on average, less than other stores in the System.

Except for the stores in Rochester, New York, all stores included in the Statements of Gross Sales did not receive any services that were not generally available to other Sport Clips stores, and each store offered similar products and services as would generally be offered by a typical Sport Clips store.

The gross sales figures included in the first Statement of Gross Sales below are based upon all 576 Sport Clips franchise stores and Company-owned stores that were in continual operation for the entire calendar years of 2009, 2010, and 2011. The gross sales figures are taken directly from gross sales reports made by the stores to the Company.

STATEMENT OF GROSS SALES YEAR 2011 GROSS SALES AS REPORTED TO THE COMPANY (576 STORES IN CONTINUAL OPERATION DURING 2009, 2010 AND 2011)		
Gross Sales	Number of Stores	Percentage of Stores/Cumulative % of stores at each level or higher
Over $500,000	42	7%/7%
$450,001 - $500,000	27	5%/12%
$400,001 - $450,000	61	11%/23%
$350,001 - $400,000	88	15%/38%
$300,001 - $350,000	106	18%/56%
$250,001 - $300,000	142	25%/81%
$200,001 - $250,000	87	15%/96%
Less than $200,000	23	4%/100%
Total	576	100%

These 576 stores had average sales of $335,905 for the entire year 2011. 246 stores had sales above this average, and 330 stores had sales lower than the average.

The gross sales figures included in the second Statement of Gross Sales below are based upon all 641 Sport Clips franchise stores and Company-owned stores that were in continual operation for the entire calendar years of 2010 and 2011. The gross sales figures are taken directly from gross sales reports made by the stores to the Company.

STATEMENT OF GROSS SALES YEAR 2011 GROSS SALES AS REPORTED TO THE COMPANY (641 STORES IN CONTINUAL OPERATION DURING 2010 AND 2011)		
Gross Sales	Number of Stores	Percentage of Stores/ Cumulative % of stores at each level or higher
Over $500,000	44	7%/7%
$450,001 - $500,000	30	5%/12%
$400,001 - $450,000	66	10%/22%
$350,001 - $400,000	93	14%/36%
$300,001 - $350,000	121	19%/55%
$250,001 - $300,000	157	25%/80%
$200,001 - $250,000	99	15%/95%
Less than $200,000	31	5%/100%
Total	641	100%

These 641 stores had average sales of $332,283 for the entire year 2011. 272 stores had sales above this average, and 369 stores had sales lower than the average.

The financial performance representations above do not reflect the costs of sales, operating expenses, or other costs or expenses that must be deducted from gross revenue or gross sales figures to obtain your net income or profit. You should conduct an independent investigation of the costs and expenses you will incur in operating your Sport Clips franchise. Franchisees or former franchisees, listed in the Disclosure Document, may be one source of this information.

In addition to actual sales, an important metric for any retail business is the growth in same store sales year-over-year. For the fourth quarter of 2011, the 707 stores that were open one year or more at the beginning of the quarter averaged $6,352 per week in sales, which annualized would be $330,300. 409 stores had average sales lower than this amount, and 298 had higher sales. This was an increase for these same stores over the fourth quarter of 2010 of 12.6%, with 6.2% of this increase coming from increases in Client counts and the remainder from increases in average tickets. Increases in average tickets came from a combination of some individual store price increases and an increase in the number of Clients who purchased a more expensive service (such as our signature MVP service) or who bought more hair care products to take home.

Expense Reports for Company-Owned Stores During 2011

The Expense Report below shows the average expenses at each store's sales level and those expenses as a percentage of total revenue in each column. It is based on 14 stores owned and operated by the Company in Austin, Texas for the entire calendar year 2011. The managers of the Company-owned stores included in the Expense Report did not receive any services

that were not generally available to other Sport Clips stores. Each store offered similar products and services as would generally be offered by a typical Sport Clips store, except for limited tests of procedures, products and/or services that may or may not be eventually incorporated into the system, depending on the success of the tests.

We owned and operated 14 stores in Austin for the entire year of 2011. We also owned one store in Jacksonville, Florida between January and March 2011. We sold that Store to a franchisee in March 2011. We have not included results for the Jacksonville, Florida store in the data below because we did not own the store for the entire year of 2011.

	Sales Less Than $300,000	Sales $300,001 to $350,000	Sales $350,001 to $400,000	Sales Greater Than $400,001	Average of all stores
Number of Stores	2	2	6	4	14
Gross Sales	$258,542 100%	$303,915 100%	$379,698 100%	$531,395 100%	$394,906 100%
Variable Costs (Note 1)	$21,178 8%	$22,596 8%	$27,398 7%	$39,232 7%	$29,205 7%
Payroll (Note 2)	$106,212 41%	$124,132 41%	$150,757 40%	$220,875 42%	$160,623 41%
Occupancy (Note 3)	$51,968 20%	$55,183 18%	$57,253 15%	$57,234 11%	$56,197 14%
Advertising (Note 4)	$21,029 8%	$18,399 6%	$22,356 6%	$25,841 5%	$22,597 6%
Miscellaneous (Note 5)	$2,061 1%	$1,374 0%	$1,424 1%	$1,612 0%	$1,561 0%
Operating Profit (Note 6)	$56,095 22%	$82,232 27%	$120,509 32%	$186,601 35%	$124,722 32%

Note 1. Variable Costs include operating supplies, cost of goods sold, bank service charges, credit card discounts, and advertising to recruit Stylists.

Note 2. Payroll includes direct payroll, including payroll for an on-site full-time manager, payroll taxes and fringe benefits except for 401K and medical insurance costs.

Note 3. Occupancy includes rent, pass-through expenses from the landlord, utilities, phone charges, repairs and maintenance.

Note 4. Advertising includes the weekly payments to the Ad Fund plus other advertising and marketing expenses for the store.

Note 5. Miscellaneous expense includes magazine subscriptions, store insurance and overages and/or shortages from the cash drawer.

Note 6. Operating Profit does not include an amount paid for royalties or weekly training fees. The numbers in the Expense Report are unaudited, but we believe that these numbers are substantially correct.

We own and operate 8 stores in the Las Vegas market, including one store that we opened in April 2011 and one store that we opened in June 2011. We are not offering franchises in this market. The results of these stores are in the data below. Results for the stores opened in April 2011 and June 2011 are not included in the data below as they were not open during all of fiscal year 2011.

The Expense Report below shows the average sales for the six Las Vegas stores and expenses that were open for the full year as a percentage of total revenue. The managers of the Company-owned stores included in the Expense Report did not receive any services that were not generally available to other

Sport Clips stores. Each store offered similar products and services as would generally be offered by a typical Sport Clips store, except for limited tests of procedures, products and/or services that may or may not be eventually incorporated into the system, depending on the success of the tests. While the results for these six stores are less favorable than for our Austin area stores, the Las Vegas economy was one of the worst, if not the worst, in the country in 2011. We are very optimistic about the Las Vegas market long-term, and see the current downturn in the economy as an opportunity for Sport Clips to strengthen our market position and increase our market share. During 2011, we relocated 2 existing stores to stronger shopping centers. We have already signed leases for 2 additional stores in that market to open in 2012.

	Sales Less Than $300,000
Number of Stores	6
Gross Sales	$264,683 100%
Variable Costs (Note 1)	$20,393 6%
Payroll (Note 2)	$116,493 44%
Occupancy (Note 3)	$53,216 21%
Advertising (Note 4)	$19,644 7%
Miscellaneous (Note 5)	$2,340 1%
Operating Profit (Note 6)	$52,597 20%

Note 1. Variable Costs include operating supplies, cost of goods sold, bank service charges, credit card discounts, and advertising to recruit Stylists.

Note 2. Payroll includes direct payroll, including payroll for an on-site full-time manager, payroll taxes and fringe benefits except for 401K and medical insurance costs.

Note 3. Occupancy includes rent, pass-through expenses from the landlord, utilities, phone charges, repairs and maintenance.

Note 4. Advertising includes the weekly payments to the Ad Fund plus other advertising and marketing expenses for the store.

Note 5. Miscellaneous expense includes magazine subscriptions, store insurance and overages and/or shortages from the cash drawer.

Note 6. Operating Profit does not include an amount paid for royalties or weekly training fees. The numbers in the Expense Report are unaudited, but we believe that these numbers are substantially correct.

A NEW FRANCHISEE'S INDIVIDUAL RESULTS ARE LIKELY TO DIFFER FROM THE RESULTS STATED IN THE STATEMENTS OF GROSS SALES AND THE EXPENSE REPORT.

Substantiation of the information contained in this Item is made available to prospective franchisees at the Company's office at 110 Briarwood, Georgetown, Texas 78628.

Other than the preceding financial performance representation, Sport Clips, Inc. does not make any financial performance representations. We also do not authorize our employees or representatives to make any such representations either orally or in writing. If you are purchasing an existing outlet, however, we may provide you with the actual records of that outlet. If you receive any other financial performance information or projections of your future income, you should report it to the franchisor's management by contacting Gordon B. Logan, 110 Briarwood, Georgetown, Texas, 78628, telephone (512) 869-1201, the Federal Trade Commission, and the appropriate state regulatory agencies.

SPRING-GREEN
America's _Neighborhood_ Lawn Care Team.

SPRING-GREEN LAWN CARE

11909 Spaulding School Dr.
Plainfield, IL 60585
Tel: (800) 777-8608, (815) 436-8777
Fax: (815) 436-9056
Email: nbabyar@spring-green.com
Website: www.springgreenfranchise.com
Nancy Babyar, Franchise Development Qualifier

SPRING-GREEN delivers lawn and tree care services nationwide. Our service is centered on the beautification of middle class and affluent neighborhoods and communities. Our customers include both residential and commercial establishments. SPRING-GREEN services include lawn, tree, and shrub fertilization, as well as disease and perimeter pest control. SPRING-GREEN has been beautifying the environment for more than 35 years as your national lawn care team.

BACKGROUND
IFA Member:	Yes
Established & First Franchised:	1977; 1977
Franchised Units:	94
Company-Owned Units:	26
Total Units:	120
Distribution:	US – 120; CAN – 0; O'seas – 0
North America:	26 States, 0 Provinces
Density:	31 in IL, 15 in WI, 10 in NC
Projected New Units (12 Months):	7

Qualifications:	4, 3, 1, 3, 2, 4

FINANCIAL/TERMS
Cash Investment:	$40K
Total Investment:	$84.2 – $94.2K
Minimum Net Worth:	$160K
Fees (Franchise):	$30K
Fees (Royalty):	10 – 8%
Fees (Advertising):	2%
Term of Contract (Years):	10/10
Average Number of Employees:	N/A FT, N/A PT
Passive Ownership:	Not Allowed
Encourage Conversions:	Yes
Area Development Agreements:	Yes
Sub-Franchising Contracts:	No
Expand in Territory:	No
Space Needs:	N/A

SUPPORT & TRAINING
Financial Assistance Provided:	Yes (I)
Site Selection Assistance:	N/A
Lease Negotiation Assistance:	N/A
Co-operative Advertising:	No
Franchisee Association/Member:	Yes/Member
Size of Corporate Staff:	22
On-going Support:	C, D, E, F, G, h, i
Training:	Initial: 1 Week Training Corp. HQ; 2 Days Field Training

SPECIFIC EXPANSION PLANS
US:	All United States Except AK, AZ, CA, CT, HI, MA, ME, MO, MS, ND, NM, NV, NY, RI
Canada:	No
Overseas:	No

We use historical financial information submitted by our franchisees to compile the information contained in these Tables. The financial information submitted by our franchisees is also used for calculating the Royalty described in Item 6. We did not independently verify the accuracy of the information. Franchised Businesses did not typically submit copies of all of the invoices for each customer or list each customer in their period reports to us. The information contained in these Tables is based upon the financial information and other data entered by each Franchised Business into the software system described in Item 11.

	Number of Franchised Businesses	Gross Sales Range	Average Gross Sales	Number and Percentage that Attained or Surpassed the Average	Average Revenue Per Customer	Number and Percentage that Attained or Surpassed the Average
THREE YEARS OF PERFORMANCE Table A Statement of Average Gross Sales and Average Revenue Per Customer for the First 3 Years of Operation for Franchised Businesses Operating in a Single Territory						
First Full Calendar Year	14	$30,210 to $118,862	$61,325	6 of 14 (43%) had higher gross sales than the average of the group	$343	7 of 14 (50%) had higher average revenue per customer than the average of the group
Second Full Calendar Year	13	$46,876 to $205,036	$115,857	6 of 13 (46%) had higher gross sales than the average of the group	$341	6 of 13 (46%) had higher average revenue per customer than the average of the group
Third Full Calendar Year	10	$54,732 to $296,554	$156,874	5 of 10 (50%) had higher gross sales than the average of the group	$356	3 of 10 (30%) had higher average revenue per customer than the average of the group

Notes to Table A:

(1) Table A includes information regarding the first calendar year of full time operation for 14 Franchised Businesses for which their first full calendar year of operation occurred during or after 2008. 4 additional Franchised Businesses had their first year of full time operations during or after 2008 but were not included because they were no longer in operation as of December 31, 2011. Each of these 14 Franchised Businesses operated in only one Territory during their first year of operation. Due to the Flex Start® Program, 13 of the 14 Franchised Businesses included in Table A began operating part-time before their first full calendar year of full-time operation.

(2) Table A also includes information regarding the second calendar year of full time operation for 13 of the 14 Franchised Businesses that had their first year of full time operations during or after 2008. 1 Franchised Businesses who had its first year of full time operations after 2008 was not included because it had not completed its second full year of full time operations as of December 31, 2011. Each of the 13 Franchised Businesses operated in only 1 Territory during their second year of operation.

(3) Table A also includes information regarding the third calendar year of full time operation for 10 of the 14 Franchised Businesses that had their first year of full time operations during or after 2008. 4 Franchised Businesses who had their first year of full time operations after 2008 were not included because they had not completed their third full year of full time operations as of December 31, 2011. Each of the 10 Franchised Businesses operated in only 1 Territory during their third year of operation.

(4) Gross Sales of the Franchised Business means the amount billed by the Franchised Business on the sales of the services and products authorized to be sold by the Franchised Business under the Franchise Agreement, whether or not sold at or from or under the auspices of the Franchised Business, including the fair market value of any services or products received by the Franchised Business in barter or exchange for services or products, but deducting: (1) customer discounts and credits; and (2) the amount of any sales, use, service, excise, or gross receipts taxes leveled directly on such sales, collected from the purchaser billed on such sales, and paid to the appropriate taxing authorities.

(5) To compute the average revenue per customer for the first, second and third full year of operations, we totaled all invoices for all services for each Franchised Business for the respective calendar year in which their first, second and third year of full-time operations occurred and divided by the number of customers invoiced during those same calendar years for a spring lawn care service application, not by the total number of customers served in the entire year.

INDEPENDENT FRANCHISE OWNERS – SINGLE TERRITORY Table B Statement of the 2011 Annual Gross Sales Results for Independent Franchised Businesses Operating in a Single Territory Consisting of Less Than 120,000 Single Family Dwelling Units and in Operation for 2 Full Calendar Years or More as of December 31, 2011		
	Average	Number and Percentage that Attained or Surpassed the Average:
Average Gross Sales Per Franchised Business	$266,874	17 of 49 Franchised Businesses (35%)
Average Revenue Per Customer	$371	23 of 49 Franchises Businesses (47%)

Notes to Table B:

(1) We compiled information contained in Table B from information for 49 Franchised Businesses that operate in only 1 Territory consisting of less than 120,000 single family dwelling units for the calendar year ending December 31, 2011 and that were in business for 2 full calendar years or more as of December 31, 2011 and operated for the full calendar year in 2011. Due to various demographic factors such as population changes, differences in climate, and the need for the services in the Territory, the Gross Sales among Territories will vary.

(2) The Gross Sales per Franchised Business for the 49 Franchised Businesses ranged from $1,107,156 to $61,949.

(3) The Revenue per Customer per Franchised Business for the 49 Franchised Businesses ranged from $831 to $209.

(4) Gross Sales of the Franchised Business means the amount billed by the Franchised Business on the sales of the services and products authorized to be sold by the Franchised Business under the Franchise Agreement, whether or not sold at or from or under the auspices of the Franchised Business, including the fair market value of any services or products received by the Franchised Business in barter or exchange for services or products, but deducting: (1) customer discounts and credits; and (2) the amount of any sales, use, service, excise, or gross receipts taxes leveled directly on such sales, collected from the purchaser billed on such sales, and paid to the appropriate taxing authorities.

(5) To compute Average Gross Sales per Franchised Business, we totaled the Gross Sales and divided by the number of Franchised Businesses.

(6) To compute the average revenue per Customer, we totaled all invoices for all services for each Franchised Business in Table B for the 2011 calendar year and divided by the number of Customers invoiced during that same calendar year for a spring lawn care service application, not by the total number of Customers served in the entire year.

INDEPENDENT FRANCHISE OWNERS – LARGE SINGLE TERRITORY & MULTIPLE TERRITORIES Table C Statement of the 2011 Annual Gross Sales Results for Independent Franchised Businesses Operating in Multiple Territories or Operating in a Large Single Territory Consisting of More Than 120,000 Single Family Dwelling Units and in Operation for 2 Full Calendar Years or More as of December 31, 2011 with Gross Sales Over $400,000 for the Calendar Year Ending December 31, 2011		
	Average	Number and Percentage that Attained or Surpassed the Average:
Average Gross Sales Per Franchised Business	$794,216	5 of 12 Franchised Businesses (42%)
Average Gross Sales Per Territory	$397,108	8 of 24 Franchised Territories (33%)
Average Gross Sales Per Full-Time Production Vehicle	$130,556	37 of 73 Full-Time Production Vehicles (51%)

Notes to Table C:

(1) We compiled information contained in Table C from information for 12 Franchised Businesses that operate a Franchised Business in more than 1 Territory or operate a Franchised Business in only 1 Territory consisting of more than 120,000 single family dwelling units and that were in business for 2 full calendar years or more as of December 31, 2011 with annual gross sales of over $400,000 for the calendar year ending December 31, 2011. These 12 Franchised Businesses operate in a total of 24 Territories with a total of 73 full-time production vehicles. Each Franchised Business reports annual Gross Sales on an aggregate basis for all Territories. Due to various demographic factors such as population changes, differences in climate, and the need for the services in the Territory, the Gross Sales among Territories will vary. Further, the number of Territories within a Franchised Business does not necessarily correlate with the Gross Sales of that Franchised Business.

(2) The Gross Sales per Franchised Business for the 12 Franchised Businesses ranged from $2,045,957 to $425,373. The Gross Sales per Territory ranged from $1,022,979 to $212,687, and the Gross Sales per full-time production vehicle ranged from $188,696 to $90,683.

(3) To compute Average Gross Sales per Franchised Business, we totaled the Gross Sales for all 12 Franchised Businesses and divided it by the 12 Franchised Businesses. To calculate the Average Gross Sales by Territory, we totaled the Gross Sales for all 12 Franchised Businesses and divided it by the 24 Territories operated by such businesses. To compute the Average Gross Sales per full-time production vehicle, we totaled the Gross Sales for all 12 Franchised Businesses and divided it by the 73 full-time production vehicles used by such businesses.

(4) There were an additional 9 Franchised Businesses consisting of 17 Territories that operated in more than 1 Territory or operated in only 1 Territory consisting of more than 120,000 single family dwelling units and that were in business for 2 full calendar years as of December 31, 2011 that had 2011 annual Gross Sales of under $400,000 as of December 31, 2011 that were not included in this Table C. For these 9 Franchised Businesses, the Gross Sales per Franchised Business ranged from $381,886 to $209,563 and the Gross Sales per Territory ranged from $190,943 to $104,781. The 9 Franchised Businesses operated a total of 23 full-time production vehicles and the Gross Sales per full-time production vehicle ranged from $209,563 to $95,391. The 9 Franchised Businesses had an Average Gross Sales per Franchised Business of $293,879, an Average Gross per Territory of $155,583 and an Average Gross Sales per full-time production vehicle of $114,996. To compute Average Gross Sales per Franchised Business, we

totaled the Gross Sales of all 9 Franchised Businesses and divided it by the 9 Franchised Businesses. To calculate the Average Gross Sales by Territory we totaled the Gross Sales for all 9 Franchised Businesses and divided it by the 17 Territories operated by such businesses. To compute the Average Gross Sales per full-time production vehicle we totaled the Gross Sales for all 9 Franchised Businesses and divided it by the 23 full-time production vehicles used by such businesses.

(5) In total, 21 Franchised Businesses operate a Franchised Business in more than 1 Territory or operate a Franchised Business in only 1 Territory consisting of more than 120,000 single family dwelling units and that were in business for 2 full calendar years or more as of December 31, 2011. These 21 Franchised Businesses operate in a total of 41 Territories with a total of 96 full-time production vehicles. For these 21 Franchised Businesses, the Average Gross Sales per Franchised Business is $579,786, the Average Gross Sales per Territory is $296,964 and the Average Gross Sales per full-time production vehicle is $126,828. 6 of these 21 Franchised Businesses (29%) attained or surpassed the Average Gross Sales per Franchised Business, 10 of the 41 Territories (24%) attained or surpassed the Average Gross Sales per Territory; and 49 of 96 of the full-time production vehicles (51%) attained or surpassed the Average Gross Sales per full-time production vehicle. To compute Average Gross Sales per Franchised Business, we totaled the Gross Sales for all 21 Franchised Businesses and divided it by the 21 Franchised Businesses. To calculate the Average Gross Sales by Territory, we totaled the Gross Sales for all 21 Franchised Businesses and divided it by the 41 Territories operated by such businesses. To compute the Average Gross Sales by full-time production vehicle, we totaled the Gross Sales for all 21 Franchised Businesses and divided it by the 96 full-time production vehicles used by such businesses.

(6) Because each Franchised Business reports its annual Gross Sales on an aggregate basis for all Territories covered by the Franchised Business, each Franchised Business' Gross Sales per Territory was calculated by dividing the Gross Sales of the Franchised Business by the number of Territories covered by the Franchised Business. Similarly, because each Franchised Business reports its annual Gross Sales on an aggregate basis for all full-time production vehicles used by the Franchised Business, each Franchised Business' Gross Sales per full-time production vehicle was calculated by dividing the Gross Sales of the Franchised Business by the number of full-time production vehicles used by the Franchised Business. Consequently, the high and low ranges for the Gross Sales per Territory and Gross Sales per full-time production vehicle provided for in the footnotes to this Table C come from these averages.

(7) Gross Sales of the Franchised Business means the amount billed by the Franchised Business on the sales of the services and products authorized to be sold by the Franchised Busi-

ness under the Franchise Agreement, whether or not sold at or from or under the auspices of the Franchised Business, including the fair market value of any services or products received by the Franchised Business in barter or exchange for services or products, but deducting: (1) customer discounts and credits; and (2) the amount of any sales, use, service, excise, or gross receipts taxes leveled directly on such sales, collected from the purchaser billed on such sales, and paid to the appropriate taxing authorities.

(8) Our affiliate operated 5 Franchised Businesses consisting of 26 Territories that were not included in this table.

INDEPENDENT FRANCHISE OWNERS AND AFFILIATE OWNED —COST AND GROSS PROFIT MARGIN Table D Statement of 2011 Gross Profit Margin Results as a Percentage of Gross Sales for 57 Franchised Businesses in Operation 1 Full Year or More As of December 31, 2011		
Line Item	Average %	Number and Percentage of Franchised Businesses that Attained or Surpassed the Average
Material Costs (See Note3)	13.72%	30 of 57 (53%) had lower than average Material Costs
Direct Labor Costs (See Note 4)	15.24%	31 of 57 (54%) had lower than average Direct Labor Costs
Cost of Sales (See Note 5)	28.96%	39 of 57 (68%) had lower than average Cost of Sales
Gross Profit Margin (See Note 6)	71.04%	39 of 57 (68%) had higher than average Gross Profit Margin

Notes to Table D:

(1) As of December 31, 2011, 120 Territories were in operation, 119 of which had been in operation for at least the full calendar year. These 119 Territories were owned by 76 Franchised Businesses (including 5 Franchised Businesses operated by our affiliate) which for reporting purposes, consolidated their financial information for all Territories operated by such Franchised Business. As of December 31, 2011, our affiliate operated 5 Franchised Businesses, and there were 26 Territories covered by those 5 Franchised Businesses. Certain franchisees also own multiple Territories, but aggregate the reporting of their financial information as one Franchised Business.

(2) We included data from 57 Franchised Businesses of the 76 Franchised Businesses in Table D. These 57 Franchised Businesses operated 95 of the 119 Territories that were operational during the 2011 calendar year. Data concerning the remaining 19 Franchised Businesses that were in operation for at least one full year as of December 31, 2011 was not included in Table D due to insufficient information from the franchisees that owned them. We do not know whether the inclusion of such data, if available, would have a material effect on the gross profit margin percentages.

(3) We attribute variances in material costs to franchisee variances in pricing of lawn and tree care applications. Addition-

ally, we believe that inconsistency in the manner in which franchisees account for their inventory purchases may contribute to the variances. Some franchisees use the "last in first out" method of accounting for inventory, and others use the "first in first out" method.

(4) Direct Labor includes compensation (excluding payroll taxes, medical insurance, and fringe benefits) for employees who perform lawn and tree care services and excludes compensation for franchisee and other administrative and office personnel. We attribute the variance in Direct Labor primarily to the extent to which franchisees employed others to perform application services. Franchisees who performed all application services themselves incurred no direct labor costs and franchisees that employ others to perform some or all of the application services incurred higher Direct Labor cost. We also believe that some franchisees may have employees who perform administrative functions as well as application functions, but charged those employees' entire payroll to Direct Labor rather than splitting out that portion more appropriately charged to administration.

(5) Cost of Sales is the Sum of Material Costs and Direct Labor Costs. However, in the High Percentage column, the Material Costs percentage added to the Direct Labor Costs percentage will not equal the Cost of Sales because the franchisee who reported the highest Material Costs is different than the franchisee who reported the highest Direct Labor

Cost. The stated High Percentage Cost of Sales is based on the number reported by the franchisee with the highest combined Material Costs and Direct Labor Costs.

(6) We obtained the stated Gross Profit Margin percentages by subtracting the Cost of Sales from the 100% Gross Sales.

(7) THE RESULTS DESCRIBED IN TABLE D INCLUDE CERTAIN COST INFORMATION FOR 57 OUT OF 76 FRANCHISED BUSINESSES OPEN FOR AT LEAST ONE FULL CALENDAR YEAR AS OF DECEMBER 31, 2011. THE RESULTS ARE FOR CALENDAR YEAR 2011. FRANCHISED BUSINESSES TYPICALLY USE THE ACCRUAL METHOD OF ACCOUNTING.

A NEW FRANCHISEE'S FINANCIAL RESULTS MAY DIFFER FROM THE RESULTS STATED IN THE FINANCIAL PERFORMANCE REPRESENTATION.

WRITTEN SUBSTANTIATION FOR THE FINANCIAL PERFORMANCE REPRESENTATION WILL BE MADE AVAILABLE TO YOU UPON REASONABLE REQUEST.

"We Make House Calls!"

TUTOR DOCTOR

2070 Codlin Crescent, Unit 1
Toronto, ON M9W 7J2
Tel: (877) 988-8679, (416) 646-0364
Fax: (416) 646-0366
Email: sfriedman@tutordoctor.com
Website: www.tutordoctor.com
Stan Friedman, Vice President of Franchising

BACKGROUND
IFA Member:	Yes
Established & First Franchised:	2007; 2008
Franchised Units:	297
Company-Owned Units:	1
Total Units:	298
Distribution:	US – 45; CAN – 1; O'seas – 11
North America:	20 States, 1 Provinces
Density:	7 in CA, 4 in IL, 3 in FL
Projected New Units (12 Months):	10
Qualifications:	5, 5, 4, 4, 4, 5

FINANCIAL/TERMS
Cash Investment:	$55.4 – $73.3K
Total Investment:	$54.7 – $137K
Minimum Net Worth:	$500K
Fees (Franchise):	$39.7 – $127.7K
Fees (Royalty):	20%
Fees (Advertising):	0%
Term of Contract (Years):	10/10
Average Number of Employees:	1 FT, 0 PT
Passive Ownership:	Not Allowed
Encourage Conversions:	N/A
Area Development Agreements:	No
Sub-Franchising Contracts:	No
Expand in Territory:	Yes
Space Needs:	N/A

SUPPORT & TRAINING
Financial Assistance Provided:	No
Site Selection Assistance:	No
Lease Negotiation Assistance:	No
Co-operative Advertising:	No
Franchisee Association/Member:	Yes/Member
Size of Corporate Staff:	15
On-going Support:	A, B, C, D, G, H
Training:	8 Days La Jolla, CA

SPECIFIC EXPANSION PLANS
US:	All United States
Canada:	All Canada
Overseas:	All Countries

As of the date of this Disclosure Document, we wish to provide you with the following information which is based on the experience of both our corporate location and our U.S. and Canadian franchisees. We do not currently require that you charge a certain minimum or maximum tutoring fee for your customers (although we reserve the right in the future to set maximum prices), so you may charge as much as you would like.

Using our weekly mini reports submitted by all reporting franchisees in North America from February 2011 up to and including July 2012, the average enrollment value in the United States was US$2,128 (expressed in U.S. Dollars). The average enrollment value in Canada was CAN$2,086 (expressed in Canadian Dollars). (As of July 30, 2012, the Canadian and U.S. dollars were almost on par: CAN$1.00 = US$0.9981.)

Notes:

1. The above figures were solely based on the results of our corporate location (in Canada) and the our North American franchisees and are for the period of February 1, 2011 to July 31, 2012. There were 115 franchisees in the United States and 55 franchisees in Canada who were operational during this entire period. Of these franchisees, there were 29 in the United States and 11 in Canada who were not included in the results because they did not adequately report information to us. Of the 86 franchisees in the United States included in the results above, 47 franchisees met or exceeded the average enrollment value in the United States of US$2,128. Of the 44 franchisees in Canada included in the results above, 19 met or exceeded the average enrollment value in Canada of CAN$2,086.

2. Tutoring costs are approximately 45% of tutoring revenues generated by the corporate location.

3. For every 10 assessments completed on average (in which the child's proficiency is assessed by the franchise manager), our corporate location has net approximately 7 student enrollments.

4. These figures and cost projections will vary from one location to another and from one geographic area to another. A new franchisee's individual financial results may differ from the result stated in the financial performance representation.

5. Hourly Rate - This is the rate which we charge families for in-home tutoring services. Typically we charge between $44.00 and $54.00 per hour (in the U.S. this is in U.S. Dollars and in Canada, this is in Canadian Dollars). The hourly rate will fluctuate depending upon the program that the student enrolls in which is determined by a block of tutoring hours purchased, for example, a 12 hour program would be billed at $54.00/hour and a 96 hour program would be billed at $44.00/hour. For the purposes of this document we took the total revenues generated and divided it by the number of hours of tutoring we sold to come up with the average hourly rate.

6. Tutoring costs - refers to the amount paid out to our tutors who deliver the tutoring service in the home. We took the average hourly rate paid to our tutors ($19.50/hour) and divided that by the average hourly rate that we charge families ($43.00/hour) to come up with this percentage.

7. The amount that you may ultimately charge your customers and your revenue will depend on numerous factors including general and local market conditions of your Business, the city in which your Business is situated, the level of competition in your Territory, the socio-economic status of the population within your Territory, how well you follow the System, your management skills, experience, business acumen, prevailing wage rates, ongoing working capital requirements, accounts receivable financing or other costs and the level of sales experienced by you (which may fluctuate over time).

8. The businesses from which data is reflected in this Item offered substantially the same products and services to the public as you will.

Other than the preceding financial performance representation, we do not make any representations about a franchisee's future financial performance or the past financial performance of company-owned or franchised outlets. We also do not authorize our employees or representatives to make any such representations either orally or in writing. If you are purchasing an existing outlet, however, we may provide you with the actual records of that outlet. If you receive any other financial performance information or projections of your future income, you should report it to the franchisor's management by contacting Frank Milner at 2070 Codlin Cres., Unit #1, Toronto, Ontario M9W 7J2 and 416-646-0364, the Federal Trade Commission, and the appropriate state regulatory agencies.

Written substantiation for the financial performance representation will be made available to the prospective franchisee upon reasonable request.

VANGUARD CLEANING SYSTEMS

655 Mariners Island Blvd., #303
Sna Mateo. CA 94404
Tel: (800) 564-6422 x414, (650) 8287-2400
Fax: (650) 591-1545
Email: elast@vanguardcleaning.com
Website: www.vanguardcleaning.com
Eric Last, Director of Franchise Development

VANGUARD CLEANING SYSTEMS has been successfully franchising in the commercial cleaning industry since 1984. VANGUARD is currently seeking unit and master franchisees in the United States and Canada. Currently, Vanguard has 2,440 franchises and 60 regional offices.

BACKGROUND
IFA Member:	Yes
Established & First Franchised:	1984; 1984
Franchised Units:	2,440
Company-Owned Units:	0
Total Units:	2,440
Distribution:	US – 2,247; CAN – 193; O'seas – 0
North America:	31 States, 3 Provinces
Density:	413 in CA

Projected New Units (12 Months):	852
Qualifications:	2, 2, 3, 1, 3, 5

FINANCIAL/TERMS
Cash Investment:	$2.5 – $30.8K
Total Investment:	$8.5 – $37.9K
Minimum Net Worth:	$2.5 – $30.8K
Fees (Franchise):	$7.2 – $34.2K
Fees (Royalty):	10%
Fees (Advertising):	N/A
Term of Contract (Years):	10/10
Average Number of Employees:	0 FT, 1 PT
Passive Ownership:	Discouraged
Encourage Conversions:	Yes
Area Development Agreements:	Yes
Sub-Franchising Contracts:	Yes
Expand in Territory:	Yes
Space Needs:	N/A

SUPPORT & TRAINING
Financial Assistance Provided:	Yes (D)
Site Selection Assistance:	N/A
Lease Negotiation Assistance:	N/A
Co-operative Advertising:	No
Franchisee Association/Member:	No
Size of Corporate Staff:	9
On-going Support:	A, C, D, G, H, I
Training:	2 Weeks+ Local Regional Office

SPECIFIC EXPANSION PLANS
US:	All United States
Canada:	All Canada
Overseas:	No

Apart from designating the Service Revenues associated with the Business Plan that you select when you sign the Franchise Agreement, Vanguard does not furnish or authorize its salespersons to furnish any information about the actual or potential sales, costs, income or profits of a franchise. Vanguard does not make any representations about a franchisee's future financial performance or the past financial performance of company-owned or franchised outlets. Vanguard also does not authorize our employees or representatives to make any such representations either orally or in writing. If you are purchasing an existing outlet from Vanguard, however, Vanguard may provide you with the actual records of that outlet. If you receive any other financial performance information or projections of your future income, you should report it to the franchisor's management by contacting Jim Foley, 655 Mariners Island Blvd., Suite 303, San Mateo, California, 94404, the

Federal Trade Commission, and the appropriate state regulatory agencies.

Vanguard works to provide you with the Account Transfer offers that, if accepted by you and fully performed, are anticipated to generate annual gross revenue in the amount specified in the Business Plan you elect to purchase as described in Exhibit A to the Franchise Agreement and Item 5 of this disclosure document. This information is only an estimate of the gross revenue that may be generated by your Business Plan Accounts if fully performed and if billings to those Accounts are fully collected. Gross revenue that might be obtained from an Account is not an assurance that you will make a particular amount of gross or net revenue. Vanguard cannot ensure that all Account Cleaning Services Agreements will be fully performed. Accounts may cancel or fail to pay all amounts due under their contract. Vanguard does not guarantee that canceled Accounts can be replaced, and there may be a delay between cancellation of an Account and securing a replacement, if any. In providing you with a particular Business Plan package, Vanguard estimates the volume based on what is provided in the Account Cleaning Services Agreements, assuming full performance at the prices specified without reduction for early cancellation, bad debt or any other reason. The information provided is not a forecast of your future financial performance. The Business Plan commitment only relates to the Accounts Vanguard agrees to initially provide to you. It does not guarantee that the Accounts will remain with you. Accounts may cancel for a variety of reasons and Vanguard does not promise they will be replaced. Your exclusive remedy in case the Business Plan gross revenues commitment is not timely fulfilled is to request a refund, as explained in Item 5 of this Disclosure Document.

In the fiscal year ended December 31, 2011, 33 of the 35 franchisees who purchased franchises in that year had either received 100% of the Business Plan Account commitment from Vanguard or were still in their fulfillment period at the end of the fiscal year. 1 franchisee requested a lower level of Service Revenues than the Business Plan originally purchased and we provided a refund for the difference. 1 franchisee requested a postponement to receiving its VCS Accounts for personal reasons.

These results only represent whether Accounts were initially offered to franchisees according to the Franchisee's selected Business Plan and do not represent whether the Accounts remained with the franchisee. Accounts may cancel for a variety of reasons and Vanguard does not promise they will be replaced. The results for this fiscal year are not necessarily a reliable predictor of Vanguard's future performance, and Vanguard does not represent that it will in all cases fulfill the initial minimum Business Plan Account/Service Revenues commitment.

ACTUAL RESULTS VARY FROM UNIT TO UNIT AND VANGUARD CANNOT ESTIMATE THE RESULTS OF ANY PARTICULAR FRANCHISE. THE VOLUME OF YOUR BUSINESS PLAN SHOULD NOT BE CONSIDERED TO BE THE ACTUAL SALES OR REVENUES YOU WILL REALIZE. YOUR RESULTS MAY DIFFER AS EXPLAINED ABOVE.

THE VOLUME OF YOUR BUSINESS PLAN DOES NOT REFLECT THE COSTS OF SALES, OPERATING EXPENSES, OR OTHER COSTS OR EXPENSES THAT MUST BE DEDUCTED FROM THE VOLUME/REVENUE FIGURES (IF ATTAINED, WHICH MAY NOT NECESSARILY OCCUR) TO OBTAIN YOUR NET INCOME OR PROFIT. YOU SHOULD CONDUCT AN INDEPENDENT INVESTIGATION OF THE COSTS AND EXPENSES YOU WILL INCUR IN OPERATING YOUR VANGUARD CLEANING SYSTEMS BUSINESS. FRANCHISEES OR FORMER FRANCHISEES LISTED IN THE DISCLOSURE DOCUMENT MAY BE ONE SOURCE OF THIS INFORMATION.

On reasonable request, Vanguard will provide you with substantiation of the data used to prepare the information in this Item.

ZIPS DRY CLEANERS

7500 Greenway Center Dr., #400
Greenbelt, MD 20770
Tel: (888) 321-9477, (301) 313-0389
Fax: (301) 345-2895
Email: zips@franconnect.com

Website: www.321zips.com
Andy Cucchiara, VP Franchise Operations

ZIPS® is "America's One Price Dry Cleaner." Our successful business model is based on the revolutionary concept of offering any garment dry cleaned for just $1.99 AND ready for pick-up the same day—that's less than half the price of today's industry average! ZIPS® is expanding, offering franchise opportunities to qualified individuals and groups. If selected, you may be part of the ZIPS® revolution with a ZIPS DRY CLEANERS® franchise of your own!

BACKGROUND
IFA Member: Yes

Established & First Franchised: 1996; 2006
Franchised Units: 35
Company-Owned Units: 1
Total Units: 36
Distribution: US – 36; CAN – 0; O'seas – 0
   North America: 4 States, 0 Provinces
   Density: 11 in MD, 6 in VA, 3 in PA
Projected New Units (12 Months): 14
Qualifications: 5, 5, 1, 1, 4, 5

FINANCIAL/TERMS
Cash Investment: $150 – $225K
Total Investment: $616.2 – $778.5K
Minimum Net Worth: $450K
Fees (Franchise): $50K
Fees (Royalty): 6%
Fees (Advertising): 4%
Term of Contract (Years): 10/10
Average Number of Employees: 4 – 8 FT, 6 – 10 PT
Passive Ownership: Discouraged
Encourage Conversions: No

Area Development Agreements: Yes
Sub-Franchising Contracts: No
Expand in Territory: Yes
Space Needs: 3500 SF

SUPPORT & TRAINING
Financial Assistance Provided: No
Site Selection Assistance: Yes
Lease Negotiation Assistance: Yes
Co-operative Advertising: Yes
Franchisee Association/Member: No
Size of Corporate Staff: 5
On-going Support: A, B, C, D, E, G, H, I
Training: 1 Week Corp. Office; 7 Weeks Existing Store

SPECIFIC EXPANSION PLANS
US: Mid-Atlantic
Canada: No
Overseas: No

Historical Financial Performance Representation for Select Franchised Businesses. Presented below are the average total income, average total cost of goods, average gross profit and average selected costs and expense data for 11 Franchised Businesses during the period January 1, 2011 through December 31, 2011. We consider these 11 Franchised Businesses to be "mature" since they have been in operation for at least 1 year. All 11 Franchised Businesses were open and operating during the 12 month period January 1, 2011 to December 31, 2011. These Businesses are located in Maryland, Pennsylvania and Virginia. The 1 Franchised Business that is not included has not been in operation for 1 year and therefore is not considered mature.

This data was compiled from unaudited financial statements submitted to us by the Franchised Businesses. We believe the information is accurate, but we have not audited or veritied the information and we cannot verify that the information was compiled using consistentiy applied accounting principles.

FRANCHISED ZIPS DRY CLEANERS BUSINESSES
Statement of Average Total Income, Total Cost of Goods, Total Gross Profit and Total of Certain Costs
(During Period January 1, 2011 to December 31, 2011)

	Average	Percentage of Total Income	Percentage of Franchised Businesses Above Average	Number of Franchised Businesses Above Average
Total Income[1]	$696,299	100%	36.37%	4
Total Cost of Goods Sold[2]	$64,267	9.23%	45.46%	5
Total Gross Profit[3]	$632,032	90.77%	36.37%	4
Total Significant Other Costs/Expenses[8]	$394,627	56.67%	45.46%	5
Labor[4]	$254,687	36.58%	36.37%	4
Rent[5]	$88,379	12.69%	54.55%	6
Repairs and Maintenance[6]	$15,886	2.28%	27.28%	3
Utilities[7]	$35,675	5.12%	45.46%	5

Notes for Table appear after next table.

Historical Financial Performance Representation for Select VDA Member Owned Businesses. Presented below are the average total income, average total cost of goods, average gross profit and average selected costs and expense data for 17 VDA Member Owned Businesses during the period January 1, 2011 through December 31, 2011. As noted in Item 1, the VDA Member Owned Businesses are individually owned and operated by VDA Members. We consider these 17 VDA Member Owned Businesses to be "mature" since they have been in operation for at least 1 year. All 17 VDA Member Owned Businesses were open and operating during the 12 month period January 1, 2011 to December 31, 2011. These Businesses are located in the District of Columbia, Maryland, Pennsylvania and Virginia. The 1 VDA Member Owned Business that is not included has not been in operation for 1 year and therefore is not considered mature.

This data was compiled from unaudited financial statements submitted to us by the VDA Member Owned Businesses. We believe the information is accurate, but we have not audited or verified the information and we cannot verify that the information was compiled using consistently applied accounting principles.

VDA MEMBER OWNED ZIPS DRY CLEANERS BUSINESSES
Statement of Average Total Income, Total Cost of Goods, Total Gross Profit and Total of Certain Costs
(During Period January 1, 2011 to December 31, 2011)

	Average	Percentage of Total Income	Percentage of VDA Member Owned Businesses Above Average	Number of VDA Member Owned Businesses Above Average
Total Income[1]	$1,285,059	100%	47.06%	8
Total Cost of Goods Sold[2]	$133,512	10.39%	52.95%	9
Total Gross Profit[3]	$1,151,547	89.61%	47.06%	8
Total Significant Other Costs/Expenses[8]	$612,806	47.69%	41.18%	7
Labor[4]	$385,119	29.97%	33.34%	6
Rent[5]	$142,798	11.11%	41.18%	7
Repairs and Maintenance[6]	$28,621	2.23%	47.06%	8
Utilities[7]	$56,268	4.38%	41.18%	7

Systemwide Historical Financial Performance Representation. Presented below are the average total income, average total cost of goods, average gross profit and average selected costs and expense data for 17 VDA Member Owned Businesses and 11 Franchised Businesses during the period January 1, 2011 through December 31, 2011. We consider these 28 Businesses to be "mature" since they have been in operation for at least 1 year. All 28 Businesses were open and operating during the 12 month period January 1, 2011 to December 31, 2011. These Businesses are located in the District of Columbia, Maryland, Pennsylvania and Virginia. The 1 VDA Member Owned Business and the 1 Franchised Business that are not included have not been in operation for 1 year and therefore are not considered mature.

This data was compiled from unaudited financial statements submitted to us by the VDA Member Owned Businesses and the Franchised Businesses. We believe the information is accurate, but we have not audited or verified the information and we cannot verify that the information was compiled using consistently applied accounting principles.

SYSTEMWIDE ZIPS DRY CLEANERS BUSINESSES
Statement of Average Total Income, Total Cost of Goods, Total Gross Profit and Total of Certain Costs
(During Period January 1, 2011 to December 31, 2011)

	Average	Percentage of Total Income	Percentage of Businesses Above Average	Number of Businesses Above Average
Total Income[1]	$1,053,760	100%	42.86%	12
Total Cost of Goods Sold[2]	$106,308	10.09%	39.29%	11
Total Gross Profit[3]	$947,452	89.91%	42.86%	12
Total Significant Other Costs/Expenses[8]	$527,093	50.02%	42.86%	12
Labor[4]	$333,878	31.68%	42.86%	12
Rent[5]	$121,419	11.53%	35.72%	10
Repairs and Maintenance[6]	$23,618	2.24%	39.29%	11
Utilities[7]	$48,178	4.57%	39.29%	11

NOTES TO ITEM 19 TABLES:

1. "Average Total Income" – This figure is an average of all income and revenue from the sale of all services and products to customers.

2. "Total Cost of Goods Sold" – The average Total Cost of Goods Sold includes the total costs of all services and products sold at ZIPS Dry Cleaners Businesses (such as alterations, supplies, leather costs, customer claims, dry cleaning and laundry supplies, waste disposal and cash overage/shortage). These costs may vary from year to year, or within a year, due to fluctuations in the prices of supplies and/or materials, transportation costs and/or shipping costs.

3. "Total Gross Profit" – This figure represents the Total Income minus the Total Cost of Goods Sold.

4. "Labor Costs" – The "Labor Costs" include salary, wages, or benefits (including vacation pay) for management personnel. Each ZIPS Dry Cleaners Business compensates its managers differently and may use varied formulas. Franchisees may compensate managers differently or may compensate one or more individual owners in lieu of one or more managers. You will set and pay compensation (and any benefits) for owners and management personnel at your Franchised Business at a rate you determine. Your benefits package to employees may include some, all, or none of the expenses incurred by the ZIPS Dry Cleaners Businesses covered in this Item 19. The total amount of salaries for your employees and managers at a particular location will vary according to local wages, the number of employees, and the number of hours that the Franchised Business is open for business. You must make la-

bor, wage, and benefit determinations based on your market, experience, and other factors.

5. "Rent" – This includes rent, property taxes and miscellaneous items. Rent consists of minimum rents, percentage rents, common area maintenance charges, and any sales or other taxes. Property Taxes are real estate taxes and assessments levied against the property upon which the business is located. The amount or rate of taxation varies from jurisdiction to jurisdiction and you should consult with your tax advisors regarding the impact that these taxes will have on this analysis.
6. "Repairs and Maintenance" – This includes equipment repair and maintenance, store cleaning, and window cleaning.

7. "Utilities" – This includes alarm system monitoring, satellite and cable costs and charges for gas and electric. The charges for water are included in either the Utilities category or the Rent category, depending upon whether such charges are payable under the terms of the lease for the particular ZIPS Dry Cleaners Business.

8. "Total Significant Other Costs/Expenses" – This is the total of all costs shown in the table including Labor, Rent, Repairs and Maintenance, and Utilities, which are explained in more detail in footnotes 4 through 7 above.

Written substantiation for the financial performance representations will be made available to you upon reasonable request. Please carefully read all of the information in these financial performance representations, and all of the notes following the charts, in conjunction with your review of the historical data.

A NEW FRANCHISEE'S FINANCIAL RESULTS ARE LIKELY TO VARY FROM THE RESULTS STATED IN THE FINANCIAL PERFORMANCE REPRESENTATION.

You are strongly advised to perform an independent investigation of this opportunity to determine whether or not the franchise may be profitable and to consult your attorney, accountant, and other professional advisors before entering into any agreement with us. You should conduct an independent investigation of the costs and expenses you will incur in operating your Franchised Business. Our current and former franchisees may be one source of this information. You should construct your own business plan and pro forma cash flow statement, balance sheet, and statement of operations, and make your own financial projections regarding sales, revenues, costs, customer base, and business development for your Franchised Business.

A franchisee will incur other expenses of doing business which are likely to be significant, and which vary widely among franchisees. You will be required to pay certain fees to us including royalty fees and advertising fees. The additional categories of expenses which franchisees may incur include, but will not necessarily be limited to, the following: additional occupancy costs; franchisee compensation over and above that earned from the operations of the Franchised Business (such as a salary that a franchisee may pay to himself/herself); additional employee benefits; debt service; Insurance; business and regulatory fees and licenses; ongoing and supplemental training expenses; recruitment expenses; and bookkeeping and other professional services.

Actual results vary between ZIPS Dry Cleaners Businesses, and we expect that they will vary from franchisee to franchisee. Your income and expenses will be affected by a variety of factors including the following:

- prevailing economic or market area conditions, demographics, geographic location, interest rates, your capitalization level, the amount and terms of any financing that you may secure, the property values and lease rates, your business and management skills, staff strengths and weaknesses, and the cost and effectiveness of your marketing activities;

- your own operational ability, which may include but is not limited to your experience with managing a business, your capital and financing (including working capital), continual training of you and your staff, customer service at your location and your business plan;

- the location of your Franchised Business, site criteria, local household income, population, ease of ingress and egress, traffic counts, parking, the physical condition of your Franchised Business, the visibility of your Franchised Business, the visibility of your signage, the quality of your staff and having the correct quantity of staff; and

- the weather, the season and periodic marketing campaigns you run and those run by your competitors

Other than the preceding financial performance representations, we do not make any financial performance representations. We also do not authorize our employees or representatives to make any such representations either orally or in writing. If you are purchasing an existing outlet, however, we may provide you with the actual records of that outlet. If you receive any other financial performance information or projections of your future income, you should report it to the franchisor's management by contacting Andrew Cucchiara, Vice President of Franchise Operations, ZIPS Franchising, LLC, 7500 Greenway Center Drive, Suite 400, Greenbelt, MD 20770. (301) 313-0389, the Federal Trade Commission, and the appropriate state regulatory agencies.

Index of Franchisors

1-800-FDD-UFOC.com

Gain insider knowledge on America's most popular and successful franchises with our library of Franchise Disclosure Documents (FDDs) and Uniform Franchise Offering Circulars (UFOCs).

www.1-800-FDD-UFOC.COM has a comprehensive library that includes both current, up-to-date filings and an archive of over 25,000 past FDDs and UFOCs dating back to 1990. Order a complete FDD/UFOC or selected items from the FDD/UFOC. Our products include:

1. Entire FDD/UFOC | Price: $220.00
   Package includes Items 1-23, as well as the Franchise Agreement, Financial Statements, Franchisee List, as well as all other exhibits and attachments.

2. **Partial FDD/UFOC | Price: $150.00**
   Package includes Items 1-23 only. Excludes Exhibits, Franchise Agreement, Financial Statements, Franchisee List, etc.

3. **All FDD/UFOC Exhibits | Price $150.00**
   Package Includes all Exhibits in FDD/UFOC, including Franchise Agreement, Financial Statements, Franchisee List, etc. Excludes Items 1-23.

4. **Item 19. Financial Performance Representations/Earnings Claims | Price: $40**
   Historical sales, expenses and/or profits on actual franchise operations, as submitted by franchisor. Over 1,000 recent Item 19s from major franchisors are available. (Note: Only 55% of franchisors provide an Item 19.)

5. **Annual Item 19 Packages for Food-Service, Lodging, Retail and Service-Based Sectors | Price: $150 - $750 depending upon package.**
   Includes packages from 2010 (371 Item 19s), 2011 (484 Item 19s) and 2012 (531 Item 19s).

Orders are usually processed within 2 hours.
PLEASE VISIT WWW.1-800-FDD-UFOC.COM TODAY!
or call (888) 612-9908 or (510) 839-5471 to order by phone.